D1453578

From Karl Mannheim

Karl Kaunhein

from
KARL MANNHEIM

Edited with an Introduction by

KURT H. WOLFF

New York
Oxford University Press
1971

Contents

Contents: Introduction

Note. The first pages of what follows are based on the "Biographische Notiz,"
in Karl Mannheim, *Wissenssoziologie: Auswahl aus dem Werk,* eingeleitet und
herausgegeben von Kurt H. Wolff, Berlin und Neuwied: Hermann Luchterhand
(Soziologische Texte, Band 28), 1964 (henceforth referred to as *Wissenssoziologie*),
p. 691. Sections I-XIII are a modified translation of "Karl Mannheim in seinen
Abhandlungen bis 1933," the introduction to *Wissenssoziologie*, pp. 11-65; of
these, Sections II and VIII, in turn, are based on "Karl Mannheim on Interpretation," *Studies on the Left*, 3, 3 (Summer, 1963): 45-49; Section XXI derives
from "Karl Mannheim's Thought," a review of *Freedom, Power, and Democratic
Planning, Commentary*, 12, 4 (October, 1951): 402-404.

*Titles preceded by * are reprinted in full in body of text.
**Titles preceded by ** are reprinted in part in body of text.
Title preceded by † is reprinted in full in Introduction.
Titles preceded by †† are reprinted in part in Introduction.

Introduction:
A Reading of Karl Mannheim

KARL MANNHEIM, the only surviving child of a Hungarian father and a German mother, was born in Budapest in 1893. There he passed his childhood, graduated from the humanistic gymnasium, and began his university studies. But then he followed friends to Freiburg, Heidelberg, and for a briefer period Paris. He married a fellow student in Budapest and Heidelberg, Juliska Láng. She was a psychologist and became his lifelong companion and adviser, surviving him by nine years.

Mannheim's earliest interest was philosophy, in particular epistemology (he wrote his doctoral dissertation on its 'structural analysis'). Among his most influential teachers were the Hungarians György Lukács and Béla Zalai and the Germans Emil Lask, Heinrich Rickert, and Edmund Husserl. In the course of his studies he turned more and more to the social sciences, especially to Max Weber, Max Scheler, and Karl Marx. In 1925 he became a *Privatdozent* (unsalaried lecturer) in Heidelberg, and in 1929 professor of sociology and economics in Frankfurt. Dismissed in 1933, he joined the London School of Economics as a lecturer in sociology. Eight years later he moved to the Institute of Education at the University of London, where he became professor of education in 1946. Shortly before his unexpected death on 9 January 1947, he was nominated director of UNESCO, a position he could no longer accept. During his stay in England he edited the International Library of Sociology and Social Reconstruction, thereby greatly contributing to the diffusion of sociology in England and its eventual acceptance as an academically respectable discipline.[1]

[1] Cf. above all the obituaries by Ernest Manheim, *American Journal of Sociology*, LII (May 1947): 471–74; Louis Wirth, *American Sociological Review*, 12 (June 1947): 356–57, and Leopold von Wiese, *Kölner Zeitschrift für Soziologie*, 1 (1948–49): 98–100.

Karl Mannheim moved from Hungary, where he gave lectures toward the end of World War I, to Germany, and eventually to England. He moved from 'Soul and Culture' (1918) to problems of interpretation, epistemology, knowledge—knowledge in general and particular kinds of knowledge (e.g., historicist knowledge, conservative knowledge)—and social processes impinging on knowledge (of generations, of intellectual competition, of economic ambition)—all of this between 1921 and 1930. In 1929, with *Ideology and Utopia*, he published his most searching and most influential work. For a while, then, he took stock, as it were, of the position he had reached (e.g., 'Problems of Sociology in Germany' [1929], 'The Sociology of Knowledge' [1931], *The Tasks of Sociology Called for by the Present* [1932]). In 1933, although his professional ground was cut from under his feet, he yet managed to gain a new perspective when he transferred to England, a perspective on a haunting landscape that he felt committed to enter: the planned society. He described what he saw, at first still writing in German (*Man and Society in an Age of Reconstruction*, originally 1935), then only in English (*Diagnosis of Our Time* [1943], and *Freedom, Power and Democratic Planning* [1950], which he finished just before his death but which was published only posthumously).

Mannheim died young, but his work is weighty and the course of its development may well concern us. To present this through the selections contained in the present volume and through this introduction, illustrates a problem with which Mannheim himself was occupied deeply and for a long time. The problem is: how can a unique human being, or group, or period, or *Weltanschauung*—how can what the Historicist School called a 'historical individual'—be presented or mediated? Fundamentally it is the problem of how to go about interpreting intellectual or spiritual phenomena. It is the more or less exclusive topic of Mannheim's review of Lukács's *Theory of the Novel* (1920) and of his essays 'On the Interpretation of *Weltanschauung*' (1921–22), 'Structural Analysis of Epistemology' (1922), and 'The Ideological and the Sociological Interpretation of Intellectual Phenomena' (1926). Further, the paper on historicism (1924), like that on conservative thought (1927), not only is an application of what he had meanwhile learned about interpretation and of what he was learning in the course of writing these papers, but it is also an interpretation of his own thought and the thought of his generation. 'The Problem of Generation' preoccupied him, not only in the essay by this title (1928), but also much earlier: in his first or second publication ('Soul and Culture') he spoke as a member, if not as the voice, of a generation in a more literal sense.[2]

The problem of interpretation is also inseparable from his sociology of knowledge, which is clearly shown in his first essay on the sociology of knowledge (1925). Sociological interpretation, he wrote a year later in his more systematic discussion of kinds of interpretation, is new—it was new for himself and, through his communication of it, for the world. It enriches 'immanent' interpretation, that is, the effort to come as close as possible to an intellectual phenomenon in its own terms. For precisely by going beyond immanent, or intrinsic, interpretation, and interpreting extrinsically, above all sociologically, we may be able to identify 'those meaningful existential presuppositions' to which intrinsic interpretation is necessarily blind. This does not mean that sociological interpretation abandons the intellectual sphere. For the 'existential presuppositions' are not 'non-intellectual' but 'meaningful', even though pre-theoretical or a-theoretical. For, as Mannheim says in the last two sentences of 'Competition as a Cultural Phenomenon' (1928)—which might serve as a motto to much of Mannheim's work—sociological interpretation does not imply

that mind and thought are nothing but the expression and reflex of various 'locations' in the social fabric, and that there exist only quantitatively determinable functional correlations and no potentiality of 'freedom' grounded in mind; it merely means that even within the sphere of the intellectual, there are processes amenable to rational analysis, and that it would be an ill-advised mysticism which would shroud things in romantic obscurity at a point where rational cognition is still practicable. Anyone who wants to drag in the irrational where the lucidity and acuity of reason still must rule by right merely shows that he is afraid to face the mystery at its legitimate place. [*Essays on the Sociology of Knowledge*,[3] pp. 228–29]

Sociological interpretation, or the sociology of knowledge,[4]

[2] Other members of this 'generation', that is, others who, like Mannheim, lectured in the field of *Geisteswissenschaften* (translated as 'the human studies' by W. A. Hodges in *Wilhelm Dilthey: An Introduction*, New York: Oxford University Press, 1944), were Frigyes Antal, Béla Balázs, Béla Bartók, Elek Bolgár, Béla Fogarasi, Lajos Fülöp, Arnold Hauser, Zoltán Kodály, György Lukács, Emma Ritók, Ervin Szabó, and Sándor Varjas.

[3] Henceforth *Soc. Knowl.* See Bibliography of Mannheim's writings, which follows this Introduction.

[4] Mannheim never analyzed the question whether the two are synonymous. Perhaps he so believed; but it could be shown even from his own writing that the matter is not so simple, if only because the sociology of knowledge is, among other things, a discipline, and sociological interpretation is, among other things, a method, even an attitude. The only hint at a distinction between the two that I know in the literature on the sociology of knowledge (and this not in reference to Mannheim) is found in Arthur Child, 'The Theoretical

is Mannheim's synthesis of two components which deeply mark his work. Genetically these two components are idealism and Marxism; systematically they are spirit and society. One of Mannheim's fundamental questions—perhaps the fundamental question—might be formulated thus: how, in the face of the demonstration that the spirit is socially conditioned, can I still do right by its inexhaustibility and unforeseeability? Or perhaps: how can I, nevertheless, save it? But also: how, in the face of the overwhelming spirit, can I ascertain as accurately as possible its intimate connection with society, and how can I proclaim this connection precisely for the sake of both spirit and society? And later, ever more urgently: how can I save society?

Let us try to understand what this means and what it may mean for us today by following Mannheim's writings in their development.[5]

1. *Soul and Culture* (1918)

In this essay—the title of which might almost be read as 'Spirit and Society'—Mannheim laments a distance that characterizes his time. This is the distance between the individual and 'objective culture' (religion, science, art, the state, forms of life) or the 'objectifications of the spirit'. It can be bridged by 'subjective culture', when 'the soul strives for its fulfillment, not on its own . . . but by way of those cultural objectifications—by incorporating them'. Or the distance can be rendered irrelevant through fulfillment 'beyond cultural appropriation', such as is practiced by Indian ascetics or Christian saints. This alternative, however, is not available to us, for if we were to take our position 'outside of what happens' (in this world), we would lose ourselves, since we are 'unredeemed', 'not elect', and must find our 'contact with life, with external reality, and time-given culture'. At most we have 'moments of such gracelike experiences, but not redemption, because our fall makes any enduring encounter with ourselves impossible'.

This means that we live in a time in which men depend on society if they would be themselves, would be worthy of being men. Did Mannheim mean that in earlier times the spirit was distributed less evenly through society, living in only a few blessed individuals, whereas its modern diffusion also has brought with it

---

Possibility of the Sociology of Knowledge', *Ethics*, 51 (1941): 417; cf. Kurt H. Wolff, 'A Preliminary Inquiry into the Sociology of Knowledge from the Standpoint of the Study of Man', *Scritti di sociologia e politica in onore di Luigi Sturzo* (Bologna, 1953), Vol. III, pp. 593–94.
    [5] Titles of writings here reprinted in full are preceded by *; if reprinted in part, by **.

its socialization, which we cannot escape except in blessed moments? If we look forward to his paper on economic ambition (1930; XIII below), to *Man and Society* (1935; XVIII), above all to 'The Democratization of Culture' (XVII: 3), then we can retrospectively recognize in such an idea a vague anticipation of what he was to say later about democratization. We also have here the earliest instance of his effort to diagnose his time. The connection between this' effort and Mannheim's 'fundamental questions' is this: I can identify spirit only in a given historical form, hence only by grasping a historical period (the influence of Hegel but also of Dilthey is evident here)—or I can identify a period only by grasping its spirit. We shall soon be more concerned with this circular statement.

And another theme that will become important in Mannheim's sociology of knowledge can already be found here: that of 'de-actualization'. We live in a time 'in which the presence of new, formlessly flashing contents de-actualizes much that is old'. Here 'de-actualization' does not refer to a process of alienation perceived in a sociological perspective. But beginning with 'The Problem of a Sociology of Knowledge' of 1925 (VII) and fully developed in the *Ideology and Utopia* of 1929 (XIV), this concept (though not the term) is transformed into an explicitly sociological tool for the perception of 'total ideology'.

While on the whole, and admittedly, 'Soul and Culture' is in the tradition of idealism, the theme of 'de-actualization' foreshadows a Marxist component. Biographically speaking, its most direct source appears to have been Lukács, a member (see n. 2 above) of the 'generation' that sponsored the series of lectures introduced by Mannheim's 'Soul and Culture'.[6]

[6] Cf. David Kettler, *Marxismus and Kultur* (Neuwied und Berlin: Luchterhand, 1967), the subtitle of which, in English, is 'Mannheim and Lukács in the Hungarian Revolutions, 1918–19' (this essay also contains many important bibliographical references), and David Kettler, 'Sociology of Knowledge and Moral Philosophy: The Place of Traditional Problems in the Formation of Mannheim's Thought', *Political Science Quarterly*, LXXXII (1967): 399–426, esp. 416–20. My indebtedness for both the knowledge and the text of 'Lélek és Kultura' goes to David Kettler, who reports on the manner in which he himself got acquainted with the pamphlet in the article just cited (p. 408 and n. 11) and gives a more detailed exposition of the pamphlet (pp. 408–13) than is given here. In addition, Kettler analyzes in the same paper two as yet unpublished manuscripts by Mannheim, 'Über die Eigenart kultursoziologischer Erkenntnis' (1921; On the Characteristics of Knowledge in Sociology of Culture) and 'Eine soziologische Theorie der Kultur und ihrer Erkennbarkeit' ('probably 1924'; A Sociological Theory of Culture and Its Knowability). Being familiar with these and other unpublished sources, Kettler throws light on several problems with which the present introduction is concerned; and his larger study of Mannheim, of which the paper under discussion is a part, will be even more illuminating and corrective.

Its religious language may surprise readers of *Ideology and Utopia* and of his essays in the sociology of knowledge; and it may interest readers of some of his writing during the English phase, notably perhaps of some of the essays contained in *Diagnosis of Our Time* (1943). The religious concern of the twenty-four year old Mannheim found only rare expression during his subsequent years in Germany, but it came out again in England, though 'de-actualized' (if we may apply this term) into attention to a sociologically interesting human dimension. Thus, part of the title footnote to 'Towards a New Social Philosophy' (early 1940's), reads:

In order to preclude any misunderstanding, and as personal feelings are more easily roused in the sphere of religion than perhaps in any other, he [the author] wishes to emphasize that he speaks as a sociologist, and as a sociologist only. The question put to the sociologist can only concern the relationship to, and the function in, society which religion has as one among other spiritual phenomena in the social process. Whatever this approach may yield, it does not judge the intrinsic values of Christianity and Christian Ethics. [*Diagnosis of Our Time*, p. 109, n]

And yet in 1933, Mannheim had written 'that achieving from time to time a certain distance from his own situation and from the world is one of the fundamental traits of man as a truly human being. A man for whom nothing exists beyond his immediate situation is not fully human'.[7] Let us remember this problem of religion in Mannheim's thought when we come to later writings where it is expressed again.

*II.   Review of Lukács's 'Theory of the Novel' (1920)

Mannheim's comments on the *Theory of the Novel*—the only book by Lukács he ever reviewed—is the earliest appearance, not of the Marxist component in his thought, but of the problem of interpretation. Mannheim here shows the exuberant curiosity of one who has discovered the inexhaustible interpretability of the world of the mind. To catch objects in their immediacy, he urges the most unconditional exposure to them possible. For this, man must overcome the deep-seated traditional way of perceiving them as things external to himself and realize that his perception of them depends on how he sees them, which in turn depends on how he looks at them. In his enthusiasm Mannheim does not stop to deal with the epistemological problem, implicit

[7] Karl Mannheim, 'The Problem of Ecstasy', a section in 'The Democratization of Culture' (XVII (3) below). ('Translator's [Paul Kecskemeti's] note: This paper was written in 1933'). In *Essays on the Sociology of Culture* (henceforth *Soc. Cult.*), p. 240. See also *Diagnosis of Our Time* (XX (2) below), p. 137, and esp. n. 91.

in his approach, of whether man's perceptual apparatus derives from the nature of objects or from the nature of mind.

Intellectual phenomena 'can be explained in more than one frame of reference'. Furthermore, Mannheim distinguishes between 'dogmatic' and 'logical' objects, or *interpretanda*, and warns against confusing them (for 'semantic' reasons, we might say). For instance, I call 'work of art' an object which I can consider in reference to the psychic development of the artist who made it, or in regard to its aesthetic character (lines, colors, motifs, structure, etc.), or in respect to its position in the history of style, as well as in many other respects. Using the same term 'work of art' in all such analyses, I may be led to believe—erroneously—that I am speaking about the same 'object', whereas it is a different one every time I change my frame of reference. It is the same only 'dogmatically', not 'logically'. Moreover, Mannheim points out, these logical objects which are covered by the same dogmatic object are ordered hierarchically. He stresses the danger of wanting to 'explain from below upward', that is, to explain the 'upper' on the basis of the 'lower', which he says is mistaken, and he argues the inverse direction, 'from up downward'. For instance, the attempt at exhaustively 'explaining' a work of art in terms of its origin is false, because in such a procedure 'work of art' is a psychological object which 'does not yet contain at all that which is hierarchically higher, namely, the spiritual element or, in our case, the art form'. On the contrary, it is correct to 'explain' or, 'in the narrower sense of the word', to 'interpret',[8] the 'work of art', that is, the logical object 'art form', by starting from the higher logical object 'spiritual-metaphysical phenomenon' or 'objectification of the spirit'. This is what Lukács does with respect to the form of the novel, which he tries to interpret 'from a higher point of view, that of the philosophy of history'. But it is 'extremely difficult to grasp' the spirit of a time 'and its ultimate points of orientation, if only because it never explicates itself in its creations but only manifests itself *through* them'. The result of such an interpretation can therefore never be directly demonstrated by means of quotations, 'for such a demonstration always presupposes the reader's capacity in a specific, separate act to read in the example presented what is essential in it'.

Still, only in this fashion, that is, in the direction opposite to that of the reductionist, is it possible to attain a total view. In other words, if we would know what is essential in an object, we must appreciate its nature and understand, in a fashion Mannheim

[8] This distinction between 'explanation' and 'interpretation' will be developed later, as we shall see.

evidently patterns after Wilhelm Dilthey,[9] how in the course of development it has come to be at the place where we find it. To see what is essential, however, is 'not a matter of construction or induction but a particular ability, which in rudimentary form is possessed by everybody'. This may hint at an elite view of men of knowledge as well as at the germ of a view of education. The first might be connected with Mannheim's later, well-known preoccupation with the 'socially unattached intelligentsia' and with elites in general[10]; the second, with his intense interest in education during the last years of his life.[11]

This short review is important not only because of Lukács's manifest influence on Mannheim's thinking about aesthetics and interpretation and because of the less manifest influence of phenomenology (compare 'the specific, separate act' in the last quotation with the phenomenological 'bracketing'), but also because it traces the outlines of a scheme of interpretation which Mannheim develops in his next paper, on the interpretation of *Weltanschauung*, and works out and applies in subsequent essays, especially those of 1925 (VII) and 1926 (VIII).

*III. *On the Interpretation of 'Weltanschauung'* (1921–22)

In this investigation, Mannheim aims at nothing less than a method for grasping the spirit of a time. Already a result of his having set this aim, there is an insight stated at the beginning of the essay that entails the remaining problems. The insight is that *Weltanschauung* or spirit is 'pre-theoretical'. This gives a new accessibility and comparability to all 'cultural fields'. The problem, however—Mannheim even believes it to be 'the central problem of philosophy today' (*Soc. Knowl.*, p. 39)—is how the a-theoretical can be grasped by means of science, which is theoretical, how it can be translated into theory. For Mannheim, it seems, this is a problem, not so much for historical, as for ontological reasons

because it touches upon a fundamental property of human life and mind, characterizing man far better than any of the findings of anthropological science can do. This fundamental trait is that man is the citizen of several worlds at the

---

[9] Cf. Wilhelm Dilthey, 'Die Typen der Weltanschauung und ihre Ausbildung in den metaphysischen Systemen' (1911), in *Weltanschauungslehre: Abhandlungen zur Philosophie der Philosophie* (*Gesammelte Schriften*, Vol. VIII [Leipzig und Berlin: Teubner, 1931], p. 87.

[10] Cf. esp. *Ideology and Utopia*, pp. 136–46, and *Man and Society in an Age of Reconstruction*, pp. 81–96.

[11] Cf. *ibid.*, *passim*, 'Adult Education and the Social Sciences' (XIX (5) below), 'Mass Education and Group Analysis' (XIX (6)), *Freedom, Power, and Democratic Planning* (XXI), Chapter 10, 'Education as Groundwork', pp. 246–65, *An Introduction to the Sociology of Education* (XXII), etc.

same time. We possess . . . the primordial stuff of experience, which is wholly indeterminate and of which we cannot even say whether it is homogeneous, in several distinct forms, as aesthetic, religious, ethical experience and also as theoretical awareness. [*Ibid.*, p. 39]

But why are we not contented with this?

Why is it, then, that we crave theoretical knowledge of something we have already possessed integrally in direct experience unmarred by the intrusion of the theoretical interest? Why do we not content ourselves with the aesthetic contemplation of the works before us? Why do we pass from the attitude of form-perception to that of cognitive analysis, an attitude essentially incongruous with the aesthetic datum? Why should 'thought' be the universal medium, burdened with the thankless role of a tool that is constantly needed and used, and yet is constantly despised and reviled? And is it even to provide the language in which it can be denounced? [*Ibid.*, p. 40]

Mannheim's passion for thinking and his praise of it, which this among many other passages reveals, does not, however, lead him to answer the questions he has just raised. Instead he points out the positive and fruitful nature of theory, which 'must achieve something else besides chilling the authentic experience with the cold blast of reflection', for 'otherwise it would be incomprehensible why the ethical, aesthetic, and religious realm (that is, the realm of the a-theoretical) is shot through with elements of theory even in its original, unreflected state' (*ibid.*, p. 40).

Thus not only is the theoretical manner of grasping the world given to man as one among other manners, but it is given to him as that which pervades all others. Mannheim's 'a-theoretical' passion for theory does not lead him, however, to ask why this should be so.

Instead the problem is, as we saw, how something a-theoretical, more precisely how a *Weltanschauung*, can become the object of scientific investigation. A *Weltanschauung* is far less an object than are aesthetic, religious, or ethical 'objectifications'. Generally speaking, an object can be given in unmediated or in mediated form. From this Mannheim draws the conclusion that the full understanding of a cultural phenomenon or object requires three kinds of understanding: that of its objective meaning, which is given immediately; that of its expressive meaning; and that of its documentary meaning. The latter two are not immediate, but mediated. In science the objective meaning is 'a theoretical proposition'; in the visual arts, a 'visual content'; in music, 'melody, rhythm, harmony, and the like'. The creator of a work aims at creating objective and expressive meaning; he is unaware of documentary meaning, which 'is not an intentional object for him'. If we would grasp the expressive meaning of a work or an act, we must 'transcend' the work or act in the direction of its creator or actor, that is to say, psychologically. The grasp of documentary meaning, on the other hand, 'is a matter, not of a temporal process in which certain experiences become actualized, but of the character, the essential nature, the "ethos" of the subject which manifests itself in artistic creation [for instance]' (*ibid.*, p. 55). In aiming at documentary meaning, that is, in engaging in documentary interpretation, we may 'gather the scattered items of documentary meaning together in overarching concepts' such 'as the "art motive" [*Kunstwollen*, artistic intention] (Riegl), "economic ethos" [*Wirtschaftsgesinnung*] (Sombart), "*Weltanschauung*" (Dilthey and others), or "spirit" (Max Weber and others), depending on the cultural fields explored' (*ibid.*, p. 58). Since it is 'profoundly influenced by the location within the historical stream from which the interpreter attempts to reconstruct the spirit of a past epoch', one readily understands that documentary interpretation 'must be performed anew in each period'. In other words, what Mannheim will call 'transcendent' interpretation is historically relative.

Expressive and documentary meaning are attained by a theoretical process. The original, pre-theoretical cultural phenomenon does not have these meanings. This is to say that the grasp of expressive and documentary meaning changes the objectively understood object. Interpretation 'brackets' (*ibid.*, p. 68) it, as Mannheim puts it in phenomenological terms, thus rendering more precise the distinction between dogmatic and logical object that he made in the preceding essay.

The question now is how to go about 'detaching certain elements or units of meaning from their concrete setting and fusing them into validly ascertainable objects of higher generality by using appropriate categories and conceptualizations' (*ibid.*, p. 73). But Mannheim interrupts himself to point to the 'paradoxical result', namely, that 'we understand the whole from the part, and the part from the whole' (*ibid.*, p. 74), the spirit of an epoch from documents, and documents from the spirit of an epoch. It is the 'circle' we encountered already in 'Soul and Culture'. Mannheim, however, does not pursue the problem further, for despite his passion for theory he yet appears to be less interested in theory than in method. What is needed, he continues, are concepts that are applicable to all fields of culture and do justice to their historicity; but instead of engaging in a search of such concepts, he criticizes 'certain attempts at constructing a historical synthesis' (*ibid.*, p. 75), namely, Dilthey's, Riegl's, and Spengler's, all of which tend, more or less, toward a philosophy of history; and those of Max Dvořák and Max Weber, who remained faithful to history itself, but whose 'methodological problem' (*ibid.*, p. 80)[12] was 'whether the unity of various cultural fields should be expressed in terms of "correspondence", "function", "causality", or "reciprocity"' (*ibid.*, p. 80). The most important distinction Mannheim makes is between interpretation from the totality of a *Weltanschauung* and causal explanation; if only the latter is considered 'explanation', he argues, the former should simply be called 'interpretation'.

Mannheim concludes his discussion in a spirit of hope, even enthusiasm. He speaks of a process of fermentation in which science and intellectual life as a whole are engaged: 'we are striving after a synthesis and would like to draw the meaning and form of pre-theoretical data within the orbit of science' (*ibid.*, p. 82). He thus names what modern efforts in certain areas he has gathered, and he recognizes, for himself and for those to whom he communicates it, something new.

IV.   *On the Problem of the Classification of the Sciences* (1922)

In this review of Erich Becher's *Geisteswissenschaften und Naturwissenschaften* (The Human Studies and the Natural Sciences; 1921) Mannheim argues the pre-theoretical givenness of the object as the basis of an adequate classification. This again leads into a circle, however, for despite the pre-theoretical givenness, a givenness, so to speak, irrespective of all points of view, a classification can be undertaken, after all, only on the basis of a point of view: 'which point of view is the most adequate depends on the nature of the object; but again, the nature of the object can be grasped theoretically only from a point of view; thus the whole problem seems to move in a circle' (*Wissenssoziologie*, p. 157). Nor can we escape this dilemma by declaring that every point of view is valid, for the relativism that such a position would proclaim violates the facts so flagrantly as to move us to the other extreme, that is, insistence on the pre-theoretical, 'ontic' grasp of objects. Methodologically speaking, 'the essence [of something] can be grasped in theory only from a point of view' (a proposition Mannheim advances against intuitionism); still, the various points of view

---

[12] Mannheim himself was later, in his papers explicitly dealing with the sociology of knowledge, concerned with an intimately related problem: that of the relations between cultural phenomena and social structure and of the categories appropriate for the analysis of these relations. He was criticized for not having overcome his unclarity in regard to this problem. Cf. esp. Alexander von Schelting, *Max Webers Wissenschaftslehre* (Tübingen: Mohr, 1934), p. 100, n. 3, and Robert K. Merton, 'Karl Mannheim and the Sociology of Knowledge', *Journal of Liberal Religion*, 2 (1941): 136 (repr. in Merton, *Social Theory and Social Structure* [Glencoe, Ill., New York: Free Press, 1949, 1957, 1968]. For an assessment of more general but related critiques, see David Kettler, 'Sociology of Knowledge and Moral Philosophy', esp. 399–400 and n. 1.

are arranged in a hierarchy which 'is oriented directly toward' the objects themselves. With these two declarations Mannheim tries to achieve two things: on the one hand, to give 'the significance of the methodological sphere' its proper right, which would be impossible if we posited an intuitive relation to objects and their essences; on the other hand, to acknowledge the realization that theoretical work 'has its ultimate check in something extra-theoretical, something which confronts us ontically'. In other words: once we take a point of view, we miss the essence of the objects seen from it; but which point of view we take depends on the essence of the objects that are seen from it. Mannheim fails to explain what, if anything, he does in the face of this circle; but it is clear that either of the two insights that make it up conceive the implied relation between individual (subject) and object as 'existential'.

Mannheim abandons the problem he has raised. He explains that even 'inadequate' classifications or inadequate knowledge can produce 'new insights' by pointing out 'that knowing is nothing but circling around a pre-theoretical vis-à-vis [*Gegenüber*] (to avoid here the word "object" [*Gegenstand*])'. Here we have a germ of the concepts of 'perspectivistic' knowledge that Mannheim will develop in his essay on Historicism (1924; VI) but above all in *Ideology and Utopia*, and for which he was to become known, if not famous or notorious. But the problem of how objective truth is possible despite the 'most various points of view', that is, despite the relativism he has just rejected, does not yet come up; it will plague him—and his interpreters—later. Had he met it already here, he could perhaps have tried to resolve it by analyzing the 'hierarchy' of the points of view that 'is oriented directly toward' the objects themselves.

At any rate, a 'fully adequate classification of the sciences would coincide with the copy-like repetition of the architectonics already present in them', for full adequacy means, in general, 'merely to understand and accept' (*ibid.*, p. 161). But in such acceptance, though we would 'have' the object, we would not know it. Mannheim, however, does not ask either how 'having' is possible or why knowing demands some kind of distance. He seems so convinced of the 'existential' relation between individual and objects that he is also convinced that a classification according to objects presupposes an ontology. Such an ontology would have to show, he writes, that 'the sciences follow the ontic structure of reality' and that it is not '"method" [which] creates the objects' (*ibid.*, p. 162). If we want to prove that the human studies (*Geisteswissenschaften*) form an ontically grounded unity, we must show that the 'psychic (temporally identifiable acts connected with a certain stream of consciousness)' (*ibid.*, p. 163) and that which these acts intend or mean, the meaning of these acts, belong in the same ontic sequence. Mannheim mentions Husserl, Rickert, and Spranger as having shown that this is *not* the case, and he could have recalled or mentioned—if not used for the analysis of the present problem—his own distinctions between the objective, expressive, and documentary meanings of intellectual phenomena, even more generally, the difference between origin and validity. It is useless to speculate why he did not; the reason just possibly is as simple as lack of space in a book review.

v. *Structural Analysis of Epistemology* (1922)

Mannheim distinguishes between the systematization, the system, and the architectonic of a philosophy and of intellectual phenomena generally. Most basic is systematization, 'the first ordering of the "elements of experience"'; it is 'constitutive' of all theoretical objects, which are conceivable only as systematized. By contrast, a 'system' is a 'reflected, methodological form', and the 'architectonic' is 'a mere mode of presentation'. The analysis of the system allows us to correct unsystematic shifts brought about by the architectonic; and if the account of a thinker's thought 'is to be more than a servile copy', it must make such 'an effort at a systematic reconstruction of this kind'.

Systematization, system, and architectonic may be understood as attributes of a thinker's approach to the world (with systematization the most unconditional of the three). But there is also the question of how and to what extent the thinker does reach the world, that is to say, whether and to what extent that which he discovers by means of his approach is valid. An atemporal sphere of validity is an undemonstrable postulate of all theory (which is presupposed in every attempt at demonstrating it). In pure logic—which deals with this sphere of validity—a subject does not yet occur. Epistemology, on the other hand, is unthinkable without a subject. But this means that epistemology presupposes pure logic, that pure logic is independent of epistemology and can say nothing about it, although in empirical thinking the two are inseparable. 'Approach to the world' and 'predication of the world' (these are not Mannheim's terms) are discussed together in the following passage:

Any systematization whatever can in the end permit but a single correct ordering of its elements [that is to say: its ultimate court of appeal is validity]. All concrete acts of thinking are searching for this sequence, and even if it cannot be found in this way, it is still the indispensable presupposition of meaning for any and every act of thinking. [*Essays on Sociology and Social Psychology*,[13] p. 30]

[13] Henceforth *Soc. Soc. Psych.*

This means: even though the 'circling around a pre-theoretical vis-à-vis' (of which we heard in the preceding essay) yields inadequate knowledge, still it ultimately guarantees valid knowledge. One might say that that which confronts us plays with us as if it were a magnet until, at the end of all days, it transforms itself into a valid object on which we are dead and caught. But perhaps such a chiliastic vision is 'indispensable', and its image is not the improper trifle we may be tempted to see in it. Moreover, such a vision is also found in Hegel and, in more 'earthly' form, in Marx, who, as we have begun to see here, had great influence on Mannheim.

What element is common to all epistemologies? An indirect answer is provided by a typology of epistemologies or, speaking in terms of an analysis of their structures, by a typology of loci where different practicable roads to knowledge are possible. Among the merits of such a typology is the separation of historical (including biographical) from a-historical elements; and this separation is governed by the rule that the more compelling and rational a thought is, the less is it caused empirically. It is understood, of course, that the historical *occurrence* of even the most rational phenomenon is subject to causal analysis. But such causal analysis, Mannheim insists (not the first time), can demonstrate neither the a-priori possibility nor the absolute truth value of its type. To do the former is instead the task of an 'immanent' structural analysis; to do the latter is the task of 'an immediate investigation of the content as such (in the case of epistemology, for example, only by an epistemological examination, not by a logical analysis of structure)' (*Soc. Soc. Psych.*, p. 37).

Here, too, Mannheim anticipates elements of his later typology of interpretations (VIII below). At any rate, a 'comprehensive explanation' (*ibid.*, p. 39; to be consistent Mannheim should have said 'interpretation') of a historical phenomenon must illuminate both its temporal genesis and its atemporal systematic origin 'in the supratemporal systematization of a sphere' (cf. *ibid.*, p. 39; *Wissenssoziologie*, p. 199). Without acknowledging it, Mannheim here parallels Max Weber's requirement for the adequate grasp of something, namely, its (causal) explanation as an event in time and its 'understanding' interpretation as a spiritual (intellectual) phenomenon.[14] And in our time, Mannheim says, we must, while interpreting, 'never lose sight of the *enormous tension* that prevails between the doctrine of a timeless validity and

[14] Cf. Max Weber's famous definition of 'sociology' in *Economy and Society* (1911–13), Guenther Roth and Claus Wittich, eds. (New York: Bedminster Press, 1968), p. 4.

the simultaneous awareness that every historical phenomenon is fast rooted in its age' (*Soc. Soc. Psych.*, p. 39, modified; *Wissenssoziologie*, p. 199).

He thus is carrying on a two-pronged venture: sociology of epistemology (later of 'knowledge') and diagnosis of his time. The thinking of this time is marked by two fundamental experiences: 'On the one hand, there is the insight that the very meaning of theory implies that there can only be a single truth; on the other, there is the recognition that anything subject to the process of becoming demands to be comprehended in terms of time' (*Soc. Soc. Psych.*, p. 40). The latter recognition, however, Mannheim says in a very important footnote on relativism, 'must not be carried over into the realm of meaning and validity'. True, we do not *have* to 'think or to engage in artistic activity; but if we elect to do so, it must be in strict conformity with the structure of the field in question'. And thus it is also true of his own present effort 'that one solution alone can be the right one', but that even if it 'should fail to lay bare the ultimately valid categories, the discovery of its erroneousness would imply the possibility of a correct solution' (*ibid.*, p. 40n.).

We thus observe that at this stage of his thinking Mannheim's famous 'relativism' is characterized by insistence on the historicity of intellectual phenomena, but at the same time, and as emphatically, on the existence of a non-relative, that is, objective or absolute, structure of the world. As we shall see, this does not change in his later writings either.

The first part of the present essay is entitled 'Of the Logic of Philosophical Systematizations'; the title of the second part is that of the whole: 'The Structural Analysis of Epistemology'. As epistemology shows, man is capable of knowing not only objects ('immanent knowledge') but also the presuppositions of knowing them ('transcendental knowledge'). The latter results from a 'free choice of reference' (*freie Blickwendung*; *ibid.*, p. 45), which is characterized by an *epoché*,[15] that is, by 'a type of suspension of the validity of a judgment' (*ibid.*, p. 46)—the most important types of such suspension 'are the Cartesian doubt (*de omnibus dubitandum*) and the Kantian transcendental question (how is [experience] possible?)' (*ibid.*, p. 45). But epistemology has not only the analytical task to 'ascertain the ultimate presuppositions of any possible knowledge,' but also the evaluative task 'to evaluate the cognitive achievement as such, on the basis of the

---

[15] Here, as he did not in his review of Lukács's *Theory of the Novel*, where the idea of *epoché*, though not the expression, already occurred, Mannheim refers to Husserl's *Ideas*. (On the influence of phenomenology on Mannheim, cf. Paul Kecskemeti, 'Introduction', *Soc. Knowl.*, pp. 8–9.)

evaluation of' these ultimate presuppositions (*ibid.*, p. 47). In trying to solve these tasks, epistemology makes use of the concrete analyses achieved by logic, psychology, or ontology. These three 'primary systematizations' serve as its 'fundamental disciplines' and furnish its three most general types. For we can—directly— inquire into the ultimate presuppositions of knowledge either genetically (how does knowledge come about?) or in regard to its principles of validity; in the first case the answer is psychological or ontological; in the second, logical. An indirect inquiry into those principles, on the other hand, concerns the primary systematization itself and decides 'which of the above systematizations is to serve as fundamental discipline for the ensuing theory of knowledge' (*ibid.*, p. 49). Such an inquiry thus makes us 'aware of the ultimate basic axioms of every possible epistemology in general' and thus of 'the ultimate presuppositions of knowledge itself' (*ibid.*, p. 52). 'There can be no doubt', Mannheim adds in a footnote, 'that this type of epistemology (whose historical realization has, after all, not yet emerged) would employ as its fundamental science just the analysis of structure as the logical doctrine of the systematizations and that it would see its ultimate presuppositions in the primordial systematization laid bare by this analysis' (*ibid.*, p. 52n., modified).

In this discussion of the problem of the fundamental disciplines of epistemology, too, we see Mannheim trying to come as close as possible to experience itself and to shape his formulations while in such close vicinity. In the present instance he 'brackets' a traditional division of cognitive approaches to the world (logic, psychology, ontology) rather than taking it for granted: he identifies the three as 'primordial systematizations' of one approach (though without analyzing them in the direction of their common unitary origin). Or to employ his much-used expression, he 'relativizes' them—not, however, with reference to history or society but with reference to the (a-historical, a-social) individual. Here he is not so much a sociologist as an existentialist.

The analysis of 'specifically epistemological concepts', that is, of the 'subject–object correlation', shows that epistemology takes its concept of the subject from its fundamental discipline. 'This as yet unfulfilled subject–object correlation is what epistemology adds *out of itself* to the elements borrowed from the fundamental science, and this is what the ultimate specificity of the formation of epistemological concepts consists in' (*Wissenssoziologie*, p. 220; cf. *Soc. Soc. Psych.*, p. 55). Epistemology thus always works with three elements: (1) the known (knowledge or cognition), (2) the knower (subject), and (3) the to-be-known (object), and concentrates on the task of resolving or bridging the correlations among them—for instance, of ascertaining, in regard to the relation between subject and object, 'the proper share of both the subject and reality in the attainment of objectivity' (*Soc. Soc. Psych.*, p. 61).

In evaluating, that is, in its endeavor to reach certainty that the 'ultimate presuppositions' are the basis of true knowledge, epistemology uses a transcendent ontological criterion of truth (namely, correspondence with reality or meaning), or a formal-logical one (namely, logical necessity), or finally, a psychological one (the feeling of complete evidence): the criterion used in the evaluation derives from the fundamental discipline adopted. But this involves a paradox:

> Epistemology sets itself the task of solving on its own the problem of the cognitive efficacy of all factual knowledge and of appraising its value; in the course of its inquiry, it pushes this question of value further and further back, until it appears as the problem of the value of the ultimate presuppositions of all knowledge; and finally, it is compelled—after analysis has laid these ultimate presuppositions bare—simply to proclaim them as value (in the case of a skeptical theory, as negative value). [*Ibid.*, p. 68]

But what this means is that the epistemological critique, 'instead of being a critique of knowledge as it pretends', is 'a new systematization of it' (*Wissenssoziologie*, p. 239; cf. *Soc. Soc. Psych.*, pp. 68–69). 'Structural analysis discloses that epistemology actually solves a problem which is entirely different from the one it has set itself. *Instead of a critique of value, it turns into a theory about how a particular value can be attained and realized*' (*Soc. Soc. Psych.*, p. 69). Seen from *within* psychology, ontology, or even logic, nothing valuable or normative is visible; this appears only from a point of view *outside of* psychology, ontology, or logic. Epistemology, which, of course, does lie outside of them, is thus not descriptive (how is it?) but 'constructive' (how must it be?).

In this manner, Mannheim here comes across what he will later call the ideological character of intellectual phenomena, including epistemology. But not yet here, for he does not argue, for instance, that the 'structural analysis' should be supplemented by a sociological analysis. He rather argues that it should be supplemented by an 'inquiry into the mode of presentation of its ultimate presuppositions' which 'could suggest a reason why divergent solutions of the epistemological problem are possible' (*ibid.*, p. 73; italicized in the original).

It is clear that of the two major components of Mannheim's thought, 'idealism' and 'Marxism', the former still dominates his analysis of epistemology, no matter how many things he has discovered in the course of it.

VI. *Historicism* (1924)

In 'Historicism' Mannheim's turn toward society and sociology announces itself by way of history; this turn will be completed in the next paper, that on the sociology of knowledge.

In the epoch following the Middle Ages and the Enlightenment, historicism has become 'the very basis on which we construct our observations of the socio-cultural reality' (*Soc. Knowl.*, p. 85). Historicism treats cultural and historical phenomena not separately or immanently but as parts of something larger, and this may correspond to the transformation of the social structure from the atomization characteristic of liberalism to a greater emphasis on collective features. Epistemology has been replaced as the 'fundamental discipline' by the philosophy of history in the sense of a 'dynamic metaphysic' (*ibid.*, p. 97).

In considering matters in relation to history, Mannheim is halfway between considering them relative to the spirit and relative to society. The 'positional determination' (*Standortsgebundenheit*; *ibid.*, p. 103), the 'perspectivism' of thinking, is still understood more historically than sociologically. But as it did before and will do later, Mannheim's position raises the problem of relativism. He claims that relativism—here the relativity of historical knowledge—by no means follows from the 'positional determination' of knowledge. For the *concrete values* which serve as a standard have *developed* in their fullness of meaning *organically out of the same historical process* which they have to help interpret. There exists, therefore, a subtle bond between thought and reality—subject and object are here essentially identical' (*ibid.*, .p. 104). This passage occurs in Mannheim's extended discussion of Ernst Troeltsch's *Der Historismus und seine Probleme* (1922), which he considers representative of contemporary thinking about the problem. (For his more mature assessment of Troeltsch see his article on him in the *Encyclopaedia of the Social Sciences*, XV.) The correct understanding of historicism is indispensable for the proper foundation of the human studies, especially sociology. How, now, does Troeltsch come to terms with the fact that what is said in the quotation just presented guarantees the applicability of standards and points of view only to the student's own culture, but not an explanation of different pictures of the same historical period that are found in various epochs? Mannheim answers:

The historical subject-matter (such as the historical content of an epoch) remains identical 'in itself', but it belongs to the essential conditions of its cognizability that it can be grasped only from differing intellectual-historical standpoints—in other words, that we can view only various 'aspects' of it. By analogy with the discovery of Husserl [*Ideas*, par. 41]—that it is a characteristic of the spatial object that we can view it only in different 'profiles' (*Ab-*

schattungen), i.e. from definite perspectives—one could, it seems to us, venture the thesis that it is part of the essence of a historico-cultural, but also of a psychic object, that it is penetrable only in 'mental and psychic profiles'. [*Ibid.*, p. 105, modified]

Here, too, then, Mannheim holds on, as we observed before, to the unchangeability of the object of cognition. He relativizes the knowing subject all the more: even its most general characteristics, the categories of reason, change. (Once more: no matter how much this reminds one of his later sociology of knowledge, the *locus* of changeability is still history rather than society.) And so also change logic and epistemology, which are the bases of the structure of thinking that dominates an epoch. Mannheim passionately affirms this changeability. Generalizing from Troeltsch, and doubtless from himself, he writes:

One might still indeed live a self-contained and unblemished life if one were to use as a foundation certain earlier positions whose residues still survive among us. But the pressures which spring from the contemporary situation, once they have penetrated our consciousness, permit now only a going to the limit. In this process, one must demolish all firm foundations under one's feet, and all one can do is to grasp the eternal as a component of the most immediate temporal problems. This means that the prophet and the leader themselves become guilty, but it may be hoped that the radicality of the commitment will compensate for the temporal limitation of the objectives. [*Ibid.*, p. 99]

Even the prophet, the leader (*Führer*), can no longer carry the banner of tradition. But the hope to find validity by the act of commitment itself—an act which is both affective and moral— would be less unclear if Mannheim had asked what it is that man can hope to find in or through such commitment and how this commitment can lead to it. But he does not ask this question, any more than he asked in connection with the previously mentioned theme what is common to the various interpretations of the same historical period that would account for their mutual understandability. In both cases a hypothesis concerning elements common to all men, by means of which they identify with one another and make allowance for the relative, appears as a promising next step.

Instead of taking this step, Mannheim turns to the 'forms of historical movement'. Earlier in the present paper, he speaks of the tendency of life 'to become itself, again and again, a system' (*Wissenssoziologie*, p. 252; cf. *ibid.*, p. 89).[16] Now he poses the question of 'how to combine psychic, that is, a-theoretical,

[16] This thought is closely akin to Simmel's concept of life as 'more-than-life' (which Mannheim does not mention). Cf. Georg Simmel, *Lebensanschauung* (1918), and Rudolph H. Weingartner, *Experience and Culture: The Philosophy of Georg Simmel* (Middletown, Conn.: Wesleyan University Press, 1960), pp. 69–71.

changes with the rational, that is, theoretical, method of intellectual development' (*Wissenssoziologie*, p. 279; cf. *ibid.*, p. 111).
But he does not make use of the results reached in the essay on the
interpretation of *Weltanschauung*—as if he had forgotten the
problem of the theoretical graspability of the a-theoretical,
which was central to that essay and which does return, though in
a subordinate position, in the present one. His answer to the
question of this graspability, which here, too, is positive ('owing
to the essential unity of the rational and irrational in human
consciousness'; *ibid.*, p. 111), sounds like an aside given on the
way to what here is Mannheim's real aim: the identification of
the types of the forms of development that we can read from
history. He modifies Alfred Weber's dichotomy between 'process
of civilization' (to which alone the idea of progress can apply)
and 'movement of culture', and adds the 'dialectic', which
characterizes 'philosophy and some related disciplines' (*ibid.*,
p. 114). Analyzing the first (e.g., technology or natural sciences)
requires no attention to one's own point of view or to that of
the period under study, which, on the contrary, is essential in
regard to existential ('*seelengebundenen*') phenomena (e.g., culture).
To illustrate, then, dialectical development, Mannheim points
to the history of philosophy, which shows that philosophical
systems do not annul or supplement earlier ones but reorganize
themselves from ever new centers, for they have a super-theoretical
or super-philosophical basis, namely, that which is located in
their life-situations—in this sense they 'express the truth of the
epoch concerned' (*ibid.*, p. 117). Every philosophy, thus, has
'a double criterion. One is that of inner truth: that is, whether
a given philosophy can give a consistent account of the scientific
and vital insights which emerge at that particular time. The
second is that of dialectical truth: that is, whether that philosophy
is more comprehensive, broader in scope than the preceding
ones' (*ibid.*, p. 118).

A philosophy of history which proceeds in corresponding
diagnostic fashion must recognize, however, a 'positional determination' in addition to the one mentioned before, namely,
the determination by certain social strata and their tendencies:
it must be enriched by attention to social differentiation—'but
we cannot pursue this subject here any farther' (*ibid.*, p. 125).
This comment is found in the beginning of a short section on
'Historicism and Sociology' in connection with a glowing reference
to Lukács's *History and Class Consciousness* (1923); it probably
marks Mannheim's earliest explicit turn toward sociology.

In the last section, 'Dynamic Standards in Thought and
Practice', Mannheim returns to the problem of relativism.

To say that the absolute itself is unfolding in a genetic process, and that it can be grasped only from definite positions within the same process, in categories which are moulded by the unfolding of the material contact of the genetic flux itself—to say this is not tantamount to professing relativism. What this position denies is only a subject which remains outside of the flux, never changes, and maintains contact with the flux only by a miracle. [*Ibid.*, p. 130]

And in a fashion similar to that in 'Structural Analysis of Epistemology', here, too, Mannheim applies what he has said generally to this very essay, which does 'not claim to have spoken the last word' on its topic; but 'truth in a perspectivic sense means that within one historical constellation only one perspectivic conclusion can be correct' (*ibid.*, p. 130).

Mannheim does not ask, whose 'historical constellation'—his own, his 'generation's', his 'time's'?

*VII.   *The Problem of a Sociology of Knowledge* (1925)

Instead, he completes the turn toward sociology that had 'announced' itself in 'Historicism' a year before. Both 'the vital and the practical as well as the theoretical and intellectual currents of our time seem to point toward a temporary fading out of epistemological problems, and toward the emergence of the *sociology of knowledge* as the focal discipline' (*Soc. Knowl.*, p. 136). Mannheim says this on the basis of his analysis of the contemporary 'problem constellation' which is 'exceptionally favourable' to the sociology of knowledge. This analysis—it could be inferred already from 'historicism'—shows that Mannheim's conviction regarding the state of knowledge in his time is an unanalyzed premise which the explication of his philosophy of history could illuminate. 'If, then', Mannheim says, 'we ask ourselves about *the ultimate, fundamental factors entering into the constellation which necessarily gave rise to the problem of a sociology of thought* [= sociology of knowledge?] in our time' (*ibid.*, p. 136), we find

(1) the self-relativization of thought and knowledge, (2) the appearance of a new form of relativization introduced by the 'unmasking' turn of mind, (3) the emergence of a new system of reference, that of the social sphere, in respect to which thought could be conceived to be relative, and (4) the aspiration to make this relativization total, relating not one thought or idea, but a whole system of ideas, to an underlying social reality. [*Ibid.*, p. 144]

Every part of this 'constellation', as well as the constellation as a whole, seems to threaten us with relativism, and Mannheim tries to meet this threat in a footnote on 'self-relativization', which clarifies the problem as it appeared at this stage of his thinking:

What we mean by 'self-relativization' is by no means epistemological 'relativism' but merely the opposite of 'autonomy'. One may very well assert that thought is 'relative to being', 'dependent on being', 'non-autonomous', 'part of a whole reaching beyond it', without professing any 'relativism' concerning the truth value of its findings. At this point, it is, so to speak, still open whether the 'existential relativization' of thought is to be combined with epistemological relativism or not. In any case, however, we would like to go on record, at this point, that we cannot share the at present widespread fear of relativism. 'Relativism' has become a catchword which, it is believed, will instantly annihilate any adversary against whom it is used. But as to us, we definitely prefer a 'relativism' which accentuates the difficulty of its task by calling attention to all those moments which tend to make the propositions actually discoverable at any given time, partial and situationally conditioned—we prefer such a 'relativism' to an 'absolutism' which loudly proclaims, as a matter of principle, the absoluteness of its own position or of 'truth in itself', but is in fact no less partial than any of its adversaries—and, still worse, is utterly incapable of tackling with its epistemological apparatus the problem of the temporal and situational determination of any concrete process of thought, completely overlooking the way in which this situational conditioning enters into the structure and the evolution of knowledge. [*Ibid.*, p. 137n.]

We notice that not only the argument of his adversaries, such as it is implied here, but also Mannheim's answer, is as vague as it is passionate. This suggests more a conflict between *Weltanschauungen* than a rational or analytical discussion. Even to clarify this conflict so that the validity claims of the two parties could be examined would require an analysis of the words both use to indicate and argue their positions, that is, a kind of 'documentary interpretation' such as Mannheim himself has described it in his essay on *Weltanschauung*. Most of his critics (e.g., those cited in n. 12 above) have instead taken him 'literally', criticizing him with considerable plausibility for being unclear or self-contradictory. To what extent and in what sense Mannheim, on his side, did *not* take his critics literally (but tried to understand or interpret them sociologically or otherwise) is another question, the answer to which would demand a special effort. The essay on interpretation which he wrote shortly after the present one (see VIII) will, if not clarify, at least drive home, the problem of 'literalness'.

The first factor, the self-relativization of thought, again brings 'the danger of a theoretical *circulus vitiosus*' (*ibid.*, p. 137): the thought which relativizes thought thereby invalidates itself. We are acquainted with this danger already from Mannheim's 'Structural Analysis of Epistemology' and from 'Historicism', where (briefly recalling) he answered that positions, though relative, are not arbitrary and can be corrected. This time, he mentions 'only one type of solution': 'if one maintains that the sphere of thought . . . is merely one of *expression* rather than of the ultimate cognitive *constitution of objects*, the contradiction, otherwise insurmountable, becomes devalued' (*ibid.*, p. 138).

In other words, Mannheim continues to hold on to the unchangeability of the objective world that we have observed more than
once before.[17]

Thought can be relativized from or to various spheres—
mystical consciousness, gnosticism, 'or by an empirically investigated sphere, subsequently hypostatized as ultimate reality, such
as the biological or social sphere' (*ibid.*, p. 138; this notion, too,
will be more systematically and completely presented in the
essay on interpretation). Several of these relativizations, Mannheim writes, are not new; what is new is relativization 'with
regard to sociological reality' (*ibid.*, p. 139)—the second factor,
we saw, of the 'problem constellation' of the sociology of knowledge. This particular kind of relativization is undertaken by the
'unmasking turn of mind', which does not aim at simply rejecting
certain ideas so much as at disintegrating them, 'and that in
such a way that the whole world outlook of a social stratum
becomes disintegrated at the same time' (*ibid.*, p. 140). It is
not a matter of *contesting* an idea, which would mean accepting
it as a thesis to be countered by an antithesis (cf. again the essay
on interpretation); instead, an idea is merely considered 'in
terms of the *extra-theoretical function*[18] it serves' (*ibid.*, p. 140).
To unmask an idea, thus, is not to refute it theoretically, but
to destroy its effectiveness; and it differs from the unmasking
of lies, because this also destroys the liar. Combined with the third
and fourth factors of the problem constellation of the sociology
of knowledge (transcendence of thought toward the social sphere
and relativization of an outlook in its entirety—Hegel's 'subjective
beliefs', Marx's 'ideology'), the unmasking of ideas represents a
new kind of interpretation.[19]

[17] A comparison between this position and Arthur Child's regarding the
problem of the categories of thought—particularly Child's concept of 'biotic
categories'—would probably show a considerable similarity between the two.
Cf. Child, 'On the Theory of the Categories', *Philosophy and Phenomenological
Research*, 7 (1946): 316–35, and Wolff, *op. cit.*, pp. 595–600.

[18] On Mannheim and functionalism, see Thelma Z. Lavine, 'Karl Mannheim and Contemporary Functionalism', *Philosophy and Phenomenological
Research*, 25 (1965): 560–71.

[19] In a footnote Mannheim writes: 'Cf. my simultaneously appearing paper,
"Ideologische und soziologische Interpretation" (*Internationales Jahrbuch für
Soziologie*, Band I)'. (In *Wissenssoziologie*, p. 35, n. 12, and in *Soc. Knowl.*,
p. 145n., this footnote is abridged and partly corrected.) The paper referred
to appeared in 1926, not 1925; in Vol. II, not I, of *Jahrbuch für Soziologie*,
and with a slightly different title (see next section and bibliography). The
footnote (in this version only in the 1925 original) does show, however, that
the paper now under discussion was written when that on interpretation,
although it appeared a year later, was completed or at least in the process of
completion.

Mannheim supplements his diagnosis of the time, undertaken in his analysis of the 'problem constellation' of the sociology of knowledge, by stating that we appear to be at that stage 'where the problem of a sociology of knowledge, which up to now belonged to the context of progressive thought, is recognized as a "stubborn reality" and is being tackled as such from other standpoints as well' (*ibid.*, p. 149, modified). It is a task with which *all* contemporary thought must come to terms. But there are above all four positions within that thought from which a sociology of knowlege can be undertaken: (1) positivism, (2) formal apriorism, (3) material apriorism (phenomenology), and (4) historicism. The decisive controversy, however, is between phenomenology (that is, Max Scheler) and historicism (that is, Mannheim himself).

Positivism treats problems, including that of a sociology of knowledge, as matters to be handled by the special sciences. It thus operates with a certain concept of empiricism and is convinced that human knowledge can do without metaphysics and ontology. But 'a doctrine which hypostatizes certain paradigmatic methods, and the reality spheres corresponding to them, as "absolutely" valid, thereby becomes a metaphysic itself—albeit a particularly limited one' (*ibid.*, p. 150). Nevertheless, positivism was 'genuine', namely, a genuine expression of the shift in the center of experience from the spiritual and religious to the social and economic, and this shift led to the discovery of the problem of a sociology of knowledge. Phenomenologically false, however, is its blindness to the irreducible difference between meaning and experience. Yet again, 'genuine' was the insistence on 'devotion to empiricism' (*Empiriefrömmigkeit*) 'which will make metaphysics in the form of pure speculation impossible for all time' (*ibid.*, p. 151). 'We assert, then, that *substantively* positivism has performed the essential turn toward a way of thinking adequate to the contemporary situation; systematically and methodologically, however, it did not rise above a relatively primitive level, since, among other things, it did not realize that its "this-worldly" orientation, too, involves a metaphysic' (*ibid.*, pp. 151–52, modified).

Here, too, an explication of Mannheim's philosophy of history would help clarify the criterion of 'genuine' and the counter-concept it implies ('vicarious'? 'false'? 'apparent'?).

The philosophy of formal validity (formal apriorism) depreciates existence compared with thought, which it tries to comprehend in its own terms, immanently. It is understandable, therefore, that it has produced only the beginnings of a sociology of *culture*, not of a concrete sociology of *knowledge*. Unlike positivism, it does recognize the difference between meaning and being, but it overemphasizes meaning metaphysically, considering formal traits of thought, such as the categories, as autonomous and super-temporal, and it thus misses the 'most essential problem of a sociology of knowledge, namely, the transmutation of the categories and the shift in the hierarchy of spheres [of value]' (*ibid.*, p. 153, modified). Instead, within the framework of this philosophy, a sociology of culture and knowledge can only 'examine the *contentual realizations* of the formal value spheres at a given time' (*Wissenssoziologie*, p. 332; cf. *ibid.*, p. 153).

By far the longest section of the paper is devoted to Scheler ('material apriorism' or 'modern phenomenology'). In his analysis Mannheim, of course, also submits his own ideas. Among them is the conviction—known to us already from the 'Structural Analysis of Epistemology', where, however, it was formulated differently—that at this time the fundamental experience, at least in the German tradition, is the tension between, on the one hand, 'a doctrine of the "timeless" essence of man; on the other . . . [of] the uniqueness of historic objects' (*ibid.*, p. 159). He now also says, after an extended discussion of Scheler, that the 'historicist standpoint, which starts with relativism, attains the point of absoluteness only because in its final form it places the absolute into history itself' (*ibid.*, p. 172, modified). And further in his discussion of relativism:

we understand, looking at things from our perspective, the possibility and necessity of the other perspectives; and no matter what our perspective is, we all experience the controlling 'stubbornness' of the data [*Gegebenheiten*]; thus, we all have every reason to assume that we move in the 'medium of reality', so that we can disclaim all illusionism. [*Ibid.*, p. 173, modified]

This passage may well be one of the most flagrant expressions of Mannheim's alienation from the world. He appears to be unable or unwilling either to take literally his own taking literally of 'naïve realism' (without taking naïve realism literally he might easily miss the train or stumble on the stairs) or to 'bracket' this realism and to consider it as only one possible point of view. He appears to need a kind of 'we-feeling' (which possibly predisposed him to his 'democratization' that is to take place later on in England) in order to intensify the 'stubbornness' of the given—it evidently is not stubborn enough for him—for it to give him a feeling of reality. His circumspection may strike us as comical, but his aloneness and dependence only on himself—perhaps related to similar features in *our*selves—may move and stir us.

He continues in epistemological terms, transforms the 'stubbornness' of the 'data' into that of 'facts', asks why we cannot, like the positivists, rest content with this stubbornness, and answers that this stubbornness consists in the check the facts exert on arbitrary constructions, not in any extra-systematic, isolated meaninglessness, hence ungraspability. But positivism does not see this.

At the end of his analysis of Scheler, Mannheim summarizes the differences between Scheler and himself. In contrast to Scheler, Mannheim considers the duality of being and meaning to be only phenomenological, not ultimate, and holds that their interaction at any given time can be ever more clearly illuminated by a combined approach of philosophy of history and sociology; this approach considers both being and meaning 'as parts of a dynamic genetic *totality*' (*ibid.*, p. 161). In regard to the specific question of a sociology of culture and of knowledge, Mannheim discusses four major differences between himself and Scheler. In the first place, for himself, in contrast to Scheler, even drives are historicized. Secondly, superstructure and substructure stand in a relation of reciprocity. Third: '*Not a pre-existing world is functionalized in history, but "changes in existence" create unpredictable changes in meaning*' (*Wissenssoziologie*, p. 366; omitted in *Soc. Knowl.*). And fourth, Mannheim works, not with epochs and 'culture areas' (*Kulturkreise*), but with social strata: the history of ideas must be supplemented by historical social-structural analysis, since every epoch contains more than one current—indeed, history of ideas becomes sociology of knowledge if it undertakes its investigation with due regard for social strata.

Mannheim acknowledges his conviction of the meaningfulness of the historical process out of which points of view grow, as a metaphysical presupposition of his thinking. 'The entire problem of absolute truth will, then, coincide with that of the nature of this unitary meaning of the process as a whole; the question is how far we are able to grasp the evolutionary goal that *can* be seen at a given moment' (*ibid.*, p. 177). Related to this: 'the mere change of function of an idea already means a change of meaning —this is one of the most essential proofs that history is a creative locus of meaningful contexts and not only the locus in which meaning contexts that are detachable from it and can be conceived as pre-existent are realized' (*Wissenssoziologie*, p. 383; cf. *ibid.*, pp. 187–88). Here, too, we witness Mannheim's endeavor to grasp what manifests itself only indirectly. In the present essay we have met this effort before in the idea of thought as only the expression, not the sphere, 'of the ultimate cognitive constitution of objects' (*ibid.*, p. 138), and have identified it, already in the beginning of this introduction, as the effort, of idealist provenience, to come as close to the spirit as possible.

The 'change of function' mentioned in the next to last quotation is a 'central concept of all sociology of culture and thought' (*ibid.*, p. 188). Mannheim distinguishes between an 'immanent' and a 'sociological' change of function, the former referring to the passing of a concept from one system of ideas to another, the latter to its passing from use by one social group to use by another. It is of particular importance for a central problem of the sociology of knowledge, that of imputation.

In fact, Mannheim begins his discussion of the problem of imputation by asking which categories may serve to connect points of view or outlooks with tendencies of social strata.[20] 'Vulgar' Marxism, in its aim at 'unmasking' ideology, knows only the category of 'interest', which, however, applies only to *homo economicus*, not to the whole person, which is what sociology wishes to understand.

Thus, we cannot assign a style of thought, a work of art, etc., to a group as its own on the basis of an analysis of interests. We can, however, show that a certain style of thought, an intellectual standpoint, is encompassed within a system of attitudes which in turn can be seen to be related to a certain economic and power system; we can then ask which social groups are 'interested' in the emergence and maintenance of this economic and social system and at the same time 'committed' to the corresponding world outlook. [*Ibid.*, p. 184]

In other words, the sociology of knowledge can proceed 'only by taking a circuitous route through the concept of the *total system* of a world outlook (by the circuitous route of a sociology of culture)' (*ibid.*, p. 184, modified). This is Mannheim's solution of the problem of imputation,[21] even though he does not explicitly so announce it. He briefly returns to the problem toward the end of the present paper. He will treat it at greater length in *Ideology and Utopia* without, however, essentially changing his position.

In concluding his essay, he formulates the task of the sociology of knowledge—which, because it must 'bring out' the 'functionality of every social, existentially involved thinking at different levels of being' (*ibid.*, p. 177, modified), should be called sociology of cognition[22]—as follows:

[20] This question and Mannheim's treatment of it are examined by, among others, Schelting and Merton in the writings cited in n. 12 above.

[21] For a survey of this problem, including Mannheim's treatment, see Arthur Child, 'The Problem of Imputation in the Sociology of Knowledge', *Ethics*, 51 (1941): 200–19, and Kurt H. Wolff, 'On the Scientific Relevance of "Imputation"', *Ethics*, 61 (1950): 69–73, and *op. cit.*, p. 603.

[22] Despite its need for being settled, the nature of the difference between the 'sociology of knowledge' (*Wissen*) and of 'cognition' (*Erkennen* or *Erkenntnis*) is hardly more than mentioned by Mannheim, and not even that in the literature on the sociology of knowledge generally. This is also true of the difference between 'sociology of knowledge' and 'sociology of thought' (cf.

The main task consists in specifying, for each temporal cross-section of the historical process, the various systematic intellectual standpoints from which people thought. Once this is done, however, these different trends of thought should not be confronted like positions in a mere theoretical debate, but we should explore their non-theoretical, vital roots. To do this, we first have to uncover the hidden metaphysical premises of the various systematic positions. After we have gained clarity on this, we must ask ourselves (precisely with the help of this metaphysical background) to the 'desires for which worlds' [*welchen Weltwollungen*], that exist within the same epoch, this or that 'style of thought' is imputable. When here, too, the correspondences have been established, we already have identified the intellectual strata combating each other ['intellectual strata' are groups with a common '*Weltwollen*'; *ibid.*, p. 186]. The sociological task proper, begins only after this immanent analysis of the *Weltanschauung*: when we ask which social strata are behind the intellectual strata ['social strata' are, following Marx, defined by their role in the process of production; *ibid.*, p. 186]. [*Ibid.*, p. 189, modified]

We shall see how Mannheim, directly after the paper on interpretation—which only works out and systematizes some of his thoughts already contained in previous writings—applies the program just quoted to a concrete historical topic: conservative thought.

*VIII. *The Ideological and the Sociological Interpretation of Intellectual Phenomena* (1926)

This is a sketch of a typology of interpretations. It begins with the distinction, which we already encountered in the essay on the interpretation of *Weltanschauung*, between the 'theoretical' and the 'pre-' or 'a-theoretical'. Mannheim here applies this distinction to that between various theoretical 'points of view', from which, for instance, one considers natural objects on the one hand and on the other a-theoretical attitude and perspectives. A point of view involves selection, an attitude or perspective, experience and penetration:

While the adoption of different natural-scientific points of view increases our knowledge of the object only quantitatively, different ways of looking at intellectual phenomena and different attitudes toward them enlarge the possibilities of experiencing them and the dimensions of our understanding them. [*Studies on the Left*, p. 56]

The reason for this is that only intellectual phenomena are 'posited' (in the widest, not only theoretical, sense of the word).

---

early in the commentary on the present paper the question [in brackets] whether the two were synonymous for Mannheim). On the unclarity of 'knowledge' in the expression 'sociology of knowledge', on the other hand, there is repeated discussion, most concisely in Robert K. Merton, 'The Sociology of Knowledge', in Georges Gurvitch and Wilbert E. Moore, eds., *Twentieth Century Sociology* (New York: Philosophical Library, 1945), esp. pp. 379–80 (repr. in Merton, *Social Theory and Social Structure, op. cit.*).

The intellectual phenomenon is a *Setzung*—one might also say with John Dewey that it is 'taken', or with certain existentialists that it is a 'commitment'. At any rate, this does *not* apply to natural phenomena, which, by contrast, are 'unmeaning' or 'given'.

Sociological interpretation, being an intellectual phenomenon, is itself a 'positing', is itself 'posited'. For Mannheim, it is based on the metaphysical presuppositions of a hierarchy of being and of two ways of knowing—ideological, on the one hand, socio-logical or dialectical, on the other—which differ according to their dignity. As we know from earlier papers, the sociological interpretation relativizes what it interprets, that is, its *inter-pretandum*. But whether it proceeds in positivist or idealist fashion, in other words, whether the sphere of reality in reference to which relativization proceeds is society, race, drives, or else spirit, mind, reason—in neither case is this sphere 'unmeaning' but on the contrary meaningful: it is the existential basis of the *interpretandum*, not its causal condition. Mannheim thus elaborates the distinction between interpretation and (causal) explanation which we encountered in his 'Structural Analysis of Epistem-ology';[23] he lists causal explanation in his typology, while insisting that it is not an interpretation because it accounts for meaning by reference to something 'unmeaning'. In other words (as was pointed out quite early in this introduction), sociological interpretation does not 'abandon the intellectual sphere'. On the contrary, by going beyond 'intrinsic' interpretation, it succeeds in seeing 'those meaningful existential presuppositions which, although the theory itself that is to be interpreted was not capable of seeing them, nevertheless were the presuppositions (albeit not immanent) of its validity' (*ibid.*, p. 60).

Aside from the typology it offers, this essay is of interest as a document of Mannheim's—and presumably not only Mann-heim's—ambivalence toward 'spirit' and 'society', 'idealism' and 'Marxism'. It is intrinsic, or immanent, interpretation which moves toward the spirit because it aims at the 'idea' of the *interpretandum* rather than at understanding it as 'ideology'. Here Mannheim's ambivalence just referred to shows itself. On the one hand, even in the title of his paper he refers to 'intrinsic interpretation' as ideological, which recalls the 'debunking' of 'vulgar' Marxism. On the other hand, he characterizes the person engaged in intrinsic interpretation as 'absorbed by the intellectual phenomenon' he wishes to interpret; he ' "lives" in it'; his

[23] Again Weber's influence is obvious but again is not mentioned. (Cf. n. 14 above.) On Weber's influence on Mannheim generally, cf. Kecskemeti, *op. cit.*, pp. 25–26.

interpretation 'involves the whole person'—which is not at all an act of debunking but, on the contrary, one of affirmation: the very enthusiastic affirmation of the possibility of grasping the object unmediated by tradition, which we may recall from his review of Lukács (suggesting the 'bracketing' of received notions). Yet he does equate 'intrinsic' with 'ideological' interpretation as if he had forgotten that intrinsic interpretation also has the element of immediacy, absorption, involvement. Whether the interpretation he refers to really is both intrinsic and ideological, and if so, how this is possible, or whether Mannheim has here lumped together heterogeneous phenomena that correspond to different 'attitudes', are questions that do not arise for him.

Thus, he writes:

If I take, for instance, a theoretical statement simply as an idea, that is, 'from within', I am making the same assumptions that are prescribed in it; if I take it as ideology, that is, look at it 'from without', I am suspending, for a time, the whole complex of its assumptions, thus doing something other than what is prescribed in it at first glance. [*Ibid.*, p. 56]

And the questions that come up are: How can I look at something 'from within' except by suspending received notions? For otherwise, I look at it, by definition, in terms of these notions, which I have received in the course of my life, rather than 'from within'. But—and this is the second question—can I look at anything if I have to do without my learning? How can I look other than with the help of the apparatus I have acquired? Thus, is 'intrinsic' interpretation possible at all? Mannheim does not ask these questions either—any more than he asked the related questions that arose for us from his analysis of commitment as a source of validity in his paper on historicism or, in that same paper, from his comments on various interpretations of the same historical period. The present questions, too, could be clarified by an explication of Mannheim's underlying conception of human nature.

The present questions are important not only as general epistemological ones but more directly in regard to Mannheim's sociology of knowledge. We saw that for him sociological interpretation has a metaphysical basis. But from this Mannheim does not draw the conclusion that to accept the findings of such an interpretation is contingent on accepting its underlying metaphysic; nor does he consider the consequences of this for the scientific or philosophical status of the sociology of knowledge. We again encounter what on the occasion of a passage from the preceding paper we called his 'circumspection' and his 'alienation from the world'. In the present essay, however, we also find additional and different features of his 'existential situation'. Thus he writes:

Whatever at a given time is the latest theory, is accepted immanently, as an idea, in the same way as those 'ideas' were once accepted that extrinsic interpretation has since relativized as ideology. That is, the most highly developed system in which we ourselves are caught at any one time can be grasped only as idea, and it takes 'existing', social and historical 'existing on', for the higher meaning of our own view of the world some day to reveal itself. [*Ibid.*, p. 61]

This is neither circumspect nor uncertain but at the same time tragic and optimistic: at no time do we know the whole truth, but we shall know ever more of it. Implied is a variant of the chiliastic vision that we met with already in the 'Structural Analysis of Epistemology' and that, once again, calls for explication, which, however, it does not receive either here or in a closely related passage to be found three years later (1929) in *Ideology and Utopia*, a passage which recommends the sociology of knowledge as a supplement, so to speak, of mere 'existing, on':

We have altogether too much the tendency to accept as 'objective', elements, categorial structures, and ultimate postulates which we ourselves have unwittingly read into our experience and which subsequently reveal themselves to the sociologist of knowledge as partial axioms that are relative historically and to the point of view of a particular current. After all, nothing is more self-evident than that precisely those forms of thought in which we ourselves think reveal themselves least of all in their particularity and that only the onflowing historical-social stream creates the distance from which the eventual particularity becomes visible. [*Ideologie und Utopie*, p. 163; cf. *Ideology and Utopia*, p. 167][24]

*IX. *Conservative Thought* (1927)

If the essay on the problem of a sociology of knowledge signifies Mannheim's turn toward sociology, that on conservative thought means a perhaps even more important turn: toward the world. No matter what the theme of the investigations was thus far, the stress always lay on the subject—'subject' in the sense all the way from Mannheim himself to the time out of which or for which he spoke. The central questions were: Where are we? How can we interpret? How must we judge or revise interpretations and types of interpretations? What does 'knowledge' mean? How am I to assess historicism, how the sociology of knowledge, as approaches to the world? And again: what different modes of interpretation are there? The accent, thus, was not only on the problem of interpretation—there, more or less, it will remain later on, too—but, within this problem, on the interpreter. That is, the decisive question did not concern that which is to be interpreted, the world, but the intellectual and emotional nature and the historical and, later, sociological origins and conditions of him who seeks to understand the world.

[24] The German edition (1929) will henceforth be referred to as *I.U.*; the English edition (1936), as *I.U.* Engl., or Engl.

In 'Conservative Thought' Mannheim turns to other people and to another time, just as in subsequent writings he treats less 'subjective' sociological problems (e.g., of generations, of cultural competition, of sociology in Germany, of economic ambition; more generally he treats our time and society with their problems and chances), even though he remains predominantly interpretive rather than explanatory.

We can only speculate on the reasons for the shift from—to put it briefly—the subject to the object. Did Mannheim feel that the work he had done had prepared him to apply its attainments so that it was time for him to try such application? In any event, not only his writing from the present essay onward witnesses the shift, but so do also his seminars at the University of Frankfurt in the early thirties— on conservatism, liberalism, etc.—in which he insisted that participants study primary sources, as well as the doctoral theses that he supervised and to a number of which he refers in his later writings.

In contrast to traditionalist thought, which Mannheim understands as a psychological trait, conservative thought is a historical and social phenomenon. Therefore, a traditionalist reaction to the new can be predicted, whereas the question of the conservative response 'can only be determined approximately *if we know a good deal about the conservative movement* in the period and in the country under discussion' (*Soc. Soc. Psych.*, p. 95).

Political conservatism is an 'objective mental structure' (*ibid.*, p. 96). Hence it outlasts the individual which temporarily adopts it but which by itself could not create it. It is a mental structure the nature of which neither nominalism nor realism do justice to. For nominalism 'always tries to dissolve the objective structure into the isolated experiences of individuals', while realism means by 'the objective' something metaphysical, independent of individuals, 'constant and normative (preexisting)' (*ibid.*, p. 96). Thus, what Mannheim means by an 'objective mental' or historic-dynamic structure is 'culture' in the anthropological sense. It is among Durkheim's 'social facts', to which Durkheim, too, did not apply the term 'culture'.

Mannheim sees the fundamental reason for the emergence of modern conservatism and for what is common to all its varieties among different nations in 'the dynamic character of the modern world' (*ibid.*, p. 101). This dynamism, in turn, derives from social differentiation, which

tends to draw the human intellect along with it and forces it to develop along its own lines; and ... the basic aims of the different social groups do not merely crystallize ideas into actual movements of thought, but also create different antagonistic *Weltanschauungen* and different antagonistic *styles* of thought. [*Ibid.*, p. 101]

This series of processes is unthinkable without class conflict. Mannheim holds, therefore, that traditionalism can develop into conservatism only in a class society.

In the first half of the nineteenth century, conservative thought in Germany is characterized above all by its emphasis on the concrete and on property. Even the Left, thus Marx, learns from the conservative complaint, which goes back to feudalistic thought, about the 'abstractness of human relationships under capitalism' (*ibid.*, p. 105). Whereas progressive or liberal thought considers the actual by reference to the possible in terms of the normative, conservatism, on the contrary, sees 'the actual as the product of real factors' and understands 'the norm in terms of the actual' (*ibid.*, p. 109). And while progressive thought derives the significance of the particular ultimately from a utopia of the future or from some higher norm, conservatism takes it from the past, from something 'pre-formed in the germ' (*Wissenssoziologie*, p. 437; cf. *Soc. Soc. Psych.*, p. 111). For the conservative the picture of things as a whole is inclusive and detailed; for the progressive it is more like a rough blueprint or groundplan. For the conservative the present is the last stage of the past, for liberalism the beginning of the future. The conservative experience of history is spatial, the successive becomes the next-to and into-one-another—and in his 'Morphology of conservative thought' (*Soc. Soc. Psych.*, pp. 102–19), Mannheim formulates comparable contrasts in regard to concepts like freedom and nation. But

the main thing is that this insistence upon 'concreteness', along with all the other features we have described, is a symptom of the conservative's experiencing the historical process in terms of relationships and situations which exist only as hangovers from the past, and that the impulses to act which spring from this way of experiencing history also are centred upon past relationships still surviving in the present. [*Ibid.*, p. 114]

In order to constitute itself as opposition to Enlightenment and liberalism, the conservative 'basic intention' (*ibid.*, p. 97) had to have been lived, experienced. The sociology of knowledge must both describe this basic intention and trace its development. Thereby the most important task

is to find out how far any new trend of thought that may happen to arise reflects the sociological characteristics of the group or individuals who stand behind it and through whom it finds expression. Phenomenological and logical stylistic analysis and sociological analysis must be used as complementary methods. [*Ibid.*, p. 119]

To illustrate such a sociological analysis, Mannheim chooses the romantic-feudalistic trend, shows how Romanticism became feudalistic, and feudalistic thought became Romantic, and how this movement in opposition to the Enlightenment became linked with historicism. In the beginning the romantic-feudalistic trend was represented by strata little involved with modern capitalism—petty bourgeois, and especially sons of Protestant parsons; in its full development, however, by 'socially freely suspended' ('socially unattached') intellectuals (Mannheim acknowledges this long-since famous expression as Alfred Weber's coinage; *ibid.*, p. 125, n. 1), many of whom were saved from starvation by entry into officialdom. They, and not those who according to their social location might be expected to be concerned with the fate of society as a whole, had the best chance of developing a perspective based on sociology or philosophy of history. Beginning in the eighteenth century,

the fate of the world of thought is in the care of a socially unattached, or barely attached, stratum whose class affinities and status in society cannot be precisely defined; a stratum which does not find the aims it pursues within itself but in the interests of strata with a more definite place in the social order. ... If ... there were no such stratum ... it might easily happen that all spiritual content would disappear from our increasingly capitalistic society and leave nothing but naked interests. [*Ibid.*, p. 128]

To Mannheim's passionate affirmation of thinking, which we encountered in his essay on the interpretation of *Weltanschauung*, he now adds that of its bearers (on which also see several passages in *Ideology and Utopia*, notably pp. 136–46, esp. p. 141). Whether their description is distorted by Mannheim's involvement must remain undecided. If it is, the turn from subject to object would not have been sharp enough to avoid it; that is, Mannheim would have gone back to the subjective, perhaps even to his own projection. This would have to be criticized, for he was presumably seeking the 'other' rather than himself. Such a critique, if it does apply here, does *not* apply to his characterization of the Romantic perspective, for this characterization concerns a possible relation of man, thus ourselves included, to the world. It takes its departure from a quotation from Novalis:

The world must be romanticized. That is the way to its original meaning. Romanticizing means nothing but *raising to a higher level of quality*. Through that operation the lower self is identified with a higher self, since our soul consists of a series of qualitatively different levels. This operation is still completely unknown. *In giving a noble meaning to the vulgar, a mysterious appearance to the commonplace, the dignity of the unknown to the known, the semblance of infinity to the finite*, I romanticize it. [*Ibid.*, pp. 128–29; Mannheim's, not Novalis's, italics]

Mannheim comments in a footnote that the Romantic perspective has not only a concealing character but also 'is fruitful in fields where interpretation is appropriate', because 'the spiritual sphere may be penetrated to various "depths"'. A 'phenomenological analysis', however, would also have to show that the romantic preoccupation with these 'depths' was not a true one. The predominance of the subjective approach introduced an arbitrary element into its interpretations and prevented the thinker from really getting inside his subject. This also explains the possibility of abuse to which the method of 'romanticizing' lends itself: the tendency to interpret, or understand 'from within', causally interrelated situations which, by their objective nature, are incapable of such interpretation, and to dignify mean and brutal power relationships by 'interpreting' them. Significantly enough, the possibility of a twofold interpretation is already contained in Novalis's definition: one which attempts to sound the 'depths' of the soul, and a second which leads to an ideological dressing-up of things as they are. The romantic movement realized both possibilities. [*Ibid.*, p. 129, n. 2]

This interpretation of the romantic perspective is, at the same time, a critique. Furthermore, as a critique it says something about the world that we had not yet encountered in Mannheim before. We have found repeatedly that his discussions of relativism presuppose his conviction of an unchangeable, identical world. What is new is the division of the world into interpretable and noninterpretable parts, and new is a methodological observation, namely, that it is erroneous to interpret the not-to-be-interpreted —the danger of concealing, 'ideologicizing' romanticization (which, in passing, he refers to as 'abuse' of 'romanticizing'). On the other hand, we have seen more than once that Mannheim warns against the danger of not interpreting what has to be interpreted (e.g., an idea, in contrast to its emergence or disappearance in space and time), but of explaining it. On such occasions, however, the bisection of the world—which presumably is to be understood ontologically—had not been developed even to the point now reached, although even now Mannheim does not think of a more explicit formulation of his ontology and epistemology. Yet he was keenly sensitive to misplaced romanticizing—witness also his insistence

that it would be an ill-advised mysticism which would shroud things in romantic obscurity at a point where rational cognition is still practicable. [Indeed:] anyone who wants to drag in the irrational where lucidity and acuity of reason still must rule by right [one variant of which is: 'anyone who wants to interpret where explaining is possible and hence required'] merely shows that he is afraid to face the mystery at its legitimate place [one variant of which is: 'where explanation, by the nature of things, is misplaced']. [*Soc. Knowl.*, p. 229]

It may be recalled that this is part of a passage (from 'Competition as a Cultural Phenomenon', XI below, a paper a year later than the one under discussion) which was quoted at the beginning of this introduction, with the comment that it 'might serve as a motto to much of Mannheim's work'.

Mannheim's comparison between French and German conservatism during the first half of the nineteenth century is a brilliant example of the synthesis between the sociology of knowledge, as the subject's *approach*, and certain historical, political, and cognitive phenomena—*objects* to which this approach leads. The French and German variants of conservatism militate against the two variants of modern rationalism: in France the examination of the roots of the Revolution focuses on 'the metaphysical and religious premises of the eighteenth century' (*Soc. Soc. Psych.*, p. 145), while the thrust of German romanticism is directed against 'the logical and methodological artifices' (*ibid.*, p. 146, modified). For in France, Catholicism supplies the metaphysical foundation of the counter-revolution, but in Germany the Catholic-Protestant split destroyed the unity of such a foundation, which resulted in a withdrawal into methodological problems. Furthermore, the Revolution had not taken place in German, where, therefore,

one could afford to thresh out differences of *Weltanschauung* on this very abstract plane. As soon as the sociological situation became more critical (after 1830) and conservatism, even in Protestant Prussia, had to retire to the stronghold of theism, considerations of dogma and metaphysics came again into the foreground. [*Ibid.*, p. 146]

The various elements of conservatism may be summarized by the idea of 'life' fighting against 'concept'. Mannheim's analysis of this phenomenon has a brilliance of synthesis similar to that of the difference between French and German conservatism, as will be illustrated by some excerpts:

Revolutionary thought derives its force from the desire to realize a rationally well-defined pattern of perfection of the social and political order. Conservative thought, opposed to the fulfilment of utopia, is forced to consider why the actually existing state of society fails to correspond to such a rational pattern. This impulse which is primarily anchored in self-interest at the same time renders conservatism sensitive to all those factors which revolutionary thought —again in its own vital interest—overlooks, viz., the non-rational factors in actual development. But whereas revolutionary thought conceives such irrationalities—where it sees them at all—as imperfections of reality compared with reason, conservative thought . . . attributes to them the character of superrationality. It is, however, not merely a question of inverted values, but rather of different categories and contents of life and experience. This is shown, for instance, by the fact that the irrationality experienced as super-rationality leads to that class of philosophies which might be called in a word 'philosophies of Life', the philosophies which put forward, in opposition to mere reason, sometimes 'history', sometimes 'spirit', sometimes 'life'. The great polarities of nineteenth-century philosophical thought: 'being' and 'thinking', 'concept' and 'idea', 'speculation' and 'praxis', even if they arose as intrinsic elements of philosophic systems, are nourished and held together as standpoints by the corresponding political polarities of the will for a liberal as against a conservative world. [*Ibid.*, pp. 147–49, modified; cf. *Wissenssoziologie*, pp. 484–85]

Despite all differences, all philosophies of life reject bourgeois rationalizing thought in its two major variants, Kantianism and positivism. Their 'great importance' consists in the urgency with which they point out

that whatever passes for 'real' in our rationalized world is merely a reflection of the specific categories of Reason of which modern man has made an idol; in other words, that this world of alleged reality is merely the world of capitalist rationalization, which as such hides a world of 'pure experience' that lies behind it. But even today the philosophy of Life betrays its conservative origin in that it constitutes a latent opposition to the rationalist world which surrounds us. Being, however, depoliticized in the largest sense of the term, it can find no direct way of changing things; it has intrinsically given up the 'becoming' world, which, to be sure, only 'becomes' along rationalized lines. Nevertheless, the philosophy of Life, in all its peculiar character, is, of course, a function of *the contemporary becoming of the world—and a very important one at that. It keeps alive a certain germ of experience; and it is the question of later syntheses which combinations it will enter. [In a footnote Mannheim points to connections between Bergson and fascism and between Sorel and syndicalist direct action.] . . . It always splits up and relativizes what we believe to be 'rational' and 'objective'. [*Ibid.*, p. 162, modified; cf. *Wissenssoziologie*, pp. 504–5]

However brilliant, this analysis also shows a strange combination of perspicacity and myopia. It is perspicacious in respect to the sphere of the spirit as that of cognitive relation to the world in which the rational and the irrational must find their proper places; this sphere is distinguished from 'life' as political reality and social and mass psychology. But saying this also signals what is myopic about his analysis: Mannheim speaks of a world in process of rationalization; he speaks of the depoliticized nature of the philosophy of life, while at the time of his writing Fascism was five years old—but perhaps it was a local Italian phenomenon, and it might not have seemed possible to Mannheim that a fanatic like Hitler, of whom he knew, of course, could mean anything like Nazism, which took power six years later. Personal and other memories suggest that he had a hard time taking Nazism quite seriously enough even in the early part of 1933.[25] The mixture of perspicacity and myopia could perhaps be described—recalling the comment on his characterization of romanticism—as being too much taken by what was to be interpreted and paying too little attention to the explanation of 'things as they are' (which in the meantime had become much clearer than they had been in Novalis's time).

A Note on '. . . the State as an Organism'

This may be the likeliest juncture for mentioning 'The History of the Concept of the State as an Organism: A Sociological

[25] When Mannheim is supposed to have said that it could last hardly two months: Heinz Maus, 'Bericht über die Soziologie in Deutschland 1933 bis 1945', *Kölner Zeitschrift für Soziologie und Sozialpsychologie*, II (1959): 72.

Analysis', because its content and concern are more closely related to the much longer essay on conservatism just considered than to any other single writing by Mannheim. This may be the reason why in the *Essays on Sociology and Social Psychology* Paul Kecskemeti has it follow the paper on conservatism; but the dating is uncertain: in his introduction to the volume, Kecskemeti only refers to it as 'an unpublished paper' and indicates that it was written in English (*ibid.*, p. 11; cf. p. 172). The only writing by himself which Mannheim mentions is 'Conservative Thought' (*ibid.*, p. 175); the latest publication referred to in a footnote dates from 1939, which proves little on the date of the essay because Kecskemeti or even Mannheim himself may have added some references that had become available since the original writing (as is true in regard to some other papers where we do know the date of publication but are not informed of the authorship of such references). As in 'Conservative Thought', Mannheim speaks of 'styles of thought' (*ibid.*, p. 165) and argues that his position is not one of relativism (*ibid.*, p. 181). He has something to say on 'distance' (*ibid.*, p. 180), on which there is much more in 'The Democratization of Culture' of 1933 (XVII (3) below), and which reminds one very much of Simmel, whom Mannheim does not mention, however. Other indications of the neighborhood to 'Conservative Thought' and other early writings may be gleaned from the final paragraphs of the paper, which at the same time give an inkling of its content:

Let me sum up in a few statements the main results of the inquiry.

1. In the development of the patterns of thinking there is a continuous interchange between the ways of thinking in the natural sciences and political thought.

2. But the nature of that process cannot adequately be understood if we confine our observation to causal influences and only think in terms of reciprocal causation. Behind the development of the two concepts [of the state], mechanism and organism, there stood the development of two corresponding styles of thought.

3. Thus the origin, unity, dissemination and decay of these styles of thought is a problem in itself and has to be investigated with the same accuracy as the various styles in the history of art or literature. This does not mean that scientific thinking is nothing but a kind of artistic activity, but only that our approach to the various spheres of reality does not emerge out of the vacuum, that it does not proceed in terms of mere accumulation, but that there is a kind of cohesion, an inner unity in the changing patterns of thinking.

4. On the other hand, this is only the subjective aspect of the process. The unifying *Weltanschauung*, the styles of thought in their turn are not absolute entities. They do not appear out of the blue, they are somewhere connected with social history.

5. Once this has been agreed the next task is to find the connecting link with social history. This cannot be found simply in the socal classes themselves, as Marxism asserts. ... The key to changes in our thought is to be found— as I have tried to show—in the changing practice both of science and politics.

If the main patterns of action are disclosed, then we can further inquire whether this was brought about by the rise of some new class or group, and its changed attitudes towards society.

6. Through the Sociology of Knowledge a new approach to the problems of political science becomes possible. [This sentence would seem to suggest the neighborhood of the paper to 'The Prospects of Scientific Politics' in *Ideology and Utopia* (XIV below).] A careful analysis of the specific nature of political practice and of its various forms might disclose the main changes in its modes of thought.

This also might throw light upon the deeper unity which underlies scientific and political development. [*Ibid.*, pp. 181–82]

x.   *The Problem of Generations* (1927)

In the article on the Sociology of Knowledge that Mannheim wrote for the *Handwörterbuch der Soziologie* (1931; XV below) and a translation of which was added to the 1936 edition of *Ideology and Utopia* (pp. 237–80),[26] he discusses 'social processes influencing the process of knowledge' (p. 240), of which competition is 'a representative case' (p. 241). For what may seem to be purely theoretical positions are the more or less direct consequences of differences in *Weltanschauung*, which, 'in turn, are invisibly guided by the antagonism and competition between concrete, conflicting groups' (p. 242). He continues:

To mention only one of the many other possible bases of collective existence, out of which different interpretations of the world and different forms of knowledge may arise, we may point to the role played by the relationship between differently situated generations. . . . From the knowledge derived from our studies on competition and generations, we have concluded that what, from the point of view of immanent intellectual history, appears to be the 'inner dialectic' in the development of ideas, becomes, from the standpoint of the sociology of knowledge, the rhythmic movement in the history of ideas as affected by competition and the succession of generations (p. 242).

Thus, as Mannheim says three years after pub ishing his paper on generations, this paper, too, belongs in the problem area of the sociology of knowledge, although we might not expect if from its title—and indeed even the text is much less persuasive on this score than is his paper on competition (XI).

The present essay begins with a history of the treatment of the problem of generation and then turns to its main task, the clarification of concepts needed for the analysis of the problem. A generation, first of all, is not a 'concrete group'; one belongs to a generation as one belongs to a social class: for reasons, though very different in the two cases, not of one's choosing; and one may or may not be aware of one's location in generation or class. Chronological simultaneity is one of two elements that constitute a 'generation status' (*Generationslagerung*; *Soc. Knowl.*, p. 302);

[26] The following page references are to this edition.

the other is belonging to 'the same historico-social space—the same historical life community' (*Wissenssoziologie*, p. 542; cf. *Soc. Knowl.*, p. 303). If a third element is added—'*participation in the common destiny* of this historical and social unit'—we have a 'generation as an actuality' (*Generationszusammenhang*; *ibid.*, p. 303). Within the 'generation as an actuality', there are 'generation units', persons united by more concrete bonds than those who generally make up the 'generation as an actuality', namely, by the fact that they 'work up the material of their common experiences in different specific ways' (*ibid.*, p. 304). For instance, both the romantic-conservative and the rationalist-liberal youth belonged in the same generation as an actuality, within which each of them, however, represented a 'generation unit'. The frequency with which the potential characteristic of a 'generation status' becomes active has to do with the tempo of social change (cf. *ibid.*, p. 309).

Generational change is one among the factors of history. Mannheim raises the question of an order of these factors,[27] which may well be not the same at all times. Generational change has different chances in different intellectual spheres: they are much slighter in the sphere of 'civilization', because of its straight-line development, than in that of 'culture'.[28]

This 'formal-sociological' (*ibid.*, p. 288) paper separates some matters that are often confused. It is more concerned with the 'world' than with the subject, and argues a cultural, rather than biological, understanding of the problem of generations, although 'culture' and 'cultural' are used as general social-scientific terms as little as they were in 'Conservative Thought'. The concepts and the distinctions among them that Mannheim develops serve the enrichment of interpretation by contributing to the articulation of the *interpretandum* (object).

As to this *interpretandum* itself, that is, substantively, the most relevant part of the paper is that which deals with the history of interest in the problem and of the various approaches to it. This relevance is well brought home in the following footnote:

It is a matter for historical and sociological research to discover at what stage in its development, and under what conditions, a class becomes class-conscious, and similarly, when individual members of a generation become conscious of their common situation and make this consciousness the basis of their group solidarity. Why have generations become so conscious of their unity

[27] Such as Max Scheler (whom Mannheim does not mention here) has sketched it: 'Probleme einer Soziologie des Wissens', in his *Die Wissensformen und die Gesellschaft* (1924, 1926) (Leipzig: Neuer Geist, 1926), esp. pp. 5–6.

[28] On this distinction by Alfred Weber as discussed in Mannheim's paper on historicism, cf. the comment in VI above.

to-day? This is the first question we [would] have to answer in this context. [*Ibid.*, p. 290]

'Today' was 1927; the time since, and especially the last few years, has greatly enlarged the material on which to draw for such an inquiry, and it has made it far more pressing.

XI. *Competition as a Cultural Phenomenon* (1928)

Mannheim meant this paper to be a contribution not only to the theme but, thereby, 'to a sociological theory of the mind' [29] (*Soc. Knowl.*, p. 191). Once more he advances his distinction between intrinsic and extrinsic interpretation, most explicitly developed in the paper of two years before, by saying more specifically:

I think a consistent application of the method of sociological analysis to mental life will show that many phenomena originally diagnosed as manifestations of immanent laws of the mind may be explained [?] in terms of the prevailing structural pattern of social life. [*Ibid.*, p. 192, modified]

And coming directly to his topic:

the so-called 'dialectical' . . . form of the development and movement of the life of the spirit can be largely traced back to two very simple structural determinants of social life: to the existence of *generations* and to the existence of the phenomenon of *competition*. [*Ibid.*, p. 193, modified; *Wissenssoziologie*, p. 569]

And in a footnote Mannheim refers to his paper on the problem of generations, which 'is closely related to the present one—both are contributions to a sociology of the mind' (*ibid.*, p. 193n.). Notice that these two exclusive 'structural determinants' become three years later (cf. the beginning of the preceding section) only examples of 'social processes'.

It was the task of a generation that had lived through the French Revolution to discover the 'phenomenology of the spirit', the philosophy of history, and thus the bearing of the *time in history* in which intellectual products originate on these products. Today at least one of our urgent tasks is to explore the bearing of *society* on intellectual matters. This proposition, evidently, is not only a piece of Mannheim's diagnosis of his time, such as we have found before (and such as here, too, demands the illumination of its presuppositions). It also shows a parallel of Mannheim's own shift, from 'Historicism' and 'The Problem of a Sociology of Knowledge', from history to society, indeed from historicism

[29] Cf. Mannheim, 'Towards the Sociology of the Mind; an Introduction' (XVII (1) below), *Soc. Cult.*, pp. 15–89, which, according to Ernest Manheim, the editor of the volume, was 'written largely during the last years of Mannheim's stay in Germany' (Introduction, p. 1, first sentence), that is, in the early thirties.

to sociology of knowledge. There is nothing to indicate that Mannheim was aware of this parallel (mirroring, reflection, projection?), which, of course, does not necessarily make it less impressive.

He says that despite the very general title of his paper (literally, 'The Significance of Competition in the Area of the Spiritual'), he will limit himself, not only to thought but, within thought, to *seinsverbundene* ('existence-related'[30]) thought, that is, historical, political, everyday thought and thought in the social sciences and the humanities; in it, 'to use Dilthey's phrase', 'the whole man' thinks. *Seinsverbundenheit* ('existentiality') or *Seinsrelativität* ('relativity to existence') means that 'certain qualitative features of an object encountered in the living process of history are accessible only to certain historico-social structures of consciousness' (in the original, italics; *ibid.*, p. 194, modified). He had said something very similar in his essay on interpretation, namely, that 'the capacity to grasp an idea as ideological is unthinkable prior to a certain time in history' (*Studies on the Left*, p. 55). But once more, this is not relativism ('under which everybody and nobody is right') but 'a *relationism* which says that certain (qualitative) truths cannot even be grasped, or formulated, except in the framework of an existential correlation between subject and object [that is, except *seinerelativ*, relative to existence]' (*Soc. Knowl.*, p. 194).

He points out that 'competition' is an economic category, which he does not hesitate, however, to apply to non-economic matters, since the social 'became visible at first in the economic sphere' (*ibid.*, p. 195)—cf. a similar thought in the essay on economic ambition (XIII) and below. That for which competing

[30] Commonly translated (e.g., *Soc. Knowl.*, p. 193) as 'existentially-determined', and the noun, *Seinsverbundenheit*, as 'existential determination', which, however, as the literal translation of *seinsverbunden* (in parentheses in the text above) indicates, is misleading, because it prejudges the relation as one of determination. The noun seems well rendered as 'existentiality', which, however, cannot, except misleadingly, be used in adjectival form. For the adjective, the literal 'existence-related', though awkward, may do, although in many cases a paraphrase can be used to avoid awkwardness without distorting sense. Elsewhere I wrote: '*Seinsverbundenheit* is an untranslatable term, a key term in Mannheim's writings on the sociology of knowledge, perhaps coined by him [or so he seems to claim: *I.U.*, p. 32, n. 3 (cf. Engl., p. 69, n. 2)]; its use abounds in [Ernst] Grünwald [*Das Problem der Soziologie des Wissens*, 1934] and other writers on the area as well. Cf. Karl Mannheim, *Ideology* and *Utopia* . . . 1936, p. 239n., where the English translation of the term as "social determination" is qualified as leaving "the meaning of 'determination' open" [determination may *not* be determination?]; "existentiality" seems better (although not usable in adjectival form)': 'Ernst Grünwald and the Sociology of Knowledge: A Collective Venture in Interpretation', *Journal of the History of the Behavioral Sciences*, I (1965): 154, n. 5.

partners struggle is the 'public interpretation of reality' (*ibid.*, p. 196; Mannheim acknowledges his adoption of this term from Heidegger), which can be attained by means of four different social processes: through *consensus* by spontaneous cooperation, by virtue of the *monopolistic position* of one group which does the interpreting, on the basis of the *atomistic competition* of many groups, and 'on the basis of a *concentration* round one point of view of a number of formerly atomistically competing groups, as a result of which competition as a whole is gradually concentrated around a few poles which become more and more dominant' (*ibid.*, p. 198). In any one period and place, more than one of these processes is usually at play, even though one tends to be dominant.

We find the first process (spontaneous consensus), which is more static than dynamic, 'in socially homogeneous strata or societies, where the range and basis of experience is uniform and where the fundamental incentives or impulses to thought tend to be the same for all individuals' (*ibid.*, p. 199). As among children and in everyday wisdom, here, too, the 'it' ('it is so', 'it shall be so') dominates thought.

The second type (monopolistic interpretation) is based on the monopolistic position of a stratum, usually a status group, such as the medieval clergy or the Chinese literati, whose position is secured by intellectual or other means or, usually, by both. While the homogeneity of opinion in the first case is spontaneous, here it is artificial. The basis of thought is given, often laid down in sacred books, and thinking largely consists in the interpretation of texts rather than of reality. The tension and conflict between the cultural elites and the aspirations of the laity in the late Middle Ages—from here on, Mannheim proceeds historically, where he had begun systematically—leads to the breakdown of the clergy's monopoly and thus to the third of the four processes, 'atomized competition', in which court nobles, patricians, members of the 'grand' bourgeoisie and high finance, and medium and petty bourgeois participate, engendering a way of thinking for which the Cartesian doubt is paradigmatic.

But just as in the area of economic competition, entrepreneurs join forces in employers' associations and workers in labor unions, so in the intellectual sphere, too, the third process, atomization, leads to the fourth, concentration around polarities. Intellectual currents spread and in so doing also absorb elements of other currents. It is

impossible to achieve an understanding of the modern process of concentration of intellectual points of view as long as one focuses only on the filiations and the interplay of particular motifs that appear on the surface, rather than on the fundamentally decisive filiations and splits in the collective will, which alone can give meaning to the partial movements of the history of motifs. [*Ibid.*, p. 210, modified; *Wissenssoziologie*, p. 590]

Although here, too, Mannheim fails to explicate his premises or to give methodological instructions on, for instance, how to distinguish between 'surface' and what is 'fundamentally decisive', this passage, nevertheless, is as timely as it was when Mannheim wrote it.

At this juncture, he again undertakes a diagnosis of his time. We find ourselves at the stage or phase (into which he has de-systematized and historicized his 'processes' in the course of this paper) of concentration, which is without any homogeneous order that could incorporate new facts. Indeed, unless consensus or monopoly are going to prevail, we shall reach a point where every new fact will call in question even this heterogeneous order. Philological and historical research into the elements of our thinking is required if we want to demonstrate that polarization is taking place in it; Mannheim instead discusses, as an ideal-typical example, the problem of 'value-free knowledge' (*ibid.*, p. 216).

He finds three positions concerning this problem: liberalism, for which value judgments must be eliminated as irrational; conservatism, for which even the rational is tied to *Weltanschauungen* and thus is irrational; and socialism, for which the opponent is irrational because bound by interests. As far as the conservative is concerned, the motives derived from interests that are at work in him, do not enter his field of vision:

For if the structure of society is such that its institutions guarantee our interests and chances, interested motives are, so to speak, appropriated by the objective structure. If I simply live according to these institutions, I never need become aware of these motives. They, then, will not be revealed by introspection. [*Ibid.*, p. 217, modified][31]

Proletarian thought has all the keener an eye for this structure of thought—in others. In respect to his own thought, the proletarian has either followed the liberal mode, absolutizing this thought, in line with the tradition of natural law, as 'pure theory', or, under the influence of historicism, has discovered that it, too, is tied to irrational interests. These, however,

---

[31] The last two sentences imply a severe critique of central aspects of Talcott Parsons's sociology (which, of course, had hardly existed at the time—the year, 1928, when the present essay by Mannheim appeared also was the year Parsons published his first paper, which he has not reprinted). Cf. esp. Parsons, 'The Motivation of Economic Activities' (1940), in his *Essays in Sociological Theory* (Glencoe, Ill.: Free Press, 1949), 1954, and *The Social System*, (Glencoe, Ill.: Free Press), 1951.

he let coincide with the idea of truth with the help of the notion of pre-established harmony. (The particular class interest of the proletariat is at the same time the interest of the whole; class consciousness is the adequately correct consciousness—the Marx-Lukács line.) [*Ibid.*, p. 218, modified; *Wissenssoziologie*, p. 600]

The polarization that Mannheim has sketched with regard to the idea of value-free knowledge characterizes most concepts and indeed 'affects the very categorial apparatus of thinking itself'. 'I could further show you', he continues,

how apparently simple, basic problems and facts—which one might think could be interpreted in only one way—such as what 'praxis' is, how its relation to 'theory' is to be conceived, are seen differently according to the pole in the social and political differentiation at which one finds oneself. [*Wissenssoziologie*, p. 600; cf. *Soc. Knowl.*, p. 218]

And at this point, he appends a note:

I try to give an extensive analysis of this example from the point of view of the sociology of knowledge in my study, 'Is Politics Possible as a Science?' [translated as 'The Prospects of Scientific Politics']. Contained in my book, *Ideology and Utopia*, in press. [*Wissenssoziologie*, p. 601, n. 17; cf. *Soc. Knowl.*, p. 218n.]

This, presumably, is the earliest reference to his first book.

Mannheim now asks whether there is for us beside polarization also synthesis, which indeed he hopes for from the perspective of the sociology of knowledge:

It seems, by the way [the whole passage quoted here is in parentheses], that the sociology of knowledge itself provides . . . a viewpoint 'farther back' from which purely theoretical philosophical differences, which in terms of their content can no longer be seen at the same time, can be seen through in their partiality and by this alone already be grasped synthetically. In the existence of this continually receding viewpoint . . . lies, in my judgment, an important problem of the sociology of knowledge that has hitherto not been broached at all. [*Soc. Knowl.*, p. 224, modified, *Wissenssoziologie*, pp. 607–8]

Even though there are no absolute syntheses, as Hegel still believed, synthesis is yet 'the best that thinking can produce from the standpoint of the socializability of knowledge' (*Soc. Knowl.*, p. 224, modified; *Wissenssoziologie*, p. 608). Still, synthesis covers up certain elements of thought that is relative to existence. In saying so, Mannheim, by implication, raises a problem that is pressing today and may become more pressing in the future: how we, despite enormous cultural differences of which, thanks to technological and attendant developments, we become ever more aware—how we can live in one world and in one that has shrunk so: which synthesis does right by all of us?

Despite divisions, there remains a fund deriving from the synthesis of all parties. For instance, sociology, which in its origins was oppositional, is 'gradually—almost secretly—adopted,

simply because in the modern situation it is the most adequate
orientation to the world' (*Soc. Knowl.*, pp. 225–26, modified;
Wissenssoziologie, p. 609). Mannheim might have recalled here
what he had said earlier in the present essay—that intellectual
currents, on spreading, absorb elements of other currents, that is,
change. This surely applies to sociology, on being officially
accepted, institutionalized, professionalized, as is probably more
conspicuous in the United States, the country of its widest
diffusion.[32]

If actually that is adopted by all which 'in a given epoch is
indispensable, hence the most useful' (*Wissenssoziologie*, p. 610;
Soc. Knowl., p. 226), then the sociology of knowledge, on raising
the obvious question whether the indispensable and useful also is
true, engages in an epistemological inquiry. Mannheim does not
here go beyond what he had attained in his 'Structural Analysis
of Epistemology', namely, the insight that epistemology is not a
critical but a justificatory discipline.

He concludes his lecture with the passage quoted at the beginning of this introduction as a possible motto for much of his
work, and in part repeated in connection with the discussion of
certain aspects of his paper on conservative thought.

XII.   Problems of Sociology in Germany (1929)

In this article, the significance that Mannheim attributes to
sociology, as we have just seen, appears as a special feature of
German sociology. The article is the answer to Ernst Robert
Curtius's attack on Mannheim ('Sociology—and Its Limits')[33] but
should actually be entitled, 'In Praise of Sociology in Germany'.
The 'new perspective' of this sociology 'broke out in the form of
a mighty eruption in the works of three great ones (to name this
time only those already dead)—those of Max Weber, Ernst
Troeltsch, and Max Scheler' (*Wissenssoziologie*, p. 614). And this
at a time when East and West, and indeed, other countries are
coming ever closer together but also into mutual conflict, so
that the old questions, 'Where do we stand in historical time?
How can our spiritual and psychic place in it be found?' (*ibid.*,
p. 615), take on new meaning and urgency.

In Germany, these and similar questions have overshot the
limits of the single disciplines toward philosophy or toward a

[32] By now this seems to be a rather widely held view, and not only in the
United States, where its first and still powerful postwar expression was probably
C. Wright Mills's *The Sociological Imagination* (1959).

[33] 'Soziologie—und ihre Grenzen', *Neue Schweizer Rundschau* (October
1929); Mannheim's 'Zur Problematik der Soziologie in Deutschland' appeared
in the next issue, November. Despite its general title, Curtius's article is a
critique of Mannheim's recent *I.U.*

'politically active world orientation' (*ibid.*, p. 615), for here sociology had a 'philosophical tradition that was alive', and there was Marxism. The philosophy of consciousness and of life flourished, while positivist epistemology had been overcome. Sociology became 'the organon of the new man': 'man is once again shedding his skin, striving after an enlarged form of his existence' (*ibid.*, p. 616).

Mannheim's 'dynamic relationism' which Curtius attacks is, 'in the interest of the self-enlargement that today is already possible', an invitation to '*every* position for once to call itself in question and to suspend the self-hypostatization that is a habit of thought self-evident to everybody' (*ibid.*, p. 620)—as Mannheim wishes to paraphrase pp. 40–41 of *Ideologie und Utopie* (Engl., pp. 75–77). And he throws out this challenge (even though in a footnote) in praise of sociology against its enemies: 'he who today means to offer the transcendence of his being in ultimate seriousness must have subjected it to the ultimate self-examination, just because the ultimate [fate] of mankind is at stake' (*Wissenssoziologie*, p. 623, n. 3). He concludes what may be called his *apologia* for sociology: 'For it is the true thinker's duty not to resist thought' (*ibid.*, p. 624).

This was in 1929, the year of *Ideologie und Utopie*, the book that aroused passionate discussion, of which this paper gives us an inkling. By then, there had been seven years of Fascism, twelve of Soviet communism, and Nazism was less than four years off—Mannheim's innocent passion and straightforwardness, but also his stubbornness, which is what had become of part of the perspicaciousness documented by the passage from 'Conservative Thought' that we singled out earlier, are moving. That perspicaciousness has decreased, and the myopia that accompanied it has grown. Mannheim's existentialist passion to interpret, which ever more urgently demanded complementation if not, at times at least, replacement, by explanation,[34] will certainly not move

[34] On this cf. Mannheim himself (about a year earlier): 'I consider it an immense danger of German thought—and this danger is only the other side of one of the greatest virtues of this thought—that in its tendency to interpret it also wants to interpret that which can only be explained . . . it wants . . . to "deepen" and make into a problem of interpretation even that which can be adequately grasped only within the scheme of "making" or of "mechanism". . . . This methodological discrepancy—that one interprets where one ought to explain—is, after all, the expression of an unpolitical attitude repeated on the methodological level and often observed in life itself': Mannheim's concluding remarks in the discussion on 'Die Konkurrenz' (which concerned more than anything his own lecture on competition—see XI above), *Verhandlungen des Sechsten Deutschen Soziologentages* (1928), (Tübingen: Mohr, 1929), p. 122. Mannheim thus repeats the plea against mystification with which he concluded the paper under discussion and which we recalled at the end of the commentary

all readers—many of us will instead be irritated and turn away, smiling perhaps and shaking our heads. The proper reaction is a serious concern of each of us.

XIII.   *On the Nature of Economic Ambition and Its Significance for the Social Education of Man* (1930) [35]

In the same year in which *Ideologie und Utopie* and the papers on competition and on sociology in Germany appeared, Mannheim gave a lecture on economic ambition,[36] working it out for publication in the following year. He addressed participants in a course given by the 'German Association for Political Education'. This may remind us of his first lecture ('Soul and Culture'), which had been directed to students and fellow educators— during the intervening eleven years he had not spoken to a similar audience or discussed a paedagogical topic. His interest in education thus is old but for many years found no expression; it was to be all the more central during his English phase.

In the present essay, he explicitly stresses the educational intent of sociology. Hitherto, he says, the means of paedagogy had been personal contact with teachers, specialized and general cultural knowledge, training, habituation, and 'life'. The sociologist replaces 'life in general' by the 'concrete form of social existence in a particular situation' (*Soc. Knowl.*, p. 232), and the sociologically oriented educator wants to know the direction in which the new generation living in the industrial world is to be educated; he strives to develop 'the existing form of society beyond itself to a further stage' (*ibid.*, p. 233). Hence his interest in the investigation of the individual's milieu, in which the economy is one, albeit a most important, factor. Max Weber had pointed out that at the stage of developed capitalism, the structure of the economy goes far in shaping the spirit; furthermore, changes in this structure can be identified with greater precision than is true of changes in intellectual life (this last proposition itself, which echoes a remark in the essay on competition called attention to in XI above, is of methodological and paedagogical relevance). With this Mannheim arrives at the topic of his paper, but at the end he comes back to its educational significance: 'A theory of economic education will more and more have to

---

on that paper. But as we now had (again) occasion to witness, Mannheim was not always consistent.

[35] A more literal translation of the title of the paper is: 'On the Nature and Significance of Economic Ambition: A Contribution to Economic Sociology'.

[36] See the title footnote in the original publication and in *Wissenssoziologie* (p. 625n.); it is omitted in the English translation (*Soc. Knowl.*, p. 230).

take into account for what scope of activity we have to educate this or that pupil' (*ibid.*, p. 274). Such a theory is not satisfied with norms that have no relation to the concrete life-space of the individual, and this discontent shows a 'major moral advance' (*ibid.*, p. 274). For it is possible to shape the economy and the society, but this requires 'exact knowledge of the world in which man lives now, at this present day' (*ibid.*, p. 275).

More clearly than in 'Soul and Culture', though perhaps not as clearly as later, we here see Mannheim the teacher. He taught uninterruptedly during roughly the last twenty years of his life, occasionally even before, mainly at the Universities of Heidelberg, Frankfurt, and London. Up to now we have met him as a thinker and have observed the shift in his interpretive point of reference from history to society and, within his interpretation relative to society, a change in focus from interpreter to *interpretandum.* But we have also observed already that, in one process, he clarified his thought to himself and to those to whom he communicated it—he discovered the new simultaneously for himself and the world. He thus was a teacher even as a thinker, more particularly a Socratic teacher—and if he were to reject this characterization, it might well make it even more probably correct.

As to his own development, as far as this can be read from the present paper, Paragraph 5 in Section V ('The Social Structure and Chances of Success') seems to anticipate the later stages of this development most clearly. In this section Mannheim discusses two elements in 'the rise of the economic sphere to dominance': 'a democratization which is more profound than its political counterpart' and which is being brought about by 'the flow of the most highly valued energies into the economic sphere', and, secondly, 'a new form of more or less calculable and controllable conduct' (*ibid.*, pp. 243–44).

The pressure exerted by the economic system, although leaving the individual formally free to act according to his own free will (he is always free to act without regard to his economic interests), nevertheless in the long run does produce a more or less determinable optimum of 'right' conduct for each situation which each individual seeks to ascertain and to achieve. In this way the formal freedom of every individual to follow his own self-interest, becomes a far more powerful means of 'domestication' or social adaptation than force, since force can never penetrate every mesh of the complicated social web, whereas the economic sphere—in the measure that it becomes dominant— tends, in view of the inter-relatedness of all rational lines of conduct, to bring all human activities into its orbit, including even actions and reactions which have nothing directly to do with economic behaviour at all. [*Ibid.*, p. 244]

The social structure can never rest on force alone but must be aided also by ideology. Modern economic society has made 'domestication', that is, social control,[37] the self-interest of the individual, which allows this society a considerable laxness in the control of ideologies. However, 'we can observe at the same time a growing prominence of the ideological factor in politics', for we have no purely economic society but instead one which must secure the power of the key positions ideologically, these positions not being purely economic but based on the mixed notion and practice of 'property'.

The relationship between power and tradition (which is simply ideology become habit) characteristic of former societies has given way in our society to a relationship between power and the economic system. Just as formerly the key positions in the traditional-religious framework of society were guaranteed by force, and the 'domestication' of man took care of the cultural and spiritual fields, it is sufficient in the modern social framework to guarantee only the key positions in the economic sphere by force; everything else is taken care of by the economic automatism (which acts, so to speak, as the extended arm of the power centres). Thus, in such an economically dominated society the striving for economic success is the motive of action which can most generally be counted upon to be operative. . . . Because in economic action, which is the dominant concern of modern society, it is possible to dispense . . . with ideological factors, it has become a habit of modern man to dismiss all 'religious' and ethical factors as 'purely ideological'. The derogatory and depreciatory nature of this characterization unconsciously reflects the ability of the modern social structure to give free rein to ideological and cultural factors over a fairly wide field, and in fact, it does confer such a freedom in many cases. Someone who experiences this without sociological understanding is inclined to believe that only the interdependent spheres of rational reactions can legitimately claim to be 'reality', and he therefore tends to regard everything 'spiritual' or 'intellectual' as 'accessory', as 'mere ideology'. [*Ibid.*, pp. 246–47, slightly modified]

This diagnosis, which does justice not only to interpretation and that which is to be interpreted but, much more than earlier diagnoses did, also to explanation and that which must be explained, appears, by hindsight, as the anticipation of much that Mannheim wrote subsequently—especially on functional and substantive rationality, on planning, or on the 'third way' besides liberalism and totalitarianism. The reason is likely to be that the passages that have been quoted here so extensively also describe Mannheim's loyalty to himself. For they, too, tell of his commitment to both spirit and society; and the anticipation of what was to come later also concerns a change in this commitment. Whereas in Mannheim's first phase, as we have seen, it consisted in his effort to grasp the spirit as accurately as possible precisely by insisting on its social conditioning and by tracing this conditioning, here we already have an indication that Mannheim

[37] Mannheim does not use this term here but will in *Man and Society* . . . (1935–40), of which a whole part is dedicated to social control (see XVIII below).

will devote himself ever more singlemindedly to thinking about the salvation of society, lest the spirit itself perish.

**xiv. 'Ideology and Utopia' (1929)

Those who know about Mannheim, however—yet this does not contradict the last sentence—will agree that *Ideology and Utopia*, his first book, also is his most important, certainly his most influential, and probably his most lasting work. Ever since its English translation appeared in 1936—enlarged by the 'Preliminary Approach to the Problem', which Mannheim wrote for the purpose, and by 'The Sociology of Knowledge', the previously mentioned dictionary article of 1931 (see XV below)—but particularly since its publication as a paperback (1955), numbers of college and even high-school students have had it assigned to them. It has attained the status of a 'classic' or a 'minor classic', perhaps also an attendant ghost-like aura. But because it is inexpensive and easily available, it will not be expounded here. Still, it probably needs being returned to the status of a work by a human being; here, however, all we can do is push in this direction by, first, making some remarks on the translation of the book and presenting a translation of the detailed table of contents of the original German edition (not preserved either in the translation or in postwar German editions), and second, tracing certain features of the work and commenting on Mannheim's introduction to the English translation.

A word, then, on this translation. It is doubtful whether a more literal version—such as has been attempted in the table of contents below and in those passages from Mannheim's work that have been and will be quoted either in fresh translations or in modification of existing ones—would have led to the success of the book in which Louis Wirth's and Edward Shils's rendition has resulted. Their version, however, replaces relatively idiosyncratic German by relatively standardized English, thus presenting us with a book of a character quite different from the original.[38] This is not said in order to criticize but to point to a

---

[38] The language may even have something to do with the striking difference between sales in Germany and the United States. Germany: The Third Reich 'forgot' to confiscate it, the remaining third surviving Nazism to be destroyed by a bombing attack in 1943. Source: Gerhard Schulte-Bulmke, Vorwort, *I.U.*, 3rd ed., 1952, p. vii. This edition, of 2,000 copies, was sold out only in 1965; the 4th ed., 1965, sold its 1,000 copies by the end of 1968; the work is now in its 5th ed., 1969. (Letter from Gerhard Schulte-Bulmke, 23 July 1969.) U.S.A.: The Harcourt, Brace hardcover edition (10 December 1936) sold 5,345 copies by June 1969; the Harvest Books paperback edition (4 August 1955), 65,707 copies by the same date. (Letter from Harcourt, Brace and World, 22 August 1969.) German figures are for both hardcover and paperback copies.

problem, which is that of the implications and consequences of choosing faithfulness as against understandability as the first criterion of a translation. One of the bases of the choice is bound to be the translator's expectation of the reader. In regard to the translation to follow (which, it should be remembered, covers what in the English edition appears as Parts II–IV, Part I there being the 'Preliminary Approach'; Part V, the 1931 article on the sociology of knowledge), I have assumed understandability that can be attained by serious attention. Of course, no table of contents is fully transparent without the text to which it refers; and what has been said about the English translation of the book will indeed become far more plausible if the reader were to compare the table of contents with it.

IDEOLOGY AND UTOPIA
(as Introduction)

The inner connection of the two studies. The ideological and utopian elements in our thinking have become transparent. The crisis resulting from this. Characteristics of experiencing and thinking consistently in terms of 'ideas'. The emergence of the fear of 'false consciousness'.

The need for a preliminary clarification of concepts. The many meanings of the concept of ideology. The *particular* and the *total* concepts of ideology. Common and distinguishing features of the two concepts.

On the history of change in meaning of the concept of ideology. An attempt at subjecting this change to a sociological structural analysis. The distrust becomes methodical. 'Ideology' as meaning a *phenomenon of deception* occurring only on the *psychological level*. History of the rise of the concept of 'particular ideology'. Bacon's 'idols'. The emergence of the suspicion of ideology in the everyday political practice of the Renaissance. The Enlightenment psychology of rational interests.

The concept of total ideology calls the noological sphere of consciousness in question. How is it that just our epoch is capable of calling its spiritual basis so radically in question? Stages in the rise of the concept of total ideology. A. The emergence of the philosophy of consciousness. B. 'Consciousness as such', first conceived as super-temporal, is historicized. The Historical School and Hegel. The national spirit (*Volksgeist*) as subject. The points of departure of these philosophical theories originally out of the life problems of the time. C. The further differentiation of the [intellectual] bearer: the social class as subject. On the possibility, which results from this, of perceiving historical events.

The problem of 'false consciousness'. The religious origins of this problem. The modern suspicion of a 'false consciousness' becomes methodical. The criterion of 'reality', too, changes in the modern period. The original meaning of the word 'ideology'. The Napoleonic use of the word. The emergence of the concept of ideology in Marxism. The diffusion of the concept among the remaining positions.

The rise of a dialectically new situation through the expansion of the concept of ideology into all camps. The change in meaning of the concept that is connected with this. The *special* and the *general* concepts of ideology. Theory of ideology becomes sociology of knowledge. A new form of intellectual history becomes possible. The tasks of a sociological analysis of meaning.

The value-free concept of ideology. Continuous relativization as method of investigation. Relationism: neither relativism nor illusionism. The constitutive impingement of the subject on the cognitive result. The conceptual framework of the knower is historically and socially relative (*gebunden*). The value of positing something as absolute becomes problematical. Everyday and political practice finds it difficult to do without such positing.

The transition from the value-free to the evaluative concept of ideology. The motivation, based on *Weltanschauung*, behind the value-free concept of ideology gradually becomes visible. The inevitability of an *ex-post* ontology. The blindness of positivism toward its own presuppositions.

Characterization of two typical ontic decisions that can lie behind the value-free concept of ideology. A. The relativization of history in favor of an ecstatic center beyond history. B. A medium in which the traces of 'becoming human' can be grasped is seen in history and in the changes in the elements of meaning. This indicates a negative attitude toward history and the social sphere in contrast to the positive one that is maintained here. The sociological diagnosis of the time.

The recurrence of the problem of 'false consciousness'. Thoughts that are 'real' and thoughts that are 'unreal' in a given time. Examples of false consciousness, (a) in the ethical realm, (b) in self-understanding, (c) in the area of orientation toward the world.

The search for reality in the ideas of ideology and utopia. The multiform nature of the ontological decision (sliding back into the value-free concept of ideology). The multiform nature of our thinking, too, is connected with the multiform nature of ontological decisions. In everyday thinking and in the special disciplines, objects are experienced only as particulars. The breakthrough of the crisis of our thinking in positive research. Methods of hiding the situation from oneself. The crisis in our thinking concerns all parties. The task of an analysis of the situation in the field of thinking.

IS POLITICS POSSIBLE AS A SCIENCE?
(The Problem of Theory and Practice)

Why has there been no political science up to now? The concept of politics. Rationalized structure and 'margin ['*Spielraum*'] of irrationality'. The concept of action. The difficulties a science of action confronts: (a) fluid objects; (b) no static effective factors; (c) the theorist is involved in the play of forces to be identified; (d) knowledge itself is politically and socially differentiated in its basic structure.

Proof of the thesis that knowing itself is politically and socially relative [gebunden] through a sociological analysis of the differences in meaning that the concepts 'theory' and 'practice' show among different parties: *The problem of theory and practice* in (a) bureaucratic conservatism; (b) historical conservatism; (c) the liberal-democratic bourgeoisie; (d) socialism; (e) fascism.

The problem of synthesis. The particularism of [all] ways of thinking. Political sociology as knowledge of the totality of standpoints. Impossibility of a super-historical absolute synthesis. An additive synthesis is unsatisfactory.

The problem of the bearers of the synthesis. It is not some super-temporal and super-social subject. The static and the dynamic form of 'mediation'. *The problem of the 'intelligentsia'.* On the sociology of modern culture [*Bildung*]. The 'center' does not have the character of a class. *Two avenues for the modern intelligentsia*: (a) a blind joining of classes and parties; (b) decision on the basis of the exact knowledge of one's own situation and mission. The intelligentsia is not a party-forming factor but the expression of a unique social position with its specific chance of insight. The possibility of choice. Partly schools and the need for a higher form of political science.

On the particular nature of political knowledge. We have an overly narrow knowledge. Our conception of knowledge is too intellectualistic and therefore conceals the structure of knowledge [operative] in practice. On knowledge which is accessible only to particularly structured subjects. The significance of participation [*Mitvollzug*] for the mediation of knowledge. The connection between perspective and decision.

On the communicability of political knowledge. The problem of the 'social equation'. The social equation is not always a source of error. The danger of the student's contemplative attitude distorting the structure of praxis. The contrast between schematic ordering and orientation toward action. The question of recruitment. Correlations between forms of groups and kinds of knowledge. The intellectualistic and the romantic form of intellectual transmission. The structure of the *studio* and the *club*. The *party school*. Discipline of the will and appeal to the free will. Political praxis is not to be identified with revolutionary praxis.

Three avenues for the sociology of knowledge: (1) The truth value of existence-related knowledge is denied. (2) The effort to salvage the value of this knowledge by trying to identify an area free from decisions of the will. The relative justification of this method. There is formalized knowledge of very different degrees which is relatively independent of standpoints. (3) Evaluation and perspective are examined in their connectedness. The '*consensus ex post*' and the ever renewed attempt at a synopsis. This solution, too, contains a decision. To know more does not render decisions superfluous; it only enlarges one's field of vision. The tendency to reduce the margin [*Spielraum*] of irrationality. The three historical types of ethics: the ethics of fate, of principle, of responsibility.

THE UTOPIAN CONSCIOUSNESS

A.   Attempt at a Clarification of Basic Phenomena: Utopia, Ideology, and the Problem of Reality

The orientation toward the transcendence of existence, and reality. The ideological and the utopian orientation. What is real? The concepts of the relatively and the absolutely utopian. Proof that already the definition of a basic concept is relative to a standpoint. Projected spaces and projected times ('*Wunschräume und Wunschzeiten*'). Changes in the substance and form of utopia. Ultimately, an effective utopia is a collective achievement. Correlations between various forms of utopia and social strata. Counter-utopias. What does 'utopian consciousness' mean? The connection between the utopian center of a consciousness and the attendant perspective. Utopia and the experience of historical time.

B.   Changes in the Form of the Utopian Consciousness and Their Stages in Modern Development

I. *The first form of the utopian consciousness: The orgiastic chiliasm of the Anabaptists.* Phenomenology of the chiliastic consciousness. Breaking into the 'here and now'. The unconscious falsification of the phenomena of chiliasm by the perspective of the history of ideas. Mysticism and chiliasm. Thomas Münzer. Stylistic parallels in the art of the time. The chiliastic can also hide behind the extreme rationalism of a closed system.

II. *The second form of the utopian consciousness: The liberal-humanitarian idea.* The utopia here appears in the form of the 'idea'. Affirmation of culture and ethicization. The historical and social locus of idealistic philosophy. The eternal and unconditional element in the 'idea'. The two-fold root of the idea of progress. The experience of historical time in the chialistic and in the ideational [*ideenhaft*] consciousness. The social backgrounds of the two utopias. The liberal experience of the unconditional.

III. *The third form of the utopian consciousness: The conservative idea.* The originally unreflective nature of the conservative consciousness. Rising strata push conservatism into a defensive position. The result: the way in which life is felt [*Lebensgefühl*] enters consciousness. The conservative consciousness of conditionality. Meeting the adversary on the level of ideas. The *ex-post* situation of conservative knowledge. The idea understood as entelechy rooted in reality, not as anticipated 'Ought'. The contrast between 'making' and 'letting grow'. The tension between Ought and Is becomes minimal. The conservative experience of time. The virtual presence of the past. The quietistic element in the development of conservatism.

IV. *The fourth form of the utopian consciousness: The socialist-communist utopia.* Positions flanking the socialist utopia. Traits it shares with the liberal idea. The discovery of the existential conditions of ideas. The analysis of ideologies as a method of destroying opposing ideas. The inversion of the ontological hierarchy. The combination of the consciousness of [the] conditionality [of ideas] with utopia. The fight against the chiliastic principle of radical anarchism. The experience of historical time in socialism and communism. The future becomes differentiated. The multidimensionality of time. The future is experimenting in the present. The space of free decision becomes narrower. The problem of the rational determinability of the place of an event in historical time. The diffusion of this 'realistic attitude' into culture.

V. *The contemporary constellation.* The gradual approximation of utopia toward 'reality'. The various forms of utopia destroy each other mutually. The typical change in the form of thinking as soon as its bearer participates in present reality. Attempt at a symptomatology of some directions within the most recent German sociology. The disappearance of historical time: American sociology, Pareto, Freud. Diffusion of the central mental attitude into art. Tendency toward un-utopian and un-ideological tensionlessness. The release of the ecstatic. The four roads 'intellectuals' ['*Geistige*'] can take: The future is impenetrable to knowledge. Discovery of the indispensability of the utopian. [*I.U.*, 'Inhalt', pp. ix–xv]

Among the reasons for the singular position of *Ideology and Utopia* in Mannheim's work are its particularly probing, passionate, and moving exploration of the author's fundamental commitments to spirit and society, and the way in which the problematic character of the relations between these commitments and their objects come to the fore. These concerns inform much of the central problem of the book, one way of formulating which is the advocacy of ideology *and* utopia versus ideology *or* utopia. There is longing for ecstasy (which will return later),[39] and there is great sympathy and feeling for chiliasm but at the same time for rationality—politically, for both revolution and reform (especially in Part IV, 'The Utopian Mentality'), with the latter (to anticipate) becoming ever more strongly emphasized during Mannheim's English period, presumably under the impact of Nazism, on one hand, and English democracy, on the other. The most concise and impressive manifestation of the difficult and passionate dual

[39] Cf. the end of I and n. 7 above. (Contrast the much more sober mood of Mannheim's article 'Utopia', written a few years later for the *Encyclopaedia of the Social Sciences* (Vol. XV, 1935), in which commitment and detachment—roughly, utopia as a mentality and as a literary or philosophical genre—do not fuse. We shall find similar inconclusivenesses in later works, thus in *Man and Society in an Age of Reconstruction* (XVIII below).

allegiance probably occurs at the very end of 'The Utopian Mentality' (the end of the original work):

> While the decline of the ideological represents a crisis only for certain strata and while the objectivity that comes from the unveiling of ideologies brings self-clarification to the whole society, the complete disappearance of the utopian would transform the very shape of the whole process of becoming human. The disappearance of utopia brings about a static objectivity in which man himself becomes a thing. There would arise the greatest paradox imaginable, namely, that the man of the most rational mastery over things would become the man of impulses; that man, who after such a long, sacrificial, and heroic development has reached the highest state of consciousness, in which history is no longer blind fate but is becoming his own creation, in giving up the various forms of utopia loses the will to history and thus his insight into history. [*I.U.*, pp. 249–50; cf. Engl., p. 236]

Here at the end of his book, a decade after World War I, Mannheim is overwhelmed by worry over man's fate in a manner that invites comparison with the way in which Max Weber ended *The Protestant Ethic and the Spirit of Capitalism* twenty-five years earlier, a decade *before* World War I:

> No one knows . . . whether . . . entirely new prophets will arise, or there will be a great rebirth of old ideas and ideals, or, if neither, mechanized petrification, embellished with a sort of convulsive self-importance. For of the last stage of this cultural development, it might well be truly said: 'Specialists without spirit, sensualists without heart; this nullity imagines that it has attained a level of civilization never before achieved.'[40]

Weber dreads 'petrification' without 'spirit' and 'heart'; Mannheim dreads 'objectivity in which man himself becomes a thing'. Weber longs for 'new prophets' or 'a great rebirth of old ideas and ideals'; Mannheim, for utopia. But 'utopia' has a protean form for him: by the end of his book it has become sheer spirit, the force which transcends existence—the same, however, as the 'scientific thinking' Mannheim relies on to grasp the nature of a time:

> At this historical moment, where suddenly all things become transparent and history almost unveils its formative elements and structures, we must be at the height of the situation with our scientific thinking, for it is not impossible that all too soon—as this has been the case in history more than once already—this transparence disappears and the world congeals into a single picture. [*I.U.*, p. 41; cf. Engl., p. 76]

A picture, that is, all perspectives on which are alike, which thus has *no* perspective; hence a world without 'existentiality' (which would account for perspectives and differences among them), thus nothing to discover, nothing into which the spirit could

[40] Max Weber, *The Protestant Ethic and the Spirit of Capitalism* (1904–5), trans. Talcott Parsons (New York: Scribner, 1930), p. 182.

gear, hence no spirit, no transcendence, no utopia, as Mannheim will say at the end of the book. In still different terms: in such a world (if we can imagine it or call it world), there would be nothing to engage thinking; and we have encountered Mannheim's passion for thinking more than once (notably in the essays on the interpretation of *Weltanschauung* and on conservative thought) and now find new instances of it, such as this:

> It is not impoverishment but infinite enrichment when we see ever more clearly a difficulty of life and thought. It is not bankruptcy of thinking when reason looks ever more deeply into its own structure; not incompetence, when an immense enlargement of vision demands a revision of the bases. Thinking is a process that is carried by real forces, continuously calls itself in question, and pushes toward correcting itself. [*I.U.*, p. 62; cf. Engl., p. 94]

This passion for thinking Mannheim now considers entrusting to the sociology of knowledge: 'Actually, in the sociology of knowledge nothing occurs but that we also let our position of thinking, which has become critical, meet us in the form of a report on the situation and penetrate relations with an intention directed toward totality' (*I.U.*, pp. 64–65).[41]

Still, as we have seen before, the utopian (elsewhere, the ecstatic), as that which transcends 'reality', 'existence', 'being', remains indispensable: could it really be, Mannheim asks desperately, that 'congruence' with existence (the opposite of transcendence of existence) can be achieved, that 'tensionlessness' and 'authenticity' can be reconciled in a *'fertig gewordenen Welt?'* This last expression, which Wirth and Shils translate as 'world which is no longer in the making' (Engl., p. 231), is a pun, as is its English translation, although neither was in all likelihood so intended. *'Fertig'* (aside from also meaning 'ready') means 'finished', that is, both 'completed' or 'done with' and 'done for'; and 'no longer in the making' means not only, as the translators undoubtedly intended, 'having ceased developing' or 'static' ('finished' in the first sense), but also 'arrested', 'truncated' ('finished' in the second sense). The pun makes Mannheim's question more poignant,[42] but the (negative and more optimistic

---

[41] In the English translation (pp. 95–96), this has shrunk to: 'The sociology of knowledge, however, aims to see even the crisis in our thought as a situation which we then strive to view as part of a larger whole'.

[42] An almost certainly equally unintended pun makes Scheler's 'solution' of the problem of relativism a shattering experience instead: we escape relativism 'by hanging up, as it were, the sphere of absolute ideas and values ... quite violently much higher [*ganz gewaltig viel höher*] above all actual value systems of history that have hitherto existed' (Max Scheler, *op. cit.* [n. 27 above] p. 14). Ostensibly, Scheler chose *'gewaltig'* for emphasis only, but in a less contextual, more literal sense, it also means 'violent'. (I am indebted to Rainer Koehne for having alerted me to this 'pun'.)

than pessimistic) answer (*I.U.*, Engl., pp. 231–35) probably less trustworthy.

The pun possibly reflects Mannheim's unclarity, or his uneasiness about it, regarding spirit as reason (science, liberalism, planning, reform) and spirit as transcendence (utopia, ecstasy, chiliasm, revolution, anarchism), or regarding their relations, differences, similarity, if not identity (cf. the quotation about 'scientific thinking' above). We saw an aspect of this unclarity in the ambivalence concerning 'intrinsic' and 'ideological' interpretation (in VIII above). Now, three or four years later, Mannheim emphasizes the 'existence-transcending' nature that ideology shares with utopia;[43] yet, at least according to the concluding lines of his book that have been quoted, he considers ideology a less indispensable transcendence than utopia— the decline of the former, we recall, would be 'a crisis only for certain strata', and its unveiling helps the clarification of all, while the end of utopia would change men into things. Ideology presupposes a point of view, whose unveiling or unmasking, which shows its partiality, clarifies matters, broadens the mind, and in the sense of the Enlightenment, can make us more mature. So far, so good. But the mistake comes in the implied identification of unveiling with abolishing: as long as there is no complete 'congruence with existence', there are points of view, perspectives, hence ideologies, the unveiled ones necessarily being replaced by others. In fact, utopia, which, compared with ideology so broadly conceived as Mannheim does here, is a much more particular kind of transcendence, can disappear without requiring the disappearance of standpoints. Hence Mannheim's alternative— the decline of one or the other—is illogical on his own terms. The correct alternatives at first glance appear to be two: first, complete congruence with existence, hence neither ideology nor utopia, as against a transcendable world, which thus has ideologies and the possibility of utopia—but since the first term is unimaginable, this alternative turns out to be a mirage and collapses. There thus remains only the alternative ideology *and* utopia vs. ideology-and-*no*-utopia, and this is not only realistic but timely today, when many believe that we have much ideology and many ideologies but no utopias. (The notion 'the end of ideology', of course, is misleading and irrelevant here, since it refers to the end of a particular ideology or particular ideologies.) The explanation of Mannheim's fictitious alternative is that 'utopia'

---

[43] This does not contradict the determination he made in 1926 of ideological interpretation as intrinsic: it participates in the 'existence-transcending' point of view of the *interpretandum*, rather than, as in sociological interpretation, critically analyzing this point of view.

figures in it as spirit, and 'ideology' as belonging in society, as society: if he has to choose between spirit and society, he sides with the spirit. Yet even in this formulation, the alternative, of course, is a false one—Mannheim's 'ecstasy' may here have got the better of him.

If such observations bring us closer to his book as the work of a human being (rather than an anonymous 'classic'), we must not let familiarity seduce us into contempt but rather lead us toward greater understanding, even if it should be accompanied by a shock of recognition. The book, however, is, of course, not only a story: it also contains many statements that are relevant today, some forty years later, at a time which in certain respects is quite different from the time in which and for which Mannheim was writing but which in some other respects, such as he identified, has not changed. For instance, the following (the passage occurs in the second section of 'Is Politics Possible as a Science?'— see (d) in this section in the Table of Contents above):

In the measure in which Marxist-proletarian strata rise, they shed the dia-lectical element in their theory and think in terms of the generalizing, law-seeking method of liberalism and democracy, whereas others who because of their position remain dependent on the revolution hold on to the dialectical element (Leninism). [*I.U.*, p. 96; cf. Engl., p. 118]

Current illustrations come to mind, such as large segments of labor in the United States.

Or note (in the first section of 'The Utopian Consciousness') the first page of a seven-page footnote (in the English edition incorporated into the text—see especially pp. 177–78) where Mannheim applies his claim that even definitions of concepts are perspectivistic, to the concept 'utopian' as used by the ideal-typical conservative and the ideal-typical anarchist. The former— not to use Mannheim's terms—says on principle 'no' to any alternative to the existing order for fear that some 'yes' might be entertainable and disquiet him; and surely there are many 'conservatives' and 'reactionaries' today who disparage any alternative as 'utopian'. Inversely the anarchist (in Mannheim illustrated by Gustav Landauer) says on principle 'no' to the existing order (which is perceived in as undifferentiated a fashion as is 'utopia' by the conservative), lest an even selective 'yes' qualify his passion to negate; and again, we know 'radicals' today who fit this description.[44]

Or read what Mannheim says on teaching (Engl., pp. 159 ff.) as it may bear on some questions concerning education today—

[44] But compare with this a 'smoother' version Mannheim added in the 'Preliminary Approach' (see next note), p. 36.

we saw his interest in paedagogy before and anticipated its growth in his later years. Altogether, there are many continuities in this book—continuations as well as anticipations; to mention only one of each: epistemological analyses (especially in Part II) and a note on rationalization (Engl., p. 101). But how did Mannheim himself present his book to the English-reading world? [45]

By starting with a bang: 'This book is concerned with the problem of how men actually think' (*I.U.* Engl., p. 1). Indeed, through most of the 'Preliminary Approach to the Problem' Mannheim refers to 'this book', which is, of course, made up of two essays to which an introductory one has been added. In the original edition (and in later German editions) Mannheim spends the first pages in pointing this out and explaining how the two papers hang together (cf. the beginning of the Table of Contents above); but in the English version these pages have been skipped (although some of their content has been shifted into the 'Preliminary Approach'). Instead, toward the very end of this 'Preliminary Approach', Mannheim introduces a justification for having written his book in essay form:

> At the present stage of development we are still far from having unambiguously formulated the problems connected with the theory of the sociology of knowledge. . . . This feeling of standing at the beginning of a movement instead of the end conditions the manner in which the book is presented. There are problems about which neither textbooks nor perfectly consistent systems can be written. . . . For such problems earlier centuries . . . invented the form of the scientific essay. . . . This form of presentation, which since has so frequently proved its worth, served as a prototype to the author when in the present volume, with the exception of the last part [the 1931 dictionary article on the sociology of knowledge], he chose to employ the essay form and not the systematic style of treatment. [*I.U.*, Engl., p. 47]

Compare the corresponding passage from the first pages of the German edition:

> The sociology of knowledge is still in that happy initial stage of not existing, even as a science, in the form of a rigid ordering scheme, of a detached result, of a precipitate of a perspective that has come to terms, if only apparently so, with its world. In the sociology of knowledge is still perceptible what in the established disciplines we often lose sight of: that looked at in total context, thinking is never its own purpose but a living organon that forms itself ever anew, shaping itself anew with the changes of the historical process, an ever becoming structure in whose medium man, too, renews himself. The following studies thus must not be lifted out of that living stream where it really is that things become problematical, where thinking is still tied to that immediate impulse which at all gives rise to reflection on experience. [*I.U.*, p. 2]

[45] He did in Part I of *I.U.* Engl., 'Preliminary Approach to the Problem', pp. 1–48, which, as Louis Wirth and Edward A. Shils inform us (p. xii), 'was especially written to introduce the present volume to the Anglo-Saxon reader'.

This surely is more honest and less 'polished' than the English comment on the nature of the book.[46]

If one reads the 'Preliminary Approach' directly after *Ideology and Utopia*, especially in its original language, the singular position of this work in Mannheim's opus, its unusually perceptive, passionate, personal, 'existence-transcending' nature, becomes even more striking. For after getting over our shock by the initial 'bang' of the 'Preliminary Approach'—which is close almost to a publicity stunt—we soon feel at home with the seriousness and intelligence we have come to know from Mannheim's papers that precede and that we read before 'the book'. For instance— but almost all of the 'Preliminary Approach' except the very beginning and the very end would do—take this passage, which could just as well occur in an earlier paper, say in the one on competition:

> The intellectual is now no longer, as formerly, a member of a caste or rank whose scholastic manner of thought represents for him thought as such. In this relatively simple process is to be sought the explanation for the fact that the fundamental questioning of thought in modern times does not begin until the collapse of the intellectual monopoly of the clergy. The almost unanimously accepted world-view which had been artificially maintained fell apart the moment the socially monopolistic position of its producers was destroyed. [*I.U.*, Engl., p. 11]

But then before we know it he leads us into the mood that makes *Ideology and Utopia* so outstanding:

> What we are concerned with here is the elemental perplexity of our time, which can be epitomized in the symptomatic question: 'How is it possible for man to continue to think and live in a time when the problems of ideology and utopia are being radically raised and thought through in all their implications?' [*Ibid.*, p. 38, but p. 3 in *I.U.*]

And he also affirms this time—when 'the unconscious' has been 'uncovered', which in life 'seems unbearable' but 'is the historical prerequisite of scientific critical self-awareness' (*I.U.* Engl., p. 42). If the end of his book recalled Max Weber's pessimistic soberness, a passage such as this recalls Weber's asceticism, as it is found especially in his conception of science ('Science as a Vocation').

As in 'the book', here too, an inspection of some passages illuminates the continuity and discontinuity of its time and ours. Thus:

> Today . . . we have reached a stage in which this weapon of the reciprocal unmasking and laying bare of the unconscious sources of intellectual existence

---

[46] Our understanding and assessment will benefit from knowledge of the circumstances in which Mannheim wrote the 'Preliminary Approach' as described by David Kettler in 'Political Theory, Ideology, Sociology: The Question of Karl Mannheim' (forthcoming).

has become the property not of one group among many but of all of them.
[This sounds already outdated, but a few sentences later we can no longer feel
so.] There is nothing accidental but rather more of the inevitable in the fact
that more and more people ... [take] flight into scepticism or irrationalism.
[*Ibid.*, p. 37]

Or take this:

In order to work in the social sciences one must participate in the social
process. ... The type of participation which the thinker enjoys determines
how he shall formulate his problems. The disregard of qualitative elements
and the complete restraint of the will does not constitute objectivity but is
instead the negation of the essential quality of the object. [*Ibid.*, p. 42]

This is still the fight against positivism, but it is doubtful whether
the affirmative if not enthusiastic tone—Dilthey's tone,[47] and
recall it from before, especially from II and VIII above—can,
with our clearest consciousness, still be sounded in good conscience, where in so many fields, unless to participate in things
means to change them, so many, instead of participating, criticize
or turn away.

Ideology and Utopia aroused considerable discussion, some of it
both passionate and incisive, when it first appeared in Germany.
The analysis of the political, as well as the substantive aspects of
this discussion, barely begun before Hitler came to power and
hardly taken up since, should be reviewed and revived in the light
of some of the pertinent events and processes that have occurred
since 1929. Such an analysis may even help us get clearer on
which of these events and processes we can answerably call
'pertinent', and what 'pertinent' means.

This, obviously, is not the place for such an effort; instead, we
continue chronologically, or rather in the present instance go
back a few years, since the 'Preliminary Approach' was presumably written in the early or middle thirties.

[47] E.g.: 'The *historical consciousness* of the *finitude* of every historical phenomenon, of every human or social situation, of the relativity of every kind of belief is
the last step toward the liberation of man. With it, man attains the sovereignty
of extracting its substance from every experience, of surrendering to it wholly,
freely, as if there were no system of philosophy or creed that could tie men
down. Life becomes free from knowledge through concepts; the spirit becomes
sovereign above all cobwebs of dogmatic thought. Every beauty, every
sacredness, every sacrifice, re-experienced and interpreted, opens perspectives that disclose a reality. And we then take into ourselves also the bad, the
terrible, the ugly as occupying a place in the world, as enclosing a reality
that is bound to be justified in the universal context. Something that cannot
be cheated away. And over against relativity, the continuity of the creative
force asserts itself as the nuclear historical fact'. Wilhelm Dilthey, 'Plan der
Fortsetzung zum Aufbau der geschichtlichen Welt in den Geisteswissenschaften', in *Der Aufbau der geschichtlichen Welt in den Geisteswissenschaften* (1910),
ed. Bernhard Groethuysen (*Gesammelte Schriften*, Vol. VII [Leipzig und Berlin:
Teubner, 1927], pp. 290–91).

xv. *The Sociology of Knowledge* (1931)

In the 'Preliminary Approach' Mannheim writes that the sociology of knowledge is 'the *systematization* of the doubt which is to be found in social life as a vague insecurity and uncertainty' (*I.U.* Engl., p. 45). One of the requirements of the sociology of knowledge is to increase its precision and refinement, which in *Ideology and Utopia* he felt confident were forthcoming if only

because nowhere can the pervasive interdependence of changes in meaning be determined with as much precision as in the field of thinking. For, thinking is a peculiarly sensitive membrane. In every meaning of a word and especially in the ambiguity of every concept operative at a given time, there vibrate the polarities of the hostile but simultaneous systems of life that are implicitly presupposed in those nuances of meaning and that fight one another also on this plane. [*I.U.*, p. 38; cf. Engl., p. 74]

He also said:

A modern epistemology which counts with the fact that all historical knowledge is relational will take its departure first of all from the circumstance that there are areas of thinking in which non-relative knowledge free from influence by standpoint is wholly unimaginable. Not even a god could formulate historical insights in terms of the $2 \times 2 = 4$ paradigm, for what is understandable can be formulated only in relation to definitions of problems and systems of concepts which arise in the flux of history. [*I.U.*, p. 34; cf. Engl., pp. 70–71]

In comparison, the 1931 article, perhaps only or largely because it is a dictionary entry, is formalized. Thus some of the precision and refinement just mentioned also appear as if transferred to the organization of the article itself, and a passionate statement on epistemology like the one quoted, while by no means absent, is also found in company of the announcement that 'the epistemological consequences of the sociology of knowledge' make up the second of its two parts, the first being the 'theory of the existentiality [*Seinsverbundenheit*] of knowledge'. How should we read this article? It is especially important to do it right because, with one brief though significant exception published posthumously,[48] this is not only Mannheim's last statement on his

[48] Letter, 15 April 1946, that is, nine months before his death, to Wolff, responding to a critical exposition (of the 'systematic' kind shown below) of Mannheim's conception of the sociology of knowledge in the 1931 article, undertaken in a seminar on the sociology of knowledge conducted in 1945–46 at The Ohio State University. The letter is reproduced in Kurt H. Wolff, 'The Sociology of Knowledge and Sociological Theory', in Llewellyn Gross, ed., *Symposium on Sociological Theory* (Evanston, Ill., White Plains, N.Y.: Row, Peterson, 1959), pp. 571–72. (If one thinks that a 'systematic' reading with attendant critical questions is appropriate, Mannheim's response is moving, even inspiring, in its modesty and honesty. If, as I now do, one thinks such a reading is a misreading, then Mannheim's acceptance of it may suggest fatigue or weakness, and his response strikes one as sad. This will become clearer presently.)

conception of the sociology of knowledge (for which, however, there will still be occasional pleas—see especially XVI (1) below), but also his last paper in the area generally—he made no more studies like, for instance, those of conservatism or competition.

One way to read it is systematically, in skeletal fashion:

(1) Nature of the sociology of knowledge, in contrast to the theory of ideology
(2) Two divisions of the sociology of knowledge: (a) theory of the existentiality of knowledge; (b) epistemological consequences of the sociology of knowledge
    (a) a. points at which existentiality influences knowledge: selection of problem, selection of data, solution of problem
        b. social processes influencing the process of knowledge: examples are competition and generations
        c. 'perspective' [*Aspektstruktur*, 'aspectual structure'], meaning how 'one views an object, what one perceives in it, and how one construes it in his thinking' [*I.U.*, Engl., p. 244][49]
        d. relationization and particularization: respectively relating of an idea to a social situation and recognizing its validity as limited to this situation
    (b) a. changes in epistemology and philosophy of science follow changes in empirical sciences
        b. discovering the activist element in knowledge ('not knowing *and* wanting, but wanting *in* knowing': *I.U.*, 1952, p. 254; cf. Engl., p. 265)
        c. objectivity means unanimity of perspective or the common denominator of different perspectives
(3) Problems of research techniques in the sociology of knowledge
    (a) imputation: it proceeds in three steps, the first two, not sociological, preparing for the third, which is
        a. imputation on the level of meaning [*sinngemässe Zurechnung*] imputes a thought, etc., to an ideal-typical world view
        b. empirical imputation [*Faktizitätszurechnung*] examines how and to what extent individual thinkers think in terms of this world view
        c. sociological imputation accounts for the nature of, and changes in, world views and the like by reference to the composition of groups or strata expressing them and by reference to the situation of a social-historical space, e.g., a nation, and its changes.

What is wrong with this reading (of which only a sketch has been given and which could be made clearer and more rewarding) is that it has not plunged into 'the flux of history' in which and out of which Mannheim wrote. It did not begin with an 'intrinsic interpretation'; it rather is a preparation for an 'extrinsic' one but

---

[49] 'Of the characteristics by which the aspectual structure of a statement can be characterized, of the criteria by which it can be identified in its imputability, we want to list here only a few: analysis of the meaning of the concepts employed, the phenomenon of the counter-concept, absence of certain concepts, structure of the categorical apparatus, dominant models of thought, level of abstraction, and underlying ontology' (*I.U.*, 1952, p. 234; cf. Engl., p. 244). (References to the German text of the 1931 article on the sociology of knowledge are to the reprint in this third ed. of *I.U.*, pp. 227–67.)

shows no sign of realizing this or of realizing why it proceeds as it does or what the outside sphere is with reference to which the interpretation is expected to be made. As soon as we say this, we can answer the questions of the why and of the outside reference; in fact, the latter answers the former: the outside sphere is an attitude—a rage for order or a wish for quick gain (synonyms?)— and it is not so much reference to this attitude as response to it which shapes the reading—a fine example of the existentiality Mannheim emphasizes. He was not himself a systematic thinker (which might justify intrinsically reading him so), though somewhat more in this encyclopedia article than usually—but this is not where his heart is.

Let us read him more patiently:

> The sociologist of knowledge has been accused sometimes . . . of not entering into the arguments, the 'subject matter' at issue at the moment but, instead, of going behind them toward the basis of the speaker's thought in its entirety in order to reveal it as *one* basis of thought among others, as a partial one. In what has just been said lies the legitimation of this non-entering into the arguments of the opponent in certain cases, namely, whenever, along with the common basis, the common 'subject matter' is missing. [*I.U.*, 1952, pp. 240–41; cf. Engl., p. 252]

Now, systematically speaking, this passage deals with the subject-object relation and says that the 'common basis', or shared subjectivity, produces a shared 'subject matter' or object. Taking the passage out of context, as we did, we read that the world is constituted by the subject (by subjects of 'like existentiality'). But in his early paper on epistemology (V above) we saw that Mannheim insisted on the existence of a non-relative world and said then that this would not change in his later writing. His problem here may be more accurately phrased as his (old and continuing) effort to ascertain beyond which point or line in the world's relativity this non-relativity can be found. In this search, he hardly went beyond a point reached a few pages later in the present article:

> Every analysis in the sociology of knowledge that follows its own intentions reaches that point at which the sociology of knowledge is more than a socio-logical narrative of how certain insights arose out of a certain milieu but also is critique because it reconstructs the grasping power and the limits of the grasping power of statements. These analyses of the sociology of knowledge thus are in this sense by no means irrelevant to meaning [*sinnirrelevant*], but neither do they completely determine meaning [*völlig sinnrelevant*], for by merely encircling the particularity of the perspective [by merely showing the partiality of a point of view], they do not replace the last direct confrontation of views nor the direct looking at things. The achievement of findings in the sociology of knowledge (this can be stated on the basis of the phenomenological analysis of its inherent intention and on the basis of the analysis of the intensity of its grasp) thus lies between irrelevance to meaning and complete relevance

to [determination of] meaning, at a mid-point hitherto not noticed. The analyses of the sociology of knowledge only prepare direct discussion—in a time which has discovered that its standpoints are split up and the basis of its thinking is inauthentic, and which strives to produce unity on a higher plane. [*I.U.*, 1952, p. 244; cf. Engl., p. 256]

That is to say: we have learned that the 'object in itself' is not as close, cannot be attained as quickly as we thought, because much more than we thought intervenes between us and the object—but this does not mean that there are no objects, that there is no world we can observe and discuss; only it is far more difficult than we have believed, than earlier times had believed, and than less 'relationized' and 'particularized' individuals are likely to believe today. We remember that a few years later Mannheim called the sociology of knowledge 'the *systematization* of the doubt which is to be found in social life as a vague insecurity and uncertainty', and we might do worse than make an attempt at such systematization or clarification—namely (for instance), give into a rage for order lest we cannot move on, that is, escape, to 'the next point'.

xvi. *Sociology* (*continued from XII*)

(1) Its Present Tasks; (2) American Sociology; (3) German Sociology during the Weimar Republic; (4) The Place of Sociology

**(1) 'The Tasks of Sociology Called for by the Present: A Teaching Program' (1932)

Mannheim's first paper on sociology (1929; XII above) was a defense of sociology in general and of *Ideology and Utopia* in particular. He next addressed himself to the topic three years later, in a lecture on 'The Tasks of Sociology Called for by the Present: A Teaching Program' at a meeting of German university teachers of sociology (28 February 1932, less than a year away from Hitler). Sociology means three things: 'general sociology', a special discipline; sociology *of* the special disciplines, or 'hyphen-ated sociologies' (in English, 'sociologies-of', e.g., of law, or 'adjectival sociologies', e.g., political sociology); and sociology of culture (we shall see a slightly different trichotomy in (4) below). General sociology, which disregards culture, can be practiced and taught in three ways: in ahistorical-axiomatic fashion, which aims at identifying the constants in socialized existence; in comparative, typifying fashion, which aims at obtaining comprehensive typolo-gies of social phenomena (e.g., the family); and in historical-individualizing fashion, which is idiographic and 'should always crown the preceding' ways (p. 9). Yet Mannheim grants all three their right, 'reflections over a considerable period of time having gradually led me from an over-emphasized historicism to the reception of the other two approaches' (p. 11)—'natural-scientific', 'positivistic', and 'generalizing' are not 'curse words' (p. 13), he writes. 'Sociologies-of' 'connect a certain intellectual area with the social process' (p. 15), such as law, religion, literature, the economy, art, language, education, knowledge. Mannheim takes time out to lecture on this last: his 'plea' is interesting because it shows how he presented the sociology of knowledge in a 'public-relations' lecture to fellow sociologists (pp. 17–21):

In connection with these special sociologies, one of them must be mentioned quite in particular, namely, the *sociology of knowledge*. Without naming it, we just noticed its significance—when we called attention to the fact that a science (in our case, jurisprudence), can be so structured that despite all mastery of relevant materials it actually covers up certain relationships by its formulation of questions and by its categories. The normative orientation of jurisprudence covers up the genesis and the real processes that lie behind existing laws. And by coining such formal concepts and categories as 'legislator', 'legal community', or 'sense of justice', it misses the concretization of problems that are possible here and that exist in reality. In this fashion, it becomes never visible *who*, for instance, in fact the lawgiver was. But such or similar coverings-up lie behind most acts of cognition. Only up to now we have not paid enough attention to them and have not had the courage systematically to make these coverings-up the topic of special study. The problem of *who* in *which* situation has formulated a state of affairs at a given time is always overlooked when utterances are taken as absolute theses. The development of a program of research which in the various sciences pursues those propositions that despite their absolutized form express particular views from certain standpoints can lead to a most fruitful revision of our knowledge in the humanities and social sciences. These disciplines will get out of their mythicizing state, which has often not yet become visible to themselves, only once this new method of self-control will be adopted. As a special discipline, it [the sociology of knowledge] has two essential areas of research:

(1) As *analysis of ideology* [*Ideologienlehre*] it must bring to the fore all those conscious and unconscious lies and misinterpretations with which vulgar everyday sociology and political and non-political groups deceive themselves and each other. For, the everyday interpretation of the world is full of concepts, schemes of thought, and myths—which are still so primitive that they can properly be understood only as rudiments of magical-mythical consciousness or which must be interpreted as consciously manipulated mendacious fairy tales serving to suppress an adequate social orientation. In this area, the sociologist has the task, which is not to be underestimated, of achieving the enlightenment that has seen for the first time that a society which struggles for self-government and self-determination and no longer simply *wants* to leave things to a transcendent power [1932!] can do so fruitfully only with the help of a critical and rational consciousness and the knowledge of social forces. Sociology must educate our and subsequent generations to be able to live in truth and to bear reality. In this connection, the analysis of ideology is not destructive, as its opponents usually call its work of clarification, but uncovering—uncovering reality, the real phenomena that surround us and in their reality are binding on us. It is an error to think that ideologies exist only in the political sphere. The Marxist unmasking of ideologies has only accidentally, owing to its special angle of vision, concentrated on this area of the social concealment of reality.

But all of our everyday reality is really blocked up, and as far as society is concerned, even the brightest among us is full of accepted inherited misinterpretations. In this sense, the rectification of the fundamental concepts and misinterpretations of everyday life, the clarification of the forces and interests that socially shape history, is a very essential paedagogic mission of sociology, especially of that branch that we have called analysis of ideology.

(2) The sociology of knowledge in the stricter sense of the term approaches this self-revision of thought on an even deeper level. Beyond the conscious and semi-conscious lies of everyday life and partisanship, it aims at identifying that constitutive false start of thought which occurs in the sciences themselves and for which the scientist as a rule can personally not even be held responsible. Its task thus lies in the removal of all those concealments that arise from particular orientations originating in the natural limitedness and restrictedness of special disciplines, social circles, and historical situations. Today we see ever more clearly that the thinking apparatus is always suited to illuminate only certain aspects and contexts of the world, namely those aspects and contexts the penetration of which from its own center of action is the task of a life situation or historico-social condition of existence. But all knowing and illuminating is at the same time a covering up, so that a way of seeing is characterized not only by what it can grasp by means of its concepts, aspects, categories, and modes of asking, but also by what it overlooks and assiduously conceals. In an age when an encounter of particular views that up to then had developed separately is unavoidable, given the expansion of communication and the growing together of life spaces,'there arises the task of confronting and connecting these views. In this situation, the sociology of knowledge must serve as a mediator by first helping to remove false views, and then by concretely demonstrating the particularity of each possible one. It tries to show how in the most various points of the encounter, there emerges at the same time the connecting and suspending of previously separated fields of vision into a more comprehensive whole, and how a higher unity of human knowledge thus begins to take shape.

So much in this context for the sociology of knowledge. I wish to add, however, that in future it will have to play a special role among the so-called 'hyphenated sociologies'. Since in all special areas of the humanities and social sciences theory rightly plays an essential role, there will unavoidably come up again and again, in the revision and typification of the various contradictory theories, the question of the social position from which they can be derived. It is already rather clear that one can analyze the various forms of particular theories of law and the state only if one is capable of analyzing them from the point of view of the sociology of knowledge. This is also true of the various orientations and schools of economics. And it will probably be similar in regard to the confrontation of the theories of the other special disciplines. Not that analysis from the point of view of the sociology of knowledge makes epistemological analysis superfluous, or that it wants to replace the direct confrontation of ideas. But from now on, it will have to be resorted to more and more in clarifying the situation of thought. For this reason, the sociologist, too, will as a matter of course avail himself of it when he wants to find his bearings in his very own realm, the area of sociological theories and views.[50]

Here, perhaps even more clearly than in his earlier statements on the sociology of knowledge, Mannheim argues for it from a diagnostic-paedagogical point of view. It is from this same point

[50] Also cf. 'German Sociology (1918–1933)' ((3) below), p. 221.

of view that he continues his general exposition as he comes to the
third sense in which sociology is practiced and taught: as sociology
of culture, when he explains and recommends the pursuit of
problems across special disciplines ('*Verklammerungsproblematik*').
For instance:

> To enter into the situation of a group, one can begin with the analysis of
> the form of the economy. From there one will always be pushed on to the
> analysis of the form of power and domination that is connected with this
> form of economy, being contained in it or made possible by it. The form of
> power and domination will influence that of the army as well as of administra-
> tion. From another side, the form of the economy will at the same time very
> largely shape also the form of the family. This, however, will quite directly
> affect education and the social cast of men. The form of the family marks the
> shape of sexuality and eroticism, hence also a very broad stratum in the forma-
> tion of feeling. From here it is possible to move into the analysis of lyrical and
> other poetry, etc. [p. 25]

To be 'able to see coherently' leads to 'problems of the structure as
a whole' as well as of 'the structure of the unique unfolding of
certain social-historical units' (p. 26). And in arguing against
'atomizing empiricism, which breaks everything up into abstract
pieces that are independent of each other', he says that this
'would be more exact than the manner of observing that preserves
contexts only, if reality itself were atomized and unstructured and
if in reality itself there were no overall connectedness of events'
(p. 27).

In addition to the three major modes of sociology, there also
are 'sociography and statistics' and *Gegenwartskunde* ('contemporary studies'), that is, the study of contemporary 'social problems',
all of them greatly developed in the United States (and indeed,
as Mannheim's paper on American sociology of the same year
will show—(2) below—synonymous, at the time in which he
wrote, with the major trend of sociology there).

No single school, let alone an individual, can act on this
'maximum' conception of sociology that comprises all of these
subdivisions. Selection is necessary, and Mannheim recommends
that it be guided by considerations of (1) 'the contemporary
situation of society in general', (2) 'the contemporary condition
of academic instruction', and (3) 'demands originating from the
contemporary state of research and the general scientific situation'
(p. 36). The first calls for mass enlightenment and education,
without which no democracy 'of reason' (*Vernunftdemokratie*;
rather than of 'mood' or 'impulse'—*Stimmungsdemokratie*—Scheler's terms) is possible.

> The more clearly the need for a *political sociology* emerges in this connection,
> the more energetically one must endeavor to present precisely these subjects

to the student in as value-free, as un-agitator-like a fashion as possible. For it would be the death of sociology if it had to become merely the agitator-like instrument of one or several parties. But it would be just as ruinous for it if, perhaps from fear of knocking against somebody or something, it assiduously and over-scrupulously wanted to avoid the political and social themes of life and of our contemporary existence and withdraw, out of sheer cautiousness, into altitudes where nothing bad could happen to it, at least in this respect. The sociologist's art consists precisely in talking about the themes of the greatest timeliness and urgency in such a way that he communicates all that can be known for the correct judgment of the subject matter, also presenting the possibilities of decision in their actual interdependence, but so that he as a teacher offers his own opinion for discussion too. The very instructive discussion of freedom from value judgments in the social sciences has in this respect shown the way how politics can be taught without suggesting and evaluating judgments. And even if the sociology of knowledge has in this connection called attention to some complications which despite complete abstinence from evaluating and complete 'freedom from value judgments' leave in every presentation a certain residue that is relative to the point of view, it has done so precisely in the interest of increased self-control and objectivity, and not in order to open the gates to arbitrariness. [pp. 39–40]

In *Ideology and Utopia* he had already written:

Nothing would be more frivolous and incorrect than to argue in something like the following manner: Since every historical-political thinking is demonstrably based to a certain extent on a meta-theoretical option, one cannot trust thinking at all; hence it makes no difference either how one argues theoretically from case to case. Thus everybody might as well rely on his instinct, on his most personal intuition, or on his interest, and opt the way it suits him at the moment. In this fashion, everybody can feel at ease in his partisanship and have a good conscience to boot.

Such a propagandistic interpretation of our analyses must be met by saying that there is a radical difference between thoughtless partisanship and an irrationalism which because it is too lazy to think limits itself to mere willful decision and propaganda, and [on the other hand] research which is radically worried about objectivity and which, after carefully eliminating all conscious valuation—which it can do without trouble by means of sociology-of-knowledge analysis—still discovers a residue of the partisan and the vital in the structure of thinking itself. [*I.U.*, p. 56, n. 1; cf. Engl., p. 89n.]

Indeed, at this time in history, only he who tries as best he can to become conscious of his social location and its perspective and thus to transcend them can be said to have convictions: 'the intellectuals' frequently observable "lack of conviction" is only the reverse side of the fact that they alone can really have convictions' (*I.U.*, p. 128; cf. Engl., pp. 141–42).

'Sociology is the adequate life orientation of man in industrial society' (p. 41). The demands placed on it, arising as they do from 'the contemporary condition of academic instruction', point to sociological culture as the modern equivalent of classical or humanistic culture. The function of the latter increasingly resembles that of a museum. Hence it should not be insisted on at all costs, for we must ask whether in contemporary man an experience of culture such as classical culture could inspire arises at all—and we must ask this especially in regard to students. Is a need for it—for 'a fruitful distance from immediacy'—not only kept alive but aroused and satisfied by the university as an institution (p. 47)? We must ask

whether one can rightly exclude the possibility that certain situations in life with a completely un-classical content also can lead to such life-distantiation and self-enlargement. Is it not possible that for other people [than those satisfied with classical culture] the ever deepening understanding of life and society can lead to a novel cultural experience? [P. 48]

Finally, the general situation of science, showing increased emphasis on the frontiers of knowledge and science, and an inter-disciplinary problem orientation (not Mannheim's term), seeks a guide to integration. This, sociology can be (three years later it will become 'the basic social science'—see (4) below), because the phenomena studied by the humanities and social sciences 'in the final analysis are held together by the fateful context of what happens in society' (p. 53). A source of contact between sociology and the most recent trends in the scientific situation is philosophy, above all by virtue of the fact that the sociology of knowledge can examine its contemporary varieties in regard to their existenti-ality. This does not mean that sociology or sociology of knowledge aims at replacing philosophy:

The loose play with the word 'sociologism' by the opponents of sociology gradually gets to be unbearable, for it always comes up when they can no longer meet sociology with objective arguments and thereupon treat the most decisive problems of the modern situation of thought as if they were problems of foreign policy, problems of border crossings between countries, or problems of departmental competence in a bureaucracy. They act as if a higher authority had issued directives concerning these matters, as if the distr ution of the competencies of the individual disciplines were regulated *a priori*, and as if one had to guard against transgressions like a border police. [P. 54]

Practically, that is, in the teaching of sociology, Mannheim solves the question of selection by arguing the individual's and the individual school's commitment to a generally accepted minimum. This would avoid 'anarchy' but at the same time secure all the more freedom in teaching and research that go beyond it. As this minimum he proposes three semester courses, general sociology, social history in its significance for the history of culture,[51] and 'contemporary studies' (*Gegenwartskunde*).

[51] Earlier in this lecture, Mannheim had said: 'Without relation to the sociology of culture and to history, general sociology dries up. It loses fullness and the stuff of experience and becomes something like a herbarium. Inversely, every sociology of culture and every consideration that focuses on the unique

without general sociology tends to absolutize particular situations that accidentally catch the eye, and to overlook the general social forces which also are at work in them' (p. 14).

(2) American Sociology (1932)

Mannheim's paper on American sociology of the same year is ostensibly a review of the *Methods in Social Science* that Stuart A. Rice had edited in 1931. In Rice's work, which he considers representative of American sociology, Mannheim praises the cooperation among scholars and the close connection between method and substantive research. But there also are features that make him unhappy. First, there are 'the limited scope of the questions' (p. 188), 'an excessive fear of theories' (this was written before Parsons and Merton), and 'a methodological asceticism'.[52]

To have nothing but theories without verifying them, to discuss theoretical dicta as a kind of mental sport serves no useful end whatsoever. On the other hand, it is a misunderstanding of positivism to try to know reality without having theories. Finally, to have theories but not to apply them to reality may be attributed to an excessive love of security which must lead to sterilization. [P. 189]

Second, there is 'a mistrust of "philosophy" or "metaphysics" '—a failure to distinguish between the merely speculative mind and the constructive mind, or to 'aim in the first place at being exact, and only in the second place at conveying a knowledge of things' (p. 189).

It is clear that some of these observations are not outdated. One of the keenest of them is this:

In one respect, American sociology is nearer to reality than German—namely as regards the solution of everyday problems. The American scholar is no bookish person; he maintains contact with criminal courts and social welfare institutions, lives with gangs, in slums and ghettos. However, as soon as political and social problems impose themselves we notice an immense reserve, a lack of social atmosphere. It looks as if science had no social background; as if groups devoted to social research cultivated no exchange of ideas on matters social and political; as if no conventicles existed in which the practical attitude of science towards such problems were discussed. [P. 191]

This pragmatic, social-work, social-engineering, liberal, ahistorical, un-Marxist approach characteristic of American sociology (and other parts of American culture) has begun to be challenged (except for such individual sociologists as C. Wright Mills) only since the mid-sixties—again, of course, along with other vast aspects of American culture—by a vaguely radical position. In his papers on sociology, and indeed in most of his later writings, Mannheim's own position, too, was liberal and reformist, since no matter how radical, how passionately pushing for the roots

[52] Cf. 'German Sociology (1918–1933)', p. 222.

he had been and still was in his investigations of epistemology and interpretation and in his substantive studies in the sociology of knowledge, he was also a professor, a member of the 'establishment' elite, and this was bound to come to the fore if in nothing else than in the choice of the topics of the four papers now under consideration—sociology in this and that country, sociology as an academic discipline, its place today, and, in the article next remarked upon, sociology in the Weimar Republic.

(3) German Sociology (1918–1933) (1934)

This is Mannheim's first writing published after Hitler came to power. 'The purpose of this paper . . . is to bring a whole spiritual constellation, which has now vanished, nearer to the foreign public' (p. 209). But this constellation is soberly and calmly described; its gist is presented thus:

> If, now, we summarize these trends of social thought, namely, the capacity for constructive thought that dates back to Hegel; the political realism that derives from Marx and Lorenz v. Stein; and the capacity for sympathetic intuition and interpretation that is found in the sociological works of Dilthey and Simmel, we have before us the mental equipment with which the modern sociologist has analysed the experiences that are met with in the present era of disintegration and dissolution. [P. 217]

This background—German idealist philosophy, Marx, and the tradition of the human studies (*Geisteswissenschaften*)—gave German sociology its 'highly developed capacity of objective scrutiny' (p. 211) in the midst 'of one of the greatest social dissolutions and reorganizations' (p. 210; originally in italics) during the years 1918–33. This was a period of instability, in which 'the individual is increasingly thrown back upon itself' (p. 213)—with which is connected the discovery of psycho-analysis and the sociology of knowledge.

Mannheim writes (but it is not clear whether he means to imply that the need should also have been felt and met during the Weimar Republic): 'Our need is neither for an abstract classificatory system nor for methodological reflections on the nature of sociology, but for a concrete analysis of past and contemporary events'.

'The man on whose work the younger generation could fall back most safely is Max Weber', in whom, as well as in Sombart, the problem of 'the rise and development of capitalism'

> was so worked out as to provide a diagnosis of the contemporary situation. What are the roots of Western society; whence do we come, whither are we going, and what is our place in the present crisis? These are the questions that are latent in Weber's empirical investigations [P. 218]—

and more explicit, indeed *far* more so, in Mannheim's own, as we have observed on several occasions. As a guide to such a diagnosis, 'the younger generation of German sociologists' has learned from Weber that both materialism and idealism broach their question wrongly and that the 'greater art of the sociologist consists in his attempt always to relate changes in mental attitudes to changes in social situations' (p. 219). This realization is another source of the 'most surprising event in the recent development of sociology', the sociology of knowledge, which has begun to do for 'different groups and periods in Western civilization' what 'the school of Durkheim and Levy-Bruhl in France did in the way of pointing out the system of logic peculiar to primitive tribes' (pp. 220–21).[53]

From some of what we have heard about the sociology of 'knowledge' and what we hear now (not all of it for the first time), it would be easier to distinguish it from the sociology of 'culture' (to which Mannheim turns next in what has by then become a survey) if it were called sociology of thinking, or of thought, or even of outlook.[54] Under the heading of sociology of culture, Mannheim points to analyses

of the genesis of love, of the meaning of the cult of friendship, about the growth and social significance of ideals of civilization, about the origin of the conception of genius, about the social genesis of public opinion, the social genesis of the *bourgeois*, etc. [P. 223]

(almost all of the works he mentions in this connection have remained virtually unknown and certainly untranslated). He refers to the 'morphological' method, developed above all by Alfred Weber, but argues that in order to

ascertain their morphological characteristics, a culture or cultures must also be *explained* in the light of their social background. Morphological analysis is a means of rendering the causal analysis more effective and richer, but is not a way of escape from historical empiricism [P. 222]—

that is to say in words we are more familiar with, as sociologists we must not only interpret but also explain—a point which has come up at least twice before, in Mannheim's review of Lukács's *Theory of the Novel* and in his 'Structural Analysis of Epistemology'.[55]

Mannheim concludes his paper by comparing German, American, and English sociology. This rewards reading, even though

[53] Durkheim plays a much slighter role in Mannheim's thought than the considerable substantive affinity of the two thinkers might lead one to expect. The above mention is the second time that Durkheim's name comes up in Mannheim's work to that time; the first time was an incidental reference nine years earlier, in 'The Problem of a Sociology of Knowledge' (VII above).

[54] On related terminological embarrassments in connection with VII, cf. n. 22 above.

[55] Cf. II, esp. n. 8, and V, esp. n. 14, above.

much of the first comparison is contained in the 'review' of the Rice compendium ((2) above). Today, almost forty years later, however, one particular passage, on Germany, may have taken on a novel significance if we now read it while asking ourselves to what extent and in what sense it does and does not apply to the United States at the present time:

As I pointed out earlier, we obtain our most important insight into the working of social forces in periods of rapid social disintegration such as that which Germany is now experiencing; for it is at such times that latent elements operative in society are revealed. The class-problem was intelligible not only to the German socialists but to all the groups of the German intelligentsia, because in recent years the latter have become increasingly aware that their fate is closely linked up with that of the groups immediately next to them. It was impossible to remedy individual defects by mere reformist measures in a society where, owing to the narrowness of the field for action, no social element could be conceived of independently of any other element. All social and political groups were therefore struggling for the radical transformation of the whole social fabric; and each group was intent on transforming it exclusively according to its own ideal pattern. Because all social groups were anxious to change the whole face of society, they were forced to concentrate on the whole social organism at once, and not only on particular parts of that organism. [P. 226]

(4) The Place of Sociology (1935)[56]

This paper was written a year later than the next publication to be discussed but is considered at this point because like the preceding three papers, it concerns sociology. In it Mannheim pleads for sociology 'as the basic social science' (p. 203). He argues, first, that there is a need for coordinating the findings of the various social sciences; for instance:

it is not the lack of substantial knowledge which prevents us from building up . . . a general theory of 'power and domination' on scientific lines, but rather the fact that there is so far not enough consistent endeavour to bring together out of the detached results of the social sciences those elementary facts which are fundamental to all of them. [P. 197]

Secondly, while

no foundation for the social sciences can be built up without combining the results of psychology and history, they themselves do not contain those points of view by which the principles of the changes in human life can be found, the latter being mostly based upon interaction and the laws of 'living together' [P. 200],

[56] The title footnote reads: 'Paper presented at a conference held under the auspices of the Institute of Sociology and World University Service, British Committee, London, 1936'. According to Adolph Lowe (letter to Wolff, 11 January 1964), the conference at which the paper was delivered took place in September 1935, and Mannheim prepared the paper in advance of it.

that is, on matters central to sociology. It follows

that co-operation between the social sciences can be established only if the
co-ordination of the problems of those sciences and the comparison of the
results reached by them is made the specific task of a scientific discipline which
has as its *raison d'être* the construction of a consistent general theory of society—
and that discipline be *Sociology* as the basic discipline of the social sciences.
Just as it would be an absurdity to study the different parts of the human organism without a knowledge of biology, so also it is absurd to expect that there
can be any organic division of labour in the field of the social sciences without
general sociology as the basic social science. [P. 203]

In its capacity of basic social science, sociology 'has three
important functions, and fulfils them on three distinct methodological planes' (p. 204): (1) Systematic or general sociology—
the 'general sociology' of the 1932 paper on the tasks of sociology
called for by the present ((1) above). 'General sociology' discovers, for instance, what 'a secret society of the so-called primi-
tives, a "guild" in the late Middle Ages, and a club' have in
common, which is that they are 'closed groups', and all closed
groups are characterized by an *esprit de corps*, by 'a complete
change in the behaviour pattern of the individual who is admitted
as a member', and by the onset, sooner or later, 'of a deadening,
stultifying tradition within the group' (pp. 204–5).[57] (2) Comparative sociology, on which the generalizations of general
sociology must be based; and (3) 'structural sociology', which
seeks to explain 'the specific, separate constellations which'
'the universally possible, ultimate elements of society' 'assume in
different societies in history' (p. 206). Structural sociology consists of statics, which 'deals with the problem of the equilibrium
of all the social factors . . . in a given social structure', and
dynamics, which focuses 'on those factors which are antagonistic
in their respective tendencies' (pp. 206, 207).

Mannheim ends his lecture thus:

I venture to assert that as long as in our research work and in our school and
academic curricula we do not introduce sociology as a basic science, so long
we shall not be good specialists—let alone be able to educate a generation of
citizens on whose correct understanding of the functioning of the society in
which they live it must depend whether the social process is in future to be
guided by reason or by unreason. [P. 208]

It is the old idea of the Enlightenment, no doubt buttressed for
Mannheim by his experience in England (and not yet shattered
by two years of Nazism nor by older practices of disbelief in
democracy and reason), which inspires this lecture but also leads

---

[57] Mannheim used the same illustration in his argument against the mono-
polization of sociology by historicism in *Die Gegenwartsaufgaben der Soziologie*,
pp. 13–14; cf. (1) above.

him to ask (while illustrating questions of static structural sociology):

> to what causes is it due that the different social strata which are engaged in economic production are moved just by those respective working-incentives which are needed in a given society? ... What social mechanism has to answer for the fact that, both in the political and in the cultural sphere, we always get (as long as a system functions at all) as much personality reserve as is required for the reproduction of the leading élites, that there is neither an over- nor an under-supply of people who have the capacity, education, and will for the guidance of a society? How does it come about that partly by spontaneous adjustment and partly by regulation, the amount of aggressive and competitive energy is just sufficiently great and is found precisely in those fields where it fulfills the functions necessary for the preservation of the social mechanism in question? Vice versa, how does it happen that, chiefly by an unobserved self-regulation of the process, there is just as much compromise and solidarity as is required by the constantly varying nature of the co-operation and the division of social functions? [Pp. 206–7]

Obviously, the questions are based on the assumption of a social balance or equilibrium, but from the discussion of neither statics nor dynamics is it clear whether Mannheim considers a society in equilibrium or one in disequilibrium the society to be taken for granted or to be accounted for (whether he holds an 'equilibrium' or a 'conflict' theory of society), or whether both need accounting for (as he might well affirm if asked in these terms)— nor how to identify equilibrium or disequilibrium nor, finally, whether the sense of the questions quoted hides a positive affect ('Behold the wonder!'), a negative affect ('What holds this miserable society together?'), or—least believably—none. But he may actually have thought that he was asking 'affectively neutral' questions in the way Simmel did when he asked, 'How Is Society Possible?', particularly since the quotation occurs a page after the eminently Simmelian, 'formal-sociological' example of the 'closed group', the frame of reference of which Mannheim might unwittingly have continued. If this or a similar interpretation does not apply, the queries quoted have the sound of a pious and question-begging 'functionalism'.

xvii. *'Essays on the Sociology of Culture'* (early thirties)

In the Editorial Note to this posthumous volume, Adolph Lowe informs us that the three essays it consists of were written in the early thirties, and that Mannheim made some major revisions during his first years in England but then set them aside. Ernest Manheim prepared the first two essays; Paul Kecskemeti, the third. 'The task to be performed', Lowe writes,

> far exceeded the scope of a routine translation. The German intellectual climate in which this book took form considerably affected not only the style

of the whole, but also the substantive emphasis which the author placed upon the individual questions raised and answers proposed. In order to make the meaning and import of the ideas comprehensible in another idiom and to the readers of a different generation raised in a different national tradition, the editors had to rethink the original text without distorting the author's intentions. Fortunately both editors possess quite special qualifications for such a delicate enterprise. . . . [P. vi]

Prolonged, even stubborn correspondence with the three scholars responsible for this volume—Adolph Lowe, Ernest Manheim, and Paul Kecskemeti—has not yielded the German manuscripts which, prepared in the fashion suggested by Lowe, make up this volume. It is thus also impossible to know how much of the volume is Mannheim, how much his translator-editors', hence how to date it with accuracy. The only clues to dating are footnotes to references published in the fifties which, though not so marked, obviously cannot be Mannheim's since he died in 1947; but we don't know whether some of the references to writings of the forties are his or his editors'.

(1) Towards the Sociology of the Mind; an Introduction (Karl Mannheim, Ernest Manheim)

Hegel's phenomenology must be replaced by the sociology of the mind, 'the study of mental functions in the context of action' (p. 20), which 'should eventually provide the wider frame of reference for our earlier inquiries in the sociology of *knowledge*' (p. 24—but on p. 81n., '"sociology of culture" or "of the mind" are used interchangeably') :

It is senseless to pose questions as to whether the mind is socially determined [what here is the German original of this expression?], as if mind and society each possessed a substance of its own. The sociology of the mind is not an inquiry into the social causation of intellectual processes, but a study of the social character of those expressions whose currency does not reveal, or adequately disclose, their action context. . . . Actually ideas take on new meaning when their social function changes, and it is this relationship of meaning and function which the sociology of the mind elaborates. This approach does not seek to relate two discrete sets of objects—the social and the mental—to one another, it merely helps to visualize their often concealed identity. [P. 44]

To 'visualize the social dimension of the mind', first,

expressions of thought, sentiment, or taste are scrutinized for their inherent or intended meaning . . . [second, the] whole gamut of social realtionships in which these utterances are conceived and made is traced and established . . . [and third, the] content analysis of the utterances is resumed in the restored context of the original interaction, and their complete situational meaning is restored. [P. 54][58]

[58] There is a footnote reference to the analysis of interpretation in the paper on the interpretation of *Weltanschauung* (III above).

While 'meaning and group relationships . . . occur in a merged state' (p. 55) and hence sociology and sociology of the mind are one and the same, abstractions are possible and useful, and three such abstractions are 'general sociology' (which deals with 'the acts of sociation conceived in relative isolation from their historical incidence'), comparative sociology, and structural sociology (pp. 56–57).[59]

One of Mannheim's recurring themes—explanation vs. interpretation[60]—comes up in this rambling paper too—as the 'explanatory' vs. the 'expository' approach (pp. 71–74, 75–77). But in the course of the discussion 'expository' becomes synonymous with 'interpretive' and 'interpretive' with 'functional'—as if there were no other modes of interpretation such as Mannheim himself had worked out in earlier papers. The present essay contains comments on a great many topics in addition to those mentioned, e.g., causation, structure, work vs. action, the genesis of the concept of the mind, and more—but they are hardly more than tantalizing hints.

(2) The Problem of the Intelligentsia: An Enquiry into Its Past and Present Role (Karl Mannheim, Ernest Manheim)

Groups, like individuals, see themselves in the perspective of some 'other'. In the Middle Ages, this 'other' was God, who subsequently was replaced by reason, then by history (historical interpretation), finally by sociology (sociological interpretation), which thus far has not been superseded: 'sociology has become the inescapable ground of self-validation for radicals, moderates, and conservatives alike' (p. 94), but it began to be such in the proletariat.

Other groups than the proletariat which have become conscious of themselves in the modern period are women and youth. In general, groups have gained social self-awareness, thanks, first, to the replacement of coercive by a large variety of non-coercive controls—'Success on the free competitive market demands a continuous awareness of social change' (p. 99); and, second, because of the considerable extent to which society has taken over controls from primary groups and communities. The 'rise of the intelligentsia' is 'the last phase of the growth of social consciousness'. The intelligentsia is the last group to attain the sociological perspective, 'for its position in the social division

[59] It will be noted that this is far more similar to the trichotomy developed in 'The Place of Sociology' of 1935 (XVI (4)) than to that of *The Tasks of Sociology* . . . of 1932 (XVI (1))—in case this might help in dating the present essay.

[60] See notes 8, 14, and 55 above.

of labour does not provide direct access to any vital and function-ing segment of society' (p. 101). It is a stratum between but not above classes, equipped 'to face the problems of the day in several perspectives and not only in one' (p. 105). The various types of intellectuals[61]—in rough historical sequence: intellectual (vs. manual) workers; members of the free professions; the educated; certified civil servants—have in common 'their differential exposure to culture' (p. 111).

There are four concerns basic to the sociology of the (post-medieval) intelligentsia, which is 'a central subject of the sociology of the mind' (p. 121): (1) the social background of intellectuals, (b) their associations, (c) their mobility, and (d) their functions in society. The paper contains keen observations, especially on (b), the longest section, and on (c), which, however, is poorly organized. The last part of the essay deals with 'the contemporary situation of the intelligentsia'; the last two paragraphs are here worth quoting from:

> What then can the intellectual do? First of all let him take stock of his limitations and potentialities. His stratum is not above parties and special interests, nor can any political programme or economic promise weld it into an action group. [By definition? Surely numbers of them have been so welded!] The only concern which this stratum has in common is the intellectual process: the continuing endeavour to take stock, to diagnose and prognosticate, to discover choices when they arise, and to understand and locate the various points of view rather than to reject or assimilate them. Intellectuals have often attempted to champion special ideologies with the self-abandon of persons who seek to attain an identity they do not possess. They have tried to submerge in the working-class movement or to become musketeers of free enterprise, only to discover that they have thereby lost more than they hoped to win. The apparent lack of social identity is a unique opportunity for the intellectual. . . .
>
> A group such as the intelligentsia abdicates only when it surrenders its self-awareness and its capacity to perform in its own peculiar way. It cannot form a special group ideology of its own. It must remain as critical of itself as of all other groups. . . . [P. 170]

These again are statements that become more significant if consulted on their applicability today. Thus the 'lack of social identity' may for some time have been replaced by a 'search for identity', and not only on the part of intellectuals but, at least in the United States, also (among others) of youth, women, and blacks. Perhaps an even sharper change is that from accepting, as Mann-heim did and urged his readers to, the proposition that 'the intelligentsia abdicates only when it surrenders its self-awareness. . . . It must remain as critical of itself as of all other groups',

---

[61] Which, Mannheim now corrects himself, he did not distinguish in his discussion of the 'socially unattached intelligentsia' in *I.U.* Engl. (pp. 106 and 111, n. 1); cf. above, XIV, Table of Contents, 'Is Politics Possible as a Science?', Section 4.

to holding, as in particular so many 'radical' students do, that even the intellectual has the more urgent duty to 'act' than to think.[62] Indeed, in this paper there is no feeling, as there seems since to have arisen in some people during their more desperate moments and as many more behave as if they acted on, that we may be living in a society in which thinking other than technical and technological has no place.

*(3) The Democratization of Culture (Karl Mannheim, Paul Kecskemeti)

The translator tells us that this paper was written in 1933. He so comments on its title and some other aspects (p. 171):

> The original title of this essay, 'Demokratisierung des Geistes', cannot be rendered exactly in English. While 'culture' has a wider meaning than 'Geist', the term 'mind' which might be used instead of 'culture' would be too narrow. The essay analyzes the historical process of 'democratization' as it manifests itself in characteristic changes in various cultural fields, particularly philosophy, art, and religion. The process itself is conceived as a social process at bottom, rather than as a self-contained process taking place in the realm of thought or mind [a position we have encountered before, most recently in the first of the three essays collected in this volume, (1) above, pp. 25–31]. Hence, the expression 'democratization of culture' seems more appropriate to designate it than the alternative expression 'democratization of mind'.
>
> The German text has been rendered in free translation, clarifying obscurities and omitting redundant passages but closely reproducing the meaning intended by the author. The omission of longer redundant or incompletely developed passages is marked by dots.[63]

Despite recent dictatorships, Mannheim diagnoses the modern period as that of democratization. The very recognition of the difficulties of democracy as a form of social existence lends plausibility to this diagnosis: democracy is no longer a far-away ideal but something we examine. We must guard, for instance, against the danger of a 'democracy of reason' degenerating into a 'democracy of impulse'[64] and indeed into dictatorship; we have also learned that democracy guarantees neither international harmony nor the flowering of individualism.

'Democracy' refers to a pervasive social and cultural structure, something far more inclusive than merely political. Its basic

---

[62] In his conflict with some German radical students, the late Theodor W. Adorno put in a passionate plea for thinking; on this point, at least, he would have applauded Mannheim. See particularly the interview with Adorno, *Der Spiegel*, 1969, No. 19, pp. 204–9, and his posthumous paper, 'Resignation', *Frankfurter Rundschau*, 16 August 1969, Feuilleton, p. IV.

[63] A more compelling reason for the title as phrased in English is that it is more accurate than the German. 'The Democratization of the Spirit' is a more literal translation.

[64] Cf. XVI (1) above.

principles are (1) 'the essential equality of all human beings' or, more precisely, 'the same ontological principle of human-ness' embodied in all men (p. 176); (2) 'the autonomy of the individual' (p. 177); and (3) a particular 'way of selecting and controlling its elites' following from the necessary 'voluntary abandonment of the individual's autonomous aspirations' (p. 179).

1. 'The principle of the ontological equality of all men' shows itself, for instance, in the democratic directive that knowledge be accessible and communicable to everybody (epistemologically founded in Descartes's 'clear and distinct' ideas and Kant's 'necessity' and 'universal validity' as criteria of true knowledge), and in the replacement of the connoisseur by the expert and of '"articulation" of a global intuition' (such as the connoisseur's) by increasingly abstract analysis (explanation).

2. 'The autonomy of the social units' (subjects, individuals) is indicated by the conception that the individual can 'gain knowledge, and criticize traditional beliefs, by a spontaneous use of his own mental energies', which Kant formulated in 'the assertion of the original *spontaneity* and *creativity* of the epistemological subject and of the act of cognition' (p. 189), and by 'faith in the all-healing virtue of free discussion' (p. 191), in which 'all participants are equally and jointly responsible for the conclusion reached' (p. 194). Such discussion, however, must not be confused with 'neutralized' discussion, in which the admission of the possibility that there are basically different opinions is only make-believe. 'Neutralized' discussion characterizes 'historical situations in which the ferment of intellectual uncertainty and of a genuine search for an elusive truth still survives from earlier ages and must be silenced in the interests of conformity' (p. 193). Although this is a generalization from a comment on scholastic writings, there is no indication that it may not be applicable to the time in which the paper was written:

Right now we seem to have reached a turning-point. When the incomplete democracy in which economic and intellectual élite strata occupy the positions of control is suddenly transformed into full democracy, the tendency towards the full autonomy of all social units goes to the limit and at the same time massification results in the self-neutralization of democracy. [P. 195]

Against this danger, which may bring dictatorship or at least regression to what (Mannheim reminds us) Durkheim called 'mechanical solidarity', where 'the individual is nothing but a specimen of his group', there is the recommendation to create 'numerous small communities' (p. 196), for 'it is futile as well as thoughtless to condemn democracy in the name of the ideal of order' (p. 197)—decades after this was written, we hear *both* comments (on 'communes' and for 'law and order') from a great many more people. Even more of them would agree with the following (though there would not be so many who would say it *and* what preceded):

Educating the mass in reality-oriented ways of thinking, that is, a real democratization of the mind, is the paramount task at the stage of fully developed democracy (p. 199). Sociology [though this is in another context] is particularly appropriate to fulfill this task in the modern world. [P. 239][65]

3. 'Democratic elites and their mode of selection', which is discussed in more detail than the first two principles, deals with elite selection (in modern society by bureaucratic advancement, which favors methodical personalities; by competition on the basis of popular appeal; or by group—party, class—pressure, with the strength of the group represented being the decisive factor); the structure of elites and their relations to other groups and to society at large; the self-evaluation of aristocratic and democratic elites; social distance and democratization; and the cultural ideals of aristocratic and democratic elites. The treatment of the last two aspects receives the greatest attention, and remarks will be limited to them.

'Social distance' may be horizontal ('at arm's length', 'aloof', 'forward') or vertical (between hierarchical unequals, as well as with reference to cultural objects, which may be 'high' or 'low' and are discussed in 'high' or 'low' speech). But there also is 'existential' distance, 'between the I and the other purely as a person', and, a variant, 'self-distantiation: the experience that I am a stranger to myself, or rather that I can be more or less close to myself' (p. 209). Democratization means vertical 'de-distantiation'. Two of many examples are the replacement of Latin by the vernacular and 'the irruption of "lower" (technological and industrial) concerns into the sacred precincts of "science"' (p. 211), but vertical de-distantiation can also be traced in the careers of fashionable terms ('progress', a key term of the Enlightenment, and the later 'evolution' are important instances) or in the shift from conservative ontology, which operates morphologically, with 'unanalysed and unanalysable given wholes in their unique *Gestalt*', to a liberal and progressive one, which 'decomposes the seemingly monolithic entities of the traditional world view into functional elements' (p. 214).[66] As

[65] As Mannheim had said, it will be recalled, in XVI (1) and, with more elaborate argument, in XVI (4).

[66] There obviously is a relation, but there also are confusions, between conservative–morphological–'expository'–interpretive–functional (?) ('Towards the Sociology of the Mind', (1) above)–'articulating' (this paper, 1. above), on the one hand, and liberal–analytical–explanatory, on the other. But this is not mentioned, let alone clarified, although it is important not only for a theory of interpretation but also from the point of view of the sociology of culture.

more and more individuals are drawn into the political process, the analytical view of things spreads, because:

For someone far removed from the governmental sphere—say, a provincial farmer—'the government' is a monolithic unit, something like a mythical figure or a person. The insider, however, has a very different picture of the whole thing—he sees intrigues, jockeying for position, competition—anything but monolithic unity. In short, the outsider must see things morphologically; the insider, analytically. [P. 214]

A conspicuous expression of the change from the morphological to the analytical, of de-distantiation, is the sociology of knowledge (p. 216), which, in addition, illustrates a related shift, namely, from 'systematic' to 'genetic' thinking.

Yet we also find as a characteristic of the process of democratization an opposite trend, namely, the distantiation of such '"abstract" collective entities' as 'state', 'party', 'class'. 'This combination of the analytical approach with distance-creating mythmaking introduces a certain ambiguity into democratic thought' (p. 219), which can be accounted for by the fact that there is no such thing as a unilinear movement from pre-democratic to democratic, but that there have also been, and are, distantiating or 're-feudalizing' trends—and 'it is a fundamental postulate of the sociology of knowledge that whatever has come into being in the cultural process cannot simply disappear; it will enter into later cultural configurations in changed form' (p. 224). Aside from this, however, there is an unresolved contradiction within the democratic mode of life, namely, between its first and second principles—equality and 'vital autonomy': 'If the field of experience is "homogeneous", if no object is respected "above" any other, how can man himself, the individual unit of society, claim any particular dignity?' (p. 226). This conflict shows itself in psychology, sociology, the experience of time, art, and philosophy.

It is differences in the selection of elites that give rise, or contribute to giving rise, to differences in 'culture' (rather than vice versa), whereby the mechanisms at work are 'unconscious'. But elites and other groups also have conscious cultural ideals, two of which, the 'humanistic' and the more democratic, are today conspicuous and in conflict.[67] The positive features of the humanistic ideal are distance from everyday life, as well as from oneself, solitude, and communion with oneself; its limitations are that it takes the sphere of the cultivated elite as 'the' world, that it lacks contact with the less refined portions of life, that it neglects the fact that literary and artistic works are created by individuals,

---

[67] Cf. XVI (1) above; but the present discussion is more detailed.

and in general, that it dislikes the dynamic and unexpected. The democratic ideal is still developing, hence difficult to characterize, but it stresses vocational specialization, even in the conception and practice of politics, and 'cultivation' in the 'deeper sense of becoming able to advance from familiarity with an immediately given concrete situation to the understanding of the structural pattern behind that same situation' (p. 237).

Yet there remains, as Paul Kecskemeti aptly says in a note (p. 239), the 'necessity to transcend the purely pragmatist and positivist approach', and this 'is the argument of the next con-concluding section', 'The Problem of Ecstasy', a concern of Mannheim's to which we called attention already in connection with his first available paper, 'Soul and Culture'.[68] Is democracy antithetical to ecstasy?

Our answer is that if we consider the potentialities inherent in the democratic approach, it will appear to be eventually conducive to a new type of 'ecstasy' and of true 'cultivation'. It may even be suggested that ecstasy can be a general, universally shared form of experience only in a democratized culture. But this democratization of culture does not attain that stage at one stroke. To begin with, radical democratization means de-distantiation; this has to be overcome before new forms of ecstasy can emerge. Democratized culture must go through a dialectical process before it can realize its full potentialities. [P. 240]

This process is discussed with regard to the relations between 'I' and object, 'I' and 'Thou', and 'I' and self.

Full democratization means de-distantiation of individuals and objects, hence 'a flat, uninspiring, and unhappy world' (p. 241). What has to be recognized is that such de-distantiation is only one approach to the world—a manipulative one; and since 'the tendency towards overcoming partial perspectives is inherent in democratization' (remember Mannheim's comments on free discussion, his faith in sociology and the sociology of knowledge, including the synthesizing function of intellectuals), there is reason to hope 'that the way will be open for new distance-creating experiences' (p. 242).

The abolition of social distance has a leveling and deadening effect, but it may also make it possible for purely 'existential' distance to come into its own: 'At the democratic stage, it becomes possible to "love" or "hate" the other as a person, irrespective of any social mask he may wear' (p. 242).

The real opportunity that democratization gives us consists in being able to transcend *all* social categories and experience love as a purely personal and existential matter. [Pp. 243–44]

[68] I, n. 7, above; the quotation presented there bears rereading now.

Indeed,

one of the reasons why we seek to subject human reality to radical sociological analysis is that we need to know the effects produced by social factors in order to be able to counteract them when they are inimical to man [p. 244],

or, in a slightly different formulation, to grasp more responsibly and knowledgeably what is universal in man (Kant's or, in a later version, Husserl's 'transcendental subject'); or finally, in terms used before, we want, with Mannheim,

to grasp the spirit as accurately as possible precisely by insisting on its social conditioning and by tracing it.[69]

Not only in some of the passages cited but also in others, the way in which concerns with our age of democratization are expressed here bears striking resemblance, in argument and illustration, to concerns expressed and, still more, acted on by youth, especially 'hippies' and related groups, a quarter of a century after the disappearance of Nazism—in the face of the beginning institutionalization of which this essay was written. This is a striking and uncanny proof of the feature common to both societies which by an undefined term is here called 'massification'. 'Hippies' would do well to learn from this paper—as its author, were he alive, undoubtedly would from them.

**XVIII.   'Man and Society in an Age of Reconstruction:
Studies in Modern Social Structure' (1940)

This book is based on *Mensch und Gesellschaft im Zeitalter des Umbaus* of 1935. The first part of the preface to the earlier work reads as follows:

The studies made into a unit in this book undertake it to render experiences of the last years accessible to a sociological interpretation. They attempt to glean from contemporary events their scientific substance. This will for research to be related to the contemporary scene springs from the feeling that it is probably not exaggerated to speak in the present situation of the moment of truth of science, and therefore it does not do to evade problems with which our life confronts us. Such a position undoubtedly has its dangers. As surely as we must from now on make the social process and politics increasingly the theme of science, as little must we allow this to result in a politicization of science itself. Today more than ever the political man in the true sense longs to escape from the various forms of influence by the politics of the day and to look the social forces directly in the eye.

The character of the studies shows that their origin, too, is tied *to* [*particular*] *situations*.[1] . . . (*p. vii*)

1 The first study ['Rationale und irrationale Elemente in unserer Gesellschaft'—Rational and Irrational Elements in Our Society] was originally given as the Hobhouse Memorial Lecture at Bedford College (University of

---

69 XIII above, toward the end.

London) and appears in English at Oxford University Press [1934]. The second study was published under the title, 'The Crisis of Culture in the Era of Mass-Democracies and Autarchies', in *The Sociological Review*, XXVI, 2 (April), 1934. The versions of the two studies contained in the present volume are much enlarged in comparison with the English texts, and the third study ['Das Denken auf der Stufe der Planung'—Thought at the Level of Planning] is published here for the first time.

The materials mentioned in this footnote developed into, respectively, Parts I, II ('Social Causes of the Contemporary Crisis in Culture'), and IV of *Man and Society*. The brief Part III— 'Crisis, Dictatorship, War'—goes back to a lecture given at the London School of Economics, published in 1937,[70] the same year in which there also appeared a short section of the much longer Part V ('Planning for Freedom').[71] The Introduction ('The Significance of the Age of Social Reconstruction'), the short Part VI ('Freedom at the Level of Planning'), and the very extensive Bibliography—together 'more than half of the present volume' (p. xxii)—are new.

The first three pages of the Introduction ('The Crisis of Liberalism and Democracy as Seen from the Continental and Anglo-Saxon Points of View'), which are reprinted in this Reader, are revealing as a document of Mannheim's change from Germany in the early thirties to England in the late thirties, from 'his deep-rooted scepticism as to the vitality of democracy' to temptation by 'an optimism which could make him forget that we all are sitting on a volcano' (p. 5).

Mannheim's position, which at the latest had begun to develop in the mid-thirties (but which may well be connected with roots planted much earlier, as David Kettler argues in his forthcoming 'Political Theory, Ideology, Sociology: The Question of Karl Mannheim'), was that of a passionate advocate of planning for whom the realistic alternatives were, not planning and no planning, but bad (totalitarian) and good (democratic) planning. For 'the clash of the principles of laissez-faire and planless regulation' is 'the main cause of the maladjustment in modern society'. Although 'planning will be inevitable' (p. 6), it will be as difficult as 'replacing the wheels of a train while it is in motion', and yet not as completely innovative as 'rebuilding a house on new foundations' (p. 12). Still, it won't be possible except 'by remaking man himself'; hence what is required is 'a psychology which

[70] 'The Psychological Aspects of the Problem of Peaceful Change', in C. W. Manning, ed., *Peaceful Change: An International Problem* (1937), pp. 101–32. This paper also forms the basis of 'Mass Education and Group Analysis', 1939; see XIX (6) below.
[71] 'Present Trends in the Building of Society', in R. B. Cattell, J. Cohen, and R. M. W. Travers, eds., *Human Affairs* (1937), pp. 278–300.

would be socially and historically relevant' (p. 15). According to such a psychology,

relationships, which are neither economic nor political but social, form the real centre of the human drama, in which social changes are directly transformed into psychological changes. Rightly understood, these non-economic yet social factors are the answer to the much-discussed problem of 'mediation' (*Vermittlung*), for they represent transmission belts which act as a vehicle by which the basic principles underlying our society (among which the economic are undoubtedly very important) are transformed into psychological relationships. [P. 21]

By this time in Mannheim's life, the social psychology he seeks has become an important heuristic principle in the service of his perpetual quest to understand social life. Thus there is, as Ernest Manheim rightly observes,[72] an important change in the way in which he pursues this quest: from society or history as that principle, to psychology. But to put it so is to underestimate (as Mannheim himself may well have done at times) the importance of precisely that which the psychology is only to help, namely, the understanding of social life. The 'social factors', we just read, 'mediate' between 'the basic principles' (they remain unspecified, they are simply 'basic') and 'psychological relationships'. This vague and vaguely put but very real quest also inspires Mannheim's related search for *principia media*,

temporary groups of general factors so closely intertwined that they operate as a single causal factor (p. 182). . . . universal forces in a concrete setting as they become integrated out of the various factors at work in a given place at a given time . . . on the one hand, reducible to the general principles which are contained in them . . . on the other hand . . . to be dealt with in their concrete setting as they confront us at a certain stage of development. . . . [P. 173]

Clearly, *principia media* are not (necessarily) psychological phenomena. They mediate between the unique and the general and are not only 'midway' between them (somewhat like 'theories of the middle range'); they mediate, one might put it, between two ungraspables or ineffables, the unique and the universal, both of which need mediation to be understood—and both tempt reason with the romantic illusion of immediacy.[73]

The central concern of Part I is the fate of rationality in contemporary society. This society is characterized by 'fundamental democratization' and 'growing interdependence' (p. 44). It therefore raises the question of how 'to attain a rational and moral way of life' (p. 51) in a historically new sense: by looking

[72] Ernest Manheim, Introduction to Karl Mannheim, *Soc. Cult.*, pp. 5–6. Cf. Wolff, 'The Sociology of Knowledge and Sociological Theory', *op. cit.*, pp. 580–82.

[73] Cf. Mannheim's discussion of romanticism in 'Conservative Thought', and comments in IX above.

to society in order to discover the roots of irrationality and of the irrational elements in morality. Before we can hope to find such social roots, we must clarify two meanings of 'rationality' itself—'substantial' and 'functional'. 'Substantially rational' is 'an act of thought which reveals intelligent insight into the inter-relations of events in a given situation', whereas 'functionally rational' is 'a series of actions' 'organized in such a way that it leads to a previously defined goal, every element in this series of actions receiving a functional position and rôle' (p. 53). Mannheim discovers that 'functional rationalization by no means increases substantial rationality' but has, on the contrary, a 'paralysing effect on the capacity for rational judgment' (p. 58). Indeed, such judgment is concentrated in a 'few organizers', and this in turn helps to account for the 'appeal to the leader' (p. 59).

The crux of what Mannheim says on 'the social causes' of rationality and irrationality thus is this:

As a large scale industrial society, . . . [industrialized mass society] creates a whole series of actions which are rationally calculable to the highest degree and which depend on a whole series of repressions and renunciations of impulsive satisfactions . . . it so refines the social mechanism that the slightest irrational disturbance can have the most far-reaching effects, and as a mass society it favours a great number of irrational impulses and suggestions and produces an accumulation of unsublimated psychic energies which, at every moment, threatens to smash the whole subtle machinery of social life. [P. 61]

The 'social causes of the rational and irrational elements in morality' (p. 66) are discussed in similar fashion. In a broad way, we can distinguish three stages of morality: that of the horde, to which Durkheim's mechanical solidarity applies; that of individual competition; and that of solidarity and cooperation, where 'the highest level of reason and morality awakens in the members of society, even if only dimly, a consciousness of the need for *planning*' (p. 70). But:

Up till now we could believe that relatively free competition between different forms of education and propaganda would, by natural selection, allow the rational, educated type of man, best fitted for modern conditions, to rise to the top. But when the instruments of propaganda are concentrated in a few hands, they may be monopolized by the more primitive types, and then the spiritual regression which has already appeared, becomes permanent. [P. 74]

Mannheim does not explain why 'the more primitive type', 'the "hand-cart mind"', should be able to control 'the mass mind' (p. 73), that is, what accounts for the seductive power of atavism. Consequently, even though we have reached the stage of planning, the question, 'in its religious and quietistic form', '"Who plans the planner?"', or in its political and realistic form: "Which of the existing groups shall plan us?"' (p. 75), is a haunting one. 'The longer I reflect on this question, the more it haunts me' (p. 74).

The vagueness of Mannheim's concepts of *principia media* and that of 'substantial rationality' are related: he is in search of the referents of both but has not found them yet. The reason for this may be, in regard to the first, the vagueness or implicitness of the conception or philosophy of history with which we have more than once seen him work before; and, for the second, the fact that he not only observes the growth in functional and the decline in substantial rationality but exhibits them: in comparison with the commonsensical and hardly theoretical definition of substantial rationality, that of functional rationality is a clear-cut application of a well-known theoretical model, that of the means-end scheme. The vagueness of formulation may well reflect the unease in front of the phenomena formulated, or in the case of substantial rationality, it may reflect their very decline. In regard to the latter, Mannheim, however, has distinguished predecessors, notably Max Weber and Pareto.[74]

Part II, 'Social Causes of the Contemporary Crisis in Culture', begins by claiming:

> So far we have discussed the symptoms of contemporary social disintegration and transformation as reflected in the psychological crises of our time. Now we must analyse the effects of social disintegration upon the development of culture. [P. 79]

The claim is more ostensible than precise, and what has been announced turns out to be likewise. More precisely than ostensibly, it is a discussion, among other things, of elites (the increase in their number, the breakdown of their exclusiveness, changes in the principles of their selection and in their composition), the public, the intelligentsia, and problems connected with regulating culture, especially in dictatorships. Part III deals with 'Crisis, Dictatorship, War', which result from 'the causes of disorganization in their most disastrous forms' (p. 117), by commenting on some widespread beliefs concerning human nature, on forms of insecurity and their impact on behavior, and on the change from unorganized to organized insecurity and the role of the leader and his manipulation of symbols in this transition. The two parts just catalogued should remind us of their (and other parts') sources in earlier papers (see the beginning of this section above) —Mannheim modified them so as to make them into a more unified structure. His pages, however, contain many striking

[74] Cf. Mannheim's own reference, which is wholly without any such accent, however, to these and other 'predecessors', p. 52n.

observations that are worth our pondering today. One will have to do:

> It is not to be expected that the old bureaucracy of the country or the former commercial and industrial leaders trained in the ways of rational calculation will find the secret of symbol-manipulation. They need an alliance with a new kind of leader, and this leader, and the petty leaders, must come chiefly from those holes and corners of society where even in normal times irrational attitudes prevailed and where the catastrophe of unorganized insecurity was most severe and prolonged. [P. 138]

The reference, obviously, is to Hitler and Nazi Germany.

In Part IV, 'Thought at the Level of Planning', this stage is contrasted with two preceding ones, those of 'chance discovery' and 'invention'. Its characteristics are treated in regard to the relations between unplanned and planned activities and between theory and practice, the nature of the individual, the importance and the difficulties of discovering the *principia media*; differences between planning, establishing, and administrating, the volitional and emotional aspects of planning, and the help of pragmatism, behaviorism, and depth psychology in transforming man. Much of this veers between a substantive and a methodological stance, that is, between speaking about the phenomena and their changes ostensibly at issue and about their study by variably suited social-scientific approaches—roughly, between praxis, involvement, judgment, and, on the other hand, Mannheim's groping for them.

The bulk of Part V, 'Planning for Freedom', by far the longest of the six and an easily separable treatise on social control or 'social techniques', is devoted to a classification of social controls (direct and indirect, with the latter in unorganized masses, concrete groups, 'field structures', 'situations', and 'social mechanisms'), their 'transmutations', and an essay on the history of parliamentary and democratic government as the history of social control. What Mannheim wants of planning—and this is related to his quest for *principia media* and other quests mentioned before—is that it be 'the rational mastery of the irrational' (p. 267), similar to making music: 'only the man who has fully mastered technique can really express the irrationality of musical experience' (pp. 267–68). Moving toward this aim, we should also see what we can learn from totalitarianism (pp. 259 ff.)[75]— not, surely, to turn totalitarian but, precisely, to become better at rationally mastering the irrational or, as Mannheim will shortly put it, at realizing 'the third way'[76] between laissez-faire and totalitarianism: the democratically planned society.

[75] Similarly in 'The Problem of Youth in Modern Society' (1941), in *Diagnosis of Our Time*, pp. 52–54 (XX (2) below).
[76] In *Diagnosis of Our Time* and *Freedom, Power, and Democratic Planning*.

The coda, Part VI, 'Freedom on the Level of Planning', once more raises Mannheim's unease and fears, as if he had not written so much of the preceding hundreds of pages to show that they can be overcome, and be overcome rationally.

> Planning raises the fundamental philosophical question: 'Is not an ideally planned society a prison, a strait-jacket, even compared with the almost intolerable life led by many classes in an unplanned society? . . . Does not the continual development of social technique lead to the complete enslavement of the individual?' The question is only too justified, and if a human solution of our present problems is to be possible at all, an answer must be found. [P. 369]

The answer, no more up to the question than before, consists in a discussion of freedom at the 'stages' of 'chance discovery' and 'invention', contrasted with that of planning, where its criterion is the control of cumulative effects from key positions.

> At the stage we have just reached, it seems to be greater slavery to be able to do as we like in an unjust or badly organized society, than to accept the claims of planning in a healthy society which we ourselves have chosen. The realization that fair and democratic planning does not involve the surrender of our freedom is the mainspring of those arguments which show that an unplanned capitalist society is not the basis of the highest form of liberty. [P. 377]

Thus do uncertainty and caution check the hope and conviction Mannheim would have characterize his answers to these excruciating questions.

XIX.   *Social Planning on the Eve of World War II*

(1) Human Valuation; (2) Mannheim's Answer to a Newspaper Poll; (3) Diagnosis of the Time; (4) Planned Society; (5) Adult Education; (6) Group Analysis.

The reasons for treating more than one piece of writing in a section of this introduction before seemed too obvious to discuss them: in regard to Section XVI it was the topic (sociology) and the temporal contiguity (1932–35); in regard to XVII, it was the (plausible) claim of Mannheim's editors that the three essays, written 'in the early thirties', belonged together.

In the present section and in the next, too, there is temporal contiguity (1936–39 and the war years), but there are additional reasons for bringing a number of essays together under two heads. One is that in comparison with earlier, particularly pre-Hitler writings, these pieces (with some reservations regarding (2)) are slighter; they show a changed Mannheim, a thinker who tries to find his bearings in a new country and in a new period. The period is new, not only because it is no longer that of liberalism, but also because Mannheim is suddenly struck by the impact the liberal period, which is past, had on his thought; now the time is closer, more urgent, of more immediate bearing on him. He no longer appears to have the leisure or the detachment which now, by hindsight, seem to characterize the writing he did in Hungary and in Germany before Hitler.

When he went to Germany, he was a young man, and Germany and German were the source of his own highest culture—Hungary had been part of it, part of the Austro-Hungarian empire until 1918. Mannheim's emigration to England had a quite different meaning; he had lost his position, a very prestigious one, in Germany; he went into a country that belonged to the West (John Stuart Mill, not Hegel or, for that matter, Marx; rationalism, pragmatism, muddling through, democracy, not German 'depth', romanticism, metaphysics, mysticism); he was adult and he was widely known; he had just begun to experience the ravages of Nazism; he must have been eager to understand English social and political life and organization; he obviously sought to become much more practically or intimately a part of it than he had ever felt the need for in Germany. Hence the eagerness with which Mannheim contributed to the discussion of urgent problems; thus the volume of his writing and its occasional hastiness and repetitiousness.

Ernest K. Bramsted and Hans Gerth, the editors of Mannheim's posthumous *Freedom, Power, and Democratic Planning* (XXI below), suggest an illuminating parallel to Mannheim's emigration to England and illuminate this emigration itself:

> In the eighteenth century, Voltaire had come to early industrial England from an absolutist state where one social stratum in alliance with one Church wielded unlimited power. What then impressed him was the peaceful pluralism of England's political and religious groups which in no way seemed to threaten the stability of the social order. Two centuries later, Mannheim, too, could not find in an England now fully industrialized any trace of that tendency toward artificial conformity which dominated totalitarian Central Europe. But he was even more surprised by the absence of that chaotic diversity of hostile groups that had destroyed the Weimar Republic. He discovered that spontaneous conformity could coexist with the freedom of many experimenting groups; genuine tolerance toward a wide variety of political attitudes and critical evaluations seemed to draw its very strength from the nationwide acceptance of certain ultimate principles.[77]

We now turn to Mannheim's first writings out of his new country.

(1) A few Concrete Examples Concerning the Sociological Nature of Human Valuations (1936)

This paper begins with a few such examples, but then pleads for theory—'There is in this country a tendency to put a premium

[77] Ernest K. Bramsted and Hans Gerth, 'A Note on the Work of Karl Mannheim', in *Freedom, Power, and Democratic Planning*, p. x.

on pure description' (p. 235): this is now said in England to an English audience, while similar remarks appear in the paper on American sociology four years earlier (XVI (2)), but they were written in a comparably detached fashion, from Frankfurt for an American learned journal. He puts forward, 'quite tentatively', some hypotheses, 'which in my opinion suggest themselves when one tries to solve the riddle of changing human valuations' (p. 236).

1. 'Valuations of human attitudes and activities . . . are originally set by groups' (p. 236). 2. The social structure, the organization, and the needs and functions of a group are reflected in the group's standards (cf. warriors vs. agriculturalists). 3. Most of the time, valuations cannot be adequately explained as subjective motivations. To try to do so 'is the mistake of the introspective psychologists' (p. 236). 4. The coordination or superimposition of groups usually makes for conflict in valuations. 5. Valuations also are relative to social strata; they are separate if the strata do not communicate (e.g., castes); they clash or mix if they do. 6. 'In a static society, which has reached a certain balance, there will always be some classes of leading groups (elites) the standards of which will become representative, and will be silently accepted even by those groups which are subjugated and essentially frustrated' (p. 237). 7. Such groups will be challenged only when there is sudden social change or mobility. 8. All groups, not just social classes, set their standards, 'which compete with each other and clash in the consciousness of the individual who participates in their activities' (p. 238); furthermore, changing valuations are often engendered also by social forces or processes, such as competition.

The subtitle of the paper suggests a second topic, the relation between psychology and sociology. This is the conclusion to which its discussion leads:

The unceasing interplay between our primary impulses which seek for satisfaction and their repudiation or remoulding by the counteraction of the already established relationships ['institutions'] makes the theme of the history of mankind. If in the observation of this interplay one is more interested in the subjective origin of these psychic driving forces and in their concatenation in the life-history of the individual, one becomes a psychologist. If one is more interested in the power of these 'established relationships', and primarily wishes to know how they react upon the newborn individual from the very first day of his socialization; and if one follows up the existing configurations of these institutionalized activities viewed from their objective function in a given society, one becomes a sociologist. [Pp. 240–41]

Anything human can be looked at psychologically (focusing on intentions or motivations)—Simmel would say from the *terminus a quo*; and sociologically, 'in terms of the social functions it consciously or unconsciously fulfils' (p. 241)—Simmel's *terminus ad quem*.

This paper, then, is a plea for theory, advanced in simple terms in the new, 'untheoretical' country, and a didactic effort to clarify, which yet in the very process of expounding finds new formulations.

*(2) Mannheim's Answer to a Newspaper Poll (1937)

A few months after publishing this paper on valuation, Mannheim answered a poll directed by the *Prager Presse* to a number of intellectuals concerning the books they considered important or that had influenced them. Mannheim's answer (*Prager Presse*, 28 March 1937) has not been republished but is sufficiently informative and interesting to warrant translation and publication in the present context.

My contribution to your inquiry is limited in a double sense. In the first place, as a sociologist I want to refer to only those books that have been of great help to me in my orientation in the contemporary world. Secondly, I will do without mentioning those works that are usually referred to as 'eternal values'. I believe that at its time, each of the real eternal values was of the greatest topicality, became famous because it had something to say to the men in their particular situation then, and will really come to life again only when mankind finds itself in a similar situation.

One can understand the contemporary world in its rapid change only if one learns to think sociologically, if one is capable of understanding changes in ways of human behavior by reference to the changing conditions of society. This, however, also requires acquaintance with recent findings in psychology and philosophy.

Our idealist philosophy has failed in the contemporary situation. When it emerged, it represented an outstanding achievement. But it had placed too much confidence in the power of 'ideas'—as if ideas by themselves were capable of transforming man and society. Today it becomes ever clearer to us that man's thought is part of his coming to terms with his society and its conditions, that the formation of consciousness is the result of his social life, and that as society changes, so does man. In this direction, books like those by J. Dewey, *Human Nature and Conduct* (New York, 1930), G. H. Mead, *Mind, Self and Society* (Chicago, 1934), J. H. Robinson, *The Mind in the Making: The Relation of Intelligence to Social Reform* (1921), and Max Scheler, *Die Wissensformen und die Gesellschaft*, are of epoch-making significance.

The American philosophers mentioned have tried to interpret man above all as an acting being and have thus made available to our time of activism a new access to the understanding of man. There is another guide to the interpretation of the changing nature of man: Nietzsche. In *Will to Power* and *Genealogy of Morals*, he knew how to peek behind the screens of consciousness and values and to clarify for us why in our world there is a collapse of the tables of values. At the same time, he penetrated to the instinctual roots of human spiritual life and thus became the forerunner of Freud and depth psychology, without which we could no longer do today. Whether the psychology of the individual or of the masses be in question, the theory of the unconscious has become indispensable. If there is still a good deal of uncontrolled speculation about in these areas, yet something truly essential has been gained by understanding man on the basis not only of his superficial reactions but also of the lower strata of unconscious motivations.

To have applied depth-psychological analysis to the understanding of politics with all its deterioration that meets us at the present time is the merit of H. D. Lasswell. In *Psychopathology and Politics* (Chicago, 1930), and *World Politics and Personal Insecurity* (Chicago, 1935), there are many good things, although the reading is often made difficult by the disjointedness of his thought.

Equipped with a novel knowledge of man's psychology, one can then move on to the study of society itself. There is a large number of sociological books, some of them very valuable; but if one wants to have the greatness of the achievement in this field fused in a single person, then one can only point to Max Weber. As an introduction, one should read his two lectures, 'Politics as a Vocation' . . . and 'Science as a Vocation'. . . . The technique of analysis and the moral position will impress the reader and effectively assist him in his own search. Then one should turn to Weber's great work, *Economy and Society* . . . and to the collected essays on the sociology of religion. . . . No easy reading; but he who has worked through it will see the world with new eyes and understand history in a new sense. Marx's great achievement—formulating the social process as a theoretical problem—is here transformed into detailed concrete research, all the while avoiding the suggestion of a political attitude by means of science. Unfortunately, Max Weber's work does not extend into the most recent period. What one can obtain from him is the equipment for understanding society; the application to our problems one must make oneself.

In order to understand the fundamental tension in which contemporary man finds himself placed—the struggle between liberalism and democracy on the one hand, fascism and communism on the other—let me point to some additional books. The venerable pair of scholars, Sidney and Beatrice Webb, have in their old age still given us an exemplary description and analysis of Soviet Russia—*Soviet Communism: A New Civilization?* (London, 1935). In the struggle between the values of a liberal-democratic culture and a planned society, the paedagogical writings of J. Dewey, in particular, are of particular value. Beatrice King, *Changing Man*, informs us, among other books, about Soviet education. The threat to the stratum of our intellectuals and to freedom of thought, further the decay of culture in the rising mass society, are the themes of some widely read books such as those by Ortega y Gasset, *The Revolt of the Masses* (1933), J. Benda, *La trahison des clercs*, and Huizinga, *In the Shadow of Tomorrow*. They touch essential danger points in the development of modern society. In decisive points, however, the lack of a genuine sociological analysis prevents them from going beyond lamentations by scholars.

I have limited myself to few books; none of them is a guide that could replace the others. Neither have I tried by this list to foist a particular political position on anybody. It has been compiled in order to help the individual with his self-orientation; nobody can today be relieved of deciding for himself.

Among the many things this letter tells us, let us only single out Mannheim's acquaintance with some of the major contemporary representatives of English and American liberalism and their attraction for him.

*(3)   On the Diagnosis of Our Time (1937)

'Zur Diagnose unserer Zeit' appeared in the first issue of the shortlived *Mass und Wert*, a journal founded and co-edited by Thomas Mann, then an exile in Switzerland. Perhaps this origin accounts for its tighter texture and its higher seriousness, compared with the other writings in the present section. As the title indicates, it is a diagnostic article, one of Mannheim's many efforts to diagnose his time. It is important also because it shows the diagnostician between his German and English phases— between the earlier *Ideology and Utopia* and the German version of *Man and Society* and the later *Man and Society* (English version), *Diagnosis of Our Time* ((4) and XX (2) below), and *Freedom, Power, and Democratic Planning* (XXI): while writing in German and thus for fellow Germans—by now above all fellow German exiles—he yet writes from England, drawing on his English experience, recommending and thus mediating it.

His—our—difficulty of diagnosis is twofold: subjectively, it derives from the end of belief in progress and increasing reasonableness and is the price we pay for our better, more sober understanding of natural science and technology; objectively, it stems from the increasingly chaotic development of our society (population displacements, planless industrialization, dissolution of family and other institutions, the problematic character of leisure). In response to these changes there has arisen 'modern social technology' (p. 106; cf. *Man and Society* above and other papers of this period below), that is, 'the practical management of mass drives' (p. 110). It originated in the United States and was taken over by the Soviet Union, then by Fascist Italy and Nazi Germany. This social technique is 'grandiose' because in its absence mass society would dissolve; it is 'inhuman' (p. 114) because it is a means, its goodness or badness depending on the purpose to which it is put and which in part depends on the psychology associated with the technique.

Mannheim advocates a 'sociological psychology', which he finds at work in 'modern social service', 'juvenile courts', 'group and individual education', and adult education (p. 116). He also tries to counteract the suspicion of planning by pointing out that the 'coordination' it involves need not be enforced against people's will but can also—and, of course, should—be understood and practiced as 'planning for freedom' (p. 119),[78] 'with which we can strive for differentiation and by which order is attained not only at the cost of restricting freedom'.

It is the freedom of a society which, disposing of the entire coordinated social technology, has itself under control, guarding itself by its own free will against the dictatorial suppression of certain areas of life, and incorporating the guarantees of these free areas into its structure and constitution. [P. 119]

[78] This is the title, it may be recalled, of Part V of *Man and Society* of 1940, a sketch of which, however, appeared in 1937, the same year as the present paper; see beginning of XVIII, and esp. n. 71 above.

It is not clear—Mannheim is not clear—how the planned society is to be brought about: on the one hand, it must follow 'the spontaneous movement of the masses'; on the other,

it must be guided by groups who proceed on the basis of a decisive political will and of corresponding psychological and sociological knowledge and do not leave the most important steps to desperadoes, military agitators, and radio managers. [P. 120]

Thus, Mannheim does not face the problems of a theory of social change, even though they had emerged already three years before[79] in the form of the 'haunting' question, 'Who plans the planner?'[80] Now the planners, simply, are individuals (intellectuals?) with a political will and with social-scientific knowledge. In the next to last paragraph, we find that Mannheim assimilates thinking to clarifying 'the struggle of contending tendencies' (p. 121) and (some pages back) that he almost substitutes it for hope in 'the countries with liberal-democratic traditions' (p. 118). This well illustrates some of the observations ventured in the introductory remarks to this section.

(4) Planned Society and the Problem of Personality: A Sociological Analysis (1938)

Under this title Mannheim delivered four lectures in 1938: 'The Age of Planning', 'The Structure of Personality in the Light of Modern Psychology', 'The Impact of Social Processes on the Formation of Personality in the Light of Modern Sociology', and 'Limits of the Sociological Approach to Personality and the Emergence of the New Democratic Idea of Planning'. In these lectures, Mannheim makes 'an attempt at a theoretical analysis of the social forces underlying the formation of the new totalitarian states and of the factors reshaping men living under the changed conditions of a new system' (*Soc. Soc. Psych.*, p. 255).

It seems that Mannheim continues to be impressed by his experience of differences among forms of society and by his insight into the pervasive impact that differences among forms of society have on their members. The first impression presumably came from his transfer to England, his acquaintance with England, his comparison of the England in which he now was living with the Weimar Republic, and his deep desire that in his new country democracy not only not suffer the fate of democracy in Germany but, by understanding itself more truly, change so as to be immune to the allurements of totalitarianism. Yet the way democracy

[79] See beginning of XVIII above, the quotation from *Mensch und Gesellschaft*, esp. n. 1 of the quotation.
[80] *Man and Society*, p. 74, quoted in XVIII.

has to change is toward a form of society of which totalitarianism is thus far the only existing instance: the planned society. This greater similarity between totalitarianism and planned society than between the latter and the only existing instance of democracy, namely, liberal democracy, may make understandable at least three passages in these lectures where Mannheim writes as if 'planned society' were interchangeable with 'totalitarianism'— passages which without such an interpretation might puzzle or alienate the reader.

The first occurs when, directly after discussing totalitarian states, Mannheim says: 'But besides war and external pressure there is an inner reason which works in favour of *planning*' (p. 258; italics added). Then there is the first sentence of his second lecture: 'Our main problem in these lectures is to find out whether the recent drift of society towards planning . . .' (p. 267); finally, there is the first sentence of the third: 'Perhaps one of the main reasons why present-day *planned societies* rely chiefly upon central regulations . . .' (p. 279; italics added).

There are two other passages in which Mannheim introduces himself—in one explicitly, in the other by inference. They may lend weight to the interpretation of his attitude toward changes in the form of society which he finds are demanded by other social changes that have taken place or are in the process of doing so:

The vantage point from which I shall present the situation is to a certain extent that of a liberal, but of a liberal whose vested interests are not so much to be found in the economic world as in his being a member of a certain type of intelligentsia whose only capital is his learning and whose fundamental demands on life are freedom of thought and free development of personality.

But this wing of the intelligentsia is liberal only so long as the future of culture and development of the personality is in question. As to the general transformations in society it is ready to see what is really happening in the world and it is not blind to the potential good in the movements of our age.

The longer we study present-day society the less can we avoid seeing that all the basic conditions of the age of liberalism are vanishing, or else transforming themselves into new ones, and that we are confronted with completely new configurations. [Pp. 255–56]

That is to say, Mannheim presents himself as a liberal in regard to culture and personality but as non-committed in regard to 'the general transformations in society' and to 'what is really happening in the world'.

The other, presumably unintended, autobiographical statement occurs in his discussion of the 'sociological meaning of personality as contrasted with the liberal interpretation' (p. 262):

5. Another root of the doctrine of the self-contained character of soul and personality is to be found in the fact that the philosophy of the liberal era, as represented by idealism and romanticism, was a philosophy of introverted intellectual strata. Particularly in Germany, these had been excluded from

practical political work, and had therefore never had a chance to combine self-observation with practical action and to follow up the ramifications of the interaction between the mind and its social environment. [P. 264]

Mannheim still belongs to these 'introverted intellectual strata' (being, as he himself said, 'a liberal . . . whose fundamental demands on life are freedom of thought and free development of personality'). But he is apparently very much more aware of it than he had been, perhaps aware of it almost for the first time, and thus more cognizant of the duty which the fact that he is an intellectual, a thinker, rather than a political activist, imposes on him: the duty is not to think about epistemology or interpretation or the sociology of knowledge but about how to save 'man and society'.[81]

By planning, obviously. Mannheim's ideas on this are similar to those developed in the preceding paper, which is briefer and more succinct; in the present lectures, however, as title and subtitles suggest, much attention is given to personality. In the first lecture, he praises 'the positive elements of pragmatism, behaviourism, Marxism, and the sociology of knowledge', which have proved 'that the evolution of mental attitudes and even of knowledge does not occur in a vacuum but is strictly linked up with action' (p. 265). Before he can discuss the sociological aspects of this linkage (third lecture), he must present the modern conception of personality, including society's psychological influences on it. This conception is largely psychoanalytical, distinguishing 'three levels of the mind': that of the *id* (drives and impulses, including 'reflex reactions', 'involuntary reactions', and 'automatic reactions, which were once learned' (p. 268); that of the ego; and that of the super-ego and the ego-ideal. The first and part of the second level are unconscious; the rest, conscious; and there are unconscious and conscious social influences. Among the former are 'spontaneous unconscious adjustments to different situations', or 'trial and error' (p. 272), but also 'conditioned reflexes and the making of habits'; and there are suggestion and hypnosis. On the other hand, there is 'the impact of society on the conscious part of the mind, which means the conscious part of the ego' (p. 273), through intelligent adjustment, learning, education in the broadest sense, and psychoanalysis. (In this discussion, it is obviously not clear whether 'conscious' and 'unconscious' are predicates of parts of the mind or of influences on it or of both.) In summing up this lecture, by 'personality' Mannheim means

that kind of organization of the mind, specific to each individual, by which, through his mutual interaction with the environment, he develops a pattern of inner organization which is unique in itself. [P. 278]

[81] Cf. the beginning of his introduction, just before I.

The third lecture, then, deals with 'social factors in the formation of personality as they worked in the liberal, unregulated society' (p. 280), particularly with 'the relation between external situations and the growth of human personality' (p. 281), namely, isolation, contact, division of labor, the democratic organization of small groups, the 'most suitable form of organization so far known making for spontaneity in its members' (pp. 282–83), and free competition. In connection with the latter, Mannheim points out:

Whereas it is the danger of competitive society that it tends to dissolve the ultimate social bond of consensus, the danger of planned society is that it extends the necessary minimum of conformity to everything, and people lose the rational and critical power without which an industrial society cannot survive. [P. 286]

And:

What the liberals did not understand and what the Russians in spite of many failures have proved by experiment is that competitiveness, acquisitiveness, and property sense are not in the least identical, but were rather an historical combination of attitudes united into one single complex in our society. [P. 287]

Mannheim then discusses 'the sociological determination of preferences and choice' (p. 288), the formation and implantation of wishes, 'the working of social forces . . . on the level of introspective and self-regarding attitudes' (p. 290) and in regard to the realization of 'the uniqueness of one's life history' (p. 292). At the end of this lecture he announces the task of the next, the last, as the effort

to answer two questions: (1) How far could planned society make use of such sociological insights into the nature of social forces and situations making for individualization, if planning were not to mean to the planners planning for conformity. (2) Secondly, we must at least touch upon the question of where the limitations of both the sociological concept of the self and of planning based upon it become apparent. [P. 293]

In this last lecture he warns against the 'limitless manipulation of the environment', which 'kills the personality centre' (p. 303), and against 'socialists and fascists', that is, advocates or practitioners of planned society, because they 'tend to become subject-blind', while the liberal's mistake was the tendency 'to be environment-blind' (p. 304). (While there is thus a further instance of the synonymous use of 'totalitarian' with 'planned'—and even of 'socialist' with 'Soviet Russian', indeed with 'Stalinist'—because of what these share in Mannheim's perception if contrasted with 'liberal', in an earlier passage that occurs in a discussion of the Soviet Union, he does ask: 'Does prevention of privacy and introversion belong to the very essence of planned society or is it

merely a Russian misinterpretation?': p. 300.) He distinguishes
between the use of sociological and psychological knowledge in
order to understand historical societies, which is beneficial, and
its use as the basis for planning society, which, far from being
beneficial, would lead to 'total regulation', 'to a deadening
mechanization of man and society' (p. 307). Planning, thus, must
not interfere where not necessary; and wherever possible, it must
replace command by spontaneity: the contrast to liberal society is
planned society, not dictatorship. To be sure, there is a 'basic
sphere without which consensus, co-operation, is impossible',
where conformity applies, and where 'some of the fundamentals
of a new common life have to be induced without necessarily
being always based upon rational argument'.

But once this minimum of conformity concerning fair play, decency,
community spirit, sense of justice, incentive for work, and the necessarily
greater conformity in the wants of the consumer is guaranteed, the social
scope has to be provided for individualization and freedom. [P. 308][82]

Here is the characteristic end of these lectures, written in unresolved anguish over the fate of both society and spirit, and
seeking its resolution in a religiously tinged, trusting hope:

The new society has to be based upon a new synthesis between the self-assertive
forces of liberal society and the over-estimated possibilities of some kind of
complete altruism. A synthesis which I have never found more exactly expressed
than in a saying of the old Jewish sage Hillel:

> If I am not for myself, who will be for me?
> If I am only for myself—then what am I for?
> [Pp. 309–10]

A trusting hope which is moving but has not led to conceptual
clarification.

(5)   Adult Education and the Social Sciences (1938)[83]

This and the next paper appear to be the last that Mannheim
wrote before the outbreak of World War II. The organization of
the lecture on adult education suffers, probably, from being an
abridgement; the footnote to this effect does not inform us who is
responsible for the shortening; thus Mannheim himself is not
excluded. The major merit of the essay is that it moves from
very broad considerations of current society to concrete questions
about adult education. 'We have to educate people to live in a

[82] Cf. Herbert Marcuse's argument against 'repressive tolerance' in his
essay by this title in Robert Paul Wolff, Barrington Moore, Jr., and Herbert
Marcuse, *A Critique of Pure Tolerance* (Boston: Beacon Press, 1965), pp. 81–117.
[83] A footnote to the title reads: 'A shortened version of a paper given at the
Annual Conference of the Tutors' Association at Liverpool, April, 1937'.

world which presents, and will in future present, situations which cannot be anticipated' (p. 27); 'our society is in a state of dissolution' and

cannot hope to recover unless the millions realise that by finding new responses to their own particular situation they are not only working for themselves but contributing to a general reorganisation;

and thus we also

have to answer the questions of adults of a new kind, who do not come to us simply because they wish to spend their leisure in a more sensible way than the rest of their comrades, but of adults who are beginning to realise the problems of a new era. [P. 28]

Mannheim talks of rising dictatorships and the interdependent world in which we live (p. 29), argues for 'a new combination between psychology and history', and praises the 'discipline which studies those most elementary processes which are present in any social system' (p. 30)—

competition, co-operation, conflict, accommodation, assimilation, division of labour, the various forms of social organisation, social control, about which we know a great deal on a comparative and experimental basis and without which any accurate study of societies is completely impossible. [Pp. 30–31]

He does not say 'sociology', but urges the synthesis of all social-scientific findings. The need for such a synthesis is also felt 'in institutions like those of adult education' (p. 31). Hence Mannheim's specific recommendation on teaching the social sciences to adults: they must be offered the choice of two curricula:

The one is by widening the scope of the existing special subjects by relating their results to the concrete setting in which they originally occur. The other way is by introducing a three year's [sic] curriculum under the heading for example of the 'Study of Society' which sets out to re-interpret the results of the special subjects as parts of social interaction and deliberately starts with a description and analysis of the social forces and social structures which underly any transformation of society. [P. 32]

To begin with, this must be an experimental undertaking, if only because 'there will be few tutors in this country who will be able to give these courses' (p. 33).

The paper illustrates Mannheim's concern with education, which we have seen before and will see again. It also contributes to the impression, voiced in the beginning of this section, that his writing in England was occasionally hasty and repetitious, in part, perhaps, because he had become widely known and was invited to speak to too many groups.

(6)   Mass Education and Group Analysis (1939)[84]

This is a second paper on education. It begins by urging its reconsideration in the light of the new totalitarian states. For education shapes man not in the abstract 'but in and for a given society' (p. 330); its basic unit is the group, not the individual; its aims must be understood in reference to a given time and place; and 'codes and norms' express the

interplay between individual and group-adjustment. The fact that norms themselves are not absolute but change with the changing social order and help to solve the tasks with which society is faced, cannot be seen from the experience of the single individual. To him they seem to be absolute and unalterable decrees, and without this belief in their stability they cannot be made to work. Their true nature and function in society as a form of collective adaptation reveals itself only if we follow their history through many generations, continuously relating them to the changing social background. [P. 331]

Here suddenly, then, in the course of a comparatively casual listing of some 'implications' of 'a sociological approach to education' (p. 330), Mannheim comes to formulate what in the meantime has become of his conception of the sociology of culture or of knowledge (see also p. 344n.): broad, casual, popular, commonsensical, confident; very different from the specific, serious, esoteric, searching, boldly hoping efforts—to characterize them by some contrasting adjectives—that he made in pre-Hitler Germany.

Indeed, he did not even interrupt himself in the listing of 'implications' of 'a sociological approach to education' to announce a view of the sociology of culture; *we* did. We must realize (he continues) that educational aims are transmitted by educational techniques, which are among the 'social techniques' and must be related to them, 'to the remaining forms of social control' (p. 332), in order to be successful. Adherents of a liberal conception of education reject the sociological conception just sketched because, among other reasons, they 'think that a knowledge of social conditions is equivalent to levelling personality' (p. 334). They thus cling to an elitist view despite the general 'moral chaos' (p. 337), in the midst of which, however,

modern sociology and psychology are making progress not only in reforming moral standards, but in finding new methods of readjusting the masses by group analysis. . . . I venture to say that we have in them a genuine alternative to the Fascist exploitation of group emotion. [Pp. 337–38]

Before coming to his discussion of group analysis, however, Mannheim inserts a section on 'Individual Adjustments and

[84] In J. I. Cohen and R. M. W. Travers, eds., *Educating for Democracy*, pp. 329–64; page references are to this edition, rather than to the reprint in *Diagnosis of Our Time* (XX (2) below).

Collective Demands' (pp. 338–50). Among a number of things, it contains a statement on 'three main criteria' of a 'successful' society. One of them is:

> Through its institutions it will help the individual to make his adjustment in the best possible way, and will come to the rescue of those who have failed in their readjustments. [P. 343]

Again, as in the quotation concerning 'codes and norms', there is the tone that was called broad, casual, popular, etc.: he speaks, or so it sounds, as a group member to fellow group members, all of whom are engaged in rescuing or at least improving society and praising each other for this laudable work. Still, Mannheim has hardly arrived; he can hardly be a *bona fide* member; rather, he plunges into the members' midst, hoping, with closed eyes, so to speak, to be accepted, to be transformed into a member and at the same time to convince the other members that his sociological insight is an asset to the group as a whole. He is a refugee from Nazism, an immigrant to England.

Group analysis, unlike psychoanalysis, does not 'tear the individual from his social setting' (p. 351); it 'refers the individual case, not only to the family constellation, but to the whole configuration of social institutions'. In discussing some attempts, which 'are still in an experimental stage' (p. 352), Mannheim also touches on 'that new branch of knowledge which is called the analysis of ideologies', that is, of

> those interpretations of situations which are not the outcome of concrete experiences but are a kind of distorted knowledge of them, which serves to cover up the real situation and works upon the individual like a compulsion. The existence of ideologies was first noticed in the political sphere. [P. 355]

And there is a footnote reference to *Ideology and Utopia*, just as if this book were not concerned with a wholly non-psychological conception of ideology[85]—just as if it were not a wholly different (by now we can perhaps say, a pre-Hitler) book.

As before, and especially in (2) above,[86] Mannheim moves toward a view of social change but does not explicitly confront the task.

> Unless a large-scale attack is made on the defence mechanisms [= ideologies] by education, propaganda, and social work the poisoned mental atmosphere of the whole nation will always be stronger than the readjusted individual or the smaller group. [And in a footnote a little later he writes that the 're-moval of these ideologies or utopias' is] not only a matter of psychological

[85] A striking illustration of the point made in the passage in XVIII above to which n. 72 refers.

[86] Recall particularly the end of the comment; also Mannheim's 'auto-biographical' statements in (4) above.

analysis but a question of changing the social and economic position. [Pp. 356–57 and 358n.]

Thus there is no mention of institutional change, because, clearly, even 'changing the social and economic position' refers to the position of the individual (to his therapeutic change of milieu). He so writes despite his insistence on the importance of the social context and despite the fact that World War II, which presumably was directed against a social system, broke out in the same year in which this essay appeared.

This essay ends by condemning 'contempt for the masses' (p. 359), emphasizing the distinction between 'crowd' and 'group' and the need for 'the creation of "institutional behavior" in the individual' (p. 362; the term is accredited to Floyd H. Allport), and with this final sentence:

The educationalist and the representatives of the new social services have the special opportunity of standing at the cross-roads where they gain insight into the working of the individual psyche and of society. They, more than others, have the power to link up the regeneration of man with the regeneration of society. [P. 364]

xx.   *World War II*

(1) Psychic Economy; (2) Diagnosis of Our Time; (3) Three Short Papers: Democratic Planning and the New Science of Society, Popularization in Mass Society, The Refugee

(1)   On War-Conditioned Changes in our Psychic Economy (1940)

Presumably this is the first paper Mannheim wrote during the war. It is not a treatment of the topic its title suggests, but a proposal for research into this topic in which sociologists and psychologists would cooperate. Mannheim argues the advantages of the cooperation and concludes with concrete suggestions. Among them, 'the writing of a war diary on which, if possible, a psychologist and a sociologist would be to record the most important collective emotional currents' and the establishment of 'a kind of clearing office for acute conflicts and difficulties' (*Soc. Soc. Psych.*, p. 251) perhaps show most clearly Mannheim's involvement in his new environment and the kind of specific tasks with which he had come to identify himself and his involvement.

**(2)   'Diagnosis of Our Time' (1943)

The writings in this collection directly reflect the war and war-time England. Except for 'Mass Education and Group Analysis' (XIX (4) above), of which the 'bibliography has been brought up to date' (p. 184, n. 1), they were written in 1940–42, although the date of 1942 is conjectural for the last, by far the longest essay, 'Towards a New Social Philosophy'.

In the 'Preface to the American Edition', Mannheim stresses the importance of consensus and the necessity of order *and* progress for planning. The greater consensus in England may make planning less difficult there than in the United States. In any event, he takes it for granted that change calls for reform, not revolution (p. viii).

The first, the title essay (January 1941),

is a brief restatement and further development of . . . [*Man and Society*; XVIII above]. Furthermore, the author is working on a book, 'Essentials of Democratic Planning' [presumably the posthumous *Freedom, Power, and Democratic Planning*; XXI below], which will deal in a more systematic manner with the different aspects of planning. [P. 179, n. 2]

The paper much resembles the four years older 'On the Diagnosis of Our Time' (XIX (2) above).

'The Crisis in Valuation' (January 1942) is concerned with the simultaneous existence in our society of several 'philosophies of life': Christian, liberal, socialist, fascist. There thus is disagreement regarding the nature of freedom, education, work, and leisure, as well as regarding the causes of the crisis, particularly between their Idealist (spiritual) and Marxist (economic) tracing. Mannheim compares

the two sociological approaches, the Marxist and that which I am to expound. According to the Marxist, you have only to put your economic house in order and the present chaos in valuation will disappear. In my view, no remedy of the chaos is possible without a sound economic order, but this is by no means enough, as there are a great many other social conditions which influence the process of value creation and dissemination, each of which has to be considered on its own merits. [P. 19]

Among these are the 'uncontrolled and rapid growth of society', our failure to come to terms with the machine, either in work or in leisure, the growing number of contacts among groups through communication and through social mobility, new forms of authority, an increasingly conscious, as against traditional, 'value appreciation and acceptance' (p. 26), all of them calling for 'a tremendous reform of education' (pp. 26–27), which also would pay due attention to 'those values which appeal directly to the emotions and irrational powers in man' (p. 27). In this respect, we can learn from the Catholic Church, 'which tried to present the truth to the simple man through images and the dramatic processes of ritual, and invited the educated to face the very same truth on the level of theological argument' (p. 28). In respect to valuation, 'the third way', or 'the democratic pattern of planning or planning for freedom', means that democracies must give up their complete lack of interest in the sphere of valuation; they must engage in self-discipline, that is, in the struggle for common valuations and for justice. Thereby they must avail themselves of the 'remedies for social evils' (p. 32) discovered by sociology (Mannheim praises *The Negro in Chicago: A Study of Race Relations and a Race Riot* by the Chicago Commission on Race Relations, 1922). Education, adult education, social work, juvenile courts, and other institutions must be subjected to a more conscious philosophy of their meaning so that we can find William James's 'moral substitute for war' (p. 34).

Youth ('The Problem of Youth in Modern Society', April 1941) is a revitalizing agent in society, provided society makes use of its marginality and outsider status. Despite its title, the subsection, 'The Special Function of Youth in England in the Present Situation', instead deals with the English anti-theoretical bias[87] and its causes: security and wealth, an influential rentier class that stifles imagination and the courage to investigate the meaning of change, the Englishman's living more in his institutions than in reflective thought, the disparagement of a free-lance intelligentsia by the rentiers, 'practical' businessmen, and certain civil servants, a system of education that stresses examinations and marks and contains no sociology, and youth's lack of a proper place and share in society. Youth, 'one of the most important latent spiritual resources for the revitalization of our society' (p. 51), must be organized. This sounds like advice imitating the totalitarians, but 'there is a way of learning from events, and even from our opponents, which is the exact opposite of imitation' (p. 52): we must 'rely on our own judgment as to the merits of an institution, and admit that many items in our opponents' methods are simply a response to a changed situation which affects us equally' (p. 53);[88] but we must not, on the other hand, 'tolerate the intolerant' (p. 55).[89] We must satisfy the need for new forms of authority by creating 'blended attitudes',

a form of behaviour which is not driven from one extreme to the other, from violent hatred to submissive guilt feelings, from an inferiority feeling through over-compensation to a superiority complex, but which is proud of a balance of the mind which can only be achieved through self-control and intelligence. [P. 56]

And education must be characterized by 'gradualism': 'first for group conformity, and then for the emergence of the many-faceted, balanced personality' (p. 57).[90]

'Education, Sociology and the Problem of Social Awareness' (May 1941) is a passionate plea for sociology as an educational

---

[87] Cf. XIX (1), p. 235, and XX (1), p. 243.
[88] Cf. XVIII, pp. 259 ff., and n. 75 above.
[89] Cf. XIX (4), p. 308, and n. 82 above.
[90] This idea, too, is anticipated in XIX (4), p. 308.

force to overcome the liberal compartmental conception and practice of education, which splits school and world, youth and the rest of life, school and home, moral and curricular concerns. In order to accelerate education becoming 'integral', integrating itself with other institutions as well as 'with respect to the wholeness of the person' (p. 61), the teacher must acquire what relevant sociological knowledge has been gathered so as to attain and impart 'awareness in social affairs', 'a comprehensive sociological orientation' (p. 67), a 'total awareness', in comparison with which class consciousness is only 'partial awareness' (p. 70). Such an awareness becomes necessary in times of rapid social change but is hampered by overspecialization in education, by misinterpreting tolerance and objectivity as neutrality, and by the fear of disturbing consensus. Yet it must be made to prevail because with World War II our choice has become that between freedom and democracy vs. dictatorship, while before it had been between capitalism and communism; and we have realized that the social struggle must be fought by reform, not by revolution. Much of this paper could indeed stimulate reform—the reform of departments of sociology that would translate 'social awareness' into the structure of their curricula.

In June 1941 Mannheim made a brief BBC broadcast on 'Nazi Group Strategy', very likely the only time he addressed himself to Nazism exclusively. He describes Hitler's procedures in disorganizing the society he is attacking, the effect of this on the individual who is moved to cooperate, indicates the second step in the strategy, the establishment of the new order, and points to the training of new leaders who are characterized by 'a strange blend of infantile emotionalism and blind submission'—while when 'Churchill says: "I have nothing to offer but blood, tears, toil and sweat", he appeals to a nation of adults' (p. 108).

'Towards a New Social Philosophy' is subtitled 'A Challenge to Christian Thinkers by a Sociologist'. It

was written for a group of British friends, Christian thinkers. . . . The group, consisting of theologians, clergymen, academic teachers, Civil Servants, writers, etc., used to meet four times a year for a week-end with the avowed purpose of understanding recent changes in society in their relevance for Christianity. Several years ago, the author was invited to join the group as a sociologist, and in this capacity he wrote the present statement. [P. 109n][91]

[91] For most of the remainder of this note, see I above, toward the end. Cf. T. S. Eliot, *Notes towards the Definition of Culture* (New York: Harcourt, Brace, 1949), Preface: 'Throughout this study, I recognise a particular debt to the writings of Canon V. A. Demant, Mr. Christopher Dawson, and the late Professor Karl Mannheim. It is the more necessary to acknowledge this debt in general, since I have not in my text referred to the first two of these writers, and since my debt to the third is much greater than appears from the

The 'need for spiritual integration in a planned society' (p. 111) has several reasons, among them the facts that without it men will not 'be capable of accepting the sacrifice which a properly planned democratic order must continually demand from every single group and individual in the interests of the whole' (p. 112), and that new issues must be emotionalized, which presupposes the redefinition of the crucial problems of life (cf. p. 115). In this process Catholicism and Protestantism, with their main emphasis respectively on institutions and the individual, have different strengths and weaknesses, namely, those of 'Thomistic' and 'Individualized Rationality'.

At present I cannot do more than point to these two types of rationality. It is very likely that the future will have to be devoted to their reconciliation, and only one thing can be forecast: a simple evasion of the calamity of the modern mind will not do [the danger of a Catholic sociology], but neither can bottomless individualism be made the basis of social organization [the danger of Protestantism]. [P. 118][92]

In as complex a society as we live in, Kant's categorical imperative, a mere formal *Gesinnungsethik*, is not enough; we need a much more concrete *Verantwortungsethik*.[93] Education for social awareness must aim at the best combination of both, of individual conscience and social responsibility: 'One cannot be a good Christian in a society where the basic rules are against the spirit of Christianity' (p. 124); theological thought must be blended with sociologcal knowledge. In discussing how this is possible, Mannheim once more formulates his view of sociology:

---

one context in which I discuss his theory'. Eliot refers to Chapter II ('The Class and the Elite') of his book, where he discusses Mannheim's treatment of this topic in *Man and Society*. Cf. Bramsted and Gerth, *op. cit.* (n. 77 above), pp. xiv–xv: 'In gradually evolving the outlines of the answer to "who is to plan the planners", which is laid down in the present book [*Freedom, Power, and Democratic Planning*], he was deeply influenced by a group of prominent Christian thinkers, among them T. S. Eliot, J. Middleton Murry, and J. H. Oldham. Over many years he met with this group for periodic discussions, he himself playing an outstanding part in reorienting the ideas of its members. Then and there be became convinced that sociology and social philosophy cannot afford to remain "religion blind" any more than a truly religious concern with the world can remain "society blind"'.

[92] 'Individualized rationality' appears to suffer from the same lack of a theoretical basis as does the 'substantial rationality' the historical diminution of which Mannheim diagnosed as a consequence of 'functional rationalization' in *Man and Society*. See XVIII above.

[93] Gerth and Mills translate these two terms, which Max Weber developed in his lecture on 'Politics as a Vocation' (1918), as respectively 'ethics of ultimate ends' and 'ethics of responsibility'. See H. H. Gerth and C. Wright Mills, trans., ed., and with an introd., *From Max Weber: Essays in Sociology* (New York: Oxford University Press, 1946), esp. p. 120.

If one takes the radical view that Christian values are eternal and pre-established, there is little chance for co-operation. Only if there is at least a limited scope left for experimentalism in the field of valuations is it possible to make use of the sociological approach. It is no good hiding the difficulties arising in this sphere, and therefore, in order to make the challenge complete, I shall represent the sociological approach in its most radical form.

Sociology in its historical origins is a secularized, perhaps the most secularized [cf. as early as VIII above], approach to the problems of human life. It borrows its strength from following up to its final consequences the immanent, i.e. the non-transcendental, approach to human affairs. . . . This becomes particularly apparent when it deals with values. . . . To him [the sociologist] it would seem unwise and methodologically inconsistent to exclude certain phenomena from the range of sociological explanation. He would not agree to a suggestion which considers certain phenomena from the very outset as being holy and therefore not open to the sociological approach, whereas others, being profane, could be more accessible to it. . . . By having carried through the sociological analysis to its final consequences . . . the sociologist himself sees where other approaches need to be called in to supplement his findings. On the other hand, before they have embodied the knowledge available through the sociological analysis, philosophy and theology seem to deal with a picture of life which is deprived of those problems and findings which are most characteristic of our age. [Pp. 126–27]

This says two things, which Mannheim does not explicate or even distinguish. One is the observation that among approaches to the world there are the theological and the sociological. They are available to man, though not actualized in all times and places. So to think is to subscribe to an essentially phenomenological view; Mannheim's failure to say so suggests that he had forgotten his early familiarity with this view.[94] The other is a historical observation (of the kind which obviously is much more pervasive in Mannheim's work): that at this time in history, the sociological approach cannot be ignored, and particularly not by those who take the other of the two singled out in his essay, the theological.

In the planned society there must be room for all 'four existential spheres of religious experience' (p. 136): in mysticism, in personal relations, as imbuing the whole social order, through conventions.[95] It is a society in which the Christian can adjust to the world and to his particular environment 'in harmony with his basic experience of life' (p. 145), his 'paradigmatic experience'

[94] Cf. V above, esp. n. 15.

[95] In defending the first, Mannheim once again—cf. in I above the quotation from 'The Problem of Ecstasy' to which n. 7 refers, and XVII (3), esp. the passage to which n. 68 refers—shows the importance he gives to the possibility of transcending the everyday world by temporary withdrawal from it: 'It will become more and more a question whether something corresponding to the monastic seclusion, some form of complete or temporary withdrawal from the affairs of the world, will not be one of the great remedies for the dehumanizing effects of a civilization of busybodies' (p. 137; also see pp. 170–73).

(pp. 143 ff.).[96] In the planned society 'the religious focus' is allowed to be what it ought to be, 'a way of interpreting life from the centre of some paradigmatic experience' (p. 146). 'If these paradigmatic experiences evaporate', Mannheim writes,

it is obvious that the problem of values contains nothing but the adjustment character of human conduct. Right or wrong only means efficiency, and there is no answer to the question: Efficiency for what? [P. 146; cf. p. 167]

In other words: 'rationality that is functional for what?' a question that can be answered only by substantial rationality, which continues to be lacking[97]—but which is needed most urgently because we 'have a new and extremely dangerous antagonist . . . Mechanized Barbarism' (p. 151; cf. the end of *Ideologie und Utopie* and the comparison it suggested with Max Weber's pessimism in *The Protestant Ethic*[98]).

Mannheim concludes his paper by discussing 'some concrete issues which are subject to re-valuation' (p. 164), namely, general ethics, ethics of personal, and ethics of organized, relations. A dilemma under the first heading is: '"What is the good of democracy if we do not survive?" or alternatively "What is the good of surviving if we lose our freedom?"' (p. 166), which Mannheim answers by saying that

we have first to make the primary choice in our hierarchy between the survival value of efficiency and democracy. Once this is settled we can turn to concrete issues and work out the casuistry of individual decisions. [P. 167]

Under 'Ethics of Personal Relationships' he deals with the problems of privacy and of mass ecstasy in the modern world, under 'Ethics of Organized Relationships' with several aspects of relations within a factory all of which, he claims, need re-evaluation. In regard to organized relations Mannheim diagnoses two tendencies:

There is a tendency to introduce into the sphere of work the military pattern of command and blind obedience. On the other hand, there are often very strong tendencies at work beneath the surface, which are at the same time anti-Fascist, anti-Communist and anti-Capitalist, representing fundamentally new strivings of men and women. They do not yet form a new system, or a coherent outlook, but it is possible to point to these trends which, particularly under the revolutionizing effect of war, are emerging here and there irrespective of the political organization which prevails. [Pp. 176–77]

[96] 'Paradigmatic experiences' are 'those decisive, basic experiences which are felt to reveal the meaning of life as a whole. Their pattern is so deeply impressed upon our mind that they provide a mould into which further experiences flow. Thus once formed they lend shape to later experiences' (p. 187, n. 7).

[97] Cf. the quotation from p. 118, along with n. 92, above, and XVIII, p. 75 ('who plans the planner?', a question that 'haunts' Mannheim).

[98] Cf. XIV above.

These are: economic organization moving 'from purely financial calculation' to '"organic welfare"'; working incentives moving 'from purely financial recompense to the motive of Service'; the emergence of an 'integrated attitude' stressing a combination of 'security for everybody' and 'collective venture'; the meaning of freedom turning from free enterprise to creativeness; and 'a move towards a true democracy' which 'allots a creative social task to everybody' (p. 177). Mannheim concludes his essay, again, with qualified hope:

> I am aware of the fact that an over-emphasis on the humanization of organized relationships in factory, Civil Service and elsewhere, without reorganizing the economic structure in its fundamentals [cf. the inconclusive section 'The Emerging Social Pattern in its Economic Aspects', pp. 156–59], might be misused by those who only want to alter human relationships on the surface without paying the price of structural reconstruction. But the only remedy for this possible misuse is social awareness. Just as it is impossible in the long run to humanize leisure and factory relationships within a dictatorial system, where the pattern of command and obedience will necessary [*sic*] break through everywhere, so it is equally impossible to humanize factory relationships as long as the basis of calculation remains efficiency in terms of money returns and profits instead of social welfare. [P. 178]

(3)   Three Short Papers (1944, 1945, 1946)

In 1944 J. R. M. Brumwell edited *This Changing World* ('A Series of Contributions by Some of Our Leading Thinkers, to Cast Light upon the Pattern of the Modern World'), to which Mannheim contributed a chapter on 'Democratic Planning and the New Science of Society' (the subtitle, supplied no doubt by the editor or publisher, reads: 'The century to come will be dedicated to the study of the social and moral sciences and to the problems of democratic planning'). Mannheim shows the merits of sociology by examples which make it plausible that individuals should be understood in terms of groups to which they belong rather than in isolation, from there moves to his arguments for planning and the distinction between fascist and democratic planning, and ends with a mixture of threat and hope: 'so long as we fail to make the democratic processes function within the framework of modern society, we shall be doomed to live either drifting in chaos or imprisoned in a cage' (p. 82).

The title footnote of 'The Meaning of Popularisation in a Mass Society' (February 1945) refers to 'Professor Mannheim's forthcoming book, *Essentials of Democratic Planning*, which he is writing for the Royal Institute of International Affairs', and in which 'the ideas expressed . . . [here] will be developed more fully'—as did a footnote to 'Diagnosis of Our Time', the first paper in the volume by that title ((2), 2nd par., above; but *Freedom, Power, and*

Democratic Planning contains nothing on popularization). Just as Mannheim had argued against the 'contempt for the masses' in 'Mass Education and Group Analysis' (XIX (3), end, above), so he now argues against the contempt for popularization, in favor of 'creative dissemination':

The future of culture depends not only on our ability to guarantee the conditions of survival for original thinkers at higher levels, but also on our inventiveness in finding new forms for the dissemination of the substance of culture without diluting it. [P. 8]

Those who succeed in the great venture of being genuine on the lower levels of communication contribute at least as much to the preservation of culture as those who keep existing fires burning in small selected circles. [P. 10]

Only those who have the capacity to communicate with any audience realize how much fertilizing power there is in saying the same thing to different people.

. . . Those who teach and have something to impart need to be trained to assimilate and to interpret correctly the minds of those to whom they speak. In this the new discipline of the sociology of knowledge, which studies systematically different existing frames of mind . . . and the sociology of education, which studies the concrete conditions in which education takes place, can be of great help. [P. 12]

Mannheim probably thought of this short paper, including the references to the sociology of knowledge, one of his old, pre-English concerns, and to the sociology of education, one of his most recent concerns in England, as a modest instance of 'creative dissemination'.

'The Function of the Refugee' (April 1945) is 'A Rejoinder' to Montgomery Belgion's short article, 'The Germanization of Britain'.[99]

Any student of sociology would have told Captain Belgion that I am one of the most ardent protagonists of the idea that there is a fundamental difference in subject matter between the natural and the social sciences. . . . His attack will have, I hope, at least one merit—that it will draw the attention of thoughtful people to Hodges' book on Wilhelm Dilthey.[100] [P. 5]

[99] *The New English Weekly*, 26 (15 February 1945): 137–38. Examples: 'A considerable number of German speculative writers . . . can be found to have let Reason founder altogether while they were enticed to their perdition as thinkers by those two Lorelei, the Extravagant and the Fanciful. Among this number we may include, I submit, the Brothers Schlegel, Goethe, Karl Marx, Schopenhauer and Nietzsche, and unquestionably the inventors of psycho-analysis'. As well as Mannheim. And 'Dilthey is as corrupting as Dr. Mannheim'. (Quotations from p. 138.)

[100] H. A. Hodges, *Wilhelm Dilthey: An Introduction*, which appeared in 1944 in the 'International Library of Sociology and Social Reconstruction', which Mannheim edited—and in the present article also defended against Belgion's critique. (In the same series Hodges published *The Philosophy of Wilhelm Dilthey* in 1952, when, after Mannheim's death, the series was edited by W. H. Sprott.)

A sociological question 'implicit in Captain Belgion's article' concerns the fashion in which refugees or, 'if I may put it more exactly', 'individuals who have assimilated two or more cultures' can 'best serve the country of their adoption'. Mannheim's answer is that such a person has the 'new constructive task' 'to serve as a living interpreter between different cultures and to create living communication between different worlds which so far have been kept apart' (p. 6). This, the article as a whole, all of these three brief papers, and indeed most of what he wrote in England, shows the difference, among other things, between his pre-Hitler thoughts about the 'socially unattached intelligentsia'[101] and himself as one of its representatives on the one hand, and on the other, himself as a refugee; 'more exactly' as one of the 'individuals who have assimilated two or more cultures'. Whatever 'assimilated', indeed whatever 'culture' may mean in this context, one aspect of Mannheim's change, intimated before,[102] is that he now used, or had to use, part of his energy in 'assimilating', while as long as he wrote in German, he had all of it at his disposal for his investigation. Now part went into assimilation, part into 'creative dissemination'; only the rest was left for his own voice, which was that much diminished for it. This also applies to the last work he wrote, the *Essentials of Democratic Planning*, posthumously published as *Freedom, Power, and Democratic Planning*.

XXI.   *'Freedom, Power, and Democratic Planning'* (1950)

While he was in Germany, Mannheim's central preoccupation had been the sociology of knowledge, that is, the effort to understand intellectual phenomena sociologically, rather than in the belief that an 'intrinsic interpretation' could be exhaustive or that referring them to other 'extrinsic', such as philosophical or religious, points of view would be adequate. Sociological interpretation was and is a stirring proposition, an easily disquieting, certainly a meaningful, experience. Mannheim explored and tried to conceptualize this experience, a shattering but intriguing onslaught of secularization, which turned out to be one of the frustrated promises of the Weimar Republic. The promise might be formulated as that of an answer to the question:

How in the face of the demonstration that the spirit is socially conditioned can I still do right by its inexhaustibility and unforeseeability? Or, perhaps: how can I, nevertheless, save it? But also: How in the face of the overwhelming spirit can I ascertain as accurately as possible its intimate connection with society, and how can I proclaim this connection precisely for the sake of both, spirit and society?

[101] Cf. XIV, Table of Contents, 'Is Politics Possible as a Science?', Section 4, and XVII (2), above.

[102] Cf. particularly the beginning of XIX above; also XIX (5).

The 'but also' in this question and what follows it is marked already by the imminent collapse of the Weimar Republic in the early thirties, when the promise had faded, then gone, and a question had risen that came to replace the promise. 'Later, ever more urgently', this question revealed itself to Mannheim in England as 'How can I save society?'[103]

Hence, his leap into Planning, Planning for Freedom, the Third Way, his trying to figure out how to put it into practice, as well as how to convince his new audience of its terrible urgency. Beginning, roughly, with *Man and Society*, and plainly in *Diagnosis of Our Time* and later writings, including the present book, sociology is primarily understood as our guide to avert our disaster and instead to reconstruct society and ourselves as individuals. Thus if the German Mannheim above all articulated sociology, he now above all promoted and applied it—while at the same time trying, as has been suggested, to assimilate his new setting as well as to disseminate what he had brought with him and was now learning. In part his energy did have to be devoted to new tasks; to put it differently, his passion was more multi-faceted than it had been. Bramsted and Gerth frame a similar observation when they say that Mannheim was

a thinker to whom 'thinking' more and more meant the unity of diagnosis and therapy. The detached critical observer has grown into the political and social strategist who tries to understand so that others may be able to act.[104]

Freedom, Power, and Democratic Planning, the preface to which is dated January 1947, the month Mannheim died, consists of three parts. The first, 'Diagnosis of the Situation', surveys social techniques that enable small minorities to exercise unprecedented power, and describes small-group and cooperative controls that have disintegrated, as well as systems of secular and religious beliefs that have lost their vitality. A review of the totalitarian responses to the crisis—the pessimistic answer of fascism and the utopian answer of communism—leads Mannheim to advocate his own response, democratic planning.

Part II ('Democratic Planning and Changing Institutions') develops what this means in regard to society, Part III ('New Man—New Values') what it means in regard to the individual. In contrast to the clarity of this overall structure, smaller units are sometimes less plausibly where they are or are less clearly pertinent. We have observed this insufficiently transparent orga-

---

[103] Cf. the beginning of this introduction, just before I above; also XIX (4), the passage to which n. 81 refers.
[104] Bramsted and Gerth, *op. cit.*, p. xii.

nization of Mannheim's work before. It may have to do with the less than transparent nature of his relation to his subject matter. This relation is composed of commitment and analysis, each of which makes Mannheim, moving back and forth between them, attract, like a magnet, bits of heterogeneous intellectual origins, among these themselves conative and cognitive ones, which in the rush of the exploration get placed sometimes more nearly wherever they fall rather than according to a plan, thus making for un-satisfactory organization.

Part II, for instance, opens with a chapter on power that is relevant to the announced purpose of the Part only here and there, especially in the last three sections. The remaining chapters of this Part deal with the ruling class (and many related phenomena) in totalitarian and democratic societies; with the 'reformation of politics', where specified controls of the social structure, the economy, the military and civil services, and of communication are advocated; and with the 'democratic control of government'. Part III discusses 'the new science of human behavior' that has begun to replace custom, introduces the concept of 'integrative behavior' (cf. the 'blended attitudes' we must foster in youth),[105] and, in connection with this, deals with subjective and objective aspects of responsibility. It analyzes the type of personality called for by democratic society and suggests measures for developing it, paying special attention to education in the more customary sense of this word. Other chapters discuss the meaning of work and leisure, and the potential conflict between freedom and discipline in planned society. The book closes with an inquiry—which supplements 'Towards a New Philosophy'[106]—into the integration of the social order through religion.

This cursory overview suggests the similarity between *Man and Society* and the present work, which, however, is more clearly written, is addressed to a wider audience, and is better worked out. The overview can also provide the context for discussing two passages from among many that serve to document our claims regarding Mannheim's way of writing and the changing style of his life work.

The first passage occurs in the chapter, 'The Reformation of Politics'. Mannheim points out that propaganda is misconceived if it is understood only as 'the fine art of spreading lies and arous-ing dangerous emotions'.[107] For it

[105] In XX (2) above.
[106] Cf. XX (2) above.
[107] There is a slight, probably remediable inconsistency when Mannheim writes: 'The propagandist skilfully plays on fears and ecstasies which block or sweep away rational thought and judiciousness' (p. 159).

can be fully appreciated only if one recognizes its most significant function, namely, the determination of the *reality level* on which people are going to discuss and act.

By 'reality level' we mean that every society develops a mental climate in which certain facts and their interrelations are considered basic and called 'real', whereas other ideas fall below the level of 'reasonably acceptable' statements and are called fantastic, utopian, or unrealistic. In every society there is a generally accepted interpretation of reality. [P. 138][108]

However 'reality level' may be defined more strictly, its determination does not define propaganda because this also is the function of religion, philosophy, and of other social institutions and customs. Nor can we assume without further argument that propaganda is found in all societies, as the passage appears to imply, rather than being a historical phenomenon. Mannheim cannot mean to identify 'propaganda' with 'a generally accepted interpretation of reality'[109] or to use 'fact', 'idea', and 'statement', etc., synonymously. The passage gives us only a vague notion of its subject matter, and this is true of many passages in Mannheim's writing— whether more or less often and in the same sense in the English as compared with the German period could be decided only by a special investigation. Obviously a far more useful response to such passages than to discard them impatiently, no matter how tempted one might sometimes be, is to use them as an opportunity to clarify what Mannheim has left obscure.

Another aspect of the passage quoted is that it simply is silent about the grave epistemological problem raised by the proposition that propaganda determines the 'reality level'. The problem, of course, is what on such a relativistic view becomes of truth—a problem that used to occupy Mannheim the sociologist of knowledge. Now his devotion is directed, not to conceptual clarity and metaphysical responsibility, but to saving the West—an effort which might be critically delayed, somebody could argue, by the time needed for doing justice to conceptual and philosophical requirements. Indeed, Mannheim himself says: 'In our approach, social theory in many ways represents only a higher elaboration of the dynamic purposes behind an endless series of experiments designed to help man in his practical life toward new patterns of action' (p. 236).

A second passage illustrates a similar shift in regard to a closely related topic. In his discussion of 'integrative behavior'

---

[108] It is perhaps strange that in connection with this last expression Mannheim does not refer to Scheler's closely related 'relatively natural *Weltanschauung*': Scheler, *op. cit.* (notes 27 and 42 above), pp. 59 f. (Scheler is not mentioned in the whole volume—nor in XI above: see next note.)

[109] On this, it may be recalled, see on a larger scale and as a central, rather than incidental concern as it is here, XI above.

Mannheim tries to clarify its meaning by contrasting it with 'compromise': 'The essence of democracy is the integration of purposes and not mere compromise', that is, mere 'rational adjustment between two or more opposing views' (p. 203). Here (as elsewhere in his English writings) Mannheim advocates a way of life and a society which would further it, and this advocacy is another variant of his change, another successor to his pre-Hitler concern with the problem of how to guarantee truth, of how to find the common element in conflicting views—a successor especially to one of his answers, the 'socially unattached intelligentsia', which we recently had occasion to recall.[110] To be practicable as a vehicle of mediation, both the old 'intelligentsia' and the new 'integrative behavior' presuppose the presence of the most important element they are designed to produce, that is, the *will* to mediate, seek what is common, integrate. In Germany as well as in England, Mannheim must have taken this so for granted that he failed to perceive the need for explicating it in his conceptualization of the mediating mechanisms. Perhaps he realized in England that in Germany he had been under an illusion, but now no longer was—now that he was 'surprised by the absence of that chaotic diversity of hostile groups that had destroyed the Weimar Republic'.[111] If so, the referent of the concept would have changed toward greater realism, but the problem of mediation in the absence of the will to it and the problem of how to create this will had remained and remains unsolved; nor had Mannheim even conceptualized these problems, or was conceptualizing them now in England.

The change, then, which he underwent as he moved from pre-Hitler Germany to England during and after Hitler was from analyst to a mixture of *engagé* and 'political and social strategist'.[112] What presumably did *not* change was his conception of sociology as 'the most secularized approach to the problems of human life',[113] nor, probably, his fascination with sociology so understood: 'Anyone who wants to drag in the irrational where the lucidity and acuity of reason still must rule by right merely shows that he is afraid to face the mystery at its legitimate place'.[114]

What evidence we have does not suggest[115] that his feeling for religion as 'mystery at its legitimate place' changed during his

[110] End of XX (3) and n. 100.
[111] Bramsted and Gerth, quoted in XIX, passage to which n. 77 refers.
[112] Bramsted and Gerth, quoted in passage to which n. 104 refers.
[113] XX (2), p. 127, quoted above and recalling VIII.
[114] This passage from 'Competition as a Cultural Phenomenon' (XI) has been referred to more than once before (quoted in the beginning, before I; quoted and interpreted in a certain perspective in IX; cited at the end of XI).
[115] Cf. I, last paragraph, above.

adult life; still, Mannheim might have accepted Albert Salomon's
description of the point that Mannheim, Salomon thought, had
reached at the time of his death:

There is no sociology of knowledge, but of error; there is no sociology of
aesthetics, but of fashions and tastes. . . . [A contrary assumption is not]
capable of motivating the principles of freedom and human dignity which
remain the goal of Mannheim's sociological theory of planning. Neither
sociological nor psychological techniques of planning are of any avail if they
do not create a frame of reference in which living and dying have some
meaning.[116]

XXII.   *Two Further Posthumous Works: 'Systematic Sociology'* (1957)
and 'An Introduction to the Sociology of Education' (1962)

Systematic Sociology appeared ten years after Mannheim's
death,[117] *Sociology of Education* fifteen;[118] and thus far, at least,
they are his last posthumous works. But this is hardly the reason
why here, too, they appear last; in fact, chronologically they
might have to be placed earlier; instead, there are other, and
interrelated, reasons. These two books come last because they are
'least': least like the first Mannheim, even less so than we have
had occasion to remark in regard to some of his other slighter
writings from his English period; least determinably by Mannheim himself, rather than by J. S. Erös and W. A. C. Stewart,
the editors of *Systematic Sociology*, and, respectively, W. A. C.
Stewart, the self-declared co-author of the *Sociology of Education*;[119]
least, finally, but most importantly, in substance. The kind of

[116] Albert Salomon, 'Karl Mannheim, 1893–1947', *Social Research*, 14 (1947):
361.

[117] 'The first three parts of this book [Man and His Psychic Equipment;
The Most Elementary Social Processes; Social Integration] are based on the
manuscript of Mannheim's lectures on systematic sociology, first delivered
during the academic session 1934–35 and, in slightly modified form, during the
following sessions. Part Four of this book [Social Stability and Social Change] is
based on some of the lectures in a course on social structure delivered during the
war years.' Editorial Preface, p. xi.

[118] 'There were few relatively complete manuscripts on which any section
of this book could be based. Many, many fragments and notes, a very small
number of complete lectures with the usual pause and accent markings, sheets
of bibliographies, schemes for lecture courses, diagrams for ideas, characteristically bold and handsome doodlings—these constituted the materials from
which the book has been constructed. Because I have had to be arbitrary in
selection and to be freer in adapting and composing the material than an
editor should be, I have coupled my name with Mannheim's as co-author.
While it is true that I have been more than an editor, it is clear that the basic
ideas in the book are Karl Mannheim's.' Introduction, pp. xv–xvi.

[119] See preceding note. The authorship of these two books appears to be
even more difficult to ascertain than in the case of *Soc. Cult.*; cf. XVII above,
introductory paragraphs.

literature both approach is that of textbooks, at which Mannheim may well impress one as rather inept. As a textbook *Systematic Sociology* is superior to the *Sociology of Education*, which seems to derive from far more fragmentary materials.

Systematic Sociology, indeed, might be considered for revision, tightening the argument and bringing references up to date, then trying it out as an introductory text. Among its advantages over many other texts that are in use is its attention to both animal sociology and psychoanalysis; its concern—in the very beginning of an introduction to sociology—with 'individualisation' (esp. pp. 65 ff.); and its wide-cast net of references (a net, however, which is not always pulled up and inspected). Among its weaknesses are the absence or the poverty of definitions and many inadequate or inconclusive discussions, such as of 'group' and kinds of groups (pp. 82, 107–12), authority (p. 129), 'values' (pp. 131 ff.), or Marx and Marxism (pp. 137, 143, 144). Here too, Mannheim is the concerned reformer who opposes revolution:

> If one takes it [the class struggle] as a tendency, there will only be struggle if through reform we are unable to remove those institutions which hamper the evolution of the modern economic system, and thus cause continuous crises in it. But on principle revolution can always be avoided if these transformations are carried out gradually and in a peaceful way. If from the very beginning we state that the struggle is, and must be, inevitable, we sap reform. On the other hand, one has of course always to be alive to the possibility that through frustration revolution may become unavoidable. [P. 145]

The last chapter ('The Future') of *An Introduction to the Sociology of Education* begins with what could serve as a motto for the book:

> No educational activity or research is adequate in the present stage of consciousness unless it is conceived in terms of a sociology of education. [P. 159]

And while Mannheim misses no occasion to persuade the reader of the relevance of sociology, the book also contains many other kinds of material, such as expositions of theories of personality and of learning theories (according to which Freud plus Hull are better than either alone: p. 67; and dynamic psychology is superior to associationist psychology: p. 83). Against much confusion, which still prevails, Mannheim clearly distinguishes (Chapter II, pp. 12–18) between training (having to do with skills), instruction (with information), teaching (with interaction between teacher and student), and education (which goes far beyond school toward life-long 'socialization', a term Mannheim does not use in this sense); this 'broader definition of education' (p. 19), he believes, has arisen because of the 'spread of democracy, the greater mastery of the social environment, and the importance

of the community as well as the home as an educational agency'
(p. 20). His concern with education is genuine, and far more so
than his concern with analyzing it—'it' referring to both concern
and education—in its connectedness with the economy and with
questions of economy:

... While everybody admits that perhaps the most pressing international
problem is that of poverty in the midst of plenty, we have to add that we
can have barbarism in the midst of educational plenty. [P. 6]

And so (for instance) he only writes (in 'Sociology for the
Educator')[120]:

The economics of a society can be pretty clearly seen in the class structure
and conflict and the importance attached to the various forms of property
control. . . . In a capitalist or mixed economy ownership is in the hands of
individuals or groups of individuals and educators have to understand the
motivations to which these different points of view give rise, because they will
help to establish the attitudes of parents and children and of the teachers
themselves, to the institution of school. [P. 151]

Basing himself on Max Weber, Mannheim distinguishes
'charismatic education', 'education for culture', and 'specialist
education' (p. 161; without relating this typology to that developed in Chapter II). 'Specialist education', he says—and
people today may well be more receptive to his words than when
he pronounced them—'produces the necessary cogs and wheels
in the social machine', but it 'disintegrates both the personality
and the mental powers for understanding the human situation
which has to be mastered' (p. 161).

XXIII. *Invitation, Not Conclusion*

This was the last thing to write about the last book which has to
do with Mannheim's own writing; and everything ends abruptly:
the section just finished, the reading of his life, his life itself. The
reading of his life is this life conceived as read, a process of
expressing an interaction with Karl Mannheim as he expressed
himself from beginning to end. There is no summing up, no
summary, no conclusion—all of this, too, instead, is in the reading,
for anybody who so wishes to tease out. And in this reading,
intensity and thoroughness, just as boredom or hurry, are responses to Mannheim's own expression, which also was variable,
although the fundamental turn occurred in 1933. A second
expression of interaction with him is the choice of his writings

---

[120] Part of a lecture, 'Sociology and Education', delivered by Mannheim
in 1943, on which, the editor informs us (p. 143n.), Chapter XIV, 'Sociology
for the Educator and the Sociology of Education', is based.

contained in this volume. But both expressions are not only the results of interaction. Obviously they also have a function: that of inviting the reader to engage in his own interaction with their source.

Newton, Massachusetts
Christmas, 1969 K.H.W.

Bibliography
of Mannheim's Writings
(following the sequence in the preceding introduction)

I. Soul and Culture. Lélek és Kultura. Programmelöadás A II.
szemeszter megnyitása alkalmából tartotta. Mannheim Károly.
Budapest, 1918. Benkö Gyula Cs. és kir. Udvari Könyvkeres-
kedése. [Soul and Culture. Programmatic lecture given at the
opening of the second semester by Karl Mannheim. Budapest,
1918. Gyula Benkö's Imperial and Royal Bookstore.] (Elöadások
a szellemi tudományok köréböl [Lectures in the field of the
human studies].) No English translation exists. German translation, 'Seele und Kultur', by Ernest Manheim in *Wissenssoziologie*,
pp. 66–84. This is the version here used.

II. Review of Lukács's *Theory of the Novel*. Review of Georg
Lukács, *Die Theorie des Romans, ein geschichtsphilosophischer Versuch
über die Formen der grossen Epik* [. . . an essay in the philosophy of
history of the great epic forms], Berlin: Cassirer, 1920. *Logos*,
9 (1920–21): 298–302. Reprinted in *Wissenssoziologie*, pp. 85–90.
English translation by KHW in *Studies on the Left*, 3, 3 (Summer
1963): 50–53. Reprinted here.

III. On the Interpretation of *Weltanschauung*. Beiträge zur
Theorie der Weltanschauungs-Interpretation. *Jahrbuch für Kunstgeschichte*, I (XV), 4 (1921–22): 236–74. Translated by Paul
Kecskemeti, in Karl Mannheim, *Essays on the Sociology of Knowledge (Soc. Knowl.)*, Paul Kecskemeti, ed. [and transl.]. London:
Routledge and Kegan Paul; New York: Oxford University Press,
1952, pp. 33–83. Both this translation and the reprint in *Wissenssoziologie* (pp. 91–154) have been used here.

IV. On the Problem of the Classification of the Sciences. Zum
Problem einer Klassifikation der Wissenschaften. *Archiv für*

Sozialwissenschaft und Sozialpolitik, 50, 1 (1922): 230–37. Reprinted in *Wissenssoziologie*, pp. 155–65. This is the text here used.

V. Structural Analysis of Epistemology. *Die Strukturanalyse der Erkenntnistheorie*. *Kant-Studien*, Ergänzungsheft [supplement] Nr. 57. Berlin: Reuther und Reichard, 1922. 80 pages. Translated by Edith Schwarzschild and Paul Kecskemeti, in Karl Mannheim, *Essays on Sociology and Social Psychology* (*Soc. Soc. Psych.*), Paul Kecskemeti, ed. London: Routledge and Kegan Paul; New York: Oxford University Press, 1953, pp. 15–73. Both this translation and the reprint in *Wissenssoziologie* (pp. 166–245) have been used here.

VI. Historicism. Historismus. *Archiv für Sozialwissenschaft und Sozialpolitik*, 52, 1 (1924): 1–60. Translated by Paul Kecskemeti in *Soc. Knowl.*, pp. 84–133. Both this translation and the reprint in *Wissenssoziologie* (pp. 246–307) have been used here.

VII. The Problem of a Sociology of Knowledge. Das Problem einer Soziologie des Wissens. *Archiv für Sozialwissenschaft und Sozialpolitik*, 53, 3 (1925): 577–652. Translated by Paul Kecskemeti in *Soc. Knowl.*, pp. 134–90. Both this translation and the reprint in *Wissenssoziologie* (pp. 308–87) have been used here.

VIII. The Ideological and the Sociological Interpretation of Intellectual Phenomena. Ideologische und soziologische Interpretation der geistigen Gebilde. *Jahrbuch für Soziologie*, 2 (1926): 424–40. Reprinted in *Wissenssoziologie*, pp. 388–407. English translation by KHW in *Studies on the Left*, 3, 3 (Summer 1963): 54–66. Reprinted here.

IX. Conservative Thought. Das konservative Denken. Soziologische Beiträge zum Werden des politisch-historischen Denkens in Deutschland [. . . sociological studies of the development of politico-historical thought in Germany]. *Archiv für Sozialwissenschaft und Sozialpolitik*, 57, 1 (1927): 68–142; 2: 470–95. Translated by Karl Mannheim and Paul Kecskemeti in *Soc. Soc. Psych.*, pp. 74–164. Both this translation and the reprint in *Wissenssoziologie* (pp. 408–508) have been used here.

The History of the Concept of the State as an Organism: A Sociological Analysis. *Soc. Soc. Psych.*, pp. 165–82.

X. The Problem of Generations. Das Problem der Generationen. *Kölner Vierteljahrshefte für Soziologie*, 7, 2 (1928): 157–85; 3:

309–30. Translated by Paul Kecskemeti in *Soc. Knowl.*, pp. 276–322. Both this translation and the reprint in *Wissenssoziologie* (pp. 509–65, 703–5) have been used here.

XI. Competition as a Cultural Phenomenon. Die Bedeutung der Konkurrenz im Gebiete des Geistigen. *Verhandlungen des sechsten deutschen Soziologentages vom 17. bis 19. September 1928 in Zürich.* Tübingen: J. C. B. Mohr (Paul Siebeck), 1929, pp. 35–83. Translated by Paul Kecskemeti in *Soc. Knowl.*, pp. 191–229. Both this translation and the reprint in *Wissenssoziologie* (pp. 566–613) have been used here.

XII. Problems of Sociology in Germany. Zur Problematik der Soziologie in Deutschland. *Neue Schweizer Rundschau*, 22 (November 1929): 820–29. Translated for this volume by KHW from the reprint in *Wissenssoziologie*, pp. 614–24.

XIII. On the Nature of Economic Ambition and Its Significance for the Social Education of Man. Über das Wesen und die Bedeutung des wirtschaftlichen Erfolgsstrebens. Ein Beitrag zur Wirtschaftssoziologie. *Archiv für Sozialwissenschaft und Sozialpolitik*, 63, 3 (1930): 449–512. Translated by Paul Kecskemeti in *Soc. Knowl.*, pp. 230–75. Both this translation and the reprint in *Wissenssoziologie* (pp. 625–87, 705–10) have been used here.

XIV. *Ideology and Utopia. Ideologie und Utopie* (Schriften zur Philosophie und Soziologie, begründet von Max Scheler, herausgegeben von Dr. phil. Karl Mannheim, Band III). Bonn: Friedrich Cohen, 1929. Pp. xv + 250. Translated by Louis Wirth and Edward Shils, with an introductory chapter by Karl Mannheim and a translation of XV below. London: Routledge and Kegan Paul; New York: Harcourt, Brace, 1936. Pp. xxxi + 318. Both the original and the translation have been used here.

XV. The Sociology of Knowledge. Wissenssoziologie. *Handwörterbuch der Soziologie*, Alfred Vierkandt, ed. Stuttgart: Ferdinand Enke, 1931. Pp. 659–80. Translated by Wirth and Shils in *Ideology and Utopia*, pp. 237–80. This translation has been used here.

Preliminary Approach to the Problem. In *Ideology and Utopia*, pp. 1–48.

XVI. (1) *The Tasks of Sociology Called for by the Present: A Teaching Program. Die Gegenwartsaufgaben der Soziologie: ihre Lehrgestalt.* Tübingen: J. C. B. Mohr (Paul Siebeck), 1932. 65 pages. Neither reprinted nor translated.

(2) American Sociology. Review of Stuart A. Rice, ed., *Methods in Social Science*, Chicago: University of Chicago Press, 1931. *American Journal of Sociology*, 37 (September 1932): 273–82. Reprinted in *Soc. Soc. Psych.*, pp. 185–94. This reprint has been used here.

(3) German Sociology (1918–1933). *Politica*, 1 (February 1934): 12–33. Reprinted in *Soc. Soc. Psych.*, pp. 209–28. This reprint has been used here.

(4) The Place of Sociology. Presumably not published prior to *Soc. Soc. Psych.*, pp. 195–208. Cf. last entry in this Bibliography.

XVII. *Essays on the Sociology of Culture*. Edited by Ernest Manheim in cooperation with Paul Kecskemeti. London: Routledge and Kegan Paul; New York: Oxford University Press, 1956. Pp. ix + 253. Translated from German manuscripts which it has thus far not been possible to trace. From the early 1930's.

(1) Towards the Sociology of the Mind; An Introduction (edited by Ernest Manheim), pp. 15–89;

(2) The Problem of the Intelligentsia. An Inquiry into Its Past and Present Role (edited by Ernest Manheim), pp. 91–170;

(3) The Democratization of Culture (edited by Paul Kecskemeti) (1933), pp. 171–246.

XVIII. *Man and Society in an Age of Reconstruction: Studies in Modern Social Structure*. With a Bibliographical Guide to the Study of Modern Society. (Based on *Mensch und Gesellschaft im Zeitalter des Umbaus* [Leiden: A. W. Sijthoff, 1935. Pp. xviii + 208]. Revised and considerably enlarged by the Author.) Translated by Edward Shils. London: Routledge and Kegan Paul; New York: Harcourt, Brace, 1940. Pp. xxii + 469.

XIX. (1) A Few Concrete Examples Concerning the Sociological Nature of Human Valuations. The Sociology of Human Valuations: The Psychological and Sociological Approach. In J. E. Dugdale, ed., *Further Papers on the Social Sciences, Their Relations in Theory and Teaching*: Being the Report of a Conference Held under the Auspices of the Institute of Sociology at Westfield College, Hampstead, London, from the 25th to the 27th of September 1936. London: LePlay House Press, 1937, pp. 171–91. The original (second) title above is the one listed in the Table of Contents. In the text it is: A Few Concrete Examples Concerning the Sociological Nature of Human Valuations; with Some Theoretical Remarks on the Difference between the psychological and the Sociological Approach. Reprinted in *Soc. Soc. Psych.*, pp. 231–42. This reprint has been used here.

(2) Untitled. *Prager Presse*, 28 March 1937. Not reprinted. Translated for this volume by KHW.

(3) On the Diagnosis of Our Time. Zur Diagnose unserer Zeit, *Mass und Wert*, 1, 1 (September–October 1937): 100–21. Not reprinted. Translated for this volume by KHW.

(4) Planned Society and the Problem of Human Personality: A Sociological Analysis. *Soc. Soc. Psych.*, pp. 253–310. P. 255n.: 'The four lectures in this section were delivered at Manchester College, Oxford, in 1938'. Not published prior to the publication in *Soc. Soc. Psych.*

(5) Adult Education and the Social Sciences. *Tutors' Bulletin of Adult Education*, 2nd. Series, no. 20 (February 1938): 27–34.

(6) Mass Education and Group Analysis. In J. I. Cohen and R. M. W. Travers, eds., *Educating for Democracy*. London: Macmillan & Co., 1939, pp. 329–64. Reprinted in XX (2).

XX. (1) On War-Conditioned Changes in Our Psychic Economy. *Soc. Soc. Psych.*, pp. 243–51. Apparently not published before.

(2) *Diagnosis of Our Time: Wartime Essays of a Sociologist.* London: Routledge and Kegan Paul; New York: Oxford University Press, 1943. Pp. xi + 180.

(3) a. Democratic Planning and the New Science of Society. In J. R. M. Brumwell, ed., *This Changing World*. A series of contributions by some of our leading thinkers, to cast light upon the pattern of the modern world. London: George Routledge & Sons, 1944, pp. 71–82.

b. The Meaning of Popularisation in a Mass Society. *The Christian News-Letter*, 7 February 1945, Supplement to No. 227: 7–12.

c. The Function of the Refugee. *The New English Weekly*, 27, 1 (19 April 1945): 5–6.

XXI. *Freedom, Power, and Democratic Planning*. Edited by Ernest K. Bramsted and Hans Gerth. London: Routledge and Kegan Paul; New York: Oxford University Press, 1950. Pp. xxiv + 384.

XXII. *Systematic Sociology: An Introduction to the Study of Society*. Edited by J. S. Erös and W. A. C. Stewart. London: Routledge and Kegan Paul; New York: Oxford University Press, 1957. Pp. xxx + 169.

An Introduction to the Sociology of Education. By Karl Mannheim and W. A. C. Stewart. London: Routledge and Kegan Paul; New York: Humanities Press, 1962. 187 pages.

OTHER WRITINGS BY MANNHEIM

Rational and Irrational Elements in Contemporary Society. Hobhouse Memorial Lecture, delivered on 7 March 1934 at Bedford College for Women (University of London). London: Oxford University Press, 1934. 36 pages. Expanded in *Mensch und Gesellschaft,* 1935 (see XVIII), and in XVIII.

The Crisis of Culture in the Era of Mass-Democracies and Autarchies. *Sociological Review,* 26, 2 (April 1934): 105–29. Expanded in *Mensch und Gesellschaft,* 1935 (see XVIII), and in XVIII.

Troeltsch, Ernst. *Encyclopaedia of the Social Sciences,* Vol. XV, 1935.

Utopia. *Encyclopaedia of the Social Sciences,* Vol. XV, 1935.

The Psychological Aspect. In C. A. W. Manning, ed. *Peaceful Change: An International Problem.* London: Macmillan & Co.; New York: Macmillan Co., 1937, pp. 101–32. Expanded in XVIII.

Present Trends in the Building of Society. Translated by H. Lewis. In R. B. Cattell, J. I. Cohen, and R. M. W. Travers, eds., *Human Affairs.* London: Macmillan & Co., 1937, Chapter XIV, pp. 278–300. Expanded in XVIII.

Les sciences sociales et la sociologie. In *Les convergences des sciences sociales* (Introduction de C. Bouglé), Paris, 1937, pp. 208–24. French version of XVI (4).

NOTE

The major sources of writings on Mannheim (not always exclusively) are contained in the following.

I.U.

Man and Society

Norman Birnbaum, 'The Sociological Study of Ideology (1940–60): A Trend Report and Bibliography', *Current Sociology: La sociologie contemporaine,* IX, 2 (1960): 127–72.

Groupe de sociologie de la connaissance et de la vie morale, 'Bibliographie de la sociologie de la connaissance', *Cahiers internationaux de sociologie,* 32 (1962): 135–76.

Kurt Lenk, ed. and intr., *Ideologie: Ideologiekritik und Wissenssoziologie,* Neuwied: Luchterhand (Soziologische Texte, Band 4), 1961, pp. 323–38; 2nd ed., 1964, pp. 381–400 *Wissenssoziologie,* pp. 699–703.

Sociological Abstracts, since 1953; consult Decennial Index (to 1962) and later indexes, entries under 'Mannheim, Karl'.

From Karl Mannheim

I
A Review of Georg Lukács'
*Theory of the Novel**

To account for the enigma of the variety of forms of art is the task of aesthetics. This variety is a historical given; the task is to interpret its meaning.

It is characteristic of intellectual phenomena that they can be explained in more than one frame of reference. An aesthetic phenomenon, for instance, can be approached psychologically, sociologically, in regard to the technique of its craft, the history of its style, the premises of its metaphysics and philosophy of history that underlie it; nor do these interpretations cancel each other out. While they refer to what is, dogmatically speaking, the same object, each approaches it from a different point of view, and thus emphasizes another side of it.

Deeper critical reflection, however, shows that all these different explanations actually correspond to different *logical* objects. Even as the logical objects of the various natural sciences are created by the methods of these sciences, the objects of the various *Geisteswissenschaften*, too, emerge only in and through their methods, points of view, perspectives, or however else these subjective-functional correlates of the changing objects may be called. Designations of these possible, wholly heterogeneous logical objects, such as 'the work of art "as a structure of experience", "as a sociological product", "as an art form"', and so on,

* The important critical study *Die Theorie des Romans* by Lukács was published in Berlin in 1920. It was republished by Herman Luchterhand in 1963 but is not yet translated into English. Mannheim's review was published in *Logos*, IX, ii (1920–21), pp. 298–302.—Tr.

From *Studies on the Left*, III (Summer 1963), pp. 50–53. Reprinted by permission of Routledge and Kegan Paul Ltd.

are inadequate because the little word 'as' involves the danger
of confusing these objects and glosses over their fundamental
differences.

We shall not be concerned here with the question whether
primacy must be given to the objects or to their subjective
correlates (point of view, perspective), with the question, that is,
whether these different objects arise by virtue of the point of
view or, rather, are logically prior to the perspective that corresponds to them and that they impose on the subject. Much more
important for us is the problem whether the possibility of several
explanations of the (dogmatically speaking) apparently identical
object does not contain the danger of confusing the various logical
objects that hide beneath it. And indeed, whenever one tries to
approach one of these logical objects motivated by an explanation
that is alien to it (even though it may be appropriate to the same
dogmatic object), a false explanation results.

For instance, when psychology undertakes to explain a work of
art by reference to the artist's psychological processes (wherein
Freudianism is now one of the preferred trends), it may under
certain circumstances yield interesting observations on the genesis
of the psychic complex it finds in its creator, but it can yield
nothing as far as the intrinsic meaning of the corresponding
aesthetic object is concerned. The reason is that its logical object
is only the work of art 'as experience'; *not* the complex of meanings
that is valid in and of itself. When it claims it can say something
concerning the latter, too, it engages in an illegitimate hypos-
tasis, and its whole explanatory procedure reveals itself as
inadequate and, all too often, ridiculous. The psychological,
experiential context yields explanations only of psychological
phenomena and explains the work of art only insofar as it contains
or suggests them. The aesthetic object, on the other hand, is
something essentially of the spirit; in relation to it, the psychic
element is mere material, to be ordered and formed. But it is
just these spiritual aspects (such as composition, etc.) that can be
adequately explained only in appropriate teleological frames of
reference. Psychology enters where the spiritual component
beyond the subject has not even emerged yet.

Among the various logical objects of the different disciplines,
there is a hierarchy (which we can merely allude to here, rather
than present in detail). What has been said of psychology applies
to all methods that attempt an exhaustive explanation of something hierarchically higher by something lower—an instance is the
sociological explanation of cultural phenomena (sociology of
culture). As long as they remain within their framework, these
methods yield extremely valuable insights even into cultural

phenomena. But when they leave their proper logical object (the cultural object 'as a sociological phenomenon'), ascend to a higher level, and there claim an *exhaustive* explanation of the intellectual phenomenon in all its uniqueness, they are mistaken.

Efforts to interpret objects, not 'from below upward', but rather 'from up downward', are quite a different matter. An example is the attempt at interpreting a form of art by an approach from metaphysics or philosophy of history. Whereas the psychological object (the experiential content hinted at in the work of art) does not yet contain at all that which is hierarchically higher, namely, the spiritual element or, in our case, the art form, the latter, in turn, is only one component of the full spiritual-metaphysical phenomenon, that is to say, of the work of art 'as an objectification of the spirit'. The form is only an abstract component of the full spiritual content of the work of art and can be adequately abstracted from an aesthetic perspective. It follows that an interpretation of the abstract part is justified and possible only by proceeding from the whole.

One can even go a step further here. Aesthetics as analysis of form can describe the formal components it abstracts and can show and, in this sense, explain their intrinsic teleological structure. But by itself alone, it can never grasp the deepest meaning of this structure. This deeper explanation can be attained only by a discipline that takes as its object the full spiritual content of the work as a whole: metaphysics or philosophy of history. We want to call this deeper kind of explanation, which tries to explain something hierarchically lower from something higher, *interpretation*, in the narrower sense of the word. It has always been felt that the purely aesthetic-poetic and the stylistic-historical explanations of a form not only permit, but demand, interpretation. And the desire to transcend explanation as aesthetic clarification of form has resulted in 'attempts at interpretation' of a psychological and sociological kind—which, however, have tried to derive something higher from something simpler and lower.

This kind of 'interpreting' quite corresponds to the tendency of the modern spirit. The Middle Ages always took the road from the higher to the lower; only Descartes established the fatal principle that the whole must be derived from its parts, the higher from the lower. Yet it was bound to become obvious, especially in the intellectual sphere, that this, in principle, is impossible, that the lower does not yet contain the higher, nor the part the whole; that, therefore, it cannot let it arise out of itself; that it thus is impossible to say anything about the higher or the whole by starting from the lower or the part. And in fact, with regard to every such effort one has the feeling that the interpreter really fails to grasp the object he claims to be speaking about, since, instead of building it up from its elements, he allows it to end in them.

Lukács' book moves in the right direction: it is an attempt at interpreting aesthetic phenomena, particularly the novel, from a higher point of view, that of the philosophy of history.

By its intrinsic methods, aesthetics, or more specifically poetics, has worked out the main forms of art—tragedy, the epic, the novel, etc.—and the history of style has described their intrinsic development. But to grasp their meaning, to grasp that higher unity from which they spring, takes a discipline that has as its object precisely the spirit as the necessary forms of which these forms of art appear. Their wealth can by no means be imputed to an arbitrary play impulse which, to amuse itself, takes on now this form, now that. Instead, in the actualization of each of these forms there is always an element of necessity, which becomes fully explicable only by reference to that spirit as the appearance of which alone it can adequately be interpreted. In this case, we seek the *principium differentiationis* of the art form, not (as so often) in the various materials of the arts, nor in their sociological preconditions, even though such endeavors have their limited justification. Rather, we posit it in the actual origin of each creative tendency, which we locate in the spirit that we can describe only metaphysically; and we derive differences among the forms from the differences among the ultimate, historically changing points of orientation of this spirit.

The prerequisites of such an interpretive effort are two. One is a descriptive and analytical poetics, which sharply discriminates the forms to be explained and their qualities according to their essential features. The other is a philosophy of history, which describes the development of the spirit in sufficient depth. However one may think about the feasibility of such a philosophical-historical enterprise, what I have tried to prove thus far is that the ultimately correct solution of full interpretation can only be attained in this fashion; that the task lies in this direction. The meaning of a form can be adequately explained only by the spiritual content that avails itself of it. It is extremely difficult to grasp this spirit and its ultimate points of orientation, if only because it never explicates itself in its creations but only manifests itself *through* them. The task here is, not to present the explicit content of works of art of a past epoch, documenting it by appropriate quotations, but to conceptualize the spirit in which these works of art originated. It follows that in such a study in philosophy of history, observations can never be *directly* documented by quotations, for such a demonstration always presupposes the reader's capacity in a specific, separate act to read in the example presented what is essential in it. Yet this says nothing against the demonstrative power of such indirect documentation. For just as we grasp the Aristotelian species along with the unique, concrete, actual object (a process with which we all are familiar), the philosopher of history sees in the actual, unique historical individual that which from his point of view is essential in it. This is not a matter of construction or induction but a particular ability, which in a rudimentary form is possessed by everybody.

It is Lukács' strength, not to proceed deductively from a few principles, nor to construct his philosophy of history from superficially, rationally plausible elements, but to grasp, with the help of a surprising capacity of interpretation, that which is essential and deepest in a form of art and in the spirit from which it must have sprung. It is for this reason that the more valuable part of his book is the second, where his argument becomes more concrete and he offers us an unusual wealth of insights into Dante, Cervantes, Flaubert, Goethe, Pontoppidan, Tolstoy, and others—insights that at first may surprise us but that are always confirmed on further reflection. Even the skeptical positivistic, or critical person who shies away from metaphysics will be carried along by this interpretation, which penetrates new depths: he will learn to understand his former readings anew.

II
On the Interpretation
of *Weltanschauung*

I. THE PROBLEM OUTLINED

IN the following study we shall try to give a methodological analysis of the concept of *Weltanschauung* and to determine its logical place within the conceptual framework of the cultural and historical sciences. It is not our intention to propose a substantive definition of *Weltanschauung* based upon definite philosophical premises; the question we should like to answer is rather the following: What kind of task is a student of a cultural and historical discipline (a historian of art, of religion, possibly also a sociologist) faced with when he seeks to determine the global outlook (*Weltanschauung*) of an epoch, or to trace partial manifestations back to this all-embracing entity? Is the entity designated by the concept of *Weltanschauung* given to us at all, and if so—*how* is it given? How does its givenness compare with that of other data in the cultural and historical disciplines? But even this is not the whole problem. Many things are 'given' of which no clear theoretical account can be rendered. And now we ask: provided that something like the 'global outlook' is already grasped—as we shall see—in pre-theoretical fashion, is there a way to transpose it into scientific and theoretical terms? Can such a 'given' ever become the object of valid, verifiable scientific knowledge?

The problem we have raised is not a matter of gratuitous speculation; it is constantly cropping up in actual research on cultural and historical subjects, and some attempts at solving it are already on record. We shall try to elucidate the methodological principles by which endeavours of this kind are guided.

To be sure, the historical disciplines within which this problem

From *Essays on the Sociology of Knowledge* (New York: Oxford University Press, 1952), pp. 33–83. Reprinted by permission of Routledge and Kegan Paul Ltd.

8

arises are not yet advanced far enough to permit us to attempt a final answer. All we can do now is to make explicit the logic behind the actual procedure followed by a few selected scholars, to evaluate the logical achievement involved in their attempted solutions; in conclusion, we shall at least touch upon the wider problems involved.

II. THE STRUGGLE FOR A SYNTHESIS

Is it possible to determine the global outlook of an epoch in an objective, scientific fashion? Or are all characterizations of such a global outlook necessarily empty, gratuitous speculations? These questions, long neglected, are again attracting the interest of scholars. This is not surprising in view of the strong urge towards synthesis noticeable in the various historical disciplines. Following a period of limited analytical research and of increasing specialization, we are now witnessing the onset of a period characterized by a synoptical approach. The preceding concentration upon analytical historical research had been a much-needed reaction against Hegel's venture in the philosophy of history which, with its ready-made assumptions, had proved premature in content and method alike; and at the same time it provided a wholesome contrast with a stream of 'universal histories' which, though they made interesting reading, fell hopelessly short of scholarly standards and presented an uncritical mixture of incongruous viewpoints, methods, and categories.

This premature synthesis had to give way before the better judgment that, while the ultimate object of historical research obviously is the historical process as a whole, no knowledge of the global process is possible without a previous investigation of its parts. These component parts, then, had to be studied first in isolation; this led to a process of specialization which is still going on. Specialization was twofold. For one thing, various cultural fields such as science, art, religion, etc., were isolated from each other and studied separately.[1] Secondly—and this is what we are primarily interested in—the isolated domains into which the whole of culture was split up were not viewed integrally as they present themselves in pre-theoretical experience, but subjected to various operations of abstraction, performed from a number of different theoretical points of view. This procedure—which had already been employed successfully in the natural sciences—proved

[1] Perhaps it ought to be emphasized that such a sharp delineation of the domains of religion, art, etc., is strictly a product of the theoretical approach to culture. The active participant in the culture experiences no such sharp divisions.

methodologically fruitful in the cultural disciplines as well; it made it possible to ask questions capable of generalization and to form well-defined concepts; as a result, the logic of the cultural sciences which we shall have one day will be in a position to assign each term used in these sciences its exact logical place, that is, to specify the problem in the framework of which alone the term in question has a meaning.

The foremost result of this second kind of specialization was—as in the case of the natural sciences—that the consistent and uniform application of specific abstractive procedures in the various specialized cultural disciplines led to each discipline constituting its own object, so to speak, by virtue of its method. Just as the 'physical object' of science is totally different from the object of immediate everyday experience and is constituted, one might say, by the method of physics, so, for example, 'style' (to take an example from aesthetics) also is a novel kind of object, brought into being by the methodical analysis of stylistic historical studies; scientific abstraction, gradually discarding all those aspects of the multiplicity of works and art forms which are not relevant to this problem, finally brings forth, as it were, the entity called 'style'.

Far more important, however, is it to note that, despite this similarity, the human studies also differ essentially from the natural sciences when it comes to the relation of their respective logical objects to the corresponding objects of pre-scientific, everyday experience. The empirical object given in the concrete fullness of actual sensual experience presents no problem for the logic of physics, since all physical laws can be expressed without reference to the global content of that sensual experience, so that physics need never concern itself with the task of reconstructing the concretely given object in terms of its own concepts, evolved as a result of methodical abstraction. For aesthetic analysis, however, the object as given in pre-theoretical, concrete experience never ceases to be a problem. In studying the historical evolution of styles, we may temporarily ignore the content and form of the individual works of the periods under investigation; we may neglect what is uniquely expressive in this or that work, and consider it merely as a point of passage in a process of transformation, reaching forward and backward beyond it in time—precisely what we call 'style'. But all the unique elements of form and content which we neglect when our interest is focused on 'style' nevertheless remain a problem to be solved by the history of art as such. Once the domain of 'nature' has been split up into the fields of physics, chemistry, biology, etc., each studied by a specialized discipline, the problem of putting together these partial fields to reconstruct a unified whole no longer arises as a scientific problem (only a 'philosophy of nature'[1] might conceivably have such an aim), whereas for the cultural sciences, the concrete experiential wholes neglected in the interests of abstraction always remain a problem. Even supposing that in the field of art history, comprehensive and logically self-contained surveys of the development of style and of subject matter have already been worked out, certain experiential wholes necessarily neglected as a result of the abstractive procedures involved in these studies would still call for scientific treatment; these include the concrete 'whole' of this or that individual work, the more comprehensive 'whole' of the *œuvre* of an artist, and the still more comprehensive 'whole' of the culture and *Weltanschauung* of an epoch.

There is still another reason why these concrete objects are of relevance to the various branches of cultural history. Since each of these branches owes its existence to an abstractive operation, none can give a full and valid account of its object within the limits of its own conceptual framework; it will be necessary at some point to refer to the concrete whole itself. Within the history of style, for instance, we have certain analytical tools which enable us to say *how* style changes; but if we want to account for the *cause* of the change, we must go beyond the history of style as such and invoke some such concept as the 'art motive' (*Kunstwollen*), as defined by Riegl, as the factor the mutations of which explain the changes in style. And in trying to elucidate in turn the causes of the mutations of the art motive, we must make reference to even more fundamental factors such as *Zeitgeist*, 'global outlook', and the like. Bringing these various strata of cultural life in relation to each other, penetrating to the most fundamental totality in terms of which the interconnectedness of the various branches of cultural studies can be understood—this is precisely the essence of the procedure of interpretation which has no counterpart in the natural sciences—the latter only 'explain' things. Thus, even a specialized discipline within the cultural sciences cannot afford to lose sight of the pre-scientific totality of its object, since it cannot comprehend even its narrow topic without recourse to that totality. That is the real reason why the historical studies of culture could not rest content with a specialized, analytic method of research. And the present trend towards synthesis is evidenced above all by the awakening interest

[1] Modern philosophies of nature seek to reconcile the explanatory principles used by the various sciences (such as the mechanical and causal principles used by physics and the teleological ones used by biology). But of course that has nothing whatever to do with the trend towards synthesis in the cultural sciences of which we spoke above.

in the problem of *Weltanschauung*, a problem that marks the most advanced point reached by efforts at historical synthesis.

This emerging set of questions cannot be treated on its merits unless one is ready to emancipate oneself from the methodological principles of natural science; for in the natural sciences, where problems of this kind are necessarily lacking, we encounter nothing even faintly analogous to the thought patterns with which we have to deal at every step in the cultural sciences. Yet the scientist's way of thinking had fascinated the analytic era to such a degree that none had dared as much as broach, let alone offer to solve, certain essential questions, for the only reason that they did not fit in with the accepted catalogue of sciences or with the general pattern of theoretic prejudice. When general questions of principle nevertheless came up in research and could not be thrust aside, the specialists of the analytic era would unfailingly refer them to the experts of some neighbouring field, who in turn would promptly pass them on with the identical excuse that it was out of place in their particular scheme of investigation. In this perpetual game of passing the buck the human studies not only risked in fact omitting to answer the most vital questions of their own field, but, which is worse, they were courting the danger of overlooking the scientific obligation to tackle these problems.

We now have evidence that the turn towards synthesis is actually taking place, for indeed specialists of late evince interest in questions of the philosophy of history. This interest manifests itself by a growing need to fit particular findings into some global historical scheme, and by the readiness to use unorthodox methods, such as that of bringing the various strata differentiated by abstraction into correlation with each other, of investigating correspondences between the economic-social and the intellectual spheres, of studying parallelisms between cultural objectifications such as art, religion, science, etc. Methodology seeks but to make explicit in logical terms what is *de facto* going on in living research.[1]

III. RATIONALISM *v.* IRRATIONALISM

The difficult and paradoxical nature of the concept of *Weltanschauung* stems from the fact that the entity it denotes lies outside the province of theory. Dilthey was one of the first to recognize

---

[1] In addition to a number of works to be discussed below, we should like to refer at this point to certain studies by Alfred Weber, who calls upon sociology to effect a synthesis; cf. among others 'Prinzipielles zur Kultursoziologie' in *Archiv für Sozialwissenschaften*, 1920, vol. 47, no. 1.

this; cf. his remark: '*Weltanschauungen* are not produced by think-ing.'[1] As far as rationalism can see, the global outlook of an age or of a creative individual is wholly contained in their philo-sophical and theoretical utterances; you need only to collect these utterances and arrange them in a pattern, and you have taken hold of a *Weltanschauung*. There are numerous investi-gations on record the object of which was to ascertain by this method the influence certain great philosophers exerted upon poets—for example, Spinoza's influence upon Goethe—and this passed for an analysis of *Weltanschauung*.

It needed the anti-rationalist movement within the cultural studies themselves, a movement which Dilthey first made a force in Germany, to make people realize that theoretical philosophy is neither the creator nor the principal vehicle of the *Weltan-schauung* of an epoch; in reality, it is merely only one of the channels through which a global factor—to be conceived as transcending the various cultural fields, its emanations—manifests itself. More than that—if this totality we call *Weltanschauung* is understood in this sense to be something a-theoretical, and at the same time to be the foundation of all cultural objectifications, such as religion, *mores*, art, philosophy, and if, further, we admit that these objectifications can be ordered in a hierarchy according to their respective distance from this irrational, then the theoretical will appear to be precisely one of the most remote manifestations of this fundamental entity. As long as *Weltanschauung* is considered as something theoretical, entire vast provinces of cultural life will be inaccessible to historical synthesis. We could at most analyse and compare the minute theoretical content that has seeped down into literature, religious dogma and ethical maxims. And it is characteristic of this conception of *Weltanschauung* and its appeal that Dilthey himself, the very apostle of the anti-rationalist approach to this problem, long remained under its spell and held that the plastic arts were outside the scope of the analysis of *Weltanschauung*.

If, on the other hand, we define *Weltanschauung* as something a-theoretical with philosophy merely as one of its manifestations, and not the only one, we can widen our field of cultural studies in a twofold way. For one thing, our search for a synthesis will then be in a position to encompass every single cultural field. The plastic arts, music, costumes, *mores* and customs, rituals, the tempo of living, expressive gestures and demeanour—all these no less than theoretical communications will become a decipherable

---

[1] W. Dilthey, 'Die Typen der Weltanschauung und ihre Ausbildung in den metaphysischen Systemen', p. 86, in *Gesammelte Schriften*, VIII. Berlin, 1931.

language, adumbrating the underlying unitary whole of *Weltan-schauung*. Secondly, in addition to widening the field of studies in cultural synthesis, this approach will enable us to look at our object from an entirely new side. For we then shall be in a position to compare, not only discursive utterances, but also non-discursive elements of form; and once we do that, we shall be bound to feel that we have come far closer to the spontaneous, unintentional, basic impulse of a culture than when we were trying to distil *Weltanschauung* merely from theoretical utterances in which the original impulse appears, so to speak, in refracted form.

Admittedly the price to be paid for this expansion of the field and the inclusion of the analysis of form is, as we have already indicated, that the entire position becomes more vulnerable in principle. The scientific investigation of culture itself belongs to the domain of theory; if, then, the global unity of culture is conceived as something a-theoretical, then the gulf separating the process of research itself from its object will become wider. Once again we find ourselves confronted by the problem of rationalism and irrationalism, or better, the question whether and how the a-theoretical can be 'translated' into theory; this is the central problem of philosophy today, and, as we see, it is equally crucial for the methodology of the cultural sciences.

Why is it that this problem, never solved, arises anew again and again, manifesting a tremendous power of suggestion? It is because it touches upon a fundamental property of human life and mind, characterizing man far better than any of the findings of anthropological science can do. This fundamental trait is that man is the citizen of several worlds at the same time. We possess the πρώτη ΰλη, the primordial stuff of experience, which is wholly indeterminate and of which we cannot even say whether it is homogeneous, in several distinct forms, as aesthetic, religious, ethical experience and also as theoretical awareness. The paradoxical nature of theoretical thought, distinguishing it from the other forms, consists in this, that it seeks to superimpose a logical, theoretical pattern upon experiences already patterned under other—for example aesthetic or religious—categories. But if this is so, we cannot accept that extreme form of irrationalism which holds that certain cultural facts are not merely a-theoretical but are radically removed from any rational analysis. Aesthetic or religious 'experiences' are not wholly devoid of form; it is only that their forms are *sui generis* and radically different from that of theory as such. To 'reflect' these forms and what is in-formed by them, without violating their individual character, to 'translate' them into theory, or at any rate to 'encompass' them by logical forms, that is the purpose of theoretical inquiry, a process which points back to pre-theoretical initial stages, at the level of everyday experience; and we cannot help feeling uncomfortable while translating the non-theoretical experience into the language of theory, since we cannot avoid the impression that the theoretical categories are inadequate and distort the authenticity of direct experience upon which they are superimposed. Why is it, then, that we crave theoretical knowledge of something we have already possessed integrally in direct experience unmarred by the intrusion of the theoretical interest? Why do we not content ourselves with the aesthetic contemplation of the works before us? Why do we pass from the attitude of form-perception to that of cognitive analysis, an attitude essentially incongruous with the aesthetic datum? Why should 'thought' be the universal medium, burdened with the thankless role of a tool that is constantly needed and used, and yet is constantly despised and reviled? And is it even to provide the language in which it can be denounced?

All this is remarkable indeed. There must be something to theory after all, something positive and fruitful; it must achieve something else besides chilling the authentic experience with the cold blast of reflection—a re-patterning of the original experience, by which light is thrown upon it from an entirely new side. Otherwise it would be incomprehensible why the ethical, aesthetic, and religious realm (that is, the realm of the a-theoretical) is shot through with elements of theory even in its original, unreflected state. Granted that ethical, aesthetic, and religious experiences have categories and forms of their own; still it cannot be gainsaid that religious experience, even though its mainsprings be of irrational character, often finds expression through the most elaborate theoretical exercises. And likewise, art, though it ultimately addresses itself to 'vision', makes use of media and materials having a strong theoretical component. Theorizing, then, does not start with science; pre-scientific everyday experience is shot through with bits of theory. The life of mind is a constant flux, oscillating between the theoretical and a-theoretical pole, involving a constant intermingling and re-arranging of the most disparate categories of many different origins. And thus, theory has its proper place, its justification and meaning, even in the realm of immediate, concrete experience—in the realm of the a-theoretical. We would like to stress this point quite strongly in opposition to the now fashionable belittlers of theory and of the rational, and to those unmitigated sceptics who flatly deny the possibility of transposing the a-theoretical into theoretical terms.

In so far as that indefinite something, *Weltanschauung*, is concerned, however, it belongs to the realm of the a-theoretical in a still more radical sense. Not only that it is in no way to be conceived of as a matter of logic and theory; not only that it cannot be integrally expressed through philosophical theses or, indeed, theoretical communications of any kind—in fact, compared to it, even all non-theoretical realizations, such as works of art, codes of ethics, systems of religion, are still in a way endowed with rationality, with explicitly interpretable meaning, whereas *Weltanschauung* as a global unit is something deeper, a still unformed and wholly germinal entity.

Aesthetic and spiritual manifestations such as works of art and religious systems are a-theoretical and a-logical but not irrational (the latter is something entirely different from the former). In fact, those manifestations are just as much based upon categorial forms, forms of meaning, as any theoretical proposition—the only difference is that in their case we have to do with a different set of basic categories: aesthetic, religious, ethical, etc., rather than theoretical ones.[1] *Weltanschauung*, however, does not properly belong to any of these fields of meaning—to the theoretical as little as to the a-theoretical ones—but rather, in a way, to all of them; for just this reason, it is not to be fully comprehended within any one of them. Unity and totality of the concept of *Weltanschauung* mean that we must go not merely beyond the

---

[1] It is submitted without further elaboration that for the purposes of this study, all objectifications of culture are considered as vehicles of meaning (*Sinngebilde*). There is no longer any need to labour this point; it is sufficient to refer to the works of Husserl, Rickert, and Spranger, among others.

It was Spranger who first utilized for the purposes of an 'interpretation' (*Verstehen*) of behaviour the unreal, non-psychological 'meaning' of which Husserl had given a systematic account in the logical and theoretical sphere, and Rickert (whose pluralism we accept in the present study) in all the various spheres of culture. (Cf. Husserl, *Logische Untersuchungen*, vol. 1, Halle, 1913. Rickert, *System der Philosophie*, pt. 1, Tübingen, 1921. E. Spranger, 'Zur Theorie des Verstehens und zur geisteswissenschaftlichen Psychologie' in *Festschrift für Johannes Volkelt*, Munich, 1918.) We take 'meaning' in a much broader sense than the above-mentioned authors do, and, as will be seen in the sequel, we introduce certain distinctions into this concept, since we are convinced that even the most elementary problems of interpretation cannot be tackled without these distinctions. Topics which may be important for philosophical analysis (such as the bearing of the problem of the timeless validity of values upon the problem of meaning) are quite irrelevant to the theory of understanding; the only thing that matters here is that—as we shall try to show by means of examples—every cultural objectification is a vehicle of meaning as to its mode of being and that it therefore cannot be fully comprehended either as a 'thing' or as a psychic content; culture, therefore, requires an ontology which is expanded accordingly. We may then very well ignore all platonizing tendencies which colour most of the philosophical attempts at analysing the theory of culture.

theoretical but beyond any and all cultural objectifications. Every cultural objectification (such as a work of art, a religious system, etc.), and also every self-contained or incomplete phase of it is, under this aspect, really something fragmentary, and the corresponding totality cannot be supplied at the level of the objectifications. For even if we could inventorize all the cultural objectifications of an epoch (we cannot, of course, since the number of items is limitless) a mere addition or inventory would still fall far short of that unity we call *Weltanschauung*. In order to reach the latter, we need a new departure in a different direction, and must perform a mental operation which will be described later, transcending each objectification as something merely itself. Only then will it become part of the totality we are concerned with here. And our task now is to define this methodological departure, to characterize the decisive step by which a cultural objectification can be looked at, as it were, from a new side, and, pointing beyond itself, can be seen as part of a new totality beyond the cultural objectification level. In themselves the objectifications of culture as they immediately present themselves to us are vehicles of meaning and therefore belong to the rational (though not the theoretical!) sphere; whereas the new totality we are seeking lies beyond all realizations of meaning, although it is somehow given through them.

But is it at all possible that something of this kind should be given? Can it become the object of scientific inquiry? This is what we must now ask—but, for the sake of clarity, we must keep the two questions apart. The first question is whether that something beyond the cultural objectification level is in fact given to us at all. That is: we know that something possessing aesthetic meaning is given to us when we approach the work of art in an aesthetic attitude, and something possessing religious meaning, when we experience the religious objectification in an attitude congruent with it; but is something else given to us in addition which we can designate as the *Weltanschauung*, the global outlook behind these objectifications? And if so, is there a specific attitude we have to adopt to grasp this new datum, an attitude different from those which enabled us to capture the original meanings? Can we describe the new type of intentional act corresponding to the new attitude?

Not until this question has been answered in the affirmative—and that can only be done by phenomenological analysis of the intentional acts directed towards cultural objects—shall we be in a position to tackle the second problem—that of the way in which contents grasped in a-theoretical experience can be transposed into theoretical, scientific terms.

IV. *WELTANSCHAUUNG*: ITS MODE OF PRESENTATION

THE THREE KINDS OF MEANING

The first question accordingly pertains to the phenomenology of the intentional object,[1] and all it asks is whether *Weltanschauung* is a possible object at all, whether, in fact, it is given at all, and in how far the way in which it is given differs from that in which other objects are given to us.

An object may be given either immediately or mediately—and this alternative is very much to the point here. If given immediately, the object is present itself, if mediately, then something mediating is present in its stead; and this 'proxy' which might be said to take the place of the object proper may play vastly different mediator-roles, of which we shall mention two as having a vital bearing on the problem under review: the function of *expression* on the one hand, and that of *documentation* or *evidence* on the other.[2]

The distinguishing mark of mediate presentation is that a datum which is apprehended as being there in its own right can, and indeed must, also be conceived as standing for something else —and this in one of the modes of mediation or signification mentioned above. Accordingly, to find out whether any object under discussion (in our case: the global outlook, the 'spirit' of an epoch) is at least given mediately, we shall have to see whether the works or objectifications which are directly given also point beyond themselves—whether we have to transcend them, to round them out, if we want to grasp their integral meaning.

We shall try to show that any cultural product can be fully understood only on the following conditions: it must first of all be grasped as a 'something itself', regardless of its mediator function, after which its mediating character in the two senses

[1] It will be obvious to anyone familiar with Husserl's work to what extent this phenomenological analysis is indebted to him, and in how far his procedure has been modified for our purposes.

[2] As a third type of mediation, *representation* may also be mentioned, but we shall not go into it any farther in this paper, since our analysis would be unduly burdened by introducing this further dimension. We shall limit ourselves to the following remark in connection with this topic which is of primary importance in other contexts: the sphere in which representation is of prime importance is that of painting and sculpture; besides shaping a visual medium and 'aesthetic space' (about which more later), a work of art in these fields also may *represent* a number of objects. The essential difference between expression and representation is that the representation and the represented object must belong to the same sensory field. Sounds can be represented only by other sounds, optical objects by other optical objects and, in general, sensory data by other sensory data; mental and psychic data cannot be represented, only expressed or evidenced.

defined must also be taken into account. Every cultural product in its entirety will, on this showing, display three distinct 'strata of meaning': (a) its objective meaning, (b) its expressive meaning, (c) its documentary or evidential meaning. First we have to show that these three strata are distinct, and that they are discoverable. If we look at a 'natural object', we shall see at the first glance that which characterizes it, and the modern scientific attitude appropriate to its study is the fact that it is taken as nothing but itself and is fully cognizable without being transcended or rounded out in the two directions of which we spoke above. A cultural product, on the other hand, will not be understood in its proper and true meaning if we attend merely to that 'stratum of meaning' which it conveys when we look at it merely as it is 'itself'—its objective meaning; we have also to take it as having an expressive and a documentary meaning, if we want to exhaust its full significance. Of course, with Nature too, it is possible to transcend the purely experiential attitude, and, attempting a metaphysical interpretation, to conceive the whole of Nature as a documentation of God; proceeding in this fashion, however, we merely shift to nature the mode of analysis properly suitable to culture. That, however, this mode of procedure is alien to the sphere of nature, while it is appropriate within the realm of culture, will easily be seen from the following negative experiment: if we abstain from transcending the objective meaning in the two directions mentioned above, the natural object will still be scientifically cognizable, but the cultural product will lose its meaning.

There is still a second difference between natural and cultural objects. The former must be conceived exclusively as something located in physical space-time or in the temporal-psychic medium, whereas the latter are invariably vehicles of meaning (in the several senses just described) and hence are not integrally located either in the spatio-temporal world (which is at most the external framework of their realization), or within the psychic acts of the individuals who create or experience them (these acts being at most necessary for the actualization of the meanings). In so far as a cultural object is concerned, its meaning is by no means an adventitious index, an accidental property of something in physical space, as though the physical were the only real existent and the cultural meaning a mere accident. The marble of a statue, for instance, merely actualizes a meaning (the work of art as such), and the 'beauty' of the statue is not one of the properties of the physical object marble, but belongs to an altogether different plane. Likewise, the genuineness of the material, 'texture' [stressed by Semper], and the treatment of architectural space, are sensual data which represent the aesthetic meaning of a material or spatial object—but precisely because they embody meaning, they belong neither to the material nor the spatial planes themselves.

To give a still clearer illustration of the 'meaning' character of cultural phenomena, and of its threefold differentiation, we shall mention a concrete example. And we have deliberately chosen a trivial example, so as to make it clear that our concept of the 'cultural' embraces, not merely cultural products endowed with traditional prestige, such as Art or Religion, but also manifestations of everyday life which usually pass unnoticed—and also that these manifestations already display the essential characteristics of meaning as such. Take the following case:—I am walking down the street with a friend; a beggar stands at a corner; my friend gives him an alms. His gesture to me is neither a physical nor a physiological phenomenon; as a datum, it is solely the vehicle of a meaning, namely that of 'assistance'. In this process of interpretation, the event which is mediated by visual sense-data becomes the vehicle for a meaning which is something entirely different from the visual data and belongs to the sociological field, where it is theoretically subsumed under the category 'social assistance'. It is only in a social context that the man at the corner will be a 'beggar', my friend 'one who renders assistance' and the bit of metal in his hand an 'alms'. The cultural product in this case is solely the event 'assistance', to be defined in sociological terms; in so far as the meaning of the event (by which it is constituted as an event) is concerned, my friend as a psycho-physical individual is quite irrelevant; he enters into the context merely as a 'giver', as part of a 'situation' that can only be grasped in terms of meaning and that would be essentially the same if his place were taken by any other person.

No knowledge of the intimate content of my friend's or the beggar's consciousness is needed in order to understand the meaning of 'assistance' (which is the 'objective meaning' of the situation); it is sufficient to know the objective social configuration by virtue of which there are beggars and people with superfluous cash. This objective configuration is the sole basis of orientation which enables us to grasp the meaning of the event as one exemplifying 'assistance'.

Now every cultural product or manifestation has such an objective meaning, and the distinguishing mark of such a meaning is that it can be fully grasped without knowing anything about the 'intentional acts' of the individual 'author' of the product or manifestation. All we need know[1] is the 'system' (used here in

[1] But it is not required, in turn, that we be able to account for this knowledge theoretically and reflectively!

a non-logical, a-theoretical sense), that context and whole, in terms of which the data we perceive coalesce into a meaningful entity.

In science, this 'objective meaning' is a theoretical proposition, and in our sociological example it has at least a considerable theoretical component. In the plastic arts, however—as the sequel will show in greater detail—the objective meaning is itself a purely visual content, the meaning of something that can only be seen, or, to use a term of K. Fiedler's, 'pure visibility'. In music, again, the objective meaning is melody, rhythm, harmony, and the like, all of which have their objective structural laws. These structures are 'a-theoretical' but not 'irrational' or 'non-constitutive' (*setzungsfremd*) in character.

However, to continue with the analysis of the example cited, it is possible or even probable that when my friend caused an event to happen the objective meaning of which was 'assistance', his intention was not merely to help, but also to convey a feeling of sympathy to me or to the beggar. In this case, the event which has the objective meaning we indicated will also be the vehicle of an entirely new kind of meaning which need not always have a terminologically fixed designation; in this case, it may be called mercy, kindness, or compassion. Now, the perceived movement, the gesture of charity, will not merely be endowed with the objective meaning 'assistance', but also with a second stratum of meaning superimposed, as it were, upon the former: the expressive meaning. This second type differs essentially from the first in that it cannot be divorced from the subject and his actual stream of experience, but acquires its fully individualized content only with reference to this 'intimate' universe. And the interpretation of expressive meaning always involves the task of grasping it authentically—just as it was *meant* by the subject, just as it appeared to him when his consciousness was focused upon it.

Now, strangely enough, this expressive content—in spite of the fact that we have no theoretical-reflective knowledge of it but merely direct, concrete, pre-theoretical experience—is still meaning, that is, something interpretable, rather than something merely psychic, a diffusely endured state. It has a certain *cachet* (even if it lacks a definite conceptual form), which makes it more than an elusive, indistinguishable phase in the flux of our consciousness. It must be noted, however, that objective meaning can be grasped by objective interpretation without recourse to what was subjectively intended, i.e. it can be treated as a problem of nothing but meaning—whereas meaning as expression, meaning as realized in direct experience, has once been a unique historical fact[1] and must be investigated as such.

With that, one might think, all possibilities of interpretation have been exhausted—but our example shows that this is not the case. For I, as the witness who interprets the scene, am in a position to go on from the expressive meaning as subjectively intended, and from the objective meaning as displayed by the act, in an entirely new direction. That is, analysing all the implications of what I see, I may suddenly discover that the 'act of charity' was, in fact, one of hypocrisy. And then it can no longer matter to me in the slightest what the friend has objectively done, nor yet what he 'wanted' or 'meant' to express by his action—all that concerns me now is what is documented about him, albeit unintentionally, by that act of his. And seeing evidence of his 'hypocrisy' in his gift, I am also interpreting his act as a 'cultural objectification', though in a new and vastly different sense than before. Whenever a cultural product is grasped not only as expressive but also as documentary meaning, it again points beyond itself to something different—with the qualification, however, that this 'something different' is no longer an intentional content actually entertained by my friend, but his 'essential character' as evidenced by his action, and revealed to be, in ethical terms, a 'hypocritical' one. Now I can apply the same technique of interpretation to every other manifestation of his personality as well—his facial expressions, his gestures, his gait, his speech rhythm; and as long as I maintain this interpretive approach, all his impulses and all his actions will exhibit a new stratum of meaning. Nothing will be interpreted in terms of consciously intended meaning, or in terms of objective performance; rather, every behavioural datum will serve to illustrate my synoptical appraisal of his personality as a whole; and this appraisal need not be limited to his moral character—it may take his global orientation as a whole into its purview.

Our first task is to make visible, and to keep apart, the phenomena relevant in this respect; it must be shown, above all, that these techniques of interpretation are always applied in cultural analysis, and that especially the last type of interpretation exemplifies an indispensable mode of understanding which must not be confused with either of the two preceding ones.

At this point, we have to note the curious phenomenon that

[1] And still it remains something unreal: meaning. We can call it factual because it is so intimately tied up with the temporal stream of consciousness of a spatially located individual that this nexus enters constitutively into the content of the meaning. 'Fact', in this terminology is not the opposite of 'unreal'.

we can, on occasion, apply this last mode of interpretation to *ourselves* as well. The expressive-intentional interpretation of our own objectifications is no problem for us. The expressive meaning we intended to convey in any one of our acts was immediately given in the living context—and we can always bring it back to consciousness (except, of course, in cases where memory fails us). But the documentary significance of an action of ours is quite another matter and may be as much of a problem for us as if in our own objectifications we were brought face to face with a total stranger. Hardly anywhere is there such a sharp contrast between the expressive and documentary interpretation as in this border-line-case of 'self-recognition'. And the totality we call the 'genius' or 'spirit' (of an epoch) is given to us in this mode of 'documentary' meaning; this is the perspective in which we grasp the elements that go to make up the global outlook of a creative individual or of an epoch.

Before discussing the difference between these three strata of meaning in more general terms, we shall examine these patterns of meaning in the field of the plastic arts; to begin with, however, we shall limit ourselves to a clear differentiation between objective meaning on the one hand and expressive meaning on the other.

In the theoretical aesthetic analysis of works of art it is customary to resort to an abstractive operation, the gist of which is a distinction between 'form' and 'content'. We have to ask, then, the following question: How does our distinction between the three strata of meaning (a distinction, by the way, which also requires abstractive operations for its implementation) relate to this distinction between content and form? Does the stratum of objective meaning perchance correspond to 'content', with the expressive and documentary meanings sharing in the 'form'? Nothing of the kind; objective meaning covers an already in-formed content, and examination will show that any aesthetic 'content' in its concrete phenomenal givenness already displays several superimposed aspects of form—even though the abstractive emphasis upon 'content' usually makes one overlook this.

If these latter are to emerge clearly, a further distinction is required, and to this end the inquiry will have to proceed in two stages; this because the distinction between 'form' and 'content' can be understood in either of the following two ways: (*a*) the representational content (subject-matter) of the picture and *its* representational form, and (*b*) the material content of the medium (marble, layers of paint) and *its* formal dimensions.

To begin with: it is immediately apparent that any representational content combines objective and expressive elements. But even if we try to isolate the representational content as such, we shall have to admit that the demarcation line between form and content is essentially fluid; for it is impossible to tell the 'story' underlying the picture (e.g. a biblical tale, or a village brawl in a Flemish painting) so dryly and soberly as to obtain mere content into which no 'form' has been injected by the reporter. Even newspaper stories are slanted and pointed in such a way that the 'forming' of the raw material is unmistakable. Thus, even in trying merely to describe what the picture 'relates', we cannot help noticing in what way the story is told. This 'representational form' is exemplified, among other things, by the following aspects of the picture: the choice of a particular visual phase of a temporal sequence of events; the arrangement of the figures—whether hieratically rigid or merely secular in its ordering; whether brought about exclusively by effects of lighting, colouring, and linear rhythm; whether animated by lifelike gestures or frozen in a static design pointing beyond mere lifelike realism; whether based upon a rhythmic-architectonic pattern or upon effects of intersection and foreshortening; whether presented as seen by the outside spectator or organized around a point of reference within the picture. All these in-formations of the representational content must be considered as objective, inasmuch as they can be ascertained merely by looking at the picture, without reference to the artist and his consciousness.

Nevertheless, the mere inspection of the representational content in all these aspects will also reveal an expressive component—there is hardly any 'story' without expressive meaning. If the Middle Ages as a rule confined pictorial representation to sacred contents (derived from the Bible), and, furthermore, to certain selected episodes, the reason is, in part, that pictorial art was supposed to convey only a limited range of moods and feelings. Thus, a certain emotional inventory of selected subjects was gradually evolved; particular scenes from the Bible absorbed definite emotive connotations into their complex of objective meaning (into the events related as such), and these connotations became so standardized that the contemporaries could not help considering certain expressive meanings as objectively inherent in certain contents. That this cannot be the case in an *absolute* sense is clear from the fact that the same events and figures were called upon in the course of history to support many different expressive meanings. For instance, certain biblical scenes which in early paintings expressed only religious exaltation later on came to acquire an 'erotic' expressive meaning. Another well-known example of a shift in expressive meaning is that of medieval plays in which the blind and the halt play a comic role, whereas, conversely, a later generation took the hero Don Quixote to be a comic figure. All this makes it clear that in interpreting expressive meaning, including that embedded in a representational content, we must seek to grasp what the artist actually intended; hence, close familiarity with the attitudes and idiosyncrasies of an epoch or an individual artist is needed if we want to avoid the risk of seriously misinterpreting his works.

When we next come to examine the way in which the material medium (the marble of the statue, the colour and canvas in the painting) is treated, it will also be immediately apparent that the visual shapes as such directly embody objective meaning, quite apart from any meaning related to the 'story' which is represented. When we look at a statue, our visual experience embraces not only sense data of sight and (potentially) of touch, but invariably also an aesthetic conception (*Auffassung*) underlying the arrangement of visual shapes purely as such. While we think we do not look beyond the purely visual, we already are dealing with relationships of meaning and form; in other words, the 'space' of the statue is not the same as the 'space' filled by a mere slab of marble would be—the statue has its 'aesthetic space' which differs from that of a purely physical space of optics in that it is structured in terms of visual meaning. This is further evidence that objective meaning need not pertain to the theoretical analysis of facts (as the meaning of an act of 'assistance' does), but may very well be something purely visual and still amenable to interpretation in terms of meaning as one of the possible ways of imparting aesthetic form to visual space. And this type of meaning can again be called 'objective', since all those factors which constitute such meaning in a work of art—the treatment of space, the mode of composition, etc.—can be grasped without reference to the artist's consciousness. Thus, we can have complete understanding of the visual, aesthetic content of primitive African works of art without being obliged to analyse what the Negro artist wanted to 'express' by them.

There can be no cultural product without some such objective meaning, and without objective visual meaning in particular there can be no work of plastic art. To be sure, it needs preparation to understand this objective meaning: a newcomer to art will be quite incapable at first of grasping the objective meaning of a painting by Cézanne (but on the other hand, it certainly will not be the subjective, psychological development of Cézanne which can teach him this, but only gradual assimilation of the preceding stages in the hierarchy of pictorial devices on which alone comprehension can be based)—and yet, all these preliminary 'learning' stages display a strongly objective orientation. That is, they are not merely stages in a purely subjective process of experience but show a complete analogy with the process of how one comes to understand a theoretical proposition such as Pythagoras' Theorem; in this latter case, too, one must first learn to understand the meaning of the concepts employed and the peculiar structure of the space (in this instance, *geometrical* space) involved.

The peculiar way in which plastic art realizes objective meaning in a visual medium compels us to distinguish between two types of objective meaning in general: the objective meaning realized by means of signs, and the objective meaning realized by way of form. In both cases, there are concrete vehicles of meaning, but the relationship between the meaning and its vehicle is unmistakably different in the two cases.

The theoretical meaning—the concept—bears no intrinsic, essential relation to its sensual vehicle, the spoken or written word; the latter is merely a *sign* for the former. On the other hand, although objective aesthetic meaning, being meaning, is not something located in space or in matter, it is yet essentially related to the sensual medium from which it cannot be detached and to which it belongs as its own visual meaning, or form. Objective meaning of the kind to be met with in the plastic arts, as form, somehow embraces the sensual medium as an essential component within the context of meaning, without becoming thereby part of the physical world. Visual meaning—what Fiedler calls 'pure visibility'—is the *meaning* of an optical datum and precisely for this reason not something optical itself.

Objective meaning, that is, meaning to be grasped by objective interpretation, is rooted in the structural laws of the object itself; certain elements and phases of sensible reality here become necessary stages in the progressive realization of meaning. All one needs for a proper understanding of this layer of meaning is an accurate grasp of the necessary structural characteristics of the sensual field in question. And indeed, the interpretation of objective meaning in art is the one least equivocal and relatively the least impaired, as the above-mentioned example of Negro sculpture has shown, by cultural remoteness and intellectual differences.

Our phrase, 'relatively the least impaired by cultural remoteness', implicitly concedes that, although objective interpretation is concerned only with objective meaning and has nothing to do with empathic probing of subjective processes, it still is far from presupposing some unique and universally valid 'visual universe' —as if the 'aesthetic space' of Negro sculpture were the same, *qua* visual universe, as that of Greek or modern sculpture. Several conceptions of space are possible—and as such no doubt amenable to a typology—even within sheer objective visibility, all of which have their inner consistency and therefore constitute visual universes: any given part of a statue, a distinctive surface, a movement, all these gain quite a different visual meaning according to whether they are comprised in this or that 'visual universe' —always provided of course, and that is most unlikely, that they can be transferred at all from one 'visual universe' to another. If these latter are to some extent commensurable, it is entirely because they may be considered as variants of 'visual treatment of space' as such; a generic concept which is supra-historic in that it provides a framework of comparison within which we can set off against each other the individual characteristics of the various historical visual universes. Because we have such a category of visual representation in aesthetic space, because we can refer certain instances of hewn stone to an aesthetic 'visual universe', we have, as it were, unlimited, ubiquitous access to this sphere of meaning which for this very reason we call 'objective'.

Now, however, it must be added that expressive meaning too is always embedded in this stratum of objective meaning—a form within a form, as it were. And it is the examination of the expressive meaning of the work of art which will bring out the full import of the distinction we made above between objective meaning realized by 'sign' and by 'form' respectively. Once we make the distinction between sign-meaning and form-meaning, it will become immediately apparent that the expressive content (usually referred to as the 'emotional' element) can be rendered far more adequately through form than through sign. Where—as in theoretical discourse—the word is merely a sign of an expressive content, we can only 'name' it—this verbal designation merely refers to it without being able to express it adequately. True expression is characterized by the fact that some psychic content is captured within a sensually formed medium, endowing it with a second dimension of meaning; and this capturing of the psychic content is possible only if the sensual medium is not treated as something secondary and exchangeable but is given its individual form valuable in its own right.

If I tell the beggar 'I am sorry for you,' or if I give him a coin as a 'sign' of my sympathy, with a gesture which is purely practical and has no aesthetic significance, then I do not, properly speaking, 'express' a feeling—I merely 'name' it, 'refer' to it. But if my gesture gives my emotion visual form, then a psychic content I experience finds real *expression*.

Accordingly, we can already distinguish two radically different types on as low a level of expression as that of the gesture: some gestures fulfil the function of sign language (e.g. the gestures of designating, pointing, blessing, or such conventional manifestations as a polite smile), but these can convey only *stereotyped* psychic contents; others have their own individual pattern which attracts attention and calls for interpretation. In the latter case, each individual pattern of movement conveys a specifically unique state of emotion, and then we have to do with a really 'expressive' gesture. As long as we have only the sign-language type of gesture in mind, we may assume that there is a 'universal grammar of expression', in terms of which certain movements may be put together in rigid combinations which correspond to certain typical patterns of emotion. But as soon as we take the second category of 'expressive gestures' into account, we shall abandon our attempt to construct such a grammar, aware of the fact that within this group we have to do with altogether different and essentially unique relationships between the psyche and the sensual medium, and that although the medium, or rather its visual meaning, is constitutive for the expressive meaning, it would yet be quite unwarrantable to assume a definite, uniquely determinable reciprocal relation between the elements of these two strata of meaning. And it is this second kind of expression that matters in art, inasmuch as the fashioned work of art is quite other than a mere indication of, or sign for, certain psychic states. Rather, each line, each form, in a word: every formative phase of the medium has at least a double significative function: on the one hand, it confers upon the medium an objective, visual aesthetic meaning or form, and on the other, it also embodies a unique subjective meaning which calls for adequate expression.

Aesthetic form, as exemplified by a work of art, goes beyond a mere expressive gesture in one respect—to wit, the subject performing a spontaneous expressive gesture is not explicitly and consciously concerned with the visual shape of the gesture and the way in which it conveys expressive meaning, whereas the artist's mind has both the shape of the work and its role in conveying expressive meaning as its intentional object. Mimic expression is something that happens, but the work of art is made. At this point I ought perhaps to make it clear that I am using the terms 'awareness', 'consciously held intentional objects', and the like, not in the possible sense of having the significant content in a definite theoretical and reflective framework, but of a non-reflective attitude, even though it be oriented towards theoretical meaning. In the case of the artist, this non-reflective attitude is one of 'making' or 'shaping'; in that of the spectator, it is one of 'understanding'. Whenever we contemplate the work of art in a direct value-orientation, we perform those acts of realization of meaning which the work calls for, but it is only in interpretation that we try to translate this experience of meaning into theoretical knowledge. It is quite legitimate, therefore, to speak of the 'intended expressive content' of a work, provided that 'intended expressive content' is to be identified with the intentional object in the artist's mind in the second sense of non-reflective awareness which has nothing to do with theoretical knowledge.

That the spectator can grasp the intended expressive content of a picture is no less and no more of a miracle in principle than the general phenomenon that we can associate the sensual content of the work with any kind of meaning-function at all.[1] Expressive meaning also is a 'given'; and if interpretation of this type presents peculiar difficulties, it is only because, unlike objective meaning (such as, for example, the composition of a picture) which is self-contained and hence ascertainable from the picture alone, the expressive meaning embodied in aesthetic elements such as the subject matter, the sweep or foreshortening of a line, cannot be established without an analysis of the historic background. ('Changes in emotive significance' are already to be met with, as we saw in connection with early representations of the blind and halt, even in the more easily comprehensible sphere of subject matter.) This difficulty, however, need not induce us to become sceptics on principle; all we have to conclude from it is that intended expressive meaning is only discoverable by factual historical research, i.e. that in investigating it we have to employ the same methods as are used in any factual historical inquiry. That the intended expressive meaning will not remain

---

[1] None will dispute this fact except those who approach matters with the pre-conceived notion that perception (*Anschauung*) is exclusively a matter of sense, without even considering the question whether it would be at all possible to explain the simplest phenomena without recognizing the existence of intellectual, or rather categorial, perception (*Anschauung*). In understanding the objective visual meaning (visual *configurations*) of a statue, this meaning must be quite as immediately before me—it must be just as immediately perceived by my mind—as the purely sensual elements ('colour', 'glitter', 'shadow') are at the same time directly perceived by my senses. Equally formative, prescriptive of meaning and immediately perceptible to the mind are the expressive (and documentary) dimensions of meaning in the work of art. The 'expressive value' attaching to a colour or combination of colours, and the individual *cachet* they possess, are so much present in aesthetic experience that we often notice them before noticing the underlying colour itself as such. Meaning, in fact, can only be given immediately; and the only reason why we can communicate with each other is that there is such a thing as categorial perception of 'meaning', i.e. of something that is not immanent to consciousness, something that is de-subjectivized and 'unreal'. Although it is true that no meaning can be communicated and understood without a sensual medium, the latter alone would never convey it all by itself. The true inter-subjective medium is meaning in its proper sense which differs from, and is more comprehensive than, the current popular definition of meaning.

inaccessible (as may well be the case with Negro sculpture) is guaranteed to some extent for those periods and cultures which are in a continuity of history with ours. The historical structure of consciousness itself is guarantee that some understanding of the intended meaning may be possible even in respect of works remote in time, the reason for this being that the range of emotions and experiences available to a given epoch is by no means unlimited and arbitrary. These forms of experience arise in, and are shaped for, a society which either retains previously existing forms or else transforms them in a manner which the historian can observe. Since historical consciousness can establish contact with works of the past in this fashion, the historian is able gradually to make himself at home in the 'mental climate' of the work whose expressive intent he is seeking to understand; thus he secures the background against which the specific intent of the work, the unique contribution of the individual artist, will stand out in sharp detail.

This analysis of 'objective' and 'expressive' meaning, and of the way in which it is conveyed by subject-matter and by form, was necessary in order to give us a clearer understanding of 'documentary' meaning, to which we now shall turn.

The incorporation and projection of both 'objective' and 'expressive' meaning is a matter of conscious effort for the artist. By contrast, the third dimension of meaning—documentary meaning—is not an intentional object for him. It can become an intentional object only for the recipient, the spectator. From the point of view of the artist's activity, it is a wholly unintentional, unconscious by-product.

Whereas objective interpretation is concerned with grasping a completely self-contained complex of meaning—pervading the 'representation' of the subject-matter as well as the 'shaping' of the medium—which is ascertainable from the work alone as such, expressive meaning, as we have seen, points beyond the work and requires an analysis of the artist's stream of psychic experience. Now documentary meaning is akin to expressive meaning in that it requires us constantly to look beyond the work; here, too, we are concerned with the man behind the work—but in an entirely different sense. Expressive meaning has to do with a cross-section of the individual's experiential stream, with the exploration of a psychic process which took place at a certain time; documentary meaning, on the other hand, is a matter, not of a temporal process in which certain experiences become actualized, but of the character, the essential nature, the 'ethos' of the subject which manifests itself in artistic creation.

The best way to get this difference clear is to imagine oneself sharing the life of an artist, spending every living minute with him, taking part in all his moods and every wish of his, constantly occupied with all the things that occupy him—all this without ever bothering about documentation. In such a case, one would understand the artist's work in the 'expressive' dimension and one would have a more or less adequate picture of the latter's stream of experience in which one would be a partner—and yet one would lack insight into the artist's personality, his *Weltanschauung*, his ethos. And conversely, another analyst with scant familiarity with the artist's work and actions, but with an acute documentary sense, could build upon the little factual material at his disposal a complete characterization of the artist's personality and outlook, not in the psychological but in the cultural sense.

Documentary meaning also is conveyed by 'objectifications'— what is 'characteristic' in the documentary sense may again be ascertained from the way in which the subject-matter is selected and represented, and from the way in which the medium is shaped. And yet in many essential respects things are not the same as in the case of expressive meaning. Both are alike in that there must be an objective stratum of meaning upon which both the expressive and the objective meaning are superimposed. But whereas expressive meaning cannot be grasped without taking the whole extent of the objective meaning into consideration, that is, in other words, whereas expressive meaning is founded upon the objective meaning as an integral whole, documentary meaning can be ascertained without considering the work in its entirety; in fact, any fragmentary aspect of a work such as a characteristic treatment of line, spatial structure,[1] or colour composition can convey documentary meaning: no need to take only concrete,

---

[1] A good example of documentary analysis of this kind, pursuing documentary evidence down to the smallest details, is provided by a lecture of Max Dvořák's ('Über Greco und den Manierismus', publ. in *Jahrbuch für Kunstgeschichte*, vol. 1 (XV), 1921/22) from which I quote the following remarks about El Greco's 'Funeral of Count Orgaz': 'Gone is the solid spatial organization, since Giotto the sacrosanct foundation of all pictorial representation. Has the space breadth? Has it depth?—who can tell? The figures are crowding on one another as if the artist had been clumsy about their grouping. Yet at the same time the flickering light and the *féerie* above evoke an impression of boundless expanse. The leading principle of the composition is old and simple, used hundreds of times before in portraying the Assumption. *Yet how is its meaning changed*, simply because the painter makes the margin cut across the figures in the forefront so that nothing is to be seen of the ground and the figures seem to spring up somewhere as if by magic . . .' (p. 24; my italics).

An exposition of the layer of objective meaning in the shaping of both the subject-matter and of the medium is immediately followed by a specification of the corresponding documentary meaning.

proper parts of the work into consideration. Expressive meaning is closely interwoven with the unitary, integrated complex of objective meaning; documentary meaning may be inherent in detachable partial aspects.

Now after the documentary meaning of one phase of a work is ascertained, we still need further evidence, in order to make the characterization of the man behind the work complete. Such evidence, however, will not be sought within one single work or one single field of objectification. We rather have to range over all comparable realizations of the same producer, in order to make him, as it were, take shape before our eyes. This confrontation of several pieces of evidence is, however, not a matter of simple addition—as if one item of evidence were part of a whole we are after—a whole which can only be put together by collecting scraps of meaning here and there. The peculiar thing is, in fact, that in a certain sense one single item of documentary evidence gives a complete characterization of the subject; if we are looking further, it is in order to have corroborating instances conveying the same documentary meaning in 'homologous' fashion, rather than in order to supplement one fragment by others. Further, whatever documentary meaning we have discovered by analysing a partial aspect of a work can be corroborated only by other items of documentary evidence; neither expressive nor objective analysis can corroborate documentary interpretation as such. We must perform a new kind of intentional act, corresponding to this new kind of intentional object that documentary meaning is, in order to separate it from the objective and expressive meanings with which it is associated. And in the end one will gain the impression that he has derived one common documentary meaning from a wide range of objective and expressive meanings. This search for documentary meaning, for an identical, homologous pattern underlying a vast variety of totally different realizations of meaning, belongs to a class apart that should not be confused with either addition, or synthesis, or the mere abstraction of a common property shared by a number of objects. It is something apart because the coalescence of different objects as well as the existence of something identical pervading an entire range of differences is specific to the realm of meaning and intention and must be kept uncontaminated by metaphors which have been derived at least in part from the working of spatial and manipulatory imagination.

Riegl's assertion that the so-called 'negative' ornaments occurring in late Roman decorative art manifest the same 'art motive' as the one underlying the architecture of the period, and his analysis of this 'art motive', so broad in its terms that it yields certain analogies with philosophical systems of the same epoch, are good examples of the documentary approach. The analyst succeeded in this case, merely by examining a seemingly insignificant procedure employed in treating the material medium, in putting his finger on something so characteristic that he was able, by following up this hunch, to bring to light the corresponding formal traits in other fields of creative activity directly relevant to the global outlook of the period. In this instance, the documentary meaning was derived from the shaping of the medium, but it obviously can be distilled just as well from the treatment of the subject-matter; every dimension of the objective stratum of meaning may become relevant to documentary interpretation if only we are able to discern its documentary import. And not the objective meaning alone but also the expressive meaning may be exploited for documentary purposes, i.e. made to yield insights into what is culturally characteristic. The most radical procedure—which, however, is applied very frequently in practice—may be mentioned briefly at this point. This consists in taking theoretical utterances, aesthetic confessions of faith, which artists make in order to explain their own formal or expressive goals; these can always be exploited for documentary interpretation. This 'documentary' interpretation of an *Ars poetica* or of an aesthetic theory put forward by an artist does not consist, however, in merely treating these utterances as authentic reflections of the author's artistic personality, of his 'art motive', or of the 'spirit' of his epoch. What we have to ask is not whether the theory is correct—nor what its proponent 'meant' by it. Rather, we must go beyond this 'immanent' interpretation and treat the theoretical confession as confession: as documentary evidence of something extra-psychic, of the objective 'art motive'[1] as a driving force, just as a doctor will take the self-diagnosis of one of his patients as a symptom rather than as a correct identification of the latter's illness.

All such attempts at documentary interpretation gather the scattered items of documentary meaning together in overarching general concepts which are variously designated as the 'art motive' (Riegl),[1] 'economic ethos' ('*Wirtschaftsgesinnung*') (Sombart), '*Weltanschauung*' (Dilthey and others), or 'spirit' (Max Weber and others), depending on the cultural fields explored. One may then also define, as a subjective counterpart to these objective cultural generalizations, the corresponding historical subject; in

---

[1] Cf. Erwin Panofsky, 'Der Begriff des Kunstwollens' (publ. in *Zeitschrift für Aesthetik und allgemeine Kunstwissenschaft*, vol. XIV, no. 4) where an analysis of Riegl's concept of the 'art motive' shows a clear understanding of what is here defined as documentary meaning.

some cases this subject is identified by the name of a historical person or collectivity, as when one speaks of the 'Shakespearian', the 'Goethean', the 'classic' spirit. Such names, however, are always used in an oblique mode, because what we mean is not Shakespeare or Goethe as real persons, but an ideal essence in which their works are epitomized. The term 'classic spirit' is less misleading in this respect because it does not suggest an existing empirical group as its vehicle.[1]

---

[1] One might ask whether the so-called 'real' subject whose existence is presupposed in intentional analysis will not turn out to be a fiction, a mere point of reference of configurations of meaning, if we apply this method of 'structural analysis' to it—so that the supposed 'reality' of the other self will dissolve itself in mere relationships of meaning. From the point of view of structural analysis, there is nothing that prevents this, for in so far as structural analysis is concerned, the supposedly real subject of expressive interpretation is on the same level as the supposedly unreal subject of documentary interpretation, and can equally be resolved into connections of meaning. Hence, if it is nevertheless posited as 'real', there has to be some further experience of it which does not pertain to meaning but is altogether ontological and immediate; its psychic existence must somehow be accessible to us without being mediated by objectively interpretable manifestations or by the manifestations of subjective experiences which are equally open to interpretation of meaning. An ontological experience of this kind in respect also of the subject of *Weltanschauung* is professed by those who would have it postulated as a metaphysical subject. And so when Hegel or Lukács talk of 'spirit' they no more think of it as a methodological device than would a man who in speaking of Goethe would indicate that he imagines being put into communication, through the works of Goethe, not only with the latter's 'ideal essence' but with his ontic reality.

Two diagonally opposed views can be taken as to how other selves present themselves to us and how they are constituted. The first reduces all our knowledge of the other self to configurations of meaning, and holds that we can have access to the psychic reality of the other only through the mediation of intelligible (*geistig*) unreality; Eduard Spranger (*op. cit.* and *Lebensformen*, Halle, 1921) leans towards this view. The second position in turn reduces all our knowledge of the other self to intuitive acts directed towards ontic reality, disregarding the supra-psychic sphere of meaning as something that can be separated from the concrete stream of consciousness; this is the view taken by Scheler (*Über den Grund zur Annahme des fremden Ich*, a supplement to *Phänomenologie und Theorie der Sympathiegefühle von Liebe und Hass*, Halle, 1913).

For once the truth seems to be half-way between these extremes. Understanding of another self must start with configurations of meaning. It cannot, however, end with it, unless we take 'meaning' in a far wider sense than usual. Up to now, the realm of meaning has been taken to include only the theoretical; or at most—if one wanted to give it a very broad construction—that range of phenomena which we designated by the term 'objective meaning'. Thus far, nobody thought of 'expressive' and 'documentary' phenomena as phenomena of meaning. It should be remembered, however, that if we are to have any access to the other subject, it can only be through these dimensions of meaning. It is impossible to see how a subject could be constituted out of objective meaning alone. But even if we add these two other layers of meaning, we shall still fall short of grasping the other subject as a psychic *existent*. Inferences by

Accordingly, one would commit the gravest methodological error if one simply equated this cultural subject (which has been defined merely as a counterpart to an objective cultural generalization) with empirical collective subjects defined on the basis of anthropological or sociological categories, such as race or class. And for this reason no documentary interpretation of the kind we have in mind can be demolished by proving that the author of a work belongs by descent or in terms of status to a 'race' or 'class' other than the one whose 'spirit' was said to be exemplified by the work. Our formulation shows that we do not object to the investigation of 'race' as a problem of cultural history, or of 'class' as a problem of cultural sociology; surely both topics designate problems which deserve to be solved; all we wanted to do was to point out certain methodological implications which apply to these lines of research. Inquiries of this sort employ two sets of concepts which the investigator must rigorously keep apart; on the one hand, a collective subject will be characterized in terms relating to the documentary interpretation of a cultural product, and on the other, we shall obtain collective subjects of a different sort by using the categories of sciences like anthropology or sociology which form their concepts in an altogether different fashion. (The concept of class, for instance, is defined in terms of an individual's role in the economic process of production, and that of race, in terms of purely biological relationships.) Between these two kinds of subject—the subject of collective spirit, derived from the interpretation of cultural objectifications, and the anthropological or sociological subject—the discrepancy due to their heterogeneous origin is so great that it seems absolutely imperative to interpolate an intermediate field of concepts capable of mediating between these two extremes. This may be the task in the solution of which the interpretive cultural psychology (*geisteswissenschaftliche Psychologie*) initiated by Dilthey will find its most fruitful application. Two important studies exemplifying this approach were published recently.[1]

analogy and 'empathy' are entirely inadequate makeshifts—Scheler has proved this much conclusively. The existential postulate of a real other self is grounded in an act of immediate intuition: When I look into the eyes of a person, I see not only the colour of his eyes but also the being of his soul.

How and on what epistemological level this apprehension of being takes place, and whether it is *always* associated with an act of interpretation of meaning or may also be completed in direct ontic communion, these are questions we need not pursue any farther, since our topic is not the problem of reality with all its ramifications.

[1] Cf. Karl Jaspers, *Psychologie der Weltanschauungen*, Berlin, 1919. Eduard Spranger, *Lebensformen, geisteswissenschaftliche Psychologie und Ethik der Persönlichkeit*, 2nd edition, Halle, 1921.

But to come back to the distinction between documentary and expressive interpretation: it is brought into fresh relief by the two types of subject we have just discussed. Both in documentary and in expressive interpretation of a work, we may refer to 'collective subjects' behind that work; but it is immediately apparent that the collective subject we mean in the one case is not the same as the one we mean in the other. Since we can assign expressive meaning only to a real subject or to his stream of consciousness, we can construe the 'expressive meaning' entertained by a group only in strictly nominalist fashion as the meaning entertained *on the average* by the individual members of the group. The characterization of a group in the light of a documentary approach, however, is a different matter; for the purposes of such characterization, we may well make use of collective subjects which are pure constructs, and whose cognitive value consists merely in the fact that they serve as the subjective counterpart of the characterological units suggested by the documentary interpretation.

Finally, we should like to mention one further respect in which the three types of interpretation differ essentially from one another—a difference which, although it does not stem directly from the different mode of 'givenness' of the three meanings, may ultimately be traced back to it. Unlike the two other types of interpretation, documentary interpretation has the peculiarity that it must be performed anew in each period, and that any single interpretation is profoundly influenced by the location within the historical stream from which the interpreter attempts to reconstruct the spirit of a past epoch. It is well known that the Hellenic or Shakespearian spirit presented itself under different aspects to different generations. This, however, does not mean that knowledge of this kind is relative and hence worthless. What it does mean is that the type of knowledge conveyed by natural science differs fundamentally from historical knowledge—we should try to grasp the meaning and structure of historical understanding in its specificity, rather than reject it merely because it is not in conformity with the positivist truth-criteria sanctioned by natural science.

To understand the 'spirit' of an age, we have to fall back on the 'spirit' of our own—it is only substance which comprehends substance. One age may be nearer in essence than another to a particular era, and the one with the closer affinity will be the one whose interpretation will prevail. In historical understanding, the nature of the subject has an essential bearing on the content of knowledge, and some aspects of the object to be interpreted are accessible only to certain types of mind—the reason for this being precisely that historical understanding is not timeless like mathematical or scientific knowledge but itself shaped by the historic process in philosophical self-reflection. To mention a simple example: we may have an entirely different personality image of our parents at 10, 20, 30, 40, 50 years of age, but this does not mean that there is no such thing as 'the' personality or character of the parents; it only means that at each age level one will grasp just that character trait or aspect which is accessible at that level, and that the characterization which has the best chance of being recognized as most 'comprehensive' (rather than 'objectively correct') is the one arrived at when the interpreter is of the same age as the person characterized. Just as one admits this, one will also admit that the temporal process of historical understanding, which does not add one item of knowledge to another but reorganizes the entire image around a new centre in each epoch, has positive cognitive value—this type of knowledge. in fact, being the only one a dynamically changing subject can have of a dynamically changing object.

That is not to say, however, that every documentary interpretation has the same claim to be accepted. For one thing, there is an immanent and formal criterion in that documentary interpretations must cover the total range of the cultural manifestations of an epoch, accommodating each particular phenomenon without exception or contradiction, and secondly, cultural products which we consider from the documentary point of view always unmistakably impose or exclude certain interpretations, so that we do have a certain control. If, then, we have several different interpretations of an epoch all of which are *correct* in this sense, we can only ask which of them is most adequate, i.e. which one shows the greatest richness, the greatest substantial affinity with the object. Where there is a seeming contradiction between correct interpretations of a given epoch or *Weltanschauung*, handed down by different generations of interpreters, what we have to do is to translate the less adequate (but still correct) interpretations into the language of the more adequate ones. In this fashion, the image obtained in the earlier, still inadequate interpretation will be 'suspended' in the Hegelian double acception of this term— that is, the earlier organizing centre of the interpretation will be *discarded*, but whatever was incompletely grasped will be *preserved* in the new centre of organization. Neither objective nor expressive interpretation show this dynamic character. To be sure, an historical preparation is necessary for objective and expressive interpretation too: we cannot properly ascertain objective meaning without exploring the historical antecedents of the emergence of certain forms, and we cannot grasp expressive meaning without being familiar with the historical development of certain psychological trends. But once this preparation is done, the conclusions are simply true or false, without any 'dialectical' ambiguity (such as the one exemplified by the Hegelian term 'suspension'). One may describe the composition of a picture correctly or incorrectly, one may do justice to the purely visual elements of a picture or not, one may re-enact the authentic emotional content of a work or not—for all this one has to know only what is already 'in' the work—but the 'spirit' or global outlook of an epoch is something the interpreting subject cannot grasp without falling back upon his own historic 'substance', which is why the history of documentary interpretations of past ages is at the same time a history of the interpreting subjects themselves.[1]

V. THE PRE-THEORETICAL STRUCTURE OF CULTURAL PRODUCTS

In the foregoing analysis, we distinguished three strata of meaning in every cultural product. It should not be forgotten, however, that the three strata we have been able to keep apart in our purely abstract account only acquire their separate identity, their neat stratification, within the framework of a theory

[1] In the previous discussion, the terms 'expressive' meaning and 'intended' meaning were used as if they were synonymous. Lack of differentiation between these two concepts cannot lead to confusion at this level of inquiry, inasmuch as 'expressive' meaning is always 'intended' meaning and can be understood only as such. Meaning which is not of the 'expressive' mode can, however, be 'intended', i.e. entertained by the subject as an intentional object.

'Intendedness' belongs to an entirely different dimension from the three types of meaning distinguished above. The counterpart of 'intended' meaning (i.e. meaning as entertained by a subject in his particular way) is the 'adequate meaning' of a cultural objectification which may inhere in the latter and can be ascertained as such by the outside observer even if the author of the cultural objectification does not entertain it consciously. The producer may (and quite frequently does) fail to grasp the adequate meaning of the product—and then there is a gap between these two kinds of meaning.

This distinction between 'intended' and 'adequate' meaning corresponds to the distinction Max Weber makes between 'actual' and 'correct' meaning (*Wirtschaft und Gesellschaft*, pt. III, sect. 1, p. 1 ff.).

This alternative, however, has little bearing upon our subject. We can, if we want to, apply this distinction to the terms of our classification of meanings and see which term permits us to differentiate between 'intended' and 'adequate' meaning. We shall then obtain:

(1) both intended and adequate objective meaning;
(2) intended expressive meaning;
(3) adequate documentary meaning (possibly recognized in retrospect by the author of the work interpreted as document).

Thus, it makes no difference to objective meaning whether it is intended or not; expressive meaning can be understood only as intended; and for documentary meaning, it is unessential whether it is 'intended' by the author of the document or not.

—i.e. an interpretive theory. It may very well be that it is only reflection which introduces this analytic stratified structure in the object which in itself is homogeneous, non-stratified; and that in the immediately given, pre-theoretical object there is nothing that corresponds to the three strata.

This point calls for some consideration of cultural products as they are given in immediacy, still untouched in so far as possible by any theorizing. Does a monadic cultural product always present itself simultaneously in terms of objective, expressive, and documentary meaning? Is it even permissible to speak at this level of 'elements', 'fragments of meaning', that can be rounded out in various directions? And further: What manner of thing is this expressive meaning? Does it appear in the cultural product in the same way as the objective meaning, and for that matter: can it even be properly described as meaning at all? There is no escaping these and similar questions, and they call for a characterization of the cultural products in their a-theoretical form, as they present themselves when we grasp them adequately as value objects in the immediate, unreflected approach to the value in question. Questions of this kind are still concerned with form. The cultural product taken in immediacy also has a structure, difficult though it be to describe it systematically. Let us, then, try to develop, albeit in fragmentary fashion, some of the characteristic features of this immediately-given structure.

1. In the first place: A cultural product in its immediate givenness does not present itself in a stratified form. In the picture, subject-matter, visual form, expressive meaning and documentary import are present all at once and together. The tones and intervals of a musical composition exhibit simultaneously an aesthetic form, a melodic and harmonic structure (objective meaning), an emotional content (expressive meaning), and the specific 'musical ethos' of the composer (documentary meaning). Now the question is whether structural stratification is irreconcilable with this psychological simultaneity. May it not be that one and the same acoustic combination of sounds can bear various meanings at once, be encompassed by several forms from the very beginning? There are some who might say that only the objective meaning (i.e. melody, harmony, rhythm, etc.) is actually present, while 'mood' and 'ethos' are introduced from without, associated and super-added, so that they cannot be considered as autonomous 'strata of meaning'. But on this reckoning, melody also should be taken as something super-added rather than actually given. For a tune is more than the individual tones and their temporal sequence. Melody is a meaning-imparting factor in the various sounds and intervals which is superimposed upon their purely

acoustic content and stamps them as an aesthetic phenomenon. But the 'mood', the emotional content in its turn is also a meaning-imparting factor in exactly the same sense—by virtue of it, each individual note becomes something over and above what it would have been if the synthesis of melody alone had given it form.

2. The prevalent inclination to regard expressive content as associated, introduced from without, is explained by the general reluctance to acknowledge it as 'meaning'. What remains after abstracting the purely musical element (acoustic organization) from a tune, from music, what is left of a picture after deduction of its objective meaning, its subject-matter and the form of the presentative medium, this residue is usually designated as 'mood', 'atmosphere', 'general tone of experience', etc. One overlooks, however, the element of 'form' or 'meaning' in this emotional tone—a form which is certainly there although it cannot be defined conceptually.

One of the reasons why the theorist of culture is so likely to miss these things is that we possess only a very few terms to designate contents of this sort. Our careless use of the word 'feeling' for anything and everything of which we cannot form some kind of image is apt to make it seem as if art and cultural products in general could only convey vague feelings and emotions. In actual fact, however, we can distinguish more shades of expressive and documentary meanings than we know how to identify by means of theoretical concepts. We can distinguish without fail the 'vital atmosphere' expressed by a work of Mozart and Beethoven respectively, although we are not yet in a position to formulate this difference theoretically. Thus even where concepts are lacking as yet, there may still be non-theoretical distinctions in meaning, and we may know how to make these distinctions in adequate aesthetic intuition. An example will show that the 'vital atmosphere' of a work of art is not merely an inarticulate subjective state but invariably a sharply patterned meaning, even though we have no concept to define it theoretically.

'Sentimentality' is a form of experience which is very frequently encountered as expressive meaning. Very often an objective meaning (e.g. a pictorial representation) is accompanied in the subjective or expressive dimension by a property we may designate as 'sentimentality'.

Now this 'sentimentality' was present and discernible even before the concept as such was coined—and certain gestures, pictorial representations and *motifs* conveyed it unmistakably, so that it was clearly differentiated from certain related emotional characteristics such as sadness or melancholia. In an even earlier period, however, this subjective pattern of experience itself had not yet come into being; not only the concept as such was lacking, but even the non-theoretical, intuitive form of experience was not there. In discussing works of this period, we cannot speak of sentimentality even in a pre-theoretical sense. In those days sentimentality could not be experienced as such; and if a person ever fell into a mental state of this sort, he or she could not identify it as a distinct species of emotion—and still less interpret other people's manifestations in terms of it. An experience as reference to the inner world can assume a specific character only if it is so sharply set off against the undifferentiated stream of experience that the subject can grasp it as meaning (though not necessarily theoretical meaning). Being set off from the mere flow of subjective states, being turned into something objective—this is what makes a meaning a meaning—whether of the objective or subjective, theoretically defined or non-theoretical variety. We must recognize this sphere of non-theoretical meaning as something intermediate between theory and intuition, if we do not want to consider everything non-theoretical as intuitive and irrational; between merely endured psychic states which are in fact irrational, and the realm of theoretical meaning, we have this broad layer of non-theoretical but meaningful patterns of experience. A good deal of expressive and documentary meaning belongs in this sphere, and it is open to understanding even while the corresponding concepts are still lacking. In the course of evolution, gradually more and more concepts are coined to designate contents of this sort, so that what was first distinguished in a non-theoretical sense later becomes also conceptually identifiable. At any rate, it is wholly inadmissible to fix the genesis of a form of experience at the moment when a concept defining it is coined.

3. The domain of meaning, however, has a wider extension than theoretical meaning together with the realm of non-theoretical meaning represented by cultural products recognized by official and academic tradition. There is a submerged culture which also is meaninglike in structure; it is set off against the mere flux, it can become an intentional object, it can be presented, it is 'unreal in the mode of meaning'—and for this very reason, it cannot yet be identified with the irrational ground of being. Here is the habitat of patterns of experience (such as, to cite a few for which we have already found some sort of a title: resentment, melancholia, acedia, *fin de siècle* mood, what has been termed the 'numinous',[1] etc.); and these, if only because they have a

---

[1] Cf. Rudolf Otto, *The Idea of the Holy* (1919), translated by John W. Harvey, Oxford University Press, 1928.

cultural history of their own, are not mere subjective events in
life but undoubtedly have meaning and stand out from the living
stream as distinctly significant entities. (Pain as a vegetative state
in which one lives has no history; sentimentality, on the other
hand, most certainly has one.) We find ourselves in the realm of
the radically meaningless, of the wholly irrational, only when we
leave all formed experience behind, when we do nothing but
function in the act which has no distinguishable meaning, when
we reach the opaque region of the unorganized. And of this
alone is it true to say we do not 'understand' it in any sense of the
word. We live in these acts, float along with them—possibly they
colour our lives, may even be the most vital part of our existence;
since, however, they do not present themselves as intentional
objects, we do not 'have' them, either in introspection or in the
observation of the other psyche. This segment of our psychic
life is the one we do not *understand*, either in ourselves or in others.
But take anything that is in any way meaningful—to grasp it we
can always rely on intellectual intuition which is just as adequate
as our grasp of theoretical word-meanings. There is only one
difference in this respect between our own and another's psyche,
namely, that we cannot perceive a meaning entertained by the
other without a sensual medium. There is a continuum between
these two poles of meaning—that of theoretical meaning which is
totally de-subjectivized, and emotive meaning which is just
barely objectified. And the nearer a meaning is to the latter, the
more subjective will be the colouring it bears and the more
intimate the nexus with the Here and Now of the individual
psychic stream.

4. We have had to deal at some length with the meaning-character
of our patterns of subjective experience, because these constitute
the stratum in which expressive and documentary meaning are
grasped. They cast in a new form the optical and acoustic material
which has already been formed by objective meaning.

Tempo and rhythm of speech, of drama and music constitute
this material—and rhythm and tempo, too, are organized units
of (objective) meaning. What are, then, the elements of this objective meaning from which the passage to expressive and documentary meaning can be effected?

In this respect, it is not the content, the 'What' of objective
meaning that is of preponderant importance, but the fact and
mode of its existence—the 'That' and the 'How'.

When I want to interpret what a friend of mine is saying in
terms of expressive and documentary meaning, I pay attention
less to the theoretical tenor of 'what' he says than to the fact
'that' he communicates just this and not some other proposition—

and also to 'how' he says what he says. Similarly, the subject-matter of a picture as a constituent of its objective meaning is relevant to its expressive and documentary meaning only in so far as the fact that just this subject-matter was chosen can be revealing. The 'how' in turn appears only in extremely subtle manifestations. In a conversation, next to the objective content, things like gesticulation, facial expression, tempo of speech may become significant; in a dialogue, it will be the way in which the exchange takes place, that is, in what relation a question stands to the answer—whether the answer 'skips' the question or 'transfixes' it, as it were.

5. As we see, meanings of formed experience re-cast the objective meaning in the mould of expressive and documentary meaning. And this gives rise to the further question: is an element grasped first as a unit of objective meaning (e.g. in a picture: as a purely visual *Gestalt*), and then additionally also as a unit of expressive documentary meaning? It follows from what was said above that these latter modes of meaning are not simply super-added to the former one: the element under interpretation becomes an entirely new unit of meaning when seen under the aspect of formed experience. The first interpretation *may* be preserved (and, indeed, must in so far as it is objective interpretation); but once we proceed to a new interpretation, we are faced with an entirely new meaning. The first one survives, not in modified, but in 'bracketed' state, and is replaced by an entirely new stratum of meaning. In the example cited above, the gesture made by my friend conveyed the objective meaning 'assistance'. Seen under the aspect of the expressive meaning 'pity', the same gesture in all its details becomes the vehicle of an entirely different meaning. And exactly the same thing happened when my friend's action was scrutinized in terms of its documentary meaning; the characterological category of 'hypocrisy' immediately informed each part anew, claiming the whole for its own. In one point only has the objective mode of meaning a certain advantage over the others, that is, it can be grasped without the others whereas the others cannot stand alone but need objective meaning to become visible, although the objective meaning immediately becomes 'bracketed' while they are being contemplated. A picture or statue must exist first *qua* organization of a visual field, before expressive and documentary meaning can take hold of it; my friend's gesture must be interpreted as an instance of 'assistance' before it can be seen as a manifestation of pity or an example of hypocrisy (and it may be pointed out in passing that in this case the gesture *qua* organization of the visual field is left out of account, since this aspect of it is quite as irrelevant as the acoustic *Gestalt*

of the uttered word is to its conceptual meaning). Objective meaning is always the first stratum of meaning to become relevant and capable of interpretation—but it need not always consist in the in-forming of a visual or acoustic substratum, as it does in art.

6. What we have to do with here, then, are not 'elements' or self-subsisting 'units of meaning' which form novel wholes when other units are added to them. It is not one and the same 'element' which enters now into objective, now into documentary and expressive meaning. To assume this is to falsify the constitution of meaning by taking a crude spatial metaphor as expressing its essence. Here there are no parts awaiting integration; on the contrary, something can only be a part by being grasped within its appropriate whole. What remains unaltered is merely the material substratum (a patch of colour, a line), and even that, in so far as it may be regarded as a definite 'something', is necessarily part of a compresent whole; and with the appearance of a novel whole, the part as such is also transformed.

The phases here described as forming a succession may of course psychologically be experienced simultaneously. I can envisage the patch of colour at once under the aspect of colour composition and of emotive value. Our tendency to break down *Gestalts* of meaning in this atomistic fashion can be explained only by the unjustifiable paradigmatic preponderance of word language. Word language gives an impression as if more comprehensive units of meaning (sentences or systems of propositions) were built up, mosaic-like, from isolated phonetic units (words with their conceptual meanings), and as if the individual concepts had their own firmly circumscribed meanings outside the systems. Well, even in theoretical language, this is never wholly so ; but whereas theoretical concepts do have a certain vestigial autonomy, it would be a mistake to suppose that meaning has ever this kind of structure in the a-theoretical realm.

Our theoretical account of the structure of meaningful objects up to now has made it appear as if there were self-subsisting 'elements' or 'units of meaning' which subsequently entered into more comprehensive *Gestalt*-like complexes. At this level of our inquiry, however, we have to get rid of this way of looking at things, and to show how each fragmentary 'unit' is already encased in a universe of interpretation (*Auffassungsganzheit*) whenever it is grasped as such—this 'universe' prescribing the pattern according to which all further units have to be fitted into the picture as it is being rounded out. This will be clearer if we think of the 'language of the body', of physiognomical interpretation, which is in far closer analogy to the structure of cultural meanings than the principal medium of theoretical meaning, word language.

In physiognomics it is plain that the whole goes before, and that it is not built up mosaic-like from self-subsisting parts. If we think of a face with its characteristic features which cannot be described in words but can nevertheless be grasped adequately in their uniqueness, such as, for example, the face of Leonardo's St. Anne, it is clear that the 'meaning' of the whole, this unique character, cannot be said to reside in the mouth or the eyes, but only in all these features together at once. The *cachet* is not pieced together from physiognomic fragments with a meaning of their own, but it is the whole which imparts to each fragment its specific function and thereby its meaning and substance.

VI. HOW CAN THE GLOBAL OUTLOOK BE TREATED SCIENTIFICALLY?

We tried in the two preceding sections, first, to show that the meaning of cultural products does possess a dimension which may be characterized as documentary meaning, and, second, to describe the way in which this documentary meaning is grasped, in pre-theoretical, direct experience. We now shall pass to a methodological discussion of certain works in which the attempt is made to give a scientific account of global outlook (*Weltanschauung*) in terms of documentary analysis. Our discussion will be confined to a few examples which seem to be typical of a certain approach; no judgment of value, however, is implied in the selection of just these examples rather than of others.

Once it is shown that in every cultural product a documentary meaning reflecting a global outlook is given, we have the basic guarantee that *Weltanschauung* and documentary meaning are capable of scientific investigation. Positivist method, correctly understood, required us to substantiate this point; for we, too, adhere to the principle that science can treat only of what is given beforehand. That documentary meaning in fact is given will be doubted only by those who confuse this correctly understood positivism with a one-sided positivism oriented towards natural science exclusively, and who arbitrarily admit as positively given only the physical or at best—an utterly generous concession, they claim—the psychic datum. As against this, we invoke the phenomenological principle that each sphere of reality has its own kind of 'givenness', and that the domain of 'meaning' is not restricted either to the sphere of physical 'things' or to the psychic events localized in one temporal sequence of individual experiences.

We may, then, take the presence of documentary meaning in each cultural product, notably in the work of art, as established; but with this, the most important condition for the possibility of scientific control of statements about *Weltanschauung* is fulfilled, since immediate intuitive perception of the datum—in our case, the direct presence of documentary meaning—is both the source of authentic richness and the basis of control of theoretical statements. Eliminate the dimension of documentary meaning, and each work loses its specific morphological character. Hence, what we have to do is only to work out the most fitting concepts, permitting the closest theoretical approximation to our object—in order to see where the difficulty of theory lies. In the direct aesthetic enjoyment of a work, we acquire 'knowledge' of it in a certain sense—such enjoyment also involves the presence of 'something out there' (to avoid the term 'object' at this point), something we can identify and recognize. But if 'knowledge' is to be defined as theoretical knowledge, encompassed by concepts and logical connections, our methodological problem will consist in trying to find out how the datum grasped in pre-theoretical intuition can be transposed into theoretical concepts.

On this point, too, those who accept the degree of precision attained in exact natural science as their standard will insist upon complete conceptualization of the object, i.e. the complete explication of the object in terms of theoretical concepts. They will not admit that we have 'knowledge' of anything unless this condition is satisfied. The categories which permit the fullest explication in terms of theory are form, relation and law. But we should be compelled to disclaim the possibility of knowledge in vast areas of exploration, if we took such a rigid standard literally, instead of calling to mind that each area, as it were, lays down the requirements, the limits, and the nature of possible theoretical analysis, so that criteria of exactness cannot be transferred from one field into another. There are data which can be treated mathematically; others may be described in terms of different but still uniform regularities; still others are uniquely individual but nevertheless display an inner law of their unique structure, an inner consistency which can be described conceptually; and finally, there are some in respect of which all theory must limit itself to an 'indication', 'approximation', or 'profiling' of certain correspondences, because their substantive characterization has already been accomplished in pre-theoretical experience.

We saw in the preceding section that immediate aesthetic experience takes note of different strata of meaning but fails to keep them apart—at this level, all strata are given in 'psychological simultaneity'. It is because immediate experience can englobe simultaneously different strata which only abstraction can keep apart that it has a richness and depth, a morphological concreteness and physiognomical *cachet*, beside which the abstractly pure sequences of one single stratum must appear as lifeless schemata. It would, however, be a fundamental misconception of the function of theory if we assigned to it (as the extreme position cited above would have it) the sole task of reproducing on the conceptual level the full wealth of what has already been grasped in immediate experience. This could be done, if at all, by art rather than by theory; and although it is characteristic of historical and critical writing at its best that it contains passages which try to evoke the full concrete richness of the works in question, it is not this 'evocation' but something else which constitutes the essence of scientific 'rationalization'. The evocative passages merely serve to make the structure of the various cultural products visible. The object of pure aesthetic intuition as such precedes theoretical analysis; it must be given before everything else, and while we are engaged in theoretical analysis, we must constantly refer back to it and renew acquaintance with it; but it is only a 'presupposition' for theory and its re-creation is never a substantive problem for science. Science seeks to account for the totality of culture as the 'work' of man, it does not seek to re-create it. We can expect neither complete rationalization nor re-creation of the past from the cultural sciences. Their tasks and possibilities point to a third way.

We saw that direct experience itself contains many elements of theoretical meaning, and that pre-theoretical perception is charged with incipient reflection which, however, need not blur the directly given intuitive *Gestalt* in any way. Certain details may even stand out more vividly, when illuminated by theory; and theory may help us to see as enduring 'facts' certain things which would otherwise fade away after the intuitive flash is over. This, then, is one thing scientific analysis can do for cultural products: it can stabilize them, make them endure, give them a firm profile.

From this point on, we shall not be concerned with cultural reality as immediately given, but with the theory of culture as such. Our problem at this point is one of the methodology of science.

Only methodological reflection will enable us to see clearly the way in which documentary meaning is differentiated from expressive and objective meaning, although, to be sure, immediate intuitive experience also gave us a certain fragmentary idea of documentary meaning.

Thus far, cultural sciences, e.g. history of art, have focused attention mainly on objective meaning. We have seen above (pp. 35 ff.) how the history of style constitutes a novel scientific object of its own by singling out certain aspects of works of art and studying them systematically, and how iconographical studies inventorize representational motifs and trace their history in philological fashion. In studies of this kind, the immediately given 'monadic' unity of concrete parts of the individual works is dissolved in an abstractive process for the purpose of constructing new objects on a higher level of generality.[1]

A scientific, systematic analysis of documentary meaning would likewise proceed by detaching certain elements or units of meaning from their concrete setting and fusing them into validly ascertainable objects of higher generality by using appropriate categories and conceptualizations. Our question is how the documentary meaning always present in the concrete works can be disentangled from objective and expressive meaning and assigned to a particular subject or ego.

Put in different words: the crucial question is how the totality we call the spirit, *Weltanschauung*, of an epoch, can be distilled from the various 'objectifications' of that epoch—and how we can give a theoretical account of it.

A somewhat similar problem is that facing biography[2]: there, too, the task consists mainly in reconstructing the inner world of a subject from its outward manifestations and the fragments of meaning contained therein. Just as in the case of biography the entire material (works, actions, records, letters) is treated as 'confessions', and the self-centred, immanent structure of each item—as determined by its objective meaning—is disrupted, so that the item in question may serve solely as an aid in reconstructing the inner world of the subject, so in reconstructing the 'global outlook', the spirit of an epoch, too, the entire material is made to serve a wholly new purpose, and the self-contained

---

[1] Thus H. Wölfflin ('Das Problem des Stils in der bildenden Kunst', *Sitzungsberichte der Kgl. Preuss. Akademie d. Wissensch.*, XXXI, 1912, pp. 572 ff.) speaks of a 'dual source' of style and develops on this basis his concept of the immanent, autonomous evolution of visual form, distinguishing this mode of analysis from one in which the concrete, integral works themselves are examined as such; this is a good example of the abstractive method we have in mind. (In a paper by Erwin Panofsky, 'Das Problem des Stils in der bildenden Kunst', in *Zeitschrift für Aesthetik und allgem. Kunstwissenschaft*, vol. X, pp. 460 ff., certain valid objections are advanced against use of the term 'visual form'.)

[2] There are two directions in which 'biography' may proceed. One kind of biography seeks to construct a personality profile of a poet from elements of his work examined in terms of documentary meaning; this is structurally the same task as the one faced in interpreting the *Weltanschauung* of an epoch. The other kind is life-history in the strict sense, and it aims at reconstructing from elements of 'expressive' meaning the actual sequence of the inner experiences of the author. On this cf. pp. 55–56 above.

'monadic' unity of the individual works is disregarded. Now just as any individual item in a biography, such as a single scene of a drama which is torn from its context and treated as a confession of the author, will gain an entirely new meaning in the light of its function in the biographic whole, any cultural object seen as the vehicle of documentary meaning will receive an entirely new meaning when it is seen within the context of the global outlook of an epoch. From this, a paradoxical result arises for all theorizing: we understand the whole from the part, and the part from the whole. We derive the 'spirit of the epoch' from its individual documentary manifestations—and we interpret the individual documentary manifestations on the basis of what we know about the spirit of the epoch[1]. All of which goes to substantiate the assertion made earlier, that in the cultural sciences the part and the whole are given simultaneously.

The methodological problem might then be formulated finally as follows: how can we describe the unity we sense in all works that belong to the same period in scientific terms capable of control and verification?

One of the difficulties has already been mentioned (above, pp. 40 f.); it is that the totality of *Weltanschauung* (that which is 'documented') is located beyond the level of cultural objectification and is not conveyed by any of the cultural spheres taken in isolation. Hence, we have to survey all the cultural spheres and compare their various objectifications in terms of the same set of documentary criteria.

Our first task, then, is to evolve concepts applicable (like a co-ordinate system) to every sphere of cultural activity alike—concepts making it possible to ask meaningful questions regarding art as well as literature, philosophy as well as political ideology, and so on.

A second stumbling-block for a comparative study of culture is the fact that culture is in process of historical evolution, so that the concepts we use in comparing various fields of cultural activity in a contemporaneous cross-section should also serve the purposes of a 'longitudinal' analysis of successive temporal stages. In other words: can we formulate a 'ubiquitous' problem and define concepts for its treatment in such a way that it will be possible to lay, as it were, cross-sections in two different directions

---

[1] In his paper, 'Das Problem des Gegebenen in der Kunstgeschichte', *Festschrift für Riehl*, Halle, 1914, Johannes Eichner makes an analogous remark about style: 'At one time, we fix the date of a certain work on the basis of what we know about the stylistic peculiarities of the period; at anothre, we use the same work to add new data to our knowledge of the style of the period' (p. 203). As we see, the same paradox arises for objective meaning too.

—once 'across' various spheres of cultural activity, and then across successive cultural stages? And if so, where are these concepts to come from—from philosophy, or from the various sciences dealing with art, religion, etc.? For the theoretical picture obtained will, in point of fact, vary, depending on the discipline from which we borrow the key concepts used in comparison. We shall now examine the methodological principles which have inspired certain attempts at constructing a historical synthesis along such lines.

The most plausible approach consists in seeing whether we can apply certain regularities and problems suggested by the history of philosophy to the examination of cultural fields other than philosophy. Thus Dilthey, whose pioneering achievement in calling attention to the irrational aspects of *Weltanschauung* we emphasized above, chose to take his departure from philosophy[1]; and although he shows great critical reserve and theoretical acumen in characterizing the various 'life patterns' (*Lebenssysteme*), the categories he uses bear the stamp of this primarily philosophical orientation. His three types of *Weltanschauung* (the systems of naturalism, of objective idealism [pantheism] and of subjective idealism) will hold good only if they prove fruitful in the analysis of the history of plastic art, among other things. This experiment was tried by one of his school, Nohl,[2] who skilfully reformulated these three types to such an extent as to be able to indicate three corresponding types in the visual universe and thus to raise the question: 'what types of visual forms correspond to the principal variants of philosophic thought' (p. 23). The author's method of inquiry is careful and accurate (he analyses pictorial subject-matter and pictorial form separately)—and it is the more disappointing that his concrete conclusions are so scanty and vague. The reason for this is, firstly, that concepts derived and sublimated from a theoretical field—philosophy—and the problem which these concepts are fit to treat can contribute but little to the elucidation of a-theoretical fields (in their case, of the visual universe). Secondly, this analysis suffers from the fact that it employs a timeless typology—styles are defined as correlates of various attempts at interpreting the universe, conceived as absolutely timeless alternatives. However, a theoretical framework which admits no dynamic (or possibly dialectical) variation is necessarily compelled to equate products of the most distant epochs—and thus to disregard precisely what is essential in them: the constitutive role of temporality.

[1] *Op. cit.*, and *Kultur der Gegenwart*, pt. I, sect. VI, pp. 1–72.
[2] Hermann Nohl, *Stil und Weltanschauung*, Jena, 1920.

The more one is impressed by the inadequacy of explaining *Weltanschauung* in terms of philosophy, the more promising will be the attempt to start from art and analyse all other fields of culture in terms of concepts derived from a study of plastic arts. The 'hierarchical level' of plastic art is closer to the sphere of the irrational in which we are interested here; and it is justified by an interest in typology, if by no other reason, to examine for once a theory of *Weltanschauung* which takes its departure from art. We should like to mention in the first place A. Riegl's study which, although not quite recent, is methodologically still challenging today. Riegl's primary objective is not to characterize the global outlook of an epoch as a whole; he merely wants to grasp the 'art motive' displayed by all four branches of visual art. These branches form a hierarchy according to the degree of distinctness with which they illustrate the 'guiding law' of the art motive. At the head are architecure and decorative art which often exemplify these 'laws' in almost 'mathematical purity'; thus we have a 'horizontal' differentiation in the manifestations of the 'art motive' of a period, to which is added a temporal differentiation of the art motives of successive periods. Antiquity as a whole has its one dominant principle, subdivided into an ancient-oriental, classical, late-antique art motive—each being sharply delimited. To illustrate the method, we have chosen Chapter V of the study[1] which deals with the correlation between the art motive on the one hand, and contemporary science, philosophy, and religion on the other, and thus expands the art motive into a kind of 'world motive' or 'culture motive'. The successive stages derived from the observation of art forms correspond to stages of religious or philosophical world interpretation. In the sequence of art forms, we have (a) separate individual forms without synthesis, (b) self-contained individual forms arranged in a purely serial rhythm, (c) aspiration toward full, three-dimensional spatiality, to be achieved by emancipation of the individual figures from the flat background. There are parallel stages in the other fields of world interpretation. Art gives clues to the necessary emergence of religious, then philosophical, and finally, towards the close of antiquity, magical thinking.[2] All stages are developed in a strict logical sequence. Thus, all of the symptomatic features of late Roman art are traced back to one supreme principle: full three-dimensional spatiality. At least in the realm of the art motive, there is a strict logical connection between such

---

[1] Alois Riegl, *Die spätrömische Kunstindustrie nach den Funden in Österreich-Ungarn im Zusammenhang mit der Gesamtentwicklung der bildenden Künste bei den Mittelmeervölkern*, Vienna, 1901, pp. 17 ff.

[2] *Op. cit.*, pp. 215 ff., and pp. 19 ff.

features as the separation of individual figures from the background, the interval as an entity in its own right, the emergence of the niche, the rhythmical treatment of colour and shadow, group composition without a collective character, objectivity, anonymity, stereotypization.[1]

Two aspects of this mighty effort at synthesis are of particular interest for us: (1) the bid for a strictly rational construction, and (2) the attempt to derive the meaningful variations of mature forms from similarly differentiated germinal forms.

We begin with the first point. The surprisingly strict rationalizing treatment of the material is explained by Riegl's desire to make the documentary meanings found by intuition amenable to objective verification. Verifiability may be ensured in two ways: (1) by the empirical confrontation of the hypotheses with the historical material; (2) by an attempt to establish logical links connecting the various symptomatic, documentary phenomena (e.g. the interval as an independent unit, or the appearance of the niche) with one another and with one guiding principle. Yet such a rationalization, it must be remembered, has nothing to do with a logical deduction of consequences from a theoretical principle—because it constantly presupposes the faculty of grasping pre-theoretical documentary meaning. As we said before: we can use an individual product of a past epoch as a corroborative instance of some hypothesis about *Weltanschauung* only on condition that we are able to perform a specific act of apprehending the a-theoretical strata of meaning exhibited by the product in question which put us in touch with its documentary import. We must already possess documentary meaning before we can bring it into correlation with other documentary meanings. Furthermore, Riegl's explanation of the separation of the figure from the flat background as an instance of the urge to achieve full three-dimensionality is more than a purely theoretical deduction. The existence of a necessary connection between these two things can only be 'seen', it is, in our terminology, comprehensible only within the categories of the 'visual universe'. Thus, the strict quasi-logical development of Riegl's exposition should not mislead us. This type of rationalization actually presupposes so-called intuition (in this case, the original a-theoretical capacity of perceiving phenomenologically necessary correlations in the purely visual content); and every step in the 'deduction' (in so far as it is objectively founded) can be verified only by reference to phenomenologically necessary correlations between units of the visual universe. To take an example from a different a-theoretical field: we cannot explain in terms of extraneous

[1] *Op. cit.*, pp. 209 ff.

categories why religious rejection of the 'world' may lead either to asceticism or to mysticism.[1] Only the form of 'alternation' is 'logical'; but in order to understand why it is the one or the other of these roads that has to be chosen, we must re-enact genuine religious experience. Similarly, it is only by 'living' in the visual universe with its specific structure that we can recognize the necessary connection between 'aspiration towards three-dimensional spatiality' and 'isolation of the figure from the flat background'.

It is no doubt profitable to show—even without 'rationalization', i.e. without demonstrating the necessity of the connection—that the same documentary meaning is conveyed by objectifications belonging to several different fields. But if we do only that, we fall short of achieving real scientific knowledge.

Thus, starting from methodologically fruitful insights (which, however, became entangled with an unfortunate brand of 'prophetic' metaphysics of history), Spengler[2] attempted to broaden Riegl's original scheme ('Euclidean man', with his corporeal world without space, as the type of antiquity which strives for self-contained individual figures) and discern this elementary pattern in all fields of ancient culture, confronting it with the modern 'Faustian' aspiration towards infinity.[3] Trying to characterize two antithetical primitive patterns of experience and cultural creation, Spengler uses the basic terms 'Apollinic', 'Euclidean', 'corporeal', 'spaceless', 'bounded', 'non-historical and mythical', 'pantomimic figure' for the one, and 'Faustian', 'infinitesimal', 'function', 'force', 'spatial', 'unbounded', 'historical and genetic', 'dramatic character', for the other. But the characterization remains fragmentary. It may be admitted that the analysis of *Weltanschauung*—intent upon giving some idea of a common background behind all objectifications—must always resort to such transpositions of concepts—and, for example, use terms taken from plastic art to characterize the music of a period, and vice versa.[4] We shall by all means take advantage

[1] The example is borrowed from Max Weber's *Aufsätze zur Religionssoziologie* (vol. 1, p. 538 ff.; Tübingen, 1920) where an attempt is made to establish a rationalized typology of the various forms of religious non-worldliness.

[2] Oswald Spengler, *The Decline of the West* (1920), translated by Charles Francis Atkinson, G. Allen & Unwin, 1926–29 (London, printed in U.S.A.).

[3] Cf. W. Sombart, *Der moderne Kapitalismus*, 2nd ed., vol. 1, p. 476.

[4] Some extreme instances of this in Spengler: 'Newton's baroque physics', 'the contrapuntal method of numbers', 'Catholic and Protestant colour', etc. It may be pointed out at this juncture that we are not concerned with the factual rightness of the findings of Spengler or of the other authors whose works we discuss; we are solely interested in the methodological procedure involved.

of the possible metaphorical and ambiguous[1] uses of words in order to formulate this 'synaesthetic' experience. All this, however, ought to be only a means, not the end of the inquiry. Since there are no terms available for a phenomenological description of Riegl's 'germinal patterns' (to which we shall turn in a moment) we must resort again and again to a specific method which may be described as the 'sublimation' of a concept (as distinct from mere 'transposition'). 'Sublimating' a concept means that a term which originally refers only to objective meaning is used to designate the documentary meaning associated with the objective one. For instance, the concept of 'baroque' is sublimated if, instead of designating a purely visual, stylistic category, it is used to refer to the general 'baroque principle', the 'spirit' of baroque, which can be grasped only by an intentional act directed to a documented essence. But it is not enough to use the right terms; we must also work out the necessary connection between 'objective' and 'sublimated' meaning, the necessary progression from one stage to the next.

Now this is precisely the heroic course on which Riegl (the discussion of whose work we now resume) has embarked; and this brings us to the second difficulty inherent in his method. He seeks to characterize *Weltanschauung* as a global entity by ascertaining certain common features in the various objectifications. All such attempts, however, fail to go beyond abstract, formal analysis. They can only succeed in bringing to light the categories and forms of experience and expression pertaining to a given period before they become fully differentiated in objectifications—in other words: all they can establish is a typology of 'initial', 'germinal' patterns of mental life. Such undertakings are neither futile nor hopeless. But it will never be possible to derive the wealth of meanings embodied in the actual works from these germinal patterns. This is the weakness common to Riegl's method and the other attempts we have reviewed so far. Complex meanings cannot be adequately grasped or interpreted in terms of elementary concepts. The common residue we are left with as the 'basic principle' of the *Weltanschauung* of an epoch is so bare

---

[1] It is too often ignored that the ambiguous use of terms—i.e. the same word used in disparate contexts—is by no means without relevance. If both a well and a tone are described as 'deep', this does not mean that a spatial category is applied to a non-spatial, musical datum, but the term 'deep' expresses in both cases the same general 'germinal' pattern of human experience which is only subsequently differentiated into separate spatial and acoustic patterns. Ambiguity expresses a relevant experience of pre-scientific language. It indicates some common underlying element. Ambiguity is an offence to the analytic mind, but a source of rich insights for the synthetically oriented scholar.

and abstract that it does not even suggest the wealth of forms we actually encounter when we look at the cultural products themselves.

The drawbacks of this method explain why certain theorists of *Weltanschauung* take a different position—I mean those who, inspired by Dilthey's fascinating example, take the *historical* approach and examine individual phenomena in all their concrete detail in order to re-create the essence of a past epoch in all its multiform variety. The former group tended, in part at least, towards a philosophy of history; the adherents of the latter aspire to be historians first and last. I have in mind 'synthesizing' historians like Dvořák and Max Weber, who, though experts in some special field, have a strong sense of universal history which impels them to correlate their chosen subject with the 'total constellation'. The methodological problem facing this type of author is whether the unity of various cultural fields should be expressed in terms of 'correspondence', 'function', 'causality', or 'reciprocity'.[1] While Dvořák decides in favour of 'correspondence' and parallelism, Weber postulates a mutual causal dependence among the various domains of culture and considers it necessary for purposes of a correct 'causal account' that the economico-material should at times be explained from the mental, and another time—as the occasion calls for—the spiritual from the material, with the reservation, however, that neither of these domains is wholly deducible from the other as if it were simply a function of it. He thinks that we can only establish certain partial determinants of the historic process in this fashion. The historians' way of proceeding clearly indicates that for them, too, the factor making for necessary connections (causality, reciprocity, and correspondence) is again the heart of the problem. The historian may have isolated with complete certainty one and the same 'documentary' symptom in several cultural domains; still, the question which form of connection should be interpolated will have to be solved separately. The category of causality—which largely governs the explanations of natural science—seems to be best suited for this task. But—even apart from the question what 'causal explanation' means in the cultural sciences and what its scope is—we may very well ask whether tracing a phenomenon back, not to another phenomenon, but to a 'global outlook' behind both, does not constitute a type of elucidation which is totally different from genetic, historical, causal explanation. If the term 'explanation' is to be reserved for the latter, we propose

[1] Cf. M. Dvořák, *Idealismus und Naturalismus in der gotischen Skulptur und Malerei*, Munich–Berlin, 1918, pp. 10 ff.; Max Weber, *Religionssoziologie*, vol. 1, pp. 12 ff., 205 ff.

to call the former 'interpretation' (*Deutung*). The theory of *Weltanschauung* is an interpretive rather than explanatory one in the sense just defined. What it does is to take some meaningful object already understood in the frame of reference of objective meaning and place it within a different frame of reference—that of *Weltanschauung*. By being considered as 'document' of the latter, the object will be illuminated from a new side.

In other words: there is no causal relation between one document and another; we cannot explain one as the causal product of the other but merely trace both back to the same global unity of *Weltanschauung* of which they are parts. Similarly, when we trace two actions of a person to the same personality trait, we cannot also treat one as being caused by the other, i.e. say that one kindness has caused another, instead of saying that two actions have been caused by the same kindness. Therefore, it seems that the form of connection chosen by Dvořák—parallelism —is the most adequate, best fitting one.[1] We cannot construct a theory of *Weltanschauung*—i.e. a pattern of necessity connecting documentary data—by explaining one as the causal product of the other, but solely by showing both to be parts of the same totality: by disengaging, step by step, the common documentary import contained in both. That, incidentally, is not to say that historico-genetic causal explanation as such has no place in the cultural sciences. Interpretation does not make causal explanation superfluous. It refers to something quite different, and consequently there is absolutely no rivalry between the two. Interpretation serves for the deeper understanding of meanings; causal explanation shows the conditions for the actualization or realization of a given meaning (on this distinction see p. 44 above). At any rate there can be no causal, genetic explanation of meanings—not even in the form of an ultimate theory superadded to the interpretation. Meaning in its proper essence can only be understood or interpreted. Understanding is the adequate grasping of an intended meaning or of the validity of a proposition (this, then, includes the objective as well as the expressive stratum of meaning); interpretation means bringing the abstractively distinguished strata of meaning in correlation to each other and especially to the documentary stratum. In the history of art, and in the cultural sciences in general, the procedures we have so sharply distinguished—causal explanation and interpretation —will, of course, both be applied *in turn* (but not in the same

---

[1] It should be stressed, however, that Max Weber's actual historical analyses do not always correspond to his theoretical precepts. In his theoretical writings, he insists upon causal explanation; in his historical works, he very often proceeds according to the 'documentary' method.

breath!) in order to give as good an idea as possible of the full, concrete variety and 'vitality' of the historical process in question —although it is also quite rewarding to analyse an epoch consistently from a purely interpretive viewpoint.

*   *   *   *

On comparing the various ways pursued by the methodology of historical research in *Weltanschauung*, we detect a gradual emancipation from a methodology oriented entirely on the natural sciences. Mechanistic causality no longer holds exclusive sway; the limits and scope of historico-genetic explanation become more and more closely defined. A new hearing is given to methods of elucidation formerly condemned. The mechanistic method by which the material is broken up into atomic constituents no longer appears fruitful when it is applied to higher-level phenomena of meaning. In the realm of the mental, we cannot understand the whole from the parts; on the contrary, we can only understand the parts from the whole. Modern nominalism seems to be supplanted by a realism which recognizes universals (such as, for example, 'spirit'), if only as methodologically warranted constructs. The concept of 'substance', which had practically been ousted by that of 'function', is again coming to the fore, and we no longer ask only about the How of things but also for a definition of What they are. Understanding and interpretation as adequate ways of ascertaining meaning have come to supplement historico-genetic explanation, and as an aid in determining the historico-mental in its temporal dimension,[1] the problem of historical dialectics once again comes into view.

But—to conclude on my part with an attempt at 'documentary' interpretation—all these things are merely the methodological repercussions of a much more far-reaching cultural transformation. The fact that natural science had to restore to history its rightful autonomy, that there is a dawning understanding of the distinctive nature of the mental and the historical, that we are striving after a synthesis and would like to draw the meaning and form of pre-theoretical data within the orbit of science—all this is a sign that science along with our whole intellectual life is in ferment; and although we see the trend of this process, we cannot

---

[1] Cf. Troeltsch's essays on methodology: 'Über den Begriff einer historischen Dialektik', 1919, in *Historische Zeitschrift*, series 3, vol. 23, no. 3, pp. 373–426; vol. 24, no. 3, pp. 393–451. 'Der historische Entwicklungsbegriff der modernen Geistes- und Lebensphilosophie',1920, in *Hist. Zeitschr.*, ser. 3, vol. 26, no. 3, pp. 377–453. 'Die Dynamik der Geschichte nach der Geschichtsphilosophie des Positivismus', Berlin, 1913, in *Phil. Vorträge der Kantgesellschaft*, no. 23.

anticipate its final outcome. History never repeats itself literally —and if we tried to speed up the process by simply taking over parallel phenomena from the past, or accentuating existing tendencies by following them as models, we would be renouncing our own destiny. The logician can but decipher what has already been achieved—science and the spirit go their own way.

III
The Problem of a Sociology of Knowledge

I. THE PROBLEM CONSTELLATION

THE term 'constellation' comes from astrology; it refers to the position and mutual relationship of the stars at the hour of a man's birth. One investigates these relationships in the belief that the fate of the new-born child is determined by this 'constellation'. In a wider sense, the term 'constellation' may designate the specific combination of certain factors at a given moment, and this will call for observation when we have reason to assume that the simultaneous presence of various factors is responsible for the shape assumed by that one factor in which we are interested. Astrology no longer has any meaning or reality for us; the category of constellation, however, has been lifted from the descriptive and theoretical context of astrology, and, having been incorporated in a new context of *Weltanschauung*, it now represents one of the most important categories we use in interpreting the world and the human mind. It has happened in other fields, too, that fundamental categories were detached from their original context which had become obsolete, to be further utilized in a new theoretical context of their own. Although little has been done thus far to study categories of this sort, and although they have been practically overlooked in methodological investigations, we may say that it is precisely these categories which constitute the most valuable set of tools we have for interpreting the world and mastering the phenomena we encounter in daily life as well as in the cultural sciences. The categories of the philosophy of history in particular (e.g. 'fate') turn out to be of continuing fruitfulness, though in ever-changing form, and our interpretation of the world is always based upon them.

The category of 'constellation', thus detached from its original

From *Essays on the Sociology of Knowledge* (New York: Oxford University Press, 1952), pp. 134–90. Reprinted by permission of Routledge and Kegan Paul Ltd.

context, has proved particularly fruitful for us in the one field in which we still can make use of a genuine metaphysical instinct today: in the contemplation of the history of thought. While nature has become dumb and devoid of meaning for us, we still have the feeling, in dealing with history and also with historical psychology, that we are able to grasp the essential interaction of the basic forces, and to reach the fundamental trends which mould reality, beyond the topical surface of daily events. In this respect, even the specialized scholar is a metaphysician, whether he wants to be or not—for he *cannot* refrain from breaking through the individual causal connections between separate events and pushing all the way to the 'driving forces' which make the various individual events possible. Obviously, this kind of metaphysics, which is the only one that suits us, differs greatly from all the other kinds of metaphysics that existed in the past—just as the category of constellation does not mean the same thing for us that it did, for example in astrology.

Our knowledge of human thought itself develops in a historical sequence; and we were driven to raise this problem of 'constellation' by our conviction that the possible next step in knowledge is determined by the status reached by the various theoretical problems, and also by the constellation of extra-theoretical factors, at a given moment, making it possible to predict whether certain problems will turn out to be soluble. In the cultural sciences especially, we are convinced that not every question can be posed —let alone solved—in every historical situation, and that problems arise and fade away in a particular rhythm which can be ascertained. Whereas in mathematics and natural science, progress seems to be determined to a large extent by immanent factors, one question leading up to another with a purely logical necessity, with interruptions due only to difficulties not yet solved, the history of cultural sciences shows such an 'immanent' progress only for limited stretches. At other times, problems not fore-shadowed by anything immanent to the preceding thought processes emerge abruptly, and other problems are suddenly dropped; these latter, however, do not disappear once and for all but reappear later in modified form. We can probe the secret of this agitated wavelike rhythm of the successive intellectual currents, and discover a meaningful pattern in it, only by trying to understand the evolution of thought as a genetic life process, thus breaking up the pure intellectual immanence of the history of thought. Here, if anywhere, we see the saying confirmed that nothing can become a problem intellectually if it has not become a problem of practical life beforehand. If we broaden our field of vision accordingly, then the problems implied by the category of 'constellation' require us not only to achieve a synoptical view of all the theoretical problems given at a certain moment, but also to take the practical life problems of the same time into account. And then, our question will assume the following form: what intellectual and vital factors made the appearance of a given problem in the cultural sciences possible, and to what extent do they guarantee the solubility of the problem?

Putting our question in this form, we may assert that the vital and the practical as well as the theoretical and intellectual currents of our time seem to point toward a temporary fading out of epistemological problems, and toward the emergence of the *sociology of knowledge* as the focal discipline—and also that the constellation is exceptionally favourable to the solubility precisely of the problems of this discipline.

We shall at first try to characterize the constellation which gave rise to the problems of the sociology of knowledge, and to describe the fundamental currents which favour this approach. It is our belief that it is no wasted effort to ask preliminary questions of this kind before tackling any problem of the history of thought. We have to ask such preliminary questions, because our horizon has become broader and because our greater reflectiveness not only enables but also obliges us to avoid asking questions just as they occur to us, in a naïve and unconscious fashion, but rather to pay conscious attention to the intellectual background of our problems, to the constellations which are responsible for their emergence. Such investigations also seem to have become necessary, owing to the particular way in which work is organized in the cultural sciences, namely the absence of any institutionally prescribed division of labour, as a result of which everyone seeks out his problems himself. In view of this, a synoptical orientation as to the status of all problems in this field becomes more and more imperative. What we need, however, is not merely a catalogue of the existing currents and trends, but a maximally radical *structural analysis of the problems which may be raised in a given epoch*, an analysis which not only informs outsiders about what is going on in research, but points out the *ultimate choices* faced by the cultural scientist in the course of his work, the tensions in which he lives and which influence his thinking consciously or unconsciously. Such an analysis of the work going on in the cultural sciences will give us the most fundamental characterization of the intellectual situation prevailing in our time.

If, then, we ask ourselves about *the ultimate, fundamental factors entering into the constellation which necessarily gave rise to the problem of a sociology of thought* in our time, the following four things appear worthy of mention:

(1) The first and most important factor which makes it possible to ask sociological questions about thinking is what may be called the *self-transcendence and self-relativization* of thought. Self-transcendence and self-relativization[1] of thought consist in the fact that individual thinkers, and still more the dominant outlook of a given epoch, far from according primacy to thought, conceive of thought as something subordinate to other more comprehensive factors—whether as their emanation, their expression, their concomitant, or, in general, as something conditioned by something else. There are considerable obstacles in the way of such a self-relativization—thus above all the paradox that a thinker who sets out to relativize thought, that is, to subordinate it to supra-theoretical factors, himself implicitly posits the autonomous validity of the sphere of thought while he thinks and works out his philosophical system; he thus risks disavowing himself, since a relativization of all thought would equally invalidate his own assertions as well. Thus, this position involves the danger of a theoretical *circulus vitiosus*. The attempt to relativize any other sphere, such as art, religion, etc., encounters no such obstacle; anyone who is convinced that art, religion, etc., depend on a more comprehensive factor, such as 'social life', may say so without having to fear being entangled in logical self-contradiction. In this latter case no contradiction can arise, because in asserting the dependence relationship in question, one does not have to posit the sphere of art and religion as something valid by virtue of that assertion; but in so far as thought is concerned, it is clear that one cannot relativize it without at the same time being a thinking

---

[1] What we mean by 'self-relativization' is by no means epistemological 'relativism' but merely the opposite of 'autonomy'. One may very well assert that thought is 'relative to being', 'dependent on being', 'non-autonomous', 'part of a whole reaching beyond it', without professing any 'relativism' concerning the truth value of its findings. At this point, it is, so to speak, still open whether the 'existential relativization' of thought is to be combined with epistemological relativism or not. In any case, however, we would like to go on record, at this point, that we cannot share the at present widespread fear of relativism. 'Relativism' has become a catchword which, it is believed, will instantly annihilate any adversary against whom it is used. But as to us, we definitely prefer a 'relativism' which accentuates the difficulty of its task by calling attention to all those moments which tend to make the propositions actually discoverable at any given time, partial and situationally conditioned —we prefer such a 'relativism' to an 'absolutism' which loudly proclaims, as a matter of principle, the absoluteness of its own position or of 'truth in itself', but is in fact no less partial than any of its adversaries—and, still worse, is utterly incapable of tackling with its epistemological apparatus the problems of the temporal and situational determination of any concrete process of thought, completely overlooking the way in which this situational conditioning enters into the structure and the evolution of knowledge.

subject, i.e. without positing the sphere of thought as something valid.

We may escape this vicious circle by conceiving thought as a mere partial phenomenon belonging to a more comprehensive factor within the totality of the world process, and particularly by devaluing, as it were, the sphere of theoretical communication in which this self-contradiction arises. To mention only one type of solution: if one maintains that the sphere of thought (that of concepts, judgments and inferences) is merely one of *expression* rather than of the ultimate cognitive *constitution of objects*, the contradiction, otherwise insurmountable, becomes devalued. To be sure, this way of doing away with the theoretical contradiction is not immanent to theory, and if one—to put it in a paradoxical way—thinks only 'within thought', he will never be able to carry out this mental operation. We have to do here with an act of breaking through the immanence of thought—with an attempt to comprehend thought as a partial phenomenon within the broader field of existence, and to determine it, as it were, starting from existential data. The 'existential thinker', however, asserts precisely that his ultimate position lies outside the sphere of thought—that for him, thought neither constitutes objects nor grasps ultimately real matters of fact but merely expresses extra-theoretically constituted and warranted beliefs. Once thought is depreciated in this fashion, inner contradictions (cf. Hegel) and paradoxes can no longer be considered as symptoms of defective thinking—on the contrary, such symptoms may be valued as manifestations of some extra-theoretical phenomenon being truly grasped in existence. Since ultimate philosophical principles are supra-theoretically grounded, the historical progress from one philosophical system to another is not limited to a kind of theoretical refutation. One never gives up such an ultimate principle because it is proved to involve contradictions; philosophical systems change if the vital system in which one lives undergoes a shift. It is, however, important to pay attention to these ultimate philosophical principles, because they are involved in one form or another in every investigation in the cultural sciences.

If we look at 'relativization of theoretical thought' from a historical and sociological viewpoint, we see that it can be carried out in a great variety of ways, depending on what the entity is on which thought is said to depend; this role may be played by mystical consciousness, by religious or any other *gnosticism*, or by an empirically investigated sphere, subsequently hypostatized as ultimate reality, such as the biological or social sphere. In all these cases, the factor on which thought is said to depend is contrasted with it as 'Being', and the contrast between 'Thought' and 'Being' is worked out philosophically following the model of Greek philosophy. In most such systems 'Being' appears as a whole, in contrast to 'Thought' as a mere part; and it is often assumed that in order to grasp Being one needs a supra-rational organ (i.e. intuition) or a higher form of cognition (i.e. dialectical as against reflective knowledge).

Now this relativization of thought is not an exclusively modern phenomenon. Mystical and religious consciousness has always tended to relativize thought in relation to ecstasy or revealed knowledge, and the doctrine of the primacy of will represents just one more way of solving this problem of relativization.

If it were only a matter of self-relativization, sociology of knowledge could have emerged at any time; the characteristic thing is, however, precisely that one single factor is never a sufficient reason for the emergence of a problem: what is needed is a whole constellation of mental and practical tendencies. The new and distinctive feature which our epoch had to have in addition to self-relativization of thought in general to make the sociology of knowledge possible was that thought was relativized in a particular direction, that is, with regard to sociological reality.

(2) In our last remarks, we specified a further factor the analysis of which will help us complete the elucidation of the total constellation in which the sociology of knowledge emerges. After the self-liquidation of medieval religious consciousness (a type of consciousness which, as we have seen, contained elements transcending pure rationality) we see as the next comprehensive system the rationalism of the Enlightenment period. This system, which was the only one endowing Reason with real autonomy, was as such least likely to effect a relativization of thought—it pointed rather in the opposite direction, that is, toward an absolute self-hypostatization of Reason in contrast to all irrational forces.

At this point, however, a completely different factor emerged, for which we can account only in terms of real, social developments rather than in terms of the immanent development of ideas, that is, to use an expression of C. Brinkmann, the constitution of the *oppositional science* of sociology. Humanism—the first instance of lay groups engaging in scientific pursuits in the Occident—already represented a kind of oppositional science; but this type of science reached the systematic stage only in the period of the Enlightenment which was about to prepare the stage for the bourgeois revolution. The systematic as well as sociological core of this oppositional science was its hostility toward theology and metaphysics—it saw its main task in the *disintegration* of the monarchy, with its vestigially theocratic tradition, and of the clergy which was one of its supporters. In this struggle, we encounter for the first time a certain way of depreciating ideas which was to become an essential component of the new constellation. *What* ideas were combated is of secondary importance; what matters is that we see here for the first time a kind of attitude toward ideas which from that point on became the hallmark of all rising classes and merely found its first conscious, reflective formulation in Marxism. We mean the phenomenon that one may call the 'unmasking turn of mind'. This is a turn of mind which does not seek to refute, negate, or call in doubt certain ideas, but rather to *disintegrate* them, and that in such a way that the whole world outlook of a social stratum becomes disintegrated at the same time. We must pay attention, at this point, to the phenomenological distinction between 'denying the truth' of an idea, and 'determining the function' it exercises. In denying the truth of an idea, I still presuppose it as 'thesis' and thus put myself upon the same theoretical (and nothing but theoretical) basis as the one on which the idea is constituted. In casting doubt upon the 'idea', I still think within the same categorial pattern as the one in which it has its being. But when I do not even raise the question (or at least when I do not make this question the burden of my argument) whether what the idea asserts is true, but consider it merely in terms of the *extra-theoretical function* it serves, then, and only then, do I achieve an 'unmasking' which in fact represents no theoretical refutation but the destruction of the practical effectiveness of these ideas.

But of this *extra-theoretical destruction of the efficacy of theoretical propositions*, too, we may distinguish several types. Thus, we may again point to a certain phenomenological difference—that between, for example, the 'unmasking' of a lie as such, and the sociological 'unmasking' of an ideology.

If we call a certain utterance a 'lie', this also constitutes no theoretical refutation or denial of what the utterance asserts; what we say concerns rather a certain relation of the subject making the utterance to the proposition it expresses. The point is to invalidate the purport of the utterance by attacking the personal morality of the person who made it. In fact, however, the theoretical purport of an utterance is not invalidated by showing that the author of the utterance has 'lied'. It may very well be that a person makes a true statement and lies at the same time—what he says is objectively true but 'in his mouth', as the saying goes, the statement is a lie. Admittedly, usage is fluctuating in this respect; the term 'lie' is often used in the sense of a false statement consciously made. But even in this case, 'lie' as distinguished from 'error' is an ethical rather than a theoretical category. The term 'lie', it appears, refers to a certain relation between real existence on the one hand and certain mental objects on the other; it means that we consider statements of a subject from the point of view of his ethical personality. Yet, it cannot be said that the 'unmasking' of a lie is the same thing as the 'unmasking' of an ideology, even though both come under the genus of the functional analysis, directed toward the unmasking of a subject, of certain theoretical complexes from the point of view of their relation to existential reality.

The essential difference between the unmasking of a lie and that of an ideology consists in the fact that the former aims at the moral personality of a subject and seeks to destroy him morally by unmasking him as a liar, whereas the unmasking of an ideology in its pure form attacks, as it were, merely an impersonal socio-intellectual force. In unmasking ideologies, we seek to bring to light an unconscious process, not in order to annihilate the moral existence of persons making certain statements, but in order to destroy the social efficacy of certain ideas by unmasking the function they serve. Unmasking of lies has always been practised; the unmasking of ideologies in the sense just defined, however, seems to be an exclusively modern phenomenon. In this case too, the fact that the social-psychic function of a proposition or 'idea' is unmasked does not mean that it is denied or subjected to theoretical doubt—one does not even raise the question of truth or falsehood. What happens is, rather, that the proposition is 'dissolved': we have to do here with the existential corroding of a theoretical proposition, with an attitude toward theoretical communications which neglects the problem of their truth or falsehood and seeks to transcend their immanent theoretical meaning in the direction of practical existence. The emergence of the 'unmasking' turn of mind (which we have to understand if we want to grasp the distinctive character of our time) is the second factor—calling for interpretation in sociological terms—which represents something radically new, due not so much to the direction as to the manner in which theoretical immanence is transcended. The practical struggle of social classes gave rise to a new type of attitude to ideas which, at first practised only with regard to a few selected ones, later became the prototype of a new way of transcending theoretical immanence in general.

(3) The emergence of the 'unmasking' turn of mind—the hidden history of which still calls for more exact investigation—does not, however, suffice to explain why we have today a constellation permitting the development of a sociology of thought. We still have to mention two further factors which contribute to

shaping the present-day variant of existentially relativizing thought.

First, relativization, as we have characterized it thus far (in terms of 'unmasking' and 'transcending'), referred merely to certain individual items of thinking—it was still partial in its intent. Secondly, we have not yet indicated the *terminus* of the transcending motion, the absolute in relation to which certain items are relativized. And yet, as we said, thought, the immanence of theoretical meaning, cannot be transcended unless we put something more comprehensive, a 'Being' in contrast with it—a Being of which the ideas are conceived to be the 'expression', 'function', or 'emanation'. But at this point, we still lack the point of reference, that ontological sphere of central importance in respect of which thought can be considered as relative or dependent. As we have said, such a centre can never be excogitated; it will always shift into that sphere of life in which the systematizing thinker as a practical subject lives most intensely. In earlier times, subjects who transcended thought 'lived' in revealed religion, in ecstasy, and so on; during the last, contemporary stage of the evolution of consciousness, however, the characteristic thing was that the sense of reality became more and more concentrated upon the historic and social sphere, and that in this sphere, the economic factor was felt to be the central one. Thus, theory in our time is not transcended in the direction of the religious or ecstatic experience; the rising classes in particular experience the historic and social field as the most immediately real one; and this is, accordingly, the sphere which is contrasted with the ideas as that of 'Being' or 'Reality', in relation to which the ideas are considered as something partial, functional, as a mere 'awareness' of something more comprehensive. This is a new type of ontological metaphysics, even though it received its sharpest formulation from anti-metaphysical positivism. That such a new metaphysics was created by positivism will, however, no longer surprise us if we remember that, after all, positivism, too, is a metaphysic, inasmuch as it lifts a certain complex out of the totality of the given and, like any other metaphysic, hypostatizes it as an ontological absolute. This hypostatized complex for positivism is that of the findings of empirical science. It is in line with the shift of the vital centre of experience into the socio-economical sphere that sociology was developed by the positivistic current. When in his later writings Saint-Simon analysed literary works, forms of government, etc., in terms of the socio-economic process, he specified that sphere which later came to play more and more decisively the role of the 'absolute' pole in the direction of which theoretical immanence was transcended. When sociology was constituted within the framework of positivist consciousness, the ontological 'terminus' of the motion transcending theoretical immanence was given.

(4) But we still lack one feature needed for the full characterization of the contemporary constellation. Before the present stage could be reached, 'unmasking' as a method had to surmount the partiality which at first kept its exercise within limits. Although the aim had been, from the very beginning, the disintegration of the total *Weltanschauung* of a ruling class, what was actually achieved was merely the disintegration of certain ideas, the 'functional' nature of which was shown in sociological terms; the ideas of God, of metaphysics, etc., were relativized in this fashion. This undertaking, however, could reach its final goal only when the interest-bound nature of ideas, the dependence of 'thought' on 'existence', was brought to light, not merely as regards certain selected ideas of the ruling class, but in such a way that the *entire* ideological 'super-structure' (as Marx would have it) appeared as dependent upon sociological reality. What was to be done was to demonstrate the existentially determined nature of an entire system of *Weltanschauung*, rather than of this or that individual idea. That one could not, in this connection, consider ideas and beliefs in isolation, but had to grasp them, instead, as mutually interdependent parts of a systematic totality, this was the lesson we learned from modern historicism. Questions of detail such as that concerning the exact contribution one or the other epoch or school made to the emergence of this total view of ideology—e.g. to what extent historicism is germinally present in 'Enlightenment', and how the romantic mind made a global view of historical wholes possible—need not be investigated here. We have to mention, however, that one most important representative of historical thought from whom Marx took over the concept of historical totality which enabled him to pose the problem of ideology referred to above—namely, Hegel. In his thinking, too, we encounter the *motif* of the self-relativization of theory, though in a peculiar modification. Thus, Hegel distinguishes 'reflective' from 'philosophical' thought; he depreciates the sphere in which the principle of contradiction is valid as compared to the true movement of the idea; he puts forward a doctrine of the 'ruse of the Idea' according to which the subjective beliefs of men are mere tools to help *real* developments along. In all these cases, if the one word 'ideology' were added, we should find the same fundamental conception as the one underlying Marxist theory. In both Hegel and Marx, we find mere 'subjective belief', as Hegel calls it, or 'ideology', as it is called in Marxian language, depreciated; this subjective sphere is deprived of its autonomy in favour of some basic reality. It is a relatively insignificant

difference that for Hegel, who stands in the idealist tradition, this basic reality is mental, whereas Marx, who shares the positivist approach towards reality, defines this basic reality as the social and economic one. Just because this structural similarity exists, the category of 'totality' could play a crucial role in both authors: the beliefs of existent persons do not depend on those persons' social existence in piecemeal fashion, but it is the totality of their mental world, the whole superstructure, which is a function of their social existence.

It is only because of this aspiration toward 'totality' that the attempt to transcend theory with the help of the technique of 'unmasking' assumes a specific new form, clearly distinguished from all earlier versions. As a result of this, we see a new type of the relativization, of the invalidation of ideas. At this point, we may relativize ideas, not by denying them one by one, not by calling them into doubt, not by showing that they are reflections of this or that interest, but by demonstrating that they are part of a system, or, more radically, of a totality of *Weltanschauung*, which as a whole is bound to, and determined by, one stage of the developing social reality. From this point on, worlds confront worlds—it is no longer individual propositions pitted against individual propositions.

As we have seen, the problem of a sociology of knowledge arose as a result of the interplay of four factors: (1) the self-relativization of thought and knowledge, (2) the appearance of a new form of relativization introduced by the 'unmasking' turn of mind, (3) the emergence of a new system of reference, that of the social sphere, in respect of which thought could be conceived to be relative, and (4) the aspiration to make this relativization total, relating not one thought or idea, but a whole system of ideas, to an underlying social reality.

When this stage is reached, the original emphasis accompanying the emergence of these new patterns of thought gets shifted, and many superficial forms of expression originally associated with the new approach fade away of their own accord. Thus, the emphasis on 'unmasking' in determining the social function of ideas can more and more be eliminated. As our theory becomes broader in scope, we are getting less and less interested in depreciating individual ideas by branding them as falsifications, deceptions, mystifications, and 'lies' of a class; being increasingly aware of the fact that *all* thinking of a social group is determined by its existence, we find less and less room for the exercise of 'unmasking', and the latter undergoes a process of sublimation which turns it into a mere operation of determining the functional role of any thought whatever. 'Unmasking' consists no longer in such

things as uncovering 'priestly fraud' and the like—one even goes
so far as to rule out conscious deception in most cases ; the goal
of the critical operation is reached when one has specified that
the 'locus' of the idea which is to be combated belongs to an
'obsolete' theoretical system, and, further, to an existential whole
which evolution has left behind.

The second 'shift' which occurs at this stage consists in a natural
broadening of the aspiration toward totality. Once we have
familiarized ourselves with the conception that the ideologies of
our opponents are, after all, just the function of their position
in the world, we cannot refrain from concluding that our own
ideas, too, are functions of a social position. And even if we refused
to admit this, the opponent would compel us to do so—for he
eventually will also make use of the method of ideological analysis,
and apply it to the original user. And this is precisely the main
characteristic of the present situation: the concept of 'ideology'
was first evolved by 'oppositional science', but it did not remain
the privilege of the rising classes. Their opponents, too, employ
this technique of thought—first of all, the bourgeoisie which has
achieved success and is stabilizing its position. Today, it is no
longer a privilege of Socialist thinkers to observe the social
determination of ideas; this has become an integral part of our
contemporary consciousness as a whole, a new type of historical
interpretation which has to be added to the earlier ones.[1] In this
connection, the salient point demanding attention is the fact that
new methods and techniques of thought emerging in the cultural
sciences have their origin in social reality, but later go through
an evolution of their own, eventually losing contact with their
social place of origin. At this stage, we have to observe how the
content and function of the new techniques change when they
lose their original social meaning. We have already seen two
examples of this: first, the modification of the 'unmasking'
attitude, i.e. the fact that certain given theoretical complexes are
surmounted by indirection, by reference to a synoptical view of
the historical process, rather than by the 'unmasking' of isolated
items; and, secondly, the fact that the choice of the social sphere
as a system of reference was first effected by an 'oppositional
science' and then gradually became more or less a common
possession of all camps.

We may mention a third aspect of the natural expansion and
evolution of ideas, i.e. the fact that the fundamental trend
toward self-relativization (a distinctive characteristic of the
modern mind) cannot stop at any given moment. Granted that

[1] Cf. my essay on 'Ideological and Sociological Interpretation', *Internationales
Jahrbuch für Soziologie*, vol. I.

ideas, theoretical complexes are relative to Being—it is still possible to conceive of this Being, either as an essentially unchanging, static, or as a dynamic one. Now it is characteristic of modern historical thought that it considers its last point of reference—in this case, Being—simultaneously also as something dynamic and 'becoming'. Not only 'ideas', but also the 'Being' on which they are seen to depend, must be recognized as something dynamic— the more so as, for those who have insight, their own standpoint, too, is undergoing constant change. This poses the task of satisfying the urge toward totality in a more radical fashion. It is not enough to see that the 'ideas' of an antagonistic class are dictated by its 'existence', it is not enough to recognize that our own 'ideas' are dictated by our own existence; what we have to grasp is that both our 'ideas' and our 'existence' are components of a comprehensive evolutionary process in which we are engaged. This overall process, then, is posited as our ultimate 'absolute' (albeit a changing and evolving one); conservative as well as progressive ideas (to use these over-simplified labels) appear as derivates of this process.[1] In our opinion, the present problem constellation necessarily implies this radical following through of these ideas to their last consequences; and the difficulties involved in this set of theses lead to the emergence of the problems of the sociology of knowledge.

We have to go back to the point where the problems arising from social reality seek a systematic solution, and to review the possible solutions available at the various stages of the evolution of consciousness.

II. THEORETICAL POSITIONS

Thus far, we have outlined the constellation of those factors which

[1] The expressions 'progressive' and 'conservative' will be used later on to characterize certain thinkers roughly as a first approximation. They are by no means meant as an exhaustive characterization of the entire political personality of the thinkers in question. In this paper, we are merely groping toward 'affinities' and 'correlations' between certain thought structures on the one hand, and certain reality-demands on the other. But it is clear to the historically minded that there can be no unchanging correspondence between a certain type of thought and a political current, e.g. between 'historic' thinking and 'conservatism'. Most types of thought admit of a multiple interpretation, either in a progressive or in a conservative sense. This, however, cannot prevent us from investigating in concrete detail how in the real historical situation certain reality-demands allied themselves with a certain style of thought, and what changes of function occurred in this connection. As these investigations are further refined, the categories of 'conservatism' and 'progressivism' must be further differentiated and treated as dynamic entities. At present, however, we are concerned, as stated above, only with a first rough approximation of the 'affinities' existing between reality-demands and thought structures.

had to be given together so that the problem of a sociology of knowledge could emerge at all. Even in this preliminary investigation, our approach has been primarily a sociological one—we showed how an oppositional current of thought led to questions concerning the sociological determination of ways of thinking. Having gone through two stages—the first or preparatory one being the thinking of the rising bourgeoisie, the second that of the next oppositional class, the proletariat—these ideas have by now acquired a scope and urgency such that no one who wants to think in categories of a genuinely global import can afford to ignore them as components of present-day thought.

If we look at history as a stream divided into several branches, and if we conceive of the history of thought as likewise split into several currents by some inescapable historical necessity (and any closer study of history can but confirm such a view), then we can easily be led to assume the extreme position that the history of ideas consists of completely isolated sequences of thoughts without the slightest intercommunication, so that, for example, conservative and progressive thinking would each have its self-contained independent tradition of world interpretation. Those who think in this fashion are likely to adopt either an extreme Right or extreme Left solution to the problem of interpreting history; taking into account nothing but the historical route traversed by their own group, and the demands raised by it, they are totally unable to do justice to the function and significance of the ways of thinking of other groups. Now it cannot be doubted that sociological and historical theories, methods, and attitudes always come into being in close correlation with the specific social position and the intellectual interests of a social class or group. Nevertheless, it must be admitted that after one class has discovered some sociological or historical fact (which lay in its line of vision by virtue of its specific position), all other groups, no matter what *their* interests are, can equally take such fact into account—nay, *must* somehow incorporate such fact into their system of world interpretation.

Once this is admitted, we must conclude that all groups, though committed to their separate traditions, nevertheless seek to develop a comprehensive picture of the world, not ignoring any of the facts brought to light by any of them. Hence, the question facing a concrete sociology of knowledge is the following one: what categories, what systematic conceptions are used by the different groups at a given stage in accounting for one and the same fact uncovered in the course of practical operations? And what are the tensions which arise in the attempt to fit these new facts into those categories and systematic conceptions? We can put this more simply if we disregard the role of the *a priori* systematic presuppositions in the thought process; what remains then is the fact that different intellectual currents do not proceed in splendid isolation but mutually affect and enrich one another, and yet do not merge into one common system but try to account for the totality of the discovered facts, each starting from different general axioms.

This view of the historical-sociological structure of the intellectual process leads us to the conclusion that at each moment there are several different systematic philosophical 'standpoints' from which one may undertake to account for a newly emerging fact, for a new facet of cognitive reality.

In fact, none of us stands in a supra-temporal *vacuum* of disembodied truths; we all confront 'reality' with ready-made questions and suggested systematizations, and the attainment of new knowledge consists in incorporating new facts into the old framework of definitions and categories, and ascertaining their place therein. We do not want to deny that 'class' or 'idea' are objective realities; still, they lack the character of 'stubborn fact' ascribed to things (also somewhat wrongly, as it seems) by virtue of which they would be given to us unquestionably exactly the way they objectively 'are'. That the concepts we mentioned ('class', 'idea') are objectively real is proved by the fact that they stubbornly withstand attempts to doubt them and irresistibly impose a *Gestalt*-like pattern upon the spectator. But the question *what* they are will be answered differently, depending on the systematic standpoint from which they are examined. This is the reason why it is so tempting to observe how the discovery of certain facts (such as 'class', 'ideology') is connected with certain systematic and social commitments; how, for instance, the concept of 'class' essentially belongs to oppositional thinking, while certain 'organic' concepts such as 'tradition' or 'protocol' have an affinity to conservative thinking. What this suggests is that certain commitments, as it were, render us sensitive to certain realities of the past, present, or future. Nevertheless, once facts have become visible, they are also acknowledged by the other currents in the specific perspective in which they appear to them. And the most tempting question is perhaps that of the way in which the systematic preconceptions of these other groups *modify* in their thinking the reality discovered by somebody else.

All this implies, of course, that even specialized scientific discoveries are bound up with certain philosophical, systematic presuppositions, and can be detached from the latter only as regards some of their partial aspects. When new 'data' are being interpreted, the recognition of new 'facts' depends on the system-making trends in a philosophical sense which just happen to prevail. As we have seen above, it cannot be stated once and for all what philosophical positions conservative and progressive thinking respectively make use of—these correlations also are dynamic in nature. It has to be investigated historically and sociologically how long and to what extent positivism is a characteristically 'bourgeois' way of thinking; what 'nuance' of positivism becomes a basis for proletarian thought; in what respects the positivism of a successfully consolidated bourgeoisie differs from revolutionary positivism and materialism; how much of 'dynamic' thought will be appropriated by revolutionary and conservative groups respectively, and so on.

We shall not try to trace the historical social *genesis* of the various standpoints from which reality is being interpreted today. Our plan is, rather, to choose one *cross-section* of contemporary standpoints arbitrarily and to find out what the different fundamental principles are on the basis of which one may try to analyse a newly emerging problem today. For we seem to have reached the stage where the problem of a sociology of knowledge, which up to now belonged to the context of progressive thought, is recognized as a 'stubborn reality' and is being tackled as such from all *other* standpoints as well. Having outlined the constellation which made the emergence of the problem possible, we now must face the further question: what are the pre-existent systematic positions in the thinking of various groups which this problem encounters at the moment when it achieves that status of 'stubborn reality' which requires every group to pay attention to it? What contemporary philosophies, what 'standpoints' permit systematic work on this problem, and what is the specific characteristic of these standpoints?

It seems that the most important philosophic-systematic standpoints from which one may undertake to work out a sociology of knowledge today include the following: (*a*) positivism, (*b*) formal apriorism, (*c*) material apriorism (i.e. the modern phenomenological school), (*d*) historicism.

Properly speaking, positivism alone has given so far an extensively developed sociology of knowledge, and this in two variants—one being the so-called materialist theory of history,[1] which belongs to the proletarian 'nuance' of positivism, and the other the 'bourgeois positivist' theory developed by Durkheim, Lévy-Bruhl, Jerusalem, etc. Formal apriorism contributed merely an initial approach to the problem of a sociology of knowledge, without engaging in detailed historical investigations. One may

---

[1] Other variants of Marxist historical theory will be discussed later.

think in this connection of the various 'nuances' of neo-Kantianism which obtained recognition partly among bourgeois, partly
among socialist democrats.

The most detailed discussion shall be reserved for the modern
phenomenological school, material apriorism, so that we shall
omit any further characterization of it at this point. A separate
discussion will also be devoted to the philosophical standpoint of
historicism which is eminently relevant to the problem of sociology
of knowledge. Among the representatives of this standpoint we
may mention Troeltsch and the orthodox left Marxist G. Lukács.

It is the debate between the last-named two schools (phenomenology and historicism) which we consider as decisive. Before
taking up these two positions, however, we shall make a few
remarks about the two schools mentioned first. Our own conception will be presented as the concluding section of this paper.

(a) *Positivism*, which is merely a philosophy of no-philosophy,
treats the problem of the sociology of knowledge as one belonging
to a specialized scientific discipline. It is, however, an essentially
deluded school, both because it hypostatizes one particular
concept of empiricism, and because it holds that human knowledge can be complete without metaphysics and ontology.
Moreover, these two principles are mutually contradictory: a
doctrine which hypostatizes certain paradigmatic methods, and
the reality spheres corresponding to them, as 'absolutely' valid,
thereby becomes a metaphysic itself—albeit a particularly limited
one. Applied in practice, the positivistic doctrine has the consequence that in each particular field of research, the scientist takes
either the 'material' or the 'psychic' substratum to be 'ultimate'
reality, to which all other phenomena (e.g. intellectual, artistic,
and other cultural ones) can be traced back. One variety of
positivism—that which takes the economic sphere to embody
ultimate reality—is particularly important for the sociology of
knowledge. The adherents of this theory—especially those·
representing 'vulgar Marxism'—argue, first, that nothing exists
except matter, and, second, that the particular stubborn-factness
of matter is exhibited, in the social sphere, by economic relationships; it is in terms of these, then, that one should account for
cultural realities.

As a response to the decisive experiences of our time, all variants
of positivism were basically genuine: from our point of view, they
represent a straightforward reflection of the fact that the centre
of our experience has shifted from the spiritual and religious
sphere to the social-economic one. It was capitalism, with the
intensification of class struggles it brought about, that was
responsible for this shift of the experiential centre to these fields,

as well as for the fact that technological and scientific thought became the only recognized prototype of all thinking. It is by no means surprising that a philosophy which sought to provide a world interpretation with this type of experience and thought as its basic frame of reference based its epistemology exclusively on natural science, and in its ontology attributed reality only to those spheres which it experienced as real—withholding full theoretical recognition from those spheres which in its practical experience appeared only at the periphery. This defect, this one-sidedness, could easily be corrected; all that would be needed would be a broadening of the horizon which would permit a transformation of mere anti-metaphysicism into the positive insight that all human thinking is so structured that it must assume absolute Being somewhere—and hence must posit one or the other sphere of experience as absolute. More grave, however, is another defect of positivism, namely, that its unconscious phenomenological presuppositions are false, so that its methods are entirely inadequate especially in treating intellectual-spiritual-artistic reality.

The positivist descriptions of reality are phenomenologically false, because its adherents—as naturalists and psychologists —are blind to the fact that intended 'meaning' is something specific, *sui generis*, incapable of being dissolved into psychic acts. They are blind to the fact that perception and knowledge of meaningful objects as such involves interpretation and understanding; that the problems arising in this connection cannot be solved by scientific monism; and, finally, that their naturalism prevents them from seeing the relationship between reality and meaning in a correct way.

Notwithstanding these strictures, we must recognize that it was positivism that first discovered and articulated the problem of a sociology of knowledge. And even though we must consider the methods and premises of positivism as no longer sufficient, because too narrow, we have to admit that this doctrine contains two points which reveal genuine experience and therefore still remain valid even for us. One is that positivism first gave a philosophical formulation of the fact that for contemporary man the centre of experience has shifted to the economic-social sphere —this is the 'this-wordly' orientation of positivism ; the other is its respect for empirical reality which will make metaphysics in the form of pure speculation impossible for all time. We assert, then, that *substantively* positivism has performed the essential turn toward a way of thinking adequate to the contemporary situation; systematically and methodologically, however, it did not rise above a relatively primitive level, since, for example it did not recognize the fact that its 'this-wordly' orientation, too, involved a hypostatization, a metaphysic.

(b) The philosophy of formal validity represents a second standpoint from which one could undertake to build up a sociology of knowledge. All that this school has achieved, however, is merely a few beginnings of a general theory of a sociology of culture; and it is small wonder, in our opinion, that this type of philosophy inspired no concrete sociological research. For the philosophy of validity depreciates Being, as against Thought, to an extent equivalent to a declaration of complete disinterestedness in Being. This school mainly seeks to comprehend thinking in terms of thinking, that is, in an immanent fashion—as well as to give a theoretical justification of this 'immanentist' position. From this immanent point of view, to be sure, the phenomenological difference between 'being' and 'meaning', to which the positivist attitude is necessarily blind, becomes easily discernible, and one will be able to do justice to the essential difference between an act of experience and the meaning intended by it. However, if one does not go beyond this immanent point of view (as is the case with the philosophy of validity), this dualism will be hypostatized as something absolute, and the second term of the relation—'meaning'—will inevitably receive an exaggerated metaphysical emphasis. The philosophy of validity is chiefly interested in rescuing 'validity' from the toils of historical and sociological genesis, in preserving it in supra-temporal sublimity. But this causes a crack in the system: the sphere of theoretical 'validity', as well as those of the other values, are hypostatized as supra-temporal absolutes, while the material substratum in which they are actualized is abandoned to the anarchic flux of Being.

This philosophy remained self-consistent as long as it had enough courage to assert—as the philosophy of Enlightenment did—its unwavering faith in Reason, and, following the example of 'natural law' theories, to declare one specific position, with the corresponding derivation of 'validity', as the exclusively 'correct' one. (Obviously, in doing this, one necessarily overlooks the fact that he is conferring 'eternal' validity upon one transitory stage of the history of thought.) But the inner consistency of this type of philosophy gets lost as soon as, under the impression of the historical variability of thought, all *material* propositions are given up as purely relative and existentially determined, but autonomy and supra-temporality is claimed for the *formal* elements of thought, such as the categories or—in newer variants of this philosophy—formal values. Sociologically, the former stage—the assertion of the exclusive truth of one material position—corresponds to the self-assurance of the rising bourgeois order which had unbroken faith in certain tenets. When, however, the bourgeoisie was later forced to adopt a defensive position, the bourgeois social order became a mere 'formal democracy', i.e. it contented itself with asserting the principle of complete freedom of opinion and refused to make a choice among the various opinions. Such an attitude corresponds to the philosophical presupposition that there can be only *one* truth, and that that truth can be expressed in only *one* form; however, the task of finding it must be left to free discussion. (In so far as this transition process within bourgeois democracy itself is concerned, it has already been described by historical analysis.)

Philosophically, the defect of this position consists in its inability to account in organic fashion for the *unity* of being and meaning—a problem which inevitably arises within any system. Moreover, to adopt this position means to render philosophically a-problematic, and to keep out of the reach of historic-sociological research, precisely the most essential problems of a sociology of knowledge, such as the problem of the transmutation of categories and of the shifts in the hierarchy of value spheres, as well as the problem whether the present assumption of isolated, self-contained 'value spheres' does not merely amount to a hypostatization of a transitory, specifically modern state of things. The only way in which adherents of this philosophical position could tackle problems of the sociology of culture, and particularly of thought, consists in examining the material substratum in which the formal value spheres are actualized.

This approach, however, could not become fruitful. For if the cleavage between 'form' and 'matter' is made as sharp and absolute as this, matter is, so to speak, left to mere chance. This is also why this school could produce no material philosophy of history. Furthermore, if 'form' is so sharply separated from material actualization, all cultural products of past epochs must inevitably be viewed in terms of a present-day 'form of validity'. Since it is only 'matter' that changes, there is only one 'art', 'religion', etc., and it is essentially always the same as today. This school overlooks the fact that—to use its terminology—the 'form of validity', actualized at a given time, is influenced by the changing material substratum, so that a transformation in the material sphere induces a transformation in the sphere of formal 'validity'. 'Art' was not always 'art' in the sense defined by the school of *l'art pour l'art*, as one is tempted to assume; and, similarly, depending on the existential context in which it emerges, a thought does not always represent 'thinking' and 'cognition' in the same sense that mathematical and scientific thinking does, as the philosophy of validity would have it—unconsciously taking the 'form of validity' of scientific thought to be that of all thought as such.

III. SOCIOLOGY OF KNOWLEDGE FROM THE STAND-POINT OF MODERN PHENOMENOLOGY
(MAX SCHELER)

After this brief survey of the contributions of positivism and of the philosophy of formal validity (neo-Kantianism) to the problem of the sociology of knowledge, we now turn to a confrontation of two other schools—modern phenomenology and historicism—which will for the first time permit us really to come to grips with the decisive problems involved in providing a solid foundation for a sociology of knowledge and cognition.

In our comparison of the two schools, we ourselves will adopt the standpoint of historicism in the form in which we think it is a valid doctrine,[1] and analyse the phenomenological approach from this point of view. Just as there are several different variants of historicism, it is possible to draw many different conclusions concerning the problem of a sociology of knowledge by starting from phenomenological premises; in our discussion, however, we shall not deal with phenomenological attitudes toward this problem that are possible in the abstract, but with the phenomenological outline of a sociology of knowledge recently published by Max Scheler.[2]

From the point of view we have adopted thus far, Scheler's study is particularly interesting as a striking illustration of our thesis that problems originally developed by a social opposition are taken over by conservative thinkers—and it also affords an opportunity to observe the structural transformation a problem undergoes when it is incorporated into the systematic framework of a theory based upon a different tradition. Here we have a concrete example of the final stage reached in the career of ideas first developed in a given social environment—a stage where, recognized as 'stubborn facts', they are taken up by the adverse movement and are transformed by it.

We may characterize Scheler's standpoint in a short formula by saying that he combines various *motifs* of the modern phenomenological school with elements of the Catholic tradition. We cannot say without qualification that phenomenology is a Catholic philosophy (although Catholic thinkers like Bernhard Bolzano and Franz Brentano are among its precursors); nevertheless, in many

[1] Cf. our essay on *Historicism* (above, pp. 84 ff).
[2] Cf. Max Scheler, *Probleme einer Soziologie des Wissens*, Munich and Leipzig, 1924.

essential points it lends itself very well to bolstering up Catholic concepts of 'timelessness', 'eternity', with new arguments. By drawing an extremely sharp line between 'factual' and 'essential' knowledge, phenomenology offers concrete evidence justifying the Catholic dualism of the eternal and temporal—and prepares the terrain for the construction of a non-formal, intuitionist metaphysics.

Phenomenology holds that it is possible to grasp supra-temporally valid truths in 'essential intuition' (*Wesensschau*). In actual fact, however, we observe considerable divergencies among the intuitions achieved by different members of the school. These divergencies can be explained by the fact that intuitions of essence are always dependent on the historical background of the subject. Most impressive among phenomenological analyses are those based upon traditional Catholic values—our civilization, after all, is very largely a product of this tradition. It must be stressed, in so far as Scheler is concerned, that he has already dissociated himself from a number of Catholic tenets. This, however, is less important in the present context than the fact that he is still profoundly attached to the formal type of thinking exhibited by Catholicism.

The main point about Scheler and his new essay is that he has a far closer affinity to present-day reality, and takes the obligation to count with new cultural developments far more seriously, than the majority of those who interpret the world in terms of the Catholic tradition. As a philosopher of a restless and sensitive turn of mind, impatient of limitations and rigid formalism, he cannot rest satisfied with a line drawn once and for all between eternity and temporality; he feels impelled to account for the new cultural factors emerging in the world. Affinity to the present, embedded in conservative modes of thought and experience, produces extravagant tensions in the structure of his arguments, so that the reader is in constant fear lest the entire edifice blow up before his eyes, the building stones flying apart in all directions. Since we are stressing precisely the complex problems inherent in the interaction of various standpoints, we are mainly interested in the way in which a modern representative of an earlier intel-lectual and emotional phase comes to grips with the new factors of cultural reality—a configuration of real symbolic significance. For the essential richness of the historic-social world process stems largely from the possibility of such 'anachronisms' as this—attempts to interpret present-day world factors on the basis of premises which belong to a past stage of thought. There is, however, a particular strain in Scheler's treatment of the problem, because he not only seeks to incorporate new factors into an old framework but even tries to present the position of 'historicism' and 'sociologism' in terms of a philosophy of timelessness.

We shall deliberately limit our discussion to this structural side of Scheler's theory, and select from the bewildering wealth of his insights only those points which are relevant to our problem of the various intellectual 'standpoints'. We are not interested in detecting errors or inaccuracies, but only in tracing the line of historical determination which made this type of thought fatefully what it is.

The main characteristic of Scheler's essay is—as stated above—the great width encompassed by his argument: he tries to analyse the sociological from the point of view of timelessness, the dynamic from that of a static system. We encounter in his theory all the points enumerated in our description of the 'constellation' underlying the emergence of a sociology of knowledge: (a) thinking conceived as relative to being, (b) social reality as the system of reference in respect of which thought is considered to be relative, and (c) a comprehensive view of historical totality. In addition to this, we can also observe in Scheler the 'shift' from the original 'unmasking' tendency to an impartial sociology; this is not surprising, since this change is even more in line with a conservative attitude than with an oppositional one. The question we want to examine is to what extent a static systematizing approach can do justice to the dynamic and sociological—i.e. whether a 'timeless' philosophy can treat adequately those problems which arise from the present intellectual situation.

Scheler, according to whom the sociology of knowledge has up to now been treated only from a positivistic point of view, proposes to approach this problem from another point of view 'which rejects the epistemological doctrines of positivism and the conclusions drawn therefrom, and sees in metaphysical knowledge both an "eternal" postulate of Reason and a practical possibility' (Preface, p. vi). For him, the sociology of knowledge is part of cultural sociology which in turn is part of sociology—the latter being divided into 'real' and 'cultural' sociology. The former examines 'real' factors of the historical process, especially 'drives' such as the sex, hunger, and power drive, while the latter deals with the 'cultural' factors. Sociology as a whole, however, has the task of 'ascertaining the types and functional laws of the inter-action' of these factors, and especially of establishing a 'law of succession' of such types of interaction. Thus, we have here, as in all sociologies of culture, a distinction of the 'substructure' and 'superstructure', but with the specific difference (this is the 'shift' characterizing Scheler's position) that (a) the 'substructure' consists of psychological factors (drives) rather than socio-economic ones, and (b) that there is a rather sharp line drawn between the two spheres, in contrast to the neo-Hegelian variant of Marxism. According to this latter view, the relation of 'substructure' to 'superstructure' is that of whole and part; both form an inseparable unity, since a certain 'ideal' configuration can emerge only in conjunction with a certain 'real' configuration and *vice versa*: a certain 'real configuration' also is possible only when the 'ideal' factors show such and such a configuration. Scheler, however, is unable to construct a historical theory of this kind, since he bases his 'cultural sociology' upon a theory of the drives and of the mind of *man* in general. This theory seeks to ascertain timeless characteristics of man, and to explain any concrete historical situation as a complex of such characteristics. And it also fails to establish a closer affinity with historicism when it examines in a 'generalizing' fashion the interaction of the 'real' and 'cultural' factors—taking it to exhibit a general law of succession, rather than a sequence of concrete, unique temporal phases. Although Scheler takes great pains to formulate a 'law' of the possible dynamic genesis of things embedded in an order of 'temporal efficacy' (p. 8), it is clear that such 'laws' can result only from the application of the generalizing categories of natural science. This sociology is merely consistent when it tries—after the fashion of natural science—to establish rules, types, and laws of the social process.

At this point, we should like to call attention to the fundamental difference between types of sociology which are possible today. The one continues the tradition of natural science with its objective of establishing general laws (Western sociology is of this type); the other harks back to the tradition of the philosophy of history (Troeltsch, Max Weber). To the former type, every historical individual is merely a complex of general, changelessly recurring properties, and the 'rest' which is not reducible to these properties is disregarded. The latter type, on the other hand, proceeds in the opposite direction. It considers historical individualities—comprising not only personalities but any historical constellation in its uniqueness—as the proper object of investigation. The individual, according to this conception, cannot be determined by a combination of abstractively distilled, unchanging characteristics; on the contrary, the historian must and can penetrate the psychic and mental core of a unique individual directly, without mediation by general properties, and then proceed to determine all characteristics and partial factors individually. This is how we proceed in grasping the physiognomy of a human face; we do not combine general characteristics (eyes, mouth, etc.), but the all-important thing is to seize the unique centre of expression and characterize the eyes, mouth, and other features in the light of this central insight. The school in question holds that this method, spontaneously employed in everyday life, has its application in science also and has in fact been unconsciously used by scientists; it is high time, then, to fix the methodological character of this type of knowledge. For it is not the case that the 'centre of expression', the particular physiognomy of a situation, the unique evolutionary line exhibited by a sequence of events can be grasped only by intuition and cannot be communicated or scientifically objectified. All such insight into wholes can be translated into controllable scientific knowledge, and the present revival of historico-philosophical modes of thought can be explained in our opinion by the desire to find a method of communicating what is unique in the historical process. In the sociology of culture, the attempt is made to analyse unique historical situations in terms of unique combinations of properties and factors undergoing a constant process of transformation—constellations which in themselves are phases in a genetic process the overall 'direction' of which can be determined.

Scheler himself seems to be aware of the fact that a sociology based upon a generalizing doctrine of the essence of man has already become a very problematic affair, since the general essences must always appear empty as compared to historical, concrete mental phenomena (one of the reasons why they can be sharply disjoined). Thus, he emphasizes (p. 13) that mind exists only in a *concrete multiplicity* of infinitely varied groups and cultures, so that it is futile to speak of a 'unity of human nature' as a presupposition of history and sociology. This means, however, that we cannot expect any essential illumination from the theory of essences, since it is now admitted that it can work out only the most general *formal* framework of the laws of intentional acts. Scheler, in fact, places himself in this fashion in the immediate proximity of Kantianism and of formal philosophy in general.

But why this summary rejection of the thesis of the 'unity of human nature', after Scheler himself proposed to base sociology upon such a highly general doctrine of the essence of man? The answer that the supra-temporal unity of man (to be treated in a general drive and mind theory) refers to the *essence* 'man', whereas the 'concrete multiplicity' merely deals with the *fact* 'man'—this answer, though expected, cannot satisfy us. To a human mind existing and developing only in a concrete multiplicity, only a *dynamic* essence 'man' can correspond; in our opinion, one cannot think in historicist fashion in factual research and remain static in essential analysis. If, however, one should nevertheless cling to such an 'essentialist' doctrine of the human mind and of intentional acts, inspired by 'supra-temporal' aspirations, then the problem still remains how one can attain concrete historical reality starting from this position. The questionable character of static generalizing and formalizing is not eliminated by restricting this mode of thought to 'essences'. Generalizing and formalizing are, in our opinion, valid 'technical' procedures and also have their uses in sociology, since they can be employed to control the multiplicity of data; for *concrete thought*, however—for the thinking of the concrete—they can serve merely as a springboard. Does, in fact, formalization not always lead to distortion, if we look at it from the viewpoint of the concrete? After all, a form is what it is only in conjunction with the concrete (historic) matter it in-forms, and it changes and grows together with change and growth of the matter. Those who engage in limitless formalization merely let themselves be guided—precisely in the sense of the distinction made by Scheler—by models and structural relationships prevailing in the dead, mechanized world of mere 'things', and the schemata so obtained obscure the peculiar nature of the living.

Thus, we are at this point in the presence of a profound conflict. On the one hand, Scheler propounds a doctrine of the 'timeless' essence of man; on the other, he is aware of, and feels responsible toward, the uniqueness of historic objects. This conflict is possibly the fundamental experience of our time (at least within the German cultural tradition).

Another thesis most characteristic of Scheler's doctrine concerns the 'law of the order of effectiveness of the real and ideal factors', already alluded to. The interaction of the two factors is described in the following way: mind is a factor of 'determination', not of 'realization'. That is, what works *can* be created by a culture is determined by mind alone, by virtue of its inner structure; but what actually *gets* created depends on the particular combination of the *real* factors prevailing at the time. Thus, the function of the real factors is to make a *selection* among the possibilities made available by Mind. Through this selective function, the real factors control the ideal ones. Both the ideal and the real factors existing at a given moment are, however, entirely powerless in face of those real factors which are in the process of emerging. Power constellations in politics, production control relationships in economy, follow their determined way in a robot-like fashion; they are subject to 'an evolutionary causality blind to all meaning' (p. 10). Human mind can at most block or unblock but never alter them.

What is fruitful in this way of looking at the problem is the fact that the peculiar phenomenological and structural character of the mental—which materialistic monism necessarily overlooks

—is well seen here. Its one-sidedness, however, consists in our opinion in this, that Scheler does not go beyond the assertion of a phenomenological separation of the 'real' and 'mental'. As a result of this, the separation, and the abstract immanence of the 'mental', remain unchallenged even when at last an attempt is made to bring about a synthesis, clarify the mutual relationship of the two spheres, and answer questions concerning their genesis.

In order to illustrate the difference between Scheler's position and the one represented by us, we shall mention an example showing two possible conceptions of the mutual relationship between the actual and the possible, the real and the mental. One of these conceptions—toward which Scheler seems to lean to some extent—is expressed by one of the characters in a play by Lessing who says that Raphael would have become just as great an artist if he had been born without hands, since it is the artistic vision rather than the visible realization that matters. For such a theory, standing in the Platonic tradition, in which ideas and models are considered as pre-existent, realization is something secondary. And it remains secondary even in Scheler's more moderate version of this conception. Obviously alluding to the example just mentioned, Scheler says: 'Raphael needs a brush; his ideas and artistic dreams do not create it. He needs politically and socially powerful patrons who commission him to glorify their ideals. Otherwise his genius cannot realize itself' (p. 10). Scheler stresses explicitly that he has no essential influence of the real factors in mind, as a result of which they would in part determine the substance of the works. This conception—which in its essence still harks back to Platonism—contrasts with another one specifically rooted in the modern attitude to life. This modern conception is expressed, for instance, in K. Fiedler's aesthetics. We may paraphrase Fiedler's theory somewhat freely in the following way: neither the creative process itself nor the work as a complex of meaning should be analysed by assuming that the artist sees models before his mind's eye before he starts working, and that he merely copies them afterwards as well as he can. The truth of the matter is that the work and its idea come into being *during* the process of creation. Every 'real factor', every line already drawn, every movement of the hand not only determines those that follow but also creates new possibilities not dreamed of beforehand. All real factors, such as the structure of the human hand and gestures, the particular texture of the material, the organic and psychic constitution of the artist are the source of meaning in this process. Their contribution to the work is not without effect upon the 'immanent' meaning it expresses. Hence, we should not merely say that the artist must exist as a man—and as this particular man—in order that an absolute possibility of the ideal world can gain shape (be realized) in the spatio-temporal world. What we should say is that the existence of the artist—determined as this particular existence—is itself a *conditio sine qua non* of the *meaning* and the idea embodied in the particular works. This new way of interpreting the correlation between 'idea' and 'reality' is also an essential component of our conception of the role of 'real factors' in cultural creation.

For us, too, there is a phenomenological separation between Being and Meaning; but this phenomenological duality can no longer be considered as fundamental when we come to examine both terms as parts of a dynamic genetic *totality*—a problem which surely has a meaning also within Scheler's system. When we reach 'existence' as an ultimate unity in which all phenomenological differences are cancelled, 'Being' and 'Meaning' appear as hypostatized partial spheres which are ultimately the 'emanations' of one and the same Life. For any philosophy or theory of culture or sociology (or whatever one may choose to call the ultimate synthesis in question) which seeks to transcend the abstract immanence of the various cultural products and to analyse them as part and parcel of an overall life process, the phenomenological duality cannot be more than a provisional device. One should not object at this point that the historian engaged in positive research is not interested in these metaphysical questions, since he need not go beyond the phenomenological separation of the spheres of 'Being' and 'Meaning' when he tries to give a historical account of the immanent evolution of ideas. This objection merely arises from a positivistic delusion which prevents us from realizing how deeply the supposedly pure scientist is engaged in metaphysics whenever he gives interpretations, establishes historical relationships, ascertains historic 'trends', or puts 'real' factors in correlation with 'ideal' ones. As soon as one attempts to explain a work in terms of facts in an artist's life, or of cultural currents of a period, and so on, he inevitably replaces the immanent 'meaning' of the works in the global framework of the life process, since he has deprived the works of their character as self-contained units and has been concerned instead with the central experience which determined the way of life and the cultural creativity of an epoch.

We have to recognize, in the light of the foregoing, that there is something true in the materialist conception of history, according to which it is Being, reality, that creates the ideal sector. The error of materialism consists merely in its wrong metaphysics which equates 'Being' or 'reality' with matter. In so far, however, as it negates the concept of the 'ideal' as something absolutely self-contained, as something that is somehow pre-existent, or unfolds itself within itself, merely on the basis of an immanent logic of meaning, or provides for historical or any other kind of reality the necessary stimulus that makes self-realization possible—in so far as it negates this concept of the 'ideal', materialism is right. And one cannot surmount this idealistic dualism if one proceeds like Scheler who combines with his idealistic theory a doctrine of 'the impotence of the mental', a thesis merely reflecting the transformation which German conservative thought underwent during the last phase of its development. Conservative thought in Germany increasingly drifted away from its humanistic origins since the inception of the trend of 'Realpolitik' and power politics, and at the same time abdicated more and more in the presence of the newly emerging social realities which did not favour the conservative aspirations. It is interesting to observe that the rising classes—whose aspirations are supported by the dominant 'real factors' of an epoch—consider *these* factors to be essential, whereas the conservatives, though they may acknowledge the importance of the real factors, can characterize their role and significance merely as a *negative* one.

In one word, as soon as we abandon the platonizing conception, the phenomenological difference of the real and ideal factors will be subordinated to the genetic unity of the historic process, and we shall advance to the point of origin where a real factor is *converted* into a mental datum. From a merely phenomenological point of view (defined as one involving nothing but straight description of the given, disregarding all those aspects which are connected with its genesis) this 'conversion' of the real into the mental cannot be grasped, since according to this view the gap between bare 'Being' devoid of meaning on the one hand, and a 'meaning' on the other, cannot be bridged. Since, however, we as interpreting subjects are existent human beings, and have an immediate experience of our 'existence' in which real factors are converted into mental data, we are able to push our inquiry to the point where the two spheres of the ideal and mental meet. As regards this conversion, moreover, it should be noted that many factors classified as 'real' are by no means completely devoid of meaning and purely 'material'. One is often inclined, for instance, to regard economic and geographical data as belonging integrally to the 'material' and 'natural' sphere. We should not forget, however—to take up only the first example mentioned, that of economics—that only the physiology of the hunger drive belongs to mere 'nature', but that this physiological substratum constitutes an element of the historic process only in so far as it enters into mental configurations, for example by assuming the form of an economic order or some other institutional form. This should not be misunderstood. We do not want to deny the fundamental role of the drives—and it is by no means our contention that economy could exist without the hunger drive; but if something is a necessary condition of another thing, it need not be unconditionally equated with the latter. What matters for us is that the various forms of economic institutions could not be explained by the hunger drive as such. The drive as such remains essentially unchanged over time, whereas economic institutions undergo constant changes, and history is exclusively interested in these institutional changes. That excess over and above the purely physiological substratum which alone transforms the drive into a historical factor is already 'mind'. It is, therefore, not enough to say that economy would not exist without mind; it should be added that it is this *mental* element which makes *economy* out of mere drive-satisfaction. If, then, we constantly lower the limit of the 'natural' by refining our distinctions, so that the 'economic' turns out to be 'mental' rather than 'material', then we must recognize two 'mental' spheres, the mutual relationship of which is that of substructure and superstructure. The question will then be how one sphere affects the other in the total process —how a structural change in the substructure determines a structural change in the superstructure. Now to be sure, if two spheres of the 'mental' are distinguished in this fashion, then we are of the opinion that the mind-in-the-substructure—involving primarily the conditions of production, *together with all concomitant social relationships*—does in part shape and determine mind-in-the-superstructure. For we should not forget that mind-in-the-substructure is the more 'massive' factor, if for no other reason, then because it is the components of this substructure which create the enduring framework of the continuous existence of human beings—that which is generally called *milieu*. And since the 'conversion' of the real into the mental (the most mysterious event in the historical process) takes place within man as a living being, the greatest determining force is exercised by those categories of meaning in which the human being lives with the greatest intensity.[1] It is by no means the case, then, as Scheler

[1] Later on, we shall qualify this broadly 'economistic' theory from the point of view of a more comprehensive doctrine, that of historicism. It will then appear as something merely corresponding to one particular phase of the historical process—inasmuch as the 'vital centre' of man moves into different spheres of activity in different epochs, and each epoch understands historical reality most clearly in connection with the sphere in which it lives most intensely. Thus, the economism which is predominant in Marxism is historically

seems to assume (if we understand him rightly), that a selection from among pre-existent mental forms takes place in the super-structure under the direct pressure of a purely 'natural' substruc-ture,[1] but rather: that which is vaguely sensed as being 'nature' converts itself into the various 'mental' configurations of the sub-structure, and in this fashion shapes, first, men as existent beings, and then, cultural reality as a whole (in analogy to Fiedler's conception of the co-determining role of the real factors).

What we are reluctant to accept, then, is, first of all, the intro-duction of the 'natural' dimension of the substructure, as a supra-temporal, unchanging entity, in terms of which the historical process is to be explained in part. For a causal factor of this kind could give rise only to combinations of elements which are other-wise unchanging. To be sure, Scheler does speak of 'changes in the drive structure', but these can be interpreted in his system only as relative shifts, that is, mere quantitative modifications; thus, he suggests that it is the 'power drive' which predominates at one time, the 'racial instinct' at another, etc. In our opinion, how-ever, 'natural' factors of this kind can be used as a dynamic principle of explanation of the historic process only if we assume that they undergo *qualitative* changes in the course of history. Such an assumption, in fact, is made plausible if we remember that the 'natural' on the various levels of its 'mental' transformations plays a different historical role every time.[2] At what time and in what form the so-called 'power drive' can manifest itself—in fact, whether it can do so at all—depends also on the total cultural constellation which the various generations find themselves con-fronted with in maturing. In this connection, too, there is no

determined. Nevertheless, it must be recognized that the fundamental explana-tory principle used by Marxism, the economic one, is rather powerful, because it characterizes the total process in terms of that factor which is the 'lowest' mental organizing principle of every social reality and hence lends itself very well to characterizing the structure of various epochs.

[1] We do not assert that the doctrine of the pre-existence of ideas we attribute to Scheler has a *metaphysical* import, and still less that it should be interpreted in the sense of *temporal* pre-existence. All we want to indicate is that Scheler teaches a logical immanence of the ideal sphere, and thus a separate and independent givenness of the ideal as something apart from the real. The function of the latter consists merely in making a selection among the ideal data, rather than in creating them in part. However, it is impossible to carry through a thorough-going parallel between our position and that of Scheler, since we draw the line between 'mind' and 'nature' at a different place.

[2] Thus a geographical fact, such as the insular position of a country, does not always have the same historical significance; its impact upon history will be different, according as we have to do with an 'early' historical epoch or with various stages of capitalistic evolution. The same natural factor performs a different function in different overall social and cultural situations; its 'meaning' for the cultural process changes accordingly.

eternally, self-identical 'power drive' as such which merely gets more or less repressed, but the identical expression 'power drive' covers a great variety of differently structured, differently experienced 'intentions of the will', having each time different objects as their correlates.

We are also reluctant to accept the positing of a mental world with an immanent logic of meaning *vis-à-vis* which the historical world with its 'real factors' plays only a selective role.

We also conceive the relationship within the 'possible' and 'actual' in a different way from Scheler. For us, too, there is at each moment that which is actual, surrounded by a horizon of possibilities; this horizon, however, is not the abstractly 'possible as such', but contains merely that which is possible in a given situation as a result of a certain constellation of factors. This 'horizon', in turn, is merely the starting-point of a new process leading to new actualities; this always involves the completely new, creative role of the moment and of the unique situation. For our conception of the world, then, it is not the abstractly possible that is higher; the value accent rests upon the emerging and the actual. The real is not, as in Scheler's system, an always inadequate selection from a transcendent treasure of forms, but a creative concretization flowing from historically unique constellations.

Only when we consider the actual *ex post*,[1] i.e. after it has emerged, rather than *in statu nascendi*, as it would be seen from the viewpoint of the creative centre of the evolutionary process—only then can we view it as having the structure of an immanent, completely self-contained complex of meaning. Only those who focus their attention exclusively upon the actual, upon the finished product cut off from all functional relationships within the genetic process, can have the impression that what happened was the realization of something pre-existent, of a self-contained,

---

[1] It seems to be generally overlooked that the subject studying and understanding history can look at the latter from various 'standpoints' which make a considerable existential difference. Thus, as suggested above, it makes a great difference whether one surveys products of the mind retrospectively as finished products or rather tries to re-enact the process of their creation. In our opinion, however, it is a mistake to adopt the 'retrospective' standpoint, and to try to account for the structure of genesis in terms of the actual as an accomplished fact, when dealing with problems of a metaphysic of the genetic process. (On the other hand, the problem of the 'standpoint' of the subject studying history is not the same as the problem of 'standpoints' in the theory of historicism. All historicism teaches a determination of thinking by the 'standpoint' of the thinker, but such historicist theories may have a conservative or progressive slant, depending on whether they are conceived from a 'retrospective' or an *in statu nascendi* standpoint.)

absolute entity. Since, however, cultural sociology is primarily concerned with reconstructing the functional relationships between the 'actual' on the one hand, and the past genetic process on the other, it is in our opinion too risky for this branch of knowledge to adopt the premise of a 'pre-existent' world of ideas, even if only in the sense of a non-temporal genesis of pure 'meaning'. It seems to us that there can be an immanent logic of meaning only for the retrospective view of the analyst of structure: once they have become actual, all works of the mind display an intelligible, meaningful structure. We want to stress in this connection that it is one of the most important tasks to ascertain this intelligible structure of meaning of a set of actual, finished works.

We discussed Scheler's conception of the relation of the substructure and superstructure in detail, and gave a full account of our contrary position, in order to show that even apparently purely formal presuppositions of historical research depend on a valuational and social standpoint; we wanted to demonstrate in detail that in this field, too, the process of cognition, far from realizing step by step problems which already are there in 'pre-existent' form, approaches from different sides problems growing out of the living experience of groups belonging to the same society. Everything that distinguishes the static and dynamic view is somehow related to this central point—that of the relationship between the ideal and real. Since for Scheler the essential ultimate is something pre-existent, floating above history, the historic process can never achieve real essentiality and substantiality in his system in which the static, freely floating entities are not really 'constituted' but merely 'realized' by the historic process. Such a sharp dualism can never lead to a real philosophy of history; and the fact that methodological decisions also are connected with metaphysical and 'vital' orientations is nowhere more clearly visible than here. For we now can understand why Scheler decided in favour of a generalizing type of sociology when faced with the choice which sociology must make today—whether to proceed in accordance with the generalizing method or seek a renewal on the basis of historico-philosophical traditions. To be sure, the case of Scheler is not quite so simple. As we have seen, a tension arises in Scheler's system owing to the fact that although his basic doctrine is one of eternal values, he yet recognizes the dynamic as particularized in various 'standpoints' and wants to account for it in terms of the basic doctrine. Both the wide scope of his plan and the unresolved juxtaposition of static and dynamic elements in his doctrine can be well seen from the following passage in which Scheler says that he intends to 'hang up', so to speak, the realm of absolute ideas and values, corresponding to the essential idea of man, very much higher than all factual value systems thus far realized in history. 'Thus, we give up as wholly relative, as historically and sociologically dependent on the particular standpoints, all orderings of *goods*, *goals*, *norms* in human societies, as expressed by ethics, religion, law, art, etc., and retain nothing but the idea of the eternal Logos, whose transcendent secrets cannot be explored, in the form of a metaphysical *history*, by any one nation, any one civilization, any or all cultural epochs that have emerged thus far, but only by *all together*, including all future ones—by temporal and spatial co-operation of irreplaceable, because individual, unique cultural subjects working together in full solidarity' (p. 14).

The tensions revealed by this passage illustrate the internal struggle between Scheler's doctrine of eternity and present-day historical consciousness; the important thing from our viewpoint is that Scheler tries to incorporate in his system, not only alien theses, but also alien systematic presuppositions. For the historicist, entities do not exist apart from the historic process; they come into being and realize themselves in it, and become intelligible exclusively through it. Man has an access to entities creating history and dominating the various epochs because, living in history, he is existentially linked to it. History is the road—for the historicist, the only road—to the understanding of the entities genetically arising in it. But the abyss between the temporal and eternal which Scheler's system assumes decisively affects his theory of the interpretation of history. The real entities are supra-historical; hence, contrary to what Scheler says, history cannot contribute anything relevant to their exploration, or, if there is a contribution which history as conceived by Scheler can make, it can only be a somewhat limited one.

History is in this system like a sea of flames surrounding the eternal entities. The flames may rise or subside; they may approach the entities or recede from them, and the rhythm of their movement, imposed by destiny, is shrouded in mystery; all we know is that some periods get closer to the entities than others. Fanatics of the Middle Ages, whose theory of history is based upon present-day romanticism, assert that the Middle Ages have marked the greatest proximity to the eternal entities, and they specify the culmination point within the Middle Ages at various moments, depending on the nature of their own subjective experience. Scheler marks a certain progress beyond this narrow glorification of one historical epoch, in that he maintains that each period and each civilization has a specific 'missionary idea' involving a close affinity to a certain set of entities which is different in each case.[1] But he still essentially cleaves to the static conception of entities, for in his view, too, the eternal entities remain cut off from the flux of historical life, their substance is alien to that of history. All that Scheler admits is a principle of 'access': some eternal entities are primarily accessible to just one cultural group, others to another. Historical 'synthesis', then, consists in a combination of all the essences discovered in the course of history. This way of looking at things, however, involves certain abrupt 'jumps' which we cannot square with our fundamental experience. Scheler's theory contains two such 'jumps'. He admits that concrete norm systems are historically and sociologically determined, and that at each moment man stands within history. But for him, all this applies only in so far as we are not dealing with an understanding of those 'entities' the realization of which is the 'mission' of mankind. In so far as these latter entities are concerned, historical man suddenly turns into a conqueror of temporality and acquires a superhuman capacity of shaking off all historical limitation and determination. This is one 'jump' in Scheler's theory. But we also may ask another question. How can we know in analysing history which of the entities proclaimed by various civilizations have been real, true entities? By what criteria can we judge that a certain civilization was mature enough to accomplish the 'mission' of humanity as regards one or the other entity? If we really want to assign such roles to all past epochs and civilizations, it is clearly not enough for us to have a valid, objective knowledge of our own entities; we must have supra-historical, superhuman intuitive powers to identify all entities, or at least those which have emerged thus far in the course of history. Thus, the historian of ideas in performing his essential intuition must twice transcend temporality: once when he identifies the eternal entities assigned to his own epoch, and for the second time when he interprets the past, trying to separate the genuine from the false, the real essence from mere subjective appearance. This, however, amounts to the postulation of an absolute intuition of essences—at least of all essences thus far discovered—at each moment in history ; or at least the postulation of the absolute character of the present moment. But then, the idea of a collective 'mission' of *all* epochs and civilizations, which

[1] Here, too, we can detect the essential difference between progressive and conservative thought. If a conservative thinker conceives an idea of humanity as a whole, his orientation is *cosmopolitic*, i.e. he calls for co-operation among different nations and civilizations, each conserving its peculiar identity. The progressive conception of humanity as a unit, however, involves *internationalism*, i.e. a negation of these national peculiarities. The conservative wants multiplicity, the progressive wants uniformity; the former thinks in terms of culture, the latter in terms of civilization.

would have afforded a starting-point for a philosophy of history, becomes lost again; the historical process as such is given up as hopelessly relative, and all absolute significance is concentrated within the second 'jump' beyond temporality. Scheler tries to incorporate historicist ideas into his theory of timelessness. and even adopts the idea of 'perspectivic' vision. But his static conception of eternity never gets reconciled with the alien 'standpoint' of historicism with which he tries to combine it.

For anyone whose fundamental metaphysical experience is of such a (static) character, the sociology of knowledge—as well as of all other spheres of culture—must become a totally secondary affair. Accordingly, the real task of a sociology of thought—which in our opinion consists in discovering the overall line of development by following the genesis of the various 'standpoints'—is never formulated by Scheler.

One more objection must be made to Scheler's doctrine of essences. He forgets that any understanding and interpretation of essences (and hence also of the essences of past epochs) is possible only in perspective fashion. Both *what* is accessible to us of the essential intuitions of past epochs, and *how* they become accessible to us, depends on our own standpoint.

Each 'element of significance' (if we can speak of such a thing in isolation) is determined by the entire context of significance, and ultimately by the vital basis which gives rise to it; this is an insight we owe to historicism. Thus, an act of understanding consists in incorporating an alien 'element of significance' into our own context of significance, cancelling its original functional relationships and working it into our own function pattern. This is how we proceed in ascertaining not only the facts, but also the intentionally assigned 'meanings' of past epochs. It would be a 'technicist' prejudice to assume that we could integrate mental data (meanings) into a totality by adding one piece to another. It should not be difficult to convince Scheler of the correctness of this view, since he himself distinguishes several types of knowledge and several types of cognitive progress (p. 23). An 'additive' knowledge of intelligible essences would be possible only if essential knowledge were of the type of technicist, 'cumulative' knowledge (as Scheler calls it). According to Scheler himself, essential knowledge belongs to a type of knowledge limited to just one culture; but if this is so, it seems to us that knowledge of the meanings and essences of past epochs can only be a perspectivic one, determined by our historic-existential standpoint on the one hand and by our basic axiom system on the other. In another paper,[1] we have already pointed out that a sharp characterization

1 'Historicism', pp. 84 ff.

of the fundamental difference between scientific-technological rationality and philosophical knowledge, and between the patterns of evolution existing in these two fields, becomes possible only if one goes back to the *systematizing structural principle* underlying them. As we have tried to show, scientific-technological thought differs from philosophical thought in that the former type of thought completes just one and the same system during successive periods, whereas the latter starts from new centres of systematization in every epoch in trying to master the increasing multiplicity of the historical world. Because it is the same system that is being built up in science in the course of the centuries, the phenomenon of change of meaning does not occur in this sphere, and we can picture the process of thought as direct progress toward ultimately 'correct' knowledge which can be formulated only in one fashion. In physics, there are not several different concepts of 'force', and if different concepts do appear in the history of physics, one can classify them as mere preparatory steps before the discovery of the correct concept prescribed by the axiomatic pattern of the system. As against this, we have in philosophy, as well as in the historic-cultural sciences which are closely related to it, the phenomenon of an intrinsically necessary *change of meaning*. Every concept in these fields inevitably changes its meaning in the course of time—and this precisely because it continually enters into new systems depending on new sets of axioms. (We may, for example, think of the way in which the concept of 'idea' has altered its meaning: what it meant for each epoch can be understood by going back to the total systems in the framework of which the concept was defined.) If we observe the historical line of evolution in these fields, as well as the mutual relationships of the meanings succeeding each other, then we can observe no 'progress' toward a unique system, one exclusively correct meaning of the concept, but rather the phenomenon of 'sublimation' (*Aufheben*). This 'sublimation' consists in the fact that in these fields every later and 'higher' system incorporates the earlier systems and functional relationships and also the individual concepts belonging to those systems. However, when this happens, the earlier principles of systematization which are reflected in the various concepts are cancelled and the 'elements' taken over from earlier systems are re-interpreted in terms of a higher and more comprehensive system, i.e. 'sublimated'. We can keep apart the two types of thought (scientific and philosophic-historical) only by paying attention to this fundamental difference in system-building; this is the only way to recognize that. A genuine historical synthesis of past cultures cannot consist in a non-perspectivic addition of successively appearing phenomena but only in an ever-renewed attempt to incorporate the entities taken over from the past in a new system. The actual, historically observable evolution of thought in philosophy (as well as in the related cultural sciences) shows a pattern contrasting—as we have seen—with the pattern of evolution in the natural sciences—we described this pattern earlier[1] as a 'dialectical' one, and Scheler now proposes to designate it as 'cultural growth by interweaving and incorporation of existing mental structures in a new structure' (p. 24). The essential point—regardless of terminological differences—is, however, that in the case under consideration human thought is *organized around a new centre in every epoch*, and even though man does 'sublimate' (in the Hegelian sense of *aufheben*) his earlier concepts by incorporating them into ever new systems, this involves a change in meaning making an additive synthesis impossible. Once it is admitted that philosophical knowledge is existentially determined and limited to one specific civilization, then it is no longer possible to assume anything but a dynamic system in this sphere of thought, for otherwise we should be dealing with concepts of one structural type in terms of a different structure. This being granted, perspectivism alone will be possible, i.e. the theory that the various essential meanings come into being together with the epochs to which they belong; these essential meanings belong to essences which have their own being in an absolute sense, but the student of history can comprehend them only in perspectivic fashion, looking at them from a standpoint which is itself a product of history. This kind of perspectivism, however, is by no means self-refuting, contrary to what Scheler says in his criticism of our views (pp. 115 ff.), because—in our opinion at least—both the various epochs and the essences coming into being in them have their own being regardless of any knowledge of them that may subsequently be achieved. As we said in a passage of our essay on Historicism quoted by Scheler: 'The historical-subject matter (the historical content, so to speak, of an epoch) *remains identical "in itself"*, but it belongs to the essential conditions of its cognizability that it can be grasped only from differing intellectual-historical standpoints—or, in other words, that we can view only various "aspects" of it' (p. 105). The italicized words of this sentence indicate clearly enough that it is not our intention to use perspectivism as a means to dissolve the real being *in se* of the objects of historical inquiry; that would, indeed, be rightly construed by Scheler as a self-refuting view. *Thus*, the essence and the actual existence of Hellenism do not dissolve themselves into the various 'perspectives' opened up by successive generations of historical scholarship. It is, in fact,

[1] Cf. the essay on 'Historicism', in this volume, pp. 84 ff.

'given' as a 'thing in itself', approached from various sides, as it were, by different interpretations. We are justified in positing this real being of the object *in se*, for even though no single perspective can do it full justice, it is still given as a control we may use in ruling out arbitrary characterizations.

To mention an example by means of which we can illustrate the meaning of perspectivism most clearly: human consciousness can grasp a landscape *as landscape* only from various perspectives; and yet the landscape does not dissolve itself into its various possible pictorial representations. Each of the possible pictures has a 'real' counterpart and the correctness of each perspective can be controlled from the other perspectives. This implies, however, that history is only visible from within history and cannot be interpreted through a 'jump' beyond history, in occupying a static standpoint arbitrarily occupied outside history. The historicist standpoint, which starts with relativism, eventually achieves an absoluteness of view, because in its final form it posits history itself as the Absolute; this alone makes it possible that the various standpoints, which at first appear to be anarchic, can be ordered as component parts of a meaningful overall process.

In fact, if we look back upon a relatively closed epoch of history, such as the period of early capitalism as far as the emergence of fully developed capitalist systems, we can perceive the meaningful direction in which the line of development points. We then can interpret all the sociological and other theoretical 'standpoints' belonging to that epoch in terms of this inherent goal-directedness. To be sure, each theory claimed absolute validity when first propounded; we, however, are in a position to estimate its relative truth and its potentiality. Fruitful past theories, however, are justified even in retrospect, because they can survive as problems and components of the more comprehensive system in terms of which we think today. At the same time, however, they are relativized, because they can survive *only* as parts of a more comprehensive system. Now we do not want to deny that historicism does encounter difficulties—and they arise precisely at this point. For while we can see the meaning, the goal-directedness of the overall development in so far as closed periods are concerned, we cannot see such a goal-meaning for our own period. Since the future is always a secret, we can only make conjectures about the total pattern of meaning of which our present is a part; and since we can have nothing more than conjectures, it is understandable enough that each current of thought assumes that the goal-meaning of the present is identical with those contemporary trends with which that current happens to identify itself. Thus, the future goal-meaning of the totality of history will be seen differently, according to what particular point one occupies in the total process; the history of philosophy of a progressive author will differ from that of a conservative one, and so on.

If we pursue this train of thought farther, we shall even conclude that epochs such as those we have just described as relatively closed and therefore transparent as to their goal-meaning (such as early capitalism) may to some extent lose their definiteness of meaning and become problematic if they are inserted in more comprehensive genetic patterns. It follows from this that each historical theory belongs essentially to a given standpoint; but this does not mean—a point we want to stress—that the whole concreteness, 'stubborn-factness' of the data and essential meanings is dissolved into a number of various perspectives. Every one of us refers to the same data and essences. To be sure, as we have seen in our introductory chapter, a given movement can discover only a limited range of facts—those which come within the purview of its reflectiveness—but once these facts have been made visible, every one is obliged to take them into account. Moreover, we understand, looking at things from our perspective, the possibility and necessity of the other perspectives; and no matter what our perspective is, we all experience the controlling 'stubbornness' of the data; thus, we all have every reason to assume that we move in the medium of reality, so that we can disclaim all illusionism.

One might ask at this point why we do not content ourselves with just recording those facts we ourselves recognize as stubborn —as positivism would have it; why we do not eliminate those 'totalities of meaning' and additions to mere factuality which alone lead to perspectivism, as a metaphysical residue which is of no concern to positive science. Our answer is that there is something peculiar about the 'stubbornness', the 'positivity' of those 'facts'. They are 'stubborn' in the sense that they constitute a control we may use in ruling out arbitrary constructions. But they are not 'stubborn' in the sense that they can be grasped outside any system, in isolation, without reference to meanings. On the contrary, we can grasp them only within the framework of a meaning, and they show a different aspect, depending on the meaning pattern within which they are apprehended. Terms such as 'capitalism', 'proletariat', etc., change their meaning, according to which system they are used in, and historical 'data' become historical 'facts' only by being inserted into an evolutionary process as 'parts' or 'stages'.

That carefree, self-assured epoch of positivism in which it was possible to assume that one could ascertain 'facts' without qualification is now over; one could assume this only because one overlooked that the positivist history of culture naïvely took just one system of meaning, one particular metaphysic to be absolutely valid—although only thinkers of that one epoch could accept them as a-problematical. Positivism could successfully conceal its own framework of meanings from itself only because it cultivated nothing but specialized research in one or the other field; under these circumstances, the fact that the metaphysical presuppositions made by specialized scientists in their particular fields were based upon a global outlook and upon a philosophy of history, no less than those of non-positivist schools, could not be noticed by anyone. We, on the other hand, can see already that at least the cultural and historical sciences presuppose metaphysics, that is, an increment that turns partial aspects into totalities; and in our opinion, it is altogether more fruitful to acknowledge than to ignore this state of things.

As stated above, however, this does not mean that we shall be unaffected by those aspects of positivism which were 'genuine', and by virtue of which it marked a real progress in the history of thought. Every metaphysics that will emerge after the supremacy of positivism will have to incorporate and 'sublimate' in some form these 'genuine' elements of positivism. This 'genuine' component, however, is not a matter of the epistemological and methodological position of positivism, but, paradoxical as it may sound, of its metaphysical intention, of the vital feeling of which it is the theoretical expression. The positivist style of thought marks in the history of theoretical disciplines the same gradual transition which, in the field of politics, is designated by the term '*Realpolitik*', and in that of art, by the term 'realism'—a transition which left its mark both upon conservative and progressive thought. These terms suggest that certain spheres of life (e.g. economics) more and more occupy the centre of experience and provide the fundamental categories in terms of which all other spheres are experienced. The transition in question means that in our experience, the ontological stress is upon 'this-worldliness', 'immanence', rather than 'transcendence'. We seek the origin of all 'transcendent' concepts in just this 'immanent' experience. It may be noted, however, that this antithesis between 'immanence' and 'transcendence' is itself still expressed in the terminology of the old vital attitude and hence cannot do full justice to what is essentially new and genuine in positivism.

What we called the positivist respect for empirical reality represents a second positivist principle which, we think, remains valid for our thinking. This respect for empirical reality (which, however, no longer means for us the belief in a non-metaphysical interpretation of mental facts) consists in this, that we cannot

conceive of metaphysical entities outside of an essential contact
with that realm of experience which for us represents the ultimate
reality of the world. This is the main reason why we cannot
accept any 'jump' beyond reality—not even in connection
with the construction of a pre-existent realm of truth and validity.
We do not claim to be able to make any deductions concerning
structures of truth and validity, except from the empirically
ascertainable transformation of the structure of the various spheres
of thought, as encountered within history. All essential types of
the new metaphysics bear the imprint of this process of transformation which results in a steady heightening of the ontological
rank of the 'immanent' and 'historical'. It was possibly Hegel who
performed the most essential step toward true positivism when
he identified the 'essence', the 'absolute', with the historical
process and tied the fate of the absolute to that of the
evolution of the world. Even though his detailed propositions
cannot be accepted, his general position is closest to our
immediate orientation.

We completely agree with Scheler, then, that metaphysics has
not been and cannot be eliminated from our world conception,
and that metaphysical categories are indispensable for the interpretation of the historical and intellectual world. We also agree
with him that factual knowledge and essential knowledge represent
two different forms of knowledge, but we do not admit an abrupt
separation of the two—what we think is rather that essential
knowledge merely goes farther and deeper in the same direction
in which factual knowledge sets out. It seems to us that a passage
from factual, empirical knowledge to intuition of essences is
taking place continually. This dualism of 'fact' and 'essence' is
wholly parallel to that of historical science and the philosophy of
history. There is a general tendency to make a sharp separation
between those two disciplines; but in our opinion, the correct view
is that a good deal of 'philosophy of history' is already embedded
in the various concepts we use in characterizing particular facts
—concepts which play a considerable role in determining the
content of 'empirical' science. We are somehow guided by a 'plan',
an 'intelligible framework' of history whenever we put the
seemingly most isolated particular fact into a context.

To assume such a continuity and interpenetration of these two
types of knowledge does not mean, however, denying that they
are different, qualitatively and hierarchically. What we object
to is merely the 'jump' between the two worlds which tears their
respective structures completely apart—a conception obviously
inspired by the idea of knowledge based on revelation.

It should not surprise us that in attempting to characterize the standpoint from which a sociology of knowledge can be constructed, we had to go into such detail in discussing systematic, philosophical presuppositions. After all, the problem before us is precisely how far the empirical, scientific treatment of a problem is influenced by the philosophical, metaphysical standpoint of the investigator.

The confrontation of the divergences between our conception of the sociology of knowledge and that held by Scheler may have made it clear that both are concerned with the same task, i.e. the task implied by the fact that mental products can be interpreted, not only directly as to their content, but also indirectly, in terms of their dependence on reality and especially of the social function they perform. This is the fact which sets us the task of developing a sociology of knowledge and culture. This task is being tackled from various philosophical standpoints, all of which can be assigned to a definite social position. Since Scheler's philosophical point of view postulates a supra-temporal, unchanging system of truths (a position which in practice always amounts to claiming eternal validity for one's own historically and sociologically determined perspective), he is compelled to introduce the 'contingency' of sociological factors as an afterthought into this immobile, supra-temporal framework. But it is impossible to incorporate the historical and sociological factors organically into one's system if this approach 'from above' is adopted. An unbridgeable gulf will then separate history from the supra-temporal.

We proceed in the opposite direction: for us, the immediately given is the dynamic change of the standpoints, the historic element. We want to concentrate our attention upon this, and exploit whatever opportunity it provides for overcoming relativism. This implies, as an initial task for the sociology of knowledge, that of giving as exact an account as possible of the intellectual standpoints co-existing at a given moment, and of retracing their historical development. For even the individual standpoints as such are not 'static', remaining changeless throughout; on the contrary, the relentless flux of the historic process brings ever new data to the surface which call for interpretation, and may lead to a disintegration or modification of the previously existing systems. Furthermore, one of the important aspects of the evolution of intellectual standpoints is the contribution they make to the overall evolutionary process within society. It is possible to show in retrospect in what way every single utopia, and also every single image of past history, has helped to mould the epoch in which it emerged. There is an existentially determined truth content in human thought at every stage of its development;

this consists in the fact that at each moment, an attempt is made to increase the 'rationality' of the social-intellectual world in a specific way, in the direction imposed by the next evolutionary step. The next task of this sociology of *cognition* (as it should be called by right) consists in working out this *functional* role of social, existentially involved thinking at the various stages of the real process. The metaphysical assumption that is involved here (and we want to emphasize that our theory does presuppose such an assumption) is that the global process within which the various intellectual standpoints emerge is a meaningful one. Standpoints and contents do not succeed each other in a completely haphazard way, since they all are parts of a meaningful overall process. The entire problem of 'absolute' truth will, then, coincide with that of the nature of this unitary meaning of the process as a whole; the question is how far we are able to grasp the evolutionary goal that *can* be seen at a given moment. We have already indicated an answer to this question: to the extent that an epoch is already terminated—it can, of course, be said to be terminated only in a relative sense, as we said—to the extent that it presents itself as a completed *Gestalt*, we can specify the functional role of thought patterns relative to the goal at which the evolutionary process had been aiming. In so far as processes just unfolding themselves are concerned, however, the goal is not yet given; and it cannot be said to exist *in se* or in some pre-existent fashion. In this respect, we are wholly *in statu nascendi* and see nothing but the clash of antagonistic aspirations. And our own intellectual standpoint itself is located within one of these rival positions; hence, we can have only a partial and perspectivic view of what is unfolding and also of the past, in so far as the interpretation of the past depends on the interpretation of the ongoing process. That this need not lead to an illusionism, to a negation of the reality of the historic process, has already been stressed. We are ready to admit that an absolutistic doctrine in the old sense cannot be evolved from these premises without a 'jump' and hypostatization of one's own position; but then, we cannot even aim at such an absolutistic standpoint which, after all, is nothing but the hypostatization of the structural pattern of a static conception of truth. In our opinion, one can still believe in a static 'truth *in se*' only as long as one fails to recognize that it is not one single system which is being gradually built up in the historic-cultural process, as is the case with the system of mathematical and natural science. Within the historic process, thought constantly takes its departure from new and ever more comprehensive central ideas. The very idea of a 'sublime dialogue' of the spirits of all ages, as Scheler conceives it, can occur, even as a utopian fantasy, only to someone who believes in *one* system of truth. Once one has recognized that a 'dialogue' of this kind cannot take place in this simple fashion, if for no other reason, because every word has a different meaning in different cultures, as a result of the fact that its existential function is a different one in each case—once one has realized this, he can at most conceive, as a 'utopian' belief, the idea that each epoch contains in itself in a 'sublimated' fashion the tensions of the entire historical process leading up to it. Thus, one can at most arrive at the belief—by extrapolating from the structural position observed today—that the present rivalry of antagonistic systems and standpoints, and their attempts at incorporating the rival positions within themselves, indicate an inherent tendency of all human thought to account for the whole of reality, a tendency which falls short of achieving its goal as long as a fully comprehensive systematic principle is not yet discovered. This, then, will be reflected in the 'finiteness', the limitation to partial perspectives, of actual thinking. So far as we can see, reality is always more comprehensive than any of the partial standpoints it brings forth. Then, if we extrapolate, we may believe that a central systematic idea will eventually be found which will in fact permit a synthesis of the entire process. But we cannot suppose this grand synthesis to be pre-existent—if for no other reason, because the *real* situation which could call forth such a synthesis has not yet materialized. Our 'utopia' of the *final* total synthesis is superior to that of the one pre-existent static truth, because it has been derived from the actual structure of historic thought, whereas the latter reflects an un-historical mind, wedded to *one* static system.

One could start from these premises, and yet overcome relativism by a 'jump', either if he proclaimed his own standpoint to be the final phase of the entire dynamic (as Hegel did), or if he assumed that thought would no longer be existentially determined in the future. This, however, would amount to the 'restabilization' of an originally dynamic conception. Once an absolute stand is taken *vis-à-vis* history, thought becomes in fact static; the point of dynamism is not to recognize that history is changing, but to acknowledge that one's own standpoint is no less dynamic than all others. For a radically dynamic conception, the only possible solution is, then, to recognize that one's own standpoint, though relative, constitutes itself in the element of truth. Or, to characterize the difference between Scheler's solution and ours by a metaphor, we might say: according to our view, God's eye is upon the historic process (i.e. it is not meaningless), whereas Scheler must imply that he looks upon the world with God's eyes.

A mere structural analysis of the two doctrines shows that neither can fully overcome the antinomies inherent in it. Scheler, who puts the absolute at the beginning, never reaches the dynamic (he cannot bridge the gulf between the static and dynamic); the other conception, which begins with the factual displacement of one standpoint by another, cannot reach the absolute—not, at least, in the self-assured form in which it was once given for a static kind of thought. But while the recognition of the partiality of *each* standpoint, and especially of his own, would make Scheler's theory self-contradictory, such recognition not only does not lead to an inner contradiction in our theory and sociology of knowledge, but constitutes a confirmatory instance for it.

Since the overall sum of knowledge existing at a given time comes into being in close dependence upon the real social process, but this process itself approaches totality through antithesis and turmoil, it is not surprising that we could directly discover only partial intellectual currents opposed to each other and define a totality only as the sum of these antagonistic partial currents. 'Where several philosophies emerge simultaneously', says Hegel, 'we have to do with distinct aspects which together constitute the totality underlying all, and it is only because of their one-sidedness that we can see in the one only the refutation of the other. Furthermore, they do not merely quibble about details but each puts forward a new principle; this is what we have to find.'[1]

In this whole discussion thus far, we have been trying to focus our attention upon the broad ultimate principles whose mutual divergences represent no 'quibbling about details' but illustrate the conflicting solutions of the particular problem before us that can be reached from the standpoints actually existing today. Our next task is to show how the problems of a sociology of knowledge can be treated from the dynamic standpoint we represent.

IV. SOCIOLOGY OF KNOWLEDGE FROM THE DYNAMIC STANDPOINT

We think the present constellation is favourable to the development of a sociology of knowledge, because the sporadic insights into the social structure of knowledge gained in earlier periods have been multiplying rapidly in modern times, and have now reached a stage where a systematic rather than sporadic and casual treatment of these problems becomes possible. And precisely because this 'casualness' is now being overcome more and

[1] *Vorlesungen über die Geschichte der Philosophie*, ed. by I. Bolland, Leiden, 1908, p. 1080.

more, attention is being increasingly centred upon the philosophical premises behind the findings of detail—premises that have not been directly explored thus far. At present, even scholars engaged in specialized studies are aware of this trend toward systematic roundedness. Scheler's essay is valuable primarily because it presents a comprehensive plan, an outline embracing various disciplines; and it has profited from the fact that the author is a philosopher who is at the same time a sociologist. Work in the field of the sociology of knowledge can be fruitful only if the philosophical, metaphysical premises of each author are openly acknowledged, and if the authors possess the ability to observe thought both 'from within', in terms of its logical structure, and 'from without', in terms of its social function and conditioning.

We shall now try to indicate the way in which a systematic sociology of knowledge can be developed on the basis of a dynamic conception. We have already outlined the basic principles of our approach; what remains to be done is to analyse the relevant methodological problems as well.

If we adopt a dynamic conception of truth and knowledge, then the central problem of a sociology of knowledge will be that of the existentially conditioned genesis of the various standpoints which encompass the patterns of thought available to any given epoch. The entire effort will be concentrated upon this one point, because the change and the inner growth of the various standpoints contains for us the whole substance of the history of thought. The sociological analysis of thought, undertaken thus far only in a fragmentary and casual fashion, now becomes the object of a comprehensive scientific programme which permits a division of labour once it has been decided to go through the intellectual output of each period and find out on what standpoints and systematic premises thought was based in each case. This, the *first* major problem of a sociology of knowledge can be tackled in conjunction with the work done in the field of the 'history of ideas', which has been extremely fruitful as regards both results and methods. In a number of fields (political, philosophical, economical, aesthetic, moral, etc.) the history of ideas shows us an extreme variety of changing elements of thought; but these labours will reach their culmination, the full realization of their meaning, only when we hear not only about changing *contents* of thought but also about the often merely implicit *systematic premises* on which a given idea was based in its original form—to be later modified so as to satisfy a different set of premises, and thus to survive under changed conditions. That is: the history of ideas can achieve its objective, that of accounting for the entire process of intellectual history in systematic fashion, only if it is *supplemented* by a *historical structural analysis* of the various centres of systematization that succeed each other in dynamic fashion. We do see beginnings of this kind of analysis (e.g. in works distinguishing 'romanticism' or 'Enlightenment' as different vital climates giving rise to different modes of thinking); and one would merely pursue these ideas to their ultimate logical consequences if one made a systematic effort to lay bare the ultimate axioms underlying 'romantic' and 'Enlightenment' thought respectively, and to define the type of system to which these patterns of thought belong with the greatest logical and methodological precision possible today. This would merely mean that one would utilize for historical analysis the logical precision which is characteristic of our time. At this point already, however, we have occasion to point out a limitation of the history of ideas—the fact that its analysis proceeds in terms of 'epochs'. From a sociological point of view, both 'nations' and 'epochs' are much too undifferentiated to serve as a basis of reference in describing the historical process. The historian knows that a certain epoch will appear as dominated by just one intellectual current only when we have a bird's eye view of it. Penetrating deeper into the historical detail, we shall see every epoch as divided among several currents; it may happen, at most, that one of these currents achieves dominance and relegates the others to the status of under-currents. No current is ever completely eliminated; even while one is victorious, all the others that belong to one or the other social sector will continue to exist as under-currents, ready to re-emerge and to reconstitute themselves on a higher level when the time is ripe. It is sufficient to think of the peculiar rhythm with which 'rationalistic' and 'romantic' phases constantly succeeded each other during the most recent period in European history to realize that we are dealing here with separate strands of evolution which nevertheless are related to each other by some higher law. However, it is not sufficient to recognize this evolution in separate strands; we also have to take into account the way in which the principal currents always adjust themselves to each other. Both these problems have to be worked out by a systematic history of ideas as the first chapter of a sociology of thought. For it cannot be overlooked, for instance, that whenever romanticism makes a new advance, it always takes into account the status of simultaneously existing and dominant rationalist thought; not only do the two schools learn from each other, but they even attempt to work out an ever broader synthesis, in order to master the new situation.

However, if we did not go any farther, we should never produce a *sociology* of knowledge. No matter how systematic it is, a purely immanent analysis of the genesis of intellectual standpoints is still nothing but a history of ideas. This preliminary systematic work in the history of ideas can lead to a sociology of knowledge only when we examine the problem of how the various intellectual standpoints and 'styles of thought' are rooted in an underlying historico-social reality. But in this connection, too, it would be a mistake, in our opinion, if one were to consider reality, social reality, as a unitary current. If within the history of ideas it is too undifferentiated a procedure to take epochs as units, then it is an equally great error to conceive the reality behind the ideological process as a homogeneous unit. After all, it cannot be doubted that any higher type of society is composed of several different strata, just as intellectual life shows a variety of currents; in our own society, stratification can best be described as class stratification. And the overall dynamic of society is a resultant of all the partial impulses emanating from these strata. The first task, then, will be to find out whether there is a correlation between the intellectual standpoints seen in immanence and the social currents (social standpoints). The finding of this correlation is the first task specific to the sociology of knowledge. The immanent description of the genesis of the intellectual standpoints may still be considered as the continuation of the work of the historian of ideas; the history of social stratification may still be seen as part of social history. But the combination of these two fields of inquiry introduces a specifically sociological approach. It is, however, important precisely at this point to eliminate naturalism, as well as those attitudes which are related to the original polemical intention of sociology. Although the problem outlined above has first been formulated in terms of the Marxian philosophy of history, we must, in studying it, be careful to renounce all materialist metaphysics and to exclude (or to reduce to the element of truth contained in them) all propagandistic considerations. First of all, even the most superficial glance at the historic data will show that it is quite impossible to identify any given intellectual standpoint with a given stratum or class—for example as if the proletariat had a science of its own, developed in a closed intellectual space, and the bourgeoisie another one, neatly separated from it. This crude propagandistic exaggeration can lead only to a faulty historical oversimplification; hence, we have to suspend belief until we have ascertained how much truth is contained in it (for it does have a certain element of truth).

Even the immanent examination of the various intellectual and cognitive standpoints, as it is carried out by a systematic history of ideas, shows that they do not float in thin air or develop and ramify purely from within, but must be put in correlation with certain tendencies embodied by social strata. At first, this 'putting in correlation' will present a certain difficulty for the sociologist. The naturalist epoch of Marxism recognized only one possible correlation between social reality and intellectual phenomena: namely, the correlation that an intellectual attitude is dictated by a material interest. It is because the initial phase of ideological research was solely motivated by 'unmasking' that being 'dictated by an interest' was the only form of social conditioning of ideas that was recognized. Not that we deny that certain intellectual positions can be adopted or promoted because this is useful either in propagating or in concealing group interests; and we admit that it can only be desirable to unmask such attitudes. However, this motivation by interest is not the only correlation that can exist between a social group and its intellectual positions. Socialist ideological research is one-sided, because it primarily concentrates attention upon that form of social conditioning of ideas which is represented by motivation by interest.

If the category of 'interest' is recognized as the only 'existential relation' involving ideas, then one will be forced either to restrict sociological analysis to those parts of the superstructure which manifestly show ideological 'cloaking' of interests, or, if it is nevertheless desired to analyse the entire superstructure in terms of its dependence upon social reality, to define the term 'interest' so broadly that it will lose its original meaning. In our opinion, neither road leads to the goal. If we want to broaden ideological research into a sociology of knowledge, and combine it with con-temporary work done in the field of the history of ideas, the first thing to do is to overcome the one-sidedness of recognizing motivation by interest as the only form of social conditioning of ideas. This can be done most easily by a phenomenological demon-stration of the fact that motivation by interest is merely one of many possible forms in which the adoption of certain attitudes by a psyche can be conditioned by social experience. Thus, it may be that we profess a certain economic theory or certain political ideas because they are in keeping with our interests. But surely no immediate interests are involved in our choice of a certain artistic style or style of thought; and yet these entities also do not float in thin air but come to be developed by certain groups as a result of socio-historical factors. In the case of ideas held because of a direct interest, we may speak of 'interestedness'; to designate the more indirect relation between the subject and those other ideas, we may use the parallel expression 'committedness'. In fact, it is one of the most striking features of history that a given economic system is always embedded, at least as to its origin, in a given intellectual cosmos, so that those who seek a certain economic order also seek the intellectual outlook correlated with it. When a group is directly interested in an economic system, then it is also indirectly 'committed' to the other intellectual, artistic, philosophical, etc. forms corresponding to that economic system. Thus, indirect 'committedness' to certain mental forms is the most comprehensive category in the field of the social conditioning of ideas.

Motivation by interest appears, then, as a partial case as compared to the general category of 'commitment', and it is the latter we have to resort to in most cases when we want to ascertain the relationship between 'styles of thought', 'intellectual standpoints' on the one hand, and social reality on the other. Whereas the method of 'vulgar' Marxism consists in *directly* associating even the most esoteric and spiritual products of the mind with the economic and power interests of a certain class, sociological research aiming at elucidating the total configuration of intellectual life will not emulate this crude approach; however, anxious to salvage the element of truth in the Marxist philosophy of history, it will re-examine each step postulated by this method. A beginning toward such revision will be made if one decides to use the category of motivation by interest only where interests actually can be seen at work, and not where mere 'commitment' to a *Weltanschauung* exists. At this point, we can draw upon our own sociological method which will help us recognize that this exclusive application of the category of interest is itself determined by a certain historical constellation, characterized by the predominance of the classic economic approach. If, however, the category of interest is elevated to the rank of an absolute principle, the result can be only the reduction of the role of sociology to that of reconstructing the *homo economicus*, whereas sociology in fact has to examine man as a whole. Thus, we cannot assign a style of thought, a work of art, etc., to a group as its own on the basis of an analysis of interests. We can, however, show that a certain style of thought, an intellectual standpoint, is encompassed within a system of attitudes which in turn can be seen to be related to a certain economic and power system; we can then ask which social groups are 'interested' in the emergence and maintenance of this economic and social system and at the same time 'committed' to the corresponding world outlook.

Thus, the construction of a sociology of knowledge can be undertaken only by taking a circuitous route through the concept of the *total system* of a world outlook (through cultural sociology). We cannot relate an intellectual standpoint directly to a social class; what we can do is find out the correlation between the 'style of thought' underlying a given standpoint, and the 'intellectual motivation' of a certain social group.

If we examine the history of knowledge and thought with such questions in mind, seeking to understand how it is embedded in the history of the real, social process, then we shall find at each moment not only antagonistic groups ccmbating each other, but also a conflict of opposed 'world postulates' (*Weltwollungen*). In the historical process, it is not only interests that combat interests, but world postulates compete with world postulates. And this fact is sociologically relevant, because these various 'world postulates' (of which the various 'styles of thought' are merely partial aspects) do not confront each other in a disembodied, arbitrary way; rather, each such postulate is linked to a certain group and develops within the thinking of that group. At each moment, it is just one stratum which is interested in maintaining the existing economic and social system and therefore clings to the corresponding style of thought; there are always other strata whose spiritual home is one or the other past stage of evolution, and yet others, just coming into being, which, being new, have not yet come into their own and therefore put their faith in the future. Since the different strata are 'interested in' and 'committed to' different world orders and world postulates, some of which are things of the past while others are just emerging, it is obvious that value conflicts permeate each stage of historical evolution.

That a 'style of thought' can be associated with the emergence of a certain social stratum is best demonstrated by the fact that modern rationalism (as was repeatedly pointed out) was linked to the world postulates and intellectual aspirations of the rising bourgeoisie, that later counter-currents allied themselves with irrationalism, and that a similar connection exists between romanticism and conservative aspirations. Starting from such insights, we can develop analyses of correlations between styles of thought and social strata—these, however, will be fruitful only if these attributions are not made in a static sense—e.g. by identifying rationalism with progressive and irrationalism with reactionary thought in every conceivable constellation. What we have to remember is that neither rationalism nor irrationalism (particularly in their present form) are eternal types of intellectual tendencies, and that a certain stratum is not always progressive or conservative respectively in the same sense. 'Conservative' and 'progressive' are *relative* attributes; whether a certain stratum is progressive, or conservative, or, worse still, reactionary, always depends on the direction in which the social process itself is moving. As the fundamental trend of economic and intellectual progress moves along, strata which began by being progressive may become conservative after they have achieved their ambition;

strata which at a time played a leading role may suddenly feel impelled to go into opposition against the dominant trend.

It is thus important at this point already to avoid interpreting such relative concepts as eternal characteristics; but we must make still another distinction if we want to do justice to the enormous variety of historical reality. That is, in establishing correlations between products of the mind and social strata, we must distinguish between *intellectual* and *social* stratification. We can define social strata, in accordance with the Marxian concept of class, in terms of their role in the production process; but it is impossible, in our opinion, to establish a historical parallelism between intellectual standpoints and social strata defined in this fashion. Differentiation in the world of mind is much too great to permit the identification of each current, each standpoint, with a given class.[1] Thus, we have to introduce an intermediary concept to effect the correlation between the concept of 'class', defined in terms of roles in the production process, and that of 'intellectual standpoint'. This intermediary concept is that of 'intellectual strata'. We mean by 'intellectual stratum' a group of people belonging to a certain social unit and sharing a certain 'world postulate' (as parts of which we may mention the economic system, the philosophical system, the artistic style 'postulated' by them),[2] who at a given time are 'committed' to a certain style of economic activity and of theoretical thought.[3]

We must first identify the various 'world postulates', systems of *Weltanschauung*, combating each other, and find the social groups that champion each; only when these 'intellectual strata' are specified, can we ask which 'social strata' correspond to them. Thus, it is possible to specify the groups of people who at a given moment are united in a 'conservative' outlook, and share in a common stock of ideas which are going through a ceaseless process of transformation; the sociologist of culture, however, should not be content with approaching this subject from this doctrinal point of view, but he should also ask himself which 'social classes' make up such an 'intellectual stratum'. We can understand the transformation of the various ideologies only on the basis of changes in the social composition of the intellectual stratum corresponding to them. The same applies obviously to the progressive types of *Weltanschauung*. The proletariat (to show the reverse side of the

[1] In *Wirtschaft und Gesellschaft*, Max Weber made an attempt to give a full account of the great variety of social stratification.

[2] This 'postulation' is no reflectively conscious 'willing' but an unconscious, latent trend, analogous to A. Riegl's 'art motive' (*Kunstwollen*).

[3] In a purely economic context, W. Sombart defines 'social class' in an analogous fashion; cf. *Sozialismus und Soziale Bewegung*, 8th edition, p. 1.

correlation we are dealing with) constitutes *one* class; but this one social class is divided as to the 'world postulates' of its members, as is clearly shown by the proletariat's following a number of different political parties. The only point of interest for the sociologist is this: what types of progressive world postulates exist at a given moment, what are the progressive intellectual strata adhering to them, and what social strata within the proletariat belong to these various intellectual strata?

The peculiar function of this intermediary concept, that of 'intellectual stratum', consists in making a co-ordination of intellectual configurations with social groups possible without blurring the inner differentiation either of the world of mind or of social reality. Further, we have to take the fact into account that at no moment in history does a social stratum produce its ideas, so to speak, out of thin air, as a matter of pure invention. Both conservative and progressive groups of various kinds inherit ideologies which somehow have existed in the past. Conservative groups fall back upon attitudes, methods of thought, ideas of remote epochs and adapt them to new situations; but newly emerging groups also take up at first already existing ideas and methods, so that a cross-section through the rival ideologies combating one another at a given moment also represents a cross-section through the historical past of the society in question. If, however, we focus our attention exclusively upon this 'inheritance' aspect of the story, and try to reduce to it the entire relationship between social reality and the intellectual process, we obtain an entirely wrong kind of historicism. If we look at the process of intellectual evolution and the role of social strata in it solely from this point of view, then it will seem, in fact, as if nothing happened except the unfolding of potentialities given in advance. It is, however, merely a peculiarity of the conservative conception of historicism that the continuous nature of all historical processes is interpreted as implying that everything has its origin in something temporally preceding it. The progressive variant of historicism looks at the process of evolution from the angle of the *status nascendi*.

This perspective alone enables us to see that even motifs and aspects simply taken over from a predecessor always become something different owing to this very passage itself, merely because their sponsor is a different one, and relates them to a different situation. Or, to put it more succinctly: change of function of an idea always involves a change of meaning—this being one of the most essential arguments in favour of the proposition that history is a creative medium of meanings and not merely the passive medium in which pre-existent, self-contained meanings find their realization. Thus, we have to add to our list of categories this central concept of all sociology of culture and thought, that of 'change of function'; for without this, we could produce nothing but a mere history of ideas.

We shall, however, distinguish two types of change of function; an *immanent* and a *sociological*. We speak of an *immanent* change of function (in the realm of thought, to mention only one of the fields in which this phenomenon may occur), when a concept passes from one system of ideas into another. Terms like 'ego', 'money', 'romanticism', etc. mean something different, according to the system within which they are used. By a *sociological* change of function, however, we mean a change in the meaning of a concept which occurs when that concept is adopted by a group living in a different social environment, so that the vital significance of the concept becomes different. Each idea acquires a new meaning when it is applied to a new life situation. When new strata take over systems of ideas from other strata, it can always be shown that the same words mean something different to the new sponsors, because these latter think in terms of different aspirations and existential configurations. This *social* change of function, then, is, as stated above, also a change of meaning. And although it is true that different social strata cultivating the same cultural field share the same 'germinal' ideas (this being the reason why understanding is possible from one stratum to the other), developing social reality introduces something incalculable, creatively new into the intellectual process, because the unpredictable new situations emerging within reality constitute new existential bases of reference for familiar ideas. Social strata play a creative role precisely because they introduce new intentions, new directions of intentionality, new world postulates, into the already developed framework of ideas of older strata which then appropriate them, and thus subject their heritage to a productive change of function.

Different social strata, then, do not 'produce different systems of ideas' (*Weltanschauungen*) in a crude, materialistic sense—in the sense in which lying ideologies can be 'manufactured'—they 'produce' them, rather, in the sense that social groups emerging within the social process are always in a position to project new directions of that 'intentionality', that vital tension, which accompanies all life. The reason why it is so important in studying 'immanent' changes of function of a given idea (the passage of a unit of meaning into a new system), also to observe the tensions and vital aspirations operative behind theoretical thought, and introducing antagonisms into the life of the society as a whole— the reason why it is so important to study these real tensions is that it is extremely likely that an immanent change of function is preceded by a sociological one, i.e. that shifts in social reality are the underlying cause of shifts in theoretical systems.

If the task of a sociology of knowledge is approached with these premises in mind, it will present itself in the following form: the main task consists in specifying, for each temporal cross-section of the historical process, the various systematic intellectual standpoints on which the thinking of creative individuals and groups was based. Once this is done, however, these different trends of thought should not be confronted like positions in a mere theoretical debate, but we should explore their non-theoretical, vital roots. To do this, we first have to uncover the hidden metaphysical premises of the various systematic positions; then we must ask further which of the 'world postulates' co-existing in a given epoch are the correlates of a given style of thought. When these correspondences are established, we already have identified the intellectual strata combating each other. The sociological task proper, however, begins only after this 'imman-ent' analysis is done—it consists in finding the social strata making up the intellectual strata in question. It is only in terms of the role of these latter strata within the overall process, in terms of their attitudes toward the emerging new reality, that we can define the fundamental aspirations and world postulates existing at a given time which can absorb already existing ideas and methods and subject them to a change of function—not to speak of newly created forms. Such changes of function are in no way mysterious; it is possible to determine them with sufficient exactness by combining sociological methods with those of the history of ideas. We can, for instance, go back to the historical and sociological origin of an idea and then, following its evolution, determine, so to speak, the 'angle of refraction' each time it undergoes a change of function, by specifying the new systematic centre to which the idea becomes linked, and simultaneously asking what existential changes in the real background are mirrored by that change of meaning.

As a rather familiar example, we may mention the change of function of the dialectical method—the *leitmotiv* of the present discussion. Dialectics was clearly formulated for the first time by Hegel within the framework of a conservative world postulate (we shall not discuss the earlier history of the method). When Marx took it over, it became modified in various respects. We want to mention only two of these revisions. Firstly, dialectics was 'made to stand on its feet rather than on its head', i.e. it was lifted from its idealistic context and re-interpreted in terms of social reality. Secondly, the final term of historical dynamics became the future rather than the present. Both shifts, which represent a change of meaning in the method, may be explained by the 'change of function' brought about under the impact of the vital aspirations of the proletariat which Marx made his own. We can explain the new features of the system by recalling that the life of the proletariat revolves around economic problems, and that its vital tension is directed toward the future. On the other hand, Hegel's system also may be shown to be sociologically determined. The fact that in this system the closing phase of the dynamism of history is the present mirrors the success achieved by a class which, having come into its own, merely wants to conserve what has already been accomplished.

If, then, we define the sociology of knowledge as a discipline which explores the functional dependence of each intellectual standpoint on the differentiated social group reality standing behind it, and which sets itself the task of retracing the evolution of the various standpoints, then it seems that the fruitful beginnings made by historicism may point in a direction in which further progress is possible. Having indicated the systematic premises characterizing historicism as a point of departure for a sociology of knowledge, we then went on to suggest a few methodological problems involved in this approach. At the same time, however, we also wanted to show the method in operation, and hence we described the principal 'standpoints' from which the elaboration of a sociology of knowledge may be undertaken in the present constellation. We thought that such an analysis of the present status of the problem in terms of the categories of the sociology of knowledge would contribute to give this discipline a clearer notion of itself.

IV

The Ideological and
the Sociological Interpretation
of Intellectual Phenomena*

WHAT follows is part of a more comprehensive study. In the preceding chapter,† the many meanings of the concept of ideology were discussed. In further developing these analyses, the following pages emphasize only one of the possible meanings of 'ideology', where 'ideological' refers to a certain way of looking at things.‡

One of the meanings of 'ideological' is a way of looking at ideas, in contrast to the sociological. Such a formulation emphasizes the possibility of two manners of viewing the same phenomenon and suggests that the difference between idea and ideology may lie in the difference between two ways of looking, two attitudes.¹ The same idea (in the sense of any intellectual-psychological content whatever toward which there is a conscious orientation)

* Translation of 'Ideologische und soziologische Interpretation der geistigen Gebilde', *Jahrbuch für Soziologie*, ed. G. Salomon. Karlsruhe: G. Braun, 1926, Vol II, 424–440. Translator's additions are marked by [ ]. Wherever possible, English translations of German works have been cited instead of the originals. Numbered footnotes are Mannheim's, except where otherwise indicated.—Tr.

† The chapter here mentioned by Mannheim was not published. It may have been among those Mannheim submitted to the *Jahrbuch* but did not get printed. See *I.U.*, p. 12, n. 1, 3rd par. (3rd ed., 1952, p. 56, n. 4); this is omitted in the corresponding footnote of *I.U.* Engl. (p. 53, n. 1).—Tr.

‡ In the original, this beginning paragraph appears as a footnote to the title.—Tr.

¹ Several lines of modern research have brought the phenomenon of attitudes (*Einstellungen*) into the foreground of interest. The phenomenological school in particular has made it the center of analysis. Cf. Husserl, *Ideas* [1913], New York, 1931, pp. 101 ff. But most especially Heidegger (in lectures); also Jaspers, *Psychologie der Weltanschauungen*, Berlin, 1919, pp. 43 ff.

From *Studies on the Left*, III (Summer 1963), pp. 54–66. Reprinted by permission of Routledge and Kegan Paul Ltd.

appears as 'idea' as long as one attempts to grasp and interpret it 'from within', but as 'ideology' when one considers it from points of view that lie outside of it, particularly from 'social existence'. In this sense, every idea (whether intrinsically true or false) may be considered both 'from within' and from 'existence'.

The peculiar phenomenon we encounter here is, first of all, this possibility of more than one way of looking at ideas, of more than one attitude toward them. A particular characteristic of intellectual phenomena becomes visible, namely, that they present themselves to us differently, according to the different attitudes with which they are approached. This is not true in respect to natural phenomena, even though, at first glance, it would seem so. Yet it can always be shown that when it does, we actually are not dealing with nature but with a pattern of meanings we inject into nature. To be sure, un-meaning natural objects, too, may be considered from different points of view. For instance, the difference between the sciences of physics and chemistry is fundamentally based on the fact that these disciplines consider the 'same objective reality' (say, a stone) *as*, respectively, a physical and a chemical object. That is, different formulations of problems and conceptual levels are brought to bear on the same things, thus producing different abstractions from them. But such different theoretical points of view are by no means identical with different attitudes and perspectives. They only produce, as it were, different selections from the same 'pre-scientific object', whereas a change in attitude and perspective (which precedes all theorizing) means a change in the way in which an intellectual phenomenon is penetrated and experienced. Our very 'experience' of it differs according to whether we understand it 'from within' or view it as ideology, 'from without', that is, from some existence that lies outside of it.

But what does this grasping 'from within' mean? It means that the subject, in a particular way, is absorbed by the intellectual phenomenon, that he 'lives' in it. In contrast to natural phenomena, intellectual phenomena are 'posited' in the widest (not only theoretical) sense of the word.[2] Their grasp 'from within', therefore, may also be defined as the unconditional fulfillment of the 'positing' that is prescribed in the intellectual phenomenon. Since nature (in the sense of that which is wholly un-meaning) is not posited, we cannot be absorbed by it, cannot identify with it, cannot (as it is sometimes put, though, in our opinion, too

---

[2] The intellectual phenomenon is a '*Setzung*'. Instead of saying 'posited', one might, with Dewey, say it is 'taken', or, with the existentialists, that it is a 'commitment'. Natural phenomena, by contrast, are 'unmeaning', are 'given'. —Tr.

narrowly) take any such stand on it. Hence to bring different points of view to natural objects is a purely theoretical affair, whereas to grasp an intellectual phenomenon 'from within' or 'from without' is pre-theoretical and involves the whole person. It thus is a mistake to think that the difference between intrinsic ideological interpretation and extrinsic sociological interpretation merely reflects a difference in point of view. What lies behind these different points of view and alone makes them possible is an antecedent difference in the experience of ideas, in the attitude toward them.

The best proof that this is so can probably be given by calling attention to the following. Whereas the capacity to conceive of a stone now as of a physical, now as of a chemical, object is purely intellectual, that is, is a capacity that, in principle at least, is possessed by everybody, the capacity to grasp an idea as ideological is unthinkable prior to a certain time in history. For, the accomplishment of this task requires the existence of different pre-theoretical attitudes toward intellectual matters, that is, the ability to place oneself outside their direct sphere of influence.

It should at once be stressed, however, that such a difference in attitudes is by no means the same as theoretical negation or doubt. To deny or to doubt still presupposes one's remaining within ideology, whereas the sudden experience of an idea *as* ideology places one outside the ideological sphere. This makes theoretical negation and doubt impossible, if only because in denying and doubting, the subject still (though with negative signs) fulfills the positing prescribed.[3] And precisely because to experience an idea as ideology differs from negating or doubting it, the phenomenon of 'extrinsic interpretation' can never be described by reference to theory alone, but only by recourse to the historical person and his attitudes as a whole.

Sociological analysis, then, places the object it interprets on a new conceptual plane, precisely that of sociological concepts. But the construction of different conceptual planes is not based on the adoption of different theoretical positions alone. For these positions themselves become possible only on the basis of a new attitude or perspective taken by the total phenomenological subject toward its object (the intellectual phenomenon). Furthermore, unlike natural phenomena, intellectual phenomena do not become visible in different cross-sections but offer us, as it were, different possibilities by which they may be intellectually penetrated. While the adoption of different natural-scientific points

[3] I have tried to give a more comprehensive analysis of interpretation from without and its distinction from related phenomena in my essay 'The Problem of Sociology of Knowledge' (1925) [Chap. IV in *Soc. Knowl.*].

of view increases our knowledge of the object only quantitatively, different ways of looking at intellectual phenomena and different attitudes toward them enlarge the possibilities of our experiencing them and the dimensions of our understanding them. In this respect, intellectual and affective contents are similar. Affective attitudes (love, hate, etc.), too, are pre-theoretical; they are the preconditions of complex affective experience. Nevertheless, while the intellectual penetration of intellectual matters is closely related to the psychological penetration of psychological matters, it is not identical with it—an example of the latter is the psychological penetrability of the other 'at first glance'.

The difference between idea and ideology, then (in the sense of the present study), is not merely one of point of view but is the result of a fundamentally different attitude toward the same intellectual phenomenon, of a fundamentally different way of looking at it. If I take, for instance, a theoretical statement simply as an idea, that is, 'from within', I am making the same assumptions that are prescribed in it; if I take it as ideology, that is, look at it 'from without', I am suspending, for a time, the whole complex of its assumptions, thus doing something other than what is prescribed in it at first glance.

Yet this change in attitude toward the intellectual phenomenon is only the first phase of what we have called the sociological consideration of an idea. For we do not stop at the suspension of intrinsic interpretation but, at the same time, relate the intellectual content to something we posit outside it, as the *function* of which it then appears. It is here that we encounter the essential problems of interpretation 'from without'. For, methodologically speaking, we obtain different kinds of extrinsic interpretation according to the level at which we relate intellectual phenomena to others. And the metaphysical position of a given thinker or current of thought, too, enters the theoretical elaboration of the extrinsic interpretation at this point. The reason is that ordinarily the level at which the intellectual phenomena are seen, the sphere as the function of which they are conceived, is at the same time experienced and postulated as the ontologically more real one (as the '*ens realissimum*'). We only have to think of Marx's first sentence analyzed in the preceding chapter. There we found a clear indication that conflicts inherent in the conditions of economic production are more real than those of which people become conscious in the legal and political, in short, 'ideological', spheres. The essentially sociological task consists in understanding ideas as the function of this sphere, which has been posited as real.

The sociological consideration of intellectual phenomena is a special class of extrinsic interpretation of ideas. In it, that which 'really is', the level at which ideas are to be functionalized, is that group of phenomena (to express it in Marx's words) which the British and French have lumped together under the name of 'civil society', and the anatomy of which, according to Marx, is to be found in political economy. The sociological consideration of ideas thus is a novel kind of extrinsic interpretation only in so far as the ontological accent in the experience of reality had shifted ever nearer to the economic-social level, and as particularly the eighteenth and nineteenth centuries moved ever closer to the conception of a 'positivistic' hierarchy of being. Thus behind the positivistic solution, too, lies a metaphysical decision, namely, the singling out of a certain order of experiences as the '*ens realissimum*'. From a formal point of view, however, this newer solution still moves in the old grooves, for it holds on to two characteristics of the earlier metaphysic: (a) the postulation of a hierarchy of being, and (b) the postulation of two ways of knowing that differ in dignity—on the one hand, the merely 'ideological' one, and on the other, the 'sociological' or 'dialectical' one (or however else it may be called).

Given the contemporary this-worldly, positivistic turn of extrinsic interpretation, the more economically conceived level at which ideas are functionalized may also be replaced by biological factors, such as race, or by psychological factors, such as drives for power, food, and others, as well as by higher psychological phenomena. But any such differences are secondary in comparison to the fact that the hypostatization of *some* 'positive factors' does produce a new understanding and a new interpretation of intellectual phenomena. Looked at in this larger context, their economic-sociological interpretation and functionalization are only a specific kind of positivistic extrinsic interpretation—just as the latter, in turn, is a special form of extrinsic interpretation, which is distinguished from what might be called 'idealistic' extrinsic interpretation. One need only recall Hegel's solution in order to see immediately that it contains the paradigm of such an 'idealistic' extrinsic interpretation which invites us to transcend the intended ideas, the 'representations', of the individual and to understand them in terms of a 'spirit' that is located outside of them and that unfolds 'behind their back'.

But if this is how we distinguish positivistic and idealistic extrinsic interpretations, we are uncritically adopting a dualism (with an ultimately ontological foundation) which contrasts 'spirit' and 'positivistic' development. Such a dualism, however, could find its legitimation only if one could show that this positivistic-naturalistic extrinsic interpretation is in fact in a position to grasp the ideas (which originally are given in their immanence), *not* by reference to a system of meanings, but by reference to 'un-meaning' positive factors. When we look more closely, however, we discover that the presumed difference between idealistic and positivistic extrinsic interpretations is not nearly so radical. For, the sphere on the basis of which intellectual phenomena are understood, in reference to which they are functionalized, is, even for the positivist, not 'un-meaning', natural, 'material', because he is forced to construct a system of meanings in his positive sphere exactly as the idealist in his. We must only recall that even the most radical 'materialistic' sociologist, if he wants to understand and interpret ideologies in economic terms, is forced to conceive of economics as such a system. He, no less than Hegel, must present economic and social history, in terms of which he interprets ideas, as a meaningful order, as a historical plan. For this reason, we do not think that the contrast between idealistic and positivistic extrinsic interpretation is, in the final analysis, philosophical; we rather consider it simply as an indication that in our time a certain type of extrinsic interpretation of ideas has been separated as 'positivistic' from the 'idealistic' type. We view this separation as expressive of the fact that a certain sphere of the given has received a special ontological accent.

Summarizing what has been said thus far: The contrast between idea and ideology may be conceived of as the contrast between ways of looking at the same intellectual phenomenon. In this sense, the intellectual phenomenon appears as idea in so far as it is considered 'from within'[4]; as ideology, in so far as it is considered 'from without' and is taken as the function of an 'existence' posited outside of it. 'Extrinsic interpretations' are either idealistic or positivistic, according to whether contexts of meaning or 'positive' contexts are posited as the ultimate existence in reference to which ideas are functionalized.

But what does this functionalizing mean? It means, in the first place, the uncovering of all existentially conditioned relationships that alone make possible the emergence and the impact of an intellectual phenomenon.

There are, however, two kinds of conditions that make the emergence of, say, a theory possible (in our examples we shall

[4] In order to avoid misunderstandings: it is because of deep-rooted linguistic usage that we, too, call the intrinsic interpretation 'ideological'. As long as one takes a purely ideological (immanent) attitude, the ideological character of intellectual phenomena does not become visible. It follows that on an ideological view, ideas appear as ideas, and only on a sociological view, as ideologies. Otto Bauer speaks of an immanent vs. a transcendent history of ideas ('Das Weltbild des Kapitalismus', in *Der lebendige Marxismus, Kautsky-Festschrift* [1924], pp. 408 f.).

limit ourselves to theories). These are purely causal preconditions, on the one hand, and presuppositions in terms of meaning, on the other. Causal preconditions of the emergence of a theory are, for instance, the existence of an intellectual apparatus that functions in a causally determined manner and by virtue of which the theory is being thought and responded to. (Among existential preconditions is the existence of a certain associative mechanism, etc.) On the other hand, the emergence of a theory has prerequisites in terms of meaning—for instance, the existence or postulation of premises whence to draw conclusions.

These two types of presuppositions, 'un-meaning' causal preconditions of genesis, and immanent presuppositions of meaning, have rightly been distinguished. It has also been properly held that it is impossible to confirm or refute the validity of, for instance, a proposition on the ground of its causal, un-meaning preconditions. But it is erroneous to locate sociological (or other extrinsic) interpretations in this sphere of un-meaning causal explanations and to apply to them the axiom that genesis can determine nothing about meaning and validity.

What must be stressed is that not all genetic 'derivations' are un-meaning: there are not only genetic *explanations*, which are, but also genetic *interpretations*. Nor are all extrinsic interpretations that functionalize meaning with reference to a given existence un-meaning and thus 'mere' causal explanations. Only if these distinctions are admitted will it not be overlooked that (for instance) the sociological functionalization of a system of meanings, though not an immanent interpretation, nevertheless is not an un-meaning causal explanation either but, on the contrary, a specific, novel interpretation of meaning with respect to existence.[5]

This assertion—that most sociological explanations represent a particular type of interpretation and cannot be considered causal explanations in terms of un-meaning phenomena—may be clarified by the analysis of a concrete example. In his *Deutsche Geschichte* (Berlin, 1922, p. 81), [Franz] Mehring writes as follows about Kant:

Act in such a way as to treat mankind, both in your person and in the person of everybody else, always as an end, never only as a means.—To the historical view, this axiom of Kant's immediately appears as the ideological expression of the economic fact that the bourgeoisie, in order to obtain an object of exploitation suitable for its purposes, not only had to use the working class as a means, but also had to consider it as an end, that is, had to free it, in the name of human liberty and dignity, from the feudal fetters of hereditary subjection and bondage. And this is what Kant has in mind, for he demands full freedom and independence only for the citizens of the state, but not for its subjects, among whom he counts the whole working class.

[5] In the original, the following three paragraphs constitute a footnote.—Tr.

Whether or not this interpretation is substantively correct may remain quite undecided here. But it may serve us as a typical scheme of sociological interpretation, which clearly shows that the intrinsic meaning of a statement (Kant's conception of freedom) is interpreted sociologically by being conceived of as part (as 'ideological expression') of a more comprehensive system of meanings (namely, of a capitalism based on free labor and class rule).

Kant's proposition receives new meaning by being shown as it functions in the service of a 'social reality' conceived of as a context of meaning. But this formal scheme characterizes most statements advanced in cultural sociology. For even if the Marxist element is removed and the economically oriented concept of society replaced by another, or if factors like race or others are postulated in the 'substructure', still, all of these can be used for a sociological 'explanation' only if they are conceived of as contexts of meaning.

Here we do not wish to examine the question whether *every* sociological explanation is an interpretation. We only observe that the great majority of them follow the abstract scheme just sketched and therefore belong (or at least, also belong) in the problem area of interpretation. Max Weber and Troeltsch viewed sociology chiefly as an explanatory science. The question how consistently such a view can actually be acted on cannot be analyzed here.

Every sociological 'explanation', then, whenever it functionalizes intellectual phenomena—e.g., those found in a given historical group—with respect to a 'social existence' that lies behind them, postulates this social existence as a context of meaning more comprehensive than, though different from, those phenomena, whose ultimate significance is to be understood in relation to this context. To give a further example: Marx[6] tried to account for the eighteenth-century explanatory method that always took the individual as its point of departure by reference to the nature of bourgeois society with its free competition. But this is not an explanation of theoretical axioms by un-meaning existence. Instead, it is the interpretation of the ultimate axioms of a historical type of thought by reference to an underlying, even more comprehensive, higher order of existence conceived of as a context of meaning.

Sociological extrinsic interpretation does not serve in this case to abandon the sphere of meaning as such. But only by abandoning *immanent* interpretation is it possible to see those

[6] *Introduction to the Critique of Political Economy* [1859], Chicago, 1904, pp. 265 ff.

meaningful existential presuppositions which, although the theory itself that is to be interpreted was not capable of seeing them, nevertheless were the presuppositions (albeit not immanent) of its validity.

The functionalization of an intellectual phenomenon with respect to an underlying meaningful existential order bestows new meaning on the phenomenon. It is the miracle of historical thinking that we are able to look back and thus, in retrospect, to grasp a past intellectual content or idea as ideology, that is, to functionalize it by reference to an existence that now becomes meaningful to us—to see new meaning in past content. Indeed, our historical thinking does not progress in the sense that we simply immanently accept or reject past contexts of meaning. Essentially it progresses in the sense that, being pushed on by history, we gain a certain distance from past contents and grasp them 'from without', where earlier we understood them 'from within'. Once they have become visible for us in their contours, we functionalize them with respect to a social-existential totality that we conceive of as a context of meaning.

To be sure, this interpretation in terms of an existence seen as meaningful is not the same as the interpretation, say, of a philosophical system in terms of another philosophical system. For this reason, we want to call the former *existential interpretation*. Furthermore, the meaning that the phenomenon to be interpreted comes to have by being functionalized is not the 'meaning' of the 'meaning' of a statement. We therefore want to call it *functional meaning*. Yet there is an essential affinity between the two because in both cases, meaning is understood in terms of meaning. This fully justifies us in talking about a form of *interpretation* [rather than explanation].

At this juncture, there arises a more profound question about sociological interpretation. It may be formulated as follows. Is a simple coordination between this functional meaning and intrinsic meaning possible? Can one be discussed in terms of the other? Can the functional meaning of an idea, of an intrinsic meaning, refute, cancel, negate, or, for that matter, support that idea? If so, the relationship between the two kinds of meaning must be ascertained; if not, they lie on different planes and are wholly heterogeneous. In this case, immanent meaning can be refuted only by immanent meaning; an idea, only by an idea.

These are the two alternatives. The first stresses the relevance of functional meaning. It insists that extrinsic interpretation, while relativizing 'immanent meaning' by functionalizing it, at the same time bestows a new sense on it, precisely by incorporating it into a higher context of meaning. If one pursues this train of thought (in line with historicism), one will have to say that whatever at a given time is the latest theory, is accepted immanently, as an idea, in the same way as those 'ideas' were once accepted that extrinsic interpretation has since relativized as ideology. That is, the most highly developed system in which we ourselves are caught at any one time can be grasped only as idea, and it takes 'existing', social and historical 'existing-on', for the higher meaning of our own view of the world some day to reveal itself.

This is the position one will adopt if one reflects on the peculiar character of historical knowledge and wants to incorporate its actual form of movement into one's conception of thought. One will also adopt this position if one takes cognizance of the peculiarity of historical knowledge which, unlike natural-scientific knowledge, does not above all develop immanently but must always pass through historical social existence. It always arises in relation to a comprehensive intellectual situation for the sake of which alone it originally exists. Precisely for this reason, theories do not refute each other simply immanently: they can cancel each other only in a 'real dialectic', that is, existentially. On this view, one intellectual existential situation overcomes another; and a theory overcomes another theory only as part of such an existential situation.

The second alternative will be proposed by those who hold that the existential element in sociological and historical thinking can be neglected and, therefore, that historical and all other existential thinking should be construed in complete analogy with purely theoretical thinking. Representatives of such a position insist on the complete separation between immanent and functional meaning and on their incommensurability. But this separation of the two kinds of meaning in turn offers two possible alternatives. One will either have to say that intellectual phenomena can be investigated in regard to their truth value and can be related to other 'ideas' only through immanent interpretation —in other words, that there is a timeless discussion of theories— in which case one will be inclined to consider functional meaning as knowable but, at bottom, irrelevant. Or, one will consider only functional meaning as valid and reject any discussion on an immanent basis as 'merely ideological'—as Marx did.

Which of the three routes indicated should be taken cannot be decided here, for this is an epistemological and logical question that need not occupy us in the present context. Here we have only wanted to call attention to the fact that the most important variant of the concept of ideology which has been analyzed in this chapter—ideology as a way of looking at things—offers a novel kind of interpretation that raises numerous unsolved questions. Although usually not thought through, these questions are always hovering about sociological interpretation.

TYPES OF INTERPRETATION

We now wish to locate the sociological among other kinds of interpretation. Since, as far as we know, no typology of them exists,[7] we must try to construct one which, it should be noted, is bound to be preliminary, rather than complete. A complete one can be established only once the different kinds of interpretation have been explored by means of numerous concrete studies in various areas of intellectual endeavor.

In order to find the most comprehensive principle of classification, we begin with the contrast that we found sketched by Marx as that between the ideological and the sociological consideration of cultural phenomena and that we have called, in an enlarged sense, their intrinsic and their extrinsic interpretation.

We have seen that intrinsic interpretation includes several types (of which more presently), just as we have observed several types of extrinsic interpretation. The first group in our list, then, contains *intrinsic interpretations*.

(1) Interpretations that try to ascertain *intended meaning*. We recall that by intrinsic interpretations we understand those ways of grasping intellectual phenomena that for this purpose do not leave the realm of the 'ideological'. Simplest among them is the type that limits itself to the clearest possible grasp of what Max Weber called the 'subjectively intended meaning'.[8] It is distinguished from the ordinary understanding of meaning only in so far as it tries to locate and critically ascertain it by comparing different passages and documents of a work. Its aim is to comprehend the 'sense' of that work, or to present a doctrine in the sense in which the author himself intended it and wanted it understood.[9]

(2) A second kind of interpretation may be called *objective*. Like all intrinsic interpretations, it does not leave the ideological level. It does not ask, however, how the author himself intended his meaning but, starting from the author's own premises, tries to

[7] In lectures to which the present analysis owes many suggestions, Dr. Adalbert Fried first tried to develop such a typology, calling attention to several of the types that follow.

[8] Max Weber contrasts 'subjectively intended meaning' with 'objectively valid meaning'. Cf., e.g., *Gesammelte Aufsätze zur Wissenschaftslehre*, p. 403 n. [also *The Theory of Social and Economic Organization*, ed. Talcott Parsons, New York, 1947, Chap. I].

[9] We limit our examples to the possibilities of different interpretations of a 'philosophical system'.

draw correct conclusions from them. (Example: 'To understand Kant better than he understood himself.')

(3) A third kind of intrinsic interpretation aims at understanding an author in terms of *another system*, or other axioms, than his own. (Example: the various interpretations of Plato on the basis of modern philosophical systems—see, e.g., [Paul] Natorp's book on Plato.)[10] Ahistorically oriented interpreters will always claim this kind of interpretation to be absolute, that is, oriented toward a system of absolute truths. Since we do not wish to enter into an epistemological discussion, we only observe that, whereas from a non-historicist standpoint, there does exist this challenge of an 'absolute interpretation', for the historicist, 'absolute interpretation' can only mean interpreting a system in terms of another.

The kinds of interpretation mentioned thus far may be contrasted as *systematic* with those that are *genetic* and to which we now turn.[11] We distinguish two general types of genetic interpretation: those undertaken with an immanent (ideological) attitude, and those presupposing a consideration 'from without'. We begin with the first type.

(4) Interpretations that try to ascertain the *genesis of a meaning*. This is one of the oldest kinds of interpretation; but in the course of intellectual history it has undergone the most varied changes. It is directed, not at the factual genesis of a given meaning, but at its origin. It is attempted in cosmogonies and mythologies and lives on, though in modified form, in the various justifications of natural right. Illustrations are Robinsonades in economic theory or contract theories in political philosophy which, properly understood, are theories concerning the genesis of meanings, not concerning origins in positive history. The same kind of interpretation obtains in the field of logic, in the attempt, for instance, at a typological derivation of all possible classes of epistemological or metaphysical theories and at the understanding of the intellectual phenomenon under analysis in terms of its 'logical locus'.[12] The same kind of interpretation, however, is possible not only in the theoretical sphere but also in art. Here an illustration is the effort to understand, say, a gate or a cupola in reference to all possible artistic solutions of the relevant, ultimately technical,

[10] E[rich] Rothacker, too, has recently called attention to this type.

[11] This bifurcation coincides by no means with the division into intrinsic and extrinsic interpretations.

[12] Examples: [Wilhelm] Dilthey, *Die Typen der Weltanschauung und ihre Ausbildung in den metaphysischen Systemen*[1911]; N[ikolai] Hartmann, *Grundzüge einer Metaphysik der Erkenntnis*, Berlin, Leipzig, 1924; K. Mannheim, 'Structural Analysis of Epistemology' [1922]; [Chap. I, pp. 15–73, in *Soc. Soc. Psych.*].

tasks, and to determine a given solution by reference to its aesthetic locus within all possible types.

(5) Distinct from the preceding class of interpretations is that which aims at genesis in the manner of the *history of ideas*. In its crude form, it is mere history of motifs; in its more complex version, history of problems.[13] Non-theoretical fields, too, may be studied from this point of view.[14] This interpretation in terms of the history of problems is distinguished from that of the genesis of meaning in so far as the factual historical genesis is wholly irrelevant for the former, whereas the latter, by contrast, largely follows positive historical developments. It tries to account for the various elements of the system to be interpreted by taking them out of the unique and systematic context by virtue of which they are imbedded in that system, and relating them to a problem unfolding in history. The answer to the question toward which problems such an approach is oriented depends, of course, on the concerns of the individual student taking this approach. In short, this interpretation, too, is genetic, but is still 'from within'.

(6) A particular transition between genetic and systematic interpretations, as well as between intrinsic and extrinsic interpretations, is made by those types of interpretation that we should like to call interpretations in terms of immanent, or *ideological*, *totality*. While not leaving the ideological plane, they do leave the specific sphere in which the intellectual phenomenon under analysis is located. Thus, a given philosophy is not understood in terms of philosophy alone, nor a given art in terms of art alone, but by reference to the ideological totality of the age concerned. These interpretations try to understand phenomena by reference to the relevant total world views. We wish to distinguish two types.

(a) One we have called *documentary interpretation* (in our essay 'On the Interpretation of *Weltanschauung*').[15] Its characteristic features are the reconstruction of the totality by means adjusted to handling the sphere of the irrational and the attempt thereby to understand and interpret the phenomenon under analysis. Spengler's morphology may serve as an example.

(b) The *rationalizing method* interprets phenomena by reference to the total intellectual process. It differs from the preceding type by creating an over-all synthesis through a rationalization so rigorous as to do violence, usually, to the specific character of concrete phenomena. In view of his method of synthesizing history

---

[13] E.g., W[ilhelm] Windelband, *A History of Philosophy*.

[14] E.g., R[udolf] Unger, 'Literaturgeschichte als Problemgeschichte', *Schriften der Königsberger Gelehrtengesellschaft*, I, 1, Berlin, 1924.

[15] 1921–22, Chap. II, pp. 33–83, in *Soc. Knowl.*—Tr.

that is patterned after the model of logic, Hegel might be cited as an example; in other respects, however, his work must be identified as idealistic extrinsic interpretation.

All interpretations discussed thus far have in common the attempt at grasping the phenomenon to be interpreted from within the ideological sphere itself. Those which remain to be dealt with have been more thoroughly analyzed in the preceding chapter. We have found them to be characterized by the interpretation of the intellectual phenomenon in terms of an *existence* postulated *outside* the sphere of the intrinsic meaning of that phenomenon.

We again wish to distinguish two types. The first tries to explain intellectual contents by reference to un-meaning existence. The other functionalizes them by reference to an existence outside them but conceives of this existence as a context of meaning.

(7) The first group—purely *causal explanations*—is listed here only because of the clear contrast with the second. For causal explanations are not, properly speaking, interpretations, but determinations of un-meaning causal nexuses. They are concerned with the ascertainment of all those processes which, in themselves un-meaning, that is, not understandable, can merely be observed in their regularity; while they are preconditions, they are not presuppositions of the context of meaning to be interpreted. Here belong the efforts of explanatory psychology, biology, etc.[16]

(8) In contrast to this group of extrinsic interpretations that try to grasp meaning by reference to un-meaning existence, there are those that we have identified as interpretations by reference to *meaningful existence*. We have distinguished the two types of them as, (a) the idealistic, (b) the positivistic, functionalization of phenomena. Sociological interpretation is a certain variant of the second of these. Among intrinsic interpretations, we have singled out those that proceed in terms of immanent, or ideological, totality. The last classes of interpretations now under analysis likewise proceed in terms of a totality, but the totality is existential. They take the entire ideological sphere, together with the social

---

[16] Max Weber, too, excludes certain explanations from 'understanding sociology': 'What interests understanding sociology in them is not, however, the physiological and the formerly so-called "psychological" phenomena, such as pulse curves or shifts in reaction time, and the like, nor the purely psychic data, e.g., the combinations of feelings of tension, pleasure, and displeasure, by means of which they can be characterized' (*Gesammelte Aufsätze zur Wissenschaftslehre*, pp. 406 ff. [*The Theory of Social and Economic Organization, op. cit.*, pp. 93 and 101 ff.]). Max Weber requires for sociology 'understandable explanation' (*Gesammelte Aufsätze zur Wissenschaftslehre*, pp. 404 ff.). The whole problem of what is meant by this, of the extent to which sociology is explanatory rather than interpretive, or where interpretation begins, cannot, as was mentioned before, be treated here, but constitutes the topic of a special inquiry.

existence that lies behind it, as a unit, and thus represent the highest stage of total interpretation as such.

Here we ought also to discuss those kinds of interpretation that try to understand and interpret a given phenomenon by reference to the context of life and experience of, (a) an individual (biographical method), and (b) a historical social group. But it would lead too far to relate 'understanding' individual and collective psychology to (for instance) economic and sociological extrinsic interpretation and to tackle the general problem of the relationship between 'understanding' psychology and 'understanding' sociology.

Instead, we now wish to group the kinds of interpretation discussed in tabular form.

I. Interpretations Based on an 'Intrinsic Consideration'
(Ideological Interpretations)
A. Systematic Interpretations
    (1) Interpretations of subjectively intended meaning
    (2) Objective interpretations
    (3) Interpretations in terms of other systems
B. Genetic Interpretations
    (a) Genetic Interpretations that Trace Meaning to Meaning
        (4) Interpretations in terms of the genesis of meaning
        (5) History of ideas
        (6) Interpretations in terms of immanent ideological totality
            1. Documentary interpretations
            2. Rationalizing reconstructions of totality

II. Interpretations Based on an 'Extrinsic Consideration'
    (b) Interpretations that Trace Meaning to Un-Meaning Existence (Causal Explanations)
        (7) Various types of causal explanation (not properly interpretations)
    (c) Interpretations that Trace Meaning to Meaningful Existence
        (8) Interpretations in terms of meaningful total existence
            1. Idealistic
            2. Positivistic (sociological)
                a. In the substructure the concept of society
                b. In the substructure drives, etc.
            3. Interpretations in 'understanding'-individual and 'understanding'-collective psychology

Even this inventory of the most important kinds of interpretation shows the peculiarity of intellectual phenomena, which is that they can be approached from many different angles. It also shows that the kinds listed, of which the most modern is the sociological, cannot be fixed for all time. For they rise and change along with the historical development of consciousness and thus offer the possibility of an ever increasing and transforming penetration of the intellectual world.

V

Conservative Thought

INTRODUCTION

1. *Styles of thought*

THERE are two main ways of writing the history of thought. On the one hand there is what might be called the 'narrative' way, which simply sets out to show the passage of ideas from one thinker to another, and to tell in epic fashion the story of their development. On the other hand there is the way with which we want to experiment here, which is based on the recently developed sociology of knowledge.[1]

At the heart of this method is the concept of a *style of thought*. The history of thought from this point of view is no mere history of ideas, but an analysis of different *styles of thought* as they grow and develop, fuse and disappear; and the key to the understanding of changes in ideas is to be found in the changing social background, mainly in the fate of the social groups or classes which are the 'carriers' of these styles of thought.

Anglo-Saxon sociology has developed a concept very similar to the German 'style of thought' in the term '*habit of thought*', and although there are considerable similarities there are also very great differences which we cannot ignore. The term 'habit of thought' simply expresses the fact that people automatically use established patterns not merely in their overt behaviour but in their thought too. In most of our intellectual responses we are not creative but repeat certain statements the content and form of which we have taken over from our cultural surroundings either in early childhood or in later stages of our development, and which we apply automatically in appropriate situations. Thus they are the products of conditioning just as are our other habits. The term is unsatisfactory, however, because it only covers

From *Essays on Sociology and Social Psychology* (New York: Oxford University Press, 1953), pp. 74–164. Reprinted by permission of Routledge and Kegan Paul Ltd.

one aspect of the phenomenon in question. Our concept of a 'style of thought' is similar to it in so far as it also starts with the assumption that individuals do not *create* the patterns of thought in terms of which they conceive the world, but take them over from their groups. But our concept is meant to imply a less mechanical attitude to the history of thought. If thought developed simply through a process of habit-making, the same pattern would be perpetuated for ever, and changes and new habits would necessarily be rare. A more careful observation of the history of thought makes it clear, however, that in a differentiated, and especially in a dynamic, society the patterns of human thought are continually changing, and if we want to do justice to these various forms of thought, we shall have to invoke some such category as 'style', since 'habit-making' will not carry us far enough.

It is, indeed, the history of art which provides us with a term capable of doing justice to the special nature of history of thought. There, too, the concept of 'style' has always played an important role, in that it made possible the classification of both the similarities and the dissimilarities of different forms of art. Everyone will accept the notion that art develops in 'styles', and that these 'styles' originate at a certain time and in a certain place, and that as they grow their characteristic formal tendencies develop in a certain way. Modern history of art has developed a very thorough method of classifying the principal 'styles' of art, and of reconstructing, within these styles, the slow process of change in which small modifications gradually culminate in a complete transformation of style. The method has become so exact that it is now nearly always possible to date a work of art accurately, simply by analysing its formal elements. The trained historian of art will always be able to say, even if a work of art is unknown to him: 'This must have been painted at such and such a date by a painter of such and such a school.' That a statement of this kind will not be mere guesswork is guaranteed by the fact that art does in fact develop in 'styles', and that within the styles there is a gradual change from one phase to another which makes it possible to 'place' an unknown work of art.

Now it is our contention that human thought also develops in 'styles', and that there are different schools of thought distinguishable by the different ways in which they use different thought patterns and categories. Thus it should be just as possible to 'place' an anonymous piece of writing as an anonymous work of art, if we only took the trouble to reconstruct the different styles of a given epoch and their variations from individual to individual.

Although the very rough division of thought into 'medieval', 'Renaissance', 'liberal' and 'romanticist' schools, as familiar

in the history of philosophy or literature, may give the impression
that the concept of 'styles of thought' is already generally accepted,
we are for the most part prevented from recognizing their existence
by two assumptions. One is that Thought is one, the same for all
men, except for errors or deviations which are of only secondary
importance. At the other extreme, there is the assumption (which
in fact contradicts the first one) that the individual thinks independently and in isolation from his fellows. Thus the unique
qualities of each individual's thought are overemphasized, and
the significance of his social *milieu* for the nature of his thought
is ignored. Applied to the history of art, this would mean either
on the one hand that there is nothing but art as such, or on the
other hand, that the individual artist is an absolutely unique,
self-contained unit. Although we can neither deny the value of
thinking about art in general, nor, on the other hand, ignore the
differences between individual artists or the particular contributions made by each of them, the most important unit must
nevertheless be the *style* of an epoch, against the background of
which the special contribution of each individual stands out and
acquires its significance.

But this intermediary level between the most abstract and the
most concrete is just what is lacking in the history of thought.
We are blind to the existence of styles of thought because our
philosophers have made us believe that thought does not develop
as part and parcel of the historical process but comes down to
humanity as a kind of absolute entity; and our literary historians
who have written monographs on the great literary personalities
like to persuade themselves that the ultimate fountainhead of all
thought is the personality of the individual. The former school
makes the history of thought appear artificially homogeneous and
indiscriminate, while the latter atomizes it. It is due to this lack
of interest in this intermediary level that our tools for distinguishing styles of thought are not developed. We do not notice vital
differences in styles of thought because we do not believe in their
existence. Were we to take the trouble to watch the innumerable
slight changes in the development of the mode of thought of a
group throughout its history, the artificially imposed homogeneity or the indiscriminate atomization would give way to a
proper differentiation.

This is exactly what we want to try to do in the pages which
follow. We want to look at the thinkers of a given period as representatives of different styles of thought. We want to describe
their different ways of looking at things as if they were reflecting
the changing outlook of their groups; and by this method we hope
to show both the inner unity of a style of thought and the slight

variations and modifications which the conceptual apparatus of the whole group must undergo as the group itself shifts its position in society. This will mean that we shall have to examine all the concepts used by the thinkers of all the different groups existing in any particular epoch very carefully, in order to see whether they do not perhaps use identical terms with different meanings. Thus the *analysis of meanings* will be the core of our technique. Words never signify the same thing when used by different groups even in the same country, and slight variations of meaning provide the best clues to the different trends of thought in a community.

2. *The relationship between styles of thought and their social background*

Before developing further our method of demonstrating that styles of thought exist as relatively independent units, we must say a few words about the social 'carriers' of these styles. Just as a style of art cannot be fully described without an account of the artistic school and of the social group it represents, so we can never really understand changes in a style of thought unless we study the social groups which are the carriers of these changes. This relationship between a style of thought and its social carrier is not a simple one. It may be true that ultimately great changes in the class stratification of society are responsible for the broader changes in styles of thought; but when it comes to more detailed changes this general hypothesis needs modification. The main indication that there is some connection between the existence and fate of social groups on the one hand, and certain styles of thought on the other, is that the sudden breakdown of a style of thought will generally be found to correspond to the sudden breakdown of the groups which carried it; similarly, to the amalgamation of two styles of thought there corresponds an amalgamation of the groups. But there are reasons for thinking that this link between styles of thought and their carriers exists not only at the turning points of history in times of great social crisis. The fate of the group is apparently reflected in even the smallest change in the development of a style of thought.

3. *'Basic intentions'*

Any study in styles of thought characteristic of the first half of the nineteenth century must start with the fact that the French Revolution acted as a catalysing agent both in relation to different types of political action and to different styles of thought.

What we have so far said implies that a style of thought embraces more than one field of human self-expression; it embraces not only politics, but art, literature, philosophy, history, and so on. It implies further that the dynamic force which is behind its changing character lies deep below the concrete surface of the various ways of self-expression.

The history of art became a scientific discipline when it became the history of *styles of art* (*Stilgeschichte*). An exact description of each different style of art only became possible when Riegl introduced his concept of 'art motive,' or *Kunstwollen*, by which he meant the striving for a certain form of art, of which every style is the expression. This concept permitted him to refer all the works of art of a particular period to a basic and for the most part completely unconscious conception, in the spirit of which all the artists of the period appear to have created their works. He did not describe these art motives, these strivings behind the different styles of art, in a vague subjective way. He showed them at work in the different works of art of the period. He analysed them carefully, showing their growth, development and decay, and showing how they sometimes fused and intermingled with each other.

The concept which we wish to introduce here of a *basic intention* lying behind each style of thought is in many ways similar to that of Riegl's art motive, although different in certain important respects. In the first place it does not refer to art, but it expresses the idea that different ways of approach to the world are ultimately at the bottom of different ways of thinking. This basic drive determines the character of a style of thought. It manifests itself in the documents and utterances characteristic of that style. But whereas to Riegl this principle of style (this art motive) is something which needs no further causal explanation and has no particular social roots, the sociologist cannot assume that the basic intentions at work in the different styles have come 'out of the blue'. We must take it as axiomatic that they are themselves 'in the making' so to speak, and that their history and fate is in many ways linked up with the fate of the groups which must be considered as their social carriers. Riegl was aiming at a pure '*Geistesgeschichte*'—a history of ideas and nothing more. Whereas in his view it was an unattached spirit which by some miracle communicated its decrees to us, the contention put forward here is that although the basic art motive can be detected in immanent analysis as the formal principle (*Gestaltprinzip*) of certain schools, it also can be shown as something ultimately born out of the struggles and conflicts of human groups. It can be used on occasion as an immanent principle to demonstrate that the mind does not work in an atomistic way, piling up shapeless experiences; but we must realize that, even in the process of experiencing, certain determining principles derived from the group are at work in the individual which shape his potential experience and knowledge. These determining principles can be approached by asking ourselves what are the social causes (lying outside pure *Geistesgeschichte*) which have produced them.

4. A concrete example: German conservatism in the first half of the nineteenth century

The next task is to find suitable material on which to try out this new method. We have chosen the development of conservative thought in Germany in the first half of the nineteenth century. This choice above all presents us with a limited task, as it focuses the analysis upon one period, one country, and one social group. This has the major advantage that it is possible to acquire all the published and otherwise accessible utterances of the group in question. Thus the continuity of the thought style can be fully and accurately reconstructed, and its connections with the social groups behind it can be more easily revealed. This choice is further justified by the fact that after the French Revolution, there developed what we may call a 'polarizing' tendency in thought—that is to say, styles of thought developed in very clear-cut extremes. The dividing issue was the political differences which developed under pressure of the events of the French Revolution. Different styles of thought developed along party lines, so that we can speak of 'liberal' and 'conservative' styles of thought, to which we shall later have to add the 'socialist' style. Now this polarizing tendency was especially marked in Germany. In Germany there has always existed a tendency to go to extremes in pushing logical arguments to their ultimate conclusions—a tendency which has not existed in such a marked fashion in the European countries outside Germany. This difference will be made clear by the example of romanticism.

Romanticism is a European phenomenon which emerged at approximately the same time in all countries. It arose partly as a reaction to identical circumstances and identical problems presented by a rationalized capitalist world, and partly as a result of secondary ideological influences. Thus the basic cause of this widespread historical factor is a common one—viz. the general similarity of the total situation in the various occidental countries. But it is never exactly the same in any two countries and always varies according to the social and cultural peculiarities of the different nations. It is striking to note, even in a comparison of different romantic writers, that, for instance, whereas the movement developed in France through the medium of poetry, in Germany it obtained its special expression in philosophy. Romantic poetry is less characteristic of German romanticism than is German romantic philosophy. This is merely a symptom of the fact that in Germany reactions on the philosophical level to changes in the social and intellectual substructure are far more intense than in other countries. As Marx already pointed out, the key to the understanding of modern development lies in a realization that Germany experienced the French Revolution on the philosophical plane.[1]

Just as the centre of gravity of German romantic idealism was its philosophy, German counter-revolution, or the 'opposite of the revolution' (to use a French traditionalist term)[2] developed its challenge to liberal-revolutionary thought in its logical and philosophical implications more completely than in any other country. If France played the role of radical reconstructor of all the enlightened and rationalistic elements in consciousness, and thus became the acknowledged bearer of 'abstract' thought, it is also possible to say that Germany played a complementary role in so far as she turned conservative, organic, historical thought into a weapon, giving it at the same time an inner consistency and logic of its own. Even this ideological difference between the two countries is rooted in certain social and historical factors.[3] It is usual to consider England as the typical home of evolutionary development, and the Romantics especially have impressed us with the conservative aspect of this gradualism by presenting England as both evolutionary and conservative. This is doubtless correct to a certain extent—especially if England is contrasted with France, which is in fact the typical radical revolutionary country of the new era. But these evolutionary features are also characteristic of the development of Germany. In Germany there has been no revolution (in the radical French sense), but at most internal growing pains and temporary disturbances. However, gradualism in England is based on the fact that the conservative strata possessed an enormous elasticity and adaptability to new circumstances, and could therefore always ensure in advance the maintenance of their power. The evolutionary character of German development, on the other hand, rested on the strong pressure of the ruling groups on the lower strata, preventing revolution. The existence of this strong barrier against internal disturbances of all kinds is almost certainly connected with the fact that the military set constituted the nucleus of the German social body. (This in its turn is connected with the geographical

1 Cf. *Zur Kritik der Hegelschen Rechtsphilosophie*, vol. I, pp. 389 ff., posthumous works by Marx and Engels, ed. Mehring.

2 Cf. de Maistre, 'Nous ne voulons pas la contre-révolution mais le contraire de la révolution.'

3 Cf. Ernst Troeltsch, *Der Historismus und seine Probleme*, vol. 1, Tübingen, 1922; *Naturrecht und Humanität in der Weltpolitik*, Berlin, 1923; P. R. Rohden, 'Deutscher und französischer Konservativismus', in *Dioskuren*, vol. 3, pp. 90–138.

situation, especially of Prussia between two enemy countries, which naturally led to the formation of a military state). And this meant a strong backing for both the conservative movement and its intellectual and emotional development.

This difference in the character of the development of the two societies, evolutionary in both cases, in so far as it was free from sudden eruptions, yet so essentially different in reality, must have had an effect on the form and structure of their respective ideologies. It is most clearly reflected in the political antagonisms as we noticed them emerge at the beginning of the period with which we are concerned. For a very long time in Germany, liberalism had no hold on conservatism, and influenced it very little. We have to wait until Stahl before we can detect the first traces of any liberal influence on conservatism. Up to that time, the two currents stood in sharp contrast to each other. On the other hand, the relations between Whigs and Tories in England up to 1790 were such that it is hardly possible to express them in German terms at all. In particular, what were known in Germany as the 'Liberals' in no way corresponded to the English Whigs. That the basic intention, the practical social motives behind conservatism were manifest in so sharp and pure a form in German thought, must be partly attributed to this almost antithetical structure of German political life, which produced a situation in which even the partial interpenetration of parties and social strata as it occurred in England was impossible. Further, of even greater importance was the ability of German conservatism to maintain itself intact in doubtful periods, and the fact that whereas, for a long time, conservatism developed quite independently of liberalism, liberalism allowed itself to be penetrated by conservative elements. So far as we are in a position to judge, England never showed such a sharp polarization into extremes, even in the later period when the French Revolution had played its part in sharpening social relations there.

Further, in Germany, quite half a century of uninterrupted intellectual development stood behind conservatism. It had therefore had time to educate itself and to equip itself philosophically without having to cope with the demands of a parliamentary life which, by continually embroiling it in factional strife, would certainly have interfered with its purity and consistency.[1] As soon as parliamentary life begins, the definite contours of *Weltanschauungen* and ideologies rapidly lose their sharpness. That they can still, though faded, penetrate through to the present, is due to the fact that the incubation period, so to speak, was a very long one, so that there was time for the ideology to

[1] A Conservative Parliamentary Party first appears at the Prussian Diet in 1847.

develop thoroughly and consistently according to its own logical principles. The magic of the French Revolution provided just the right stimulus to induce people to occupy themselves with these political and philosophical matters, while the hard facts of reality were not yet mature enough to demand action which inevitably leads to compromise and logical inconsistency.

This then is the situation: under the ideological pressure of the French Revolution there developed in Germany an intellectual counter-movement which retained its purely intellectual character over a long period and was thus able to develop its logical premises to the fullest possible extent. It was 'thought through' to the end. The counter-revolution did not originate in Germany; but it was in Germany that its slogans were most thoroughly thought out and pursued to their logical conclusions.

The main stimulus actually came from England—much more politically developed than Germany at that time. It came from Burke. Germany contributed this process of 'thinking through to the end'—a philosophical deepening and intensifying of tendencies which originated with Burke and were then combined with genuinely German elements. Even the way in which Burke is received and dealt with is characteristic, however. Burke was anything but what his first German translator Gentz and his friend A. Müller believed him to be.

Müller makes him a reactionary, whereas Burke, although increasingly conservative as he got older, still retained so much of the concept of Liberty, that even the modern English liberals can quote him to their own advantage.[1]

In other words, Germany achieved for the ideology of conservatism what France did for the Enlightenment—she exploited it to the fullest extent of its logical conclusions. The Enlightenment started in England, in the most forward and progressive area of capitalist development. It then went over to France—there to achieve its most radical, abstract atheistic and materialist form. Counter-revolutionary criticism of the French Revolution originated in the same way in England, but achieved its most consistent exposition on German soil. The really basic elements of thought, for instance of 'historicism,' are to be found in embryo in Burke. Yet 'historicism', as a method and a philosophical outlook, appears to be a product of German conservative thought, and when it ultimately appears in England, it is as a result of German influence. Maine, in his *Ancient Law* (1861), is the disciple of Savigny.[2] That conservatism in Germany was worked out to

---

[1] Cf. Fr. Meusel, *Edmund Burke und die französische Revolution*, p. 141, Berlin, 1913; Friedrich Braune, *Edmund Burke in Deutschland*, Heidelberg, 1917.

[2] Cf. Ernest Barker, *Political Thought in England*, pp. 161 ff.

its logical conclusions, and that the antitheses in the predominant *Weltanschauung* of the time are so easily visible, can be attributed partly to the lack of an important middle class, able to maintain an independent social balance and thus to pursue an independent intellectual synthesis between the two extremes. In so far as such a middle class existed at all, it either developed intellectually *within* the framework of conservatism, where it played a moderating role of which we shall have to speak again later; or it lapsed into an extreme, liberal scholastic dogmatism which again only went to sharpen the extremes.[1] To this already existing impetus to separation into extremes was added another geographical one. Whereas the Rhineland and South Germany came under the direct influence of France, and were thus the seat of German liberalism, Prussia and Austria were the main citadels of conservatism. This geographical difference, to say nothing of the economic differences, also went to sharpen the antithesis.

Thus it is clear, taking all these factors together, why the antithesis between liberal and conservative thought is to be found in its sharpest and most logically consistent form in Germany in the first half of the nineteenth century, and why sociological forces here enabled a social development which remained at a complex and confused stage in France and England to achieve the greatest logical and structural consistency. This is why it is just in this German period that we can follow in the sharpest outline the impact of social forces upon the very logical structure of thought, and why we chose this topic as a starting-point of our analysis of the significance of political elements in the development of thought.

Our choice has the disadvantage, however, that it suggests that political action is always the centre around which styles of thought crystallize. This is not necessarily the case. Our contention is only that in the first half of the nineteenth century politics gradually became the centre around which the differences in both the fundamental attitudes and the *Weltanschauungen* of various social groups developed. In other periods, religion might have been the crystallizing agency, and it only requires further explanation to show why in this period politics were so decisive in the formation of

---

[1] It is not correct to say that 'German thinking' as such is conservative, or that 'French thinking' as such is oppositional and liberal. What can be maintained is only that conservative thought was most consistently developed in all its implications in Germany, owing to certain peculiarities in the German sociological situation; the same applies, *mutatis mutandis*, to rationalism and libertarianism in France. A. de Tocqueville already pointed out that the predominance of general ideas and deductive systems in French pre-revolutionary political writings was due to the particular sociological position of the French *literati* of that period, rather than to some intrinsic quality of the '*esprit français*' (cf. *L'Ancien Régime et la Révolution*, 8th ed., p. 217, Paris, 1877).

styles of thought. In spite of this, however, it would be wrong to draw too clear-cut a distinction between politics and philosophy and to regard political thought as socially determined but not philosophy or other types of thinking. Such distinctions between philosophy, politics, literature, etc., only exist in textbooks and not in real life, since, given that they belong to the same style of thought, they must all emanate from a common centre. If only one penetrates deeply enough, one will find that certain philosophical assumptions lie at the basis of all political thought, and similarly, in any kind of philosophy a certain pattern of action and a definite approach to the world is implied. From our point of view, all philosophy is nothing but a deeper elaboration of a kind of action. To understand the philosophy, one has to understand the nature of the action which lies at the bottom of it. This 'action' which we have in mind is a special way, peculiar to each group, of penetrating social reality, and it takes on its most tangible form in politics. The political struggle gives expression to the aims and purposes which are unconsciously but coherently at work in all the conscious and half-conscious interpretations of the world characteristic of the group.

We do not mean that every philosopher is nothing but a political propagandist, or even that he himself is necessarily committed consciously to a certain political point of view. A philosopher, or even an isolated thinker, may be quite unaware of the political implications of his thought, and yet develop attitudes and categories of thought, the social genesis of which can be traced to a special type of political activity. Kant, for example, is the philosopher of the French Revolution, not primarily because he was in full sympathy with its political aims, but because the form of his thought (as reflected for example in his concept of the *ratio*, in his belief in gradual progress, in his general optimism, and so on), is of the same brand as that which was a dynamic force behind the activities of the French revolutionaries. It is the same form of active penetration into the world. It is this which unconsciously produces the categories and ways of interpretation common to those who are bound by the mutual bond of a common style of thought.

SECTION 1
Modern Rationalism and the Rise of the Conservative Opposition

Social differentiation reflects itself not only in different currents of thought but also in a differentiation, on a more general plane, within the mental climate of the age. Not only thought, but even the ways in which people experience things emotionally, vary with their position in society.

It has often been pointed out that the most characteristic feature of modern thought is its attempt to achieve a thorough rationalization of the world. The growth of natural science is nothing more than a consistent pursuit of this aim, which no doubt existed in earlier times. No one could deny the presence of some rational element in medieval Europe or in the civilization of the Far East. But rationalization in those cases was only partial, since it tended to merge too readily into irrationality. The characteristic quality of capitalist bourgeois consciousness is that it knows no bounds to the process of rationalization.

Modern rationalism as a method of thought finds its clearest and most radical application in the modern exact sciences. In that form it mainly arose in opposition to two main streams of thought—medieval Aristotelian scholasticism on the one hand, and the philosophy of nature of the Renaissance on the other. There is no better way of understanding the novel element in the rationalism of modern science than to investigate the aspects of these two streams of thought which it chiefly opposed.

The Aristotelian conception of the world was opposed because of its qualitative approach, because it held that the form of a thing is determined by a teleological aim which inheres in it. The new thought strove for a conception of the world which would explain the particular in terms of general causes and laws and present the world as a mere compound of physical mass and physical forces. It was their desire to overcome qualitative thinking that impelled modern scientists to turn to mathematics and to make it the basis of their analysis of nature.

The philosophy of nature of the Renaissance which at first continued to exert a considerable influence on the pioneers of scientific rationalism was opposed because of its magical elements and its tendency to think in terms of analogies. This side of the struggle reveals another aspect of modern rationalism. Rationalization as an opponent of qualitative thinking and rationalization as an opponent of magical and analogical thinking are two fundamentally different phenomena which were then only accidentally united.

But behind both there stands a basic attitude which holds them together. It is the desire not to know more about things than can be expressed in a universally valid and demonstrable form, and not to incorporate them into one's experience beyond that point. One tries to exclude from knowledge everything that is bound up with particular personalities and that can be proved only to narrow social groups with common experiences, and to confine oneself to statements which are generally communicable and demonstrable. It is therefore a desire for knowledge which can be socialized. Now quantity and calculation belong to the sphere of consciousness which is demonstrable to everyone. The new ideal of knowledge was therefore the type of proof which is found in mathematics. This meant a peculiar identification of truth with universal validity. One started out from the wholly unwarranted assumption that man can know only where he can demonstrate his experience to all. Thus, both anti-qualitative and anti-magical rationalism, from a sociological point of view, amount to a dissociation of knowledge from personalities and concrete communities, to its being developed along wholly abstract lines (which, however, may vary among themselves).

The characteristic of this conception of knowledge is that it ignores all concrete and particular aspects of the object and all those faculties of human perception which, while enabling the individual to grasp the world intuitively, do not permit him to communicate his knowledge to everybody. It eliminates the whole context of concrete relationships in which every piece of knowledge is embedded. The theory, in other words, takes into account only general experience, an experience which is general in a twofold sense. It relates to many objects and is valid for many subjects. The theory is interested only in the general aspects of objects and appreciates in man only that which 'generalizes', i.e. socializes him, that is to say, Reason.

This 'quantitative' rationalist form of thought was possible because it arose as part of a new spiritual attitude and experience of things which may be described as 'abstract' in a related though not altogether identical sense.[1] A symptom of this change is the decline, or eventual repression of pantheism which accompanies the tendency to 'quantify' nature.

It has often been pointed out that the rationalism of modern natural science has its parallel in the new economic system. With the substitution of a system of commodity production for a subsistence economy there takes place a similar change in the attitude towards things as in the change-over from qualitative to quantitative thinking about nature. Here too the quantitative conception of exchange value replaces the qualitative conception of use value. In both cases therefore the abstract attitude of which we have been speaking prevails. It is an attitude which gradually comes to include all forms of human experience. In the end, even the 'other man' is experienced abstractly. In a patriarchal or feudal world the 'other man' is somehow regarded as a self-

[1] For an analogous 'quantifying' tendency in ancient thought, see Erich Frank, *Plato und die sogenannten Pythagoreer*, pp. 143 ff., Halle, 1923.

contained unit, or at least as a member of an organic community.[1] In a society based on commodity production, he too is a commodity, his labour-power a calculable magnitude with which one reckons as with all other quantities. The result is that as capitalist organization expands, man is increasingly treated as an abstract calculable magnitude, and tends more and more to experience the outside world in terms of these abstract relations.

The psychological possibility of approaching men and things differently of course remains, but now the possibility exists of treating the world abstractly in a systematic and consistent manner. As to the sociological factor which accounts for the growth of this consistent rationalism, the common view is no doubt correct, that it is the rising capitalist bourgeoisie. This must of course not be taken too crudely. It is not that every individual bourgeois approached the world in this way continuously and at all times, but merely that the social aims of the bourgeoisie as the propagators of capitalism made such a consistently abstract and calculating form of experience possible. Other social strata could of course share and absorb this attitude to the world and to their environment. But it became really overwhelming and repressed all other tendencies, in those social strata whose daily life and work was immediately bound up with relations of this kind.

Most attempts to describe the general development of modern thought tend to pay exclusive attention to the growth of rationalism. The result is a picture quite incompatible with historical facts and the world as we know it. In fact, this mechanized world, this abstract form of experience and thought by no means exhaust what we know of our surroundings. A complete view of the present situation will reveal the falsity of a one-sided emphasis upon rationalism; it will lead us to recognize that the intuitive, qualitative, concrete forms of thought which rationalism repudiates have by no means disappeared altogether.

Our problem begins at this point and the study of conservative thought takes on a practical importance. We want to know: *what became of all those vital relationships and attitudes, and their corresponding modes of thought, which were suppressed by the rise of a consistent rationalization?* Did they merely sink into the past, or were they in some way conserved? If they were conserved, in what form have they been handed down to us?

As one might expect, they did in fact persist, but as is usually

[1] Cf. Marx on human relations in the Middle Ages: 'The social relationships of persons engaged in production appear, at any rate, as their own personal relationships, and not disguised as social relations of things, of products of labour' (*Das Kapital*, 9th ed., p. 44, Hamburg, 1921

the case in history, they were submerged and became latent, manifesting themselves at most as a counter-current to the mainstream. They were taken up and developed further, at first by those social and intellectual strata which remained outside the capitalistic process of rationalization or at least played a passive role in its development. The personal concretely human relations which previously held sway were kept alive in varying forms and degrees primarily in the peasant strata, in the petit-bourgeois groups which had descended directly from the handicraftsmen of earlier times, and in the aristocratic tradition of the nobility.

In particular, we find that the unbroken tradition of the religious sects like the Pietists[1] maintained ways of life, attitudes and ways of experiencing things, particularly in their spiritual life, which were bound inevitably to disappear from the lives both of the bourgeoisie as it became more and more drawn into the capitalist process and of the industrial working class.

Even these strata, however, bound up as they necessarily were with the rationalizing process of capitalism, did not entirely lose their original way of life. It merely disappeared from what we may call their *public* and *official* life. Their *intimate* relationships, in so far as they remained untouched by the capitalist process, continued to develop in a non-calculable, non-rationalized manner. They did not become abstract. In fact, the phenomenon to which Max Weber also refers, the gradual *recession into privacy* of certain spheres previously public (the spheres of life in which personal and religious feelings prevail), is in the nature of a compensation for the increasing rationalization of public life in general —in the workshop, in the market-place, in politics, etc.

Thus the irrational and original relation of man to man and man to things is driven henceforth to the periphery of capitalist life—and this in two senses. In the first place it is driven to the periphery of the individual's life in so far as in contrast to the increasingly rational development of the more representative spheres of life only the more intimate and private of human relations remain vital and alive in the old sense. Secondly, from the narrower point of view of social stratification: it is the representatives of the new social order, the bourgeoisie and the proletariat, which become more and more immersed in the new modes of life and thought, and it is only at the periphery of the new society—among the nobility, the peasants, and the petit-bourgeois—that the old traditions are kept alive. Here, at the periphery in both these senses, slumber the germs of a style of thought and life which at one time dominated the world. For a long time these germs remained hidden, and did not emerge as a 'trend',

[1] Cf. G. Salomon, *Das Mittelalter als Ideal der Romantik*, pp. 118 ff.

as something conspicuous, until they became relevant to the social struggle and were adopted by the counter-revolutionary forces, who inscribed them on their banner.

The sociological significance of romanticism lies in its function as the historical opponent of the intellectual tendencies of the Enlightenment, in other words, against the philosophical exponents of bourgeois capitalism. It seized on the submerged ways of life and thought, snatched them from oblivion, consciously worked them out and developed them further, and finally set them up against the rationalist way of thought. Romanticism took up just those spheres of life and behaviour which existed as mere undercurrents to the main stream of bourgeois rationalism. It made it its task to rescue these elements, to lend them new dignity and valué and to save them from disappearance. 'Community' is set up against 'society' (to use Toennies' terminology), family against contract, intuitive certainty against reason, spiritual against material experience. All those partially hidden factors at the very basis of everyday life are suddenly laid bare by reflection and fought for.

It is well known that romanticism developed from the Enlightenment as antithesis to thesis.[1] No antithesis escapes conditioning by the thesis it sets out to oppose, and romanticism suffered the same paradoxical fate; its structure was fundamentally conditioned by the attitudes and methods of that very movement of Enlightenment in opposition to which it originally developed.

Romanticism tried to rescue these repressed irrational forces, espoused their cause in the conflict, but failed to see that the mere fact of paying conscious attention to them meant an inevitable rationalization. Romanticism achieved a rationalization which the bourgeois Enlightenment could never have carried through, not only because its methods would have proved inadequate to the task, but also because the psychic material in question would never have been significant enough for it to pay lasting attention to it. Irrationalism, like everything else in a given period, can only be understood in terms of the prevailing intellectual climate. When this general climate is rationalist, then even irrational elements have to be submitted to rational reflection if they are to be understood. Thus romanticism may be interpreted as a gathering-up, a rescuing of all those attitudes and ways of life of ultimately religious origin which were repressed by the march of capitalist rationalism—but a gathering-up and conserving *at the*

---

[1] Franz Oppenheimer calls romanticism an 'intellectual counter-revolution' and explains its genesis in terms of an '*imitation par opposition*' in Tarde's sense (cf. *System der Soziologie*, vol. 1, pp. 4 ff., Jena, 1922). Romanticism, however, was no mere negation of the revolution; it had a positive content of its own.

level of reflection. What the romanticists did was not to reconstruct or revive the Middle Ages, religion, or the irrational as the basis and foundation of life; it was something entirely different: a reflexive and cognitive comprehension of these forces. This was by no means the original aim of romanticism; but, as it happened, it worked out suitable methods, modes of experience, concepts and means of expression for all those forces which were for ever inaccessible to Enlightenment. Thus all those ways of life and attitudes to men, things, and the world, which for almost a whole epoch had been largely invisible were once more brought to the surface. They were brought to the surface not, however, in their old form as the natural basis of social life, but as a task, as the content of a programme.

Sociologically, these factors, once brought to the level of reflection, tended to link themselves up with certain anti-capitalist tendencies.

All those social strata which were not directly interested in or were perhaps even menaced by the capitalist process and were, moreover, bound by tradition to the lost ways of life of the various pre-capitalist stages of social development, made use of their discoveries against the bourgeoisie and industrialism. The historical alliance of the enlightened monarchy and the entrepreneur meant that both were interested in rationalism, while the feudal powers, small peasant proprietors and the petit-bourgeois strata which sprang from the old craft-guilds were all interested in varying degrees in romanticism.[1] As these romantic elements emerged in a conscious, reflexive form, these strata all contribute something of their own to them. Especially, however, when it comes to a struggle round cultural questions in which these elements are consciously exploited, these strata invariably plunder romanticism for certain elements which they then incorporate into their own ideology.

The task of our investigation then is as follows. We have to show how the political and social 'right-wing opposition' not merely took up arms against the political and economic domination of rising capitalism, but how it opposed it intellectually too, and gathered up all those spiritual and intellectual factors which were in danger of suppression as the result of a victory for bourgeois rationalism, even to the extent of working out a 'counterlogic'.

It is generally believed that the socialists were the first to criticize capitalism as a social system; in actual fact, however, there are many indications that this criticism was initiated by the right-wing opposition and was then gradually taken over by the left opposition; we must, of course, try to find out what shifts of

[1] Cf. G. Salomon, *op. cit.*, p. 111, pp. 118 f.

emphasis made this reception of 'right-wing' *motifs* by the 'left-wing' opposition possible.

In fact, the type of thought which arose in conjunction with the proletariat and its social aims has much in common with the type associated with the right-wing opposition, but the essential structural differences between them must not be overlooked. The proletariat has grown out of capitalism; it is its own peculiar creation and has no tradition behind it outside capitalism itself. The 'fourth estate' is no estate but a class. Its adherents have become blended into a unified class by having been torn out of the old background of 'estates' and 'organic groups' in which their ancestors had lived. With the rise of the new world, estates tended to be eclipsed by classes, which increasingly took over the function of articulating collective action. Yet many groups, especially those with strong local, non-urban roots, performed the transition only gradually, and among urban groups, artisans retained many features of the old guild-mentality. The proletariat alone, herded together in factories, developed from an inchoate mass into a completely new class with its own traditions. In so far, however, as this new social entity emerged within the rationalist epoch itself, it tended to exhibit rational characteristics of thought to a greater degree perhaps even than the bourgeoisie. Yet it would be a mistake to see in proletarian rationalism nothing but a variant of bourgeois rationalism.

Its own dynamic, the logic of its own position, easily impels this type of rationalism to transform itself into a peculiar kind of irrationalism.

The proletarian mode of life is essentially rational because its position in the world compels it to plan revolution on a calculatory basis even more than the bourgeoisie had done. The proletariat makes even revolution a matter of bureaucratic administration and transforms it into a 'social movement'. Yet its brand of rationalism and bureaucratic management has very little in common with that desire for calculability characteristic of the successful bourgeoisie. Proletarian rationalism in fact, so long as it is in opposition, can never do without the irrational element at the basis of all revolutionary action. The utopian ideal of the bourgeois is to make every enterprise so calculable that every element of risk is completely eliminated. That this ideal is not realized, and that risk and uncertainty still adhere to capitalist enterprise, is due simply to the fact that the capitalist world is only partially rationalized, only partially based on a planned economy.

On the other hand, even when the percentage chance of success can be assessed, say in the case of a strike, by the use of strike statistics, and similar analyses, action is still not wholly dependent on a favourable outcome to the calculations, since the chances of defeat are not really determinable in so far as revolutionary *élan* always remains an uncertain factor.

At this point it becomes quite clear that the social position of the proletariat forces it into irrationalism. The attempt at revolution, however planned and 'scientific' it may be, inevitably produces an irrational 'chiliastic' element. Here lies its essential affinity with the 'counter-revolution'.

Proletarian thought has in many ways a significant affinity with conservative and reactionary thought. Although deriving from entirely different basic aims, this affinity nevertheless unites the two modes of thought in opposition to the aims of the bourgeois capitalist world, and the abstractness of its thought. A further investigation—which cannot here be undertaken—of the fate of these inherently irrational 'chiliastic' elements in proletarian thought would have to show that they derive in the last resort from what may be called the 'ecstatic consciousness'. One would have to show how from their beginning in the peasant revolts of the sixteenth century they became the germ of all revolutions, and how they were even retained as part of the otherwise extremely highly rationalized proletarian outlook on the world. Here then we are confronted with a combination of the most extreme rationalism with some of the most extreme irrational elements; this shows that the 'irrational' proves on closer observation more complex than we are at first inclined to imagine.

An exhaustive analysis would need to show the very fundamental difference between the irrational elements produced by the 'ecstatic consciousness', and that other type which we have hitherto for the sake of brevity described as the remains of the old religious tradition and frame of mind, and towards which Romanticism tended in a later epoch.

At yet another point, however, the proletarian revolutionary consciousness is directly connected with the conservative tradition—i.e. in dialectics. There was an inner necessity in Marx's taking over the idea of dialectic from the conservative Hegel. The concept of dialectic—the logical sequence of thesis, antithesis, and synthesis—seems, on the surface, extremely rationalist, and indeed it was an attempt to condense the whole process of development into a single logical formula, and to present the whole of historical reality as rationally deducible. Yet this type of rationalism is nevertheless completely different from that other type which finds expression in the bourgeois ideal of the natural sciences. The latter seeks to establish universal laws of nature; it is a democratic, non-dialectical type of thought. It is not surprising, therefore, that the latest, democratic and 'scientifically minded' generation of socialists did their best to eliminate the dialectical element from Marxism altogether.

Thus, closer observation of rationalism shows that it has different variants which we have to keep apart, just as we above found it necessary to distinguish between 'chiliastic' and contemplative mystical (romantic) irrationalism.

As a matter of fact, as we shall see more clearly later on, the dialectic in Hegel serves to solve problems which are really romantic problems, and which live on in the historical school.

The chief function of the dialectic is to provide a rational understanding of the 'historical individual'—i.e. of the individual in all his historical diversity and uniqueness. In the rational search for universal laws and generalizations the individual tends to be lost altogether; but the dialectical approach restores him as a component part of a unique process of historical growth and development. Thus the attempt to understand the essentially irrational, historically unique individual in rational terms constitutes a paradox within dialectics, since it produces a form of rationalization which must involve the supersession of rationalism itself.

The second function of all dialectics which relates to its inner meaning rather than to its external formula is to trace the 'inner line' of growth of a civilization. Here again, therefore, it rationalizes what is essentially irrational and foreign in every way to non-dialectical, naturalist thought.

In the third place, dialectics is a form of approach which seeks to find a meaning in an historical process. It is a philosophical rationalization of history. It therefore involves a form of rationality which it is very difficult to reconcile with the positivism of natural science, to which all ethical evaluations and metaphysics in general are completely alien.

Taking all this into consideration, we are forced to admit that already through Hegel a close alliance is effected between rationalism and conservative thought—notwithstanding the fact that the latter is far removed from that form of naturalist rationalism which considers everything as calculable. That Marxism could go such a long way with the Hegelian school of historical thought, that it was at all possible that it should oppose the natural-law tradition in bourgeois thought in the same way as did the historical school, although from a different point of view, indicates that both had factors in common which must not be overlooked.

Nevertheless, in spite of all these affinities and similarities between proletarian and conservative thought, the basis of the proletarian mentality is strictly rational and fundamentally related to the positivist trend of bourgeois philosophy. This positivist basis is clear in the way in which the proletarian philosophy of history derives the dynamic of events from the social and economic spheres and interprets the movement of ideas in terms of a social movement centred round the economic organization of society. At this point, proletarian thought therefore embodies the gradually developed bourgeois concept of the primacy of the economic sphere. Proletarian thought is therefore rational in so far as it must pass through capitalism as a necessary phase in historical development; in a certain sense it is even more rational in that it has not merely to accept the process of capitalist development, but actually to accelerate its tempo. To the same extent, it is, however, irrational in so far as it is forced to rely on a 'self-reversing' tendency in capitalism; this self-reversal represents an element of irrationality or even 'super-rationality' as opposed to the directly traceable particular causal relations of bourgeois rationality.

However, it is not our task here to follow all this out in detail. We found it necessary to refer to proletarian thought in order to be better able to understand our historical period.

Our own field now narrows itself down. We shall be dealing with a strictly delimited phase in the development of thought. Our problem then is to trace the development of conservative thought in the first half of the nineteenth century in Germany, and to relate this development to the social background of the time.

SECTION 2

The Meaning of Conservatism

1. *Traditionalism and conservatism*

Let us begin by analysing more exactly what we mean by 'conservatism.' Is conservatism a phenomenon universal to all mankind, or is it an entirely new product of the historical and sociological conditions of our own time? The answer is that both sorts of conservatism exist. On the one hand, there is the sort that is more or less universal, and, on the other hand, there is the definitely modern sort which is the product of particular historical and social circumstances, and which has its own peculiar traditions, form and structure. We could call the first sort 'natural conservatism',[1] and the second sort 'modern conservatism', were it not that the word 'natural' is already heavily burdened with many different meanings. It will perhaps be better therefore if we adopt Max Weber's term '*traditionalism*' to denote the first

1 Cf. Lord Hugh Cecil, *Conservatism*, Home University Library of Modern Knowledge, pp. 9 f., New York and London.

type; so that when we speak of 'conservatism' we shall always mean 'modern' conservatism—something essentially different from mere 'traditionalism.'

Traditionalism signifies a tendency to cling to vegetative patterns, to old ways of life which we may well consider as fairly ubiquitous and universal. This 'instinctive' traditionalism may be seen as the original reaction to deliberate reforming tendencies. In its original form it was bound up with magical elements in consciousness; conversely, among primitive peoples, respect for traditional ways of life is strongly linked with the fear of magical evils attendant on change.[1] Traditionalism of this kind also exists today, and is often similarly connected with magical hang-overs from the old consciousness. Traditionalism is not therefore necessarily bound up, even today, with political or other sorts of conservatism. 'Progressive' people for instance, regardless of their political convictions, may often act 'traditionalistically' to a very large extent in many other spheres of their lives.

Thus, we do not intend the term 'conservatism' to be understood in a general psychological sense. The progressive who acts 'traditionalistically' in private or business life, or the conservative who acts 'progressively' outside politics, should make the point clear.

The word 'traditionalist' describes what, to a greater or less degree, is a formal psychological characteristic of every individual's mind. 'Conservative' action, however, is always dependent on *a concrete set of circumstances*. There is no means of knowing in advance what form a 'conservative' action in the political sense will take, whereas the general attitude implied in the term 'traditionalist' enables us to calculate more or less accurately what a 'traditionalist' action will be like. There is no doubt, for instance, what the traditionalist reaction to the introduction of the railway will be. But how a conservative will react can only be determined approximately *if we know a good deal about the conservative movement* in the period and in the country under discussion. We are not concerned here to enumerate all the different factors which go to produce a particular type of conservatism in a particular country at a particular period. This much is clear, however, that acting along conservative lines (at any rate in the political sphere) involves more than automatic responses of a certain type; it means that the individual is consciously or unconsciously guided by a way of thinking and acting which has its own history behind it, before it comes into contact with the individual. This contact with

[1] Cf. Max Weber, *Wirtschaft und Gesellschaft*, p. 19, Tübingen, 1922. (This 'traditionalism' obviously has nothing to do with the French 'traditionalism' of a de Maistre or de Bonald.)

the individual may under certain circumstances change to some extent the form and development of this way of thinking and acting, but even when the particular individual is no longer there to participate in it, it will still have its own history and development apart from him. Political conservatism is therefore an *objective mental structure*, as opposed to the 'subjectivity' of the isolated individual. It is *not* objective in the sense of being eternally and universally valid. No *a priori* deductions can be made from the 'principles' of conservatism. Nor does it exist apart from the individuals who realize it in practice and embody it in their actions. It is not an immanent principle with a given law of development which the individual members of the movement merely unfold—possibly in unconscious fashion—without adding anything of their own. In one word, conservatism is not an objective entity in any rightly or wrongly understood Platonist sense of the pre-existence of ideas. But as compared with the *hic et nunc* experience of the particular individual it has a certain very definite objectivity.

In order to grasp the peculiar nature of this objective mental structure, we must first draw a careful distinction between eternal validity and objectivity. A content may be objective in the sense that it exists apart from the *hic et nunc* experience of the individual —as something intended by him—and yet it need not be a timeless content. A structure may be objective—it may transcend the individual which it has temporarily caught up in the stream of its experience—yet it may at the same time be restricted in its validity, subject to historical change, and merely reflect the development of the particular society in which it is found. An *objective* mental structure in this sense is a peculiar agglomeration of spiritual and intellectual elements which cannot be regarded as at all independent of the individuals who are its carriers since its production, reproduction and further development depend entirely on the fate and spontaneous development of these latter. The structure may nevertheless be objective in the sense that the isolated individual could never produce it alone, since he can only belong to some one phase of its historical development, and in the sense that it always outlives its individual carriers. Both nominalism and realism miss the essence of the objectivity of a mental structure in this sense. Nominalism never gets to the root of the matter because it always tries to dissolve the objective structure into the isolated experiences of individuals (cf. Max Weber's concept of 'intended meaning'), while realism never gets there because by 'objectivity' and 'validity' it understands something merely metaphysical, entirely independent of the nature and fate of the particular individuals and carriers, something constant and normative (pre-existing). Between these extremes there is, however, a third alternative which is neither nominalism nor realism. This is what I call a dynamic, historical structural configuration; a concept implying a type of objectivity which begins in time, develops and declines through time, which is closely bound up with the existence and fate of concrete human groups, and is in fact their product. It is nevertheless a truly 'objective' mental structure, because it is always 'there' 'before' the individual at any given moment, and because, as compared with any simple range of experience, it always maintains its own definite form—its *structure*. And although at any given moment such an objective mental structure may show the existence of some ordering principle in the way in which the experiences and elements of which it is composed are related, it must on no account be regarded as 'static'. The particular form and structure of these related experiences and elements can be indicated only *approximately* and only for certain periods, since the structure is *dynamic* and constantly changing. Moreover, it is not merely dynamic, but also historically conditioned. Each step in the process of change is intimately connected with the one before, since each new step makes a change in the internal order and relationships of the structure *as it existed at the stage immediately before*, and is not therefore entirely 'out of the blue' and unconnected with the past. Thus we can speak of a growth, of a development. It is a development the inner meaning of which, however, can only *subsequently* be grasped.

Within every dynamic historical structural configuration, we can discern a distinctive 'basic intention' (*Grundintention*), which the individual makes his own in the measure that his own experience becomes determined by the 'structural configuration' as such. Even this 'kernel', this basic intention, however, is not eternally valid regardless of time and history. It too has arisen in the course of history and in close connection with the fate of concrete, living human beings.

Conservatism is just such an historically developed, dynamic, objective structural configuration. People experience, and act, in a 'conservative' way (as distinct from a merely 'traditionalist' way) in so far, and only in so far, as they *incorporate* themselves into one of the phases of development of this objective mental structure (usually into the contemporary phase), and behave in terms of the structure, either by simply reproducing it in whole or in part, or by developing it further by adapting it to a particular concrete situation.

Only when the peculiar nature of the objectivity of a dynamic structural configuration has been grasped can one be in a position to distinguish 'conservative' from 'traditionalist' behaviour.

Traditionalist behaviour is almost purely reactive.[1] *Conservative behaviour is meaningful*, and moreover is meaningful in relation to circumstances which change from epoch to epoch. It is therefore clear why there is no necessary contradiction in the fact that a politically progressive man can react in an entirely traditionalist way in his everyday life. In the political sphere, he lets himself be guided more or less consciously by an objective, structural configuration; in his everyday life, his behaviour is merely reactive. Two points now arise. Firstly the term 'conservatism' must not be assumed to be a purely political one, although on the whole, as we shall see, its political aspect is perhaps the rather more important one. Conservatism also implies a general philosophical and emotional complex which may even constitute a definite style of thought. Secondly, conservatism as an objective historical structural configuration must not be assumed to include no traditionalist elements within itself. Quite the contrary. We shall see, in fact, that conservatism takes a particular historical form of traditionalism and develops it to its logical conclusions.

Nevertheless, in spite of this apparent overlapping of the two phenomena, or maybe even because of it, the distinction between merely traditionalist and conservative behaviour is a very clear one. Precisely because of its purely formal, semi-reactive nature, traditionalist behaviour has practically no traceable history, whereas conservatism, on the other hand, is an entity with a clear historical and social continuity, which has arisen and developed in a particular historical and social situation, as the best of all guides to history—language—clearly demonstrates; the very word 'conservatism' is a new one of comparatively recent origin.

It was Chateaubriand who first lent the word its peculiar meaning when he called the periodical he issued to propagate the ideas of the clerical and political Restoration, *The Conservative*.[2] The word entered into general use in Germany in the thirties,[3] and was officially adopted in England in 1835.[4] We can take the emergence of a new terminology to indicate the emergence of a new social phenomenon, although of course it tells us little about the latter's actual nature.

2. *The sociological background of modern conservatism*

Modern conservatism differs from traditionalism primarily in that it is a function of *one particular* historical and sociological

[1] *Ibid.*, p. 2.
[2] Cf. the article 'Konservativ' by Rackfahl in *Politisches Handwörterbuch*, ed. P. Herre, Leipzig, 1923.
[3] *Ibid.*
[4] Cf. Lord Hugh Cecil, *op. cit.*, p. 64.

situation. Traditionalism is a general psychological attitude which expresses itself in different individuals as a tendency to cling to the past and a fear of innovation. But this elementary psychological tendency may attain a special function in relation to the social process. What was formerly merely a psychological characteristic common to all men, under certain circumstances becomes a central factor lending coherence to a *particular trend* in the social process.

This development of the traditionalist attitude into the nucleus of a definite social trend does not take place spontaneously: it takes place as a response to the fact that 'progressivism' had already constituted itself as a definite trend.

Traditionalism is essentially one of those dormant tendencies which each individual unconsciously harbours within himself. Conservatism, on the other hand, is conscious and reflective from the first, since it arises as a counter-movement in conscious opposition to the highly organized, coherent and systematic 'progressive' movement.

The emergence of a conscious conservative movement is therefore already an indication that the modern social and intellectual world has developed a particular structure of its own. The mere existence of conservatism as a coherent trend means that history is developing more and more in terms of the interaction of such comprehensive 'trends' and 'movements', some of which are 'progressive' and further social change, while others are 'retrogressive' and retard it.

That such 'trends' can arise is explained by the fact that society today is gradually achieving a new dynamic unity, at the expense of all the old, scattered, self-contained provincial feudal units which are increasingly absorbed into national units; these latter may later coalesce further into supra-national ones. Although at first nations remain to a large extent socially and culturally autonomous, the fundamental economic and social problem in all modern states is so structurally similar that it is not surprising that parallel social and intellectual divisions are reproduced in them all.

These structural problems common to all modern states include the following: (I) the achievement of national unity, (II) the participation of the people in the government of the country, (III) incorporation of the state in the world economic order, (IV) solution of the social question.[1]

They appear to be of such importance for the social as well

---

[1] Cf. L. Bergsträsser, 'Geschichte der politischen Parteien in Deutschland', *Schriftenreihe der Verwaltungsakademie Berlin*, No. 4, 2nd ed., p. 5, Mannheim, Berlin and Leipzig.

as for the intellectual life of the community that there is a marked tendency for all divisions within it to develop in close relation to the tensions arising from attempts to solve these fundamental problems of social structure. Religious struggles have gradually been transformed into political struggles, and in the English Revolution political divisions can already be clearly seen through the guise of religious divisions. The nearer we approach the nineteenth century, the more does this become true of other intellectual phenomena as well, and the more easily can they be described along party lines, in terms of their direct or indirect relation to social and political problems.

Accordingly, at the same time as a conscious, functionalized, political conservatism emerges as a distinct political force, conservatism transcends the political sphere proper and comes to imply also a *particular form of experience and thought*. At approximately the same time as, or perhaps even a little earlier than, political conservatism, there emerged a corresponding *Weltanschauung* and conservative mode of thought. 'Conservative' and 'liberal' in our terminology, in relation to the first half of the nineteenth century, signify something more than different political aims. The terms imply in each case a quite specific affinity with quite different philosophies and therefore also imply quite different modes of thought. Thus the word 'conservative' connotes, so to speak, an entire, comprehensive world structure; the sociological definition of this word (which necessarily includes more than its historical political definition) must therefore take into account that historical configuration which brought forth a new term as the expression of a new fact.

To find out why 'modern conservatism' emerged so late in history, we must turn to the various historical and social factors the conjunction of which provided the prerequisite conditions for its development. The following factors occurring together would appear to create the necessary historical and sociological conditions for the rise of conservatism:

(i) The status of historical-social forces must cease to be a static one. It must become a dynamic process of oriented change. Individual events must to an increasing extent in every sphere point to the key problem of the growth of the social body. At first this will happen unwittingly; later, however, it will become conscious and voluntary, and at the same time the exact importance of each element for the development of the whole will become clearer. The number of isolated self-sufficient social units which previously existed will also diminish accordingly. The most commonplace action, however unimportant in itself, will now contribute something to the general process of development, and either further or hinder it[1]: and it becomes increasingly possible to describe every event and every attitude in terms of its function in relation to the development of society as a whole.

(ii) Further: the dynamics of this process must to an increasing extent derive from social differentiation. Different classes must arise ('horizontal' social groupings, reacting to events in a more or less homogeneous way). Some will tend to push social development forward, while others will hold it up, or even consciously work to set it back.

(iii) Further: ideas must also be differentiated along these lines, and the major trends in thought, whatever mixtures and syntheses may be produced, must correspond to the broad lines of this social differentiation.

(iv) Finally: this social differentiation (into groups with different functions in relation to the social process—some forwarding and others retarding it), must take on an increasingly political (and later even a purely economic) character.[2] The political factor must be autonomous, and must become the primary nucleus around which new groupings crystallize.

To put it briefly, the development and widespread existence of conservatism, as distinct from mere traditionalism, is due in the last retort to the dynamic character of the modern world; to the basis of this dynamic in social differentiation; to the fact that this social differentiation tends to draw the human intellect along with it and forces it to develop along its own lines; and finally to the fact that the basic aims of the different social groups do not merely crystallize ideas into actual movements of thought, but also create different antagonistic *Weltanschauungen* and different antagonistic *styles* of thought. In a word—traditionalism can only become conservatism in a society in which change occurs through the medium of class conflict—in a *class society*. This is the sociological background of modern conservatism.

[1] In medieval times, too, there existed progressive centres, bearers of a dynamic principle: the towns. They were, however, isolated within a static world. So far as we can see, the international culture of the Middle Ages, as represented by the Church, lacked this element of 'oriented change' in which every event assumes a function affecting the whole. On the difficulties of forming parties in a feudal world, cf. K. Lamprecht, *Deutsche Geschichte*, Suppl. II, second half-volume, p. 53, Freiburg im Breisgau, 1904.

[2] Cf. Emil Lederer, 'Das ökonomische Element und die politische Idee im modernen Parteiwesen', in *Zeitschrift für Politik*, vol. 5, 1911. Intellectual life in Germany is definitely split up into a liberal and a conservative current only after 1840. The existence of a conservative and a liberal 'style of thought', however, had been apparent much earlier (in fact, from the French Revolution onward). Ideological trends in Germany somehow antedated the emergence of the corresponding social structures.

3. *Morphology of conservative thought*

Conservatism can be studied from two points of view. Either one can regard it *as a unit*, as the relatively self-contained and fully developed result of an evolutionary process, or one can emphasize its dynamic aspect and study the genetic process which gives rise to that final product.

We shall have to utilize both approaches. For the moment, however, our task is to arrive at a general descriptive characterization of the style of thought underlying German conservatism, and we shall therefore take its historical development for granted, and consider it in its final form. We shall deal with its historical development in the next section, but this historical analysis cannot be attempted before we have examined certain fundamental factors, which determine the process.

Our first task then, to which we now turn, is to give a relatively undifferentiated description of early nineteenth-century German conservative thought. This must be divided into two stages. Firstly we must deal with the inarticulate group experience which provides what we have called the *basic intention* out of which the style of thought first grows. Then we can turn to the fully articulated theoretical statements expressing the conservative style of thought, and try to work out that *key problem* which gives this style of thought its theoretical unity, determines its growth, and makes its interpretation possible.

(a) *The basic intention behind conservative thought*

One cannot help pushing one's analysis of a style of thought right back to this basic intention, and there is only one safeguard against arbitrary constructions with no basis in reality. As far as possible, we must always adhere strictly to the authentic manifestations of the trend of thought which we are analysing.

This inner core, this drive at the heart of conservative thought, is undoubtedly related to what we have called traditionalism. Conservatism in a certain sense grew out of traditionalism: indeed, it is after all primarily nothing more than traditionalism become conscious. Nevertheless, the two are not synonymous, since traditionalism only takes on its specifically conservative features when it becomes the expression of a very definite, consistently maintained way of life and thought (which first develops in opposition to the revolutionary attitude), and when it functions as such, as a relatively autonomous movement in the social process.

One of the most essential characteristics of this conservative way of life and thought seems to be the way in which it clings to the immediate, the actual, the *concrete*. The result is a quite new, very definite feeling for the *concrete* which is reflected in the modern use of the term 'concrete' with anti-revolutionary implications.[1] To experience and to think 'concretely' now comes to mean to desire to restrict the range of one's activities to the immediate surroundings in which one is placed, and to abjure strictly all that may smack of speculation or hypothesis.

Non-romantic conservatism always starts with the particular case at hand, and never broadens its horizon beyond its own particular surroundings. It is concerned with immediate action, with changing concrete details, and therefore does not really trouble itself with the *structure* of the world in which it lives. On the other hand, all progressive activity feeds on its *consciousness of the possible*. It transcends the given immediate present, by seizing on the possibilities for systematic change which it offers. It fights the concrete, *not* because it wants to replace it merely by another *form of the concrete* but because it wants to produce another *systematic starting-point* for further development.

Conservative reformism consists in the substitution of individual factors by other individual factors ('improvements').[2] Progressive reformism tends to do away with an undesirable fact by reforming the entire surrounding world which makes its existence possible. *Thus progressive reformism tends to tackle the system as a whole, while conservative reformism tackles particular details.*

The Conservative only thinks in terms of a system as a reaction, either when he is forced to develop a system of his own to counter that of the progressives, or when the march of events deprives him of all influence upon the immediate present, so that he would be compelled to turn the wheel of history backward in order to regain influence.

This contrast between concrete and abstract thought, which is primarily one of the ways of one's experiencing his environment, and only secondarily one of thought as such, together with the fact that in its modern form it is based on a difference of fundamental political experience, supplies a crucial instance of styles of experience becoming socially functionalized.

The emergence of a specifically modern society seems to depend on whole classes devoting themselves to the disintegration of the

---

[1] On Burke's definition of 'abstractness', see Meusel, *op. cit.*, pp. 12, 137. Hegel characterized 'abstract' freedom as 'negative freedom', the freedom of (mere) rationality, and ascribed a destructive tendency to it (*Philosophie des Rechts*, § 5). Cf. also Fr. J. Stahl, *Die Philosophie des Rechts*, 4th ed., vol. 2, p. 38, Heidelberg, 1870. The socialist 'left' later adopted the category of the 'concrete' as a basic category for the interpretation of society; for this group, the 'concrete' coincides with the class struggle.

[2] As a Prussian jurist, Bekker, expressed it: 'We placed a good administration above the best constitution.' Quoted in G. v. Below, 'Die Anfänge der konservativen Partei in Preussen', in *Internationale Wochenschrift für Wissenschaft, Kunst und Technik*, 1911.

existing social structure. Their thought is necessarily abstract—it lives on the potential and possible; whereas the thought and experience of those who seek to preserve the present and retard progress is necessarily concrete, and fails to break through the existing structure of society.

The peculiar nature of conservative concreteness is perhaps hardly more clearly to be seen than in its concept of *property*, as contrasted with the ordinary modern bourgeois idea of it. In this connection there is a very interesting essay of Möser's in which he traces the gradual disappearance of the old attitude towards property and compares it with the modern concept of property which had already begun to show its influence in his own time. In his essay 'Von dem echten Eigentum'[1] he shows that the old 'genuine property' was bound up with its owner in an entirely different way from property today. Before, there was a peculiarly vital, reciprocal relationship between property and its owner. Property in its old 'genuine' sense carried with it certain privileges for its owner—for instance, it gave him a voice in affairs of state, the right to hunt, to become a member of a jury. Thus it was closely bound up with his personal honour and so in a sense *inalienable*. When, for example, the owner of the property changed, the right to hunt did not go with the property to the new owner, and the retention of the right to hunt by the original owner was a living testimony to the fact the new proprietor was not the 'real' one. Similarly, a man of ancient nobility who might purchase property from a mere *homo novus* was equally unable to transfer to his newly acquired estate the character of 'true' property merely by virtue of his own fund of personal nobility. Thus there existed a completely non-transferable, reciprocal relationship between a particular piece of property and a particular owner.

In Möser's time the feeling for this relationship still existed, although all linguistic trace of it had long since disappeared. He laments its loss when he says: 'How imperfect is the language and philosophy that no longer has any special way of expressing these fundamental distinctions.'

Here we see clearly what a wealth of pre-theoretical, inarticulate experience, embodying relationships of a most concrete kind between person and property, there was in feudal society, in place of which the abstract concept of bourgeois property emerged, suppressing the old concreteness of experience. Later theories, especially the romantic-conservative type, all reach back towards this feudal conservative concept of property, the essence of which Möser caught, so to speak in its last moments.

[1] Cf. Justus Möser, *Sämtliche Werke* (Complete Works), ed. B. R. Abeken, vol. 4, pp. 158 ff., Berlin, 1842–43.

A. Müller[1] regards possessions as extensions of the limbs of the human body, and he describes feudalism as the amalgamation of person and thing. He attributes the decline of this relationship to the adoption of Roman law, and speaks of a 'Roman French revolution' (*op. cit.*, vol. 1, p. 281) on which he lays all the blame.

These are all mere echoes of the past in an openly partisan vein. Their significance lies in the fact that such living relationships extending to things did once exist. This emphasis on the 'intimacy' between property and owner continues right down to Hegel.

For Hegel the essence of property is that 'I make a thing the vehicle of my will',[2] and 'the rationale of property consists, not in that it satisfies our needs, but in that it helps personality become something more than mere subjectivity.'[3] It is also interesting to note here something which we shall have occasion to observe again later—how the Left opposition to bourgeois capitalist thought learns from the Right opposition to bourgeois thought. The abstractness of human relationships under capitalism which is constantly emphasized by Marx and his followers was originally the discovery of observers from the conservative camp.

We are not suggesting that this distinction between the concrete and abstract approach was never known in earlier times: we are merely pointing out that two quite different ways of experiencing history have gradually developed at opposite extremes and have been embodied in the general form of experience characteristic of different groups according to their position in the dynamic social process.

Another key concept for any analysis of different styles of thought and ways of experiencing is that of *Liberty*.

Revolutionary liberalism understood by liberty in the economic sphere the release of the individual from his medieval connections with state and guild. In the political sphere they understood by it the right of the individual to do as he wishes and thinks fit, and especially his right to the fullest exercise of the inalienable Rights of Man. Only when it encroaches on the liberty of fellow citizens does man's freedom know any bounds according to this concept.[4] Equality, then, is the logical corollary of this kind of liberty— —without the assumption of political equality for all men it is

---

1 Cf. Adam H. Müller, *Die Elemente der Staatskunst* (1809), ed. J. Baxa, vol. 1, pp. 156, 162 f., Vienna and Leipzig, 1922.

2 *Philosophie des Rechts*, ed. Lasson, p. 302.

3 *Ibid.*, p. 297.

4 Cf. the French 'Declaration of the Rights of Man and of the Citizen': 'Liberty consists in doing anything that does no harm to others; thus, the only limits to the natural rights of any man are those which guarantee the same rights to the other members of society. These limits can only be fixed by law.'

meaningless. Actually, however, revolutionary liberalism never thought of equality as anything more than a postulate. It certainly never took it as a matter of empirical fact, and indeed never demanded equality in practice for all men, except in the course of economic and political struggles. Yet conservative thought twisted this postulate into a statement of fact, and made it appear as if the liberals were claiming that all men were in fact and in all respects equal.

Nevertheless, out of this sociologically determined misunderstanding there grew, as often before, a new insight into the actual differentiation of trends of thought. Just as in the case of the concept of property, conservative thought once more rescued an earlier, almost submerged way of thinking and experiencing things, and, by making it explicit, enabled it to play an active role in the dynamic process.

Political necessity compelled the conservatives to develop their own concept of liberty[1] to oppose that of the liberals, and they worked out what we may call the *qualitative idea* of liberty to distinguish it from the revolutionary equalitarian concept. The counter-revolutionary opposition had a sound enough instinct not to attack the idea of freedom as such; instead, they concentrated on the idea of equality which stands behind it. Men, they claimed, are essentially *unequal*, unequal in their gifts and abilities, and unequal to the very core of their beings. Freedom therefore can only consist in the ability of each man to develop without let or hindrance according to the law and principle of his own personality. A. Müller[2] for instance says: 'Nothing could be more inimical to freedom as I have described it . . . than the concept of an external equality. If freedom is simply the general striving of the most varied natures for growth and development, nothing more contradictory to this could be conceived than a false notion of freedom which would remove all the individual peculiarities, i.e. all the heterogeneity of these natures.'

This is also the romantic conservative idea of liberty, which now acquires political point. The revolutionary liberal, thinking abstractly in terms of the possible and not the actual, clings with an 'abstract optimism' to the principle of universal equality, or at least of equal opportunity among men, and conceives of no bounds to an individual's liberty except those set by the existence of other men. But the romantic thinker sees freedom limited by what Simmel called 'the individual law' of development within which each must find defined both his potentialities and his limitations.

This kind of liberty, vested in the nature of individuality, is typically romantic, and hence dangerously close to a kind of anarchistic subjectivism. Although the conservatives succeeded in subjectivizing the problem of liberty (thus blunting its revolutionary edge), the subjective anarchy with which they replaced the external *political* anarchy created by the liberal concept still contained a potential menace to the security of the state. The realization of this caused an immediate tendency in romantic thought (then in the process of becoming conservative) to detach the concept of 'qualitative liberty' from the individual and to transfer it to the so-called 'true bearers', the 'true subjects' of liberty, namely the larger collectivities, 'organic communities', *the estates*. Henceforth the estates became the bearers of that inner principle of growth, in the unrestricted development of which lies liberty. This makes it clear that the qualitative concept of liberty derives at least in part from feudal thinking. The 'liberty' of the different estates under feudalism which meant their 'privileges', and the distinctly qualitative and non-egalitarian flavour which was contained in the medieval concept, is here revived once more.[1] Even in its new form, however, the concept is still fraught with danger to the state and the position of the ruling groups within it, as later conservatism is well aware. Hence, an attempt is later made to select qualitatively different individual or corporative 'liberties' in such a way that they can subordinated to a higher principle, representing the whole of society. The historical school, Hegel, Stahl and others, differ among themselves only in their conception of this overarching totality; the formal structure of their various solutions to the problem is the same.

The solution was to make liberty a matter concerning the private, subjective side of life only, while all external social relations were subordinated to the principle of order and discipline. But then comes the problem: what is to prevent a collision between the two spheres, subjective Liberty and external Order? A solution is found in the assumption of a kind of 'pre-established harmony' which is either guaranteed directly by God, or by the natural forces of society and the nation. Here conservatism has clearly learned something from liberalism, from which it has taken over both the concept of 'separation of spheres' and of the 'hidden hand' which makes for universal harmony.

The historical school uses primarily the concept of 'the nation'

---

[1] Cf. A. v. Martin, 'Weltanschauliche Motive im altkonservativen Denken', in *Deutscher Staat und deutsche Parteien, Festschrift für Meinecke*, p. 345, Munich and Berlin, 1922.

or 'national spirit' to provide that necessary wider whole which prevents the liberty of the individual or group from degenerating into mere anarchistic caprice. Rothacker has shown how in Ranke's writings the concept of the state gradually overshadowed that of the nation.[1] In any case, the solution of the problem offered by Ranke and Savigny is to shift this qualitative freedom from the individual and the estates to the nation and the state respectively. Only the state, developing freely according to its own laws of growth, is ever really free. The individual is bound, and can only achieve usefulness within these wider units.

The tension between order and liberty is at its greatest in Hegel, who, as always, tries to preserve both factors. For him, what he calls the revolutionary, abstract concept of freedom becomes an intermediary stage in the progress towards truth: 'Negative freedom, or freedom of mere rationality, is one-sided. Yet this one-sidedness contains an essential feature, it is not to be discarded. But the defect of mere rationality is that it mistakes a partial and one-sided characterization for the final and comprehensive one.'[2] What he means by 'negative abstract freedom', however, becomes rapidly clearer if we follow him further: 'A more concrete manifestation of this freedom is the fanaticism of political and religious life. Of this nature was the terroristic phase of the French Revolution, which sought to slur over all distinctions in talent and authority. That was a time of tremor and commotion which was intolerant of anything that set itself off against the general. Fanaticism seeks abstract equality rather than differentiation; wherever it encounters distinctions, it finds them antagonistic to its indefiniteness and levels them down.'[3] Hegel then arrives at a third principle which holds the middle way between 'abstract freedom' and mere 'heteronomy'. This principle is that of 'concrete freedom'.[4] He says: 'The third step is that the will, while limited by the other, should yet remain by itself. While it limits itself, it yet remains with itself and does not lose its hold of the universal. This is then the concrete conception of freedom, while the other two aspects may now be seen as thoroughly abstract and one-sided.'[5]

Stahl also had to struggle with the romantic concept of liberty.[6] He, like Hegel, tried to incorporate the whole conservative tradition, and based his solution of the problem on the principle of

---

[1] *Op. cit.*, p. 433.
[2] *Philosophie des Rechts*, Addition to § 5, ed. Lasson, p. 287; cf. footnote 1, p. 103. Müller (*op. cit.*, vol. 1, p. 313) also speaks of 'negative freedom'. Cf. G. Rexius, 'Studien zur Staatslehre der historischen Schule', in *Hist. Zschr.*, vol. 107, p. 499, 1911.
[3] *Op. cit.*, p. 288.
[4] *Ibid.*, addition to § 7, p. 288.
[5] *Ibid.*, pp. 288 f.   [6] *Op. cit.*, vol. 1, pp. 143 f.; vol. 2, pp. 26 ff.

authority (*Obrigkeitsgedanke*). Hence the following conclusion: 'Freedom is not the ability to act in this or that way according to fundamentally arbitrary decisions; freedom is the ability to behave and live in accordance with one's innermost self. Now the innermost self of man is to be sure his individuality which accepts no external law and regulation. Nevertheless, individual rights such as those safeguarding an independent private sphere,[1] as well as those granting the individual a share in determining state policy, are an essential ingredient of political freedom. But the innermost self of man is not only his individuality but also his moral essence.'[2] This, then, leads to Stahl's final solution of the problem of freedom: 'The aim of politics, then, is to ensure this material [as against merely formal] freedom. It must not separate the individual from the physical power or from the moral authority and the historical tradition of the state, so as to found the state upon mere individual will.'[3]

Enough examples for the present. All these solutions of the problem show the same fundamental tendency, the same drive towards the 'concrete' and 'qualitative': The terms used are always 'material freedom' (Stahl), 'concrete freedom' (Hegel), 'positive freedom' (A. Müller), just as in the case of property. 'Concrete' and 'qualitative' are nevertheless expressions which by no means adequately describe the basic intention lying behind all these sequences of thought. The examples we mentioned merely serve to adumbrate something fundamental of which they are the manifestations: a harking back to an earlier way of life.

There is another pair of contrasts besides 'concreteness' and 'abstractness' (and a closely related one), which is also relevant to basic conflict between progressivism and conservatism. Progressive thought not only sees the actual in terms of its potentialities, but also *in terms of the norm.* Conservative thought on the other hand tries to see the actual as the product of real factors; it also tries to understand the norm in terms of the actual.[4]

---

[1] Note the infiltration of liberal ideas into the conservative system of thought.

[2] Fr. J. Stahl, *Die gegenwärtigen Parteien in Staat und Kirche*, pp. 5 f., Berlin, 1863.

[3] *Ibid.*, p. 10.

[4] Cf. Hegel's comment in the Preface to the *Philosophy of Law*: 'To understand what is, is the task of philosophy, since what exists *is* Reason. As to the individual, every one is a son of his epoch anyway; and thus philosophy, too, is nothing but the epoch grasped in thinking. It is just as foolish to imagine that a philosophy can reach beyond its contemporary world as to believe that an individual may skip over his own time—beyond Rhodes, so to speak. If a theory goes beyond the existing world and builds up a world *as it should be*, then this world will exist, to be sure, but its existence will be a purely mental one,—it will exist in a yielding medium in which anything may take shape.' In contrast to this, Hegel in his revolutionary youth wrote to Schelling: 'With the idea of how everything should be gaining universal acceptance, the indolence of settled people who take everything as it is will disappear' (quoted in F. Rosenzweig, *Hegel und der Staat*, vol. 1, p. 31, Munich and Berlin, 1920). In Stahl, Justification of the 'existing' rests on a religious basis; in *Philosophie des Rechts*, vol. 2.

Here too, in the last resort, we are faced with two ways of experiencing things and the environment out of which subsequently two styles of thought arise. One has a quite different attitude to things, persons, and institutions, if one always looks at them *with a demand*, with a 'So it *should* be', at the back of one's mind, instead of treating them as the finished and inevitable products of a long process of growth. If we adopt the first attitude, we shall find ourselves barely glancing at the given realities of our surroundings, never achieving any attachment which would make us indulgent towards their imperfections, nor any feeling of solidarity which would make us concerned with their survival. But the second attitude will lead us to accept the present, with all its defects, uncritically. The first attitude means that one always experiences and judges institutions *as a whole*, the second always involves losing oneself in a mass of detail. To understand the significance of these attitudes, we must first be clear that it is one of the characteristics of mental phenomena that they cannot be understood in isolation, but only as functional parts of a wider whole. If, however, we want to interpret something in terms of what it means—and all mental phenomena *are* only in so far as they *have meaning*—we must grasp it as a phase in some goal-directed endeavour.

The conservative, with his fundamental attachment to the principle of *quieta non movere*, would like to avoid recognition of meanings in this sense,[1] by looking at the actual simply as something that exists; this results in a streak of fatalism.[2] The conservative interpretation or imputation of meanings arises as an antagonistic reaction to the revolutionary mode of conceiving the meaning of things. The conservative, too, can only impart meaning to a thing by 'rounding it out' and fitting it into a wider whole. *But the process, the 'method' of rounding it out is entirely different from that used in liberal revolutionary thought and experience,* which is another indication that in this sphere, ways of experiencing things also develop in close connection with the social background. The peculiarity of the conservative way of putting things into a wider context is that it approaches them in some way *from behind*, from *their past.* For progressive thought, everything derives its meaning in the last analysis from something either above or beyond itself, from a future utopia or from its relation to a transcendent norm. The conservative, however, sees all the significance of a thing in

---

1 In Ranke's 'Political Dialogue' Friedrich, the spokesman of conservatism, declares: 'I hope I did not express myself as if I had wanted to describe the ideal state. I merely wanted to characterize the one we have' (*Das politische Gespräch*, etc., ed. Rothacker, p. 29, Halle, 1925).

2 This fatalism may assume various forms; it appears successively as theological, scientific and historical fatalism.

what lies *behind* it, either its temporal past or its evolutionary germ. Where the progressive uses the future to interpret things, the conservative uses the past; the progressive thinks in terms of *norms*, the conservative in terms of *germs*.

This idea of 'the past which lies behind' can thus be interpreted in two ways: as a temporal past, or as an antecedent evolutionary phase which can account for any particular detail of the actual. Looked at from the former point of view, everything has meaning because it has arisen out of a temporal process of development; from the latter point of view everything that exists historically has meaning because it exhibits the same fundamental drive, the same basic trend of mental and spiritual growth.

Thus the particular thing in this latter case is understood 'physiognomically', as the manifestation of a basic intention, as a particular 'aspect' of a totality represented by a germinal beginning. Both these conservative ways of 'rounding out' an object and giving it meaning thus tend to a total view, and the wider whole which is reached in this way is usually *an intuitively reached whole*.[1] On the other hand, the wider wholes into which the progressive places things are derived from a rational utopia, and this leads to a *structural* view of existing and developing society. A simile may help to make matters clear. The conservative picture of things as a whole is like the inclusive sort of picture of a house which one might get by looking at it from all possible sides, a concrete picture of the house in all its detail from every angle. But the progressive is not interested in all this detail; he makes straight for the ground plan of the house and his picture is suitable for rational analysis rather than for intuitive representation. And within this difference of ways of fitting individual things into their wider context, there lies a further radical difference between progressive and conservative patterns of experience— this time *a difference in the way of experiencing time*.[2]

Briefly, this difference may be expressed as follows: the progressive experiences the present as the beginning of the future, while the conservative regards it simply as the latest point reached by the past. The difference is the more fundamental and radical in that the linear concept of history—which is implied here—is

[1] Cf. F. C. v. Savigny on law, language, customs, constitution as integral wholes; in his work *Vom Beruf unserer Zeit für Gesetzgebung und Rechtswissenschaft* (1814), new ed. 1892, p. 5. Hegel praises Montesquieu for having seen legislation and laws as 'an independent phase of a totality in correlation with all the other characteristics of a nation and an epoch; they will receive their true significance and their justification from this context only' (*op. cit.*, p. 21).

[2] It is not meant, of course, that every conservative experiences time in a different fashion from a liberal; such an assertion would be completely unverifiable. What we do say is that in conservative utterances time as a category appears in a role different rom the one it plays in progressive utterances.

for the conservative something secondary. Primarily, the conservative experiences the past as being one with the present; hence, his concept of history tends to be spatial rather than temporal; it stresses co-existence rather than succession. We may understand this better, if we recall that for typically feudal groups (aristocrats and peasants) history is rooted in the soil; the individuals are nothing but passing Spinozistic 'modi' of this eternal 'substance'.

Land is the real foundation on which the state rests and develops, and only land can really make history. The transient individual is replaced by the more durable factor, land, as the foundation of events. As Möser says in the important introductory sentences of his *Osnabrückische Geschichte:* 'In my opinion, the history of Germany would take an entirely new turn if we traced the fate of the landed estates as the real component parts of the nation through all its changes, considering them as the body of the nation, and their incumbents merely as good or bad accidents as they may happen to the body.'[1]

Every isolated individual and event is regarded as purely incidental and fortuitous as against this compact, territorial substructure. This space-like ordering of events in time is evident in A. Müller, who with the linguistic virtuosity characteristic of all romantics coined the conservative counter-term 'conspatiality' as against the democratically coloured term 'contemporaneity'. In his answer to the question, 'What is a nation?', he repudiated the concept that a given nation, say, the French, consisted of 'the beings with heads, two hands and two feet, who at this insignificant moment happen to be standing, sitting or lying on that part of the Earth's surface which is called France.' As against this, he defined the nation as 'the sublime community of a long succession of past, present and future generations . . . having its tangible appearance in a common language, in common customs and laws, in a host of beneficial institutions . . . in long-lived families and, finally, in the one immortal family . . . of the ruler. . . .'[2] Here he emphasizes the participation of past generations in the present, and he regards the cross-section of time we call the present as a quite unimportant phase in the development of history. This use of time-transcending, spatially determined, material entities as the basis of history is a characteristic which conservative thought has in common with the proletarian and socialist thought which developed later. Proletarian thought also rejects the idea that the individual is the real basis of historical development, and introduces instead entities like 'conditions of production' and 'classes'. There is also a good deal

1 Works, vol. 6, pp. ix f.
2 *Elemente der Staatskunst*, I, pp. 145 f.

of sociology in Möser's statement, if we mean by 'sociology' the ability to understand individual happenings in terms of the more comprehensive factors lying behind them.

But these two 'non-individualistic' interpretations of history differ essentially from each other in that the conservative tends to trace history back to *organic* entities (of which the family is the prototype), whereas the proletarian sees newer forms of collective entities which are primarily, though not exclusively, *agglomerative* rather than organic in character, i.e. classes, as the motor forces of history. The place occupied by the family and corporation in conservative thought is occupied by classes in socialist thought; and in the same way, industrial and productive relations take the place of land.

Only bourgeois thought, standing midway between the two, and starting at that point in history where the old associations are already in dissolution, while the new stratification is still in its infancy, sees society in terms of the isolated individuals of which it is composed, and achieves a picture of the whole which is merely the sum of its parts. The bourgeois-democratic principle which corresponds to this view of society dismembers time in the same way: it experiences movement, but is only able to master its dynamic in so far as it is able to split the movement up into cross-sections of time (*Momentanquerschnitte*). What the 'general will' is is indicated, for each moment in time, by a ballot taken. Thus, in the bourgeois-democratic society, the temporal continuity of the existence of society is atomized in the same way as the national 'community' is broken down into individual atoms; we can reconstruct both only by approximation if we add together the various cross-sections representing successive temporary states. No 'totality' of the collective existence of society can be grasped, except as a sum.[1]

Thus, conservative thought concentrates upon the past in so far as the past lives on in the present; bourgeois thought, essentially devoted to the present, takes its nourishment from what is new now; and proletarian thought tries to grasp the elements of the future which already exist in the present, by concentrating upon those present factors in which the germs of a future society can be seen.

At this point, we at last reach the root of the difference between conservative and progressive forms of experience. It becomes increasingly clear with every case one analyses, that there are at present many different attitudes in the light of which one can experience and understand historical and social events. Each of

[1] On other characteristics of the democratic mind, see Carl Schmitt, *Die geistesgeschichtliche Lage des heutigen Parlamentarismus*, p. 15, Munich and Leipzig, 1923.

us can view them, so to speak, from a different point in the stream of history itself. There are ways of acting in the present which are based upon patterns of response appropriate to past conditions but still surviving today. Others have arisen during the struggle for mastery of the present situation, while yet others, although generated in the bosom of the present itself, will only become dominant formative factors at some future time. The important thing is which of these attitudes determines our evaluation of the historical process.

So far then, we have gathered together a number of character-istic features of the conservative form of experience and thought. We have discussed its *qualitative* nature; its emphasis on concrete-ness as against abstractness; its acceptance of enduring actuality, as compared with the progressive desire for change; the illusory simultaneity it imparts to historical happenings as compared with the liberal linear conception of historical development; its attempt to substitute landed property for the individual as the basis of history; and its preference for organic social units rather than the agglomerative units such as 'classes' favoured by its opponents. All these individual traits, however, are not meant to add up to a concept which will represent 'conservatism' as such. They are merely examples which somehow adumbrate one basic intention, the fundamental impulse lying at the roots of this style of thought. Our aim is to look beyond the examples at this basic intention itself, to follow up its unfolding, and finally to understand its functional importance in relation to the general social process. For the main thing is that this insistence upon 'concreteness', along with all the other features we have described, is a symptom of the conservative's experiencing the historical process in terms of relationships and situations which exist only as hangovers from the past, and that the impulses to act which spring from this way of experiencing history also are centred upon past relationships still surviving in the present. To see things authentically as a conserva-tive, then, is to experience events in terms of an attitude derived from social circumstances and situations anchored in the past,[1] an attitude which changed comparatively little right up to the birth of modern conservatism, because the groups cultivating it had not yet been affected by the specifically modern trends of social evolution. Authentic conservative thought derives its rele-

---

1 Cf. the following phenomenological distinction between 'recollection' and 'tradi-tion', made by Max Scheler: 'In effectively "traditional" behaviour, the past experi-ence is not present in its individuality; its value and meaning, however, appear as "present" and not as "past", as is the case with "recollection" ' (*Vom Umsturz der Werte*, vol. 2, pp. 202 f., Leipzig, 1909). Similarly, 'progressive' behaviour, for Scheler, is distinguished from 'expectancy': in the former, the future pattern of events becomes effective without explicit anticipation (*ibid.*).

vance, its dignity as something more than mere speculation, from the fact that vital attitudes of this character still survive in various sectors of our society.

These older ways of experiencing the world alone impart to conservatism its distinctive character. Hence, we can best study authentic conservatism in those social spheres where the traditional continuity of the concrete groups with a naturally conservative way of life is not yet broken. On the other hand, conservatism first becomes conscious and reflective when other ways of life and thought appear on the scene, against which it is compelled to take up arms in the ideological struggle. This is the first stage in the formation of a definitely conservative ideology; it is also a stage of methodological deliberation in which conservatism tries to become conscious of its essence. Subsequently, it becomes the destiny of conservatism that it can increasingly maintain itself only on the plane of conscious reflection. Möser, who marks this first stage in the development of conservatism in Germany, still lives entirely within the bounds of tradition; nevertheless, he does try to grasp the nature of this authentic conservatism in a reflective manner.

In the measure, however, that specifically modern social structures not merely co-exist with old ones but draw them into their orbit and transform them, authentic conservative experience tends to disappear. The simple habit of living more or less unconsciously, as though the old ways of life were still appropriate, gradually gives way to a deliberate effort to maintain them under the new conditions, and they are raised to the level of conscious reflection, of deliberate 'recollection'. Conservative thought thus saves itself, so to speak, by raising to the level of reflection and conscious manipulation those forms of experience which can no longer be had in an authentic way.

Here, at the stage where experience based on mere tradition began to disappear, the meaning of history was first consciously discovered, and every effort was bent towards the development of a method of thought by which the old attitude towards the world could somehow be rescued. This method of reviving old attitudes gave rise to an entirely new way of interpreting the genetic process of history. Our position, then, is that old ways of life and thought do not become superfluous and merely die off, as would be assumed by someone thinking in purely 'progressive' terms. On the contrary, in so far as these elements of the past are really alive and have a real social basis, they will always transform and adapt themselves to the new stage of social and mental development, and thus keep alive a 'strand' of social development which would otherwise have become extinct.

In order, therefore, that modern conservatism could develop as a conscious political philosophy opposed to the liberal philosophy of the Enlightenment, and play a dynamic role within the modern struggle of ideas, its germinal 'basic intention' had to exist as an authentic style of experience within certain traditional groups. Hence, we cannot neglect the task of exploring the conservative 'basic intention' in its unconscious, unreflective form; this is why we often return to the writings of Justus Möser who represents authentic conservatism, not yet at the level of 'recollection' and reflection, a conservatism—in fact, rather a kind of feudal 'traditionalism'. Only when this authentic conservatism is uprooted and detached from its original social foundations and takes on a reflective character, does the problem arise of its transformation into an urban current of thought with fixed maxims and methodological insights of its own.

(b) The theoretical core of conservative thought

Now comes the second stage in our analysis. We have described the basic impulse behind conservatism in its pre-theoretical, primitive form. We must now ask whether there is not some theoretical core, some problem at the centre of conservative thought in its more developed form, an analysis of which will provide us with a clear view of its major methodological characteristics.

Such a key problem for conservatism does exist. Conservative thought emerged as an independent current when it was forced into conscious opposition to bourgeois-revolutionary thought, to *the natural-law mode of thought*. What had up to this point been a more or less latent impulse in thought now found a theoretical nucleus around which it could crystallize and develop. Its opponent had a 'system', and conservatism was thus compelled gradually to develop its own 'counter-system'. It is important, of course, not to fall into Stahl's error by thinking that two distinct cut-and-dried systems of thought now confronted one another. Conservative and liberal-bourgeois thought are not ready-made 'systems' in this sense; they are *ways of thinking* in continuous process of development. Conservatism did not merely want to think 'something different' from its liberal opponents; *it wanted to think it differently*, and that was the impulse which provided that extra touch which turned it into a new form of thought.

The key problem for conservatism was opposition to natural-law thought. We shall therefore classify all the features which distinguish natural-law thought in the eighteenth century as a style of thought, and compare them with the corresponding characteristics of conservative thought. Our classification is divided into features of content and features of form, or methodology.

A. *The contents of natural-law thought*

    i. The doctrine of the 'state of nature'.
    ii. The doctrine of the social contract.
    iii. The doctrine of popular sovereignty.
    iv. The doctrine of the inalienable Rights of Man (life, liberty, property, the right to resist tyranny, etc.).

B. *The methodological characteristics of natural-law thought*

    i. Rationalism as a method of solving problems.
    ii. Deductive procedure from one general principle to the particular cases.
    iii. A claim of *universal validity* for every individual.
    iv. A claim to universal applicability of all laws to all historical and social units.
    v. Atomism and mechanism: collective units (the state, the law, etc.), are constructed out of isolated individuals or factors.
    vi. Static thinking (right reason conceived as a self-sufficient, autonomous sphere unaffected by history).

The most satisfactory way to get at the essentials of conservative thought is to see how it opposed each of these aspects of natural-law thought in turn.

The conservatives attacked the *content* of natural-law thought, questioned the idea of a 'state of nature', the idea of a Social Contract, the principle of popular sovereignty, and the Rights of Man.

They attacked it methodologically along the following lines:

(i) The conservatives replaced Reason with concepts such as History, Life, the Nation.

This produces philosophical problems which dominate the whole epoch. In their abstract formulation, these philosophies deal with such old problems as that of 'thinking' and 'being'; but it is possible to interpret this discussion in a thoroughly concrete fashion, that is, in terms of the overwhelmingly powerful experience of the French Revolution. Sociologically speaking, most philosophical schools which place 'thinking' above 'being' have their roots either in bourgeois revolutionary or in bureaucratic mentality, while most schools which place 'being' above 'thinking' have their origin in the ideological counter-movement of romanticism and especially in the experience of counter-revolution.

(ii) To the deductive bent of the natural-law school, the conservative opposes the *irrationality of reality*. The problem of the irrational is the second great problem of the period; it too, in the form it assumed at the time, has its sociological roots in the French Revolution. The problem of the relation of genesis to validity attains its modern significance in these ideological struggles.

(iii) In answer to the liberal claim of universal validity for all, the conservative poses the problem of *individuality* in radical fashion.

(iv) The concept of the social *organism* is developed by the conservatives to counter the liberal-bourgeois belief in the universal applicability of all political and social innovations. This concept has a special significance, since it arose from the natural conservative impulse to stem the spreading tide of the French Revolution by pointing out the impossibility of transferring political institutions arbitrarily from one nation to another. The emphasis on the qualitative which is so characteristic of conservative thought also arises from the same impulse.

(v) Against the construction of collective units from isolated individuals and factors, the conservative opposes a kind of thought which starts from a concept of a whole which is not the mere sum of its parts. The state or nation is not to be understood as the sum of its individual members, but the individuals are to be understood only as parts of the wider whole (cf. the concept of 'folk spirit'). The conservative thinks in terms of 'We' when the liberal thinks in terms of 'I'. The liberal analyses and isolates the various cultural fields such as Law, Government, Economy; the conservative seeks a synoptical and synthetic view.

(vi) One of the most important logical weapons against the natural-law style of thought is the *dynamic conception of Reason*. At first, the conservative merely opposed the rigidity of the static theory of Reason with the movement of 'Life' and history. Later, however, he discovered a much more radical method of disposing of the eternal norms of the Enlightenment. Instead of regarding the world as eternally changing in contrast to a static Reason, he conceived of Reason and of its norms themselves as changing and moving. In this way, the impulse to oppose natural-law thought had really contributed something new, had achieved new insights which played a momentous role in later evolution.

As we have already mentioned, nowhere do we find any conservative thinker making a systematic attack on natural-law thought as a whole; each deals with and criticizes certain aspects of it only. Thus it is impossible to juxtapose two static, completely developed systems of thought. All that can be done is to demonstrate the two ways of thinking, the two ways of tackling problems. The analysis of its pre-theoretical and theoretical elements which we have given is in our view the only legitimate substitute for a definition of conservative thought.

In the following section we leave this general description of conservative thought and turn to a more detailed historical and sociological analysis.

SECTION 3

The Social Structure of Romantic and Feudalistic Conservatism

Having described the general character of a certain historical mode of thought, our next task is to investigate its concrete development, in all its different currents, from the point of view of its social structure and stratification.

The most important aim of such an analysis is to find out how far any new trend of thought that may happen to arise reflects the sociological characteristics of the group or individuals who stand behind it and through whom it finds expression. Phenomenological and logical stylistic analysis and sociological analysis must be used as complementary methods.

Here again—as has already been mentioned—not more than one selected section of a complex historical situation will be presented. From the numerous currents which can be distinguished in the general flow of conservative thought, the romantic and feudalistic trend has been chosen for this purpose.

We can best give an overall characterization of the mental climate of a country at a given time, without entering upon a detailed analysis, by indicating the way in which it absorbs and transforms foreign cultural influences.

An investigation, from this point of view, of the intellectual atmosphere of Germany in the period which has been selected, viz. the decades following the French Revolution, shows as the most significant fact that the revolution produced in Prussia, the outstanding centre of conservative thought, an antagonism between the older feudalistic tendencies and the bureaucratic rationalism of the eighteenth-century monarchy. The French Revolution no doubt had a revolutionary influence on the Prussian bourgeoisie. But perhaps even more significant was its effect in weakening, for a time, the spiritual and political alliance between the absolute monarchy and the nobility which Frederick the Great had made one of the corner-stones of his social policy.[1] Not that the middle classes were inaccessible to the liberal ideas of the

[1] Frederick the Great wrote in his Political Testament of 1752: 'One object of the policy of the king of Prussia is the preservation of nobility. For, whatever changes may come about, he may perhaps find a richer, but he will never find a more courageous and loyal nobility. In order to assist the nobility in maintaining their property, commoners should be prevented from acquiring titled estates. They should be encouraged

revolution; we know very well the enthusiasm with which the widest circles of the German intelligentsia greeted the outbreak of the revolution in France.[1] The careers of most conservatives and reactionaries show revolutionary periods in their youth. We know also that there was a surprisingly large number of men with liberal ideas among the higher officials, and that the 'reforms from above' which were carried through after the battle of Jena were due to these influences. Yet this liberal response to the revolution was in the main ideological in its nature; it was largely reversed by the subsequent development of the real historical factors.

That fact in itself need not surprise us. The complex intellectual pattern of any age is historically and socially conditioned. It is therefore one of its characteristics that it reacts to external ideological influences in a definite manner which reflects its own specific structure, and that it re-moulds them to fit the direction of its own development. The ideas of 1789 demanded, in contrast to the theory of royal absolutism, that the state should be constructed 'from below' instead of 'from above'. When they penetrated into Germany, they could only set in motion and bring to life those elements of the German, and more specifically the Prussian, body politic which happened to exist there as historically and socially relevant forces. They were the estates of which in turn one alone was politically effective, the nobility.[2] Every other influence was at that time bound to remain merely 'ideological'.

We may see in the first decades of the nineteenth century in Prussia a sociological experiment, as it were, which shows what happens when ideas which have genuinely grown up in a more advanced stage of social development enter a socially backward but culturally mature society. Germany, and especially Prussia whose fate was decisive for conservative thought, were many decades behind the Western countries in the economic development towards capitalism. We need not accept Frederick the Great's estimate of Germany's backwardness in his time.[3] But

to invest their capital in trade so that only a nobleman may buy an estate, should another be forced to sell' ('Friedrich der Grosse, Die politischen Testamente', *Klassiker der Politik*, ed. Meinecke, Oncken, vol. 5, p. 33, Berlin, 1922). For the later development, *vide* F. A. L. v.d. Marwitz, *Ein märkischer Edelmann im Zeitalter der Befreiungskriege*, ed. F. Meusel, 2 vols. (in 4 half-vols.), vol. 2, pp. 80 ff.

[1] Cf., for example, Venedey, *Die deutschen Republikaner unter der französischen Republik*, Leipzig, 1870.

[2] Cf., for example, E. Jordan, *Die Entstehung der Konservativen Partei und die preussischen Agrarverhältnisse vor 1848*, pp. 9 f., 1914. Also G. Kaufmann, *Geschichte Deutschlands im 19. Jahrhundert*, p. 48, Berlin, 1912.

[3] Cf., for example, E. v. Meier, *Die französischen Einflüsse auf die Staats- und Rechtsentwicklung Preussens im 19. Jahrhundert*, vol. 1, p. 6, Leipzig, 1907. Meier considers Frederick the Great's remark that the intellectual condition of Germany corresponded to the condition of France under Francis I correct if applied to the early years of Frederick's life.

Marx's view is probably correct; and he held that the social condition of Germany in 1843 corresponded roughly to that of France in 1789.[1] At the time of the French Revolution neither Germany nor *a fortiori* Prussia possessed a real equivalent to the third or fourth 'estate'. The transformation of the feudal society of estates into a class society was still in its early stages. The proletariat consisted of handicraftsmen who still lived to all intents and purposes in a system of guilds and did not react to external pressure as a class. Nor did the '*Mittelstand*' really correspond to the '*tiers état*'; as Sombart has shown, it was as yet by no means a bourgeoisie.[2] Socially and politically immature, it still lacked clearly defined aims and a conscious purpose; it was at the mercy of a variety of ideological currents and cross-currents. The *Mittelstand* had as yet no precise place in the social system, a place defined by its own interests. As a result, most of its members were politically indifferent. They were quick to welcome new ideas; but also unstable and ready to change their moods when things went wrong or not in accordance with their abstract expectations. All these characteristics were clear symptoms of the fact that the diverse interests of the *Mittelstand* were not yet integrated along class lines. The reason for the relatively weak revolutionary influence of the French Revolution is therefore that it evoked a purely ideological response: the bourgeois element was at that time less capable of political action than any other social stratum in Germany.

An active response to the revolution came only from those strata in Prussia which their own history and the nature of the social order enabled to be politically effective, the nobility and the bureaucracy. If we may put it in an exaggerated form: For our purposes, the most important effect of the French Revolution is that the French conflict between king and people is here reproduced on a 'higher' level. It takes the form of a struggle between the estates (the nobility), which form and build up the state 'from below', and the monarchy, ruling the state 'from above' and represented in Prussia by its bureaucracy. The result is a curious interplay of influences. The revolutionary impulse proper in the French upheaval gives life and meaning to the aims of the

---

[1] K. Marx, *Zur Kritik der Hegelschen Rechtsphilosophie*, vol. 1, p. 385.

[2] 'The *Mittelstand* united in those days everyone who did not belong either to the nobility or to the lower classes. It did not have the character of a class in our sense of the term. Sometimes it appeared as the group which comprised all the moderately well-to-do; sometimes more as the educated sections of the population' (Sombart, *Die deutsche Volkswirtschaft im 19. Jahrhundert*, p. 444, Berlin, 1921). Cf. also K. F. Moser's frequently quoted remark: 'We lack that mediatory power which Montesquieu considered the support and defence of a good monarchy: le *tiers état*.'—For reasons of space we cannot enter upon a more thorough-going economic analysis of the social system of the time.

nobility who wish to form and rule the state 'from below', insists upon the privileges of the estates, and seeks an 'organic' society, a desire to revive the corporative structure of medieval society.[1] The mechanistic, rationalist, and centralizing impulse in the French Revolution, on the other hand, finds its exponents in the bureaucracy and is used by them as a weapon against the nobility. What complicates the situation further is the fact that in Prussia the revolution was at first really imposed 'from above'. (The expression 'revolution from above' was coined by von Harden-berg.) Reforms which the development of the state towards capitalism required were carried out by the absolutist state, supported by its bureaucracy. They were carried through only partly in the interests of the masses. To a certain extent they were directed against the nobility.

In France the revolution had brought about a defensive alliance between the nobility, the monarchy, and the Church. In Prussia the *real* pressure from below was negligible. The result was there-fore a partial weakening of the alliance between the nobility and the bureaucracy. The situation found its ideological expression in a feudalistic reaction. It was a movement which in its thought and ideas belonged to the nineteenth century. With the most advanced ideological weapons it fought for aims which were determined by the social position of the nobility. It expressed therefore in modern terms purposes which had their social basis and justification in an age long gone by. The ideological reaction to the Enlightenment was combined with the social reaction of the nobility. Romanticism took on a feudalistic character; the feudalistic conservatism of the nobility assumed a romantic colouring. From this combination arose the peculiar features which to the present day characterize the 'German' mind.[2] What

---

[1] The following sentences from v. d. Marwitz may serve as an illustration: 'However active and benevolent a government may be, it is useless to the state, unless the governed understand and share [*miterleben*] its activities' (*op. cit.*, vol. 2, p. 58), or (*ibid.*, footnote): 'The state does not consist of men who *live side by side*, and of whom some rule and the others obey; it consists of men who live *within each other*, it is the *unified* spiritual direction of their will'. ('Der Staat ist nicht ein *Nebeneinandersein* von Menschen, deren einige befehlen, die anderen gehorchen, sondern das *Ineinandersein* dieser Menschen—die *gemeinschaftliche* geistige Richtung ihres Wollens . . .').

[2] We cannot accept the view of those who think of national ways of thought as ultimate and unanalysable data which are to be deduced directly from 'national characters' and who speak in that sense of the 'French', 'German' or 'English' mind. It is possible that sociological study may in the end come up against some irreducible residuum of national character, although even that residuum could not be considered as unchangeable in the course of time. But one must first take into account all those factors which can be deduced from the history and social structure of the nation. Once one adopts this approach, one will realize that those who speak of a 'national' way of thought are in fact thinking of the thought of a particular period of national life, and within that period only of the thought of a particular social stratum which happens to have a decisive influence on the national culture in that period. They take this socio-logically and historically closely definable way of thought for the way of thought of

strikes us as the 'German' way of thinking is the predominance of these 'romantic' elements, supplemented by 'historicist' ones which arose at the same time and in the same constellation of historical forces and which became a powerful factor in the alliance between romanticism and feudalistic conservatism.

In order to understand this peculiar combination it is necessary to look more closely at the social character of the strata which took part in this ideological struggle. Let us begin with the romantic opposition. It consists, first, of the nobility, and secondly, of the 'idéologues', middle-class literati and literary aristocrats, who became the spokesmen of the movement.

The romantic movement, considered as an *ideological* force, began as a reaction against the Enlightenment. Its *social* basis seems to have been—especially in the period of *préromantisme*—in social strata which stood apart from the general current towards modern capitalism. They may perhaps be defined as the petty bourgeoisie (*Kleinbürgertum*). In this connection the Protestant parsonage seems to have played a particularly important part.[1] It is especially the son of the Protestant parson in whom the Enlightenment stirs doubts of the traditional religion, but who does not therefore succumb to the opposite extreme of an abstract rationalism. He experiences a transformation of his religious attitude. All his traditional habits of thought and emotional reactions which were fostered by the religious life in the parsonage survive the impact of the Enlightenment. Deprived of their positive content, they are directed with redoubled strength against the rationalist atmosphere of the time. The new approval of irrationality for its own sake was made possible by the preceding tendency to concentrate and emphasize the rational elements of the mind. A compact

the whole nation at all times. In this form the view is mistaken. What is true is that certain epochs and in these epochs certain social strata may have a lasting effect on the habits of thought of a nation, especially if the epoch is a decisive one for the development of national history and culture. In this sense, A. de Tocqueville (*L'ancien régime et la révolution*, 8th ed., p. 217, Paris, 1877) deduced the French tendency towards abstract thinking quite correctly from the sociological importance of the pre-revolutionary era—and the mentality of that era, in turn, from the cultural predominance of an intelligentsia which was excluded from the government and administration of the country. To the same extent, but in the opposite direction, the years of the Napoleonic wars and of the subsequent period of reaction have been decisive for the character of German thought. The 'German' mind has ever since been so completely romantic and historicist that even its own opposition which grew up in that atmosphere could never quite free itself from its habits of thought. Heine was a romantic despite his opposition to the romantic school; Marx a historicist despite his opposition to the historical school; etc.

[1] Cf. the thorough investigations of H. Schöffler in his *Protestantismus und Literatur*, 'Neue Wege zur englischen Literatur des achtzehnten Jahrhunderts', Leipzig, 1922.— For the precursors of the romantic movement see also Paul van Tieghem, *Le Préromantisme*, 'Études d'histoire littéraire Européenne', Paris, 1924; and A. Weise, *Die Entstehung des Fühlens und Denkens der Romantik auf Grund der romantischen Zeitschriften*, Diss. Leipzig, 1912.

ideological counter-movement of irrationalism could only arise because the Enlightenment had carried the tendency towards rationalization to the utmost extreme. It had managed to conceive the world in a radically and consistently rational manner. It thereby excluded at every point irrational factors; but with them it threw out elements of human nature which by that very process of exclusion were welded together and became the nucleus of a counter-current. They became the object of special attention and affection to all those who by reason of their personal history and social tradition were still able to think and feel in such terms—just as in the opposite camp the rationalist current had found its exponents in the progressive bourgeoisie, the monarchy, and the bureaucracy.

With the political trends of the time the romantic movement was at first but loosely connected. All we can say is that revolutionary sympathies prevailed in harmony with the predominant mood of the pre-revolutionary period. After the French Revolution the various national sections of the romantic movement went their own ways, each in accordance with the social structure of the country. The special conditions of Germany explain why German romanticism turned to conservatism and reaction.[1] In any case, this development meant a reinforcement of all those trends within the romantic movement which were from the beginning opposed to the new world of capitalism and liberalism. The peculiar characteristic of German romanticism is therefore that it increasingly unites the ideological and the political opposition against the modern world.

This ideological and political antagonism against the basic forces of the modern world must, however, not be allowed to conceal the fact that the romantic movement is not just a purely retrogressive reaction. The romantic mind has already absorbed and neutralized the contribution of modern rationalism. It is not adequate to think of romanticism simply as a diametrically opposed and entirely heterogeneous counter-movement to rationalism. It should rather be compared to the swing of a pendulum —a sudden reversal from an extreme point reached in one direction. The change-over from rationalism into irrationalism—both in the emotional life and in the intellectual activities of the individual—occurs even among the chief representatives of the Enlightenment itself. Thus in Rousseau and Montesquieu an extreme rationalism and its opposite exist peacefully side by side.[2]

[1] For the situation in France cf. C. Schmitt-Dorotic, *Politische Romantik*, Munich and Leipzig, 1919, especially the introduction.
[2] A. Wahl, 'Montesquieu als Vorläufer von Aktion und Reaktion', in *Historische Zeitschrift*, vol. 109, 1912.

In Germany the precursors of the romantic movement, the men of the '*Sturm und Drang*', Hamann and Herder appear already in the heyday of the Enlightenment. Only the swing of the pendulum which derives its impetus from the same forces as the rationalist movement explains why—in spite of undeniable radical contrasts—romanticism shows qualities which recall the rationalism of the eighteenth century: among them, its excessive subjectivism, admittedly a form of subjectivism very different from the subjectivism of the Enlightenment; also, its tendency—co-existing with a pronounced programmatic irrationalism—to rationalize all those irrational forces of the mind which the rationalism of the Enlightenment with all its abstract methods could never really have apprehended.

By the time this romantic current takes on the form of a 'movement' its exponents are to be found chiefly among the 'socially unattached intelligentsia'.[1] Thus, it has its social basis in the same stratum as the Enlightenment. But there is also a difference. In the Enlightenment, that stratum and its philosophical spokesmen were still, as it were, in touch with their social and historical origins. The bourgeois writers of the Enlightenment could still lean on the ideological support of the bourgeoisie. The conversion to romanticism meant for the intelligentsia an increasing social and philosophical isolation.[2] Nowhere is it more apparent to what extent the intelligentsia constitutes a distinct sociological phenomenon whose place within the social organism is so difficult to determine just because of the instability of its social condition and its lack of a secure economic position. The German intelligentsia, as far as it was socially unattached, was indeed very badly off during that period. Newspapers in our sense there were none, and the last years of Kleist's life show what it meant to keep alive a journal like the *Berliner Abendblätter*.[3] One could try to exist as an independent writer, a profession which was then of but recent origin. Klopstock, Lessing and Wieland were in fact the first German writers who tried to make a living by literary production alone.[4] In view of these difficulties which life as an independent intellectual involved it is not surprising that the lives of most literary men of the time show, after a period of violent youthful

---

[1] An expression of Alfred Weber's.

[2] The son of the parson becomes an independent writer, etc.

[3] Cf. the vivid account in R. Steig, *Heinrich v. Kleist's Berliner Kämpfe*, Berlin and Stuttgart, 1901.

[4] Cf. Lamprecht, *Deutsche Geschichte*, vol. 8 (I), p. 209. Lessing's other literary contemporaries, Weisse, Engel, Moritz, Dusch, soon took refuge in safer means of earning their living. Compared with Lessing's time conditions had improved only at the time of Schlegel and Novalis. Cf. W. Dilthey, *Leben Schleiermachers*, vol. 1 (2nd ed.), pp. 193, 255, Berlin and Leipzig, 1922.

opposition to the world and their environment, the tendency to take refuge in the haven of officialdom.

This combination of an unstable economic position with an intellectual horizon which went far beyond their own narrow sphere of life produced in the romantic writers an enormous sensibility coupled with moral uncertainty and a constant readiness to become adventurers or mercenary pamphleteers. They cannot earn a living by their own unaided effort in their 'unattached' state. They sell their pen to one government or another[1]; they oscillate between Prussia and Austria, many of them landing at that time with Metternich who knew well how to make use of their services. Never properly employed as officials, chiefly used for secret or propaganda services, their thought assumes that semi-concrete quality which stands halfway between the idealist's remoteness from the affairs of the world and the official's exclusive concentration on concrete tasks. They are neither abstract dreamers, nor narrow-minded practical men. They are characteristically interested in exploring the specific marks of their age[2]; they are born philosophers of history. This, in fact, is the positive side of their activity, for there must and should always be men who are sufficiently free from the ordinary ties to shoulder cares other than that for the common routine of life[3]; and the more involved the social process becomes, the greater the need for such men who are in a position to throw light on its course. At the beginning, or at least at an important juncture of that development, which represents, as it were, the creation by history of an organ of self-observation, stand the speculations of the Enlightenment on the philosophy of history. Romantic thought fulfils the same function, although the value standards it applies are diametrically opposed to those of Enlightenment. From this source, too, German sociology has derived its predilection for problems of the philosophy of history, a predilection which, in contrast to Western sociology, it still maintains as its characteristic quality. This is the positive element in romantic political thought. Its negative quality is its readiness to justify any cause and any condition.

[1] Adam Müller even makes an offer to Hardenberg to edit, in the service of the government, a government *and* an opposition paper at the same time.

[2] An essay by Friedrich Schlegel was entitled 'Die Signatur des Zeitalters'.

[3] If one attempted to speculate *a priori*, without taking historical experience into account, at which point in the social structure a philosophy of history (in other words an interest in the totality of the process of history) is likely to arise, one would think it probable that those would reflect on these general aspects who, by their social position, are responsible for the whole—high officials, diplomats, kings. Experience, however, shows that this conjecture is only partially correct, if at all. High civil servants possess the necessary practical experience and knowledge of the forces at work; but their general point of view tends to see society in terms of administration or

These unattached intellectuals are the typical advocate-philoso-phers, *ideologues* who can find arguments in favour of any political cause they may happen to serve. Their own social position does not bind them to any cause, but they have an extraordinarily refined sense for all the political and social currents around them, and the ability to detect them and enter into their spirit. By them-selves they know nothing. But let them take up and identify themselves with someone else's interests—they will know them better, really better, than those for whom these interests are laid down by the nature of things, by their social condition.

Sensibility is therefore also the peculiar quality of their thought. Their virtue is not thoroughness but a flair for events in the spiri-tual and intellectual life of their society. Their constructions are therefore always false or even deliberately falsified. But there is always something that is astutely observed. Herein lies the fruitfulness of the romantic movement for the social sciences.[1] It threw up problems for discussion; it discovered whole new spheres of study. But it was left to later research to sift the facts from mere

---

power politics. Such a perspective can never give rise to a philosophy of history or sociology. The 'unattached intelligentsia' is no doubt liable to hatch out empty specula-tions. Yet the best chance for the achievement of comprehensive views of the whole course of history appears when intellectuals who are gifted with an instinct for concrete matters and who are, to start with, socially unattached, ally themselves with the aims of real existing social forces. (It is, in this context, at first irrelevant whether the real forces which they join show society from above, as with Ranke or Treitschke, or from below, as with Marx.) The first generation of the romanticists still lacked this sense of the concrete. Even in its later period (Fr. Schlegel, A. Müller) abstract speculation and awareness of real forces are to be found side by side but unrelated. Ranke, Treitschke, Marx show a much more powerful fusion of both faculties; it is almost possible to speak of progress. How much even the 'first servant of the state' is prevented by the peculiar character of his social position from reaching a proper philosophical or sociological insight into the general structure of society—even where he is personally endowed with a gift for 'philosophy'—some sentences from Frederick the Great's Political Testament of 1752 may serve to illustrate. He writes: 'Too ambitious and complicated political schemes are no more successful than excessively ingenious movements in a war. . . .' He gives some historical examples and then continues: 'All these examples show that grand schemes which are tackled too soon never come off. Politics is too much subject to accidents. It gives the human mind no power over future events and over anything that belongs to the realm of chance. The art of politics consists more in utilizing favourable opportunities than in bringing them about by careful planning in advance. For this reason I advise you not to conclude treaties which refer to uncertain events in the future, but to preserve your freedom of action so as to be able to take your decisions in accordance with time, place, and the state of your affairs: in one word, as your interests will require at the time' (pp. 61 f.). Even the 'political reveries' which follow do not break through the 'tactical approach'. The agent himself stands much too close to be able to see behind the appearances of men and affairs and to penetrate to the structural relationships.·

[1] For the importance of romanticism for historiography, cf. v. Below, *Wesen und Ausbreitung der Romantik*, supplement to his book *Über historische Periodisierung* (*Einzel-schriften zur Politik und Geschichte*, ed. by H. Roeseler, no. 11, Berlin, 1925). Also v. Below, *Die deutsche Geschichtsschreibung von den Befreiungskriegen bis zu unseren Tagen*, 2nd ed. (*Handbuch der mittelalterlichen und neueren Geschichte*, Munich and Berlin, 1927).

intellectual constructions. The 'enlightened' intellect of the French *philosophes* had to substitute wit and *esprit* for the scientific foundation which it lacked. With the romanticists this wit becomes a specific form of sensitiveness—a faculty for detecting fine shades of quality, supreme mastery in the art of emotional sympathy and appreciation. Thus the intellectual current of literary *esprit* and romanticism produces one component of what one might call 'qualitative thinking'. Its other component sprang at the same time, though in a wholly different way, from the attitude of feudalistic conservatism.[1] It was due, as we have seen, to their lack of any firm roots in the social structure that the romanticists were excluded from an understanding of ultimate ends, that their thought was full of direction but without starting-point, that they defended causes which had their social basis elsewhere—in strata of greater social vitality. Their fate is typical of the fate of the intelligentsia in the modern world—clearly traceable since the eighteenth century. The fate of the world of thought is in the care of a socially unattached, or barely attached, stratum whose class affinities and status in society cannot be precisely defined; a stratum which does not find the aims it pursues within itself but in the interests of strata with a more definite place in the social order. This fact is of the greatest importance for modern thought, because the ultimate directions and aims of ideological movements are determined by their social background. If even these ultimate aims were surrendered into the hands of that socially unattached intelligentsia they would soon be scattered and frittered away. If, on the other hand, there were no such stratum of socially free and unattached intellectuals, it might easily happen that all spiritual content would disappear from our increasingly capitalistic society and leave nothing but naked interests. For it is the latter which are at the basis of ideas as well as ideologies.

If one wants to carry the description of the peculiar character of the thought of these romantic writers beyond the two qualities which have already been mentioned (their interest in the philosophy of history and their sensitiveness to qualitative differences) one could hardly find a better definition of the romantic element than that which was given by Novalis himself. He declares: 'The world must be romanticized. That is the way to its original meaning. Romanticizing means nothing but *raising to a higher level of quality*. Through that operation the lower

[1] When two currents of thought merge into each other, it is the task of the sociology of knowledge to discover those elements in both which showed an inner resemblance even *before* the synthesis and which thus made the synthesis possible. This is one of the guiding considerations in this part of our analysis. The methodological problem has been suggested previously, in a similar sense, by Max Weber, in his *Religionssoziologie*, vol. 1, p. 83.

self is identified with a higher self, since our soul consists of a series of qualitatively different levels. This operation is still completely unknown. *In giving a noble meaning to the vulgar, a mysterious appearance to the commonplace, the dignity of the unknown to the known, the semblance of infinity to the finite,* I romanticize it.'[1] We should like to redefine this 'technique' of thought by saying that it finds a higher level of cause and meaning for the facts of a given situation than is usually associated with them. We believe that this merely expresses in different words what Novalis said in the above quotation. It shows, at the same time, that the facts of a situation are not created or discovered by the romantic thinker. He merely receives them from somewhere. A typical instance of this method of 'romanticizing' is the romantic treatment of Catholicism or of the nobility. The existence of the nobility is an empirical fact. Assuming all the historical faults and virtues of the nobility as known and given, romantic thought contributes its share by discovering a 'principle', and representing the historical development of the nobility as a struggle between conflicting principles. The facts which in themselves are merely parts of a causally interrelated situation, especially in the eyes of a person with a positivist approach, are thereby given a new interpretation as aspects of a meaningful whole. Such 'romanticizing' no doubt sheds new light on the facts ('something is always astutely observed') but it conceals the real relationships.[2]

It would not be necessary to spend much time on this method of 'romanticizing' if it were confined to the political sphere. The peculiar thing is, however, that this method led to the re-discovery and understanding of an older *mode of thought* which would otherwise have remained latent. Just as romantic thought failed to find its political aims within itself, so it took over, at a certain

---

[1] Novalis, *Schriften*, ed. by J. Minor, vol. 2, pp. 304 f., Jena, 1907.   My italics.

[2] We emphasize in the text the concealing character of romantic thought. It could, however, be shown that the romantic method of thought is fruitful in fields where interpretation is appropriate. The reason is that the spiritual sphere may be penetrated to varying 'depths'. The positive meaning of Novalis's remark and of the whole romantic mode of thought lies in the fact that, in contrast to the Enlightenment, it was aware of these different depths. For reasons of space we have to refrain here from a phenomenological analysis which would show this in detail. But such an analysis would also have to show that the romantic preoccupation with these 'depths' was not a true one. The predominance of the subjective approach introduced an arbitrary element into its interpretations and prevented the thinker from getting really inside his subject. This also explains the possibility of abuse to which the method of 'romanticizing' lends itself: the tendency to interpret, or understand 'from within', causally interrelated situations which, by their objective nature, are incapable of such interpretation, and to dignify mean and brutal power relationships by 'interpreting' them. Significantly enough, the possibility of a twofold interpretation is already contained in Novalis's definition : one which attempts to sound the 'depths' of the soul, and a second which leads to an ideological dressing-up of things as they are. The romantic movement realized both possibilities.

stage of its development, certain fundamental ideas opposed to the Enlightenment from the inventory of ideas of *feudalistic conservatism*. It 'romanticized' certain tentatively elaborated conservative theses into a full-fledged methodology, and adapted them to political purposes.

At the important juncture in the history of German social thought where the romanticism of the intellectuals (as the ideological reaction against the Enlightenment) joins hands with the current of feudalistic conservatism stands Adam Müller with his *Elemente der Staatskunst* (Elements of Politics). Adam Müller is not an author who deserves attention on account of his creative originality or the solid worth of his achievement. But he is one of those historical figures who have done a great deal to shape the thought of their age, or at least of one of its predominant movements. He is the born *ideologue* and romanticist in the sense which has just been defined; receptive rather than creative, but at the same time a connoisseur, endowed with an exquisite flair for gathering up what belongs together from the teeming welter of contemporary ideas.[1]

Since we are here concerned only with the main trends of thought, we cannot discuss in detail the beginnings of political romanticism, and little need be said about the early political writings of Novalis and Friedrich Schlegel. Everything they contain that became relevant for the subsequent development of thought is somehow or other worked into Adam Müller's system. Novalis's beautiful essay 'Christendom or Europe' (1799) stands out, but it is a poetic dream rather than political thought.[2] Its ideological point was discovered by Müller: its criticism of Protestantism and its praise for the Catholic hierarchy. With Novalis came into the open that curious Protestant longing for the deserted Church which led to a considerable movement of

---

[1] The literature on romanticism is too extensive to be given here in full. Some of it is collected in J. Baxa, *Einführung in die romantische Staatswissenschaft*, pp. 176 ff., Jena, 1925, and in the second volume of Baxa's edition of Adam Müller's *Elemente der Staatskunst*. The relevant chapters in Meinecke, *Weltbürgertum und Nationalstaat*, and Troeltsch, *Der Historismus und seine Probleme*, are useful. Of recent works may be mentioned, for example, the special volume on romanticism of the *Deutsche Vierteljahrsschrift für Literaturwissenschaft und Geistesgeschichte*, 2. Jahrg., Heft 3, Halle, 1924; R. Aris, *Die Staatslehre Adam Müllers in ihrem Verhältnis zur deutschen Romantik*, Tübingen, 1929; I. Petersen, *Die Wesensbestimmung der deutschen Romantik*, Leipzig, 1926; S. v. Lempicki, *Bücherwelt und wirkliche Welt.* 'Ein Beitrag zur Wesenserfassung der Romantik', in *Deutsche Vierteljahrsschrift für Literaturwissenschaft und Geistesgeschichte*, pp. 339 ff., 1925; G. A. Waltz, *Die Staatsauffassung des Rationalismus und die Romantik und die Staatsidee Fichtes*, Berlin, 1928. The best brief account in English of the political thought of the German romanticists is to be found in R. Aris, *History of Political Thought in Germany 1789–1815*, part 2, London, 1936.

[2] There is an early English translation by J. Dalton, London, 1844. For Novalis, see R. Samuel, 'Die poetische Staats- und Geschichtsauffassung Fr. v. Hardenbergs, (*Deutsche Forschungen*, vol. XII), Frankfurt, 1925.

conversion and which had its sociological basis in the interests of Austria, in the Holy Alliance, and in ultramontanism.

One element of the early period of romantic thought was taken up by Adam Müller and acquired an immense importance for the formation of the romantic attitude. It is the element of *pantheism* which, as an intellectual attitude, formed a curious contrast with the hierarchic structure of the Catholic conception of the world and of Catholic thought.[1] Pantheism appeared for the first time in the modern world in the Renaissance, whose philosophy of nature was an intellectual reflection of the pantheist attitude to life. As a wide stream of thought it was vanquished by the growth of natural science. But there were apparently thousands of small rivulets in which it had survived. The *Sturm und Drang* period marks its first powerful reappearance. It is well known how much it colours Goethe's thought.[2] This attitude to life became part of early romantic thought, and there seems to be some truth in the epigram: when Protestantism becomes atheist it tends to turn to pantheism; when Catholicism becomes atheist it turns into materialism.[3] The pantheist attitude dominates the early period of romanticism and lends it a special colour. As its most pronounced feature appears the feeling or idea that God not only stands at the beginning and is not experienced only as the Creator, but lives in every particle of nature.[4] In a sense, both the generalizing, inductive, and positivist thought of natural science and the conceptions of Catholic dogma are opposed to this type of thought, however much they may differ from each other.

For the Catholic Church and scientific positivism resemble each other in that both conceive the immanent world as rational and therefore as rationally intelligible. They are, for that reason, well able—as has often been observed before—to join forces. The miracle (the irrational) stands for Catholic thought at the beginning as the creator and the act of creation; for natural science the irrational has either completely disappeared or it has been relegated to a kind of transcendental sphere of things-in-themselves—at any rate, both systems of thought possess a purified

---

[1] For the history of pantheism cf. W. Dilthey's essays in vol. 2 of his *Gesammelte Schriften*, Leipzig and Berlin, 1914; and the relevant portions of his Life of Schleiermacher; see also H. Ritter, *Die Halbkantianer und der Pantheismus*, Berlin, 1827.

[2] Cf. F. Bulle, 'Zur Struktur des Pantheismus: Die Kategorie der Totalität in Goethes naturwissenschaftlichen Schriften', in *Euphorion*, vol. 21 (1914), pp. 156 ff.

[3] This connection was already noticed by Fr. Schlegel ('Signatur des Zeitalters', published in *Concordia*, a journal edited by him .pp. 45 f., 1820–23). Also Stahl, *Gegenwärtige Parteien*, lecture 27; cf. v. Martin, *Weltanschauungsmotive*, pp. 374 f.

[4] A passage may be cited which illustrates the mood as well as the structure of pantheist thought: 'Feel how a spring day, a work of art, a loved one, how domestic bliss, civic duties, human deeds weave you, in all the dimensions of the globe, into the Universe, where one art follows the other and the artist lives for ever . . .' (A. Müller, *Die Lehre vom Gegensatz*, book 1, 'Der Gegensatz', p. 92, Berlin, 1804).

sphere which is thoroughly amenable to rational analysis. In contrast to all this, the pantheist feels Life and God everywhere. He feels a vitality which is inaccessible to the rigid intellect with its abstract generic concepts. Thought, where it plays a part at all, undergoes here a change of function. Its task is no longer to recognize and register the rules of the game, the general laws which govern the world, but to move in harmony with the growth and fluctuations of the world. Two tendencies of thought arise from that pantheism. One is the tendency to think in terms of analogies[1] which existed already in medieval alchemy and astrology, reappeared later in the romantic speculations on nature, and was finally introduced into political philosophy. This mode of thought conceives the world as thoroughly alive, but it assumes that one can find in it hidden sequences and analogies. The tendency to think in terms of analogies is still not wholly opposed to the ordinary method of thought which looks for generally valid laws in the world, since—in its own curious way—this form of thought, too, endeavours to find general laws—that is, morphological laws of succession. This thought becomes really pantheistic when it abandons even the analogy as a pattern of regularity—when it experiences every moment as something unique and incomparable, any genesis as the manifestation of a life force, and assigns thought the task of following the rhythm of the world. Thought must not *portray* the world; it must *accompany its movements*. From this tendency arises everything that we call 'dynamic thinking'. The pantheism of the nineteenth century represents a special form in that it became a historical pantheism—as the highest experience of the essence of life appeared the experience of history.

We shall later on pursue in detail the varied fate of romantic pantheism. For the present it is enough to state that the pantheist dynamic style of thought was the most important heritage which Adam Müller received from the early period of romanticism. At the same time, it is interesting to observe the struggle which takes place in his thought between the hierarchic and static principle of Catholicism and the new dynamics. It is almost possible to put one's finger on the exact spot in the *Elemente der Staatskunst*[2] where the pantheist conception of things gradually dies down and gives way to the hierarchic mode of thought. Later on, we shall have to consider two other influences which

---

1 Carl Schmitt, in his *Politische Romantik*, analyses that tendency to think in terms of analogies and the technique of 'removing dualities by means of a higher *tertium quid*' very cleverly from the Catholic point of view. We feel that Schmitt does not do justice to the essential dynamic element which is contained in this type of thought.

2 Cf. A. Müller, *Elemente der Staatskunst*, half-vol. 1, p. 218, and Baxa's marginal comment to the passage.

left their mark upon the *Elemente:* Edmund Burke and Justus Möser.

Before turning to the analysis of these additional influences, it is necessary to investigate the concrete sociological situation in which the *Elemente der Staatskunst* were written and which alone entitles us to consider the work as historically representative. As the title-page announces, the book consists of lectures which had been delivered in the winter of 1808–9 in Dresden 'before His Highness, Prince Bernard of Saxe-Weimar, and a gathering of statesmen and diplomats', and were printed in the same year in lecture form. It anticipates a state of mind which did not find expression in practical politics until the rise of the aristocratic opposition against Hardenberg in 1810–11.[1] The main theme of the book is a plea for the nobility and the whole feudalistic attitude. This is the nucleus around which the author develops a whole system of political philosophy—with much brilliant argument and unrivalled intellectual virtuosity. The immediate occasion for the choice of the subject was a pamphlet by the liberal writer Buchholz, 'Concerning the Hereditary Nobility', which, according to the testimony of Gentz, aroused immense consternation among the older nobility.[2] We do not wish to linger on the much-discussed fact that Gentz encouraged Müller in his letter to write a refutation of Buchholz's book and promised him an 'exceedingly pleasant existence' as the reward.[3] For us that fact is important only because it shows clearly that the alliance between romantic and feudalistic thought was causally determined by real social relationships. Two currents of thought which already possess an inherent affinity are here induced to merge and coalesce by the influence of external social conditions.

After these comments on the real sociological situation we may now return to the analysis of the two non-romantic contributors to Adam Müller's thought we have mentioned, Burke and Justus Möser. The influence of the former is much more obvious, not only because Müller frequently refers to him and praises him to the skies, but because there is material evidence of his influence, i.e. one can show without difficulty that certain ideas are derived from Burke. The influences of the feudalistic element on Müller's work, on the other hand, lie much deeper; and that is perhaps the

---

[1] Cf. W. Steffens, 'Hardenberg und die ständische Opposition 1810–11', in *Veröffentlichungen des Vereins f. Geschichte d. Mark Brandenburg*, Leipzig, 1907; also F. Lenz, *Agrarlehre und Agrarpolitik der deutschen Romantik*, Berlin, 1912; H. Sultan, 'Rodbertus und der agrarische Sozial-Konservatismus', in *Zeitschrift f. d. ges. Staatswissensch.*, vol. 82, pp. 71 ff., 1927; A. Lewy, *Zur Genesis der heutigen agrarischen Ideen in Preussen*.
[2] Cf. *Briefwechsel zwischen Friedrich Gentz und Adam Heinrich Müller, 1800–29*, p. 140, Stuttgart, 1857.
[3] *Ibid.*

reason why they are much harder to establish by 'positivistic' methods. Adam Müller does not quote Möser once.[1] Yet, reading Müller after Möser, one cannot help noticing how the former reproduces Möser's attitude on a romantic plane; and that Möser's writings contain, in a naïve (unromantic) form, modes of thought and older feudalistic ideas which reappear on a romantic 'level' in Müller. That influence is so fundamental that the individual does not matter. In other words, what matters is not whether Müller derived that attitude from Möser himself, but whether Möser does not represent a type of thought which was so common in his time that it may have acted on Müller through quite different intermediaries.

We will begin with the less problematic of the two influences, with Burke.[2] Here again the first thing to do is to determine his sociological position. The importance of Burke lies in the fact that he was the first influential author who attacked the French Revolution. He was the initiator of modern anti-revolutionary conservatism, and all those who later on criticized the French Revolution from the conservative side were somehow influenced by him. It was Burke who, more than anybody else, supplied the anti-revolutionary camp with ideas and slogans. His 'Reflections on the Revolution in France' was published as a pamphlet against the pro-revolutionary societies and clubs which which were growing up in England. His comments are therefore the spontaneous outgrowth of that definite historical situation. That nonetheless—and in spite of the speed with which they were written—so many points of principle, so much that was to recur again and again, became visible to Burke can only be explained by the fact that he was already able to look at the revolution from a vantage point which virtually forced fruitful insights on the spectator. For a proper political understanding of the revolution England offered so favourable a perspective that every particular observation turned of itself into a statement of principle, it became 'philosophical'—even for a mind which was, by any serious standards, so essentially unphilosophical as Burke's. Herein

---

[1] Cf. Baxa, 'Justus Möser und Adam Müller', in *Jahrbuch für Nationalökonomie und Statistik*, series 3, vol. 68, Jena, 1923. Baxa confines himself chiefly to an elaboration of the similarity of *ideas*, while we must attempt to discover much more fundamental similarities, viz. in the general mode of thought.

[2] It is impossible to give here a comprehensive survey of the literature on Burke. For our purposes the most useful works are: A. Cobban, *Edmund Burke and the Revolt against the Eighteenth Century*, London, 1929; J. MacCunn, *The Political Philosophy of Burke*, London, 1913; M. Einaudi, *Edmondo Burke e l'indirizzo storico nelle scienze politiche*, Torino, 1930; F. Meusel, *Edmund Burke und die französische Revolution. Zur Entstehung historisch-politischen Denkens, zumal in England*, Berlin, 1913; also *Early Life, Writings and Correspondence of Edmund Burke*, ed. by A. R. I. Samuels, Cambridge, 1923; J. Morley, *Burke*, London, 1888; R. H. Murray, *Edmund Burke*, Oxford, 1931.

lies the peculiar feature of that 'philosophy' (and this is the only real point of resemblance between Burke and Möser as opposed to Müller), that in the case of the former it is an involvement in political practice which yields philosophical insights, whereas, in the case of Müller, philosophical principles are to be applied so as to master practical problems.

It is in itself an interesting spectacle to observe how England provides the first impressive picture of revolutionary France, a picture which guided whole generations. It is as if England takes revenge for the conventional portrait of herself which the Frenchman Montesquieu originally painted and which was, for a long time, decisive for the judgment of England abroad.[1]

To the question, which aspects of Müller's thought are already present in Burke's, the answer must be that it is simply the specifically conservative attitude which Müller took over from Burke. It is primarily the idea of 'history', if it may be so called. Looking at it more closely one finds that 'history' in Burke's thought is not yet that complicated, profoundly romantic, transcendental construction which confronts us in the writings of Müller, and also of Savigny. It is only one element of this complex whole, though an important one, the element of 'continuity.'[2] Burke profoundly stimulated conservatism to think about the

---

[1] The German idea of England naturally changed in the course of time. The Anglomania of the young Adam Müller emphasized the feudal structure of English society. The same Adam Müller characteristically abandoned his favourable attitude towards England as a result of the changes in English foreign policy. (Cf. F. Engel-Jánosi, 'Die Theorie vom Staat im deutschen Oesterreich 1815-48', in *Zeitschrift f. öffentl. Recht*, p. 386, footnote 3, 1921.) It is interesting to observe the widespread appeal which England made at that time to the minds of contemporary Germany. At the time when capitalist England experienced its first crisis (1815-19), risings of the working classes, the agitation for parliamentary reform, and the first wave of serious criticism of its social and political system, German contemporaries were still full of praise for England, although each for different reasons. Thus the young Adam Müller sees in England the example of an anti-revolutionary organic social order; F. J. Stahl praises the English constitutional system; Fr. List, the economist, looked at England as the *nation prédominante*; the liberals from Kraus to Prince-Smith glorify England as the home of Locke and Adam Smith; and even Marx takes English development as the pattern for his analysis.

[2] Some characteristic passages from the 'Reflections' may be quoted: 'You will observe, that from Magna Charta to the Declaration of Right, it has been the uniform policy of our constitution to claim and assert our liberties, as an *entailed inheritance* derived from our forefathers, and to be transmitted to our posterity' (Burke, *Works*, vol. 5, pp. 77 f., London, 1801-27). 'The policy appears to me to be the result of profound reflection; or rather the happy effect of following nature, which is wisdom without reflection, and above it. . . . The people of England well know, that the idea of inheritance furnishes a sure principle of conservation, and a sure principle of transmission; without at all excluding a principle of improvement' (*ibid.*, p. 78). 'You [the French] had all those advantages in your ancient states; but you chose to act as if you had never been moulded into civil society, and had every thing to begin anew. You began ill, because you began by despising every thing that belonged to you. You set up your trade without a capital' (*ibid.*, p. 82).

historical nature of society. But his is not yet the attitude to the historical factor which gives rise to refinements of historical method, which attributes an unchangeable place in the historical scale of values to every product of organic growth. He does not yet realize all the complications of the problem of value standards and fails to grasp the fruitfulness of the relativistic method which, arising out of historicism, makes even the position of the observer a relative one within the general process of historical development. He is unaware of the depth of the organic conception of society and of the synoptic view of the whole. All he sees is that one will achieve more useful results if one allows institutions to grow gradually than if individuals set about to construct them in a day. He is aware of the continuity, the gradualness of historical development; he stresses the gradual accumulation of the historical forces of the past (compare the typically English simile of 'capital'). He shows that reverence towards the past which one feels in a gallery of ancestral portraits. 'By this means our liberty becomes a noble freedom. It carries an imposing and majestic aspect. It has a pedigree and illustrating ancestors. It has its bearings and its ensigns armorial. It has its gallery of portraits; its monumental inscriptions; its records, evidences, and titles. We procure reverence to our civil institutions on the principle upon which nature teaches us to revere individual men; on account of their age; and on account of those from whom they are descended.'[1] All these, however, are relatively unemotional statements of principles, rather than expressions of a new fundamental attitude. At most, one can consider them as the first appearance of the phenomenon which may be called a 'positively historical' conception of history, as opposed to the 'negatively historical' conception of the Enlightenment.[2] To the Enlightenment the gradual continuity of historical development appeared as a purely negative element. It would not be true, then, to say that conservatism discovered history as such; but it did discover a specific *meaning* of growth, viz. its aspects of tradition and continuity. This example clearly shows the value 'social attachment' has for the understanding of history. Historical thinking is fructified by the vital relationship in which the knowing subject stands to the historical process. One cannot understand history without wishing something from history. The sympathetic[3] grasp of the nature of historic growth which Burke achieved would never have been

1 *Ibid.*, p. 80.
2 Cf. G. Rexius, 'Studien zur Staatslehre der historischen Schule', in *Historische Zeitschrift*, vol. 107, p. 500, 1911.
3 Gentz, in the comments to his translation of Burke's 'Reflections', speaks of an 'affectionate return to the past' (Burke, *Betrachtungen über die französische Revolution*, transl. by Fr. Gentz, new ed., vol. 1, p. 408, Hohenzollern, 1794).

possible had not certain strata felt that their social position was threatened and that their world might perish.

Historicism is, as we have seen, an exceedingly complex and many-sided phenomenon, both in its internal structure and in its sociological foundation. But in its chief points it is of conservative origin. It arose everywhere as a political argument against the revolutionary breach with the past. A mere interest in history becomes historicism when historical facts are not merely lovingly contrasted with the facts of the present, but where 'growth' as such becomes a real experience. This is the common meaning of Burke's 'continuity', French traditionalism[1], and German historicism. This fundamental experience, as the common element, on the other hand, is accompanied by several more complex factors which account for the detailed ramifications.[2] With the fact of growth, of continuity as such, as the basic experience of the historicist, there goes always, as a second element, the preference for a particular epoch and a particular social stratum in history. Here again Burke set the example for Müller in his preference for the Middle Ages and his conception of the nobility as the chief makers of history.

An analysis of the significance of the historical phenomenon 'nobility' was an important problem for the conservative forces after the revolution. But only in exceptional circumstances are the outlines of a form of social life visible to those who are born into that form. Sociology, even a sociology which serves merely to 'interpret' and to bolster existing institutions, needs a suitable perspective, involving a certain 'distance' but also a certain amount of solidarity with some of the factors involved. We have mentioned before the value of a 'socially unattached' intelligentsia for making the structure of society transparent. The

---

[1] Rohden, in his introduction to the German edition of J. de Maistre's *Considérations sur la France* ('Betrachtungen über Frankreich', *Klassiker der Politik*, ed. by Meinecke and Oncken, vol. 2, p. 24, Berlin, 1924), analyses the fundamental experience of the French traditionalists, the '*durée*', and goes on to show that it is conceived, not 'dynamically' but 'statically'. Following up this idea, we see the essence of German historicism in the fact that it had become 'dynamic' and was able to take full advantage of the fruitful potentialities of conservative thought.

[2] The historical and sociological explanation of the 'dynamic' character of historicism in Germany is probably (I) that in Germany conservatism in its chief trends and in the historically decisive period under discussion, had no need to become reactionary since there was after all no revolution in its own country. For a counter-revolution has to confront reality with an ideal just as rigidly utopian as that of a revolution. The revolutionary attitude, on the other hand, favoured the growth of a 'dynamic' historicism. (II) The German middle class with its static natural-law conceptions had no part in German conservatism for the simple reason that it had not yet become politically relevant. (III) German historicism was able to develop to a large extent independently of Roman Catholicism and could therefore also avoid the static approach of the latter. (This independence of Catholic influence has also been pointed out by Rohden.)

example of Burke merely confirms that view. Burke was not a member of the nobility himself, he was a self-made man who sought admission to the inner circle of the aristocracy; his own social status thus was a mobile one. For that very reason he was able to determine in an exemplary fashion—although with an apologetic intention—the social significance and peculiar character of the nobility. In Germany, too, a member of the middle class, Adam Müller, became the interpreter of the nobility. France alone provides an example of a nobility who themselves became aware of the significance of their social position.[1] The explanation is, of course, to be found in their emigration during the years of the revolution. The detachment from their accustomed mode of existence which fate forced upon them gave them also historical and sociological insight. It is during ascent or descent in the social scale that the individual achieves the clearest view of the social and historical structure of society. In the ascent one understands what one is aiming at, in the descent what one is losing.

What is true of the evaluation of different social strata is equally true of the evaluation of different epochs of the past. With the defence of the nobility goes an apologia for the Middle Ages—focused less upon the medieval status and guild system or upon medieval mysticism than upon the element of chivalry.[2] Burke, however, achieved little more in this respect than a sympathetic treatment of the Middle Ages at a time when they were simply the 'Dark Ages'. Nothing in his writings betrays that emotional sympathy which is characteristic of historical thinking, as opposed to a mere 'attribution of positive value' to historical facts. Nor do they show that urge to rekindle the embers of the past that are still aglow in the present which alone makes possible a socially relevant revival of the past. In Burke's thought the defence of continuity, of the nobility, of the Middle Ages has too much of a rhetorical flavour. All these things are indeed only of the nature of 'reflections', they do not yet constitute a distinct mode of thought.

To turn now to Möser[3]—a writer who may be considered a

---

[1] Rohden points out that French traditionalism had its origin without exception in the landed nobility and he attributes a special importance to that fact (introduction to 'de Maistre', *loc. cit.*, p. 14).

[2] Cf., for instance, the famous passage from the 'Reflections': 'The age of chivalry is gone. That of sophisters, economists, and calculators has succeeded; and the glory of Europe is extinguished for ever. Never, never more shall we behold that generous loyalty to rank and sex, that proud submission, that dignified obedience, that subordination of the heart, which kept alive, even in servitude itself, the spirit of an exalted freedom' (Burke, *Works*, vol. 5, p. 149). The guild system of the Middle Ages found its apologists in Tieck and Wackenroder.

[3] For Möser, cf. the introduction by K. Brandis to the selection from Möser in the series *Der deutsche Staatsgedanke*, first series, vol. 3, Munich, 1921. A detailed bibliography of Möser, *ibid.*, pp. 265 ff. Cf. also H. Baron, 'Justus Mösers Individualitätsprinzip in seiner geschichtlichen Bedeutung' in *Historische Zeitschrift*, vol. 130, 1924.

good representative of the feudalistic trend of thought. The first thing that strikes one is the great difference between his general attitude and that of the romanticists. One might call his conservatism a 'primitive' conservatism, implying by that term that it is the first stage in the transition from a mere traditionalism into a self-conscious conservatism.[1] There is here none of the reflectiveness and introspectiveness of romantic conservatism. The frontal attack of the French Revolution against the inherited, traditional attitude is still in the future. The *leitmotiv* of Möser's reflections is, first of all, praise of the 'good old days'.[2] Somehow he stands completely in the atmosphere of the Enlightenment. His grandfatherly wisdom is sober, practical, rational. Yet his rationalism—and here we realize that there are also several variants of rationalism —is not the calculating, abstract rationalism of the bourgeoisie.

As long as planned economy has not yet unified the world, capitalism will always show a double mentality.[3] One representative type of capitalism is the meticulous keeper of accounts; the other is the pioneering adventurer who takes incalculable risks. Möser's sober wisdom has much more of the rationality of the peasant farmer. It is not a constructive calculation of abstract factors. It is the method of carefully reckoning up the concrete factors of a situation. It has its origin in caution and a mental agoraphobia which refuses to face any dynamic factors. This rationality refuses to leave for one moment the sphere of direct experience, it revolts against any invasion by elements from other worlds. It is afraid of the disintegration of the conventional moral ties which make the environment what it is. It is a conservatism which does not want to engage in experiments beyond its ken. That this primitive conservatism becomes reflective at all in Möser is due not to any sudden shock, but to the gradual infiltration from France of 'new-fangled' ideas and attitudes. It does become reflective. But Möser never 'romanticizes' what has happened. He may, and in fact he constantly does, interpret history involuntarily in the light of his own aims[4]; but he never tries, consciously or unconsciously, to justify something by means of far-fetched and extraneous arguments, or to save it by investing it with a 'higher' meaning.

The romanticists were full of enthusiasm for the Church, for the Middle Ages, and for the nobility, because something in their

---

[1] Cf. Sec. II, p. 116, above.

[2] Cf. 'Die Spinnstube', a local story in *Works*, 1, p. 24.

[3] Sombart distinguishes the 'mentality of the entrepreneur' from the 'middle-class mentality' ('Victorian') and analyses the two separately as component parts of the 'mentality of the bourgeoisie' (Sombart, *Der Bourgeois*, Munich and Leipzig, 1920).

[4] The *Osnabrückische Geschichte*, though based on original sources, is largely a tissue of more or less gratuitous explanations.

own wish-dreams had brought these things nearer to them. They sought in them compensation for some of their own troubles. The relation between the romanticist and his ideal is never one of intensive study. Led on by a wish-dream inside him he merely grazes the surface: 'Those were lovely, glorious times when Europe was a Christian country; when *one* Christendom inhabited this human corner of the world; when *one* great bond of common interest joined the remotest provinces of this far-flung spiritual realm'—these are the opening lines of Novalis's essay 'Christendom or Europe'. They suggest the fundamental mood, and in the remainder of the essay it is that mood, not the subject, that is developed.

Möser's attitude is completely different. He does not *approach* his subject, he *lives* in it. He does not go back to the past, he lives in the remnants of the past which still exist in the present. He lives in them and his thought arises out of them. The past is not something that lies behind him; it is an integral part of his life, not as a memory and a return, but as the intensified experience of something that he still possesses and is merely in danger of losing.

This type of conservatism which still lives in the heritage of the past, for which the past is not yet a memory and an object of reflection, has already been mentioned in our general discussion of the conservative attitude. We pointed out that Möser exhibits it in its purest form. It merely remains to illustrate that assertion.

The following passage serves well to characterize Möser's standpoint. 'When I come across some old custom or old habit which simply will not fit into modern ways of reasoning, I keep turning around in my mind the idea that, "after all, our forefathers were not fools either," until I find some sensible reason for it. . . .'[1] Now compare this with Novalis. Möser starts out from the concrete datum, an old custom, an old habit, and tries to discover its meaning. In the case of the romanticists the thinker is, so to speak, the starting-point, and all his efforts are directed to discover, if possible, a world that will satisfy him. 'Turning around and around' an object is as characteristic of Möser's thought as is his peculiar rationalism which must somehow find a 'sensible reason' for the behaviour of the forefathers.[2] Only the blind reliance on everything old and inherited is irrational, not a reluctance to attack traditions. Moreover, he looks for a 'sensible reason', not for some 'higher' far-fetched, metaphysical justification. Of course, one may keep 'turning around' real objects and yet arrive at romantic or paradoxical conclusions. Of the French traditionalists, it has been well said that they were 'rationalists

---

[1] *Works*, vol. 5, p. 260.
[2] Cf. also H. Baron, *op. cit.*, p. 49.

with irrational axioms.'[1] A writer like Kierkegaard, for instance, also practises some of that paradoxical sophistry which makes use of a trenchant rational logic to demonstrate an irrational position. Möser is paradoxical only in order to surprise,[2] not in order to invent irrational explanations. He merely intends to recover the lost 'sensible reason' for the inherited traditions. What is irrational in his thinking is only his conviction that the ancients must have acted sensibly, not, however, the explanations he is trying to find.

Bourgeois calculation is always abstract. Things and human beings appear solely as figures in an intellectual operation. Möser's 'reckoning' is always concrete. He really *reckons* with things, not simply by counting them or treating them as functions in a calculable process, but because he believes that they demand his attention as concrete parts of a definite social context.

From that attitude arises also the concept of 'practice', as he calls it, the eternal praise of practice as opposed to theory (a feature, by the way, which we shall find again, on an entirely different level, with the romanticists). He wrote an unfinished polemical essay against Kant with the title 'Theory and Practice'. Its salient passage runs: 'Real events often form a sounder basis for correct conclusions than far too exalted [*gar zu hohe*] premises.'[3] He fights against constructive thinking from 'far too exalted premises' in the name of concrete thinking which holds on to the data of experience: 'Practice which clings to each individual circumstance and knows how to use it must surely be more competent than theory which in its high flight is bound to overlook many circumstances.'[4]

The purpose of the essay is a justification of serfdom. It is of special interest because it shows clearly how the immediate occasion, the desire to defend an old institution, gives rise to a struggle between two methods of thought and thus brings out in full relief the differences between them which were to engage conservative thought for a long time to come. It is the contrast

[1] Rohden says: 'If the traditionalist asks the question: "What is a nation?" the naïve reader necessarily expects the answer, which to de Maistre represents the banal solution, "The totality of all citizens." The traditionalist answer, on the contrary, is: "The king and the bureaucracy." The art of the traditionalist thinker consists in taking a problem from the armoury of the adversary and connecting it by a logical argument with the solution which is supplied by his own attitude to life. The discrepancy between the expected "enlightened" answer which is constantly present in the reader's subconsciousness and the answer which he in fact receives produces a state of anxious tension' (Rohden, introduction to his edition of 'de Maistre', *loc. cit.*, p. 23).

[2] The above-quoted sentence from Möser is taken from a fragment of his entitled 'The Right of Man: Serfdom'. Referring to that title the fragment begins: 'Indeed a paradox! many a reader will think when he reads this title.' To that extent Möser, too, uses the method mentioned by Rohden.

[3] *Works*, vol. 9, pp. 158 f.

[4] *Ibid.*, p. 168.

between the method which starts out from normative and constructive premises and that which proceeds concretely from the given data. The tension is increased by the fact that Möser, in his justification of serfdom, still thinks in terms of natural-law ideas, since he starts from an original contract. Underneath that justification in terms of natural law, however, works the fundamental intention to deduce the validity of the institution, not from normative premises, but from the living, practical interplay of social and historical phenomena.

Another example may be mentioned which illustrates how much Möser is constantly occupied with the tension between concrete and abstract thinking. He wrote a short essay called 'The Moral Point of View'.[1] In it he tries to show, from an entirely different angle—in the moral sphere—that the value of a thing cannot be grasped on the basis of general principles, because measured by such excessively high standards everything must appear imperfect. Instead one should realize that everything carries within itself the point of view from which it can be adequately apprehended: 'Can you tell me one single beautiful object of the physical world which retains its beauty under the microscope? Does not the most beautiful skin get knolls and furrows? the loveliest cheek a horrible mildew? the rose quite a wrong colour? Everything therefore has its own point of view from which alone it is beautiful.' And at the end of the essay he says: 'Let us be honest, and see the virtue of a thing only in its usefulness or its inherent quality. In this sense, a horse, and iron, have their virtues, and so has the hero who has his due share of steel, hardness, coldness, and heat.'

Möser's thought contains still further elements which became the intellectual heritage of conservatism and were taken over by romanticism as parts of the feudalistic trend of thought. One is generally inclined to consider the tendency towards extreme individualization, the demand that every man and every thing should themselves provide the clue for their understanding, as a typically romantic trait. An analysis of Möser's thought shows, however, to what a large extent that tendency is already inherent in the aims of feudalistic thought. It displays already the preference for 'qualitative thinking' as a method of thought. It is already concerned with the problem of making the individual element accessible to thought. Already we find a close connection between such reflections on the method of thought and political aims. Our task is therefore to show that the feudalistic conception which still constitutes the framework of Möser's point of view produced modes of thought which were just then being attacked by the bourgeois world; and that it was due to that attack that this thought became reflective and aware of its own character.

Some examples may now be quoted which disclose the *political* significance of Möser's desire to experience every thing as individual, to understand it in terms of its specific 'usefulness'. In his essay which bears the title 'The Modern Taste for General Laws and Decrees is a Danger to Our Common Liberty' (1772)[1] the feudalistic origin of the emphasis on individuality, as opposed to the generalizing tendency of the bureaucracy, is clearly apparent. Right at the beginning he declares: 'The gentlemen of the *Generaldepartement* [central administration], it seems, would like to see everything reduced to simple principles. If they had their way, the state would let itself be ruled according to an academic theory, and every councillor would be able to give his orders to the local officials according to a general plan. . . . That means in fact a departure from the true plan of Nature who shows her wealth in variety; it paves the way for despotism which wants to force everything by means of a few rules and in doing so loses the wealth of variety.'

One can see here quite clearly how the political struggle against the centralizing and rationalist bureaucracy gives rise to insights into problems of method. Möser clearly recognized the spiritual affinity between the centralizing bureaucracy and the enlightened monarchy, and saw the essence of despotism[2] in that it wants to force everything by means of a few rules. He calls the tendency towards uniformity and generalization a 'new-fangled way of thinking'[3] which may be used as a technical expedient but never as a standard of judgment in a concrete case. Every native inhabitant should be judged according to the laws and customs of his locality. In fact, he sees the meaning of liberty in the observation of these local differences. Voltaire had made fun of the fact that someone lost a case by the law of one village which he would have won by the customs of the neighbouring village. Möser has something to say even for that paradox: 'Voltaire need not have troubled to think the difference between two neighbouring villages ridiculous; he could have found the same diversity between two families living under the same roof.'[4] If the decrees of the state are not obeyed the reason is that 'we are trying to cover too many things by *one* rule and deprive Nature of her wealth rather than change our system.'[5] Having observed the sense for variety

1 *Works*, vol. 2, pp. 20 f.
2 This goes back to Montesquieu.
3 *Works*, vol. 2, p. 21.
4 *Ibid.*, pp. 23 f.
5 *Ibid.*, p. 26.

and diversity, individuality and peculiarity arising from a feudalistic and particularist conception of the world (which becomes merely reflective in Möser) we are not surprised to hear that, in his opinion, every little town should be given a constitution of its own.[1]

Nor is it surprising, in view of that tendency which had its roots deep in the thought and experience of feudalistic conservatism, that the Prussian nobility were slow in their appreciation of the idea of the nation state; and that, for a long time and even during the high tide of national patriotism in the first decades of the nineteenth century, their path to it was beset with difficulties and antagonistic emotions. Not until one has got to know the incredible particularism of the feudalistic attitude in its original form does one realize that, compared with the provincial particularism of that period, nationalism is already a stage in the transition to internationalism. Here is a passage from v. d. Marwitz which illustrates the *Prussian* variety of this particularist individualism: 'Prussia is not a nation which has always been what it is now, uniform in language, customs and laws. It is a conglomerate of provinces each of them very different from the other in its laws and habits. Nor can it ever become a nation. For every province has for its neighbours other provinces which are not part of its own state but to which it feels at bottom more closely related than to the remote and unknown other provinces of the Prussian state—Brandenburg, for instance, to Saxony, Silesia to Bohemia and Moravia, East Prussia to Courland and Lithuania. To propose to merge them into one means depriving them of their peculiar character, turning a living body into a dead carcass.'[2] There are many sociological differences between v. d. Marwitz and Möser apart from the interval of two generations.[3] There is first the fact that v. d. Marwitz was a *Junker*, landlord of Friedersdorf, and spokesman of the nobility of one of the oldest provinces of Prussia (Kurmark). Möser's father, on the other hand, had been a councillor in the chancellery of Osnabrück who had done so well later on as a middle-class lawyer that he had actually governed the country for a time side by side with the aristocratic 'privy councillors'. As the son of a patrician Möser showed no more sympathy towards the nobility than was necessary in his position.[4] He believes in the corporative feudal state, even though

---

1 Cf. the essay 'Sollte man nicht jedem kleinen Städtchen seine besondre politische Verfassung geben?', *Works*, vol. 3, p. 67.

2 Quoted by W. Steffens, *Hardenberg und die ständische Opposition*, p. 30. Cf. also *ibid.*, footnote 2, where it is pointed out that there was *some* national feeling, however overlaid by antagonist emotions.

3 Möser was born in 1720, Marwitz in 1777.

4 'Too many princes, too many noblemen, too many scholars, are the ruin of the state' (*Works*, vol. 5, p. 37).

he may date back his Golden Age to the days of ancient liberty and common property.[1] But just because he does not defend the nobility but rather the medieval social system with its relatively high degree of integration, with its hierarchic stratification[2] and feudal structure, as a whole, and takes a special interest in the attitude of the old peasant strata, we may accept the agreement between the two as typical. It confirms the assumption that at least one of the roots of Müller's emphasis on individuality, quality and peculiarity is to be found in the older 'feudalistic' trend of thought. Similarly, the emphasis on 'life' and variety, as the elements which a bureaucratic rationalism is bound to neglect, anticipates a line of thought which is crystallized as a definite trend, at first in opposition to bureaucratic centralization, later in opposition to revolutionary natural-law thought—and points to later 'philosophies of life'. The older forms of thought and experience were being subjected to an attack from all sides by bourgeois, absolutist, and bureaucratic forms of rationalism and were in danger of dying out. They were saved by their meeting and alliance with romanticism which revived them and equipped them with a modern theoretical foundation.

The earliest stage of conservative thought, represented by Möser, is no longer a primitive traditionalism. It has assumed a social function in the shape of its antagonism against the 'enlightened' tendency towards bureaucratic centralization. Under the direction of romanticism its political significance changes. Its enemy is now the natural-law thought of the revolutionary bourgeoisie.

To their conservative adversary the two variants of modern rationalism now appear interlocked. Under the influence of the French Revolution conservatism begins to acquire some insight into the character of bourgeois thought as well. The times called for resistance to it too. In their efforts to lay bare the ideological roots and causes of the revolution the French traditionalists concentrated on the metaphysical and religious premises of the eighteenth century, and made them bear the brunt of their attack.[3] In Germany, in contrast, romanticism tends rather to

[1] Cf. the introduction by Brandis to his selection from Möser's works, p. xxi; also O. Hatzig, 'Justus Möser als Staatsmann und Publizist', in *Quellen und Darstellung zur Geschichte Niedersachsens*, vol. 27. For v. d. Marwitz, see the essay by Fr. Meusel in vol. 1 of his edition of v. d. Marwitz's works; also W. Andreas, 'Marwitz und der Staat Friedrichs des Grossen', in *Historische Zeitschrift*, vol. 122, pp. 44 ff., 1920.

[2] Cf. 'Der Staat mit einer Pyramide verglichen. Eine erbauliche Betrachtung' ('The State Compared to a Pyramid, An Edifying Reflection') (1773), in *Works*, vol. 2, p. 250.

[3] A typical example of the character of the campaign against revolutionary thought which was carried on by the French traditionalists may be seen in de Bonald's interesting essay 'De la philosophie morale et politique du 18e siècle' (1805), in *Œuvres de M. de Bonald*, pp. 104 ff., Paris, 1819. He tries to draw parallels between theism,

make the logical and methodological aspects of liberal thought the objects of its criticism. The reason is that in France the counter-revolution found its metaphysics ready-made in the dogma of Roman Catholicism; whereas in Germany—as often has been observed before—the schism between Protestant and Catholic dogma rendered the metaphysical foundations heterogeneous and therefore unsafe. As a result, one withdrew into considering problems of method. Moreover, since the revolution was not taking place *intra muros*, one could afford to thresh out differences of *Weltanschauung* on this very abstract plane. As soon as the sociological situation became more critical (after 1830) and conservatism, even in Protestant Prussia, had to retire to the stronghold of theism, considerations of dogma and metaphysics came again into the foreground. There was a feeling that the pantheist and methodological ground of romanticism was no longer safe. It is Stahl's achievement to have satisfied that demand by establishing the monarchical principle once more on theistic foundations.

For the time being, however—during the first decades of the nineteenth century—the pantheistic and methodological variant of counter-revolutionary thought was still able to develop freely, and thus to determine the character of German conservatism for a long time to come. Adam Müller can claim to have drawn on both the feudalistic and romantic sources and thus to have given internal consistency to the ideological struggle. His *Elemente der Staatskunst* reveals, for the first time, the full importance and force of the fight against natural-law thought. Here grows up that phenomenon which, under the name of 'philosophy of life' (*Lebensphilosophie*), has ever since, and today with renewed vigour, assailed rationalism in all its diverse forms.[1]

atheism, deism and the various forms of government. A few passages may be quoted which indicate his conclusions: 'Democracy furiously casts out from political society all visible unity and focus of power; it sees the sovereign only in the *subjects*, or the people: just as atheism rejects the original and prime cause of the universe, and sees it only in its effects, in matter. In the system of the latter, matter has done everything; in the system of the former, the people have the right to do everything. In fact, one might call the democrats the atheists of politics, and the atheists the *madmen* or *jacobins* of religion' (pp. 128 ff.). 'Royalism' has its counterpart in 'theism or Christianity', and this is what he says about the centre: 'The "*impartial*" moderates and constitutionalists of '89 take their stand between the democrats and the royalists, just as do the deists between the atheists and the Christians; one might therefore reasonably apply to the constitution which they have invented the name "*monarchical democracy*". They want a king, but a king without a will of his own, without the right to independent action; and a king who, as the scholar of the party, Mably, told the Poles, *receives the highest respect but has only the barest shadow of authority*. By these signs one can recognize the ideal and abstract God of deism, without will, without action, without presence, without reality' (pp. 129 ff. De Bonald's italics).

1 Cf. Baxa's comments to the *Elemente der Staatskunst*, vol. 2, p. 293. Rothacker points out the roots of the concept in the historical school (*Einleitung in die Geisteswissenschaften*, pp. 62 ff., especially p. 71, footnote 2, Tübingen, 1920).

Having analysed one by one the most important currents which converge in the thought of Adam Müller we may now inquire which new and comprehensive political impulses brought about the ideological unification of all these different tendencies in a single *Weltanschauung*.

At this stage, conservative thought derives its impulse to emphasize Life, as opposed to concepts, no longer, as in the case of Möser, from the reaction against bureaucratic rationalism alone, but also from the reaction against the other contemporary variant of rationalism, the rationalism of the bourgeoisie.[1] If we were to speculate *a priori* about which group emphasizes Life and which builds on abstract, unchanging concepts, we should answer: it is obviously the progressives who favour Life, the conservatives who rely on rigid norms and abstractions. But if we look at history empirically, we see that it was the other way round. The reason is that the revolutionary thought of the bourgeoisie arose in alliance with rationalism. The reaction therefore naturally adopted the contrary ideology for the sake of mere opposition if for no other reason. But interpretation can penetrate even deeper. Revolutionary thought derives its force from the desire to realize a rationally well-defined pattern of perfection of the social and political order. Conservative thought, opposed to the fulfilment of that utopia, is forced to consider why the actually existing state of society fails to correspond to that rational pattern.[2] This impulse which is primarily anchored in self-interest at the same time renders conservatism sensitive to all those factors which revolutionary thought—again in its own vital interest— overlooks, viz., the non-rational factors of organic reality. But whereas revolutionary thought conceives such irrationalities— where it sees them at all—as imperfections of reality when measured by the standard of reason, conservative thought— indulging in one of its favourite means of expression, the paradox —attributes to them the character of super-rationality.[3] It is, however, not merely a question of inverted values, but rather of different categories of life and experience. This is shown, for

---

[1] Concerning the nature of modern rationalism cf. the works of Max Weber (especially his remarks on rationalism in legal thought in *Wirtschaft und Gesellschaft*, pp. 394 f., and on the form of rationalism which is produced by the socialization of the market and by the institution of the contract, *ibid.*, p. 394), Sombart, Simmel (*Philosophie des Geldes*, Leipzig, 1900), Lukács (*Geschichte und Klassenbewusstsein*, Berlin, 1923, especially the essay on 'Die Verdinglichung und das Bewusstsein des Proletariats').

[2] That is the stage which German conservatism has reached, for example, in Hugo, *Lehrbuch des Naturrechts, als einer Philosophie des positiven Rechts, besonders des Privatrechts*, 1st ed., 1798.

[3] It is not our task as sociologists to decide whether interpretation in terms of 'suprarational' categories is objectively correct or not. *Our* opinion on the value of irrationality must be left aside.

instance, by the fact that definition of irrationality as super-rationality leads to that class of philosophical systems which might be called in a word 'philosophies of Life', the philosophies which put forward, in opposition to mere reason, sometimes 'history', sometimes 'life' or sometimes 'the spirit'. The great polarities of nineteenth-century philosophical thought: 'reality' and 'thought', 'concept' and 'idea', 'theory' and 'practice', often arose as integral parts of philosophical systems. But they were always nourished and their sociological significance was preserved by the corresponding political polarities of liberalism and conservatism.

The most primitive form of the struggle against destructive rationalism through the appeal to Life consists in contrasting the 'written constitution' with a reality richer and more alive than the written word.[1] Frederick William IV's phrase about the 'mere scrap of paper' which was coined to ridicule the idea of the constitution goes back to this most primitive form of the fight against 'rationalization'. But if we look more closely, we notice that it expresses a contrast which can be defined in philosophical language as the contrast between 'norm' and 'being'. What conservative thought objects to in this context is that such reflections, as for instance in the Declaration of the Rights of Man, start out from the 'rights of man as such'.[2] The conservative is shocked by this procedure, by the application of the deductive

---

1 This was formulated in a typical manner by de Maistre in his *Considérations sur la France* (1796): 'No constitution has its origin in a mere decision. The rights of the people have never been written, or at least, the articles of the constitution and the written fundamental laws are never more than plain declarations of previously existing rights of which nothing more can be said than that they exist because they exist.' Or: 'A written constitution of the kind that rules France today is nothing but a mechanism which appears to be alive.' In his struggle for the idea that it is impossible to construct anything according to a rational plan from the beginning he works out for himself the difference between 'creating' and 'changing': 'In his sphere of action man can change everything but he creates nothing.' Here again the emphasis on 'growth'. He goes so far in his aversion to planned creation as to prophesy: 'I do not believe in the durability of the American government; nor do I trust the peculiar institutions of English America. The cities, for instance, have not been able to agree where the Congress should sit; none of them would leave that honour to another. They therefore decided to build a new city which should become the seat of government. The most favourable situation by a broad river was chosen and it was decided that the city should be called Washington. The site of all public buildings is already fixed, building operations have begun, and the plan of the "queen of cities" already circulates throughout Europe. There is nothing in the idea as such which is beyond human power; it is certainly possible to build a city. But there is too much deliberate decision in the thing, too much that is human; and one could offer a bet of a thousand to one that the city will not be built, that it will not be called Washington, that Congress will not sit in it.' It is fortunate for de Maistre that he did not make that bet. Cf. for the struggle against 'artificial creation' also Burke: 'The very idea to manufacture a new government is repulsive to us Englishmen', quoted in A. Wahl, *op. cit.*, p. 550.
2 'The constitution of 1795 is, like its predecessors, made for men. But there is on earth no man as such. I have seen in my lifetime Frenchmen, Italians, Russians, etc.

method, and the idea that a perfect state can be developed in this fashion; he casts about to find a different method. In the course of his search, in his opposition to the oppositional forces, he remembers how hitherto the state and society, law and regulations, have come about. He realizes that now it is discussion and the vote which decide matters, that now 'reason' wants to make reality, whereas formerly everything grew gradually and was preserved by custom. With that realization the logical and the historical starting-points fall apart. In natural-law thought logical and historical origins were still conceived as identical; the theory of the social contract was at once a logical construction and a historical fiction. Not until Kant were the two quite clearly separated. Once the separation was made, the relation between being (growth) and norm became a vital problem for the collective thought of the whole epoch.

The feudalistic opposition was faced with the bureaucratic form of rationalism; hence, the aspect of modern rationalism it criticized was mainly its questionable tendency towards generalization and mechanization. The appearance on the scene of a more radical form of rationalism in the shape of the revolutionary rationalism of the bourgeoisie widens the basis of attack of the anti-rationalist campaign. Bureaucratic rationalism consists, on the whole, of little more than the tendency to 'equalize' (the abolition of territorial and later of feudalistic social differences). Apart from that, it does not advance beyond a narrow sphere. Bourgeois rationalism, on the other hand, is revolutionary and radical just because it wants to rationalize the whole social order right from the beginning in a systematic manner. It opposes to the world as it has grown up a single rigid and static political system (in the form of written plans or constitutions). In reply, conservatism puts into the foreground, next to the struggle against generalization, the struggle against systematic thought, against thought as a static system.[1]

Thanks to Montesquieu I even know that one can be a Persian, but I declare that never in my life have I seen a man—unless indeed he exists unknown to me' (De Maistre, *Considérations sur la France*, Germ. ed., p. 72). Here again the intellectual attitude is transferred to the left-wing opposition : 'But man is no abstract being, sitting outside the world' (K. Marx, *Zur Kritik der Hegelschen Rechtsphilosophie*, ed. Fr. Mehring, vol. 1, p. 384).

[1] The paradox that the progressive, the liberal, who after all proved in fact surely more open to the new elements of growth than the conservative, appeared to his contemporaries as 'rigid', while the conservative and the old traditional forms of development appeared as mobile and 'alive', is due to an illusion to which those who took part in the process (the contemporaries) were bound to succumb. Lukács (*Geschichte und Klassenbewusstsein*, p. 109) tries—with reference to law—to suggest a solution to a similar paradox: 'Thus arises the apparently paradoxical situation that the law of primitive forms of society which has hardly changed for hundreds, in some cases even for thousands, of years possesses a fluid irrational character, continuously reborn in judicial decisions, whereas modern law which undergoes continuous and violent

Rigid and immobile thought having been confronted with dynamic Life there were now two possibilities: Either one re-nounced all thought, denied its significance and returned to irrationality; or distinguished a rigid from a mobile form of thought, the latter being able to keep step with the mobility of life because it is itself dynamic. The historical school chose the first path by combining the experience of dynamics with a thorough-going irrationalism. Adam Müller, on the other hand, combined the dynamic experience he derived from practical politics with certain sociologically related trends he observed in contemporary philosophy, and thus came to conceive the idea of '*dynamic thinking*'. In this mobile thought he saw the solution to the political problems of the time. This leads us to a funda-mental methodological conception, the distinction between 'idea' and 'concept'.

The antithesis between 'idea' and 'concept' which Adam Müller elaborates in the *Elements of Politics* is in his case the fruit of earlier reflections on logic the beginnings of which are to be found in his work *The Theory of Antithesis* (1804). The development of his thought brings out most clearly the consecutive stages of the elaboration of 'dynamic thinking'. The most important stages might be described as (*a*) thinking in terms of antitheses, (*b*) dynamic thinking, and (*c*) dialectical thinking.

The first stage is the attempt to oppose to linear deduction from an axiom the method of thinking in terms of polarities.[1] The rigidity which lies in the method of linear deduction is here overcome by dissolving all positions into antitheses. The thought of the Enlightenment proceeded in straight lines[2]; where an

transformations appears rigid, static and complete. The paradox proves illusory when it is realized that it only arises from the fact that the same situation is seen, in one case, from the standpoint of the historian (who stands outside development as far as his method is concerned), in the other, from the standpoint of the person who stands within the process, from the standpoint of the impact of the existing form of society on his consciousness.' To this undoubtedly correct observation may, however, be added that the thought of the complete, static system is *in fact* more rigid than that which its romantic opponents opposed to it as more 'alive'. If conservative thought proved none the less more impervious to the 'new', the reason must be sought not in the *forms* of con-servative thought but in the fact that this current closes its eyes to the new *contents*. That is the other aspect of the paradox which has just been discussed: the contem-poraries paid attention to the manner of thought (the forms of thought), whereas we as historians concentrate on the contents.

1 Here is an example for the early stage: 'The listener is the true counter-speaker; which of the two we call the active, which the passive partner or counter-agent in the process, who is called object and who subject, is completely arbitrary. One thing alone is essential: if one of them is called object, the other must be called subject' (A. Müller, *Die Lehre vom Gegensatz*, pp. 38 f.).

2 The excessively 'unilinear' form of rationalism itself gives rise, at a certain late stage, to a tendency towards antithetical thinking. Since 'unilinear' thought splits up everything into sets of exclusives, it contains within itself the elements which eventually carry evolution beyond it. In this sense Lublinski points out correctly that at a late

attempt was made to construct a philosophy of history, development was always conceived as the unfolding of a single principle. The idea of progress has its roots in a 'unilinear' construction— just as, in another sphere, the rights of man are to be deduced from a single idea, the 'idea of man'. Such a construction, however, is remote from reality, because the world cannot be understood in terms of a single principle. To try to think from more than one position and to comprehend the world by means of several principles increases the efficacy of thought and is therefore the first step towards improvement. This method of thinking in terms of antitheses and polarities is a romantic heritage. It is a method of thought which endeavours to reach some degree of mobility while remaining within the static framework.[1]

Adam Müller demonstrates the possibility of the two alternative methods of thought by two alternative methods of definition. He calls the first (the rigid one) the 'atomistic', the second the 'dynamic' definition. The former consists in describing 'the nature of the thing to be defined in isolation, its qualities, the parts of which it is composed, the symptoms by which it is recognized. The dynamic definition consists in mentioning some other known

stage of the Enlightenment a position beyond mere Enlightenment was sought and found in the Enlightenment itself. He shows how both Kant and Schiller attempted, in different spheres, to overcome 'unilinear' thought by means of the category of 'interaction'. In Lublinski's view, Schiller's endeavour to portray the hero as bound up with his environment by mutual relations and 'interaction' represents the same emergence of a new attitude as Kant's endeavour to establish the category of interaction in thought. In both cases, the point is that instead of merely placing correlated entities side by side, thinking sees the elements of experience as interrelated. Here once again it appears that new forms of thought are emanations of a more comprehensive factor, of new forms of experience. Cf. S. Lublinski, *Literatur und Gesellschaft im neunzehnten Jahrhundert*, 4 vols., vol. 1, p. 57, Berlin, 1899–1900.

[1] Metzger (*Gesellschaft, Staat und Recht in der Ethik des deutschen Idealismus*, pp. 260 f., Heidelberg, 1917) points out the romantic roots of this dynamic thinking. He mentions Friedrich Schlegel's *Ironie und antithetische Synthesis* (*ibid.*, footnote 1). Meinecke (*Weltbürgertum und Nationalstaat*, p. 131, footnote 2) refers to Fichte for its origins. H. Heller (*Hegel und der nationale Machtstaatsgedanke in Deutschland*, pp. 139 f., Berlin, 1921) tries to establish Hegel's influence on Müller through Schelling, on the one side, and Gentz, on the other. The only influence which is certain is that of Schelling's philosophy of nature which is mentioned by Metzger (*ibid.*, footnote 2) who follows A. Friedrich's book *Klassische Philosophie und Wirtschaftswissenschaft* (Gotha, 1903). Müller himself acknowledges this influence when he writes about antithesis in his essay on 'The Nature of Definition' (published in the review *Phoebus*, ed. by H. v. Kleist and A. Müller, and republished in *Neudrucke romantischer Seltenheiten*, 1924, p. 37) : 'It was in 1803 when I succeeded in the chief step of constructing a dynamic logic, the need for which I had felt in the name of the philosophy of nature.' (Cf. also *Die Lehre vom Gegensatz*, pp. 9, 11.) For the sociologist the determination of priority does not possess the cardinal importance that it has for the pure historian of ideas. For isolated discoveries are for him always expressions of general social trends. It is not important for us whether the dynamic logic which was achieved at about the same time by Hegel, Schelling and Müller, was arrived at independently or under mutual influence. What is important is to find the sources in the social and intellectual life of the time from which arose the impulse to search for a dynamic logic.

thing which stands in direct opposition to the thing to be defined',[1] e.g. heat through cold, love through hatred, masculinity through femininity. Nature herself is, on this view, nothing but 'a whole [organism] composed of an infinite number of antitheses'.[2] This type of dynamic thinking remains, in any case, still deeply bound up with the speculations of pantheism and the philosophy of nature. The element of analogy competes with the intention to think dynamically and the dynamic quality of the method does not really come to life until this type of thought turns from the philosophy of nature to historical reality.

The second stage of the dynamic conception of thought finds expression, in Adam Müller's system, in the correlation between *concept* and *idea*. One of the most important passages in the *Elements of Politics* runs: 'The State and all great human affairs have the characteristic quality that they can in no way be enveloped or compressed in words or definitions. . . . Such stiff forms, designed once for all for the State, for life and for man, as the ordinary sciences carry and hawk around are called *concepts*. But there *is* no concept of the State.'[3] One asks, what *is* there of the State? He answers promptly: 'If the thought which we have entertained of such a sublime object expands; if it moves and grows, as the object moves and grows; then we call the thought, not the concept of the thing, but the *Idea* of the thing, of the State, of life.'[4] The difficult question of how to treat thought once it has become evident that there is a discrepancy between flowing reality and rigid thought is thus not solved here by simply rejecting thought altogether. The solution consists rather in calling only one type of thought rigid and hence inferior, and opposing to it the idea of a mobile form of thought (the 'Idea'). The Idea too is a product of rationalization, but of a dynamic rationalization. It is admitted—and the above-mentioned sentences show that Adam Müller realized this—that thought need not necessarily comprehend the live object under a rigid concept fixed at a given moment of time. The single concept may always be static and rigid. But thought is a process, and this process can participate in the changes of the object. The theory demands that thought should move and grow—a demand which already goes far beyond the first step towards dynamic thinking,

---

1 A. Müller, *Vom Wesen der Definition*, p. 37.

2 *Ibid.*

3 A. Müller, *Elemente der Staatskunst*, vol. 1, p. 20.

4 Cf. S. T. Coleridge, who developed the theory of the Idea which he had probably taken over from Schelling in a manner very similar to that of Adam Müller and who gave it a very important place in his philosophy. He defines the notion of the Idea as 'that conception of a thing, which is not abstracted from any particular state, form or mode, in which the thing may happen to exist at this or that time; nor yet generalized from any number or succession of such forms or modes; but which is given by the knowledge of its ultimate aim' (*Church and State*, pp. 11 f., 1852).

the method of merely thinking in terms of polarities. It is no longer a question merely of grasping the object through its no less rigid opposite. The wish to make thought just as mobile as life itself breaks through here.

The difference between this solution and the solution of the same problem by Savigny and the historical school is that the romantic solution does not destroy the eighteenth-century faith in reason. It merely modifies it. The faith in the power of reason, in the achievement of thought, is not abandoned. Only one type of thought is rejected, the immobile thought of the Enlightenment which argues deductively from one principle and simply puts together rigid concepts. Only as compared with that type of thought does a widening of the horizon of potential thought take place. Here again romantic thought (unintentionally perhaps) merely continues, though more radically, and with new methods, the same process which the Enlightenment had already hoped to complete—the thorough rationalization of the world.

What is rational and what is irrational is, after all, really a relative question, or rather—and this is a point which we have to get clear—the two terms are correlative. Under the rule of the generalizing and rigidly systematic thought of the Enlightenment the limit of the rational had coincided with the limit of that thought. Everything that lay beyond had been conceived as irrational, as Life, as a residuum which, from the point of view of the Enlightenment, was irreducible. The idea of dynamic thinking pushed the limit of the rational a good deal further. Romantic thought therefore solved a task of the Enlightenment which the latter with its own instruments could never really have solved. Adam Müller acquired access to the dynamic experience, partly from the pantheistic sources of romanticism, but also largely from a revived experience of the old conservative attitude to the world. He saved this old mode of thought from decay by equipping it with new instruments of thought which corresponded to the most modern stage of consciousness—with instruments of thought, in other words, which not only incorporated but also made considerable advance on the thought of the Enlightenment. He helped to raise to a modern stage of consciousness a mode of experience and thought which historically preceded the Enlightenment.

It would none the less be one-sided to pretend that the above quotation adequately represents Adam Müller's conception of idea and concept. It presents only the dynamic intention of thought, clear and freed from romantic oddities. If further passages are adduced in order to observe the method of thinking with 'ideas',[1]

[1] Cf., e.g. Müller, *Elemente der Staatskunst*, vol. 1, pp, 351, 354, 355, 356.

it becomes apparent that he relapses again and again into the romantic tendency to think in terms of analogies. Every concrete event is understood by him only by presenting it as an 'interplay' of several forces which are mostly opposed to each other on the analogy with the sexes.

In one place he himself gives a good brief description of the method which he actually uses: 'I had to show the nature of the State. Without any definitions which are the poison of science, I described the interplay between the four eternal estates, the clergy, the merchants, the nobility and the professions [*Bürgerschaft*]; I mediated [!] between the necessary differences of age and sex, and there developed—more clearly and precisely than would have resulted from the astutest analysis, and now moreover alive—the nature of the State.'[1]

It is a matter of portraying the interplay of living forces as the 'mediation' between differences. Everything that lives is conceived as alive by presenting it always as a tension between several antagonistic principles. Every moment, every situation in life is on that view nothing but a momentary mediation, a neutralization of ever-present tensions. The following sentence from Adam Müller stands wholly under the influence of that conception; at the same time it reveals the political point, the political origin, of that mode of thought: 'The social contract is therefore not a contract concluded at some definite time in some definite place; it is the Idea of a contract which is continuously and at every point being concluded, a contract which is at every moment renewed by the new freedom that begins to stir at the side of the old, and which is thus preserved.'[2]

Here again it is quite apparent that the desire to think dynamically has its sociological roots in the opposition to bourgeois natural-law thought and hopes to overcome the latter not only as to its content but also as to its method of thought. Nowhere else can the fundamental difference between the two forms of thought be seen more clearly. In bourgeois natural-law thought the state is established by a settlement (contract) between the contracting parties recognized for all time as just. In feudalistic, romantic thought the state is an ever-fluctuating dynamic settlement between antagonistic groups. Something in that conception sounds familiar to us. Today we are quite accustomed to interpreting the historical process in terms of such polar and counteracting factors, and to conceiving any one situation of the present as a synthesis (mediation) of co-existing but dynamically changing factors. This mode of

1 *Ibid.*, vol. 2, p. 178.
2 *Ibid.*, vol. 1, p. 147. Cf. Coleridge who speaks of the Idea of an 'ever-originating contract' (*The Friend*, 2 vols., vol. 1, p. 191, 1863).

thought which has become almost axiomatic for us arose here in reaction to the 'unilinear' construction of eighteenth-century rationalism. In the method of thinking with Ideas (to use Adam Müller's terminology) romantic and feudalistic 'philosophy of life' did indeed create an instrument for the orderly arrangement of flowing historical growth and for the understanding of history as a totality.

The third stage in the development of conservative dynamic thought is represented by the stage of the dialectic. It must be analysed in connection with Hegel, whose complex sociological position leads to a very special intellectual solution.

We must now turn to a third important category of Müller's thought which can only be understood in relation to the contrast between 'concept' and 'idea'.

In the discussion of Müller's dynamic conception of the Idea we have several times come across a favourite concept of his, the concept of 'mediation'. 'Mediation' is a category characteristic of the romantic-feudalistic synthesis. All thought is, however reluctantly, analytical; and it has the task to reunite the parts of reality which it has broken to pieces. But the peculiar character of a mode of thought is never more apparent than where it is faced with the task of synthesis. The rationalist thought of the Enlightenment analysed by taking to pieces and atomizing things. Its synthesis accordingly consists in addition. Feudalist-romantic thought, as it has just been described, analysed by dividing a living totality, life or the state, into polar movements of its various parts. The question would have to be: How can one reach a living dynamic synthesis? The answer to the problem lies in the concept of 'mediation'.

The word recalls sometimes the common Christian idea of the 'mediator', sometimes the specifically Catholic idea of the mediating role of the Church.[1] But here it is really rather a special romantic creation which receives its peculiar modern meaning from the fundamental tendency of romanticism which has already been described, the striving for dynamic thinking and for an intellectual comprehension of the polyphony of life. But at the same time the concept contains also the other component which is derived from the feudalistic attitude, the antipathy to the subsumption of the individual and particular under one general principle. Feudalistic conservatism somehow strives for some other definition of the relation between whole and part, between particular and universal, than those of subsumption and addition. This impulse is here incorporated in Müller's solution.

---

[1] One passage in the *Elemente* (p. 175), recalls the religious context. Cf. for the religious origin of the term 'Mediator', P. Kluckholn, *Persönlichkeit und Gemeinschaft. Studien zur Staatsauffassung der deutschen Romantik*, p. 17, Halle, 1925.

In order to understand the meaning of the concept of 'mediation' in Adam Müller's system—its meaning in connection with the fundamental notions of 'concept' and 'idea'—one has to return once more to the basic attitude which holds that every living totality is always developing and unfolding itself, that it is a dynamic product of antagonistic forces and principles. Sometimes, as has been seen, the antithesis lies between the different estates that fight each other, sometimes it is the conflict between the family and the individual,[1] or between eternity and the moment.[2] It is the task of the agent, of the judge or of the thinker, not to conceive any given concrete situation as the special case of a general rule or or a general concept, but to experience the constantly changing situations as the neutralization of the changing elements of the process, and to understand them and deal with them as such. Rationalistic, generalizing thought works with the correlation: general law—particular case. Its methodology is based upon the category of subsumption. Dynamic thinking grasps the Idea, i.e. the inner aim and purpose of the concrete whole, and conceives the particular as a part of this dynamically changing whole. Its methodology is based upon the category of 'mediation', as illustrated by the role of the judge who 'mediates' between a law and a concrete case under dispute. 'The highest judge of your land', says Adam Müller, 'should represent, not the whole as such, but the aim and purpose of the whole. In a small way and within his own limited sphere he should stand—like the Sovereign in his large and wide sphere—between the demands of the forefathers and the needs of the contemporaries, between law and dispute, carrying out a vital mediation, not making lifeless comparisons and calculations.'[3]

The sociological root of this tendency of thought to which we have already alluded is here clearly visible. The threatened patrimonial jurisdiction of the lord, for example, is contrasted as a higher form, a 'mediation', with the jurisdiction of the bureaucratic administration which merely subsumes individual cases under the general law.[4]

It is not an accident that the judicial decision is here taken as the model. Rationalism was implicitly concerned with the purely thinking, theoretical, contemplative, inactive individual who makes no decisions, who merely assents or denies (which is not the same as making decisions). The model of dynamic thought,

---

[1] Müller, *Elemente der Staatskunst*, vol. 1, p. 179.
[2] *Ibid.*
[3] *Ibid.*, p. 143.
[4] For further passages containing the term 'mediation', see *ibid.*, pp. 148, 205. Note in the latter passage the expressions 'calculating wisdom', and 'not only weighed and decided by quantity . . . mediated'; also pp. 206, 286, 305 ('continuous peace-making'), and again applied, by analogy, to money (p. 361).

in contrast, is the man who decides, judges, mediates. The purely contemplative, theoretical, individual subsumes under general rules. The individual who stands in the midst of the conflicting polarities of life decides and mediates. The concept of dynamic synthesis, 'mediation', therefore contains already a *breach with the contemplative attitude*.[1] Dynamic thinking grasps the particular by decision and mediation. It should gradually become clear that the manifold forms of thought which the levelling effect of the written word has largely blurred for us are here still visible. 'Thought' is not always the same thing; thinking differs from thinking, depending on the living function which it fulfils. Both the man who subsumes and systematizes and the judge who decides *think*; yet, 'thinking' as a function in the judicial decision is something completely different from contemplative subsumption.

For a proper understanding of the difference between the inductive rationalism of the Enlightenment and the dynamics of feudalistic romanticism it is not sufficient merely to elaborate the dynamic quality. One has to penetrate to those ultimate sociological foundations which in practice determine the varying forms of the relation between theory and practice. By the way, the adherents of both modes of thought also reflect on this very problem of the relation of theory to practice, and they reach, of course, different conclusions.

Before turning to this problem of the relation between theory and practice, it is, however, necessary to say a word or two about the subsequent fate of the category of 'mediation'. Already in the *Elements of Politics* (where, as has been mentioned, the pantheist and dynamic begins, at a certain point, to fade before the Catholic and hierarchic element) there are passages which represent mediation not as an automatic mutual combination of dynamic polarities, but in the new meaning of *reconciliation*. The tribunal of reconciliation which is set up above the dynamic elements is the Catholic clergy. The clergy is said to be a 'mediatory apostolic estate' whose task it is to provide a bond between the various national states, to mitigate the contrast between poverty and excessive wealth within the states, and to preserve the spirit of 'moral equilibrium'.[2] The function of mediation is therefore here assigned to a special institution. That this is the Catholic clergy follows naturally from the pro-Catholic tendency of romanticism which began with Novalis.

[1] Here again a far-reaching agreement between the 'left' and the 'right' opposition to the bourgeois rationalist world. Cf. for instance the condemnatory reference to the calculating and contemplative character of the capitalist attitude also in the legal sphere in Lukács, *op. cit.*, p. 109.

[2] Müller, *Elemente der Staatskunst*, vol. 1, p. 288.

Once again we can observe clearly that even the most fundamental categories of thought, the special forms of synthesis, differ as and when the conditions of thought change in their sociological and historical structure. The same thinker constructs different syntheses on a romantic-feudalistic and on a Catholic foundation. Even the formal categories of the synthesis change with his answers to the main problems. As long as thinking remains pantheist in inspiration, the antagonistic poles reach a synthesis by themselves, without an extraneous mediating force. Now the Catholic tradition also contains philosophies based upon the idea of polarity, as the Jesuit scholar Przywara[1] has penetratingly shown. In Pascal one finds a philosophy of polarities, the same as in Newman's doctrine of 'opposite virtues'. Genuinely Catholic thought, however, has the tendency to join the polar elements by means of some higher factor to which they are subordinated. Originally it was God. But his place may also be taken by the Church. With Novalis romanticism already shows this hierarchic junction of polarities: 'It is impossible that mundane forces should of themselves find their equilibrium; a third element, at once mundane and supermundane, can alone solve this task.'[2]

The more this feudalistic, romantic and pantheist thought moves across into the Austria of Metternich with its largely Catholic traditions the more the first layer of dynamic ideas is overlaid by a second Catholic layer which may briefly be called hierarchic. The Idea and 'mediation' receive a new meaning.[3] Since we are here concerned only with romantic and feudalistic thought, the subsequent fate of 'mediation' cannot be dealt with here, and we must resume the analysis of the problem of the relation between theory and practice in feudalistic romanticism.

The respective attitudes of bourgeois rationalism and feudalistic conservatism to this problem have been discussed in connection with the polemic between Möser and Kant.[4] The former takes

[1] Cf. his preface to A. Müller's *Schriften zur Staatsphilosophie* (Theatiner-Verlag, Munich), pp. vi f.
[2] Novalis, 'Die Christenheit oder Europa', in *Schriften*, ed. by J. Minor, vol. 2, p. 42, Jena, 1907.
[3] Hence, Baxa (see his Comments on the *Elemente der Staatskunst*, vol. 2, p. 292 f.) is wrong when he tries to interpret the notion of Idea in the *Elemente* by means of quotations from Müller's later works, such as the *Theologische Grundlagen*; for in the latter the 'Idea' has already received a platonistically 'archetypal', theological meaning. A similar mistake was committed by Gentz, who tried to explain the 'Idea' of the *Elemente* simply on the basis of Müller's work of 1804 (cf. Fr. v. Gentz, *Schriften*, ed. by Schlesier, vol. 4, p. 359, 1838-40). The point is to see even the thought of a single author dynamically. It must always be the task of the sociologist of knowledge to observe how the thought of the same thinker is modified when it moves from one sociological position towards another within the same social environment. On the other hand, it will be necessary to observe in what forms certain fundamental concepts like 'Idea' and 'mediation' appear in other currents of conservative thought.
[4] Cf. Sec. III, p. 111, above.

practice as his guiding principle and makes theoretical reasoning follow practice; the latter separates the two spheres and subsequently establishes a relation between them. It has also been seen that the 'practice' which Möser contrasts as the living element with theory is not only free from all mystic elements but that it is something exceedingly sober—just as his custom and habit, religion and tradition are in no way the irrational factors which they became in the hands of romanticism and the historical school.

From feudalistic conservatism romantic conservatism derived merely the denial of the autonomous nature of theory and the conception of thought as embedded in life. The peculiarly irrational, fluid element is an independent contribution of urban middle-class romanticism. Thus the romanticism of Adam Müller possesses, in place of Möser's sober 'practice', a concept of 'life' in which the 'practical' element is mingled in a peculiar manner with emotional elements and with remains of the contemplative mystic consciousness.

The mere men of practice can satisfy Müller just as little as the mere theorists, because the former 'are confined to such narrow spheres of action, are oppressed by such petty conditions, and shut up in such narrow-minded localities that they find it just as hard to escape pedantry as it is for our theorists to escape visionary enthusiasm [*Schwärmerei*].'[1] Whereas for Möser a narrow sphere of action had still meant living contact, Müller sees in the man of practice the danger of pedantry. He now begins from two sides the process of mystifying, irrationalizing, 'romanticizing' practice. On the one hand, he stresses that aspect of practical thought which later on came to be admired as 'the sureness of instinct'. He sets out to prove that 'principles are of no use, only the feeling for what is advisable and good which has been gathered by long experience'.[2] Möser, too, had been aware of this—but his conception of practice was a different one. The second aspect under which he introduces irrationality is that of pure change and becoming, the protean quality which according to him characterizes Life and Practice or whatever else he may call the antagonist to rigid systematic theory: 'The kind of politics to which I refer should treat of the State as *flowing, living, moving*, not merely throw laws into it and then wait leisurely to see what is going to happen. The statesman should be the ever-present soul of civil society and act at once martially and peacefully.'[3]

Thus there is superimposed on the sober 'practice' of Möser the experience of the dynamic factor. It is the sheer flow and movement

---

[1] Müller, *Elemente der Staatskunst*, vol. 1, p. 15.
[2] *Ibid.*, Introduction, p. xii.
[3] *Ibid.*, vol. 1, p. 11. (My italics.)

in the concept of life which Müller wants to grasp.[1] Practice is characterized not only by the factors of concrete circumstance and locality (a concept, by the way, which appears both in Möser's and Müller's thought). For the romanticist, 'practice' does not mean day-to-day activity but that pure 'becoming' which can only be experienced from within. The emphasis upon the concrete by which the conservatives reacted to the revolution is here made an 'internal' affair and at the same time combined with a form of experience which in a religious age appeared as mysticism and in an atheistic or pantheistic one as pure dynamism.

This conception of life (a mixture of 'practice', 'concreteness' and 'pure movement') is none the less related to Möser's conception. For it too gives absolute value to something that stands outside theory and in relation to which theory is seen as something secondary. Thought is here a function of life and practice, and not vice versa; practice a mere application of theory to the immediate situation. It is not the case that the theorist decides and the practical man carries out the decision, but the decision actually lies in the comprehension of the concrete; this is the mediation performed by the living, practical participant and agent. Cognition is action and at the same time the knowledge that arises out of action. While, therefore, the consciousness of the Enlightenment which concentrated on theory was inclined to conceive even action as a kind of subsumption (in other words, concealed even action under the categories of 'theory') it is now possible that a vital concept will serve for the understanding of the concrete object. The synthesis is not a matter of joining or adding, but a mediation carried out from within.

The most important phases of feudalistic romanticism thus complete a circle: a special conception of thinking in terms of Ideas, of the relation between theory and practice, and the concept of mediation mutually explain each other as parts of dynamic thought and experience. At the same time one can isolate the dynamic element in Adam Müller's thought (which, as we have seen, is clearly distinguishable from 'practice' in Möser's sense), and thus grasp the conservative origin of the modern idea of 'life' which has its roots in the conservative's experiencing of 'pure becoming' as an Absolute.

In Müller's case, we can often observe how he strains to grasp the concrete object in its concreteness; yet he never achieves a proper realism. At the point when he should become really concrete he goes off into declamations about 'life', 'becoming', the 'Idea', and his discussions are no less abstract (though in a different

[1] For further examples of the pure experience of dynamics see *ibid.*, pp. 4, 144, 115, 193, 348, 365 f.

way) than the 'normative' abstractions of the Enlightenment to which they were supposed to be the reaction. And yet, this forced and at first merely programmatic striving for dynamics gave rise to an important aspect of the modern philosophies of Life.

The realism of the second half of the nineteenth century included a romantic conservative element which corresponded to this intense preoccupation with Life. This dynamics was at first experienced in isolation; in its German development it later took a twofold direction. In its romantic direction it gets more and more 'internalized'. In Adam Müller's thought it is—in intention at least—still in alliance with the desire for the concrete, practical and sober. Later, however, it becomes more and more separated from it and is experienced by itself in all its purity. There arises a kind of realism which does not look for 'reality' in the empirical object, in 'everyday life', but in pure 'vital experience'. This new direction, after having been temporarily eclipsed by materialism, especially during the capitalist boom of the eighteen-seventies, received a new impetus from the vitalist philosophy of Bergson, whose notion of *'durée réelle'* is really a revival of the romantic conception of pure dynamics. Many currents from the history of German thought find their way to Bergson, and German intellectual life received back from him, though at a later stage of development, much that had formerly been its own.[1] The impulse that came from Bergson combined in Germany, on the one side, with currents which converged in the *phenomenological* school; on the other, it entered into an alliance with the revived historicism of Dilthey.

The peculiar qualities of the different variants of modern philosophies of life can be defined in accordance with the different tendencies which they have absorbed. However much the various forms of this 'vitalism' may differ from each other, they all betray their origin in (counter-revolutionary) romanticism by their common opposition to both Kantianism and Positivism, the two variants of bourgeois rationalism which both endeavour to preserve and uphold as the exclusive model of all thought general concepts and the inductive method of natural science, though on different epistemological foundations. All philosophies of life are romantic in origin, because they keep alive the opposition against general concepts and because they look for reality in 'pure experience', free from conceptual constructions and rationalization. Today[2] one can no longer speak of them as counter-revolutionary,

---

[1] For the existence of the conception of *'durée'* in French traditionalism, see P. R. Rohden, *J. de Maistre als politischer Theoretiker*, p. 217, Munich, 1929; see also Brinckmann's review in the *Deutsche Literatur-Zeitung*.

[2] This was written in 1925. Since then, various counter-revolutionary movements in Germany and elsewhere have made use of 'vital' categories in building up their ideologies.—Ed.

since they have mostly become politically indifferent. But the aims of their thought and experience originally sprang, in the romantic period, from the basic aims of conservatism. Just because this originally romantic current lost its political foundation (and with it all immediate efficiency, all concrete touch with its real environment) it could isolate the 'life' and 'pure dynamics' of romanticism from Möser's 'practice' and give it a more and more 'purely internalized' meaning.

The great importance of the philosophies of Life consists in their constant emphasis on the limitations of bourgeois rationalism which in its expansion threatens gradually to obscure and devitalize everything that is alive in the world. The philosophy of Life is never tired of pointing out that whatever passes for 'real' in our rationalized world is merely a reflection of the specific categories of Reason of which modern man has made an idol;[1] in other words, that this world of alleged reality is merely the world of capitalist rationalization. As such it conceals behind it a world of pure 'vital experience'. But even today the philosophy of Life betrays its conservative origin in that it constitutes a latent opposition to the rationalist world which surrounds us. But, having lost all political interest and significance, it can find no direct way of changing things; it exalts the idea of 'becoming' in the abstract but has severed all connection with the actually 'becoming'—though rationalized—world. Nevertheless, philosophies of 'Life' are an integral part of present trends of evolution—in fact, a very important part. They serve to keep alive a certain form of experience; it is an open question to what social trends they will ally themselves in the future.[2] As a position from which to understand the world, the philosophy of Life is a useful counterpart to the currents of thought which stand under the spell of an absolute rationalism. For it teaches us again and again to put aside the rationalizations which conceal the real nature of things and to avoid shaping our consciousness to the pattern of the theoretical attitude alone. It always splits up and relativizes what we believe to be 'rational' and 'objective'.

The romantic experience of pure dynamics followed another path in the hands of Hegel. Opposed to the method of 'internalization' he sought an 'objective' standpoint and thus combined the dynamic element with the concrete problems of the political and

---

[1] Here again parallels, though of a very different structure, can be found in the left opposition; cf. Lukács, op. cit., Das Problem der Verdinglichung, passim.

[2] As far as it is possible to judge at present, it has the tendency—when it regains political significance—to provide an ideological foundation for the modern eruptive activist currents (whether in a reactionary or progressive sense). This at any rate is true of the Bergsonian trend which provided the impetus both for Fascism and for the direct action of syndicalism (Sorel).

historical world. That meant that he gave up the purely 'internal' experience of dynamics; by means of a new process of rationalization, he transformed it into 'dialectics'. But at the same time he preserved the lasting conservative discovery of movement by turning it into a method of understanding the growth of history. The dilemma, rigid thought-irrational dynamics, which appeared in the open at the beginning of the new century, he solved by the answer: There is a higher order of rationality than that of abstract, rigid thought; there is *dynamic thinking*. That answer constituted the final triumph of the tendency which has been observed before in Adam Müller, i.e. the tendency to extend the sphere of potential rationalization and to use the new method for the understanding of history. That Hegel succeeded in this, that he did not, like the romantics, lose touch with the real world and take refuge in mere 'internalized' experience, was due to the fact that he clung, with indomitable perseverance,[1] to the historical reality which was then the basic reality for conservatism.

Adam Müller's type of romanticism developed at first in alliance with the feudalistic opposition; but, since the latter could not maintain itself in the long run, it was soon left without any real social backing and had in part to escape into the Austrian camp in order to keep alive at all. That, however, meant the destruction of all that had arisen organically out of it, that gave it meaning and derived its meaning from it. As a visible 'movement', it did not even last as long as Metternich. For as a living influence in intellectual life, it had been done with in the forties; a critic like Heine had completely seen through it as early as in 1833, and still more in 1839.[2]

But in turning the mere experience of dynamics into a rational method of thought of a higher order, Hegel at the same time sets the problem of dynamic thinking and the whole complex of questions concerning truth and a standard of value, which occupy us to the present day. We cannot here describe this whole range of problems and analyse the social background of Hegel's thought. It is important only to show that it is the 'objective dynamics' of Hegel which is absorbed in the synthesis of Marxism. Marxist proletarian thought has therefore also a dynamic and dialectic conception of reality. Hegel and Marxism have this in common with

[1] The following passage from the *Rechtsphilosophie* (add. to § 13, p. 290) sounds like a confession in this direction: 'A will which decides nothing is no real will. . . . Only by means of decisions does man enter reality, however hard it may be. For laziness will not venture beyond a state of solitary brooding in which it keeps open an unlimited possibility. But possibility is not reality. A will which is sure of itself is not therefore lost in the thing it determines.'

[2] Cf. for instance Heine's *Romantische Schule* (1833), or the essay 'Der Protestantismus und die Romantik. Zur Verständigung über die Zeit und ihre Gegensätze', a manifesto publ. in the *Hallische Jahrbücher für deutsche Wissenschaft und Kunst*, 1839.

the philosophy of Life, that they, like the latter, are able to relativize 'everyday', 'static', 'abstract' thinking, and to do so on a dynamic basis. But whereas in the 'internalized' philosophy of Life the dynamic foundation is something that precedes all theory (i.e. the pure '*durée*', 'pure vital experience'), in Hegel's philosophy the dynamic basis in respect of which he relativizes 'ordinary', 'abstract' thinking is an intellectual basis (rationality of a higher order), and in proletarian thought, it is the class war and the economically determined social process itself.

It is not necessary to go into all the details which might be mentioned. Our purpose was merely to show that not only the content of thought, but even the conceptions of reality of the twofold opposition against bourgeois rationalism were formed in direct reaction against it; that the product of the struggle was a concept of life which was characterized by movement, by dynamics; and that both the vitalist and Marxist conceptions of reality developed in clear continuity from this romantic opposition.

Apart from these two directions in which the romantic-feudalistic element developed there is a third path which was chosen by the historical school. It solves in a specific way of its own the conservative problem of the relation between norm and history, between thought and existence. The determination of its sociological position presents quite a distinct problem; it occupies a place between romanticism and Hegel. But a discussion of this important current of conservative thought must also be left aside.

VI
Competition as a
Cultural Phenomenon

T HIS paper is meant as a contribution to two closely connected problems. Firstly, the intention is to illustrate further
the problem of competition, and secondly to make a contribution to a sociological theory of the mind.

As regards competition, I hope that my paper will serve as a
supplement to that of the previous speaker, Professor Leopold von
Wiese,[1] who gave a systematic discussion of competition as such from
the viewpoint of formal sociology. I, on the other hand, propose
to discuss the problem from the angle of *applied historical sociology*.

I am glad to say I am in complete agreement with Professor von
Wiese's talk in so far as it touched upon my subject, and I shall
simply build upon his conclusions without further discussion.

Thus, I shall simply submit without discussion the correctness
of his main contention that competition must be regarded as a
feature not merely of economic life, but of social life as a whole,
and I propose to outline its role as a determinant in intellectual
life, where its importance has so far been least recognized.

What is meant by saying that competition acts as a 'determinant' in intellectual life? The term is meant to suggest that competition does not operate merely at the margin, as a stimulus, an
inducement, a sporadic cause of intellectual production (which in
any case would be admitted by everyone), but that it enters as a
constituent element into the form and content of every cultural
product or movement.

This recognition of the role of competition as a determinant in
intellectual life is not meant, however, as a declaration of faith
in unbridled 'sociologism'. I am far from suggesting that it is
possible merely on the basis of a sociological account of the

From *Essays on the Sociology of Knowledge* (New York: Oxford University Press,
1952), pp. 191–229. Reprinted by permission of Routledge and Kegan Paul Ltd.

genesis of a mental pattern or product to draw direct conclusions concerning its truth or validity.

There are two extreme points of view regarding the role of competition in intellectual life. There are those who refuse to ascribe more than a peripheral role to it, over against those who see in cultural creations nothing but a by-product of the social process of competition. My own position is somewhere in the middle between these two extremes. To give a more exact idea of my position with regard to these extreme views: while the first school of thought considers the role of competition in intellectual life as peripheral, and the second as determinant, in my own view, it is *co-determinant*.

I do not propose, however, to pursue this train of thought any farther, although the epistemological problems just alluded to are certainly germane to my subject. For reasons of economy and to keep the discussion at a factual level, I would suggest disregarding all questions of epistemological validity for the time being. I shall make a few remarks about these things at the end of my talk, but I would ask you to pay attention in the first place to what I have to say about the purely sociological aspects of my subject.

My assertion that the form which competition among intellectually creative subjects assumes at a given time is a co-determinant of the visible cultural pattern is closely connected with a more sweeping conviction many of you share, namely, that not only competition, but also all other social relations and processes comprising the prevailing pattern of social life are determinants of the mental life corresponding to that particular social structure. To use a somewhat bold shorthand formula: we recognize here the problem of *sociology of the mind*, as one capable of unambiguous formulation and of detailed empirical examination.

Whereas the generation which lived through the French Revolution and went through the corresponding process of reflection had as its task the development of a 'phenomenology of the spirit' and of a philosophy of history showing, for the first time, the dynamics and the morphology of the mind and the role of the historical moment as a co-determinant of the content of intellectual products, it seems to me to be at least one of the primary tasks devolving upon our generation, owing to the historical circumstances of our time, to promote understanding for the role of the life of the social body as a determinant of mental phenomena.

Certain problems of hoary antiquity assume a surprising meaning if seen in this new context. Thus problems such as those which Wegelin had already pondered—what intellectual currents really are, what factors determine their inner rhythm—for the first time become to a large degree amenable to a solution if viewed from this angle.

I think a consistent application of the method of sociological analysis to mental life will show that many phenomena originally diagnosed as manifestations of immanent laws of the mind may be explained in terms of the prevailing structural pattern of determination within society. It seems to me, then, that I am not following a false trail if I assume that the so-called 'dialectical' (as distinct from the unilinear, continuous) form of evolution and change in mental life can be largely traced back to two very simple structural determinants of social character: to the existence of generations,[1] and to the existence of the phenomenon of competition with which it is our task to deal here.

So much for introduction, as a preliminary survey of the subject. After this more general discussion, however, I hope you will bear with me if I go on to examine only a rather narrowly circumscribed segment of the field to which my subject belongs. In the interests of concreteness, I shall now formulate my problem in more specialized terms. First I shall make a few preparatory remarks.

To begin with, I should like to delimit, examine, and describe, somewhat in the manner of a physician, the area of demonstration, the field in which competition is to be shown to operate.

I do not propose to determine the role competition plays in mental life as a whole, but only in the realm of *thought*, and even here, I shall not be concerned with all thought, but only with a special kind of thought—not that of the exact natural sciences, but only a particular kind of thought which I would like to call *existentially-determined*. Within this concept of existentially-determined thought are included historical thought (the way in which man interprets history, and the way in which he presents it to others), political thought, thought in the cultural and social sciences, and also ordinary everyday thought.

The simplest way to describe this type of thought is to contrast it with thought as it appears in the exact natural sciences. There are the following differences;

(*a*) in the case of existentially-determined thought, the results of the thought process are partly determined by the nature of the thinking subject;

(*b*) in the natural sciences, thinking is carried on, in idea at

---

[1] Cf. *'Das Problem der Generationen'* (this volume, pp. 276 ff.). This paper is closely related to the present one—both are contributions to a sociology of the mind.

least, by an abstract 'consciousness as such' in us, whereas in existentially-determined thought, it is—to use Dilthey's phrase—'the whole man' who is thinking.

What does this mean more exactly? The difference can be shown very clearly with a simple example. In the thought '$2 + 2 = 4$' there is no indication as to who did the thinking, and where. On the other hand, it is possible to tell in the case of existentially-determined thought, not only from its content, but also from its logical form and the categoreal apparatus involved, whether the thinker has approached historical and social reality from the point of view of the 'historical school', of 'Western positivism', or of Marxism.

Here arises an important point. We shall see in this a defect of existentially-determined thinking only if we adopt a methodology based upon the exact natural sciences as a model. I would urge, as against this, that each type of thinking should be understood in terms of its own innermost nature. That certain items of knowledge are incapable of an absolute interpretation and formulation does not mean that they are abitrary and subjective, but only that they are a function of a particular viewpoint or perspective; that is to say, that *certain qualitative features of an object encountered in the living process of history are accessible only to minds of a certain structure*. There are certain qualitatively distinguished features of historically existing objects that are open to perception only by a consciousness as formed and devised by particular historical circumstances. This idea of the 'existential relativity' of certain items of knowledge—which the phenomenological school, along with a few others, is now developing with increasing clarity —is far from implying a relativism under which everybody and nobody is right; what it implies is rather a *relationism* which says that certain (qualitative) truths cannot even be grasped, or formulated, except in the framework of an existential correlation between subject and object. This means, in our context, that certain insights concerning some qualitative aspect of the living process of history are available to consciousness only as formed by certain historical and social circumstances, so that the historico-social formation of the thinking and knowing subject assumes epistemological importance.

So much for existentially-determined thought: our area of demonstration at present. Now for the problem: what are we maintaining as our thesis? Firstly, that in thought (from now on, this term always means existentially-determined thought) competition can be shown to operate; and, secondly, that it can be shown to be a co-determinant in the process of its formation. The first question which confronts us as we try to develop these theses is the following: does the process of thinking, of struggling for truth, involve at all a competition?

We can be certain that our formulation of the problem will expose us to the criticism that we are projecting specifically economic categories into the mental sphere, and our first task must be to meet this criticism. This reproach, however plausible it may seem at first sight, and happily as it meets the view of those who like to see in the kingdom of the mind the unchallenged domain of absolute unconditional creation, must be rejected as beside the point. Actually, it seems to me that the reverse is the case. Nothing is being generalized from the economic sphere: on the contrary, when the Physiocrats and Adam Smith demonstrated the important role of competition in economic life, they were in fact only discovering a *general social relationship* in the particular context of the economic system. The 'general social'— meaning the interplay of vital forces between the individuals of a group—became visible at first in the economic sphere, and if we deliberately adopt the course of employing economic categories in the formulation of social interrelationships in the mental sphere, this is because until now the existence of the social was most easily discerned in its economic manifestations. The ultimate aim, however, must be to strip our categorial apparatus of anything specifically economic in order to grasp the social fact *sui generis*.

To accept the proposition that the phenomenon of competition is also to be found in the mental sphere, does not imply that *theoretical conflict* is nothing but the reflection of current social competition, but simply that theoretical conflict also is a manifestation of the 'general social'.

Phenomenologically speaking, theoretical conflict is a self-contained sphere, as is also social conflict in the more general sense. It is not enough, however, always to keep things apart and to keep watch over the jurisdictions of the various spheres. We must explore the interpenetration, the togetherness of these 'planes of experience', the separation of which is merely a matter of phenomenality and often does not go beyond the immediate datum. Once this is seen, the question becomes: how is theoretical conflict related to social conflict?

The correctness of our thesis that competition does operate in mental life—that is, in existentially-determined thinking—can perhaps be shown in the easiest way by demonstrating some of the generally typical features of competition as such in intellectual life.

In the first place, it is clear that in the case of historical thought, as in that of all existentially-determined thought, we are faced with rivalry between different parties seeking an identical goal, and also with what von Wiese has called 'a discrepancy of the lowest degree'.[1] Other general characteristics of competition can also be shown to be present in existentially-determined thinking, the tendency either to degenerate into conflict, to turn into fight, or to change into a relationship of association. It would not be difficult to demonstrate in existentially-determined thought also the two types of competition defined by Oppenheimer[2]—hostile contest and peaceful rivalry. Finally, as regards the social agents of competition, individuals, groups, and abstract collectives can all take over this function, and it could be shown how far thought, and the principle of competition operative within it, assume different forms according to whether the competing parties are groups or individuals. The American writer Ross[3] has put forward some very useful observations on this point, in particular as to competition between institutions.

It is thus clear that the characteristics of the general socio-logical phenomenon of competition are also to be met with in existentially-determined thought. There is only one difficulty—how can we show that, in existentially-determined thinking, the various parties seek identical goals? What is the appropriate formulation of competition in the sphere of thought? How can we define existentially-determined thought in such a way that the sociological factor of competition comes to the fore? Further, what can we take to be the identical goal sought by competitors in the sphere of existentially-determined thought?

It appears that the different parties are all competing for the possession of the correct social diagnosis (*Sicht*), or at least for the prestige which goes with the possession of this correct diagnosis. Or, to use a more pregnant term to characterize this identical goal: the competing parties are always struggling to influence what the phenomenologist Heidegger[4] calls the 'public interpretation of reality'. I do not suggest, of course, that Heidegger, as a philo-sopher, would agree with the sociological theory I am pro-pounding.

Philosophy, ladies and gentlemen, may look at this matter differently; but from the point of view of the social sciences, every historical, ideological, sociological piece of knowledge (even should it prove to be Absolute Truth itself), is clearly rooted in and carried by the desire for power and recognition of particular

[1] Cf. *Beziehungslehre*.

[2] Oppenheimer, F., *System der Soziologie*, Jena, 1922–27. Vol. I, pp. XIV, 348, 370.

[3] E. A. Ross, *Foundations of Sociology*, New York, 1905, pp. 285 ff.

[4] M. Heidegger, 'Sein und Zeit', *Jahrbuch für Philosophie und phänomeno-logische Forschung*, Halle a.d.S., 1927. Vol. VIII.

social groups who want to make their interpretation of the world the universal one.

To this, sociology and the cultural sciences make no exception; for in them we see only the old battle for universal acceptance of a particular interpretation of reality, carried on with modern scientific weapons. One may accept or reject the thesis that all pre-sociological interpretations of reality were based on gratuitous belief or superstition, and that our concept of reality is the only scientific and correct one. But even those who accept this thesis unconditionally must admit that the process in the course of which scientific interpretations gain ascendancy in a society has the same structure as the process in the course of which pre-scientific modes of interpretation had achieved dominance; that is to say, even the 'correct', 'scientific', interpretation did not arise out of a pure, contemplative desire for knowledge, but fulfilled the age-old function of helping some group find its way about in the surrounding world. It emerged and exists in exactly the same way as the pre-scientific modes of orientation—that is, as a function of the interplay of vital forces.

The nature of the generally accepted interpretation of the world at any given time is of decisive importance in determining the particular nature of the stage of historical evolution reached at that time. This is not merely a matter of the so-called 'public opinion' which is commonly recognized as a superficial phenomenon of collective psychology, but of the inventory of our set of fundamental meanings in terms of which we experience the outside world as well as our own inner responses.

Man, when he lives in the world rather than in complete aloofness—and we will not discuss here whether any such complete aloofness, involving complete indifference toward the prevailing interpretation of reality, is at all conceivable—does not exist in a world in general, but in a world of meanings, interpreted in a particular way.

The philosopher Heidegger calls this collective subject who supplies us with the prevailing public interpretation of reality '*das Man*'—the 'They'. This is the 'They' that is meant in the French expressions—such as *Que dit-on*, or *Que dira-t-on*—but it is not merely the collective subject responsible for gossip and tittle-tattle, but also that profounder Something which always interprets the world somehow, whether in its superficiality or its depths, and which causes us always to meet the world in a preconceived form. We step at birth into a ready-interpreted world, a world which has already been made understandable, every part of which has been given meaning, so that no gaps are left. What Life means, what Birth and Death mean, and what one's attitude toward

certain feelings and thoughts should be—all that is already more
or less definitely laid down for us: something—this 'They'—has
gone before us, apparently determined that nothing should be left
for us to do in this respect.

The philosopher looks at this 'They', this secretive Something,
but he is not interested to find out how it arose; and it is just at
this point, where the philosopher stops, that the work of the
sociologist begins.

Sociological analysis shows that this public interpretation of
reality is not simply 'there'; nor, on the other hand, is it the result
of a 'systematic thinking out'; it is the stake for which men fight.
And the struggle is not guided by motives of pure contemplative
thirst for knowledge. Different interpretations of the world for
the most part correspond to the particular positions the various
groups occupy in their struggle for power. In answering the
question how this 'They', this publicly prevailing interpretation
of reality actually comes into being, I would mention four kinds
of social process as generating factors.

The public interpretation of reality can come about:

(1) on the basis of a *consensus of opinion*, of spontaneous *co-
operation* between individuals and groups;

(2) on the basis of the *monopoly-position* of one particular group;

(3) on the basis of competition between many groups, each
determined to impose on others their particular interpretation
of the world. (We shall call this case '*atomistic competition*', although
we must add that a point is never reached where atomization is
complete, so that individuals compete with individuals, and completely independent thinking groups with others equally isolated);

(4) on the basis of a *concentration* round one point of view of a
number of formerly atomistically competing groups, as a result of
which competition as a whole is gradually concentrated around a
few poles which become more and more dominant.

As you see, public interpretations of reality, just like any other
objective cultural product, come into being through the intermediary of social relationships and processes.

Our next task is to give concrete examples illustrating these
four typical cases, and at the same time to show that the socially
determined genesis of any conception of the world so profoundly
influences its inner structure that, once our sociology of knowledge
has completed its systematic analysis of these correlations, any
expert will be able to indicate, on the basis of a simple inspection
of any given world conception or thought pattern, whether it has
come into being, as a result of atomistic competition between

individual groups, on the basis of a consensus, or of a monopoly of a dominating group.

One further preliminary remark is necessary. The four types mentioned are *pure types*. In actual societies in every age, provided they have reached a minimum degree of development, several pure types will be found to co-exist and to blend together; one type, however, will tend to predominate. This will be the 'dominant pattern of interpretation' of the society in question.

Let us take up the four types of thinking one by one.

The first type—based on consensus—is to be found in its pure form in socially homogeneous strata or societies, where the range and basis of experience is uniform, and where the fundamental incentives or impulses to thought tend to be the same for all individuals.

The main prerequisite for the emergence of this mode of thought is that social relationships should be static. This makes it possible for schemes of experience once laid down and confirmed to be used again and again; the traditional wisdom is always appropriate to the environment, and any small adjustments in the inherited modes of experience which may be necessary even in such a static environment, are easily accomplished without ever having to be made conscious and reflective.

A further prerequisite is that there shall prevail genuine intellectual democracy of the kind characteristic of primitive, archaic societies, where everyone is able to grasp the wisdom handed down by tradition and to adapt it to changed conditions: every individual carries the same traditional dispositions for perception. The external characteristics of such a type of knowledge are exemplified by myths, proverbs, and other samples of traditional folk wisdom. One is struck primarily by their undialectical character. The 'it' in us observes and rules the world. '*It is so*', say the proverbs (at least this is the implication of the way in which they address us); they are the reflection and expression of an unambiguous, undialectical experience of life. '*It shall be so*', is the straight message contained in the prescriptions of traditionally sanctional usages and customs.

This type of thought never really dies out, and it exists even today in our own society in strata which have succeeded completely or in part in keeping themselves aloof from the overpowering dynamic of the modern era. But—and this is still more important—even in our own consciousness, already made thoroughly dynamic, there exist forms of thought and experience which are adequate in responding to certain elements of our cultural environment which have not yet been drawn into the dynamic of the modern era, and are not affected by it.

Common sense, which formulates the principles of our dealings
with the simplest things, possesses this 'it' character. The majority
of proverbs are of this type; they should be included in the consensus type of thought, even if it turned out that the theory of
'cultural sedimentation' (as put forward, for example, by H.
Naumann[1]) would apply to many of them. This theory maintains
that proverbs, with the greater part of the rest of folk-culture, are
the 'sediments' of a culture shaped by past ruling strata, and that
the 'people' as such have only taken over and transformed these
cultural creations after a certain time-lag. Whether this is true of
any individual proverb or not, and whether proverbs in general
travel in an upward or downward direction, they appeal in any
case to just one mechanism of our consciousness. Our theory by
no means ignores the mental attitude corresponding to this
mechanism which we may term 'the primitive community spirit'.
The *form* of the proverb, no matter where its contents come from,
corresponds to the consensus principle of formulating experience
which in my view still dominates popular consciousness almost
completely, while the consciousness of higher and more intellectualized strata is only partly under its sway.

Since the child's world is made up entirely of the very simple
relationships which underlie proverbs, we may say that the
consciousness of the human individual initially acquires this type
of 'it' structure; and it reverts to this 'it' structure even at a later
stage of its development, whenever it becomes confronted with
such archaic relationships. To be sure, we often have the impression that the ever-advancing dynamism of our age engulfs the
totality of our vital relationships (and hence also the totality of
our mental life); but this is not altogether true, and a closer
examination shows that it is at least not true to the extent assumed.
Despite all dynamic, even for the urban type (who is most exposed
to dynamic influences) there remains untouched a substantial
layer of these primitive relationships, with their corresponding
primitive attitude patterns. The truth of a common-sense statement such as, for example, that when two people fight, a third
will reap the advantage, remains as unchangeable in the face of
all dynamic as are, for example, the emotional patterns of mystery
and of primeval fears which hardly change in the course of dynamic
development. Our feeling of security, however, is based precisely
upon this relatively constant layer of our experience; the dynamic
movement and instability of our relationships in general would
have unbalanced us long ago but for the relative stability of these
original, primitive relationships. The difficulties of complicated

[1] H. Naumann, *Grundzüge der deutschen Volkskunde*. Leipzig, 1922; pp. 1 ff.,
137 ff.

relationships can be tolerated so long as primitive relationships manifest a certain security and stability, or at least so long as they create the illusion of such a security and stability.

The second type presents that sort of thought which is based on the monopoly position of one group (generally a closed status group). The medieval-ecclesiastical interpretation of the world and the tradition cultivated by Chinese *literati* belong here.

A monopoly position of this type may be secured by purely intellectual means, or by non-intellectual instruments of power: in general, however, both are being employed. In the Middle Ages, the monopoly of the clergy rested on a very simple basis: in the first place, only they could read and write; secondly, Latin was the language of education; and thirdly, only masters of both these accomplishments were in a position to have access to the source of Truth—the Bible and tradition.

This type of thought has certain external features in common with the consensus type. Both have the same prerequisite for their existence—*viz.* a structurally stable social body, by which is not meant that nothing ever happens in such a society, but merely that the basis of all thought is homogeneous, and that the range of sensitivity is strictly delimited.

By 'range of sensitivity' I mean the extent and contents of that area of experience in which intuitive acts preceding all knowledge and providing conceptual material for it occur automatically, reliably, and on the whole, in such a way that every individual is capable of performing every intuitive act within the range. Thus, a hunting or a peasant community, for instance, has such a de-limited range of sensitivity with regard to natural objects; or a craft guild, with regard to instruments and artificial objects; a particular community with regard to certain inner experiences leading to ecstasy. The difference between the uniformity of a community of experience based on a monopoly situation and one based on a consensus, seems to lie in the fact that the former preserves its uniform character by artificial means, while the latter is able to maintain its uniformity, homogeneity, and inner stability by virtue of socially-rooted factors of an organic kind.

The basis of thought in a monopoly situation is *externally given*, i.e. laid down in sacred works. Thought is largely directed toward the interpretation of texts rather than toward the interpretation of reality. If it does concern itself with this latter task, the results are likely to be assimilated to textual interpretation. The essence of thought here is that every new fact as it arises has to be fitted into a given, pre-existent *ordo*; this is achieved, for the most part, by interpreting or re-interpreting the 'facts'.

Thus it is easy to recognize the theological and interpretive character of this kind of thought. The best example of such an *ordo* is perhaps the *Summa* of Thomas Aquinas.

The way in which the thinking of St. Thomas embraces the whole of the *ordo* is grandiose. What strikes us first in his system is its seemingly dialectical method. The way in which theses are confronted with counter-theses is at least reminiscent of dialectic. Nevertheless, this does not seem to be a genuine dialectic in the sense that the different theses represent antagonistic social factors locked in real struggle; on the contrary, it seems that the apparent controversies merely serve to eliminate those inconsistencies that may still have remained from the previous stage of competition, when there were numerous groups competing to impose their interpretation of the world, and the monopoly position of the view which later achieved predominance had not yet been established.

In judging these matters, there is an important point which must not be disregarded. Uniformity of the basis of thought and experience does *not* imply the absence of strife and controversy. On the contrary, in the Middle Ages people were always engaged in the most violent controversies—only with the qualification that controversy had to be kept within certain previously established limits. Certain religious claims are left unchallenged, and a certain method of formulation and statement is to a large extent codified. It must always be remembered how much, in spite of all conflict, is silently taken for granted.

Both types of thought just described (based on consensus and on a monopoly position respectively) co-exist in the Middle Ages. Both can develop side by side, because, as we said before, the common prerequisite, structural stability of the social body, is given. As long as society remains static, these two types of thought divide the mental field among themselves.

Even at this stage, however, we encounter certain complications which have a decisive importance for later developments. The prevailing interpretation of the world already assumes a dual character. We distinguish, on the one hand, an official, academic (*bildungsmaessig*) interpretation, and, on the other, an everyday, consensus-like one. This duality in its turn manifests itself in two ways. One of its symptoms is a social differentiation. There are groups the main activity of which consists in the official, academic interpretation of the world; others do not go beyond the spontaneous, consensus-like interpretation customary in their *milieu*. And the same duality can also be shown to exist in the consciousness of individuals. The individual lives potentially on either plane —he responds to his situation at one moment in academic terms, and at another in the spontaneous traditional ways built up in the life of his particular social stratum. We may mention, for instance, the specifically 'aristocratic' and urban 'guild' mentalities, which in the Middle Ages existed side by side with the ecclesiastical interpretation of the world.

Later developments, however, hinged precisely around the transformation of the reciprocal relationships of these two ways of thinking (the monopolistic, ecclesiastical, and the consensus-like non-institutionalized one). The ecclesiastical official interpretation was unable to maintain its monopoly position; it was shattered by the tensions prevailing in an increasingly dynamic society. At the moment of the catastrophe, however, successors appeared from two sides: firstly, there was the new *élite* of Humanists, which claimed the monopoly of the academic interpretation of reality; the interpretation was to be given in secularized terms, but the full distance between the educated and uneducated was to be maintained. Secondly, however, an ideology representing the unschooled wisdom of the common people, a consensus-like democracy of thinking, also appeared on the scene, and made a bid to supersede the official interpretation of reality.

Continually changing interrelationships of various intellectual élites, opposed by the aspirations of the spokesmen of the common people, are the principal feature of the following epoch, in which thought has the basic structure of the next type to be discussed.

This third type is that corresponding to *atomistic competition*. As has been already mentioned, this type of thinking is representative of the period following the breakdown of the ecclesiastical monopoly, and is characterized by the fact that many isolated concrete social groups bid fair to take over the inheritance of the official interpretation of the world. An absolute monopoly in the sense that *all* opposition was disposed of had never been achieved by the Church, even at the height of her power. For instance, there always were opponents within the Church who had to be kept under control. In their case, we may speak of an encysted (*eingekapselt*) opposition; one could mention, as examples, opposition groups within the Church such as the mystics, the Franciscans, and so on.

How even at this stage different lines of thought were correlated with differences between the competing social groups behind them is shown in Honigsheim's observation[1] that the adherents of the two philosophical schools, Realism and Nominalism, were recruited among members of different, well-circumscribed social

---

[1] P. Honigsheim, *Zur Soziologie der mittelalterlichen Scholastik. Die soziologische Bedeutung der nominalistischen Philosophie*. In the *Erinnerungsgabe* for Max Weber, Munich-Leipzig, 1923. Vol. II, pp. 175 ff. Cf. also the various essays by Honigsheim, in the symposium *Versuche zu einer Soziologie des Wissens*, edited by M. Scheler, Munich-Leipzig, 1924.

groups. Realism was the style of thought of the Church, possessor of central power over the most inclusive organized body of the time. Nominalism, which developed later, found its adherents among lower ranks in the Church hierarchy, that is, at the levels of the bishopric, of the parish, etc. The correlation between styles of thought and competing groups is visible even at this stage— the antagonists in the social struggle are the same as the antagonists in the ideological sphere. But all this is merely a preamble to a social and ideological differentiation which will be far more fully developed during subsequent centuries.

The Church was met by a formidable opponent in the rise of the absolute state, which also sought to monopolize the means of education in order to dispense the official interpretation of reality; this time, however, the chief educational instrument was to be science. Honigsheim points out the essential similarity between this kind of thought and ecclesiastical scholasticism, and on the basis of their structural similarity he even gives the name 'scholastic' to this state-monopolized form of thought.

Universities and academies (on the sociology of the latter, Dilthey's investigations[1] have produced interesting material), from now on claim a rival 'monopoly' besides the older monopoly of the Church.

But the importance of these institutionally protected types of thought was greatly overshadowed by others arising among concrete social groups which played an increasingly important part in shaping the public interpretation of reality.

Earlier, too, as we saw, there had existed an 'unofficial', everyday type of thinking, which showed marked variations from one social group and region to another. However, as long as the monopoly of the Church remained intact, this type of thinking did not aspire towards the dignity of the official interpretation of reality.

There is a democratizing tendency in the mere fact that the secular interpretation of the world as put forward by the lay mind claims recognition as an official interpretation. This movement is most clearly to be observed and understood in the claim of the Protestant sects to interpret the Bible in their own fashion. It is not the place here to enumerate all those various concrete social groups which from now on play an increasingly important role in shaping the public interpretation of reality, and, in fact, vie with each other in trying to make their own interpretation the dominant one. These groups never ceased to multiply from the break-up of the ecclesiastical monopoly to the time of the French Revolution.

At one moment it is the Court and the so-called 'Court nobility'

[1] W. Dilthey, *Gesammelte Schriften*, Berlin-Leipzig, 1927, vol. IV.

associated with it, who seek to set the tone for the prevailing way of life and thought; at another it is the patriciate, the 'big' bourgeoisie, and high finance which try to dictate the fashion through their salons; these groups imitated the Court and the nobility in certain things, but for the most part, conscious of their birthright, they developed a mental attitude appropriate to their circumstances, and a way of thinking to match it. Later on, the middle and small bourgeoisie enter the scene; at their social level, the parsonage had emerged, some time before, as the centre of a specific style of life. These, however, are just a few summary examples selected from a large variety of groups of different character which arise side by side as society becomes more complex and differentiated. We will omit the detailed description of this world with its many competing groups and will try instead to outline the basic characteristics of the kind of thought corresponding to this particular mode of competition.

What strikes us first is a negative characteristic of this type of thought: it is, for the most part, no longer concerned with fitting new facts into a given *ordo*. Carried to its extreme, it brooks no dogma and no authority when it comes to judging things.

Descartes' method is paradigmatic in this respect. To doubt everything which cannot maintain itself before the tribunal of reason, to be able to account for one's thinking as a whole, beginning with its most fundamental postulates, this is the Cartesian ideal—an attitude which puts a premium on epistemology.

Men wanted to think free of all presuppositions, that is, free of all but the indispensable assumptions necessitated by Reason as such; and the attempt was made to find what these ultimate assumptions actually were. The programme was only slowly fulfilled; but the more it was realized, the more clearly a fact nobody had thought of before became visible—namely, that people actually did not think along the same lines. It became clear, for instance, that people in Manchester did not think like people in German Pietist circles, nor, again, people in the French salons like people in the German universities. Every concrete group had its own perspective, different from the others.

Translated into terms of logic, this has the following implication for each of the styles of thought in question: for every concrete group with its particular perspective, another sphere of reality will become paradigmatic, and acquire the ontological dignity of the actually existing.[1] Every area of reality, however, fosters one

---

[1] On the subject of social differentiation in ontology, cf. K. Mannheim, 'Das Konservative Denken'. *Soziologische Beiträge zum Werden des politisch-historischen Denkens in Deutschland. Archiv für Sozialwissenschaft und Sozialpolitik.* Vol. 57, pp. 489 ff. (to be published in a later volume of this series).

particular cognitive attitude, one mode of thought—that which is most appropriate to the task of exploring the area in question. Just as certain areas of existence acquire a particular ontological dignity, certain types of cognition acquire a particular epistemological dignity. In our times, for instance, the epistemological primacy belongs to the type of knowledge represented by exact natural science.

Concrete thought is really much more varied than textbook logic would have us believe. It is impossible fully to characterize actual thinking with the principle of contradiction, and a few related formal propositions. Even in its formal structure, actual thought is infinitely varied; and this variety is rooted in the fundamental patterns thought develops in its efforts to master one particular area of reality. Different modes of thought are characterized in the first place by concrete schemata or 'models' (e.g. those of which physicists speak), and these models differ according to the area of reality which served as frame of reference to the primary act of orientation which gave rise to the model.

While in Manchester (the name, of course, stands only as a symbol of a certain turn of mind) economy was the field of primary experience, providing frames of reference and dominant thought patterns particularly suited to this medium, in pietistic circles in Germany the primary, paradigmatic experience was the experience of religious revival. In a group whose primary orientation is economic, attempts to grasp the structural laws of history are also based on economic thought patterns; in Germany, on the other hand, interpretations of history are inspired by experiences of revival (e.g. Johannes von Müller, Ranke, Hegel, etc. The religious origins of the Hegelian categorial scheme used in interpreting history were clearly brought to light by recent research).

In addition to these paradigmatic experiences peculiar to the various concrete groups—which we mention only as examples, without seeking completeness—there also were others, partly carried over from an early period and partly quite new—thus, we find side by side thinkers who use the category of 'mechanism' and 'organism' respectively, each trying to make *his* principle of explanation *the* universally valid one. The various concrete groups put forward different schemata of orientation, and so in the end we find that methodological differences reflect the struggle between different primary paradigmatic experiences peculiar to various concrete groups.

. It is part of the process of democratization of mental life that each particular perspective aspired to become the universally accepted frame of reference, and it is the task of a sociology of the mind to show that even in methodology itself, in the guise of the various patterns of thought, what are, ultimately, in conflict are social forces and social impulses.

This process of atomistic competition among concrete groups, which resulted in an increasingly radical rejection of an externally given *ordo* (as recognized by the monopolistic type of thought), and in the aspiration to base thinking upon rational assumptions exclusively—this process in the end has led to the following results, which have only just become clearly visible to us, after being denied by many: once this genuinely modern stage is reached, there exists (*a*) no universally accepted set of axioms, (*b*) no universally recognized hierarchy of values, and (*c*) nothing but radically different ontologies and epistemologies.

Everything seemed to go to pieces, as though the world in which one lived were not the same. In place of the old *ordo*, we now have the multi-polar conception of the world which tries to do justice to the same set of newly emerging facts from a number of different points of view.

As a reaction to the increasing fragmentation brought about by atomistic competition, a fourth type of competition developed, which is the dominant type in our era—a process of *concentration* of the competing groups and types of orientation.

Here again, we can best elucidate the mental aspects of our problem by pointing to analogous processes in the economic sphere. Just as, through the agency of competition, different markets (originally self-contained and isolated) become inter-dependent (a fact which is expressed in the increasing uniformity of price-levels), or, to take another example, just as in the labour market, organizations of employers and workers tend to emerge in place of individual bargainers, so in the intellectual sphere we find that the many local and fractional conflicts on the one hand tend to become increasingly interdependent, and, on the other, to be polarized into extremes. This kind of polarization process is exemplified in the growing consolidation of two camps we may already identify by their mottoes: rationalism and irrationalism. We can observe the details of this process of consolidation—e.g. follow the way in which different types of 'irrationalism' merged and established a common front against 'rationalism' (these different types of irrationalism include: the particularism of feudal estates in their struggle against centralistic absolutism, romantic irrationalism glorifying individuality and personality, pietistic irrationalism, opposed to the institutional discipline of the Church, etc.).[1]

---

[1] A more detailed examination of this can be found in my paper on 'Conservative Thought'. See footnote, p. 205.

While those who lack expert economic knowledge see only individual local markets with which the individual now deals directly and will continue to deal in the future, the economist can already visualize the emergence of an integrated world market. In analogous fashion, the sociologist must look beyond the direct relationships in which individuals are engaged and discover the decisive polarities behind the controversies of the various schools of thought, and attempt to grasp the ultimate important extremes behind the various local conflicts. The partial antagonisms, in which one school or concrete group is pitted against another, are being gathered up into decisive major intellectual currents and countercurrents combating one another.

This brings us to the problem of the function of doctrinal currents (*Geistesströmungen*). There had been doctrinal currents in earlier times too, but they were more in the nature of reflections and reproductions of certain fundamental attitudes, modes of interpretation, and the like. It is also true that these currents even in earlier times gave rise to countercurrents. But none of these earlier currents was so unequivocally functional in nature, and none of them reflected so closely a process of concentration and polarization of concrete groups, as contemporary doctrinal currents.

And this is comprehensible. The world, after all, had never before formed, under the organizing influence of economic forces, a unified coherent whole, and consequently, groups with a structurally analogous position could never before be encountered in every region of the world. The new function of doctrinal currents, then, consists in enabling spatially separated groups of structurally analogous position to coalesce, by giving currency to ways of life and attitudes which originally arose within a narrow group and there proved helpful in solving or at least artistically expressing some typical problem. All other groups beset by similar problems then will tend to adopt the basic attitude in question, while groups which have the opposite outlook and interests will be the more strongly impelled to project their antagonistic attitude by creating or joining a doctrinal countercurrent.

Two important groups of phenomena (or what may be called a dual movement) are called forth by this situation. On the one hand, a doctrinal current, expanding from the nucleus of the concrete group within which it originated, tends to mediate among the impulses and modes of interpretation of the other groups that join it—groups with an analogous position but yet with a different concrete experience. On the other hand, in the measure as it 'travels'—i.e. as it is adopted by people adhering to various ways of life—the doctrinal current will absorb ingredients from all these alien substances, from the different local environments.

Thus, doctrinal currents make for uniformity—but also for a conservation of the peculiarities of local conditions.

The Enlightenment, for instance, arose in England as the expression of a mental and spiritual attitude most nearly appropriate to a capitalist society. A typically modern conception of the world was projected from within a very narrow sphere and expanded into France, where it roused all those groups and individuals whose position was analogous. In so far as the characteristic elements of English thought were seized upon by these French groups, the latter necessarily sacrificed certain ways of thinking more congruent with their situation; but in so far as they transformed the alien stimulus and added certain specific elements (such as a greater radicalism) to it, they endowed the current with a distinctive national note. A specifically French 'Enlightenment' arose. The same process of incorporation and modification went on in Germany; there, as is well known, the Enlightenment was theologized.

This is how the formal structure of a 'current', as such, brings about a concentration of impulses formerly fragmentated in atomistic competition. An even greater integrative force, however, lies in the fact that political life since the French Revolution has imposed increasingly clear-cut decisions and a correspondingly effective polarization of modes of thought and attitudes—and this not only in the narrowly political sphere.

While in the case of Montesquieu and Herder it is hard to ascertain whether their type of thought stands for progress or reaction (Wahl, for example, has shown a duality in this respect in the work of Montesquieu[1]), inasmuch as their styles of thought and mode of experience are to a large extent ambivalent, the revolutions of 1789, 1830, and 1848 have brought about an increasing polarization of society in nearly every respect. Not that ambivalent thought disappears altogether (especially if we take ambivalence to mean that one and the same philosophy can become associated with more than one political trend—or *vice versa*, that one and the same political trend can be combined with more than one philosophy); but there is a decreasing scope for such ambivalences. As the process of concentration goes on, it becomes easier and easier to identify a certain attitude as to whether it is 'liberal', 'conservative', 'socialist', etc.

Moreover, it is fundamentally false to suppose—as unpolitical observers, who are unaware of the volitional basis of every theory,

[1] Wahl, A., 'Montesquieu als Vorläufer von Aktion and Reaktion', *Historische Zeitschrift*, vol. 109, 1912.

are tempted to do—that all that happens in this connection is that existing political movements cast about for a philosophical companion with which they can ally themselves. In fact, if these combinations merely depended on a process of concentration in the political and related spheres, the whole phenomenon of concentration we are examining here would merely concern the study of 'ideologies', and it could be said that these phenomena may be observed in politics, but cannot affect intellectual life in its 'higher objectivity'. It would follow that a philosophy which linked itself with a political tendency would be degraded into a mere 'ideology'; *real* philosophy, in its purity, however, could have nothing to do with the influence we have shown social factors to exercise upon the mental sphere. If someone thinks along these lines, if he looks at things in such a non-activistic, non-political spirit, then it is difficult to make him *see*. All one can do is to make him realize in case after case that philosophy—just any particular philosophy not yet deliberately allied to any political cause—is always *the product of a particular mentality*, and that already at its birth, before ever any clear relation to politics is developed, a philosophy already reflects a peculiar direction of the interpretive impulse; a peculiar style of thought, which in most cases stems from a deeper root that this philosophy has in common with the corresponding political trend with which it later becomes associated. When Liberalism links up with the Enlightenment, it is just like the reunion and mutual recognition of long-separated children of the same mother. Thus, it is utterly wrong to apply an atomistic method to the history of ideas and concentrate exclusively upon combinations and reciprocal influences ascertainable between ideas and thought *motifs* as such; what we have to do is to observe how the synthesis in the realm of ideas is determined by a primary concentration in the realm of the thought impulses. It has been said that we must learn to think in terms of 'economic systems' (Sombart, speaking at the meeting of the *Verein für Sozialpolitik*). I would urge in the same vein, that in dealing with the history of ideas, we had better think in terms of *styles of thought*. I mean to say that it is impossible to achieve an understanding of the modern process of concentration in the realm of doctrinal currents as long as one concentrates exclusively upon the filiations of *motifs* one can observe at the surface, instead of employing the fundamentally decisive processes of integration and division at the level of the group will which alone can give a meaning to the secondary processes making up the history of *motif* filiations.

After this short account of the polarizing and concentrating functions of modern doctrinal currents, we must ask the question whether there are no mental processes making for concentration *besides* the doctrinal currents. On closer inspection, it is clear that a 'current' as the vehicle of a 'polarized' mental attitude cannot carry ways of thinking from their region of origin into other regions unless the polarization had somehow been accomplished in the region of origin. Before, then, the doctrinal current can start on its way, there must be, in its source region, a process bringing about an initial concentration and polarization.

It therefore becomes our task to examine this process of initial polarization more closely. The question facing us is how such a polarization can come about before any doctrinal current makes itself felt. What is the method Life applies when it merges many particular volitional positions into one comprehensive platform?

The method used by Life, the process through which the existentially-determined positions of thinking subjects become amalgamated, is, once again, competition, which in this case operates to select out the impulses that are to be retained.

In a recent essay making an important contribution to this subject, Thurnwald[1] proposed to substitute the term 'sifting' for 'selection'; and Münzner[2] also made use of a selective or 'sifting' mechanism in explaining the propagation of 'public opinion'.

Our theory, to say it again, is concerned with something far more fundamental than the formation and propagation of public opinion, which in itself is only a superficial feature of intellectual life. The point I want to make is that processes of change in the deepest strata of world interpretation, modifications of the categorial apparatus itself, can to a large extent be explained in terms of competition. That men at a given place and time think in terms of such and such concepts and categories becomes for us a problem calling for, and capable of, explanation in concrete detail, rather than a brute historical fact we merely have to record.

Similarly, the principle of competition and the related principle of selection will be found to furnish the most natural explanation for certain facts recorded by the history of ideas—that, for instance, certain political and philosophical positions become polarized and maintain themselves in the course of development, while others fall by the wayside or are caught up by the countercurrents. As evidence for my thesis, I shall mention a concrete example of the formation of an ideological 'platform' on the basis of competition and selection—i.e. the genesis of the ideological platform of the German Conservative Party. Here, as always, it can be seen that an intellectual or volitional position, as any type of interpretation

---

[1] Thurnwald, R., 'Führerschaft und Siebung', *Zeitschrift für Völkerpsychologie und Soziologie*, Jahrgang II, 1926.

[2] Münzner, G., *Öffentliche Meinung und Presse*. Karlsruhe, 1928.

of reality, does not suddenly come from nowhere, but is arrived at through a process of selection from a variety of beliefs and impulses of competing groups.

What can here be shown as true of the formation of a political platform, applies also, *mutatis mutandis*, to all existentially-determined thought. We are of the opinion that one runs far less risk of going astray if one proposes to explain intellectual movements in political terms than if one takes the opposite course and from a purely theoretical attitude projects a merely contemplative, internal, theoretical thought pattern on to the concrete, actual life process itself. In actual life, it is always some volitional centre which sets thought going; competition, victory, and the selection based upon it, largely determine the movement of thought.

It is not intended to give the impression that mental life as a whole is a purely political matter, any more than earlier we wished to make of it a mere segment of economic life; we merely want to direct attention to the vital and volitional element in existentially-determined thought which is easiest to grasp in the political sphere, and to place it in a proper light, thus counteracting the misleading influence of the German historical tradition with its one-sided emphasis upon a contemplative approach.

The process of formation of a conservative platform began with the emergence, here and there, of groups impelled to adopt a defensive position in face of the new social reality that was arising. Firstly, there were the old feudal circles, then certain literary groups more and more leaning towards reaction, then the representatives of bureaucracy, and certain university circles became more and more conservative, and so on. Each of these groups brought with it a way of thinking, capable of exact stylistic analysis, which was specifically adapted to its own situation, traditions, etc.; and each experienced its opposition to the gradually emerging modern world in a specifically different fashion. Each discovered this opposition at a different point in the process of internal and external change, and each produced a different ideology to express its opposition.

At first, these different oppositions emerged as isolated and atomistic units, but they tended to amalgamate as soon as they came up against a common opponent. Liberalism first found theoretical expression in a coherent statement of its aims; this statement necessarily elicited from Conservatism the formulation of a programmatic counterstatement. That this was 'necessarily' the case is implied in the structure of the competitive situation. A sort of 'competition on the basis of quality', which forces each party to catch up with its opponent, and to duplicate the latter's achievements (Sombart) forced the Conservatives, although systematic thought is by no means their *forte*, to produce a systematic theoretical platform.

This is not achieved so easily, however. Many decades pass before its completion. The delay is partly attributable to the difficulties of reaching an agreement: each faction, each individual group wants to have its particular point of view accepted as the official creed of the Conservative Party.

Stahl was the first person to achieve a synthesis of the competing conservative ideologies in his system of the philosophy of law, and through his practical work on the programme of the Conservative Party: and, curiously enough, his system as an amalgam of disparate intellectual elements is an exact replica of the equilibrium achieved by the competing social groups within the conservative camp. The same is true, not only of the structure of the political platform, but also of the philosophical substructure underlying the conservative interpretation of the world. The complete rejection of Hegelian pantheism was a direct answer to the adoption of this pantheism by the left-wing groups of the 'young Hegelians'; the victory of personalistic irrationalism was a result of the increasingly thorough elimination of all liberal-rational elements from the interpretation of the world, now deliberately restricted to irrationalistic terms. A complete analysis of this example—which, however, we cannot attempt at this juncture[1]—would yield the conclusion that, whenever a comprehensive movement comes into being as a result of the banding together of formerly isolated groups, it is possible to follow up to the highest level of abstraction the process of how a mixture of various ways of thinking comes about, showing the same strands and proportions as the concrete groups participating in the new movement.

Observation of the genesis of the Marxist platform of the socialist movement would reveal the same structural phenomena we saw associated with the genesis of the conservative platform. It will be sufficient to mention one sequence of events which best illuminate our thesis—the struggle between Marx and Bakunin.

That the official programme of Socialism finally was couched in 'dialectical' terms, that it completely rejected the mental attitude corresponding to the eruptive anarchistic way of acting and made short shrift of the anti-historical, eschatological view

---

[1] Because of the impossibility of a detailed analysis, I must refer again to the paper on 'Conservative Thought', in which I have tried to show in detail the intermingling of the fundamental conceptual systems of two concrete groups engaged in the process of merging their differences in a common movement.

according to which anything may happen at any moment—this intellectual event is merely the reflection, in the logical sphere, of the massive political fact that Marx's faction was victorious over that of Bakunin.

The victory of the logical category of *dialectic* as a key to the interpretation of history over a non-historical, eschatological doctrine which recognizes no definite articulation in history and hence has no use for the concept of evolution but considers revolution as possible and necessary at any instant—this doctrinal victory reflects the victory of one faction over another, the success of one competitor in the struggle over the question of whose philosophy will serve as the party's official interpretation of reality.

But even where the impulse for the merging of positions is not a political one, we find that there is always a volitional element at the bottom of such phenomena. Positions are—as we said above—never combined through the simple summation of elements of thought, but always as a result of the meeting of fundamental impulses of will, modes of interpretation, conceptions of reality. The merging of these positions is achieved, not by the contemplative subject within us (if it is at all legitimate to distinguish a contemplative from an active subject), but by the active and ultimately—in so far as activity directed at changing the world is in the end political—the political one.

If, therefore, in analysing the fusion of ideas, we focus our attention upon their volitional source rather than their manifest content, and try to find out what controls the combinations into which thought impulses enter, we shall find that in the last analysis the movement of thought depends upon the tensions which dominate the social sphere.

After this general characterization of the fourth type of competition, that corresponding to the stage of concentration, we again have to ask: What is thinking like at this stage of evolution? How is the structure of our society and intellectual culture reflected in the situation facing our thinking?

In the first place, we find ourselves today with no uniform basis for thought. It is not merely that we have no uniform *ordo* into which we can fit every newly-emerging fact, but we are approaching a situation in which the exact opposite will be true.

This new situation has arisen in three stages. The first stage was, as we saw, the multipolarity of the basic positions. Concentration of these positions gradually produced the second stage, where we can speak of positions merged to form a few rival platforms. These platforms, however, must not be imagined as in any way static or unchanging, but always as dynamic. That is to say, they always adjust themselves in form and structure in response to new situations as they arise. This historical transformation is for the most part unknown to the various individuals who adhere to the platform in question. Only the historian, able to look back over long stretches of time, is really in a position to say what changes Liberalism and Socialism, Positivism or Historicism have undergone since their inception.

The individual who approaches the facts in terms of a definite platform does have an order pattern at this stage; it is only the 'public' as a whole that no longer sustains the same *ordo*: the old, coherent picture of the world is shattered and split into fragments.

If this dynamic movement continues at the same rate (and if no stabilizing tendency prevails, resulting either in a consensus, or in the emergence of a monopoly situation), then a state of affairs will arise in which thinking will no longer consist in fitting facts into a preconceived *ordo* but quite the contrary, in challenging the validity of any order pattern into which new facts do not readily fit.

To those who are conversant with the existential relativity of knowledge, and who reserve their position rather than commit themselves unconditionally and exclusively to one particular doctrine, the situation facing our thinking today appears as follows: various groups are engaged in existential experiments with particular order patterns, none of which has sufficient general validity to encompass *in toto* the whole of present-day reality. Against the thrust of every individual position seeking to achieve predominance over all others, there seems to be only one compensatory influence at work, that is the fact that positions do get fused in spite of everything—as if life itself, seeking to gain clarity about itself, tried to do justice to the growing complexity of the historical situation by constantly broadening the basis of thinking.

However, we had better not probe too far ahead of the situation as it exists today, or treat plausible hypotheses as if they were realities. Let us take up a purely factual problem instead.

Is it possible to demonstrate the truth of our statement that at the stage of concentration in the evolution of competition a polarization of forms of thought takes place? A really exact and stringent proof could be given only on the basis of a philological and historical analysis. Such an analysis would have to examine the most important elements of our thought (concepts, images, and categories) to see whether any tendency towards polarization could be found in them, that is, whether it could be shown that the Conservative tends to see problems differently, to use concepts with a different meaning, or to order the world in categories different from the Liberal or the Socialist, and so on.

Such proof can obviously not be put forward here in a complete form—even for a single case. What we can do is to illustrate rather than prove our thesis by pointing out a few examples of typical polarizations in modern thought, standing in visible affinity to polarization in the social and political field. Needless to say, these examples will all be 'ideal types'—ideally-typical concatenations of motives. Every concrete case is likely to have its own peculiarities, and if it cannot be completely fitted into any one of our types, it should not be put down as an instance invalidating our thesis. The point I want to make is that those polarizations which I shall mention represent the historically decisive trends; if this is true, it follows that any seeming exception must be explained in terms of particular constellations and specific conditions.

The greatest clarity can be achieved in studying polarization if we examine various typical attitudes toward one and the same problem. I choose one of the most important and instructive problems in this context—that of value-free knowledge (*Wertfreiheit*).

The ideally-typical attitudes to this problem of the different parties can be briefly outlined as follows:

A. *Liberalism*:—was characterized from the very beginning by a typically intellectualistic approach, and sought to achieve a clear separation of the rational from the irrational. Alfred Weber once said that the outstanding mark of modernism in thought was the endeavour to purge all thinking of its irrational elements. It is admitted, of course, that living (undisciplined) thought is a medley of theory and a-theoretical, purely volitional elements, but it is believed that if one tries hard, one can purge the theory of all admixtures of volitional impulse, irrationality, and evaluation. One was primarily interested in being able to argue (Carl Schmitt, following Donoso Cortes,[1] has declared this to be the really distinguishing characteristic of the Liberal bourgeoisie), and in genuine intellectualistic fashion, one believed that rational tensions grounded in existential differences could be reduced to differences in thinking which, however, it was possible to iron out by virtue of the uniformity of reason.

That Liberals and Democrats are middle-of-the-road parties is another reason why they are interested in creating a platform for discussion and mediation where the other parties can meet. This faith in mediation and discussion is incompatible with admitting the existence of irreconcilable differences, of conflicts

[1] Carl Schmitt, *Politische Theologie. Vier Kapitel zur Lehre von der Souveränität*, Munich-Leipzig, 1922; pp. 52 ff. Cf. also by the same author: *Die geistesgeschichtliche Lage des heutigen Parlamentarismus*, 2nd edition, Munich-Leipzig, 1926.

that cannot be settled by purely intellectual means. Since this theory holds that evaluation can be separated from theory as a matter of principle, it refuses from the outset to recognize the existence of the phenomenon of existentially-determined thought —of a thought containing by definition, and inseparably, irrational elements woven into its very texture.

B. *Conservatism*, as the right-wing opposition combating modernism, insists precisely on the primacy of the irrational. From the conservative point of view, the irrational is essentially the core of one's fundamental convictions (*das Weltanschauliche*). The Conservative is amenable to the idea that all thinking is nourished by a set of fundamental convictions, and tends to trace back to such convictions even things seemingly completely devoid of irrationality, such as exact mathematical knowledge, or capitalistic accounting and calculation. The conservative type of thinking attains its most pointed expression when it offers proof that even the most rational phenomena of modern culture are at bottom irrational—that, for instance, capitalistic reliance on calculation is itself not based upon calculation but upon a fundamental conviction which, although beyond rational proof, expresses itself in highly rational terms.

C. *Socialism* represents a third position with regard to irrationality—it qualifies the thinking of the *adversary* as irrational. It is significant to note, however, where the irrational manifests itself according to the Socialist view. The irrational which is inextricably interwoven with the rational, and prevents the latter from manifesting itself in its pristine purity, is not some fundamental conviction but *interest*—and collective, class-determined interest at that. To understand this difference of interpretation we must again consider the concrete group situations of the members of both parties, and the way in which these situations determine experiences of the latter. When the Conservative looks at himself introspectively, he sees—quite truthfully—still unquestioned religious, traditional, and hierarchical motives which hold his thinking in their grip. As to the interested motives underlying his actions, which for the most part operate unconsciously, he is at first completely unaware of them. For if the structure of society is such that the existing institutions automatically promote our interests and guarantee the satisfaction of our aspirations, interested motives are, so to speak, appropriated by the objective social order itself. If I simply live in the framework of these institutions, I never need become aware of these interested motives, as a conscious part of my personal experience. They, then, will not be revealed by introspection. Thus, for example, the patriarchal squire of an estate, so long as there is no question of any challenge to his rights over his property and his control over his tenants, will discover by introspection only his benevolent patriarchal feelings. And, from this point of view, we can understand how certain very rich people (especially women) can entertain a completely sublimated, un-egoistic attitude. The structure of society, so to speak, takes care of the egoistic motivations they need to preserve the style in which they live.

But with the proletarian awakening to class-consciousness, it is quite different. Just because in all situations the opposition he meets is of this kind, he will tend to discover the hidden determining class interest at every point of the social structure. The irrationalities of the various sets of fundamental convictions do not interest him; he either overlooks them deliberately, or translates them willy-nilly into class-interests.

We have called 'interest' in this connection 'irrational', because it is a factor alien to and disrupting the self-sufficient abstractness of 'pure theory'. Proletarian thought, then, discovers—as noted before—situationally-determined (here, interest-determined) thought in the adversary. But what of its own thought? There were two possibilities: proletarian thought could go the way of Liberalism and, remaining within the tradition of natural law, interpret itself as 'pure theory'; or it could—in countries where thinking was more influenced by historicism—recognize its own irrationality (dependence on interests), but then have recourse to a theory of pre-established harmony so as to make itself coincide with the idea of truth. (That is, the particular class-interests of the proletariat are identified with those of society as a whole: proletarian class-consciousness is the adequate and right consciousness, as with Marxian tradition in the form given it by Lukács.)

The polarization which we have just tried to demonstrate in relation to the problem of value-free knowledge reappears in connection with nearly every important and controversial concept; this polarization affects the very categorial apparatus of thinking itself.

I could even go farther, and demonstrate to you that even seemingly primitive fundamental concepts such as what 'practice' is and how it is related to 'theory'—concepts which, one might think, can be construed in only one way—are seen in a different light, depending on the pole of the social body at which one is situated.[1] To mention only one final example instead of many, showing how even the categorial apparatus of thinking has become

---

[1] I have attempted to give an extensive analysis of this example in terms of the sociology of knowledge in my investigation: 'The Prospects of Scientific Politics', to be found in my book 'Ideology and Utopia'. London, 1937, Kegan Paul.

socially and politically differentiated as the result of competition at the stage of concentration: The greatest difficulty besetting our thinking today is, one might say, that we can make use of a number of entirely different categories in giving a scientific account of a given historical event. The chief damage to objectivity and impartiality does not lie in the fact that historians are taking different sides on political matters, or other matters of value. Such differences could be eliminated by a strict abstention from any evaluation; in this fashion, one would obtain a corrected field of positionally neutral theory. The danger, however, lies much deeper than that, and it seems to me that the usual formulation of this problem, which mainly stresses abstention from value judgments, fails to do full justice to the difficulties involved. The real danger lies in the fact that one can use fundamentally different order patterns and categories already in isolating one's material, in defining one's subject-matter.

Thus, since the political and social polarization of thinking set in, we have had the contrast between a 'synthesizing' and an 'analytical' presentation of history, or, to put it more sharply: we have had at the one extreme, an interpretation of history based on analysis, and at the other, an interpretation based upon morphological intuition. This is a very fundamental antithesis. Its antecedents reach far back into the past history of thought. But what is of importance for us in the period under discussion, is that carried over into the field of historical and political interpretations of the world, this antithesis tends to an increasing extent to become the basis of that modern differentiation into opposing 'platforms' of which we spoke above. The decisive importance of this antithesis is due to the fact that it plays a large role even in the original delimitation and definition of the subject-matter; even in dealing with a single object (be it an individual human being, or an event) one's conclusions depend to a decisive extent on whether one is practising the 'morphological' or 'analytical' approach.

It makes a great difference to the way in which we conceive and present the history of a series of events or the deeds of an individual, whether we regard them as developments of a pre-existing 'germ' (tending, so to speak, towards a predestined goal), or whether we consider everything as constituting a particular complex of general characteristics which in other circumstances could be differently combined.

In the morphological attitude, which sees the object as the product of an inevitable development towards a prescribed goal, from a germ already inherent in it, there lies a deep-lying conservative impulse, aiming at continuity and persistence which is more fundamental than mere political Conservatism; this is the gesture of benediction of one who feels that what is, is good. If the contemplation of Being is placed higher than its breaking down by analysis, a peculiar feeling of stability results. Then, whatever is here and now will tend to be taken as 'Being as such'. This need not happen in every case, because even this type of intuitive thinking may manage to reject a 'bad' reality through the expedient of distinguishing between essence and mere contingent factuality. But this is an exceptional case which we need not consider further, since we are dealing here with the fundamental 'ideal types' of sociologically determined thinking rather than with its detailed historical description. It is sometimes useful for the coherence of scientific research to neglect exceptions and concentrate upon the main trends of evolution.

Intuitive contemplation itself is not without an analytical component—but this is fundamentally different from the sort of analysis we mentioned above, which comprises the two separate processes of dissection and recombination. The kind of analysis inherent in intuition follows the natural articulation of the object: it senses its general structure without splitting it up. If it is a question of a development through time, this sort of analysis traces the development as at each stage it permits the anticipated developmental goal to emerge more clearly. The moment we conceive reality, the given, in morphological, intuitive terms, we have virtually immobilized it even before anything has been said. This is, at least, what we observe at the moment of the original parting of the ways between Conservative and Progressive thought—at that point in the historical evolution, it was Conservatism which made use of this intuitive approach towards reality.

Exactly the opposite is the case with the dissecting type of analysis. As soon as the object is conceived in analytical terms, it no longer is what it was as a correlate of intuitive contemplation. It is already cancelled in its phenomenal immediacy. The way in which an object or a meaningful complex appears to us intuitively, what it communicates, or what it claims to be or mean, is already overlooked, corroded and relativized by virtue of the subject's analytical approach. The hidden premise of this type of thought is: *everything could be otherwise*—and the existing reality is broken down into its elements from which—if necessary —new realities may be put together. This kind of approach in itself breaks up reality, makes it fluid; at least, this was the role played by analytical thinking when it first came upon the scene during the period we are studying.

This contrast between intuition and analysis corresponds to

another alternative which was recognized as fundamental and served to differentiate between the opposing groups at the very beginning of the process of the polarization of platforms (i.e. in the discussions at the beginning of the 19th century), the alternative between 'making' and 'letting grow'.

'To make' and 'to grow' are two of those fundamental schemas we spoke about before, which exercise a decisive influence on people's views of the world, and which are responsible for different people's professing different philosophies. Those who study history with the pattern of 'making' in mind, break its substance up beyond recognition; those, on the other hand, who see history under the category of 'growth' are impressed with its finality—possibly with the finality of some single event, but mostly with that of the historical process as a whole. The concepts 'to make' and 'to let grow' represent two extremes in the broad field of possible approaches to history; according to what side he is on in this great struggle between historical and political forces, an individual thinker will consider a larger or smaller part of reality as final or as fluid respectively, and this will determine the extent to which he will be said to belong to the one or the other style of thought. We must content ourselves with these two examples of ideal types of polarized thinking.

We must now ask: Does competition at this stage only bring about polarization, or *does it also produce synthesis?* All those for whom it is a foregone conclusion that every social tension is beyond conciliation on principle, will cling to that one phase of our argument where the tendency towards polarization was brought into sharp relief, and interpret it in an absolute sense. These are, in the first place, the spokesmen of extreme social and intellectual doctrines—including, on the one hand, those who, as mentioned before, deny as a matter of principle that any existential or intellectual tension can be mediated, and, on the other, those who interpret the class-determined interest-bound irreconciliability of theoretical differences in an absolute sense.

In our view, these two extreme groups merely catch sight of a partial, though relatively justified, aspect of a global situation; we, on the other hand, must be open-minded enough to recognize the synthesis as well which may come about, in spite of the polarizing process. We hold, in fact, that syntheses do arise in the process, and that precisely the syntheses play a particular important role in the evolution of thought.

Syntheses owe their existence to the same social process that brings about polarization; groups take over the modes of thought and intellectual achievements of their adversaries under the simple law of 'competition on the basis of achievement'. Sombart[1] differentiates in the economic sphere, as is well known, between competition on the basis of achievement, of suggestion, and of force. Here too, it could be shown how these forms of competition are moulded by the general principles of social competition, and that they also occur in the region of thought. We will not pursue this line of thought farther, however, but will merely point out that in the socially-differentiated thought process, even the opponent is ultimately forced to adopt those categories and forms of thought which are most appropriate for orientation in a given type of world order. In the economic sphere, one of the possible results of competition is that one competitor is compelled to catch up with the other's technological advances. In just the same way, whenever groups compete for having their interpretation of reality accepted as the correct one, it may happen that one of the groups takes over from the adversary some fruitful hypothesis or category—anything that promises cognitive gain. Here too, instead of demonstrating our thesis, we can only illustrate it with one single, though classic, example of a synthesis of this kind—i.e. Hegel. Hegel's thought can be considered with some justification as a synthesis between the thought of the Enlightenment with its absolutist bent, and the thought of conservative Romanticism and Historicism, oriented towards the phenomenon of historical change. In the first third of the 19th century, two extreme types of thought were facing each other. On the one hand, we find the thought of the Enlightenment, with its claim to be determined solely by principles of 'rightness' not subject to historical change. For this type of thought, it was possible to deduce by pure reasoning the principles of the only right solution for any problem; everything which opposed this supposedly 'right' solution was felt to be merely an impediment, an absolute error. This attitude rendered this kind of thought as a matter of fact incapable of perceiving the phenomenon of historical genesis and growth. On the other hand, there was the historicism of the Conservatives who, for their part, denied precisely the possibility of deducing by pure reasoning a system of solutions right in themselves. The Conservatives opposed every system—they opposed systems as such. They were extremely sceptical with regard to Reason, and doubted whether the deductive-constructive method could ever produce anything either true or applicable. For them, there existed only the object gradually developing through time, and the meaning contained in this process of becoming—in the last resort, nothing but individual, completely self-contained epochs.

[1] Cf. W. Sombart, *Das Wirtschaftsleben im Zeitalter des Hochkapitalismus.* Munich-Leipzig, 1927. II. Halbband, pp. 557 ff.

Truth could only be formulated as relative to this historical reality, but never in any absolute way. Ranke provides the classical expression of this approach with his remark: 'Every epoch is God's own' (*'Jedes Zeitalter ist unmittelbar zu Gott'*).

Here again, therefore, we have to do with a case of sharp polarization, and the function of Hegel's thought, seen within the framework of our subject, consisted precisely in overcoming this tension.

He tried to find a position from which both kinds of thought could be envisaged in their partial correctness, yet at the same time also interpreted as subordinate aspects of a higher synthesis. Unfortunately, I cannot give here more than a bare outline of his solution: every epoch is a self-contained entity which can and must be understood in terms of a standard immanent to it. Historical development as a whole, however, the series of these individual epochs, represents an approach in progressive stages to an Absolute. According to Hegel, this terminal stage of the Absolute as an actuality was reached in his time, both in the State and in his own philosophical thinking. If we try to interpret this concept of the present as the actuality of the Absolute in concrete sociological terms, we shall find that it is nothing but the Prussian State of Hegel's time, from the standpoint of which he was in fact thinking.

It is not our task here to take our stand for or against this solution, but to see how it embodies the attempt to reconcile in a synthesis the historical and the absolutist forms of thought. After Hegel, it became possible to combine these two thought patterns —something nobody had dreamed of as long as the polarization tendency alone held sway. The trend towards synthesis of which this is a decisive manifestation permeates Hegelian thought throughout. Not only is the basic constructive principle he applies the reconciliation of antithetical forces in a higher synthesis; even in questions of detail, he nearly always synthesizes disparate tendencies of his time. His relationship to rationalism and irrationalism is just such a synthesizing one: it would, therefore, be wrong to range him either with the rationalist or with the irrationalist forces of his time. What he is seeking is a synthesis in which thesis and antithesis cancel out.

Let me now make a further assertion. Sociologically speaking, it is by no means accidental that Hegel and no one else should have been the discoverer of dialectics. By 'dialectics' I mean here, not a schematic logical discipline, but a concrete pattern of living history by virtue of which there arise, at first, sharply antithetical, polarized tendencies, which then are reconciled in a higher synthesis. That Hegel in particular should have discovered this is in part explicable by the fact that he and his time for the first time in history experienced a period of strict polarization (as a result of competition at the stage of concentration), followed by a short phase of freedom of decision, issuing in the first overall synthesis.

Actually, Hegel discovered in dialectics (its religious origins, recently investigated, are not under discussion here) the law of the structure of his own thought, and at the same time the fundamental structural law of his time.

It is indeed significant that about the same time, in France, Comte was seeking a synthesis in a similar way. This synthesis of course, relating as it does to a quite different situation in France, is quite differently constituted in its contents and in its various details; nevertheless, Hegel and Comte as intellectual phenomena, if envisaged from the point of view of the common rhythm of intellectual movements in modern Europe, represent roughly the same stage. Oppenheimer[1] has recently attempted to analyse Comte's thought sociologically as an example of synthesis, and it would be both interesting and valuable to subject the Hegel-Comte parallel to an exact sociological analysis, not only in respect of their similarities, but also in respect of the differences between them.

There are periods in modern history during which a representative generation becomes free to achieve a synthesis. Such generations take a fresh approach in that they are able to envisage from the higher platform of a synthesis those alternatives and antagonisms which their fathers had had interpreted in a dogmatic, absolute sense. Then, if there are existential problems not yet ripe for a solution, such a generation will experience them in entirely different contexts; the old antagonisms, however, become less sharp, and it will be possible to find a point, so to speak, farther back, from which partisan positions can be seen as merely partial and relative, and thus transcended.

(It seems, by the way, that the sociology of knowledge itself provides just such a viewpoint 'farther back' from which theoretical philosophical differences which cannot be reconciled on the level of manifest content, can be seen through in all their partiality and therewith made amenable to a synthesis. The existence of this continually receding viewpoint—which one might be tempted to interpret inaccurately as a sign of an ever-increasing reflexiveness—presents us with a hitherto untouched but nevertheless important problem of the sociology of knowledge.)

The problem of synthesis is far too complicated to allow us even to approach its solution here.

---

[1] Oppenheimer, *Richtungen der neueren deutschen Soziologie*, Jena, 1928.

It must suffice for us to see that syntheses do exist, and that the history of thought in modern times provides instances not only of polarization, but of association, crossing-over, and synthesis. One thing, however, we must not lose sight of: the syntheses are not confined to purely intellectual currents; they also represent interpretations of social forces. A pure historian of ideas would present Hegel's thought as a cross between the 'Enlightenment' and historicism; but we must go farther, and on the basis of an analysis of the genesis of these types of thought, and of their further development, always ask questions like these: which groups and strata stood behind historicism? How can we make an exact sociological diagnosis of the situation in which synthesis becomes possible? Syntheses, too, do not float in an abstract space, un-influenced by social gravitation; it is the structural configuration of the social situation which makes it possible for them to emerge and develop.

It is thus clear that we believe in no absolute synthesis—one which can transcend the historical process and, so to speak, with the 'eyes of God' directly comprehend the 'meaning of history'. We must steer clear of this self-deception to which Hegel had completely succumbed, even if we regard a synthesis as the best thing that thought can produce from the point of view of the socially unifying function of knowledge. (I repeat: from the point of view of the socially unifying function of knowledge. The plan of this lecture does not permit me to develop here the comple-mentary idea—suggesting the necessary limits of all synthesis—that certain existentially-determined elements in thinking can never be divested of this character; nor should they, since their proper meaning would be obliterated if they were to be engulfed in a synthesis.) The instability and relativity of any synthesis is shown by the emergence, in place of the homogeneous Hegelian system itself, of right and left Hegelianisms.

If one analyses this schism, however, one sees that there remained for both parties an a-problematical residue of the Hegelian synthesis, an inventory of concepts and thought-patterns which in the previous epoch had themselves been the object of strife. Through a process of selection, a certain residue separates itself from the mass of problematical material around which the main struggle was conducted, and is incorporated almost unnoticed into the outlook and primary orientation of *all* parties. In exactly the same way, many alleged discoveries and new categories are quietly dropped. We can see quite clearly today, for example, how the sociological approach—originally sponsored by the opposition and combated by dominant groups addicted to an ideological orientation—has gradually, almost secretly, become generally adopted, simply because it affords the most reliable primary orientation pattern in the contemporary situation.

In a word, then: *synthesis means selection.* The polarization process is accompanied, step by step, by a corresponding counter-movement aiming at synthesis. We have already seen that even at the party level, a platform is able to emerge only through synthesis, that a synthesis is needed to consolidate the partial perspectives of individual groups and factions into a party pro-gramme exercising a strong enough appeal to give rise to a broad 'current'; and we have also seen that beyond the scope of these intra-party syntheses, there are constant attempts to mediate in an overall synthesis the greatest tensions arising in the historical-social process. And finally, we saw that although this major synthesis is never really achieved, efforts undertaken towards it in the end result in the selective accumulation of a common inventory of concepts, as it were in a *consensus ex post* reached by the various parties.

In addition, then, to the primitive consensus, represented by the inherited fund of anxieties, emotions, and common-sense wisdom, we have to do with a latter-day consensus *ex post*, born of tension and gradually consummating itself in strife. Between these, however, lies the turbulent, problematical region of life itself within which everything still is open to question.

Now we have to ask: What is the principle underlying this selection? How large a part of the original party platform will survive the factional strife within the party, and how much of the previously held doctrine will be irretrievably lost in the process? Further, what is it that all parties will tacitly take over one from the other? What, in the long run, tends to establish itself over and above the party consensus as the consensus of an entire historical community?

Evidently that which is most applicable—that is, that which *each* party needs for orientation within the contemporary situation. Now this common fund of knowledge which imposes itself as a tacit consensus shared by all is largely existentially determined —albeit existentially determined on a higher, more abstract level.

The stream of history, then, tends to sift out in the long run those contents, patterns, and modes of experience that are of the greatest pragmatic value.

At this point, however, the question arises inevitably: Is the pragmatically valuable necessarily also the true? With this ques-tion, our problem, originally stated as one concerning the sociology of knowledge, is transformed into an epistemological one. The epistemological problem, however, cannot be disposed of in the present context. On the other hand, it is out of the question that a certain analysis should be stopped short once and for all at the most crucial point merely because the recognized domain of a different scientific department allegedly begins there (a mode of procedure typical of the bureaucratized organization of science).

At this point, I would like at least to suggest how problems of these various fields come together in one living context. Having allowed ourselves to be carried along by the stream of spontaneous doubts, having reached this level of analysis by following the inner dialectic of the problem, we should at least take a look to inspect the landscape around us. Please allow me to open for a moment a window overlooking this landscape of the epistemological problems.

Is the pragmatically valuable also necessarily the true? This being an epistemological question, the answer cannot be arrived at by the method of the sociology of knowledge. Whereas the sociology of knowledge has to do with questions of *fact*, epistemology deals with questions of *right*. Whereas any finding of the sociology of knowledge embodies an assertion of fact which can be invalidated by a contradictory factual record, the solution of an epistemological problem is always largely dependent on the concept of truth presupposed and used in the discussion. The sociology of knowledge, however, is in a position to provide a peculiar kind of factual information concerning the various truth concepts and epistemologies—factual information which itself has epistemological implications that no future epistemology may overlook.

Notwithstanding its claim to be the fundamental science and the critique of all experience as such, epistemology in fact always exists only as a justification of a mode of thought already existing or just emerging.[1] Let a new code of cognition with a new formal structure arise, such as, for instance, modern natural science, and epistemology will try to explain and justify it. Epistemology would like to be taken for a critical science, whereas in fact it represents an underpinning and justifying sort of knowledge. It finds its truth-model externally given, and this partial model will serve it as a total pattern of orientation; its concept of truth will also be the product of this *ex post* situation. Viewed historically and factually, epistemology stands in the same relationship to any given mode of thought as, for example, the philosophy of law does to the prevailing legal system. It demands to be recognized as an absolute standard, a tribunal, a critique, whereas in fact

[1] Cf. 'Strukturanalyse der Erkenntnistheorie', *Kantstudien, Ergänzungsheft*, No. 57, Berlin, 1922, pp. 72 ff. (To be published in a later volume in this series).

it is an adventitious structure, a mere system of justification for an already existing style of thought.

From the point of view of the sociology of thought—a discipline which always has the entire historical configuration within its purview—the main point is that it is not, as one would be tempted to assume at first sight, one epistemology that struggles with another, but the struggle that always goes on between existing modes of thought and cognition which the various theories of knowledge only serve to justify. In the historical and social framework, theories of knowledge are really only advance posts in the struggle between thought-styles.

What the epistemological implications of these factual findings of the sociology of knowledge are, what relevance they have to the problem of validity, I do not propose to examine here; I simply throw these questions at you, in the hope that you will bring them nearer to solution. I am fully aware, of course, that in doing so, I am simply unburdening myself of a rather difficult problem at your expense.

This question, however, lies beyond the scope of our original topic—the role of competition in the intellectual sphere. The discussion of the sociological problems involved reached its conclusion with our analysis of the Hegelian dialectics, in the course of which we tried to show that the pattern of dialectics with its movement between antithesis and synthesis can in part be explained by the modern polarization tendency of intellectual currents in the stage of concentration. With this conclusion, we really return to our starting-point, the concept of a sociology of the mind which, so we hope, will elucidate from a new aspect the riddles of the dynamics of the mind, the problem of the function of doctrinal currents.

Whatever your own attitude to Hegel and to the sociological interpretation of dialectics may be, I hope at least to have adumbrated within the limits of this necessarily short and compressed exposition that the social structure is certainly a co-determinant of the concrete shape of existentially-determined thought; that, in particular, the various forms of competition (including their extreme forms) tend to leave their mark on the thought structure with which they are correlated; and finally, that in attempting to bring a certain degree of clarity into the present intellectual situation (which often confronts one with sheer despair, and especially threatens the scientific outlook with disaster), we cannot dispense with a sociological viewpoint—in this case, with the technique of the sociology of knowledge.

This does not mean to say that mind and thought are nothing but the expression and reflex of various 'locations' in the social fabric, and that there exist only quantitatively determinable functional correlations and no potentiality of 'freedom' grounded in mind; it merely means that even within the sphere of the intellectual, there are processes amenable to rational analysis, and that it would be an ill-advised mysticism which would shroud things in romantic obscurity at a point where rational cognition is still practicable. Anyone who wants to drag in the irrational where the lucidity and acuity of reason still must rule by right merely shows that he is afraid to face the mystery at its legitimate place.

VII
Problems of Sociology in Germany

T HOUGH belatedly, sociology *is* entering Germany's official consciousness. Unofficial, uninvited, an intruder, it had long been present, but rather as an outsider to ordinary thought, most of the time no more than the bearer of social opposition.

Not as a means in the fight against clergy and royalist reaction as in France, nor in the spirit of pure agitation, but already in the hour of its birth uniting in itself the world views of two possibilities of the modern vision, the 'bourgeois' and the socialist, the new perspective broke out in the form of a mighty eruption in the works of three great ones (to name this time only those already dead)—those of Max Weber, Ernst Troeltsch, and Max Scheler. One cannot proclaim it loud enough—for even in Germany there are only few people who know it—that what we have here by way of the depth of problems treated, of substantive accomplishment, and of methodological mastery surpassed in one stroke the level of Western sociology (even though a good many choose not to be acquainted with the latter but to think little of it just the same), and that these works may well contain an extraordinary legacy, a tradition of the last generation that must absolutely be continued and developed. What is the exceptional nature and depth of this retarded breakthrough of sociology? The person

Translated from 'Zur Problematik der Soziologie in Deutschland', in Mannheim, *Wissenssoziologie: Auswahl aus dem Werk*, eingeleitet und herausgegeben von Kurt H. Wolff, Berlin und Neuwied: Luchterhand, 1964 [Soziologische Texte, Band 28], pp. 614–24 [originally, *Neue Schweizer Rundschau*, 22 (November 1929): 820–29], by Kurt H. Wolff.

who thinks about sociology to the end and is willing to relate it to himself and to take it on, finds himself in a critical situation, for this science has from its beginnings been an organon of self-reflection and self-enlargement.

In Germany the new sociology arose at an hour when the economy broadened into a world economy, when nations and countries were brought closer, but also were ranged against one another, when the occident broke into the orient in order definitively to decompose it in its traditional form—but what became questionable at the same time was one's own position. Who are we in this world? Max Weber thought our situation through on a terrestrial scale, and Max Scheler saw man as finding himself in the 'era of adjustment'.

But there also was an essential enlargement in sociology's own sphere: social strata and classes which in decisive matters were previously present only in a passive capacity and whose will, range of instincts, thoughts, and habits had been passed by, broke into the power structure and into the sphere of consciously attended culture with claims of their own. Where the world widens its social and terrestrial dimensions, we must not be surprised if the historical depth opens itself to entirely new approaches. The question 'Who are we?' is being addressed not only to races and cultures, to social strata and classes, but also to our own past. Where do we stand in historical time? How can our spiritual and psychic place in it be found? Already Troeltsch aimed at gathering the various strands of the problem that rises with such penetrating of the historical dimension. At the same time he tried to inquire what meaning the ever more clearly emerging fact of the *gliding basis* of being human and of thinking might have for philosophy.

But what is decisive is that in Germany this possibility, which exists for almost all men now living—namely, to enlarge one's view of the world and to this end avail oneself of the method of sociology—eventually exceeds the problem area of this special discipline. The sociological problem constellation in the narrower sense transcends itself in two directions—in the direction of philosophy and in the direction of a politically active world orientation. The fact that it succeeded in this, that the enlargement of the horizon that is urged on all of us who are now living has not been received only with an aesthetic gesture, that we did not simply enjoy new exotic colors nor merely abandon ourselves to the contemplation of *Gestalten*, nor finally experience the widening of the world only as an enrichment of classical knowledge is due to the circumstance that here sociology met philosophical tradition that was alive, as well as Marxism as a perspective that was politically activated in all its elements. Max Weber caught the thrust of the latter, stressing in the political aspect of Marxism not that which is only evaluative and agitatorial (and for which science has no place), but its living, spiritually timely relevance.

This sociology transcended itself in the direction of philosophy already, though unadmittedly, in Max Weber; but quite openly and consciously, in Troeltsch and Scheler. This surpassing itself toward philosophy, however, by no means implies giving up the duty to supply evidence imposed on us by the methods of empirical research. It only means combining the 'devotion to empiricism' ['*Empiriefrömmigkeit*'] with questions that always aim at more than a given body of material and its intrinsically irrelevant lawfulness. Because in Germany the philosophic impulse was alive in the form of the philosophy of consciousness and of life, while the epistemology of positivism had already been overcome, here every accretion to knowledge and every enlargement of the horizon could become topical in its philosophical relevance. Thus, to know more did not simply become a mere additional enrichment of experiences of existence. Instead, the three-dimensional deepening of vision—in the direction of the terrestrial, the social and the historical—has, in the form of a sociology that reaches into questions of philosophy, become the organon of the new man, the breakthrough of a new feeling of life: man is once again shedding his skin, striving after an enlarged form of his existence.

The converging forces thus were fundamentally heterogeneous. On the one hand, there was a historically incomparable social and political constellation; on the other, a very particular location in intellectual history. In Germany the late emerging sociology, born out of this convergence, became an instrument for the enlargement of consciousness and soul and, inevitably in the process, a radical revision of all those particular possibilities of existence which had previously posed as absolute. This destruction of false absolutizations of the very simplest facts of limited milieus, in the name of which men puffed themselves up, lived past each other and in wartime even aimed at exterminating one another mutually, came about naturally from the experience of a widening horizon. It was deepened into a systematically applicable method thanks to the availability of a philosophical tradition skilled in analyzing structures of consciousness. For the formulation of problems could not stop at the questioning of this or that alleged absolute but concerns *every* absolutizing method of thinking which plays one particular datum off against another and thus prevents us from true attention to a fellowman and from perceiving the overall context. One day, the question of how men think and the extent to which their thinking is connected with the particular situation in which they (and very often also the presumptive 'metaphysicians') find themselves, had to be posed radically and without reservation so as to call in question one's own position too.

With the discussion of these last problems I have already touched on some themes which characterize my particular approach within the sociological and philosophical development. Up to this point it has been rather precarious to characterize exclusively one trend (though a most significant one) as German. And yet, in what follows I shall have to narrow the field of vision even further and to talk only about certain problems which, moreover, have the awkwardness of being characteristic of my own position alone.

I am forced to this narrowing of the field of vision, to this unpleasant retreat into myself (as will have hardly escaped the reader of this periodical) by the fact that the present considerations spring from a specific situation; they are not only a statement but a rejoinder and a self-defense. In his latest essay. 'Sociology—and Its Limits',[1] E. R. Curtius has done me the honor of almost identifying me with the new situation in German sociology. And since he attacked me and my latest book[2] in order to strike that sociology, it now is appropriate to make clear distinctions, to do nothing in what follows but to fall back to the line of self-interpretation, that is, to ignore other important positions since these are not being attacked this time.

Thus far, my statements had the purpose of presenting, in the form of a situational analysis, a too little known development. What follows has the task of supplying a background for particular questions yet to be treated, as well as of throwing a different light on Curtius's report on the situation. For the fact that his observations and accusations miss the point is obvious already from what has been said.

Presumably it is evident by now that the structure of the trend in German sociology that Curtius attacks is not at all so simple; nor can it by any means be compared with French sociology (which in its political constellation belongs in the Third French Republic). It is also clear that the psychic and spiritual attitude which Curtius finds represented in my book does not have its origin, as he would have us believe, in the 'shock neurosis' of the last fifteen years, but that it in all its elements is most intimately tied up with the fundamental structure of our social and spiritual

[1] Published in the October issue of this *Rundschau*. (Henceforth 'C'. will stand for 'Curtius'.)

[2] *Ideologie und Utopie*, Schriften zur Philosophie und Soziologie, Bd. 3, Bonn, 1929 ('*I.U.*')

existence—that it would not even be possible if the broad-gauged development of one of the most important components of the German tradition, to which it owes almost all its decisive impulses, did not stand behind it.[3]

Neither will the reproach that I of all people represent a 'tendentious sociology' be easily sustained before a scientific public. For the sociology of knowledge such as I practice it has been initiated for the purpose of showing by means of *empirical research* those positions in all tendencies of thought in the humanities, social sciences, and in politics which have their roots in the irrational and, by means of conclusive analyses, of pursuing the question how taking such positions comes through even in the categorial apparatus. (Cf., among other places, *I.U.*, pp. 77–113 [English transl., pp. 104–130].) The sociology of knowledge recognizes the inevitable nature of the element of *Weltanschauung* as to a certain extent a structural determinant of a particular area of thought: so-called 'existence-related thinking'. But the cautious character of this attitude even goes as far as to make an attempt at mastering this existentiality by taking it into consideration as a determinant stemming from irrationality and *Weltanschauung* and to raise it to consciousness in a specific act of knowing. That is to say, it tries to determine with precision and by scientific methods the onesidedness of certain aspects of *all* points of view and of all parties. The most essential center of my efforts lies in the fact that I have undertaken to formulate the task of studying the *factual* thinking of men not only programmatically, but gradually to work out a method to the purpose and to test it in historical empirical studies. This striving for objectivity has gone so far as to make me analyze my own standpoint in regard to the question of what that ineradicable remainder of perspectivism consists in in me, and I have not hesitated carefully to analyze the particularity of certain of my concepts (e.g., *I.U.*, p. 75n. [Engl., p. 103n.], p. 175n. [ff.; Engl., pp. 177 ff.]),

---

[3] The fact that the approach to problems that characterizes my book is directly affiliated with the approaches of Max Weber, Troeltsch, and Scheler had thus far been observed by almost all critics, who are knowledgeable in the history of sociological ideas and approaches. For the latest extensive treatment, see [Karl] Dunkmann, 'Ideologie und Utopie', *Archiv für angewandte Soziologie*, September, 1929, pp. 71–84.

The sociologist of knowledge must note here in passing that his critic— an all too well known optical illusion—feels everything to be anti-traditional that does not belong precisely in the line of his own particular tradition. It also is striking how he, the programmatic representative of the doctrine of the autonomy of the spirit, interprets everything without exception from the point of view of psychopathology as soon as the topic is developmental contexts that are not in his line.

always calling the reader's attention to the as yet problematic and unresolved (such as the problematic character of the 'concept of reality').[4]

Now I should like to enter into two further objections by my critic. I must deal with them explicitly also because the first in particular aims at charging me also 'morally', and both of them may be of more general interest and wider significance. The two reproaches concern my alleged 'nihilism' and anti-idealism (C., pp. 729, 732) and the problem of the relation between philosophy and sociology.

The dynamic relationism for which I stand has nothing whatever to do with nihilism. It has grown out of tendencies to overcome, as far as this is possible at all, the narrow-mindedness and encapsulation of standpoints. It is, in the first place, a method of seeking, which expressly does *not* despair of the solubility of the crisis of our existence and thought, and which for this reason alone cannot be nihilistic (*I.U.*, p. 5). On the contrary, in the interest of the self-enlargement that today is already possible, it invites *every* position for once to call itself in question and to suspend the self-hypostatization that is a habit of thought self-evident to everybody (*I.U.*, pp. 40 f. [Engl., pp. 75 f.]). In my analysis I have seized upon the existence of that crisis, as well as on the fact—in and of itself most upsetting—that the method of studying ideologies is so advanced that almost all historical and social positions can be shown up in their existentiality. If Curtius is not disconcerted by this crisis, I take notice of it, of course. But if his position—treating me, who has not created this crisis but merely expresses and analyzes it for the sake of overcoming it (*I.U.*, pp. 54 [ff.], n. 1, 56 ff. [Engl., pp. 88 ff., n. 1, 89 ff.]), as if I were responsible—should win out, it can only lead to academic life in which intimidation makes us silent about what really concerns us. It won't do to hold the doctor who makes the diagnosis responsible for the disease.

The readers of this periodical will not find it too difficult to realize what is at stake here, for Max Rychner's essay and the 'Fragment über die neue Denkmethode' [Fragment on the New Method of Thinking], which happen to appear in the same issue as Curtius's essay, represent a point of view closely related to mine. What is in question in both cases is 'a newly forming type of man' (Rychner, p. 722), an 'attitude toward the world'

---

[4] The sociologist of knowledge overcomes partially irrational ties by methodically raising them to consciousness. As far as his critic is concerned, he is, unfortunately, obliged to observe here that he calls everything mere *Weltanschauung* with which *he* does not agree: instead of objective refutation, there only are subtleties and personal findings of a lack of substance.

that is no longer caught on 'irresolvable contrasts'; and Rychner says quite clearly, speaking for himself:

What is at stake is a new way of thinking. To overcome dualistic thought does not mean scorning the things and circumstances previously arranged in dichotomies. If by strenuous intellectual exercise I come to negate the alternative vegetarian diet vs. fleshpots of Egypt, I do not impugn either the dignity of a fruit salad or that of the *Tournedos à la Rossini*, but only their confrontation that is based on *Weltanschauung* [Rychner, p. 724].

I would say that I impugn only such claim to absoluteness as is self-evident to each of the two taken singly. Really, we still have to practice this method of thinking, and we shall learn then that the capacity to call even oneself in question if need be is no 'spiritual spinelessness' (C., p. 729); that an attempt, in the spirit of Descartes's methodical doubt, to apply this approach to all positions within reach is no nihilism.

All true thinking and living entails a certain risk; but he who would not risk himself and his habitual world view is not fit for thinking or true existence. By doubting, Descartes, too, risked a world view, but what was lost in the doubt was only scholasticism and its stock of scientific dogmas; what was gained was controllable science. Surely, such questioning involves a certain uneasiness, and surely there also is a parallel to that renunciation which abandoning belief in the geocentricity of the universe meant in the natural sciences. Indeed, on the ground of the kind of attack made by Curtius, who would almost introduce an academic vice squad to control teachable logical methods of thinking, it would not be difficult for me to rise to the pathos of an '*eppur' si muove*'. But for the time being, we don't want to be martyrs.

If every word of my critic did not express the sincerity of his outrage, I should, in view of his well-known sublimated power of empathy, be puzzled—I must say this—by his managing to understand the exact opposite of almost every sentence of mine. Thus, my alleged anti-idealism: this interpretation is based on his reading all sentences in which I speak of a so-called idealism, an idealism in quotation marks (so printed), as an attack on the authentic possibilities of idealism and on his even taking it amiss, at one point, that I advocate the 'destruction of mendacious ideologies' (C., p. 732).[5]

[5] I am forced to point to the fact that the sentences cited by Curtius change their proper sense or often turn into their opposite by being torn out of their original context (not to mention the total meaning context of the book). For reasons of space, I can present only three examples.

(1) Above all, the passage on idealism mentioned in the text (C., p. 732; *I.U.*, p. 52 [Engl., p. 86]). If one reads the quotation in its original context (at least from p. 49 [Engl., p. 84] of my book), it is perfectly clear that I am talking about *inauthentic* forms of idealism, about the reveling in myths, and that

And now in the end I still come to the question which cannot be settled here; but I feel the need to specify my position on it. It is the problem of the relation between sociology and philosophy. First, what must be said quite clearly is that I do not wish to replace philosophy by sociology—philosophy in itself constitutes

---

I condemn this, and not the authentic possibilities of spiritual existence. In addition to this unambiguousness that in my opinion results from the larger context, the fact that I place the words 'myth', 'greatness in itself', *and* 'idealistic' [Engl., 'ideals'] in quotation marks indicates that I have in mind a *so-called* idealism. Curtius *omits the quotation marks around the word 'idealistic'*, which results in a complete inversion of the meaning. A minimal oversight, which nevertheless has grave consequences, since just this word and this inversion of meaning provide him with the stepping stone for his sally.

(2) On p. 732, Curtius reproaches me for accepting certain tendencies of the new 'matter-of-factness'; thus, he disliked the passage, also mentioned in the text above, where I assert that this tendency toward 'matter-of-factness' 'is in large measure to be welcomed . . . as the transformation of utopianism into science, as the destruction of the deluding ideologies which are incongruent with the reality of our present situation' [Engl., p. 230]. If this, too, is misleading, then I must try to argue *e contrario*: should by any chance, according to Curtius, utopia be in the place of science even today, and is he out to conserve deluding ideologies? The passage is on p. 243 of *I.U.*, and right afterward—which we do not learn from my critic—I say that at the next level of analysis *I too* condemn this 'new matter-of-factness'. Has he not read this?

(3) Finally, I mention the passage in which Curtius reproaches me for imputing 'egoistic motives' to people who think differently' and for being against 'every dedication to an absolute' (C., p. 731). In context, this passage, too, shows quite a different face. What is at issue is not the prevention of authentic dedication but a complaint that the erroneous method of thinking, which absolutizes everday accidentals, benefits those comfortable souls who do not wish to see 'life's abyss' [Engl., p. 77, 'look life in the face']. In this context, the term Curtius objects to, 'comfortable and smug under conditions as they are' [Engl., p. 78], or the expression 'need for . . . certainty' [Engl., p. 77], has nothing to do with imputing material or otherwise gross motives, for the course of thought moves on a plane on which . . . [these terms] refer to the fear of the average man of 'life's abyss'. For these decisive words, 'life's abyss', are in the text (*I.U.*, p. 42) but are *missing* in Curtius's quotation; only the dots indicating the omission point to the fact that for *his* interpretive context they are irrelevant. If one reads a few sentences further on, one comes to the following passage [*I.U.*, p. 43]: 'Thus we are faced with the curiously appalling trend of modern thought, in which the absolute which was once a means of entering into communion with the divine, has now become an instrument used by those who profit from it, to distort, pervert, and conceal the meaning of the present' [Engl., p. 78]. This one sentence alone ought to be enough to prove to Curtius that, indeed, I am not indifferent to the truly spiritual and that what is to be fought are its decadent forms. Curtius is likely to interpret this, too, to the effect that what matters to me is to find not the authentic but the destructible. Let him open the last two rows [?] of my book and take cognizance of the fact that I consider a life without transcendence of existence the worst imaginable deficiency of being human. But he who today means to offer the transcendence of his being in ultimate seriousness must have subjected it to the ultimate self-examination, just because the ultimate [fate] of mankind is at stake.

a particular problem level. Furthermore, I am not only not against but expressly *for* metaphysics and ontology, and even teach their indispensability for an existence-related empiricism (*I.U.*, pp. 43–45 [Engl., pp. 78–80]); I am only opposed to the presence of metaphysics which is not recognized and thus can serenely absolutize particulars. In its plight, the sociology of knowledge, too, comes upon an ontology that is presupposed by it. Its relationizing enables philosophical ontology to revise particulars previously posing as absolutes, thus cutting the ground from under the feet of the pseudo-metaphysicians who weigh on our political and sociological thought. In this context, the struggle for an ontology, such as Heidegger, for instance, represents, is actually one of the most decisive achievements of contemporary philosophy. That further problems must result from the question of statics and dynamics goes without saying: but such as yet unresolved problems only spur and enrich the honest will to clarification.

Further—to come back to the problem of autonomy and touch on this point too—I am not at all for mixing disciplines in education, and against everything that lessens the methodical rigor of schooling. But this structural autonomy of the philosophical level of problems (and the needs of education) must not be interpreted to mean that the practitioner of a 'special science' is forbidden to enter these regions or inquire into their elements.

Among the dogmas and suggestions of the older philosophy of science—already surpassed by the methods of the human studies developed in Germany—there is the cry of 'sociologism' or 'psychologism', which is sounded every time the range of questions of a special science transcends itself—when, for instance, as we saw, intellectual history, sociologically considered, reveals the dynamically gliding basis of human knowledge and the tendency to hypostatize particulars, or a 'sociology of the mind' (as I envision it) becomes topical. It would be spiritual suicide if at such points some methodological prejudice were suddenly to make one close off the context of questions and shy away from pursuing their philosophical relevance. In such cases the true philosopher—and this exactly describes Max Scheler, whom my critic sets up against me—must have a keen ear for the impulses that arise out of life and out of scientific research and must meet them eagerly. For it is the true thinker's duty not to resist thought.

VIII
The Democratization of Culture

I. SOME PROBLEMS OF POLITICAL DEMOCRACY AT THE STAGE OF ITS FULL DEVELOPMENT

1. A democratizing trend is our predestined fate, not only in politics, but also in intellectual and cultural life as a whole. Whether we like it or not, the trend is irreversible, and hence it is the supreme duty of the political thinker to explore its potentialities and implications. Only in this way will it be possible to influence the trend of democratization in a desirable sense.

The assertion that the dominant trend of our age is toward an ever fuller development of democratic patterns of thought and behaviour may sound paradoxical in view of the frequency with which dictatorships nowadays are superseding democracy.[2] These dictatorships, however, constitute no proof that political reality is becoming less and less democratic in its essence. Dictatorships can arise only in democracies; they are

[1] Translator's Note: The original title of this essay, 'Demokratisierung des Geistes', cannot be rendered exactly in English. While 'culture' has a wider meaning than 'Geist', the term 'mind' which might be used instead of 'culture' would be too narrow. The essay analyzes the historical process of 'democratization' as it manifests itself in characteristic changes in various cultural fields, particularly philosophy, art, and religion. The process itself is conceived as a social process at bottom, rather than as a self-contained process taking place in the realm of thought or mind. Hence, the expression 'democratization of culture' seems more appropriate to designate it than the alternative expression 'democratization of mind'.

The German text has been rendered in free translation, clarifying obscurities and omitting redundant passages but closely reproducing the meaning intended by the author. The omission of longer redundant or incompletely developed passages is marked by dots.

[2] Translator's note: This paper was written in 1933.

From *Essays on the Sociology of Culture* (New York: Oxford University Press, 1956), pp. 171–246. Reprinted by permission of Routledge and Kegan Paul Ltd.

made possible by the greater fluidity introduced into political life by democracy. Dictatorship is not the antithesis of democracy; it represents one of the possible ways in which a democratic society may try to solve its problems.

A plebiscitarian dictatorship may be characterized as the self-neutralization of political democracy. As political democracy becomes broader and new groups enter the political arena, their impetuous activity may lead to crises and stalemate situations in which the political decision mechanisms of the society become paralysed. The political process may then be short-circuited so as to enter a dictatorial phase. This is a danger that threatens precisely those societies in which political democracy suddenly reaches its full development.

At the early stages of democratization, the political decision process was controlled by more or less homogeneous economic and intellectual élites. Since suffrage was not yet universal, the masses could not influence governmental policies. Those who actually wielded political power knew from long familiarity with governmental problems what was actually feasible; they did not embark upon utopian schemes. But when suffrage becomes universal, groups not yet familiar with political reality suddenly become charged with a political function. This leads to a characteristic discrepancy: strata and groups whose political thinking is reality-oriented have to cooperate with, or contend with, people experiencing their first contact with politics—people whose thinking is still at a utopian stage. The bourgeois élite, too, had passed through that stage, but that was about a century ago; in our age, when full democratization sets in, groups are yoked together in the political process whose outlook is not 'contemporaneous'. This must lead to disturbances.

Democratization, then, means a loss of homogeneity in the governing élite. Modern democracy often breaks down because it is burdened with far more complex decision problems than those facing early democratic (or pre-democratic) societies with their more homogeneous ruling groups. Today we can see the full extent of these problems; precisely because democracy has been realized in our age, for us it is not merely an ideal but a reality which has its bright and dark sides. We can no longer view democracy as the sum-total of ideal aspirations contrasting with an imperfect reality. The adequate attitude towards democracy is no longer one that equates it with every perfection that free-floating fantasy can conceive of. Rather, the required attitude is one of sober stock-taking, involving an awareness of the possible defects of democracy as a prerequisite for correcting them.

2. It is one of the characteristics of our age that believers in the ideal of democracy tend to be repelled and disappointed by its actuality. They discover to their dismay that in a political democracy the majority need not be 'progressive' in its attitudes and aspirations. While the democratization of political life at first actually favours 'left-wing' tendencies, it may happen that 'conservative' or 'reactionary' currents get the upper hand as a result of the free play of political forces.

Before democracy was achieved and tested in its actual functioning, it was customary to expect that it would necessarily usher in the rule of Reason or at least tend to confer political power upon people whom one considered 'rational'. When these prophecies were first made, they were not unrealistic. At that time, the distribution of social and political forces was such that irrationalism and conservatism went hand in hand with the rejection of political democracy, while pro-democratic attitudes were associated with belief in the rule of Reason. This distribution of roles had persisted for a number of generations. Eventually, however, it became evident that besides the 'democracy of Reason' there was also a 'democracy of Impulse', to use Scheler's terminology (in German: 'Vernunftdemokratie' versus 'Stimmungsdemokratie'). Democracy, as we now see, is not necessarily a vehicle of rationalizing tendencies in the society—on the contrary, it may well act as an organ of the uninhibited expression of momentary emotional impulses.

Likewise, democracy at one time was viewed as an instrument guaranteeing international harmony. We now see that the opposite tendency, too, is inherent in democracy: national self-assertion and aggressiveness may thrive precisely in a democratic soil. A similar ambivalence is apparent in the relation between democracy and individualism. On the one hand, democracy fosters the freedom and development of the individual personality; it stimulates individual autonomy by giving each person a share in political responsibility. On the towards democracy is no longer one that equates it with every perfection that free-floating fantasy can conceive of. Rather, the required attitude is one of sober stock-taking, involving an awareness of the possible defects of democracy as a prerequisite for correcting them.

2. It is one of the characteristics of our age that believers in the ideal of democracy tend to be repelled and disappointed by its actuality. They discover to their dismay that in a political democracy the majority need not be 'progressive' in its attitudes and aspirations. While the democratization of political life at first actually favours 'left-wing' tendencies, it may happen that 'conservative' or 'reactionary' currents get the upper hand as a result of the free play of political forces.

Before democracy was achieved and tested in its actual functioning, it was customary to expect that it would necessarily usher in the rule of Reason or at least tend to confer political power upon people whom one considered 'rational'. When these prophecies were first made, they were not unrealistic. At that time, the distribution of social and political forces was such that irrationalism and conservatism went hand in hand with the rejection of political democracy, while pro-democratic attitudes were associated with belief in the rule of Reason. This distribution of roles had persisted for a number of generations. Eventually, however, it became evident that besides the 'democracy of Reason' there was also a 'democracy of Impulse', to use Scheler's terminology (in German: 'Vernunftdemokratie' versus 'Stimmungsdemokratie'). Democracy, as we now see, is not necessarily a vehicle of rationalizing tendencies in the society—on the contrary, it may well act as an organ of the uninhibited expression of momentary emotional impulses.

Likewise, democracy at one time was viewed as an instrument guaranteeing international harmony. We now see that the opposite tendency, too, is inherent in democracy: national self-assertion and aggressiveness may thrive precisely in a democratic soil. A similar ambivalence is apparent in the relation between democracy and individualism. On the one hand, democracy fosters the freedom and development of the individual personality; it stimulates individual autonomy by giving each person a share in political responsibility. On the process, we may take the clue provided by the sociological analysis of the democratization of politics, and formulate our question as follows: *How does the shape, the physiognomy of a culture change when the strata actively participating in cultural life, either as creators or as recipients, become broader and more inclusive?*

2. Before we try to answer this question, we have to meet a possible objection. Is it at all justified to speak of a 'democratizing' tendency beyond the sphere of politics proper? In a society whose tradition is essentially idealistic in the German sense, this objection will carry much weight, for such societies are wont to look upon their culture as divided into separate, watertight compartments whose self-contained autonomy must never be questioned. To a German idealist, the suggestion that a mundane thing like political democracy might represent a tendency also operating in the sacrosanct realms of art or philosophical thought will sound like blasphemy. But what if it could be shown that political democracy is merely one manifestation of a pervasive cultural principle? This is in fact the thesis we propose to defend.

That there are certain essential differences between the artistic or intellectual products of aristocratic and democratic cultures was noticed by Nietzsche; he made many penetrating observations along these lines, even though his comments show a pronounced élitist bias and a strong resentment of democracy. Nietzsche's romantic disciples as a rule do not go beyond trivialities—democracy levels everything, it ushers in the dominance of mediocrity and the mass, and so on. Such judgments may have their partial justification, but they do not go beneath the surface. The real task, in fact, is to push through to the fundamental, structural differences between aristocratic and democratic cultures. This is a problem in comparative sociology.[1]

3. Our next task, then, is to indicate the nature of democracy as a structural, sociological phenomenon, one that can be

[1] We recall the distinction made in the first essay of this volume between general and historical sociology. We shall treat the problem of democracy as a formal, structural phenomenon, rather than as a historical one. That is: we shall not inquire into the conditions of the genesis of certain historically existing democracies like the Greek *polis* or the late medieval commune; we shall try to identify the essential traits that distinguish each and every democracy from a non-democratic ordering of society.

studied in the narrow sphere of politics as well as in the broad context of the cultural process as a whole.

To start with political democracy: its basic, formative principle is obviously that all governmental power emanates from the people. Every individual is called upon to contribute his share to the determination of governmental policies. This implies a basic attitude which reaches beyond politics proper and shapes all cultural manifestations of societies of the democratic type. Political democracy, in fact, postulates the sharing of governmental power by all because it is convinced of the essential equality of all men, and rejects all vertical division of society into higher and lower orders. This belief in the *essential equality of all human beings* is the first fundamental principle of democracy.

This principle of the essential equality of all men and the actual behaviour patterns reflecting it in society have two roots: an ideological and a sociological one. Ideologically, the belief in the essential equality of all men derives from the Christian conception of the brotherhood of all men as children of God. Without this conception, our society could never have developed a political order granting equal status to all. On the other hand, however, this teaching could not have informed social reality if it had not been for certain favourable shifts in the social and political structure of Western societies. The pressure of broad middle and lower strata gaining an increasing share in social and political influence was needed to transform the Christian principle of the equality of all human beings into an institutional and political reality. The idea as such had existed before, but it had little political relevance as long as it was understood only in relation to religious experience and found no application to things of the world. The equal treatment of all individuals as a basic feature of modern society was imposed by the growing power wielded by lower social strata.

The principle of the essential equality of all human beings as such does not imply a mechanical levelling, as hasty critics of democracy are prone to assume. The point is not that all men are equal as to their qualities, merits, and endowment, but that all embody the *same ontological principle of human-ness*. The democratic principle does not deny that under conditions of fair competition some individuals will turn out to be superior to others; it merely demands that the competition be fair, i.e. that some people be not given a higher initial status than others (e.g. in the shape of hereditary privilege).

4. This takes us to the second fundamental principle of democracy: the recognition of the *autonomy of the individual*, of the vital selfhood (*Eigenlebendigkeit*) vested in each and every person as the atom of society. In pre-democratic societies, social coordination was based upon the fact that most individuals were denied an autonomous life of their own. The social will was not shaped by impulses contributed by the many; it was determined from above, either by an absolute monarch and his staff of bureaucrats, or by powerful feudal coteries. Democracy, however, is essentially predicated upon the mobilization of all individuals as vital centres, not as a mere ideological or abstract principle, but as a living reality. We see in this the creative, vitalizing function of democracy and, at the same time, the potential danger inherent in it; for the life of a democratic society always skirts chaos owing to the free scope it gives to the vital energies of all individuals. . . .

The process of the release of individually centred vital energies has an interesting counterpart in the history of ideas. The modern concept of the 'organism' could be developed only at a time when society itself was transformed into a system in which the individual particles, though interdependent, also had their own, self-centred life. As the philosopher Erich Kaufmann has shown, the term 'organism' came to be used first in a political and social rather than biological context.[1] In this as in other cases, concrete social experience has furnished those categories which could then be used for the analysis of natural phenomena.

Kaufmann has traced the specifically modern concept of 'organism' to Kant. The term itself had already been used by earlier legal thinkers, but in a sense more akin to our own concept of 'mechanism': it denoted a system put together by a craftsman for some specific purpose, rather than a living being evolving spontaneously and seeking to maintain its internal balance. May we suggest that absolutist society in fact

[1] Cf. Erich Kaufmann, *Über den Begriff des Organismus in der Staatslehre des 19. Jahrhunderts*, Heidelberg, 1918.

corresponded to the paradigm of 'mechanism', and that society entered the stage of self-steering, 'organic' life only in the age of democracy? (It may be added that eighteenth-century Deism had also conceived of God as a craftsman who moved the universe 'from without'.)

In our age, the social process draws its energy from living cells rather than from passive, inert particles. This remains true even in the dictatorial degeneration of democracy. Modern post-democratic dictatorships essentially differ from earlier authoritarian regimes. For the latter, exacting obedience from the mass was no problem, since they could always rely on the docility of the common man. The former, however, must first mobilize mass forces in order to gain power, and then take drastic steps to counteract the potential adverse effects of the wide diffusion of vital energies throughout the society.[1]

5. All this indicates an inner contradiction inherent in the democratic organization of society. Democracy must mobilize the vital energies of every individual; but having done so, it must also find a way to dam up and in part neutralize these energies. Orderly social life would become impossible if every individual constantly made full use of his right to influence public decisions. This would spell the end of all social cohesion. Hence, all democratic societies need certain neutralizing devices involving undemocratic or anti-democratic potentiali-

---

[1] 'Docility' in aristocratic-authoritarian regimes and 'self-neutralization' in democracies correspond to two types of socially induced stupidity. The former consists in the mass of people being prevented from learning, from acquiring new knowledge. Aristocratic societies are set in their thought-ways; they do not advance towards new knowledge, much in the way in which old people refuse to learn. According to Lichtenberg, old people are immobile in their thinking, not because they are biologically unable to learn new things, but because their claim to authority would be weakened if they conceded that they are not omniscient. Aristocratic élites wielding traditional authority often refuse to admit new knowledge for similar reasons.

In democracies, on the other hand, we often observe failure to think and learn due to the fact that the people let some organization or machinery do their thinking for them. One may mention in this connection the tendency observed in American social science to develop new knowledge without 'thinking' about reality, relying solely upon routines of fact-finding, questionnaires, etc. Carl Becker related this to the 'talent for "organization", which is so characteristic of Americans' (cf. *The United States, Experiment in Democracy*, 1920, p. 180).

ties. These devices, however, are not imposed upon democratic society from without; they consist essentially in a *voluntary* renunciation by the mass of the full use of its energies.

This voluntary abandonment of the individual's autonomous aspirations may assume many forms. There is, for example, that susceptibility to propagandistic manipulation which we observe precisely in fully developed mass democracies. One may see in this and related phenomena signs of the degeneracy of democracy; when this trend goes to the limit, as it does in the cult of a 'leader', society ceases to be democratic altogether, since the institutions that enable the individuals to shape political decisions 'from below' are abolished. However, even a healthy democracy requires a certain self-limitation on the part of its individual members. Thus we see that *direct* democracy cannot exist in societies of large size. The governmental system of modern territorial states of democratic character is *representative* democracy. That is, the actual shaping of policy is in the hands of *élites*; but this does not mean to say that the society is not democratic. For it is sufficient for democracy that the individual citizens, though prevented from taking a direct part in government all the time, have at least the *possibility* of making their aspirations felt at certain intervals.

It is in politics as in culture at large: democracy does not imply that there are no élites—it rather implies a certain specific principle of élite formation. Pareto is right in stressing that political power is always exercised by minorities (élites), and we may also accept Robert Michels' law of the trend towards oligarchic rule in party organizations. Nevertheless, it would be wrong to over-estimate the stability of such élites in democratic societies, or their ability to wield power in arbitrary ways. In a democracy, the governed can always act to remove their leaders or to force them to take decisions in the interests of the many.

Democracy, then, has its own way of selecting and controlling its élites, and we can take this to be the *third* fundamental characteristic of democracy both in a narrow political and a broad cultural sense.

6. In the following parts of this paper, we shall discuss the way in which the cultural process as a whole is shaped and influenced by the three fundamental democratic principles we have

distinguished, that is (1) the *potential ontological equality of all individual members of society*, (2) the recognition of the *vital selfhood* of the components of society, and (3) the *existence of élites* in democratic society, together with *novel methods of élite selection*. We shall treat these points, not as ideal desiderata, but as features to be detected in actual social reality. In other words: we shall not attempt to prove that in all democracies, all individuals are actually treated on an equal footing, or that their autonomous vitality is always respected. Our point is, rather, that the actual social process in societies evolving towards democracy cannot be understood without assuming formative trends putting 'horizontal' equality in the place of 'vertical', hierarchical inequality, and so on. . . The scientific, sociological problem consists in seeing this process as a whole, a *Gestalt*, and also in validating this synoptic view by a detailed analysis of the myriad small changes entering into it. 'Morphology', distinguishing large *Gestalt*-like entities, as wholes, and 'analysis', dividing them into their smallest components, must go hand in hand.

B. THE PRINCIPLE OF THE ONTOLOGICAL EQUALITY OF ALL MEN

1. In pre-democratic society, all social authority is inextricably linked to the idea of the ontological superiority of the wielder of authority. No person, family, or institution can exert authority without being regarded as made of 'higher' stuff than the ordinary run of humanity. We may think in this connection of the magic origin of the institution of kingship.[1]

It will be seen that our methodological position is, so to speak, double-edged. Here as elsewhere, we reject the whole-

[1] Thomas and Znaniecki (*op. cit The Polish Peasant*, vol. I) have postulated a certain correlation between magic on the one hand, and authoritarian control on the other: magic practices essentially consist in issuing commands to nature. (Later addition.) This analogy, however, is of problematic value: magic is in all probability not of authoritarian origin. The magician usually seeks to restore a normal condition disturbed by extraordinary influences, e.g. he tries to produce normal rainfall after a period of drought. In other words, he enters upon the scene in emergencies for which the normal institutions of society are not sufficient. Magicians are also competent to deal with the uncontrolled region beyond the confines of the group, in trade or war with others. . . .

sale denial of the legitimacy of the morphological, 'Gestalt' approach in the cultural disciplines (cf. on this Karl Mannheim 'On the Interpretation of Weltanschauung', in *Essays on the Sociology of Knowledge*, London and New York, 1952, pp. 33 ff.). But, on the other hand, we also maintain that a purely morphological approach is not sufficient for the scientific treatment of any subject. A more 'microscopic', causal, functional, analytical approach is also necessary to supplement global, 'morphological' insights. The slogan that 'mechanistic' theories are appropriate in the natural sciences but are out of place in the cultural sciences misses the point. The radical application of 'mechanistic' causal analysis was successful in the natural sciences, not because inorganic nature alone is congenial to this approach, but because such analysis is essential to all scientific endeavour. We merely maintain that in the cultural sciences one must go beyond causal and functional analysis and combine it with a morphological approach.

We now take up the cultural implications of the three 'fundamental principles' of democracy one by one, beginning with the principle of 'equality'.

2. In the process of the democratization of politics, authority does not disappear, but it no longer involves a qualitative jump from the lower orders of mankind to an élite deemed higher in essence. At most, there is a quantitative, non-essential difference between the leaders and the led. The same transition from qualitative, essential distinctions to quantitative, non-essential ones, however, can also be observed in other fields than that of politics, and this change in the evaluation of human models is one of the chief characteristics of the process with which we are concerned, that is, the democratization of culture. In pre-democratic cultures, for example, talent or genius is considered as an irreducible datum—something like a magic charisma that sets off certain individuals from the ordinary run of mankind. Pre-democratic education works very largely with such concepts of human excellence. It considers the man of genius as he appears at the full height of his powers; his genius is an ultimate datum, unrelated to the facts and circumstances of life in terms of which the development and maturing of ordinary individuals may be understood. The authoritarian, pre-democratic mind shuns the idea of process and genesis in

favour of static, hierarchically ordered models of excellence. The democratic mind, on the other hand, stresses the plasticity of man.

When Goethe says, 'This is what thou art—thou canst not escape thyself,' he voices a pre-democratic sentiment. The typically democratic mood, however, is one in which we feel that 'everything could be different'. The democratic type of mind, then, is prone to explain phenomena in terms of contingency rather than essence. Now there is nothing in this style of thought (the one that prefers contingent to essential explanation) that is manifestly and explicitly related to the democratic attitude towards equality and authority. Yet, to the sociologist of culture, the two things are closely interrelated. Not that the democratic thinker necessarily denies human 'greatness'; he merely re-interprets it, seeing in it a manifestation of that human perfectibility which is the universal heritage of man. The 'great man' is great, not because he is different from others in his primordial substance, but because he has had greater and better opportunities to develop himself.[1]

3. It is interesting to see how the democratic attitude is penetrating into a field traditionally dominated by the authoritarian outlook, that of musical education. The essential difference between the musically gifted and ungifted has always been treated as a fundamental datum in the teaching of music. Recently, however, pedagogues like Jacobi have come to deny a fundamental distinction of this kind. According to this new doctrine, every child is potentially 'musical'; manifest differences in musical gifts are merely due to early experiences.[2]

Whether these theories are correct or not does not interest us here; we have mentioned them merely as examples of a 'democratic' approach towards education. According to this

[1] Landsberg makes a good distinction between two versions of the democratic doctrine of equality. The first version is that of Rousseau; it postulates equal perfection *innate* in every human being. The second is found in Locke and Helvetius; according to it, the equality of all men is based upon the fact that they have no *innate* properties whatsoever.

[2] A similar position is being taken in psycho-analytic circles towards the problem of intellectual gifts in general; a periodical for psycho-analytical pedagogy devoted in this sense a special issue to the problem of 'intellectual inhibitions'. (Cf. 'Intellektuelle Hemmungen', *Sonderheft der Zeitschrift für Psychoanalytische Pädagogik*, vol. 4, Nos. 11-12, 1930.)

approach, proficiency in music or other arts is not the appanage of exceptional individuals; the ability to acquire it is no less universal than the ability to learn to speak. Children become 'unmusical' because they have been discouraged from making music. They then do not develop beyond a primitive, infantile level of musicality. Similarly, if some people draw figures in a primitive, infantile fashion, it is because they have been discouraged from cultivating their artistic ability.

The point of these theories is that they do away with the idea of essential differences between human beings by tracing manifest differences to environmental factors. The underlying belief in the plasticity of man (pedagogical optimism) is a typical democratic trait. Pedagogical pessimism on the other hand is related to a pre-democratic, aristocratic outlook.[1]

4. We can observe the difference between pre-democratic and democratic patterns in the relationship between teachers and pupils in general. In pre-democratic school systems, the teacher is placed high above the pupils. The latter must look up to the former in every respect. In a democratic school system, however, the excellence of the teacher consists in meeting the pupils on their own level. Meeting half-way those who do not yet know is the modern pedagogic principle. This principle may be misunderstood and wrongly applied to the content of that which is to be taught. When this happens, vulgarization will be the result; anything that is not easily assimilated by the untutored mind will be put aside. The correct application of the principle, however, consists in a patient articulation of the material of study until the average intellect can grasp it. Moreover, the modern educator will always pay attention to the psyche and also to the social background of the pupil. Formerly, 'learning in school' involved in the main an obedient acceptance of things that were over the heads of

[1] In evaluating the merits of pedagogical optimism versus pedagogical pessimism, we may start from two different questions. On the one hand, we may ask whether the new pedagogical postulates are valid, i.e. whether some or many or all manifest differences in intellectual or artistic proficiency can be traced to environmental factors. On the other hand, we may also treat those postulates as heuristic principles suggesting that it is better to try to treat as many fields of endeavour as possible as open to improving influences than to recognize insuperable limits set by heredity. Is pessimism not a pretext for evading the challenge of educational problems?

the pupils. Later, perhaps, when they are fully educated and become worthy of what is being transmitted to them, they will grasp its full meaning. Modern education, however, shuns this awestruck approach. Instead, it starts from the postulate that anything that is transmitted in the process of teaching can be reduced to crystal-clear simplicity, with no 'higher' obscurities left to admire without comprehension. As we see, the democratic mind puts its trust *a priori* in that which is transparent and clear, whereas aristocratic cultures prize the recondite and the obscure, e.g. in the shape of the over-refinement and over-specialization of scholasticism. For the aristocratic mind, that which is culturally valuable must exist on a higher level, not accessible to the ordinary run of mankind. We can see, here as elsewhere, that people's attitudes towards cultural objects follow the paradigm of their basic social relationships. Where the political and social order basically rests upon the distinction between 'higher' and 'lower' human types, an analogous distinction is also made between 'higher' and 'lower' objects of knowledge or æsthetic enjoyment. . . . .

5. The dominant epistemologies of different ages show the same difference. When Descartes proclaims 'clear and distinct' ideas as necessary for true knowledge, or when Kant specifies 'necessity' and 'universal validity' as the essential characteristics of scientific judgments, they apply 'democratic' criteria to epistemology. These criteria imply that nothing can be accepted as true unless every human mind can grasp it. For the authoritarian, aristocratic mind, however, it is axiomatic that only sublime intellects and superior individuals can attain truth, or that God will reveal Himself only to chosen persons. Obviously, *this* concept of 'revealed truth' is inconsistent with democracy.[1] The democratic mind rejects all alleged knowledge that must be gained through special channels, open to a chosen few only. It accepts as truth only that which can be ascertained

[1] (Translator's Note: The author seems to have had in mind the Hebrew prophets as chosen mouthpieces of 'revealed' truth—a sociological type studied by Max Weber. In the theological doctrine of nearly all Christian churches and denominations, the revealed truth as held by the Church is addressed to all men and can be accepted by all. That this 'universal' truth is revealed first to chosen instruments is less important, in this theological context, than the expected universality of its acceptance. In Thomism, man is 'by his nature' destined for the acceptance of revealed truth.)

by everybody in ordinary experience, or that which can be cogently proved by steps that everybody can reproduce.

Clearly, this definition of truth is closely related to the fundamental democratic principle of the essential equality of all men. In addition to this, however, the modern concept of knowledge also reflects another aspect of democracy: its demand for unrestricted publicity. According to the dominant epistemology of the modern age, valid knowledge refers to the public world. Just as in politics, every individual has a claim to a share in control, in the field of knowledge every item must be subject to scrutiny by all individuals. Consequently, democratic cultures have a deep suspicion of all kinds of 'occult' knowledge cultivated in sects and secret coteries.

6. Unlimited accessibility and communicability, then, characterize the democratic ideal of knowledge. There are, however, limits to accessibility and communicability, even in democratic cultures. There is much knowledge that is accessible to, and communicable among, experts and connoisseurs only. And the case of the 'connoisseur' in the field of art is even more extreme than that of the scientific 'expert' and specialist. In order to be a connoisseur of art, one must be immersed in a historic tradition and cultivate a specialized taste. All this had a certain affinity to pre-democratic types of knowledge. The devotees of art form a closed community within society at large; their experiences are not generally communicable.

Scientific experts, too, develop a language of their own, incomprehensible to outsiders. But the scientific community is not as radically separated from society at large as is the community of æsthetic connoisseurs. Scientific thinking, in fact, is highly formalized and supremely objective; it leaves no room for subjective, purely private experiences. In principle, every scientific theory and finding could be grasped and reproduced by every normal individual. If the non-expert cannot follow the scientist, it is not because the latter's experiences are beyond the range of the former's receptivity, but because the layman rapidly loses his way in the intricacies resulting from the repetition and combination of basic mental operations that are simple in themselves. As against this, critics and historians of art derive their insights from a type of experience that cannot be shared by all men. Theories developed in these fields cannot be formalized and objectivized in such a way that every individual can reproduce them in his own mind. Connoisseurship (which is indispensable to the historian or art) is not teachable in the way in which natural science is teachable. The learning of formalized procedures of research does not suffice to make one a connoisseur. In order to become one, the student must come into contact with the works themselves, and be stimulated by them to the depths of his personality, emotionally, intellectually, and spiritually. Such experiences are not fully and readily communicable. They may even be confined within the limits of an epoch of art; connoisseurs of modern art may be insensitive to the specific values of Renaissance art, and *vice versa.*

7. We may say in this sense that certain types of knowledge are non-democratic in character, since they are accessible only to the élite of connoisseurship. Now it is interesting to observe what happens to these types of knowledge in a democratized culture. The first reaction will be to devalue them. Even though the connoisseur's judgments are undeniably 'empirical' in a certain sense, they do not represent 'exact' knowledge, since nothing is 'exact' unless it is fully communicable and demonstrable. (One may well doubt, by the way, that the current definition of exactness in terms of communicability and demonstrability is the only possible one.)

The second response of a democratic culture to this type of knowledge will occur within the disciplines in question themselves: they will try to satisfy the dominant, generally recognized criteria of exactness by adopting more 'objective' methods. For example, the attempt will be made to *articulate* the connoisseur's response to the work of art more and more, in the hope of obtaining a number of demonstrable, controllable observations instead of an unanalysed, global intuition.

This 'articulation' of a global intuition must be distinguished from 'analysis', even though these operations are often confused. When we 'analyse' a complex object, we are interested in discovering the simple, elementary parts of which it is composed. The object as a whole disappears in this process: it will no longer be recognizable from the elements brought to light by the analysis. 'Articulation', on the other hand, while it also seeks to discover simple components of a complex whole, never loses sight of the way in which the parts combine to make a whole. The complex object always remains in sight during the process. For example, I may point out the details of a façade one by one, calling attention to the various features of the windows, balconies, doors, etc. This is 'articulation', for the detailed observation of the parts merely serves to attain a fuller understanding of the whole.

Everyday, pre-scientific experience has always made use of the procedure of 'articulation', while the natural sciences, afraid of remaining on a 'pre-scientific' level, have abandoned 'articulation' and cultivated 'analysis' exclusively. Articulation, however, must be recognized as a legitimate method. There are certain cultural objects which we cannot study satisfactorily without learning to see how the whole emerges from the parts.

By refining and developing their methods of articulation, those cultural sciences which have to do with æsthetic and similar objects achieve a gain in communicability. They can in this way become more and more attuned to the democratizing trend of our culture, even though the communicability they can attain must remain limited.

8. In the foregoing discussion, we have stressed the contrast between analysis and articulation. From a sociological point of view, however, their parallelism is more important. The dominant impulse in both is to enhance the communicability of knowledge—and both achieve it through increasing abstraction, though in different ways.

There is an intrinsic correlation between the increasing abstractness of the symbols used in communication, and the democratic character of the culture. Élites which are not impelled to make their knowledge generally accessible will not engage in formalization, analysis, and articulation. They will content themselves, either with unanalysed intuition, or with sacred knowledge reserved for an élite and handed down among its members *en bloc*.

The urge towards abstraction and analysis is not imposed by the things themselves. Its origin is a social one; it arises from the size and structure of the group in which knowledge has to be shared. When knowledge must be communicated to many persons of different position and background, it must be couched in 'abstract' terms, for 'concrete' communications are intelligible only to those whose experiences and associations are very similar.[1]

9. We may conclude that a democratic society is more likely than an aristocratic one to discover 'abstract' relationships among things. At the same time, such a society will tend to bar qualitative elements from its experience and to minimize the value of qualitative knowledge.[2] This, to repeat, is an outgrowth of the trend towards greater communicability, which is in turn a manifestation of the democratic ontological principle of human equality.

C. THE AUTONOMY OF THE SOCIAL UNITS

1. We shall now try to show how the second formative principle of democracy, that of the vital autonomy or living selfhood of the individuals as social units, manifests itself in cultural domains usually seen as far removed from the political and social arena. We shall begin with modern epistemology; it seems, in fact, that the democratizing trend in culture finds its earliest fully conscious realization in epistemological reflexion.

We have already seen how 'ontological equality' as a fundamental democratic principle reflected itself, say, in the Kantian criterion of 'necessity' and 'universal validity' as defining genuine

---

[1] It would be an exaggeration to say that the size of the inter-communicating group and its heterogeneous composition in themselves are sufficient to explain the degree of abstraction of communications. The process of increasing abstraction has other aspects as well; the necessity of communicating with many heterogeneous elements is only its group origin.

On social mobility as a general source of abstractness in thinking and communication, see W. I. Thomas, *Source Book for Social Origins*, Boston, 1920, p. 169.

[2] How tendencies out of tune with the dominant social process can nevertheless maintain an underground existence is a complex problem that we cannot take up here. It may be mentioned, however, that certain forms of experience doomed by the dominant trend of culture, such as the aesthetic, qualitative experiences mentioned in the text, may save themselves by becoming objects of reflexion. While aesthetic creativity and receptivity are weaker in our time than in earlier ages, our historic sense and proficiency in articulation are greater. When there is a great deal of talk about 'Gestalt', quality, and concreteness, this does not mean that these things are experienced very strongly; they are objects of reflexion, which is a different thing altogether. . . .

knowledge. In addition to this, however, there is a doctrine which first appears in Western philosophy with Kant and separates post-Kantian from pre-Kantian thought; this is Kant's version of epistemological idealism. Its essence is the assertion of the original *spontaneity* and *creativity* of the epistemological subject and of the act of cognition. This is the philosophical formulation of our second fundamental principle of democracy.

In earlier philosophies, whether 'idealist' or 'realist', the knowing subject appears as essentially dependent on the object of cognition. The former merely reflects the latter; it does not create the object. In these philosophies, social experiences of dependence and hierarchy are drawn upon in order to characterize and account for the act of cognition. After all, epistemology can derive its basic concepts only from pre-theoretical, social experience.[1] In pre-democratic cultures, the average individual is debarred from conceiving the idea that he could gain knowledge, and criticize traditional beliefs, by a spontaneous use of his own mental energies. Even charismatic leaders of opinion such as prophets and the like do not, in such cultures, proclaim new truths in their own name; they either transmit messages directly inspired by God, or demand a return to the purity of an earlier, sacred tradition that is neglected or violated by a corrupt generation.

It is when society changes and new groups become politically active that more and more individuals are induced to interpret reality from their own personal viewpoint. During the Renaissance period, for example, certain individuals not exercising any traditional authority could rise to positions of political power as professional military leaders (condottieri) or as successful capitalistic entrepreneurs. Their experiences awakened in them feelings of self-asserting independence; the type of the 'heroic' individual was born, and this eventually opened up paths towards independent, not tradition-bound, modes of thinking. There was a long and arduous way, with many backslidings, from this to a general recognition of each individual's claim to autonomous thought and to a re-interpretation of human cognition as a creative rather than passive, receptive

[1] Cf. the paper on 'Structural Analysis of Epistemology' in Karl Mannheim, *Essays in Sociology and Social Psychology*, London and New York, 1953, pp. 15 ff.

activity. At long last, however, the process reached its culmination in the new epistemological idealism associated with Kant's name. In one of his essential activities, cognition, man developed a radically new image of himself.

The point we want to stress is that it was not the new philosophy which regenerated social reality. It was the other way round: society changed by making more and more individuals capable of exercising autonomy, and it was this process which made the new conception of knowledge as a spontaneous and creative act possible.

2. Kant's concept of natural law, which is derived from his idealistic principle of the creative role of consciousness, offers a striking parallel to the democratic idea of social law. In Kant's system, the 'lawful' regular character of the natural processes is guaranteed by the fact that the fundamental laws of the process are those of Reason itself. When the knowing subject discovers regularities in nature, he merely comes face to face with laws originating within his own reason. Likewise, the democratic citizen encounters in society no laws except those which he himself has enacted as legislator. In both cases, the law is seen to exist and to be binding because, rather than being imposed by an outside authority, it has been formulated by the same consciousness which must abide by it. It must be added, however, that in Kant's philosophy, consciousness as the source of the law is not the empirical consciousness of each and every individual. It is a more abstract consciousness-in-general ('*Bewusstsein überhaupt*') which is present in each individual as a creative faculty of knowing.

It goes without saying that this 'consciousness-in-general' implies the ontological equality of all men; it is a symbol of the identical 'human-ness' which makes man what he is. It is, however, characteristic of the Kantian, idealistic version of this egalitarian principle that 'consciousness-in-general' as the symbol of man's ontological essence is not conceived in empirical, psychological, or anthropological terms. It is, rather, seen as a Mind writ large, an impersonal force responsible for knowledge as such, of which the individual minds are merely the vehicles. All this has to do with the spiritualistic background of this type of idealism; it is unrelated to the specifically democratic character of Kantian thought with which we are here concerned. Yet, within that spiritualistic tradition, the concept of 'consciousness-in-general' represents a democratizing development. In the earlier spiritualistic tradition, the Spirit was essentially superhuman and supernatural. In Kant, it appears thoroughly humanized. It is, further, a 'democratic' feature of the Kantian consciousness-in-general that its authority and dignity rest precisely upon the fact that the experiential forms, categories and ideas involved in consciousness-in-general engender universally shareable and communicable knowledge. Kant's thought is focused upon the 'transcendental' (defined by him as that upon which the possibility of experience is grounded) rather than upon the 'transcendent' (that which lies beyond experience).

3. There is only one step from the Kantian consciousness-in-general to a characteristic feature of modern, democratic society: its faith in the all-healing virtue of free discussion. Carl Schmitt was not wrong in describing this faith as fundamental to modern parliamentary democracy.[1] He was also right in pointing out that people expected so much from discussion because they believed that articles of a universal 'Reason' were present in the mind of every individual and that therefore a wholly reasonable conclusion would necessarily emerge when individual minds were rubbed together.

Pre-democratic ages have had no use for discussion. They recognized, as ways to truth, only conversion or illumination. Those who refuse themselves to the true faith are simply lost; one cannot argue with them. Likewise, in early forensic practice, 'proof' based upon orderly deduction from general principles is unknown. Judgments are 'found', either by a kind of magic, formalistic ritual, or by intuition, by appeal to a sense of justice.[2]

[1] Cf. Carl Schmitt, *Die geistesgeschichtliche Lage des heutigen Parlamentarismus*, Munich, 1923.

[Translator's Note : It is noteworthy, however, that Schmitt, following Donoso Cortés, referred to this faith in discussion in order to heap scorn upon democracy. To these anti-democratic thinkers, "discussion" was the epitome of futility.]

[2] On this early forensic practice, see Justus Möser's paper (1770), 'How Our Ancestors Shortened Trials' (Möser, *Collected Works*, Berlin, 1842–43, Vol. 1), taken up by the leader of the 'historical school' of German jurisprudence, C. von Savigny, in the school's manifesto, 'Vom Beruf unserer

Genuine 'discussion' as a way of discovering truth is found
first in a typically urban milieu, among the sophists of Greece
and in Socrates. The essential preparatory stages were scepticism and systematic doubt. When nothing was taken for
granted, one could try to find truth only by carefully defining
terms and agreeing on rational methods of deduction. In such
discussion, partners could be chosen at random (a good
argument had to be convincing to anyone); thus, Socrates
talked to anyone he met in the market-place and appealed to
the spontaneous reasoning faculty present in him. This is how
the first genuine discussions of which we have a record came
about; their essential scheme has remained unchanged to our
day.

The essential feature of genuine discussion is that no argument from authority and no dogmatic assertion based upon
mere intuition is admitted. Truth can emerge only from radical
doubt, as the residue which is left when anything that can be
doubted has been eliminated. The final conclusion must not
be held as a dogmatic belief in advance: the *possibility* of its
falsehood must be admitted, if there is to be any genuine proof.
4. The type of argument we find in the writings of the Schoolmen is, therefore, no genuine discussion in our sense. The
conclusion is given in advance; it is firmly held in an attitude
of faith. If over and above the certainty of faith rational proof
also is sought, this represents a concession to a mentality
entirely different from that of the believer. Since the 'democratic' approach of antiquity still survived in the medieval
world, demanding rational proof, the Schoolmen undertook to
provide it, i.e. to prove that which is not provable. But the
'discussion' launched under such auspices was a sham. To the
democratic mind, all initial positions have the same right to be
considered; they are all on the same level. In the scholastic
discussion, however, the initial admission of the possibility of
adverse positions was nothing but make-believe. A real latitude
existed, of course, regarding questions not decided by dogma;
but on the important issues on which the dogmatic position of
the Church was clearly defined, argument merely served to

Zeit für Gesetzgebung und Rechtswissenschaft' (1814). Cf. E. Rothacker,
'Savigny, Grimm, Ranke', in *Historische Zeitschrift*, Vol. 128 (1923), pp.
415–445.

justify an already existing belief, rather than to establish original truth.

We find such a 'scholastic' type of discussion, using rational argumentative steps to justify an independently held and dogmatically sacrosanct position, in historical situations in which the ferment of intellectual uncertainty and of a genuine search for an elusive truth still survives from earlier ages and must be silenced in the interests of conformity. We may call this the 'neutralized' type of discussion.

The sophists still lived in the element of genuine quandary and radical searching.[1] Socrates basically belonged to this type, even though his goal was to overcome uncertainty and to find final truth. In Plato, we already see the 'romantic' reaction to the rationalistic ferment of the age of the sophists—in the dialogues, the free-wheeling, unconstrained method of discussion is sometimes used to demonstrate definite theses, initially held to be certain.

5. A notable example of silencing genuine discussion by using its formal schema in order to justify a conclusion given in advance is provided by Hegelian dialectic. All the antithetical positions developed by the age of the Revolution and rationalism on the one hand, and that of the Restoration and romanticism on the other, whether in logic, or in politics, or in private experience—all these positions are represented in the theses and antitheses dialectically marshalled by Hegel. The discussion, however, is being steered towards a predetermined solution. In fact, it appeared, in Hegel's time, that a new stability, a new synthesis was emerging from the conflict of two worlds—that of feudalism and of the bourgeois. The new stability was to be based upon the consolidated position of the victorious bourgeoisie (one could not know, at the time, that this stability would soon be challenged by the new radicalism of proletarian revolutionary movements). This expectation, that of a world in which past conflicts are resolved in a higher harmony, provides the content of the Hegelian conclusions; in the dialectic, discussion 'neutralizes' itself.[2]

---

[1] Cf. the preceding chapter, 'The Problem of the Intelligentsia', in this volume.

[2] [Translator's Note: This is true of Marxist no less than of Hegelian dialectic.]

6. In genuine discussion, all participants are equally and jointly responsible for the conclusion reached. This equal distribution of *responsibility* is one of the characteristics of democratic society. It contrasts sharply with the pre-democratic order of things in which responsibility is concentrated in one point. In the old Chinese monarchy, for example, the Emperor had to be deposed if grave misfortune befell the people under his rule: this was a sign that the Emperor's life was not according to the Way (the 'tao'). In early society, responsibility is borne by charismatic personalities, prophets or saints. Later, traditionally entrenched power groups may act as guarantors of the 'correctness' of the social process. In the traditional system, the correctness and truth of the prevailing order seem to be guaranteed by the long duration of its existence. Romanticism also sees in mere 'growth' a criterion of value and rightness. It is common to all these pre-democratic patterns of order that the source of social authority is not the autonomous life of the units of society but something outside and above it—either direct divine revelation or—at times when divinity can no longer be consulted directly—tradition, time, the imperceptible 'growth' of institutions.

Authoritarian ages do not recognize the joint responsibility of all. Something like joint responsibility does, however, exist in primitive democracy (i.e. in homogeneous primitive communities). This primitive, pre-individualistic democracy must, of course, be distinguished from modern, mature democracy in which all citizens share in responsibility as autonomous agents. It is true that in the primitive democracy, authority is not hierarchically graded; all are on the same level. But at the same time, the individual is wholly controlled by the group— he cannot act or think except according to the group's directives. . . . Durkheim speaks in this sense of a 'mechanical solidarity' as characteristic of primitive societies.[1]

In modern, mature democracy, solidarity is not automatic; it must be realized anew all the time through conflict and stress. Since all social units are fully autonomous agents they would

[1] Cf. Emile Durkheim, *De la division du travail social*, Paris, 1922, esp. chaps. II and III of Book I; also P. Fauconnet, *La Responsabilité, Etude de Sociologie*, Paris, 1920, and R. Hubert, *Manuel élémentaire de Sociologie*, Paris, 1925, pp. 301 ff.

prefer to go their own way. As long as acute massification does not set in, however, a middle road on which all can agree can always be found. Impulses coming from below find adjustment in compromise expressing the representative will of the moment. At this point, only norms endorsed by all are valid; they must be constantly scrutinized, revised and reasserted from below. In this way, responsibility becomes individualized; it is, as a rule, not only implicitly assumed but also consciously experienced as such.

7. We cannot say at present whether this individualized responsibility represents the final stage of democratic development. Right now we seem to have reached a turning-point. When the incomplete democracy in which economic and intellectual élite strata occupy the positions of control is suddenly transformed into full democracy, the tendency towards the full autonomy of all social units goes to the limit and at the same time massification results in the self-neutralization of democracy.

In the incomplete democracy, the enlightened self-interest of the leading groups is tempered by the voice of conscience. While this does not result in perfect social justice, it does have the result that the individual has well-defined rights which are generally respected. This balance between morality and self-interest, however, is overthrown when propagandistic dictatorial movements come to the fore. The individual then counts for nothing. Large groups make themselves homogeneous and clash with other groups equally moving under centralized command. All the gains made in the moral sphere, such as the refinement of conscience and the tempering of interest by rational, impartial morality, are lost. Only large collective welfare interests, statistically determined, can get a hearing, aided by the aggressive élan of competing leader cliques.

8. Such things as the making, enforcement, and administration of law undergo decisive changes under the impact of the self-neutralization of democracy. Under incomplete democracy, the trend was towards an ever-growing refinement of the ethic of intention ('Gesinnungsethik') according to which the individual must be judged according to the *intent* behind his actions rather than the *effect* produced by them. This had the result that nearly every action, when sufficiently analysed and understood,

had to be excused; in the end, hardly any lawbreaker could be punished, since psychology and sociology jointly demonstrated that he could not help acting as he did. At the dictatorial stage, however, subjective intentions become wellnigh irrelevant. Nothing counts except the objective outcome of the action to be judged. Did it, or did it not, interfere with the optimal functioning of the body social?

The law at this stage has little to do with justice as a moral category. The question before the legislator is how to frame commands which, given the probability distribution of the foreseeable responses of the individuals, will minimize the likelihood of anti-social behaviour. The law, coupled with propaganda, thus becomes an instrument of social manipulation. The judge, on the other hand, will have to determine the degree of liability to punishment, not in terms of subjective intent but in terms of the actual effect that an action had upon the integrity of the existing social order. We are, in this way, thrown back to the stage of the 'mechanical solidarity' of primitive democracy—the individual is nothing but a specimen of his group.

9. Will this be the eventual consummation of the development of democracy? Nobody can tell. The phenomena we just described may well present a transitional stage. That stage may be of long duration—it will last as long as massification prevails. It must be stressed, however, that 'massification' cannot be overcome by reducing the number of individuals actively participating in the political process. The solution, in other words, cannot be found in a return to the élitist pattern of predemocratic societies or of incomplete democracy. Our culture can overcome massification only by getting away from the compulsion to integrate people in huge, homogeneous masses, in which their autonomous individuality is drowned.

The first step towards overcoming massification might consist in the creation of numerous small communities providing all their members with an opportunity to arrive at responsible, individual conclusions. In this way, the large numbers of people who participate in the political life of fully developed democracy could become rounded individuals, as were the responsible élite members at the stage of incomplete democracy. If these communities of autonomous individuals could achieve a balance among themselves, self-neutralization would gradually recede and disappear. We may look towards the emergence of such a higher type of fully democratized but no longer massified society as an ideal. In practice, however, we cannot expect such a process to unfold itself painlessly. Social learning is likely to be accomplished in painful convulsions, precisely at the stage of democracy when social energies are fully mobilized.

10. As we said in the opening section of this study, democratic society always lives under the shadow of possible disorder and chaos, since in principle all social units have a claim to assert themselves and there is no certainty that they will compromise their divergent interests and aspirations before their conflict becomes acute and violent. The democratized individual, too, is constantly aware of chaos lurking in the depths of his own personality. There is no pre-existent pattern of order guaranteed for ever in a democratic world; order and integration must always be created anew. This is essential to democracy as a way of life; it is therefore futile as well as thoughtless to condemn democracy in the name of the ideal of order. Order and fluidity, discipline and openness are antithetical human ideals which find their embodiment in different social systems of authoritarian and democratic character respectively. Neither type of society can be properly judged from a viewpoint firmly anchored in the other's basic ideals. Thus, an authoritarian thinker will be apt to be irritated by the lack of discipline and order in a democratic system and by the many abuses to which this gives rise. At the same time, however, such a critic will overlook the positive elements inherent in the very openness and formlessness of democracy.

Human existence may fall short of realizing its full potentialities if it is too systematically disciplined. If socially imposed taboos and inhibitions bar all access to the unconscious, mental and emotional life may be frozen in a rigid cast. The order thus achieved, however, will be superficial rather than real. For the forces of chaos and the impulses of the unconscious do not cease to exist when they are banished from consciousness and deprived of expression. Rigid authority, particularly in its dictatorial form, can hide them; beneath the surface, however, they will be active and may burst forth in a sudden explosion. In a democracy, potential crises announce themselves at an early stage; in this way, society is forewarned and the various social strata can immediately react to change in the pressures to which they are subjected. We may say in this sense that democracy is the most elastic (and hence adaptive) of all social systems. The impression of 'chaos' and disorder may even be wholly misleading: what appears as chaos may be, in reality, a quick, instantaneous adjustment to a series of changes. . . .

11. Full self-expression, with its positive and negative, adaptive and chaotic, potentialities, is not attained simultaneously by all social strata. It may be observed at the early stages of democratization that groups enjoying the privilege of security become fully 'mobilized' and autonomous in their thinking while the bulk of the population still persists in its tradition-bound attitudes and behaviour. Such differences in the degree of autonomy are apt to be transitory; it is a mistake to assume that they are necessary features of every social order (or, as Michels says, that all groups are necessarily and always governed by oligarchies). The long-range picture may be very different from the short-range one. In the short run, however, the differences may be very real.

We know that the thinkers of the Enlightenment felt that the common man was not yet ripe for their own rational way of thinking. Religion, they thought, was necessary to keep him within bounds. At a much later stage, when democracy degenerates into dictatorship, we see something similar. The élites at the top are purely power-minded, disillusioned, and cynical about all ideologies, including their own official one; at the same time, they see to it that the masses' faith in the official myth is kept unimpaired. The leaders' thinking is wholly reality-oriented and rational, except for the one irrationality of their lust for power; that of the masses is drugged and controlled by demagoguery.

12. Society can be governed for long stretches of time on the basis of an uneven distribution of autonomy and responsibility. Such regimes may even appear to have discovered the secret of stability, since they can manipulate their masses so well. And the masses will be quiet and contented, as long as a modicum of prosperity is maintained; what price they pay for this prosperity and order will not be immediately evident to them. The reckoning, however, will come eventually. It may come in

chaotic, irrational fashion; society may blindly stagger from one extreme to another, since the masses, unable to assign responsibilities correctly, act from mere emotional impulse. Scheler, as we noted above, expected this dominance of blind impulses to be the final stage of democratic development. It may, however, be something different—a stage in a painful learning process. For eventually, the masses which had been kept out of contact with reality will come face to face with it. They will learn to appraise policies in terms of what they do to their own interests. To be sure, an enormous price in suffering may have to be paid before the masses shed their illusions and become as enlightened, as reality-oriented, as the élites had been.

13. A more even distribution of clarity and enlightenment may also come about in a different fashion. Leading groups may discover that it is to their own interest to accelerate the process of enlightenment and learning, in view of the dangers inherent in the existence of large masses swayed by blind emotion. Educating the mass in reality-oriented ways of thinking, that is, a real democratization of the mind, is the paramount task at the stage of fully developed democracy. A certain gain in this direction could be achieved even if, at first, schools were established by the different parties to study social reality from their own partisan point of view. Teaching in such schools would be one-sided to begin with, but a less partisan approach would eventually impose itself. There are many reasons for this: the need to understand the opponent; the need to win over opponents and uncommitted groups; the need to form coalitions with others; and the need to find a common ground among major rivals who in a democracy must expect to alternate in the government and therefore must get away from the idea that once in power, they can and must make society over completely in their own image. Finally, as I said elsewhere,[1] the coexistence of rival schools of thought in itself tends to slough off whatever is extreme, one-sided and irrational in each of them.

Clearly, education in realism in this less painful fashion can be undertaken only in democracies whose functioning is not yet dominated by dictatorial and self-neutralizing forces.

[1] Cf. Karl Mannheim, 'Competition as a Cultural Phenomenon', in *Essays on the Sociology of Knowledge*, London and New York, 1952, pp. 191 ff.

D. DEMOCRATIC ÉLITES AND THEIR MODE OF
SELECTION

1. Is it not a contradiction in terms to speak about 'élites' in a democratic society? Does democratization not do away with the distinction between 'élite' and 'mass' altogether? We need not deny that a trend towards levelling, towards the abolition of élite strata, is inherent in democracy. But it is one thing to say that a trend exists, and another to assume that it must go to the limit. In all democracies that we know, it is possible to distinguish leaders from led. Does this mean merely that the democracies that have come into being thus far have been imperfect or imperfectly democratic? Should we not say, rather, that there is a democratic optimum of the élite-mass relationship which falls far short of the complete disappearance of the élite? An optimum need not be a maximum; if democracy involves an anti-élitist trend, this need not go all the way to a utopian levelling of all distinction between leaders and led.

We assume that democracy is characterized, not by the absence of all élite strata, but rather by a new mode of élite selection and a new self-interpretation of the élite. In periods of rapid change, there must be small groups that explore new cultural possibilities, and perform experiments in living for others. In this fashion they create new types of experiences which may later become the general pattern. What changes most of all in the course of democratization is the distance between the élite and the rank-and-file. The democratic élite has a mass background; this is why it can mean something for the mass. Now it may happen that, after some time, this élite abdicates its role again. The mobilized mass will then recapture the experimenting élite, and will regress to a primitive level instead of forging ahead towards a richer life. If, on the other hand, the vanguard succeeds in transmitting its new insights, first to intermediate groups and ultimately to the mass itself, the democratization of culture will be a levelling-up process rather than a trend in the direction of equalitarian mediocrity.
2. One may study the genesis and the role of élites in democratic societies from various points of view; we shall mention five important areas of research in this field. Presumably, con-

siderable research effort will be devoted to these problems in the future. In the present paper, we shall content ourselves with more general considerations of an introductory kind, without trying to treat any of the problems fully.

The problems we propose to discuss are the following:

(a) The mode of selection by which élites are recruited from the mass.

(b) The inner structure of various élite groups, their mutual relationships, and their relation to society at large.

(c) Their self-interpretation and self-evaluation, and their assessment by outsiders.

(d) The social distance between élite and mass, understood primarily as the function of élite consciousness.

(e) The cultural ideals produced by various élite groups.

We shall discuss the first three points briefly, reserving the last two for a fuller treatment.

(a) Élite Selection and Democracy

1. Élite selection assumes many forms in different societies. There are numerous shadings from unrestricted competition to rigid monopoly, as exemplified by feudal or caste stratification.

In some societies, conditions are so fluid that any individual may attain any position. The basis of selection is broadcast in pioneering societies at the earliest stages of their development. Self-governing societies of farmers usually impose few restrictions on the choice of leaders.[1] The American colonies, New Zealand, Australia, South Africa, and to some extent Brazil offer examples of this. Expanding bureaucratic empires frequently use commoners of ability in preference to hereditary privileged classes (Russia, 7th-century China, Egypt, the Roman Empire under Justinian). Commercial aristocracies (England, the Italian Renaissance cities) have often absorbed selected commoners in their élite strata while maintaining rank distinctions. In other societies, certain conditions (such as economic or military pressure) have led to rigid caste stratification, barring practically all vertical mobility; examples of this may be found from early Indonesia and India to Ethiopia and the Sudanese empires.

[1] James J. Leyburn, *Frontier Folkways*, New Haven, 1935.

2. In modern society, élite selection takes three major forms: (i) bureaucratic advancement, (ii) unregulated competition, (iii) class pressures. People who rise into élite positions show marked differences, depending on which of these three mechanisms was operative in their ascent.

The bureaucratic type of élite selection favours methodical workers who have a flair for meeting every situation in terms of prescriptions previously laid down. Their perspective must be limited to rules and regulations; individuals who show free-ranging interests and propensities for improvisation are passed over in promotion.

As against the systematic and prearranged pattern of bureaucratic advancement, competition for leadership in political arenas such as nineteenth-century parliaments is unregulated. The essential thing for the seeker of political prominence in that milieu was not proficiency in some special field, but a generalized popular appeal and magnetism, compounded of oratorical ability, stamina, identification with collective causes, intellectual resourcefulness, and so on, down to such elusive but important things as erotic glamour.

With the rise of class parties in the 20th century, political success began to depend to a lesser extent on personal magnetism and more on party regularity. Not the personal endowment of the individual but the strength of the group which he represents is basic for advancement into political élite positions.

3. In so far as the difference between democratic and non-democratic élite selection is concerned, the most important thing is obviously the *breadth of the basis* of selection. A system is democratic only if élite recruitment is not limited to members of a closed group. But even where élite recruitment is democratic in this sense, élites different in their structure and self-interpretation may be formed, depending on certain aspects of the *mode* of their recruitment.

There is a characteristic difference in this respect between the mode of recruitment of liberal and labour leaders. The former rise in the political world individually, that is, the degree of influence and of political power that they achieve does not depend on the increase in power of any given social stratum. A labour politician, however, rises in the political world only if, and because, labour as an entire group rises. This difference in the origin of the élite position of the two types leads to characteristic differences in their mentality.

Before labour parties appeared on the European political scene, the rise of politicians to prominence and power was largely an individual affair. When a politician achieved fame and influence, he did not feel that he owed this to his being associated with a distinct stratum or interest group. Had he chosen to represent another interest group (e.g. protectionists instead of free-traders), he would have made his mark nevertheless; it all was a matter of his own superior gifts. Such personal histories tended to produce a 'heroic' posture and a general outlook according to which one's career depends on his own endowment rather than on the impersonal social configurations within which destiny has placed him. 'Life', according to this philosophy, gives the same opportunities to everyone; there are everywhere chances to be exploited.

Against such a background, rise into an élite position (not only in political careers but also in a competitive economy) appears like the fruit of personal achievement. Newcomers who enter the ranks of the élite by such a route tend to believe in the decisive role of the exceptional individual in human affairs. In drama, they look for strong-willed heroes; in history, for great personalities. Nor can we say that, as professed by this type, individualism is a mere ideology, unrelated to real life as he experiences it. This individualism is a straightforward enough distillation of a peculiar kind of life experience, even though it is wholly inadequate as a general theory. For a sociologist, it is easy enough to see the working of social configurations where the naive individualist perceives only personal merit and achievement.

This 'heroic' type of individualism is capable of great spiritual sublimation. In German idealism, the individualist outlook of the liberal bourgeoisie has achieved depth and moral dignity. Yet idealism and its successor, existentialism, also tend to isolate the individual from his fellows, and to make him blind to man's dependence on fellowship and communication. In their metaphysics, these types conceive of man as a non-intercommunicating monad. What one man can mean to another finds no recognition in this philosophy of the self-made man.

The typical outlook of labour politicians achieving élite positions is entirely different. It is not true, of course, that the group they represent rises together with them; on the contrary, they enter a higher social stratum when they become influential. Yet they cannot forget for a moment that their own rise in society has been indissolubly linked to their identification with a particular group interest and with the relative increase in that group's influence. Even when they leave their original social peers far behind and ascend to a lonely peak of eminence, they are not likely to generalize this experience in terms of a 'great man' theory of history. They are far likelier to hold that group forces and collective factors are behind the achievement of the individual. As we see, élites differing as to their mode of recruitment are apt for this very reason to adopt a different outlook towards 'life' and 'destiny'.

An analogous difference may be seen in the attitudes of these two types of élite member towards culture and civilization. In keeping with their 'heroic' and individualistic outlook, élite members who rise individually are likely to feel that the highest peaks, the great masterpieces are the essential content of culture. The works of supreme geniuses determine the value of a culture as a whole. Culture appears here, not as a continuous flow of cooperative achievement, but as a discontinuous series of sublime moments of creation. The average, the day-to-day effort of the many is devalued. This is, however, what élites recruited by a collective mechanism view as the essence of the cultural process. Their self-esteem is rooted in modesty. They like to contemplate the gradual accumulation of small gains, the confluence of many tiny streams into a mighty river. Continuity in space and time is what they value, and they emphasize transitions and differences in degree where the other type focuses upon qualitative, essential differences. In education, they hold the good average to be more important than the top achievement; in history, they maintain that the destiny of groups, and of mankind as a whole, depends more on the steady efforts of the anonymous mass than on the awe-inspiring flights of rare genius.[1] Needless to say that it is the outlook

[1] [Translator's Note: While such typical differences in outlook probably did exist in nineteenth- and twentieth-century Germany, nothing corresponding to them is likely to be demonstrable in modern American society. For

of the collectively recruited élite which corresponds to the 'democratizing' trend with which we are concerned in this paper.

(b) Group Structure and Relation to Other Groups

The inner organizational structure of élite groups and their relative position towards other groups also have important consequences for their interpretation of man and the world. For example, in the Middle Ages, the intellectual élite of university teachers was organized in corporations and thus had the same position within society at large as any other officially recognized autonomous occupational group. In the 19th century, on the other hand, the social position of a large sector of the intellectual élite was that of the bohemian, without corporate ties, without a well-defined place in society; the members of this group lived in a curious milieu in which self-styled or genuine men of genius were thrown together with black sheep from aristocratic or bourgeois families, déclassé drifters, prostitutes, matinée idols, and other fugitives from organized society. Even for young men who later were content to enter well-regulated bureaucratic or professional careers, it was customary to spend a few anarchic and unregulated years while they were students. All this exerted a considerable influence upon their thinking. Where intellectual élite groups exist outside normal society, the ideas produced by them are likely to have a 'romantic' tinge. Such intellectuals will cultivate a set of values far removed from the concerns of ordinary people. As artists, they will become aesthetes dedicated to the cult of *l'art pour l'art*; as thinkers, they will seek the abstruse and the esoteric. This is inevitable in a society which has no need for the services of the intellectual in pursuing its 'serious' business. But the scene may change. During periods of acute social conflict, political ringleaders may become acutely aware of the propagandist potential of art. They will then take the artist seriously and give him a 'responsible' job; the artist may respond by

one thing, America lacks a political élite group of labour background, since there is no labour party contending for governmental positions on the national scale. For another, the philosophy of the American self-made man involves no excessive admiration for political, artistic, scientific, or philosophical genius.]

becoming politicized and adopting the belief that only 'socially significant' art is good art.

We assume that 'democratization' involves a lessening of the distance between intellectual élite groups and the other sectors of society. As democratization progresses, the ties between intellectual strata and society at large are likely to become closer and more organic. This need not mean that art will become crudely propagandist, but only that it will have a more organic function in life than '*l'art pour l'art*' has had.

(c) The Self-Evaluation of Aristocratic and Democratic Élites

The problem of the self-evaluation of intellectual élite groups has been treated in detail elsewhere.[1] From the point of view of the 'democratization' of culture, the important thing is to see how the self-evaluation of cultural élite groups changes as the culture becomes more democratic.

Intellectual groups existing in an aristocratic environment are apt to see themselves as they appear to their social superiors. The self-esteem of the artist depends on his success in acquiring aristocratic patrons; that of the teacher, on the relative number of his aristocratic pupils. Gradually, however, these groups develop standards independent of the verdict of the socially dominant groups. How intellectual peers judge each other will be more important than how they are judged by outsiders. Finally, the standards in terms of which the cultural élite judges itself become less exclusive and narrow. Intellectual prowess which sets the élite apart from the uninitiated both in high and low social groups will no longer be treated as the supreme human value. The intellectual will no longer look down upon the manual worker, just as he is not looking up to the aristocrat. He will treat his speciality as being essentially on a par with other skills—possibly superior to others in quantitative terms as involving more knowledge and training, but not superior in an essential and qualitative terms, as the realization of a higher human type.

(d) Social Distance and the Democratization of Culture

1. The word 'distance' designates in ordinary usage spatial

[1] See the essay on 'The Problem of the Intelligentsia' in this volume.

distance between things.[1] In the present context, however, we shall apply the word (metaphorically) to social rather than spatial relationships, and we shall be interested not so much in static distances as in acts *creating* distance (as when a thing is moved *away from* another). Distance as a social phenomenon is *produced by* agents who are interested in maintaining social distance between themselves and others, precisely when they live closely together in a spatial sense.

Social 'distantiation' in this sense is akin to, but not identical with, 'alienation'. The latter consists in the cooling off of emotional relationships. When we become 'alienated' from someone, we undo ties of identification that formerly had bound us together. Similarly, we may become 'alienated' from places or groups in which we had once felt at home. But this is not what makes the essence of distantiation.

The element of spontaneous activity 'creating' a distance is well brought out in a visual example used by Bullough.[2] A ship is approaching port: the town can be seen quite distinctly. Then mist descends and the town again 'recedes into the distance'. This is 'distantiation', for the town remains spatially near; it becomes more distant only in a psychological sense. Of course, however, it is not the subject's social act which creates the distance; the subject merely registers greater distance because his sight is blurred by mist.

In the social field, 'distantiation' may well express itself, quite literally, in a movement away from the other, as when we keep ourselves at a distance from a threatening individual. Such behaviour is often found in animals.[3] In Révész' observations on monkeys, the first few times the animals were fed, each

[1] On the problem of social distance, cf. G. Simmel, *Soziologie*, Leipzig, 1908, pp. 321 ff. and 687 ff. R. E. Park, 'The Concept of Social Distance', *Journal of Applied Sociology*, vol. VIII, No. 6, E. S. Bogardus, 'Social Distance and Its Origin', *Journal of Applied Sociology*, 1925, W. C. Poole, Jnr., 'Distance in Sociology', *American Journal of Sociology*, Vol. XXXIII, 1927. R. E. Park and E. W. Burgess, *Introduction to the Science of Sociology*, London and Chicago, 1924, p. 440. L. von Wiese, *System der allgemeinen Soziologie*, 2nd ed., pp. 160 ff. A. Walther, 'Soziale Distanz', *Kölner Vierteljahrshefte für Soziologie*, 1931, pp. 263 ff.

[2] Cf. E. Bullough, 'Psychical Distance as a Factor in Art and an Aesthetic Principle', *British Journal of Psychology*, vol. V, 1912–13, pp. 87 ff.

[3] Cf. Géza Révész, 'Sozialpsychologische Beobachtungen an Affen', *Zeitschrift für Psychologie*, vol. 118, 1930. The author points out that there

monkey sought to fight off all others, but as soon as one animal established its superiority over all others, all except the weakest and hence privileged 'baby' kept a safe distance from the champion, particularly at feeding time. Dominance and fear imposed both spatial and social distance.[1]

We assume that social 'distantiation' first appears in the form of avoiding actions actually creating spatial distance. Later, social distantiation becomes more 'sublimated', no longer necessarily requiring *spatial* avoidance. Certain types of distance-creating behaviour, however, are still being characterized in everyday speech by means of spatial metaphors, as when we speak of somebody being kept 'at arm's length'. Such expressions have the connotation that a distance greater than normal, or than expected by the subject who is kept 'at arm's length', has been created. Within each social milieu there is a 'normal' distance which interacting individuals are supposed to observe. Deviations from the norm are noted as undue 'aloofness' or as uncalled-for 'forwardness'. Metaphors involving spatial distance are typically used to characterize such infringements of rules for social behaviour. The ritual of social intercourse changes when we pass from one degree of intimacy to another; when, in a situation calling for the observance of one ritual, a person incongruously applies another, our feeling is that he is 'too close' or 'too distant'. In the case of objects of everyday use or works of art, too, we may speak of the 'normal' distance at which they should be located.

Another important example of social distance is the vertical distance between hierarchical unequals: the distance created by power. This is reflected in an enormous number of behaviour patterns developed by hierarchically stratified societies. We may mention differences in dress from one caste or class to another, differential modes of address, ceremonials of deference, gestures of submission, and so on. In the sociology of culture, and in such a study as ours in particular, the problem of vertical

are 'fundamental social power relationships which come into being regardless of the intellectual level of the species in question' (p. 148).

[1] For similar observations, cf. S. Zuckerman, *The Social Life of Monkeys and Apes*, London and New York, 1932; C. R. Carpenter, 'Field Study in Siam of the Behaviour and Social Relations of the Gibbon', *Comparative Psychology Monographs*, vol. 16, No. 5, December, 1940.

distance and distantiation is, of course, paramount. It is important to see that vertical distantiation may concern, not only the
mutual relationship of two groups, but also the relationship
between a person or group and inanimate objects of cultural
significance. There is, in other words, a difference of 'high' and
'low' among cultural products. This spatial metaphor is neatly
illustrated by cases in which things of 'high' significance, like
objects of worship, are placed so high that one has to look up
to them. In speech also, there is a difference between 'high'
and 'low'. Certain 'high' subjects demand a solemn vocabulary
and cadenced delivery, while 'lower' topics can be treated in
a less strait-laced fashion. In the erotic sphere, the difference
between 'high' and 'low' is particularly conspicuous: idealizing
'love' comes into being through a 'distantiation' of sexuality,
and the object of such love is put on a 'pedestal', just as the
experience itself is of a 'higher' nature. . . .

Beyond 'social' distantiation, whether in the sense of vertical
distantiation or degree of intimacy, one may discern a more
fundamental type of distance between man and man that we
may call 'existential' distance. This is the distance between the
I and the other purely as a person, regardless of conventional-
ized social relationships. Sometimes the other himself, as a
person, is extremely vivid for me in an upsurge of empathy; at
other times, he recedes into an existential distance, he is not
real and present to me as a person. A particular variant of
existential distantiation is self-distantiation: the experience that
I am a stranger to myself, or rather that I can be more or less
close to myself. Like other forms of existential distantiation,
self-distantiation cannot well be observed in isolation from its
concrete, social, and historical context. There are cultural and
social constellations which virtually impose self-distantiation;
others make it possible to overcome self-distantiation, to recover
oneself. During such epochs, many individuals seek to restore
the integrity of their existence, to get closer to the real core of
their being. . . .

The various types of 'distantiation' we have just distinguished
are subject to change in the course of history, and it is the task
of cultural sociology to ascertain the regularities involved in
this process. Our own leading hypothesis is that the most
fundamental, causally decisive type of distantiation is the social

one. How the pattern of distantiation of cultural objects (see p. 207 above) changes will be determined by what happens in the sphere of power, that is, of vertical distantiation. In fact, the fundamental character of a culture as an aristocratic or democratic one depends primarily on its vertical distance patterns. Democratization means essentially a reduction of vertical distance, a de-distantiation.

2. Let us consider, for example, a pre-democratic (aristocratic or monocratic) culture. Its essential feature is the 'vertical distance' between the rulers and the ruled—and we mean this in the sense that innumerable psychic acts asserting and acknowledging that vertical distance are the chief mechanism through which the rulers wield power. Of course, the rulers control a great many material instruments that help them maintain their power (e.g., weapons and means of communication), but it is not these material things that endow them with power. It is, essentially, their subjects' propensity to look up to them, to consider them as higher beings.

Hierarchically organized groups within the larger society, such as armies and bureaucracies, may also be considered in this sense as products of acts of distantiation. The regular and reliable occurrence of these acts makes these organizations what they are. Vertical distance is the constitutive principle in which the very existence of such groups is grounded.

In the aristocratic society, the ruling strata 'create' a distance between themselves and the lower groups by meeting the members of the latter, so to speak, from a higher level. Every contact between 'high' and 'low' is made subject to a highly formalized ritual. Dominating the lower groups is not merely a matter of giving orders and enforcing obedience. It consists, to a very large extent, in the maintenance of a vertical distance which becomes an organic part of the thinking, not only of the rulers but also of the ruled. This psychic distantiation is just as much a part of the aristocratic hierarchical order as is the uneven distribution of advantages and risks.

Strict standards of conduct, prescribing a formal etiquette for every occasion, are a powerful instrument for maintaining distance. Aristocratic cultures frown upon spontaneous, impulsive behaviour which is deemed vulgar. They adopt such behavioural ideals as the Greek 'kalokagathia' or the medieval

German *mâze* (measure); we may also mention in this context the code of chivalrous conduct worked out by the Provençal nobility which became a universal norm. These examples show that aristocratic cultures tend to maximize distance not only in the vertical dimension, i.e., between 'high' and 'low' groups, but also among equals. The typically aristocratic attitude is 'distance' and formality even in the intimate circle.

Distantiation in the hierarchically organized society affects not only inter-personal relations but also attitudes towards cultural objects. Certain social norms and institutions are endowed with absolute authority—critical thoughts concerning them are tabooed. Aristocratic societies have their official philosophy which must on no account be questioned.

Aristocratic élites typically seek to create an 'élite culture' of their own. They see to it that certain essential features of their group culture, such as forms of social intercourse, pastimes, patterns of speech, but also various techniques and systems of knowledge, shall be unshareable by the many. (Intellectual élite groups of the aristocratic type, such as priestly castes, adopt in this vein sacred languages of their own such as Sanskrit or Latin.)

The adoption of the vernacular for literary or liturgical purposes is, considered from this angle, an important vehicle of the democratization of culture, and so is the irruption of 'lower' (technological and industrial) concerns into the sacred precincts of 'science'.

Aristocratic speech is typically formal, stereotyped, and stylized. Its horizon is severely limited: certain 'low' objects are excluded from it. Things which have the greatest urgency for strata struggling for bare existence, such as food and money, and the means of satisfying elementary needs in general, must not be mentioned. On the aristocratic level, one pretends not to notice such elementary concerns. This finickiness and delicacy becomes more extreme as an aristocratic group grows older, and comes to consist of members who have inherited (but not created) their privileged position. A 'first generation of a ruling group which has a direct experience of risk and struggle in war or in finance does not yet possess this extreme delicacy. Its descendants, however, tend to look away from the 'facts of life' until they no longer live in the world of real things but in a second world of artificial symbols.[1] The 'cultivated' speech of these sheltered upper strata separates them from the common man; this is one of the most important social barriers between classes in stratified societies. Where 'high' and 'low' speech exist side by side, full intercommunication is no longer possible. To the common man, elegant speech appears unnatural and hypocritical; to the upper strata, popular speech is coarse, brutal, and degrading.

One of the symptoms of distantiation is the tendency of terms designating lower social groups to acquire a pejorative value connotation. A well-known example is the change in the meaning of the word 'villain' in English and 'vilain' in French. Originally, these words designated the 'villager'; in modern English, the word is a synonym of 'rogue', and in French, it means 'ugly'.[2] Words originally referring to élite strata tend to change their meaning in the opposite direction (cf. 'courteous').

We may see a further characteristic of aristocratic speech patterns in their tendency towards rigid regularity; they seek to exclude the 'chaotic' and irregular. Fulfilling the requirements of an aristocratic society, the French Academy in the 17th century undertook the standardization of the French language. The French linguist Brunot made a painstaking study comparing the *Dictionary* of the French Academy (1st ed., 1694) with a later, unofficial and 'democratic' document, the French *Encyclopedia*.[3] He found that the *Encyclopedia* used an infinitely richer vocabulary, since it treated in systematic fashion a large number of technological and industrial processes which the Dictionary had excluded from consideration. According to Brunot, the difference is not one of subject matter only; the entire use of the language is a different one, since the 'new' language is replete with metaphors and turns of phrase inspired by 'vulgar' concerns, while the 'old'

[1] On this difference between generations, cf. Richard Hamann, *Die Frührenaissance der italienischen Malerei*, Jena, 1909, pp. 2 ff.

[2] On the changed meaning of 'villain', see Carl Brinkmann, *Wirtschafts- und Sozialgeschichte*, Berlin and Munich, 1927, p. 40.

[3] Cf. Frédéric Brunot, *Histoire de la langue française des origines à 1900*, vol. VI, Paris, 1930.

one largely limited itself to courtly, refined phrases and metaphors.[1]

3. The study of certain changes in fashionable vocabulary enables us to follow the process of democratization of culture. It is a symptom of democratization that certain key terms antithetical to the static and hierarchical spirit of aristocratic culture become fashionable in times of transition. We have already referred to the changed meaning of the term 'organism' in a similar context. Brunot, in the work cited above, refers to the vogue enjoyed by the term 'fermentation' as one of the symptoms of the change in outlook described by him. Other words which (although coined earlier) come into general use during the 18th century include 'social' and 'civilisation': their new vogue reflects a general re-orientation of thinking, a branching out into new realms of experience. 'Progress', of course, is a key term summarizing one of the chief aspirations of the Enlightenment period.[2] Together with the related term 'evolution', it signalizes nothing less than the advent of a new ontology, of the rethinking of the sum and substance of human experience from a radically new viewpoint. The static ontology which equated 'real' being with what is unchanging and permanent is replaced by a dynamic one, intent upon seizing 'real' being precisely in whatever is going through a process of change.[3]

[1] [Translator's Note: It should be noted that the change in question was one of content and style, rather than of linguistic form. The Encyclopedists expressed their unorthodox views in an academically correct language. Throughout the literary and political upheavals of recent times, the standardization of the French Language, initiated before the foundation of the Academy but codified by the latter, has remained virtually unchallenged.]

[2] On the history of the idea of progress, cf. Jules Delvaille, 'Essai sur l'histoire de l'idée de progrès jusqu'à la fin du XVIIᵉ siècle', Doctorate thesis, Paris, 1910; V. de P. M. Brunetière, 'La formation de l'idée de progrès au XVIIIᵉ siècle', in Études critiques sur l'histoire de la litterature française, 5me série, Paris 1902–07, 6th ed., 1922 ; J. B. Bury, The Idea of Progress, London and New York, 1932.

[3] On these implications of 'progress' and 'evolution', cf. F. Brunot, op. cit., pp. 107 ff.; John Dewey, 'Progress', in International Journal of Ethics, vol. 26, 1905; A. J. Todd, Theories of Social Progress, New York, 1918; W. R. Inge, 'The Idea of Progress', in Outspoken Essays, London and New York, 1922; W. H. Mallock, Aristocracy and Evolution, London and New York, 1898; W. F. Willcox, 'A Statistician's Idea of Progress', International Journal of Ethics, vol. 23, 1902.

It is one of the characteristics of this new ontology that it puts 'function' and 'process' in the place of 'Gestalt'. Conservative thought is 'morphological'. It explains the world in terms of unanalysed and unanalysable given wholes in their unique *Gestalt*. As against this, liberal and progressive thought is analytical; it decomposes the seemingly monolithic entities of the traditional world view into functional elements. The sociological explanation of this dichotomy is a complex and difficult matter, but one aspect of it at least may become clearer precisely through the use of our concept of distantiation. '*Gestalt*', in fact, is the product of a specific type of distantiation. A social entity like a group or an institution will appear to me as a static whole, a *Gestalt*, only if I am far enough removed from it, that is, from a distance. If I am a part of the group myself, I can see from within both its internal divisions and the mechanism that makes it run. For someone far removed from the governmental sphere—say, a provincial farmer—'the government' is a monolithic unit, something like a mythical figure or a person. The insider, however, has a very different picture of the whole thing—he sees intrigues, jockeying for position, competition—anything but monolithic unity. In short, the outsider must see things morphologically; the insider, analytically.

4. If we combine this conclusion with some of our earlier findings concerning different modes of élite selection, it will be seen immediately how democratization entails a shift from the morphological to the analytical outlook. In status-bound societies without vertical mobility, the morphological view is practically all-pervading. The mass of people is in the position of the outsider, contemplating from afar the central authorities like the Papacy or the Empire. These powers have their unique, *Gestalt*-like concreteness; the people experience them through the medium of their symbolism and their ritual. What actually goes on 'within' the precincts of power is shrouded in mystery. The secret was pierced for the first time in the West during the Renaissance period, when in the course of social changes new élites penetrated into the top region and came to see the actual process instead of the stereotyped symbol. We may mention Machiavelli as one of the first writers to analyse events in the highest strata of society in terms of a mundane power process,

stripped of their metaphysical aura of mystery. This disillusioned, realistic, analytical attitude towards 'high politics' eventually became quite universal in the 17th century. It came to be taken for granted that the substance of politics is a struggle for power in which everything is calculable and nothing is sacred.

The same sequence, running from the mystifying concealment of the realities of the power process to their disrespectful debunking, repeated itself in more recent times. During the age of absolutism, the disillusioned and analytical attitude towards the political facts of life was in no way prejudicial to authoritarian rule, because that attitude was largely confined to the wielders of power themselves. They could afford to look at their world without prettifying illusions, since their authority was unchallenged. The people did not participate in the political process and was not aware of its inner mechanism; again it perceived the central authorities as a towering *Gestalt*. When the process of democratization began, however, large groups of outsiders became interested in the governmental process and challenged the authority of the rulers. Public opinion demanded an accounting for the exercise of authority, and a wholly realistic account, admitting that all was merely a matter of power and nothing else, would have been quite unsatisfactory. It became necessary to idealize the process, and to provide ideological justifications of power. It was at that time that the theory of the state as a civilizing agency was developed.[1] This corresponded to the novel need felt by the bourgeois middle class and the professional bureaucracy to experience authority, not as naked power, but as an instrument of the universal good. Such ideologies of power, however, lost their suggestive force when very large numbers of people, formerly excluded from political influence and from higher education, penetrated into the sphere of government and of official culture. As they took cognizance of the inner workings of the system of which they previously had only seen the symbolic façade, their awe and respect were gone. Democratization,

[1] Cf. Friedrich Meinecke, *Die Idee der Staatsräson in der neueren Geschichte*, Munich, 1925 (English Translation, London and New Haven, 1956), p. 353; also Karl Mannheim, *Ideology and Utopia*, London and New York, 1936.

in fact, means disillusionment; it is often pointed out that democratic parliamentary regimes cannot command respect because the public is constantly aware of the non-edifying bickering among parties that makes up much of the parliamentary process. We may also mention in this context the 'iconoclastic' aspects of the sociology of knowledge. The latter, in fact, refuses to contemplate the representative works of a culture 'at a distance' and adopts an analytical attitude towards them, exploring the minute interrelationships among the myriad impulses impinging upon the cultural process. Thus, the advent of mass democracy puts 'analysis' in the place of 'Gestalt', just as the novel analytical methods discovered by Machiavelli's generation did. There is, however, a difference between the two epochs; during the Renaissance, only a few exceptional intellectuals practised the 'analytical' view, whereas in the age of modern mass democracy, this approach is universally shared. The secret of political analysis is no longer confined to 'manuals for the Prince' or to 'Political Testaments' for the use of the élite but becomes altogether public.

When this happens, the emphasis is placed in the beginning upon the ressentiment-laden 'unmasking' of the evil practices of power-holders. Such a response is understandable when people see for the first time the profane reality behind the sacred symbols that they had been led to adore from afar. The joy of debunking, however, is of short duration; in time, the realities of the power process come to be taken for granted. The dominant feeling then tends to be one of concern about this Leviathan, together with a sense of responsibility for taming him. In pre-democratic times, the masses, while reduced to a passive role, had also the advantage of not being burdened with responsibility for the shaping of their own destiny. The world was simple, traditional routine took care of most economic and social problems, and where decisions had to be made, these could be entrusted to a central élite. Democratization, on the other hand, seems to be associated with a growing complexity of the social and economic process, involving the necessity of making choices and of applying analysis instead of just trusting in the automatic working of tradition.

All this does not mean to say that the advent of the modern analytic approach is solely a matter for the broadening of the élite. In fact, it may happen that participation in the decision-making process becomes broader and more democratic without a noticeable advance in analytical thinking taking place. For the latter to come about, a certain maturity of critical intelligence is needed, an ability to overcome the suggestive power of symbols, resulting from 'distantiation'. But mere change in social location does not necessarily create this ability; the latter must have other sources as well. We may say, however, that greater proximity to the seat of power is *necessary* (without being sufficient) for the discovery of its inner mechanism.

5. A contrast similar to the one just discussed is that between 'genetic' and 'systematic' thinking. The modern, analytic mind prefers to use the 'genetic' approach, whereas authoritarian cultures recoil from it and seek a system of timeless truth, untouched by historical changes and vicissitudes. To the authoritarian mind, 'validity' must be independent of 'genesis'.[1]

This contrast again seems to be analysable in terms of 'distance'. Traditional authority, perpetuating itself through a series of generations, gradually pushes its origin back into a mythical distance. Such distant origins are incommensurable with anything that can be observed here and now; authority, then, comes to be experienced as timeless and existing by necessity. Traditionally sanctioned authority leaves no room for the idea that 'things could be otherwise'; its wielder acts as if he were just a timeless embodiment of superiority. When a new generation grows up in a traditionally governed society, it will tend to grant these claims of the authority-wielders, since its members cannot remember any time when things were different. Such generations, then, are not likely to think in 'genetic' or analytical terms. Sceptical, 'destructive', analytical thinking is likely to be found among the members of generations that had gone through radical changes in the realm of power.[2]

It is clear from the preceding discussion that the traditional way of thinking, while antithetical to the genetic method, does not ignore the problem of the origins; what it does is to place them at a mythical distance where they are no longer subject

[1] Cf. Karl Mannheim, *op. cit.*

[2] Cf. 'The Problem of Generations', in Karl Mannheim, *Essays on the Sociology of Knowledge*, London and New York, 1952, pp. 276 ff.

to realistic analysis. The origin of power is not laid bare but concealed in a sacred myth. A later variant of the conservative philosophy of history replaces the supra-rational myth by a rationalistic interpretation. History appears as meaningful, as the unfolding of a rational plan. Such interpretations serve as a justification of the prevailing authoritarian order. How power is generated—this question remains unexamined; it is banished from consciousness. A democratic society, however, cannot well ignore the problem of the genesis of power, since its mechanism involves precisely the generation of power in the course of the democratic process.

Nevertheless, this point is not valid without qualification. In democratic societies, too, the origin of power and authority is subject to a certain amount of distantiation, in keeping with our general point that democracy reduces vertical social distance without completely eliminating it. Distantiation does not disappear in democracy; it merely assumes a different form. Accordingly, democracy does not dissolve *every* problem of social authority into a problem of genesis. It uses genetic analysis to discredit pre-democratic authority, but its own basis of authority is also 'distantiated' in a certain way. How does this democratic distantiation differ from the traditional one? Primarily, one may suggest, through its *impersonal* character.

Traditional authority is centred in persons or families elevated above the rest of society and endowed with personal or hereditary charisma. The origin of this authority is often spelled out in myths: the Japanese Mikado as 'Son of Heaven', the high castes of India as 'Sons of the North'. Democratic authority, however, is not bound to any person as such. It is conferred only temporarily and conditionally upon certain individuals. But while the mythically sanctioned distantiation of persons is absent in democracy, the fundamental institutions do become 'distantiated'. They are elevated to symbolic dignity as myths. The electoral procedure or basic documents like the Constitution come to play such a mythical role.

Under certain conditions, individuals do achieve a heightened position in a democratic society as stars, idols, and popular heroes; but this is due to specific factors that need not detain us here. Myths that are organic to democracy grow up around collective concepts like Rousseau's 'volonté générale'. We look at this in an un-mythical, realistic way, as a certain mechanism of social integration; for Rousseau himself, however, the concept has a transcendent meaning.

6. We may mention, as a typically democratic instance of 'distantiation', the treatment of 'abstract' collective entities ('abstrakte Kollektiva' in L. von Wiese's terminology) as concrete, active subjects: the 'state', the 'party', the 'class', and so on. Similarly, processes are sometimes transformed into substances: 'socialism', 'romanticism' as substance-like entities. The treatment of business corporations as 'juristic persons' illustrates the same tendency. It is characteristic that conservative thinkers have vehemently opposed the 'distantiation' of such abstract and rational entities as 'the state' or 'law'. For these thinkers, a collective entity *could* be endowed with authority, but only if (like the Church) it presented itself in a rich garb of symbolism that put it above and beyond everyday reality. No authority could accrue to mere 'profane' instruments of social integration.[1] The modern mind, however, tends to isolate certain strands of social reality and endow them with a higher, metaphysical dignity (cf. the Marxist treatment of History as a dialectical drama enacted by antithetical social forces).

This combination of the analytical approach with distance-creating myth-making introduces a certain ambiguity into democratic thought. We find an integrally analytical, nominalist outlook in democratized groups only when they are in the opposition. And even this is not true of all of them. Liberals and anarchists lean towards integral nominalism, but the Marxists oppose their own brand of 'realism' (the term is used here, of course, in the sense of the medieval dichotomy of realism v. nominalism) to the conservative brand. All that we can say is that the analytic and nominalist approach is likely to come to the fore when the democratizing trend is dominant, so that eventually the democratic 'distantiation' of abstract entities, too, will be subjected to critique. But critical analysis cannot hope to eliminate *all* distantiation whatever.

[1] The clash between the conservative view and the modern 'distantiation' of rational, social instrumentalities is vividly illustrated in Hegel's polemic against the conservative von Haller, cf. *Philosophy of Law*, pars. 257–59.

In the above, we contrasted pre-democratic distantiation (putting persons or concrete groups upon an inaccessibly high pedestal) with democratic distantiation (personifying and hypostatizing abstract entities). The latter is, in fact, far more characteristic of our own age than the former. Nevertheless, it would be a mistake to see in Western history a unilinear progress from the 'pre-democratic' to the 'democratic'. What is 'later' is not necessarily more 'democratic'. Thus, we may already look upon the Middle Ages as driving underground the earlier, typically urban and rationalistic tradition of the Greek city states. As against this, the dominant culture of the Middle Ages stressed irrational, mystical, 'primitive' thought patterns, even though elements of the rationalistic tradition of antiquity were preserved precisely in learned clerical circles. Further, a genuine process of cultural democratization set in during the late Middle Ages when urban groups became culturally dominant in Europe. After this early upsurge of democratization, a retrograde tendency set in, and European society became 're-feudalized'. We shall now discuss these phenomena in some detail.

7. We shall turn first to the democratizing tendency as it manifested itself in the late Middle Ages. The underlying social change—i.e., the growing strength of urban groups—was accompanied by radical stylistic transformations in the realm of art, literature, and religion. To begin with art: contrasting with the highly stylized, unrealistic character of earlier medieval painting and sculpture, late medieval art about 1370 begins to be dominated by what might be called 'intimate realism' ('Nahrealismus'). The essence of this new style is that all things are represented as they appear in the context of man's everyday activities. In this we see a radically new attitude, a revolutionary self-assertion of man who discovers the dignity of his normal, ordinary activity. The phenomenon can best be characterized as one of *de-distantiation*. Sociologically, it is intimately connected with the rise of urban democracy in which the individual found an ever-widening scope for influencing political, economic, and cultural life. The distance separating the average individual from the central authorities became less; culture responded to this by boldly adopting the everyday perspective of the average individual as the one valid for art and religion.

The perspective of everyday life had, of course, existed before, but it could not be culturally representative; this became possible only when the changed social background resulted in a shift of the ontological accent towards what was experienced as 'real' in everyday life.

An analogous trend may be observed in church architecture. Early medieval churches show in their architecture maximal 'distance' between the faithful and the priest; the altar, scene of the central act of the Catholic cult, is placed at the end of parallel naves, symbolizing the 'infinite' distance between man and the object of his faith. Late medieval churches, however, have a more intimate character. They serve for private worship as well as for the exceptional solemnity of high mass.[1] The layman plays a more conspicuous and active role in the Church, and the interior of church building visibly reflects this: the lateral naves disappear, and the interior becomes an undivided hall.[2] The altar can be seen from every point. There is no longer one exclusive, privileged perspective pointing towards the altar; it may now be viewed from every direction. In this lack of a privileged axis of orientation we see an expression of a new attitude. It reflects, not chaos and disorder, but a novel desire for clarity which is characteristic of the new urban middle class. It must be possible to grasp the entire space from every point. This transparency of the surrounding space reflects a changed attitude of faith. The earlier sense of awe-inspiring, inscrutable mystery gives way to a sense of security and confidence. The 'distance' between the average individual and the central symbols and objects of faith diminishes. Religion becomes less anxiety-laden. We can observe a parallel change in medieval social relationships; while feudal authority is distant, mysterious, and anxiety-provoking, the social climate in the cities is characterized by far greater rationality and security. Social distance between the élite and the people again tends to become greater during the subsequent period. The culture of the Baroque age is far more aristocratic than that of the late medieval urban culture. But at any rate late

[1] Cf. Dehio, *Geschichte der deutschen Kunst*, Berlin-Leipzig, 1919, vol. II, p. 135.

[2] On this change, cf. Bechtel, *Wirtschaftsstil des späten Mittelalters*, Munich-Leipzig, 1930, pp. 59–66.

medieval church architecture with its development of the undivided hall shows a maximum of security within the community.

Did this change in church architecture precede or follow an analogous transformation of the social structure? The historian Bechtel, whom we have been following in our discussion of late medieval church architecture, comes to the conclusion that the change in architectural forms antedated the corresponding change in economic life.[1] The artist according to him creates new forms in his medium before society at large changes its character; economic changes are determined by changes in the realm of ideas, not *vice versa*. This conclusion, however, is open to doubt. To be sure, we see a fully developed economic system based upon new techniques and concepts only after the parallel transformation of art has run its full course. But this does not mean to say that the original impulse has come from art or from other purely spiritual or intellectual forces. In our view, the first impulse comes from social reality, from the changed relationships (particularly the changed 'distance') among social groups. These impulses produce their effects, so to speak, in microscopic fashion, long before large-scale cultural changes, either in art or in economic life, become visible. It may well be that artists appear in the van of social change, but if they are 'pioneering' in this fashion, this merely shows that they are quicker than others to react to social changes and to give them visible expression.

In the fourteenth century, religious life underwent a momentous transformation that reflected itself in a changed relationship between laity and clergy. In the early Middle Ages, the emphasis was placed upon the liturgy of the mass. In this, the community played a passive role, in keeping with the authoritarian, 'distantiated' role of the Church. In the late Middle Ages, however, the sermon begins to play a preponderant role. The Church speaks to the faithful as thinking individuals; their 'vital selfhood', to recall one of our categories of the process of democratization, must be appealed to. Preaching becomes a kind of agitation.[2] At the same time, confession also gains in importance: the priest enters into contact with the faithful as

[1] Cf. Bechtel, *op. cit.*, p. 244.
[2] Cf. Karl Lamprecht, *Deutsche Geschichte*, vol. XII, p. 40.

adviser on an intimate scale, and not only (or predominantly) in his liturgical role.

Another significant religious phenomenon of the same period is the growth of mysticism. The mystic seeks, and achieves, a more intimate union with God; here again, religious life shows a pattern of de-distantiation. What is most characteristic of the period in question is, however, that mystical contemplation is no longer practised by monks alone. In German mysticism, the artisan who withdraws into his room to practise mystical contemplation (e.g. Jakob Boehme) makes his appearance. Religion is no longer exclusively a matter of the community. It becomes privatized, solitary contemplation. The intimate life space of the individual becomes the vehicle of his religious experience; the four walls of his abode are transmuted, so to speak, into a soul-space.

We have already touched upon this heightened dignity of the space of everyday experience in connection with the 'intimate realism' of late medieval art. At this point, we may mention a related cultural symptom. Painting during the period we are discussing definitely severs its earlier close connection with architecture, and easel paintings (of religious subjects) make their appearance in private homes as well as public offices, e.g., of gilds.[1] Easel paintings require a 'distance' that is most appropriate to a 'democratized' public; the earlier media of painting —the monumental mural on the one hand, the miniature on the other—called for a distance that was either too great or too small. Monumental paintings as well as miniatures were removed from the everyday environment of the average individual. The former decorated the public buildings in which the exercise of authority in the hierarchial, stratified society was centred; the latter could be seen only by one individual, that is, an aristocratic collector. Easel paintings, however, may be placed where people congregate in their everyday pursuits —in homes as well as in the offices of autonomous corporations.

A final point concerning the manifestations of a 'dedistantiating' trend in late medieval art: the discovery of true perspective in painting falls into the same period. Early medieval painting is two-dimensional. The figures represented are removed from the space of everyday experience. They stand in

[1] Cf. Dehio, *op. cit.*, vol. IV, p. 296; also Bechtel, *op. cit.*, pp. 271, 274 ff.

a mystical, metaphysical space of their own, and their appearance stresses their attributes as divine or holy personages. The background is often a flat expanse of gold. Later, the figures become three-dimensional and their background also acquires depth. In this illusionistic style, the pictorial space is a continuation of the spectator's own space. A direct connection is established between the spectator and the object represented, a connection that does not break up the continuity of ordinary, everyday experience.

8. As we pointed out above, the democratizing tendency of the late Middle Ages (and of the early Renaissance) later gave way to a retrograde movement towards 're-feudalization'. The distance between élite and mass grew immeasurably with the advent of absolutism. It must be noted, however, that retrograde movements of this kind neither revive the hierarchial forms displaced by the earlier democratization nor eliminate the cultural results of the preceding democratizing process completely. The 're-feudalization' of European society during the 16th and 17th centuries by no means restored early medieval feudalism; it rather combined feudal elements with novel forms of stratification and novel techniques of control. In so far as the cultural evolution is concerned, it is a fundamental postulate of the sociology of knowledge that whatever has come into being in the cultural process cannot simply disappear; it will enter into later cultural configurations in changed form. Thus, the authoritarianism of the Church reasserted itself in the Counter-Reformation, and in politics the absolute monarchy became dominant at the same time. Both these authoritarian control systems, however, made use of the achievements of the preceding rationalistic eras. In art and science, the Baroque is a continuation of the Renaissance. What the new age did was to neutralize the effects of the earlier conquests of the *Ratio*, by blunting its cutting edge where it could be a menace to the new absolute authority. This was done, for example, by introducing new 'supra-rational' elements into the rational system of the Renaissance.

Baroque religion is ecstatic, not in the manner of the mystic contemplation practised by isolated monks and artisans, but in the form of an intensification of fervour beyond all measure, in a kind of overheated and sublimated eroticism. Baroque art, on the other hand, does not abandon the earlier illusionistic realism of the Renaissance; on the contrary, it exaggerates it to the point of of extreme naturalism, but for the purpose of conveying a transcendent, metaphysical message.

The supra-rational principle of the Baroque is the heroic and superhuman. The emphasis is upon the incomparable power of the ruling individual. At the same time, Baroque art, and Baroque culture in general, emphasizes rational calculation and classic measure. Classical conventions and models predominate, guiding imagination in pre-existent channels. Baroque art is cool, conventional, and yet fervent and declamatory. It depended on circumstances which aspect of this culture—the rational or supra-rational one—became dominant. The calculating rationalism of its ruling groups could produce a wholly this-wordly, critical state of mind from which some of the impulses responsible for the Enlightenment flew.

Also, Baroque society was by no means wholly permeated by the authoritarian and aristocratic spirit. The middle class, though crushed and overawed by the enormous prestige of the aristocracy, lived its own life, had its own corporate institutions, and cultivated its own intellectual and artistic taste. Besides official, heroic art, there is also the intimate art of the Dutch painters, and some of the writers of the period show considerable acumen in their ironic, disillusioned analysis of society.[1] . . .

9. Our contemporary culture is characterized by a radical negation of 'distance' both in social relationships and in the realm of culture. Our field of experience tends to become homogeneous, without the earlier hierarchical gradations between 'high' and 'low', 'sacred' and 'profane'. In all earlier ages, such divisions were all-pervasive. In the medieval university, branches of learning were divided into 'higher' and 'lower'. In ancient Greece, as Zilsel has pointed out, poetry was considered infinitely more honourable than plastic art, simply because the sculptor and painter had their social origin in the class of craftsmen who were often slaves.[2] In pre-modern times, among topics of knowledge, 'high' was sharply separated from

[1] [Translator's Note: At this point, three pages are missing from the manuscript. The context indicates that these must have dealt with the Enlightenment period and the nineteenth century.]

[2] Cf. H. Zilsel, *Die Entstehung des Geniebegriffes*, Tübingen, 1926, Part I.

'low', knowledge of divinity and metaphysics belonging into the former category, knowledge of the objects of everyday experience into the latter. In art, too, representations of ideal beauty ranked high above portrayals of everyday objects, and this distinction was reflected in the formal structure of academic paintings. Their very composition revealed a hierarchical structural principle—the things represented were arranged in a more or less regular design enhancing the dominant position of the central figures. In these academic paintings, the haphazard, random arrangement of things as we encounter them in real experience is replaced by order. As against this, impressionism strives for a 'photographic' effect, reproducing the unregulated, spontaneous freshness of momentary combinations of things. Photography, indeed, expresses well the spirit of modern 'de-distantiation'. It marks the greatest closeness to all things without distinction. The snapshot is a form of pictorial representation that is most congenial to the modern mind with its interest in the unretouched and uncensored 'moment'. (It may be added that, in keeping with the general rule that 'distantiation' always reasserts itself, composition and design tend to reappear in modern, post-academic art.)

In the modern, homogenized field of experience, every single thing is an appropriate object of scrutiny; none has a greater dignity than any other; the study of theological ideas is on a par with that of chemistry or physiology. This, however, leads to a characteristic difficulty which is inherent in the process of democratization. If the field of experience is 'homogeneous', if no object is respected 'above' any other, how can man himself, the individual unit of society, claim any particular dignity? The principle of equality thus comes into conflict with that of vital autonomy—a contradiction which is as yet unsolved. If we stress the one, we can hardly avoid slighting the other. The ideal of 'freedom', of the autonomy of vital selfhood, is difficult to reconcile with the ideal of 'equality', the assertion of the equal to value of all social units. We have to do here with a contradiction, an antinomy that reveals the deep inner conflict of our age.

This conflict manifests itself with particular sharpness in those sciences which deal with man—psychology and sociology. Psychology as a natural science works with a completely homogenized field of experience. It is not only that all individuals are treated on the same footing; in addition to this, classes of psychic phenomena which for the experiencing subject have very unequal value and dignity are just data, without any difference of rank, for the scientific psychologist. Sense data or religious striving—for psychology, they are just empirical phenomena subject to ascertainable laws. In this way, forms of experience are 'de-distantiated', just as individuals and objects are. This is inherent in the scientific attitude, but it leads to a discrepancy between the image of man as drawn by science, and the self-image of man as given in immediate experience.

In sociology, similar problems arise in connection with the problem of freedom. Sociology seeks to ascertain regularities of behaviour in a homogenized field. Now if these behavioural regularities alone are observed, disregarding individual choices and their meaningful *rationale*, all human groups will begin to resemble calculable mechanisms. But if we start from the individual and his vital selfhood, we shall discover that there is another side to behaviour, and that human actions considered in themselves result from choices due to autonomous initiative. Each individual is the centre of his own universe, and is free in this sense. It is difficult for behaviour science, with its predominant interest in observable regularities of behaviour, to render justice to this other side of the problem. We cannot undertake here to solve this antinomy; all we can do is to call attention to it.

The homogenization of the field of experience is by no means a matter of the scientific approach only. We can observe it also in everyday experience. Just as science obliterates the differences of rank among different classes of objects and phenomena, the modern attitude towards time tends to disregard the distinction between 'working day' and 'holiday'. The articulation of time in terms of periodically recurrent, 'distantiated', sacred dates has not for modern man the decisive importance it had for earlier generations. 'Holidays' tend to acquire a purely utilitarian, functional character as times for rest and recreation, even when they coincide with religious dates. (In Soviet Russia, an attempt was even made to do away with this coincidence, by substituting staggered rest days on the basis of a five-day week for the Sunday rest—a reform which, by the way, did not take root.)

Analogous trends can be observed in art and philosophy. It is characteristic of modern art that it stresses the 'how', the manner of representation, instead of the 'what', the represented object. A still life of vegetables may be just as 'high' art as a Madonna—it is all a matter of the quality of painting. The world of the objects represented is 'homogenized'; this is one of the principles of 'l'art pour l'art'. But we must enter a *caveat* at this point. The motto of 'l'art pour l'art' itself shows that for the artist the field of experience is by no means wholly homogenized. Art as such has a high dignity of its own; it is 'distantiated'. (The same is true of science as an activity.) What we observe here is not that *all* distantiation is done away with, but that distantiation is limited to the general type of activity that one is engaged in—an activity which, while itself 'distantiated', treats all its objects as being on the same level.

In philosophy, too, we may observe the levelling of the objects of speculation. The modern line of evolution in philosophy leads from theism to deism, pantheism, naturalism. One of the characteristic features of modern philosophy is its rejection of the 'reduplication of Being' ('Seinsverdoppelung'). Pre-modern philosophy tended to distinguish between purely phenomenal Being (the world of tangible and observable things) and true, noumenal Being (the metaphysical Essence). This introduced a hierarchy into the world of things: they could be ordered according to their distance from 'true' Being. Now we cannot say that all metaphysics, all 'reduplication of Being', is of aristocratic origin, just as it is wrong to assert that 'distantiation' arises only in aristocratic cultures. It is, however, correct to say that whatever tendency towards 'reduplication of Being' exists is very sharply threatened by the democratization of culture. The origin of this threat lies in the propensity of the democratized mind to homogenize the field of experience.

In the history of metaphysical thought, the idea of a personal God, God the Father, marks the maximum of 'distantiation'. (This corresponds to the steeply hierarchical, 'distantiated' character of patriarchal cultures.) From this, the trend goes in modern times towards a growing stress upon 'immanence'. The divine principle increasingly loses its transcendent character, until—passing through the phase of Deism with its minimization of the transcendent and personal traits of Divinity—we reach pantheism. In this philosophy, God is wholly immanent in Nature, and every existing thing acquires a particle of the divine essence. From a certain point of view, this represents the culminating point of the democratizing tendency, for it is here that the 'vital selfhood' of all elements receives its fullest recognition.

The modern evolution, however, does not stop here. Relentlessly, it pursues its path towards ever more complete 'de-distantiation'. The metaphysical aura which surrounds the things of the world in pantheism is dispersed in modern naturalism, positivism, and pragmatism. As a result of this radical this-worldiness, the mind of man becomes perfectly congruent with 'reality'—'reality' being understood as the sum of manipulable things. We have to do here with a radically analytical and nominalistic outlook that leaves no room for the 'distantiation' and idealization of anything. The modern type of distantiation mentioned above—that in which group integration mechanisms and institutions were treated as embodying 'higher' principles—tends to be corroded by this radical nominalism. The metaphysical concepts of People, History, and State succumb to its critique. This is inevitable in the long run, for two reasons. For one thing these concepts become party labels and thus must undergo the invidious scrutiny of the adverse party. For another, the thinking of democratized élites tends to become more and more analytical, and they therefore cease to believe in metaphysical 'substances'. The mythical image of institutions is decomposed; they are broken down into a mass of observable, empirical facts. All the rest is treated as mere 'ideology'.

(e) The Cultural Ideals of Aristocratic and Democratic Groups

1. In the preceding section, we tried to show how different principles of élite selection (the aristocratic and the democratic) give rise to characteristic differences in the 'culture' of the societies in question in such fields as art, philosophy, and religion, as well as in the current everyday interpretation of life. The underlying mechanism at work here is an 'unconscious' one in the sense that the subjects engaged in creation and interpretation need not have an awareness of the sociological

background and of the 'aristocratic' or 'democratic' origin of their impulses and activities. The uncovering of such more or less unconscious mechanisms of the cultural process does not, however, exhaust the matter. Basic cultural aspirations and norms ('Bildungsideale') are also entertained by various groups on a conscious level, and it is to such cultural ideals[1] of an aristocratic or democratic nature that we now turn.

In our own society, there is sharp conflict and competition between two such cultural ideals, a relatively aristocratic and a more democratic one. The former is the 'humanistic' ideal; the latter, a democratic one that seeks to displace it. It will be useful for understanding if we can demonstrate that the rival ideals are those of two different, and differently constituted, élite groups.

2. The humanistic cultural and educational ideal by no means represents an extreme type of aristocratic thought. It is too universalistic to be tailored to the needs of small and closed privileged castes. Relatively speaking, however, it is still the ideal of an élite group, that of the 'cultivated' bourgeoise, an élite that seeks to distinguish itself from the proletarian or petty bourgeois mass. As we shall see, the humanistic ideal has marked 'aristocratic' traits in this sense.

The humanistic ideal is, first of all, steeped in the values of classical antiquity. It finds in antiquity, on the one hand, those elements which are best suited to developing harmonious, integrated and many-sidedly cultivated personalities, and on the other, a universe of 'pure' ideas that can help modern man to rise above the sordid and profane concerns of everyday life. In both these aspects of the humanistic ideal one may perceive the aristocratic principle of 'distantiation' at work.

In order to become a universally cultivated, harmonious and integrated personality, one needs leisure. This is an ideal of ruling groups. The average man who must work for a living cannot become a harmonious and many-sided personality; specialization is his destiny. He has no time to devote himself

---

1 [Translator's Note: The German terms 'Bildung' and 'Bildungsideal' are difficult to render in English. What they designate partakes of both 'culture' and 'education'. 'Bildung' comprises whatever makes a 'cultivated' man. The 'ideals' discussed in the text refer to the image that various societies and groups have of what it takes to be 'cultivated'].

to the acquisition of social graces characteristic of aristocratic cultures (see p. 208 f., above).

The lack of specialization, the many-sidedness of the humanistic ideal might suggest, at first glance, something like the impartial openness of the democratic mind to which all things are equally interesting and absorbing. In reality, however, the humanistic many-sidedness has nothing to do with this, for its objects of interest, though manifold, are severely selected. Not all manifestations of life are worthy of interest and exploration, but only their most sublimated aspects, and, in particular, their reflection in the world of ideas. Things are admitted to consciousness only as embalmed in the flawless creations of classic art or poetry. There is no risky experimentation with real-life impulses. There is a closed horizon beyond which one is forbidden to venture.

The modern form of humanism has a twofold nature. As against the 'courtly' ideal of the aristocrat and cavalier, it is decidedly democratic. It does not stress social graces and elegant speech alone. It strives for 'cultivation' in a higher sense, in the sense of spiritualization. But this ideal is not fully democratic either. It neither wants to nor could be a possession of all men. We find its devotees among sons of upper-middle-class parents as well as among literati; but it is also worth noting that the pioneers of this cultural ideal (Shaftesbury, Humboldt) came from the nobility. The cultivated, intellectualized aristocrat was the first model for the upper middle class.[1]

This humanism creates a 'distance' from everyday life and hence unavoidably, whether intentionally or not, a distance from the common man, the mass, also. To this it adds another aristocratic trait: that of 'self-distantiation'. The humanist aspires to be, above everything else, a 'personality' in his own right. He does not turn to classical antiquity for its own sake, like a specialized historian. He needs the classical background in order to enhance his own personality, to set it off against the uncultivated. There must be a foil, a backdrop against the contemporary world; in order to be a 'personality', one needs that second world in order to feel elevated beyond the contingent circumstances of one's everyday situation.

[1] Cf. W. Weil, 'Die Entstehung des deutschen Bildungsideals', in *Schriften zur Philosophie und Soziologie*, vol. IV, Bonn, 1930.

This is a genuine, universal aspiration that we find in all ages in many varied forms. It finds its mythical expression in most religions. In fact, images of the Beyond and of salvation reflect man's striving to overcome the contingencies of his life. The mystics, and particularly the 'urbanized' mystics of the late Middle Ages, were a typical 'cultivated élite' in this sense; their ecstatic contemplation helped them overcome the limitations of everyday life. They, of course, strove for communion with God—they did not want to become 'personalities'. Yet their solitary ecstasies differed essentially from the collective ecstasies of rural 'folk' groups. In their way they were just as individualistic as the later literati who also cultivated a kind of solitary, ecstatic contemplation. For all humanists, the deepest fulfilment is found in occupation with things of the intellect and of the spirit, in seclusion from this world.

Solitude, then, becomes for the humanist of the secular type, the type which no longer seeks communion with God, something positive rather than the merely negative lack of human company. Its essence is 'communion with oneself' and enrichment through that communion. Through this self-cultivation, the humanist becomes more than himself, more than one or the other of his potentialities, more than the concrete situation in which he finds himself.

We had to stress these positive aspects of the humanistic ideal (today critically menaced if not already doomed) before discussing some of its limitations. If the humanistic ideal is about to be discarded by our culture, it is not because of the inadequacy of its ultimate aspirations but because it cannot provide enrichment of life for broader masses. Because of the conditions of mass existence, the humanistic ideal in its present form cannot be meaningful for the average man. Nevertheless, it is our opinion that this ideal contains elements indispensable for a full and rich life, and cultural ideals of a more universal appeal should make use of these elements in changed form.

We shall now turn to some of the limitations of the humanistic ideal as we see them; they are:

(a) Its confusion of its own élite sector with 'the' world itself. The humanist pretends that he is 'universally' interested, while in reality he is interested only in the world of his own educated sector. Within this universe, the humanist has an abnormally acute sense for nuances of meaning. Beyond it, he lacks the most primitive understanding of elementary facts. Men of a radically different background are needed to compensate for the one-sidedness of this so-called 'universal' outlook. The humanist cannot get over this limitation by himself.

(b) Its lack of contact with the stark realities of life. 'Cultivation' can become a prime object in life only for people who are never confronted by matters of life or death, safety or disaster, triumph or decline. For groups always faced by such realities, the ideal is too soft. They cannot understand why contemplation and book learning should be the finest things in life and why the vital struggle in itself should be considered ignoble. For these latter groups it may be a good thing to practise contemplation or to play with pure ideas once in a while, but they can have no truck with people who feel so secure that they can only make words about the tragedies of life.

(c) Its purely aesthetic relationship to things. Art has a universal function in neutralizing the sense of doom that threatens all human existence. But when art becomes the be-all and end-all of life, as it does in groups addicted to the cult of Art for Art's sake, it shuts out that sense of doom from awareness altogether, instead of merely sublimating and counterbalancing it. This attitude again is possible only for groups far removed from the rough-and-tumble of life, and wholly secure in a rentier's, patrician's, or aristocrat's existence. The reaction against this among groups fully engaged in struggle in the social arena is understandable. The latter want no 'pure' art but art carrying a practical message. This attitude threatens to abase art and to turn it into propaganda; but we should not forget that the opposite extreme, art for art's sake, also drains the life-blood out of living art. The really great art of classical Greece, for example, had an organic function in the life of the *polis*.

(d) Its neglect of the personal, biographical, and contingent element in literary or artistic creation. The *person* of the creative artist was completely neglected in favour of the 'work' as such. Works, then, did not appear as the products and manifestations of life; life was conceived as a means to produce works, and the latter alone deserved attention. Interest in the personal, biographical background was denounced as a profanation, as base 'psychological curiosity'.[1]

(e) Its antipathy towards the dynamic and unexpected. In its endeavour to produce 'harmonious', 'integrated' personalities, humanism was led to turn its back upon human potentialities whose manifestations could not be fully anticipated. Its classical canon claimed to encompass every human potentiality worthy of notice, and to provide a valid model for every situation. In this, humanism profoundly misunderstood life. One of man's supreme faculties is that of mobilizing entirely new potentialities in meeting new and critical situations. Life, then, cannot be hemmed in by the regulations and restrictions of any pre-existent canon. In defending the orderliness of its world, humanism merely betrayed a desire to maintain a wholly artificial security, based upon entrenched economic privilege.

3. It is not easy to give an idea of the contrary ideal of democratized groups, for this is still in the process of emerging and cannot be reduced to ready-made formulas. All we can do is to enumerate some of the symptoms of these novel cultural aspirations. In doing so, we shall pay particular attention to potentialities inherent in the new outlook that are not yet generally recognized.

As we shall see, the various elements of the new cultural ideal are sharply antithetical to the dominant features of humanism. Here as elsewhere, life works with antitheses; when new groups enter the arena and want to express themselves, they begin by rejecting what they find entrenched. The new is complementary to the old; this is how the historical process seeks to achieve totality.

The following points about the democratic cultural ideal deserve especial mention:

(a) In contrast to the humanistic ideal, it stresses the ideal of *vocational specialization*. Humanism is the ideal of an élite that does no specialized work, and considers such work (echoing in this the mentality of classical antiquity) as beneath its dignity. Man can become 'cultivated' only if he does not 'work'

---

[1] [Translator's Note: This criticism is directed against the school of 'Geistesgeschichte', and in particular against the literary historian Friedrich Gundolf.]

but merely 'occupies himself' with things. The new ideal, however, is work-oriented. Man can become 'cultivated' only through and within a concretely goal-oriented practice. (Political 'cultivation', too, is seen in contemporary groupings to be linked to participation in active political work, rather than to mere familiarity with doctrines.) The emphasis is upon the concrete situation, calling for active intervention, in which the individual happens to find himself. While the humanist, so to speak, hovered above the situation, the new democratized type recognizes the compelling force of the moment. In the 'homogenized' experiential field of this type, any concrete vocational task may provide equal fulfilment.

Pure specialization has traditionally been considered as antithetical to 'cultivation', and we have to admit the truth contained in this traditional view. Mere specialization as such cannot make one 'cultivated', even in a thoroughly democratized world. According to the democratic cultural ideal of which we are speaking, however, specialization as such is not the sole content of personal culture. The democratic type, too, strives to broaden his horizon beyond his specialty; he is fully aware of the fact that one cannot be a cultivated man without this. But he goes about it in a different way than did the humanist, for he starts from his concrete situation and never loses sight of it, whereas the humanist, in order to be cultivated, severed all connection with his own concrete situation.

This can be illustrated by a concrete example. A necessary phase in the acquisition of 'cultivation' in the humanistic sense is the 'grand tour' or educational trip. One has to go to Italy and Greece and see the monuments of classical antiquity. One's profession or occupation is entirely irrelevant in this respect; the prescription is the same for the student, the business man, and the lawyer. And this neutrality towards the professional horizon of the various individuals 'cultivating' themselves is essential, for the practice described unconsciously serves a very definite purpose. This consists in providing a common universe of communication among the different sectors of the cultivated élite as differentiated from the mass. To have made the grand tour was the entrance ticket to this select circle. Communication was achieved in terms of a second world besides the workaday one.

For the democratic type, too, cultivation reaches beyond specialization, but the process of cultivation starts from one's everyday occupation and remains organically linked to it. This is exemplified by the skilled worker who takes an extension course in order to gain more knowledge about his speciality, or who studies economics and management in order to have a clearer idea of where he stands in his social environment. Some workers study in order to become trade union functionaries. These people do not seek to 'cultivate' themselves in a free-floating sense; they want to be better able to control their situation and to broaden their own perspective in the process. There are no limits set to this gradual and organic process; there is a way from the trade union branch into municipal and national politics, or into the international labour movement. In any case, the process of self-cultivation is deliberate and continuous, rather than dictated by 'a priori' concepts or sudden, subjective impulses or mere curiosity.

It is an advantage of this self-cultivation programme that thought becomes congruent with life—one does not acquire knowledge about things that do not matter to one. The man who follows this path will be able to live the things he is talking about, while the man who follows the humanistic course will often repeat things that he knows about only at second-hand and that have no personal meaning for him.

(b) Politics, in the pre-democratic world, was no specialized vocation. Political offices were filled by amateurs who did not 'work' at politics but merely 'occupied themselves' with it.[1] In the age of early, pre-democratic parliamentarianism, we see epic rivalries arise between fashionable coteries and old aristocratic houses. In their oratory, the politicians of that period draw upon classical erudition and general philosophical principles; they seek to persuade, to obtain the adhesion of uncommitted individuals, free to decide for themselves. Clearly, the political struggle does not yet reflect a clash of massive economic interests. When these begin to dominate politics, a specialized knowledge of the economic effects of governmental

[1] Cf. Max Weber, 'Politik als Beruf', translated as Ch. IV in H. H. Gerth and C. Wright Mills, *From Max Weber: Essays in Sociology*, London and New York, 1946. For a good characterization of this type of politician, see R. Lennox, *Edmund Burke und sein politisches Arbeitsfeld in den Jahren 1760–1709*, Munich and Berlin, 1923.

and legislative action becomes indispensable. The political amateur, the orator dealing with universal principles and generalities, must then yield to the specialist. The real political decisions are taken in closed committee, on the basis of bargaining among interest groups; the plenary sessions of the parliaments with their set speeches are mere make-believe, staged for the benefit of the rank-and-file.

The committees and caucus rooms are an excellent school for party functionaries rising from the ranks. As they advance into higher policy-making bodies, their perspective becomes broadened. Assuming larger responsibilities, they lose the one-sidedness of their original orientation which was circumscribed in narrow geographical or class terms. In this process, the politicians of the new era typically expose themselves to the charge of being renegades and traitors; their rank-and-file suspects them of having 'sold out' to the 'interests'. But this need not be the case at all. The politician's evolution from a narrow particularist to a responsible statesman may represent the genuinely democratic type of political 'self-cultivation'.

(c) In essence, the type of 'cultivation' attained by the specialist consists in his acquiring a deeper and more adequate understanding of his own particular position, by learning to approach it from different sides. In this respect, the specialized man of the modern age is better off than the specialized man of earlier ages. For the latter, it was difficult indeed to transcend the narrow limits of his specialization, or, if he was a politician wedded to very narrow interests, to achieve a more comprehensive perspective. In modern society, however, specialization both can and must go beyond itself, for the interconnectedness and interdependence of fields of specialization and of particular interests becomes more and more evident. This is why today 'specialization' can be a good starting-point for 'cultivation', whereas this was not the case in earlier ages. Today one may become 'cultivated', not in the purely quantitative sense of acquiring more knowledge, but in the deeper sense of becoming able to advance from familiarity with an immediately given concrete situation to the understanding of the structural pattern behind that same situation.

While the humanist achieved 'cultivation' by advancing from everyday reality to a 'higher' reality of the world of Ideas, modern man attains the same goal by advancing from immediate experience to a structural view of reality. The realm of 'structure'[1] is no 'second world' of pure Essences behind the real world. It is immanent in reality, and achieving 'structural' understanding is not a matter of going beyond reality but rather of the intensity with which one experiences reality. In every field of specialization, there are people who have a merely routine interest in their activities, besides others who are so passionately interested that they have a need to penetrate to the underlying mechanism; for example, bankers who are mere technicians of finance, as against others who try to *understand* finance. Or, to return to the field of educational theory and practice: there are routiniers of education who want to know only how to keep discipline in the classroom and how to transmit the required amount of knowledge, as against true educators for whom each child represents a unique challenge. For the true educator, the pupils are not identical targets of 'education', but individualities with their own social backgrounds and their psychologically and biologically determined needs, demands, and potentialities. Such an educator will seek to fulfil his task by achieving insight into the underlying structural pattern of the schoolroom situation.

Adherents of the humanistic educational ideal often deprecate 'vocational' education as lacking in the elements of 'cultivation'. These humanists do not know how truly 'cultivated' practitioners of real stature can be. Above all, they overlook the fact that thought rooted in actual practice is likely to be more genuine than thought developed around mere topics of 'cultivated' conversation. In contrast to purely verbal knowledge, knowing achieved by doing establishes an organic relationship between the knower and the known. If such knowledge transcends one-sidedness by a broadening of the knower's perspective, it will be more truly many-sided and universal than the purely verbal universality of humanistic 'cultivation'. This type of knowledge also has the best chance of escaping the danger of becoming an 'ideological' screen for unavowed and unrealized self-centred and group-centred interests.

[1] [Translator's Note: For the role of the concept of 'structure' in Karl Mannheim's thinking, see the Introduction to *Essays in Sociology and Social Psychology*, London and New York, 1953.]

All this should not be taken, of course, as an advocacy of purely vocational education or of a cult of mere technical expertness. We do not hold that children should be taught only 'what they will need to know in practical life'. Such a view completely misses both the real nature of specialized knowledge and the educational aims and potentialities of an organic connection between 'knowing' and 'doing'. If education transmits a lot of 'practical' knowledge but still fails to enable the pupil to become oriented in his own life environment, it is in no way superior to purely verbal, humanistic education. Specialized vocational education in this sense is a symptom of decadence rather than of progress.

Hence, modern education can approximate to an ideal of 'cultivation' only by giving more than specialized knowledge, narrowly circumscribed. Such knowledge must be supplemented by more general disciplines that have orientation in life and in social reality as their subject matter. Sociology is particularly appropriate to fulfil this task in the modern world. Traditionally, philosophy was entrusted with the task of providing general principles of orientation, and we do not assert that the philosophical approach has become valueless or that philosophy should be banished from the curriculum. The dominant tradition of Western philosophy, however, is still that of idealism, of the 'reduplication of Being', of seeking a second world behind reality; such a philosophy is not able to give modern man the orientation that he needs. The idealistic tradition, on the other hand, is being more and more corroded within modern philosophy itself, as the recent trend towards pragmatism and positivism shows. There is hardly any conflict in principle between these philosophies and the sociological approach.[1]

E THE PROBLEM OF ECSTASY

In so far as 'cultivation' means a broadening of one's existential perspective, the democratic cultural ideal seems to be superior to the humanistic one: as we have seen, it achieves that broadening in a more organic fashion. Cultivated existence,

[1] [Translator's Note: The necessity to transcend the purely pragmatist and positivist approach is the argument of the next concluding section of this paper.]

however, also has another aspect: that of self-distantiation. This is an organic part of the cultural ideal of the humanistic élite, whereas the modern, democratic concept of cultivation seems to offer little in the way of 'self-distantiation' and 'ecstatic' contemplation. Is this a shortcoming of the modern ideal, or was self-distantiation an unjustified aspiration of old élites? Such questions about ultimate values are difficult to answer, and it is still more difficult to give a reasoned argument for and against the possible answers. We shall therefore state our position without entering into its pros and cons; it is that achieving from time to time a certain distance from his own situation and from the world is one of the fundamental traits of man as truly a human being. A man for whom nothing exists beyond his immediate situation is not fully human. But even the 'democratized' way of cultivation discussed above, which consists in gaining an increasingly broader situational perspective, does not suffice. We inherited from our past another need: that of severing from time to time *all* connection with life and with the contingencies of our existence. We shall designate this ideal by the term 'ecstasy'. Supposing that this ideal is a valid one, and that 'ecstasy' is a necessary element of true 'cultivation', the question facing us is this: Is it true that the democratic cultural ideal is antithetical to ecstasy and offers no avenues towards it?

Our answer is that if we consider the potentialities inherent in the democratic approach, it will appear to be eventually conducive to a new type of 'ecstasy' and of true 'cultivation'. It may even be suggested that ecstasy can be a general, universally shared form of experience only in a democratized culture. But this democratization of culture does not attain that stage at one stroke. To begin with, radical democratization means de-distantiation; this has to be overcome before new forms of ecstasy can emerge. Democratized culture must go through a dialectical process before it can realize its full potentialities.

We shall examine this dialectical process under three headings, that is, from the point of view of the new, democratic relationship between (*a*) the 'I' and the object, (*b*) between the 'I' and the 'Thou', and (*c*) between the 'I' and the 'myself', that is, self-distantiation.

(*a*) *The I-object relationship.* As we have seen, full democratization means, to begin with, radical de-distantiation of all objects, non-human as well as human. This makes for a flat, uninspiring, and unhappy world. There is no Beyond; the existing world is not a symbol for the eternal; immediate reality points to nothing beyond itself. At the stage of full democratization, human types who experience reality in this flat and uninspiring perspective do, indeed, abound. They are found among business men and scientists, educators and politicians. Their thinking is fully congruent with their doing, since they seek nothing beyond what they can actually achieve by practical manipulation. In this sense, they describe themselves as 'realists': after all, they have done away with all myths, with all concepts that are not fully operational. But are these people truly realists? We hold that they are not. For 'realism' cannot consist in doing away with all historically given forms of distantiation and then equating the remainder with 'the' world itself. There is more to the world and, in particular, to man as a real being than is open to manipulation. It may be extremely useful for a man who wants to achieve control over things and other men to consider them all for a while as if they consisted in nothing but a bundle of responses. We understand quite well that our modern culture, driven by an overwhelming need to perfect techniques of control, comes to reduce both things and men to their regular patterns of responding to stimuli. In this context, the achievements of the behaviouristic approach must be recognized. But one cannot say that this particular perspective exhausts the full reality of man. Man cannot be reduced to the sum of his responses to stimuli. Some aspects of human reality call for intuitive 'understanding' ('Verstehen'), even if we may be driven for a while to ignore these aspects for technical and methodological reasons.

The danger inherent in the modern ontology, then, is that it tends to succumb to the temptation to take its specific perspective, that of the manipulator, to be that of absolute truth. A true ontology cannot be such a partial, perspective-bound one. We have to show these 'realists' and pragmatists that they do not yet face 'the world' but only a limited segment of it, the segment corresponding to practical manipulative operations. When they equate this segment with the whole, their thinking is not 'realistic' but very 'unreal'.

Such self-deception is possible only for a human type which has suppressed his essential human-ness in his approach towards reality. This ontological error has to be corrected by the recognition of the *partial* nature of the manipulative approach. When this is achieved, the specialist will cease to take himself seriously as an arbiter of ontological truth. Since, however, the tendency towards overcoming partial perspectives is inherent in democratization, we may indeed expect that the ontological error will eventually be corrected, and that the way will be open for new distance-creating experiences.

(b) *The I-Thou relationship.* Democratization implies that all purely *social* distance between 'high' and 'low' tends to be levelled. This levelling may produce a colourless monotony. All individuals then will appear as interchangeable; the 'other' will play a purely instrumental role in the individual's life. When social distance is abolished and no other form of distantiation takes its place, there is a void in inter-human relationships: no person as a person can mean anything to another. In this respect, however, we shall also discover, if we look more closely, that democratization involves not only a danger but also, and more importantly, a supreme opportunity. In fact, the levelling of purely social distance may enable the purely 'existential' distance[1] to come into its own. When I am no longer compelled to meet the other in his role as a social superior or inferior, I can establish pure existential contact with him as a human being. And this form of relationship between the 'I' and the 'thou' can become a general pattern only on the basis of democratization. We perceive in this sense, at the stage of the democratization of cultures, the emergence of new forms of distance, just as in earlier ages purely spatial avoidance may have yielded to more sublimated psychic distance and to vertical social distance. At the democratic stage, it becomes possible to 'love' or 'hate' the other as a person, irrespective of any social mask he may wear.

Creating a basis for purely existential human relationships is the greatest potential achievement of democracy. In earlier ages, existential, supra-social, person-to-person relationships did exist. But as a rule, they were embedded in social, vertical relationships. Thus, to mention one example, the priest did

[1] Cf. above, p. 207.

speak to the penitent as a person, and his words at times stirred the soul of the believer in its innermost depth. Yet, at the same time, the priest was also the representative of social authority. In all such relationships, a purely personal appeal could make itself heard only through the impersonal medium of authority and vertical social distance.

The emergence of sublimated erotic 'love' in the knightly culture of the Middle Ages was one of the most important chapters in the history of the I-thou-relationships. The troubadours of Provence created an image of the beloved that reflected a purely 'existential' relationship; in their poetry, love was a way to self-purification and salvation. And yet, one can observe, in this as in other cases, that 'existential' relationships do not have a language of their own. They speak the language of purely 'social' distance. The troubadours represented themselves as the 'servants' of the beloved lady, in a kind of feudal relationship, and we still echo this in the ritual and language of our own sublimated erotic relationships. We even use the feudal metaphor of 'courting'. (In other 'existential' relationships, too, we tend to use the vocabulary of vertical social distance, e.g. when we designate our purely ethical appreciation for another as 'respect', although it has little to do with 'respect' for social authority.) It is, in fact, difficult for us to express our experience of existential 'distance' in non-social terms. In recent times, ritual and language begin to change, and we hear complaints about the matter-of-factness of modern erotic relationships, about the decline of 'romantic' love. In the course of social de-distantiation, the beloved woman no longer is seen as a 'higher' being. People who consider themselves 'advanced' welcome this rejection of romantic 'sham'. According to them, love relationships should be matter-of-fact and natural; they also hold that in a democratic world, man and woman ought to consider themselves as 'comrades' and 'collaborators', even in their erotic relationship with each other. This, however, is a misunderstanding. The true potentialities inherent in democratization are not yet realized when we put *horizontal* social relationships in the place of *vertical* ones in expressing our person-to-person attitudes and feelings. The real opportunity that democratization gives us consists in being able to transcend *all* social categories and experience love as a purely personal and existential matter.

It becomes apparent, then, that the 'sociological' orientation we are advocating by no means implies that we recognize 'sociological' categories as the only ones in terms of which human experience can express itself. On the contrary, one of the reasons why we seek to subject human reality to radical sociological analysis is that we need to know the effects produced by social factors in order to be able to counteract them when they are inimical to man. The positive type of modern thinker, in our view, will become increasingly sociological in his thinking, not in order to deify the social, but in order to neutralize its negative effects concerning ultimate human values.

(c) *The I-myself relationship*. The primary business of man is to come to terms with the outside world and with his fellows. Gradually, however, he becomes aware of the need to know himself and to develop an idea of his own being and aspirations. Every culture has, in this sense, its own characteristic conception of man's relationship to himself, in addition to its characteristic I-object and I-thou relationships. In hierarchically organized societies, however, man tends to think of himself in terms of his place in the social hierarchy. He is compelled to experience himself, not as a person, but as the specimen of a social category. The 'personality' ideal, the wish to achieve unique dignity as this person, is specifically modern. This aspiration is closely related to the 'existential' I-thou relationship just discussed, for a man can become a 'person' *for himself* only to the extent that he is a 'person' for others and others are 'persons' for him. In fact, to our view, the 'existential', personal I-thou relationship is fundamental to the development of a personal self-image. We hold it to be an idealistic delusion that man first becomes a person in his own, individual self-assessment and then proceeds to meet others as persons. It is the other way round: man's human and social environment must first develop in such a way that he can become a person for others and be addressed as such on numerous occasions before he can see himself as a person.

It follows that a democratic social order, with its tendency to minimize vertical social distance, provides the most favourable conditions for the development of 'internalized' personality. This is misunderstood by the modern intellectual élite whose members are proud of being able to see themselves in purely existential terms but ignore the fact that they owe this to a social trend they instinctively reject, that of social levelling. It is because the hierarchial, social evaluation of man no longer is all-pervasive and dominant that he can, from time to time, possess himself as he is in his supra-social essence, stripped of conventional and social masks, and unconstricted by his contingent social situation.

It is in this way that democratic social reality opens up new avenues towards the age-old goal of escaping the contingency of the world, of achieving ecstasy. This was, at bottom, the meaning of the aspirations of all *homines religiosi*. Escape from the world and from the contingent situation was first achieved by the use of intoxicants, later by asceticism, and finally through solitary contemplation. In all this, freedom from the tyranny of the contingent world was achieved, but not as yet a purely existential relationship to the self. The experience of salvation was articulated through mythical and religious symbols—symbols which often were the projections of social authority relationships. In this way, man who sought to escape contingent, everyday social reality was led back, in roundabout fashion, to that which he hoped to escape. A more radical liberation from contingency has become possible only in the modern age.

Whatever one may say against the modern cultural type, one cannot deny him one virtue, that of truthfulness. Other cultures may have had more sublime ideals, more challenging utopias, a more colourful reality, a greater wealth of nuances. Our modern age has sacrificed all that, for the sake of possessing truth unadorned and unfalsified. It wants to stand in its own undistorted reality; this is why it has done away with all distantiation. The individual of this culture also wants to be 'himself' as he is, not as he appears clothed in the trappings of his social status. Therein lies the greatness that the modern individual may achieve—the dissatisfaction with a socially determined relation to himself. He must pay for this, however, first of all, by the loss of that sense of security which only well-defined status can give. Orientation in status-bound societies is easy; everybody knows what he can aspire to and what he can expect. As against this, modern life no longer offers sure expectations but only an infinite challenge. In earlier times, only the poor had infinite dreams, since they could not expect finite rewards.[1] In this sense, we have all become poor. *Insecurity as a general destiny, no longer limited to submerged strata, is one of the characteristics of the modern age.* Former élites may deplore this. To be exposed to insecurity is a tragic experience. But it also opens up an avenue towards moral and cultural growth. It is wholly wrong to interpret the collapse of old hierarchies and patterns of order as a symptom of moral and cultural decay. We must see in this, on the contrary, a potentially positive factor in the education of mankind. If society with its fixed hierarchies no longer can give us a safe orientation and a basis for self-evaluation, we must for that very reason meet the challenge of developing a new pattern of orientation based upon a deeper and more genuine human truth.

This is the real task of the democratized age, and this task is yet to be done. The modern mind misunderstands itself if it assumes that by becoming wholly thing-oriented and operational it has fulfilled its potentialities. If we probe deeper, we shall see that this culture will not be able to maintain itself unless it breaks through the screen of purely social self-assessment and achieves communion with the existential self, stripped of all social masks.

[1] According to Max Weber, only oppressed strata developed a missionary consciousness, cf. *Gesammelte Aufsätze zur Religions-soziologie*, 1920–21, vol. I, p. 248.

IX

The Crisis of Liberalism
and Democracy as Seen from
the Continental and
Anglo-Saxon Points of View

THE German edition of this book was dedicated to 'My Masters and Pupils in Germany'. Thus it was originally dedicated to those who had experienced in their own lives the tremendous changes of an age of transformation. If this book appears in English, its function alters automatically. It is no longer an attempt at self-enlightenment, made for the benefit of those who have actually lived through these experiences; it attempts to explain the standpoint of these people to a world which has only hearsay knowledge of such changes and is still wrapped in an illusion of traditional stability.

We should not try to belittle or conceal the difference between these points of view. It is most clearly expressed in the fact that to the Western countries the collapse of liberalism and democracy and the adoption of a totalitarian system seem to be the passing symptoms of a crisis which is confined to a few nations, while those who live within the danger zone experience this transition as a change in the very structure of modern society.

For those who are spared these convulsions it is consoling to think that the world is still suffering from the effects of the War. They are glad to soothe themselves with the reflection that dictatorships have often been established in the course of history as temporary solutions in an emergency. On the other hand those who have had first-hand knowledge of the crisis, even if they are keen opponents of dictatorship, are united in the belief that both the social order and the psychology of human beings are changing through and through, and that if this is an evil it is

From *Man and Society in an Age of Reconstruction* (New York: Harcourt, Brace & World, 1967), pp. 3–5. Reprinted by permission of Harcourt Brace Jovanovich, Inc.

an evil which sooner or later is bound to spread. They are convinced moreover that we should not let ourselves be duped by this momentary lull, but should use it to acquire the new techniques, without which it is impossible to face the new situation. The difference in experience is irreconcilable; it colours both the interpretation of isolated facts and the diagnosis of the position as a whole. Where human and social problems are concerned there ought to be a continuous exchange of ideas between different countries and groups. It is only too easy for a nation to drug itself with false assumptions or to distort the meaning of events to fit a frame of reference which is justified, not so much by the facts themselves as by the mood prevailing in the country. Here exaggerated pessimism can be just as dangerous as exaggerated optimism. The task of those to whom destiny has given the opportunity of living in many different countries and of identifying themselves with various points of view has always been to consider this conflict of attitudes and to work it out for themselves, in a form where differences of opinion can either be diametrically opposed or blended in a new synthesis.

The author has derived the greatest profit from learning to think about this very matter both from the German and the English points of view. This book in its present form has been influenced first by his experiences in Germany and later by the English way of thinking, and is an attempt at reconciling the two.

To this book the old saying, *'Habent sua fata libelli'* can be truly applied. When the different chapters of this book were written its author was completely under the influence of experiences bred by the disintegrating tendencies of liberal democratic society. His attention was primarily directed to the failure of the liberal democratic machinery in the Weimar Republic; he had witnessed its impotence to solve the problems of modern mass society. He saw how, under certain social conditions, the planlessness of the liberal order turned into anarchy, how the principle of *laissez-faire*, which once maintained the balance of the social process, at this stage of development resulted in chaos, both in political and in cultural life.

Owing to these experiences he realized that *laissez-faire* in the old sense would no longer work; but that at the present stage of industrial society planning in some form or other was inevitable. He was not at all clear what form this planning ought to take, if it were not to do violence to the spontaneous forces of society. He had not at that time much hope of learning anything from a study of the liberal and democratic countries, for he involuntarily shared the feeling prevalent in Central Europe that the democratic system had already run its course.

This sceptical outlook was not in keeping with his private inclinations. This book was written, even then, from the point of view of a man for whom freedom and personal responsibility were the highest of all values. But he, and those like him, were anxious to guard against self-deception. A realistic description and a theoretical analysis of what was happening in the crisis of liberal democracy seemed to him more important than a mere ideological assertion of the merits of freedom and self-determination.

The concrete analysis of this failure would—he thought—at least draw attention to the cause of the evil. The social organism cannot be cured by pure enthusiasm, but only be a sober investigation of the causes of the disease.

The German edition of this book is in this sense complete in itself, and represents a stage in the writer's attempt to explain the working of modern society. The English edition, compared with the German, is almost a new work; partly because it contains new chapters, but also because the original sections have been redocumented and further elaborated. The most important difference in outlook—as already indicated—is that recently the writer has been living in a country where liberal democracy functions almost undisturbed. This gave him the opportunity of studying the effects of its principles at close range. Although it helped him to enlarge the framework of his experience and to free himself from his deep-rooted scepticism as to the vitality of democracy in our age, in the new surroundings he encountered certain facts which he did not wish to face in the spirit of a mere inquirer. He was constantly tempted, owing to the temporary security of this country, to give way to an optimism which could make him forget that we all are sitting on a volcano, and that those who have actually experienced the eruption have a greater knowledge of the nature and depths of the crater which is yawning beneath our Western society.

X

On the Diagnosis of Our Time

To make a clear diagnosis of the development of society is particularly difficult for our generation. The difficulty, of course, is felt only by those who are not committed dogmatically from the start. Those who prefer to pass their wishful imagery off as the future, imagine that they know where the course of events leads to. Only they run the danger of standing there helplessly just at the decisive moment when everything turns out different. Others who have a good chance of being wrong are those who pay attention to facts and draw conclusions about the future from the developmental tendencies of forces in existing society. Their error, however, will be scientific and thus can be revised rationally.

Our reserve and uncertainty in the field of the scientific diagnosis of a period has a twofold root: a subjective one in our spiritual disposition and an objective one in the particular nature of the forces of society themselves, which always point in several, often contradictory directions. The subjective root of our uncertainty about the future shape of our society is connected with the fact that the developmental scheme, which the last generation still thought to have identified, has begun to lose public credit. The generations that preceded us were convinced that despite all vacillations and relapses, mankind progresses and turns more and more toward reason. Those generations were the direct heirs of the eighteenth century, according to whose world view we every day smash prejudices of the past and are capable of subjecting previously unmastered depths of the soul to our control.

Translated from 'Zur Diagnose unserer Zeit', *Mass und Wert*, Vol. I, September–October 1937, pp. 100–121, by Kurt H. Wolff. Reprinted by permission of Routledge and Kegan Paul Ltd.

People lived confident that it was only a question of time before they could apply the methods of the natural sciences to man, that is, to society. It was precisely the circumstance, however, that they hoped for the progress of human society from the progress of technology alone which has eventually led to disillusionment. It became ever clearer that technology only is a means and leads to progress only if society transforms itself according to the new technological achievements. To be sure, technology saves man a great quantity of time and energy in his struggle with nature. But a great quantity of the free time gained and of the added energy given us by improved technology is absorbed in solving the social and spiritual problems created by that technology. This observation must not be understood as a new invitation along the line of the romantic 'back to nature', for the social and spiritual problems engendered by the progress of technology and their solutions have in the meantime become cultural values, thus containing at the same time losses and gains. The reference to the burden technology and culture impose on us is only meant to throw light on the fact that every technical innovation complicates the organization of society. Thus far the burdens that necessarily arise in the process have always been pushed on to particular classes—in primitive patriarchal society to women; in general, to slaves and half-free people. In our society, it is in the first place the unemployed who are the victims.

Technological achievements themselves do not signify social progress. Only a society that, in its entire organization, even in its psychological structure, receives enrichment without loss, keeps pace with technological innovations. Two events of an almost symbolic nature may illustrate this. First, there is the paradox that our society with its unlimited technical possibilities has created millions of unemployed; and then there is the example that has become famous: that wheat, which thanks to technological improvements in agriculture is produced in abundance, must be burned up to keep prices high and thus get the stagnated circulation of offer and demand moving again. These two facts are of a symbolic nature, for they make the falling apart of the technical and the social good visible to everybody. Those who base their faith on technology must necessarily turn skeptic, unless they first learn to think sociologically. All such disturbances of equilibrium and all such temporarily damaging reactions which uninterrupted progress brings with it must be handled by a society that is guided by justice and according to a plan in such a way that from the beginning newly arising burdens are distributed equally among all citizens. As long as a society introduces technological innovations without planned foresight, functional disturbances often will affect those strata and organs of society which politically and economically can resist them the least. Only the person who can calculate in advance, with more or less exactness, the consequences and effects of technological progress in the social system pursues rational thinking to the end.

The spiritual members of our generation have presumably lost their faith in progress above all precisely because they have not been able, or have not wanted, to raise that rational energy of following thought to its end. We can observe in everyday life how one who is most consistently rational in the technological and economic area becomes all too easily irrational in social matters; unconsciously he gives in, partly to a kind of indolence of the intellect, partly to socially effective inhibitions. Knowledge of social structure fails, not because of the limits of the human capacity to think, but because of the unwillingness of the individual, of a class, or of a generation to put social transformation into practice. The courage to think, which has led technology and the study of nature to such heights, must not fail when it comes to society. Our incapacity to diagnose future possibilities thus has, subjectively, its cause in the collapse of our faith in the socially redeeming force of technological progress. This collapse, however, is nothing else than the consequence of the incapacity to think sociological causal series, as clearly as technical ones, through to their end.

Let us turn now to the objective causes of our failure. Here the reason for the difficulty of anticipating certain tendencies is that the development itself becomes ever more confused and chaotic. If we realize the enormous shifts taking place in the demographic basis of society and the catastrophic blockages arising simultaneously against group movements and migrations that have become necessary, then the most elementary, but also most hidden cause of the disturbance of social circulation becomes visible. But the blocks to migrations, the task of which it is to relieve countries and create balances, is only a symptom of societal failure. Closely connected with it is the planlessness in the growth of industries. The diffusion of the general process of industrialization into new countries creates mass armies of the unemployed in the old industrial countries. In order to integrate these masses that have suddenly lost their bread as well as their function, war industries are launched. The dynamite thus created and accumulated waits to explode, creates general insecurity, and transforms even the remaining nations, which are still in balance, from work communities into war-capitalistic enterprises. These are the links of a chain; their connection makes the proliferating effect of a fundamental societal disturbance visible in its main phases. All this decay in the midst of growing absolute wealth, of increased inventive power, and of the infinite possibilities of a further differentiating division of labor—this, indeed, is a conflict between basic tendencies where every positive possibility produces an equally powerful negative one.

We come to a similar conclusion if we look more carefully at the immense processes of dissolution within social bodies. Ever since the World War [I] even the layman has been able to see clearly that the family is losing its inner consistency, and this in proportion to the social dissolution of a given country. In part this must be attributed to the loss of its former functions, for it increasingly leaves the tasks of production, consumption, education, etc., to institutions independent of it. On the other hand, the methods of forming men which are its disposal are no longer commensurate with the profoundly changed public life. Today a man thinks back to his education and his home with resentment because he can use the values, feelings, and thoughts he has absorbed in the family much less than could the citizen of earlier societies for whom home and world constituted an organic unity.

Psychoanalysis with its revelations of the psychic mechanisms which, full of resentment, dominate family life is only one of the forms in which we become aware of this conflict between home and world. Suddenly the psychic attitudes the home produces seem exclusively negative because they turn out to be unsuited to prepare one for contemporary public adulthood. For a patrician son there was no contrast between his home and the 'world', for the public sphere in which he had to prove himself was comparable to an enlarged family. This is also true for the nobleman, the craftsman, etc. They did not dash out of the private seclusion of the home and against the public world of the mass: in growing up, the individual moved step by step into participation in the public life of the time. In this gradual enlargement of the home, customs characteristic of a given landscape played a special role, but the various institutions of the life of the community added their share: habits and usages, pastor and teacher, parish and festivities, church and tavern made the individual a burgher, peasant, or beggar. The process of dissolution of traditional forms of society can be observed also in the failure of these institutions to resist. The ease with which they can now be overrun shows that they were hollowed out even before the advent of the totalitarian state. The forms of life held together by landscape, tradition, and community have only rarely withstood its organized centralism. The diagnosis that the churches in these countries (Russia, Turkey, Germany,

Spain, etc.) resisted impotently is not refuted by the heroic courage of some individuals. There is something in the psychological technique of the churches' influence over souls that does not withstand the forms of mass society which are now spreading everywhere.

What is at issue is shown even more clearly by the gradual disappearance of the old forms of using leisure. Not only in cities but wherever the psychic correlates of industrialized life penetrate, people are attracted much more by a use of leisure that creates a hunger for stimuli than by the traditional forms of sociability which aimed at keeping the whole personality in equilibrium. But it would be rash to conclude from this tendency that the man of the mass and the machine strives only for distraction and not for the integration of his personality. It is possible that his preference for the modern psychic stimuli is based on the instinctive knowledge that they do not spring from an anachronism but agree with the rest of his life. This is more important to him than are older forms of balance which have not yet come to terms with the tensions of modern life. The same is true of the ethical norms which, inherited from earlier times, correspond less and less to man's life and actions in the contemporary social structure. Here, and not in a general decadence, lies the cause why the mass is losing its belief in norms generally. The same phenomena can be observed also in the field of thought. The rupture in the basis of thought, disagreement concerning ultimate presuppositions, the decomposition of a unifying picture of the world have become so general that not only intellectuals but also ordinary men no longer dare have a consistent conception of life but see a special virtue in the lack of principles—in more solid societies only the feebleminded would be given credit for this absence of a world view. All these and many other tendencies must be related to one another. It then is difficult to decide whether we approach a general dissolution—a predatory capitalism organized by the state—or an absolutely new birth of the social order. In the latter case, however, it is to be feared that the new birth, like that of the phoenix, will be from its ashes.

Not independently of the factors just listed but almost as a response to the dissolution described, a new phenomenon has entered the play of social forces. It must be treated separately because of its far-reaching consequences. I mean the emergence of *modern social technology*. This new technology, working in a new field, has as far-reaching and significant consequences as has technology applied to nature; nor is it any less two-edged in its results. By social technology I mean the ever more conscious manipulation, direction, and interrelation of human drives and ways of thinking and reacting in modern mass society. By virtue of it, society changes into a kind of machine.

Up to now, too, society has been based on its influence on the modes of human conduct (although this was possible only within limits): education in the home, customs, school, church, and the organs of community life and of the formation of public opinion sought to exert their influence and to form a type of man according to known ideals. But this influence stopped at a stage which in the field of technology approximately corresponds to that of handicraft. Its methods were founded in everyday practical rules for the most part applied unconsciously. They were almost always taken over from the past, modified in accordance with the time, only quite rarely oriented rationally toward a desirable aim, let alone thought through. And yet they were effective. That they were is due, among other things, to the very slow development of traditional societies. Economic progress that was only slight, changed societies in a hardly perceptible fashion. The inherited educational methods of the family, the ideal images of the church, and the public customs had time to unfold and by slow selection separate viable forms of experience from unsuitable ones. Thus developed a traditional type of man whose forms of acting and models of thinking were homogeneous enough to guarantee the smooth course of the social process. At the same time they were sufficiently elastic to leave the individual enough freedom for his own attempts at adjusting to unexpected situations. The principle alive in these forms and models thus resembled that of handicraft: traditional uniformity with individual modifications that despise mechanical precision. The fact that in forming men, earlier society got along with a social technology arrested at the stage of handicraft is due, in addition to the slow growth of society, to the relatively limited social mobility of its members. By and large, people spent their lives in the groups for which they were educated. Wandering from one place to another or the rise and fall between classes took on large dimensions only exceptionally. Hence no conflict could arise between the limited nature of the traditional educational models and any rapid changes.

To be sure, the age of 'liberalism' experienced a far-reaching dynamicization of the economic bases, but the illusion of constancy long remained unaffected in large circles. In comparison with our epoch, the psychic concussion that accompanied the age of Enlightenment was still limited, because the stratum that produced economic growth was relatively thin: only entrepreneurs, intellectuals, and part of the bureaucracy were actively involved in change. Nevertheless, a subtle ear will hear in the changes of our time the same pulse beat as in the commotion of the people of the Enlightenment and of Romanticism. In the setting of their aims one can see the beginning of a process in which the traditional forms of life and experience were gradually made the theme of a rational critique. The attack on the traditional forms of experience and social structure did not yet become radical then also because the disturbances in the economic and social equilibrium were experienced and balanced out by small, adaptable social units. In the struggle for a new order of the economy and of life no organized masses were yet involved but rather small enterprises and organically grown groups. These can more easily adapt to new needs than can mass organizations which, once they are accustomed to a model, follow the blind law of inertia with all their force. In addition, the integration of the new strata making for trouble was much easier in a society in which small units freely competed: scattered, non-cartellized entrepreneurs, reformers fighting alone without organized following, and single intellectuals found their places in society after a shorter or longer period of struggle. With their integration, often their minor or major proposals for reform, too, entered the social process in the form of new institutions. The traditionally and slowly flowing course of social and intellectual life is capable of resisting smaller gusts of wind; the waves enrich its surface; but the river does not yet overflow its banks.

Today, hundreds of thousands are dragged from one place to another according to the laws of the labor market; more extraordinary structural changes take place in ten years than formerly in a hundred; the number of new psychic stimulants is greater in a week than before in decades. The individual experiences greater tension in worlds existing next to one another than did, let us say, a Christian knight on a Crusade who got to know the Oriental world. In such a world, one cannot work effectively with a social technique that corresponds to the developmental stage of the small enterprise of the craftsman. Just as the craft economy can—irrationally—satisfy only a small circle of customers, so is the traditional formulation of men inadequate to the new age of immense technology.

The groups that first experienced the full weight of control of the mass society in their own bodies were also the first to grasp the necessity of coming to terms with these new problems. We might think here of the medieval church as an antecedent; but despite its will to direct the feelings and ways of thinking according to a plan, it is not a fit example, for in a world essentially agrarian and without developed social technology, it had to leave too much to the power of tradition. In addition, it was not yet sufficiently in control of rationalized methods to figure as the real beginning in the history of the development of society as a machine. It was the army of the absolutist states which was the first great institution that devised rational methods not only as a guarantee of the physical maintenance of its battalions but also for educating large masses (which usually came from ruined strata) to act homogeneously and if possible even to acquire attitudes according to prescription.

This army worked out some social-psychological patterns of obedience and loyalty which have come up again and again whenever it has not been necessary to hide the coercive character of sociation. The organizational models of the Prussian army, for instance, have again and again proved more powerful—especially in times of crisis when democratic forms have failed—than all other integrative methods of the large society. Nevertheless, in the long run, the all too authoritarian-military procedure has not been the most usable one. In bureaucratic organizations, force which is too visibly in the foreground requires too much energy for control and espionage A growing and spontaneously expanding society needs pioneers; the spirit of a mass technique that is too centralized and too much oriented toward discipline limits individual adaptability too much for it to be equal to the tasks imposed by the expansion. For this reason, the techniques and administrative forms developed by American mass society in its growth have had a much more lasting success than had the merely military forms of obedience. The American technique of mass propaganda has found the most usable psychological rules on the basis of direct experience and has thus created the democratic pattern of influence over the mass. America had no feudalism; from the outset, therefore, the power of many territorial traditions and customs could not arise. Such customs did not have to be taken into account and, in case local traditions arose nevertheless, could, if need be, easily be broken. The mighty waves of immigrants of the most diverse nationalities into the newly available areas of settlement made 'Americanization' a mass-psychological problem. One had to proceed 'democratically', not only because in the beginning there was no effective central power but also because the immigrants represented precisely the human type of greatest originality and strongest initiative. Since this technique had originated in a democratic country, there was no thought of imposing the desired psychic modes of conduct dictatorially. One was satisfied to promote or gradually modify, when the need arose, attitudes that already existed.

This knowledge originating in America of the practical management of mass drives in a society in flux, was first utilized by Russian propaganda, which made it a part of the dictatorial enlightenment of the masses. In America, the difficult task of the new social technology was the corrective influence on men by psychic mass manipulation and social welfare. The psychic influences of home and community had been dissolved by the extraordinary restlessness of the society; by means of the social technology of men one had to see to it that the conformity necessary to build a society was produced to a degree, if only *post factum* and artificially. By contrast, Russian dictatorial enlightenment had the task of transforming, in an incredibly short period, peasant masses into industrial human types who were not only reliable in their new work but also had to adopt the rational world view that in the machine age is required for the maintenance of a planned state. In America, propaganda had to solve the problems of how differently prepared masses without tradition could be made to feel and act alike in elections and on other occasions. In comparison, Russian social technology had much more difficult tasks, namely gradually to transform occasional, merely emotional loyalty into an educational campaign which would seize the whole person and make him into the citizen of a new society.

This could not be brought about by emotional propaganda alone. What is new in all this is the following: in addition to the consciously calculated impact on the emotions, the total state has at its disposal all other means of psychic control. Besides the propaganda apparatus, there is the whole school system, and behind the political coordination of the mentality, more or less based on imitation, there is the coordinating violence of anxiety, inspired by the power organization of the state. The aim is always to transform shortlived moods into lasting effects on outlook. Nursery, kindergarten, school, and university deepen the effect that the propaganda apparatus has only occasionally. But the other areas of social life, too—workers' groups, leisure-time management, the press—serve the same aim: to develop social technology to the utmost. In its methods, this technique is more rational than earlier traditional schools, churches, and national organizations, which worked with a vague popular psychology and with unclear aims. It is more effective also because it coordinates its means and does not permit its institutions to work at cross-purposes.

As regards world view and power politics, in earlier traditional society, the church, with its religious impact, was usually not in the same hands as the state schools—and this led to the mutual destruction of the effects the two achieved. Confronting both was 'life' with its conflict mechanism which justified egoistic drives and aimed at stunting the moralistic elements that home, school, and church together represented, despite all differences among them. Looked at purely from the one-sided point of view of efficiency, liberal social technology wastes enormous energy because by its planlessness it weakens, if it does not destroy, effects in one place that it achieves in another. There is no doubt that the coordination of lines of influence saves expenditure and energy. One may well admit this even while disagreeing with the aims or arguing that this gain is canceled by deeper injuries.

In any case, the Russian state has put this recognition into practice by using its coordinating social technique to push the rationalization of influence over men to its extreme. In addition to the conscious manipulation of psychic effects, this coordination of social forces, which approaches machinelike precision—and not the fact that the state aims at influencing its citizens at all—is the decisive novelty modern society has brought about. Even if it is correct to observe that the invention and use of instruments which spread outlooks and opinions—such as telephone, telegraph, radio, and popular press—fall in this period, still, these are only mechanical facilitations of the new spirit and of the will to organize the influence over men as a large-scale operation and according to plan.

Italian and German fascism simply took over this large-scale enterprise of coordination from Russia—with one difference. True, they, too, are penetrating the schools and are trying to have more than a propagandistic effect; but they are incapable of transforming the technique of social influence into a work of true enlightenment. And this for a simple reason: in such work, Russian industrialization and socialization can tolerate a considerable amount of rationality, although in that society, too, many areas of thinking are taboo. By contrast, fascism must become irrational and emotional in all decisive phases of life and social organization because its system does not resolve but only covers up the fundamental difficulties of the new economic and social structure. In one respect, however, the fascist countries are superior to the liberal states: forced by their crises, they try somehow to come to terms with the *psychological* problem of modern mass society, in the first place with that of unemployment. To be sure, thus far fascism has not been able to overcome economic crises, let alone bring about prosperity and a lasting rise in the standard of living, even by the artificial means of war industry. Quite on the contrary, its economy is going downward. But at least it tries, even if with the most brutal of means, to get the psychological consequences of unemployment under control. In its social technique it surely chokes off the enlightenment of the masses and addresses itself to the most primitive instincts; but at least it occupies itself, even in this distorted form, with questions that every future mass society will have to solve.

This is the point where the prosperous mass states of liberalism and democracy threaten to lag behind. They too have structural unemployment and, as long as the tempo of world industrialization keeps on, will in all likelihood continue to have it. But in these states, there is not yet any understanding of those problems. Aside from unemployment, the circulation of society is rather smooth; and this conceals the difficulty of the phenomenon to all who are still well off and make the decisions in these countries. Although the fascist work camp is a most unpleasant solution of the psychic crises to which the permanently unemployed is exposed, still, social-technologically it is at a higher level than that of the liberal practice of trying to solve the social-psychological problem of unemployment by subsidies.

Thus, for instance, the fact that the English middle-class observer, too, already lives in a mass society remains largely hidden to him. He does not yet see the symptoms of mass existence in his country because except for minor frictions, the traditional modes of forming men—from Puritanical home to public school to university—still function. The existence of a world empire, which again and again creates escapes from economic and social difficulties, has prevented more than one dark symptom of the problem of mass society from becoming suddenly visible. But this does not mean that England and other countries favored by prosperity will be saved from the problem of mass society; perhaps, however, they will be in the fortunate position of studying these problems by observing the experiences of other peoples and of passing from the stage of social technology characteristic of domestic economy and handicraft to that of large-scale organization. This gain in time should be used for the thorough investigation of aim-directed methods. Countries such as England, which have not yet permitted their liberal and democratic institutions to be destroyed and which want to maintain them even when the new social technology develops mass dimensions, set new tasks for themselves.

Above all, we must not stand in front of modern social technology devoid of understanding and see in it only propaganda. We must not judge it exclusively from the aristocratic point of view of a minority culture, the aim of which was to have a few outstanding individuals while merely tolerating the dull masses. Modern social technology is a necessity of life of every industrialized mass society. It is just as necessary for the psychic maintenance of this society as economic technology is for its economic maintenance. Scorning it does not enable us to do without it; and left to itself it becomes a blind force that destroys everything. It shares with the other kinds of technology both their grandeur and their inhumanness. It is grandiose because it resolves difficulties of impressive dimensions. We have only to imagine how a mass society, with its tendencies that contradict one another and push toward dissolution, could exist if it were not capable of placing its entire technique of influencing people on a new basis. In view of the chaos in which the church, the home, and the school lose their power of shaping men, the invention of planned influence over people is a salvation, even though in its present form only a makeshift. This technology is inhuman because, being an idling machine, it is neither good nor bad. Its effect always depends on the aim in the service of which it is used. Its positive power is highlighted by the fact that Germany, the moment its rulers considered it useful, managed instantaneously to stop the hatred of the Poles. This hatred is one of the most deep-rooted collective feelings; and even if not all Germans suddenly are in love with the Poles, it remains sociologically significant that attitudes of hatred can be guided in such a way that they do not integrate sociologically and thus do not become politically effective either.

What relief would come to man's social life if this power of planned influence could be used, not for the artificial instigation of conflicts, but for the cultivation of attitudes on the existence of which every peaceful cooperation and understanding is based! We should tolerate a good many planned interventions by those in authority if these were limited to the spheres of human conduct in which peacefulness, readiness to understand, and decency have their roots. An agreement among nations to coordinate education and propaganda in the sense that men would consider a minimum of decency as indispensable would be a kind of conformity against which we have no reason whatever to rebel. At the moment, we need not decide what other preconditions of an economic and political sort would have to be met to bring about such a social re-education of men on an international scale: it is enough to realize that it is neither large masses nor well developed social technology, but the manner in which technology is directed at the present time, that creates evil.

In order fully to appreciate the possibilities of the new social technique we must bear in mind that its contemporary form continues to work with an all too primitive psychology. This psychology rests on the collection of rules of thumb that correspond to the horizon of the agitator, officer, or sales manager of a large-scale organization, and for this reason is still far from having attained the refinement from which its real power could be inferred. The propagandist works with a very superficial analysis of human possibilities. Beside this psychology, however, there is emerging in our society a much more subtle sociological psychology, a science the wealth of which has not yet been fully utilized. We have in mind the enormous progress that it has made in connection with modern social service, with juvenile courts, and with group and individual education. We have in mind experiments known in behaviorism as 'reconditioning', which make it possible to free damaging habits originating in early childhood from their rigidity, or to restructure them in fruitful ways. We have in mind the results of adult education, which show that most traits generally interpreted as character defects or lack of talent are early milieu damages. The almost pathological arrest at a primitive stage of development of the drives and of spiritual life can in such cases be corrected by later education.

These experiments in later education also throw light on the people's political conduct that is often so senseless. Instead of explaining this by means of LeBon's lay psychology of mass behavior, it is more promising to point out that people who have had no occasion to act politically in responsible fashion will necessarily react in a senseless manner as long as no gradually accumulating practice in the political field teaches them step by step to learn from experience and thus brings them to the level of action of a fully adult person. Why should the individual instantaneously, without previous schooling and opportunity of practice, be equal to normal demands just in the field of politics? Nobody would expect a man to be able to drive a car without previous training, or a layman to pass a reasonable judgment on complex business affairs. In this list of refinements in psychological techniques, mention may finally be made of depth psychology. Its disclosure of the unconscious opens up insights which, even though for the present they have all too much the nature of constructions, will in time subject a new psychic dimension to control.

If we consider all these positive possibilities of social technology, the next task emerges as that of their careful observation and the progressive disclosure of their real meaning. The fundamental error that blocks the road to an adequate understanding of modern social technology is most clearly revealed on analyzing the linguistic expression—the word—by which it is usually referred to. It is most characteristic that in the atmosphere of mass dictatorships, 'coordination' has been translated as *'Gleichschaltung'*, although the two words have totally different meanings.

Coordination signifies the meaningful relating one to the other of all means at one's disposal, the harmonizing of many instruments in an orchestra. Such attuning, however, leaves the road open to either monotony or polyphony. Now it is indeed most significant that coordination has been interpreted, without much hesitation, in the sense of monotony, as *Gleichschaltung* for the purpose of producing bleak conformity. But if we think the matter through to its end we see that *Gleichschaltung* does not necessarily follow from the existence of a centralized social technology, that this technology need not be used for the creation of uniform, herd-like people. The extant social experiments represent only mutilations of the possibilities implicit in the idea of coordination. In the social sphere, exactly as in the orchestra, coordination only signifies that the available means—in our case, the psychological means of influence, such as family, school, leisure-time activities, etc.—are not allowed to work at random but that the formative forces contained in them are attuned to one another. Whether they are used for the purpose of creating the uniformity or on the contrary the many-sided differentiation of individuals depends on the will of the planners.

To be sure, access to this insight is blocked not only to dictatorial levelers but also to those who believe that a completely free play of social forces without coordination and planning is still within the realm of the possible. These liberals of an older stamp must be reminded, however, that there is no return to such a conception of freedom. At the stage of mass society, the planless play of social forces, unrestrained liberalism, does not lead to freedom but, with the first radical convulsion that comes along, to chaos. Just out of such a chaos of uncontrolled groups fighting each other in mass society, each wanting completely to suppress the other, there have grown in times of crisis, as a reaction, the will to manipulate by violence all available means of influence and to conceive of planning as leveling and suppressing all spontaneity. In this early phase, in which men for the first time encounter the great power implicit in the coordinating manipulation of social technology, the thought that optimal planning does not mean planning for uniformity must prevail in due course. Otherwise, the development will irresistibly lead to such mass enslavement of mankind that it hardly makes a difference under whose banner it is consummated. Even a social order which has rational aims and foundations and is capable of functioning, but which abandons its citizens institutionally, will in time fall victim to the technicians of the social machine, the bureaucrats.

I therefore believe that the countries with liberal-democratic traditions must, at this moment when they enter the age of mass society, use their particular traditions to interpret the problem of mass education in a more correct sense than the dictators have done. The first step to this end is to separate the idea of planning and coordinating from the idea of *Gleichschaltung*. In our time of collectivism, true liberalism has the complementary task of calling attention to those possibilities of social technology and planning with which we can strive for differentiation and by which order is attained not only at the cost of restricting freedom.

Planning in this sense means planning for freedom. This means to control those fields of social growth on the security of which depends the smooth functioning of the apparatus of society, but at the same time consciously to leave free those areas that contain the greatest opportunity for creative development and individualization. This freedom, however, it not the freedom of *laissez-faire*, *laissez-aller*, which can no longer exist today. It is the freedom of a society which, disposing of the entire coordinated social technology, has itself under control, guarding itself by its own free will against the dictatorial suppression of certain areas of life, and incorporating the guarantees of these free areas into its structure and constitution.

He who plans freedom, that is, assigns self-determination free spaces in the regulated structure, must plan, to be sure, also the conformity needed for the life of the society. The liberal epoch could calmly direct all its attention to the diffusion of the idea of freedom, for it could rely on that substructure of traditional conformity which the preceding communal culture of the middle ages had passed on to it. In the immediate future we shall have to devote much energy to substituting a new conformity for the traditional one, which is in process of dissolution. In this effort we shall rediscover values that we had forgotten in the age of unlimited competition: identification with the other members of society, collective responsibility, and the obligation following from it to possess in common with the others a basis of attitudes and ways of behavior. But once this necessary solidarity with the new collectivity is secured as the fundamental outlook—a conformity to which we could hardly object—there is no reason why on this basis there should not occur variety which in natural gradation goes all the way to the individualized personality, and why the road to such variety could not be prepared in terms of the structure of the society, of plans for education, etc. This conscious creation of opportunities for personality formation is the more possible, the more in other areas of life modern social technology makes available far more certain guarantees of smooth functioning than were at the disposal of societies of an older stamp.

The fact of large numbers does not exclude the capacity of there being integration in small groups in which initiative and individualization have their social locus. In these small groups, in which everyone once again has the feeling that much depends on what he himself does and in which he learns to act on his own responsibility, instead of wholly losing himself in the anonymity of the mass, there emerge those social constellations in which individualization is most likely to unfold. Today sociology has already reached the stage where it is possible to indicate which social forces and constellations have typically promoted individualization in the course of history. Here, too, planning for freedom does not refer to the concrete shape of the personality that one may wish to prescribe for the individual. What it means is to know from experience and science which kinds of education and which social constellation and tasks offer the greatest chance of kindling initiative and the will to determine and shape oneself.

This development of the possibilities contained in coordination cannot succeed, however, if we glide into the next phase of society formation blindly. True, the transition from the old to the new state of society must occur following the spontaneous movement of the masses. At the same time, however, it must be guided by groups who proceed on the basis of a decisive political will and of corresponding psychological and sociological knowledge and do not leave the most important steps to desperadoes, military agitators, and radio managers.

Certainly, this requirement only hints at the political task and is far from solving it. But once we gain clarity on what we actually want and have sociologically clarified knowledge of the means contemporary society makes available, the solution is within the realm of the possible.

Today we do not believe that thinking alone can solve the problems of the development of society but—after the experiences of the last decades—even less that the inner dynamic of the social process relieves us of the obligation to think critically, or that faith alone leads to everybody's salvation. Instead, we have realized that we must constantly observe what is happening and quickly learn from changing experiences, but that in this process we cannot rely by any means on the dogmas of a party. In the long run, history is not made by one group alone but is born out of the struggle of contending tendencies in which human intelligence and unhampered thought are the clarifying power and can become leading if they intervene in the right places and knowledgeably identify existing forces.

What is urgently needed, therefore, is that particularly those groups become socially conscious whose complementary function it is to help the values of individualization, of the undogmatic approach to things, and of humanity to gain recognition in the approaching age of a new collectivity. As long as they do not learn correctly to assess the meaning of the new forces, however, their struggle will equal in hopelessness that of the craftsmen in the age of emerging modern technology, the machine wreckers. Like them, they run the risk of destroying the new machine of the society in a blind struggle, rather than in their knowledge becoming its master.

XI

Education, Sociology and the Problem of Social Awareness

I. THE CHANGING FEATURES OF MODERN EDUCATIONAL PRACTICE[1]

ONE of the most important changes in the educational field seems to be the gradual change from the compartmental concept of education, as it prevailed in the age of laissez-faire, to the integral concept. The first concept treated education as a more or less self-sufficient compartment of life. It thought in terms of schools and classes where teachers instructed boys and girls in subjects specified by the curriculum. The progress of the students, and indirectly the capacity of the teacher, was assessed by a system of marks. There were written examinations, and if these were passed to the satisfaction of the examining body, the aim of education had been achieved. Some may consider this to be a caricature, but others will blame me for characterizing this method as belonging to the past only. They may feel that too many still act and think in these terms. However this may be, even if it is a caricature, it represents in an exaggerated form the tendency toward compartmentalization.

Education was a compartment because the school and the world had become two categories not complementary but rather opposed to each other. Education was a compartment up to that age limit at which a human being was expected to be accessible to educational influence. Up to a certain age educational institutions tried to impress you and to impress your behaviour, whereas

[1] To supplement what has been said in the text I mention some of my other publications on the function and shape of sociology:
K. Mannheim, *Die Gegenwartsaufgaben der Soziologie* (The Task of Sociology

From *Diagnosis of Our Time* (New York: Oxford University Press, 1944), pp. 59–79. Reprinted by permission of Routledge and Kegan Paul Ltd.

after the age limit you were free. This tendency towards compartmentalization has been broken by the revolutionary concept of adult education, extramural education, refresher courses, which familiarized us with the idea of post-education and re-education. It is equally due to the healthy influence of adult education that we acknowledge the fact that education ought to go on for life, that society is an educational agent, and that education at school is good only if in many ways it embodies the educational technique of life. From now on, the aim of the school is not only to impart ready-made knowledge but to enable us to learn more efficiently from life itself.

But it is not only getting rid of the bookish scholastic concept of learning which abolishes the barriers between school and life. The same tendency works equally strongly in other directions. In former days there was an absolute cleavage between home and school. Now attempts are made to bring together parents and teachers and to co-ordinate influences coming from school with those coming from home. The growth of social work, the study of juvenile delinquency, threw new light upon the share that various compartments of life have in the building of the character of the young. It became evident that if the home, the school, the child guidance clinic, the social worker, the juvenile court work only for themselves, they disregard each other's

in the Present Situation). Opening lecture at a conference of German University teachers of Sociology, held in Frankfurt a. M. in February 1932 (published in German only: Tübingen, 1932).

———, 'The Place of Sociology', in *The Social Sciences: Their Relations in Theory and in Teaching* (London: LePlay House Press, 35 Gordon Square, 1936).

———, 'Adult Education and the Social Sciences', in *Tutors' Bulletin of Adult Education*, Second Series, No. 20 (February 1938).

———, 'German Sociology, 1918–33', in *Politica* (February 1934).

Cf. also M. Ginsberg, 'The Place of Sociology'; A. M. Carr-Saunders, 'The Place of Sociology'; T. H. Marshall, 'Report on the Teaching of the Social Sciences', in *The Social Sciences: Their Relations in Theory and in Teaching* (London: LePlay House Press, 35 Gordon Square, 1936).

C. A. Beard, 'A Charter for the Social Sciences (Report of the Commission on the Social Studies)', in *American Historical Association* (New York, 1932); L. C. Marshall and R. M. Goetz, 'Curriculum-Making in the Social Studies—A Social Process Approach (Report of the Commission on the Social Studies)', in *American Historical Association*, Part XIII (New York, 1936); E. Horn, 'Methods of Instruction in the Social Studies (Report of the Commission on the Social Studies)', in *American Historical Association*, Part XV (New York, 1937); and the excellent volume, *The Social Studies in General Education*, Report of the Committee on the Function of the Social Studies in General Education for the Commission of Secondary School Curriculum (New York and London, 1938); Frederick William Roman, *La Place de la Sociologie dans l'Education aux Etats-Unis* (Paris, 1923); A. Walther, *Soziologie und Sozialwissenschaften in Amerika* (Karlsruhe, 1927); F. B. Karpf, *American Social Psychology: Its Origins, Development and European Background* (New York, 1932).

influence; thus a tendency to integrate their work was bound to follow.

But this realization of the need for integration in life had its influence on the work of the school in a different way. It led to an integral concept of the curriculum. This can best be shown in our changing concept of moral education. Formerly the moral self was to remain compartmentalized, and one thought to have paid due tribute to it if one inserted into the curriculum religious or moral education. To-day we know that this religious or moral education is bound to remain ineffective unless it is related to the other parts of the curriculum. Everything we teach, and even more how we teach it, has an impact upon character formation. Whereas formerly we thought that the mysteries of character training could be solved by games or the boarding-school system, to-day we know that the kind of games one plays and the intimate details of school organization are more important than the actual labels given to these games or school systems. The social organization of the school, the kind of social rôles one has an opportunity to play, whether competition or co-operation prevails, whether there is more opportunity for team work than for solitary work, all contribute to the type of man which will grow up in these surroundings.

These integrating trends in the curriculum are themselves nothing but an expression of a deeper psychological insight, namely, that personality is one and indivisible. If we give up the previous rigid concept of school subjects and try to relate the knowledge gained in one course to that of the other courses, it is because we know to-day that only a co-ordinated attack on the mind of the individual will be effective. The efficacy of our teaching depends on how we relate new experience to the already existing background of the individual. Ultimately the ideal teaching of a human being would take into account the whole life-history of the individual and many of the social factors which operate on him apart from the school. Thus education is becoming integral in two respects: (*a*) by integrating its activities with the activities of other social institutions; and (*b*) with respect to the wholeness of the person.

But the peak of the integrating tendencies is reached when not only in our practice but also in our theory we plainly admit that education is only one of the many social agencies influencing human behaviour, and as such, whether we want it or not, always serves a social purpose and is deliberately aiming at moulding certain human types.

In the previous age, the age of laissez-faire Liberalism, educational practice was over-compartmental; the main shortcoming of its theory was that it was society-blind. It could not see, or did not want to admit, the existence of society as a relevant factor in human affairs. It did not want to assess the impact of society upon the aims and methods of education.

In its theory, traditional education had an extreme idealistic philosophy and insisted upon the statement that the basic values and the aims of education were eternal, and the final and exclusive purpose of education was the fostering of the free development of personality through the unhampered unfolding of innate qualities. The integral theory of education, in its sociological aspects, does not object to that theory as such; it does not doubt the fact that some ideals may be stated which survive the ages and are the basis of any decent way of life and social organization. What it objects to is that this theory is too aloof from history to be really helpful in concrete situations. Whoever tries to state such eternal values very soon realizes that they are bound to be too abstract to lend concrete shape to education at a given moment. In the same way, if the final core of the self is something that is eternal and beyond environmental influence, we still have to consider that more empirical and historical attire in which we meet our fellowbeings as citizens of a given state, as workers in factories, as clerks in an office, as human beings striving for such satisfactions as are available in a given social order.

II. SOME REASONS FOR THE NEED OF SOCIOLOGICAL INTEGRATION IN EDUCATION

Our fathers and forefathers could do without sociological theories, for the interdependence between the institutions and human activities in a village or small community were too obvious and could be seen by everybody. In the age of our forefathers sociology was on the whole a part of common sense, but the immense growth of industrial society, the invisible operation of its forces, made society most enigmatic to the individual. Even the most careful observation of the immediate surroundings cannot disclose to the untrained mind what is going on beneath the surface, how effects accumulate and react upon each other.

The belief that one could settle the most important problems of education and social work on the basis of common sense alone was shaken whenever the different functionaries of society had to meet in connection with the same case. This revealed that the schoolmaster, the judge, the social worker, the public servant relied upon a completely different kind of common sense. The rule of thumb was different in the departments of administration, in education, the courts, etc., according to their peculiar traditions and the ideologies which prevailed in these circles. They very often held different views as to the effect of punishment, for instance, or assessed differently the effects of environmental influences upon the individual.

Fortunately, during the last decades a great deal of knowledge has been accumulated in the various branches of psychology and sociology. Child psychology, educational psychology, criminology, experimental psychology, psychoanalysis collected a whole store of material which was ready to be co-ordinated and integrated into a Science of Human Behaviour. From another angle sociology made its contribution to science. It observed man's behaviour in different societies, in primitive societies, in different phases of history, in different classes and in the social surroundings of our own society. It observed the effect of different social institutions such as the family, the community, the workshop, the gang, upon behaviour. It observed man under the conditions of social security, when he is craving for gradual improvement in his economic conditions, in his status or his enjoyment of leisure, but it also observed him under the conditions of social insecurity, social unrest, revolution and war.

Thus in the long run it became impossible to deal with the innumerable cases of personal and social maladjustment, as they followed from the growth of industrial society, disregarding that accumulated knowledge which characterizes human nature and its conditioning. This branch of sociology is another integrating link between the disciplines dealing with human affairs, and it is impossible to think of a teacher who does not, day by day, meet with behaviour difficulties in the child which, properly observed, are but symptoms of conflicts within the family, in the community, conflicts between age-groups, etc.

There is yet another sphere of sociological information which has to be acquired by the teacher, if his aim is not to educate his pupils in the abstract but for life in an existing society. As contrasted with those problems which grew out of the difficulties of the individuals to adjusting themselves to their immediate surroundings, there are maladjustments more comprehensive in scope. Here I have in mind the cultural crisis through which our society is passing, the spiritual changes in society at large, which certainly have their impact also upon the behaviour difficulties of individuals in their everyday life. I am thinking of those epoch-making changes caused by industrial civilization, such as the partial, sometimes total disorganization of our customs, habits and traditional valuations. I think of those social processes which very often disintegrate the family or the community. I think of the changed nature of work and leisure, and their impact upon personality formation or their disintegrating effects. I think of those tendencies in modern society which lead to a deterioration in our cultural life, to the lack of contact between the thinker, the artist and the community, the lowering of the standards by which we judge public affairs, the causes of the power of propaganda, the effects of commercialization, overorganization, etc. It is even more absurd that the teacher should be unaware of the sociological investigations concerning the place of Youth in modern society and of observations which show how biological fermentation and social unrest work together to create a generation which, if left to itself, will be unable to stand the strain of an age to come. In one word, it is impossible that the teacher should have no knowledge of these fundamental tendencies of deterioration, their causes and the remedies which have been tried with more or less success. It is impossible that we should return from the present war, the most inhuman in history, to peace-time conditions without having the assistance of the teachers in attacking these disintegrating tendencies. To-day no one can think of the peace after this war just as a going back to pre-war conditions. There will be too much upheaval and, therefore, an urgent need for a fundamental regeneration of our society. In the society of the past it was possible to hand down habits, customs and an established philosophy of life, which enabled the individual to play rôles in society which were more or less fixed in advance. In a changing society like ours only an education for change can help. The latter consists in an undogmatic training of the mind, which enables the person not to be driven by the current of changing events but to rise above them.

This is no longer possible through *ad hoc* improvised pseudo-sociological interpretations. There must be an informed mind which can discriminate between those genuine elements in the tradition which are still alive and make for emotional stability, and those human attitudes and institutions on the other side which decay because they have lost function and meaning in a changed society. It is our ignorance of the dehumanizing effects of industrial civilization upon the mind which allows the growth of that void into which the witch-doctors of propaganda pour their poison. If the modern teacher will think of himself not so much as a schoolmaster but as a lifemaster doing from another angle what the social worker does in his sphere, then he will be striving for all the knowledge available which could help him in this task. He will try to educate a generation of Youth which combines emotional stability with a flexible mind; yet he will only succeed if he is capable of seeing each of the problems of the new generation against the background of a changing world.

To sum up: we have so far met with sociology as an assistance to the teacher to overcome compartmentalization and the limited scholastic concept of education by orientating most of the things we teach to the needs of society. Then we met sociology as a help in co-ordinating the work of education with influence coming from institutions other than the school, i.e. from the family, the church, social work, public opinion, etc. We saw that the real meaning of education can only be assessed if its work is based upon a thorough study of human behaviour in its sociological aspects. Again, we met sociology as a help in interpreting many of the psychological conflicts and maladjustments of the individual as reflections of maladjustments in his immediate and the social surroundings. Finally, sociology appeared as a help in the understanding of the deeper sources of deterioration in our moral and cultural life, caused by the disintegration of tradition and the prevailing social structure. To express it in the language of academic subjects, courses on (1) Sociology of Education, (2) Science of Human Behaviour, (3) Sociology of Culture, (4) Study of Social Structure, ought to assist the training in education proper.

In all the functions analysed so far, sociology served as a help to make education more human, more social. We saw that in a modern, complex and quickly changing society education is only adequate if the teacher knows the social world from which pupils come, for which they have to be prepared, and if he is capable of assessing most of the things he does in terms of social results. In all these aspects sociology is a necessary supplement to education in our age, in whatever country or in whatever social system we may live. The question emerges whether in addition to these services sociology has something special to give to education of the Democracies and at this moment.

III. THE RÔLE OF SOCIOLOGY IN A MILITANT DEMOCRACY

The same problem can be put in other words. Is there an aspect of sociology in which it not only gives information about isolated facts, certain causal sequences and trends, or is it also capable of giving, apart from surveys, descriptions or monographs, a synthetic picture of the present situation? Is there an integration of the empirical information available which can answer questions like these: 'Where do we stand?' 'Where do we go?' 'Can sociology become an asset in framing our general policy?'

Before the outbreak of the war there would have been some obstacles in the way of accepting these synthesizing aspects of the teaching of sociology. One would gradually have admitted that some piecemeal information about society was a necessary subject in the curriculum, but one would have shrunk from drawing conclusions in terms of an approach aiming at a synthesis.

To-day there is nothing more obvious to thoughtful people than the need for a consistent and objective outlook concerning society and its present and future possibilities. The main difference between our pre-war democracy and the present one is that the former was a democracy on the defensive, which was mainly concerned with maintaining its equilibrium, whereas now we know that we can only survive if we are able to transform ourselves into a dynamic and militant democracy which will be capable of bringing about the necessary adjustments to the new situation from within, and at the same time express the nature of the changes required in terms of constructive ideas. These ideas must be true and timely and must appeal to the imagination of our younger generation, which has to fight for them, as well as to the peoples of the subjugated countries of Europe, who wait for such a lead.

One of the outstanding problems of the hour is, therefore, the lack of awareness in social affairs, which in one way is nothing but the lack of a comprehensive sociological orientation. Let me, therefore, make the question of awareness and of the causes of its suppression one of the main subjects of the following discussion.

By 'awareness' I do not understand the mere accumulation of rational knowledge. Awareness means both in the life of the individual and in that of the community the readiness to see the whole situation in which one finds oneself, and not only to orientate one's action on immediate tasks and purposes but to base them on a more comprehensive vision. One of the ways in which awareness expresses itself is the correct diagnosis of a situation. An otherwise able Civil Servant may know all the technicalities which are needed to put into practice an administrative regulation, but he may be unaware of the configuration of the political forces which were responsible for the creation of the law and of the possible social effects that law will have on certain prevailing tendencies in society. These political and social realities lie in another dimension, beyond the range of his awareness. To give another example: A young man may be very clever, well trained and equipped for certain purposes, but still be quite unaware of those hidden anxieties which again and again interfere with his actions and defeat his purposes. By becoming aware of his psychological type or the deeper sources of his anxieties he gradually can gain control over factors which controlled him in the stage of unawareness. Awareness, therefore, is not measurable in terms of the acquired knowledge only, but in terms of the capacity of seeing the uniqueness of our situation and, let us add now, in terms of getting hold of facts which are on the horizon of our personal or group experience, but only enter into our consciousness through a special effort. This was the case of the young man who became aware of his unconscious fears. Awareness does not claim the knowledge of transcendental things which are beyond human experience, such as ghosts, spirits or even the divinity, but of facts which are ready to become part of experience yet do not enter into the picture because somehow we do not want to take cognizance of them.

To the real educationist this sphere of the knowable but not yet known should constitute a very important realm, worthy of his attention. My general attitude concerning the degree and quality of awareness is not that one should aim under all circumstances at the highest degree of awareness, but that it depends both on the situation of the individual and of a group, such as a nation, how much awareness is wanted, how much of it can be achieved and how it should be achieved.

Once more a simple example will make clear what I have in mind. An old peasant may be a wise man who by experience, by intuition and habit knows what he has to do in any given situation of life. Young peasant boys and girls may ask him for advice on all sorts of affairs of their lives, concerning love, work, family, etc. He will always know how to deal with them, both in terms of custom, tradition and in terms of his own personal judgment. He will be able to give the right advice without being able consciously to define the whole situation in which he and his fellow-villagers live. The best test of his lack of awareness is that he will take it as a matter of course that the rules he applies are the rules of life in general and not only of the limited social world in which he happens to live. But an awareness of the situation might come to him as a revelation, if through a sudden removal from the village into a town he noticed that his wisdom and knowledge fail to cope with the new situation. First he would feel completely lost, not only because his habits and unconscious expectations are completely adjusted to a social world entirely different from the new one, but also because his ways of thinking and valuations are different from those which prevail in a town. His survival in the new surroundings will henceforth mainly depend on his ability to conform to their new demands, and this, in turn, will depend on his awareness. Awareness in his case will consist in the realization of the existence of two worlds side by side (the rural and the urban), each of which has its proper way of acting and thinking. That means that from now on most of the things he does must be accompanied by an awareness of the social frame of reference, by an awareness of the situation into which his responses will have to fit. This awareness will not hamper, as many people think, either his spontaneity or the development of his habits. Just the opposite holds true: awareness will assist him in reorganizing his behaviour and in reorientating his unconscious expectations.

But it is not only a change of environment which calls for awareness; any other change that leads to new conditions will make for a revision of habits, reorientation of expectations and for a search into the current changes. If an adolescent passes through the age of puberty and is being tormented by psychological and social conflicts, guidance consists in making him aware of the new situation. The very fact that he is able to define the situation in which he finds himself is very often an essential help in the search for a new equilibrium. In this connection it is not without interest to notice that if an adolescent passes through the age of puberty without developing the necessary awareness of that stage, it is very likely that he will be lacking in that quality up to the end of his life, although under specific conditions a kind of post-education even in this case may be of some help.

The need for awareness in society varies mainly with the rate of change and the nature of individual and group conflicts which go with it. As long as slow, gradual development and security prevail, there is no need for an excessive amount of awareness. If sudden changes occur, it is impossible to find the right way of action without reference to the meaning of change. Especially those who usually are expected to give lead to thought and action, the leaders in the various walks of life, will lose their followers if they are unable to define the situation anew. Sociology in terms of a thorough survey, a description of facts, will still be necessary in such an age of change, but the gist of its contribution will consist in a search into the new direction of events and into their new requirements.

Awareness is not to be mixed up with class-consciousness in the Marxian sense. Although the latter is a very important form of awareness it is only a special elaboration of it. Class-consciousness is awareness of those factors which make a social group or class ready to fight against another class or the rest of society covering up all other aspects of the whole situation. Class-consciousness deliberately blinds itself to those factors which, in spite of the prevailing conflicts, are making for cohesion and co-operation in society. Class-consciousness is the social world seen in the perspective of a fighting group.

Class-consciousness is partial awareness, whereas the awareness I have in mind is total awareness: awareness of the total situation, as far as that is humanly possible, at a given stage of history. It is a synthesis that emerges after the different aspects of partial group experiences have been confronted and integrated.

The specific feature of this country has been great security, wealth, gradual change. Thus there was no need for a continual revision of the situation, and social awareness could remain more or less undeveloped. It is only now that the rapid changes brought about by the war, and the even more rapid changes which will follow, make it a vital necessity that at least the leaders of the nation, and among them the teachers, should be educated in a way which will enable them to understand the meaning of change.

Whether under the pressure of changing events a complete psychological upheaval or reasonable reform will follow, depends mainly on whether there are leaders all over the country who are able to understand the situation in which they and their fellow-men find themselves, and whether they are able to present the pattern of reasonable adjustment. Where there is no reasonable pattern as an alternative to passing customs and habits in times of rapid change it is only natural that things go wrong and people go mad.

As awareness is not knowledge as such but an attitude of the mind, its development does not depend on instruction only but also on the removal of certain obstacles, such as unconscious fears. The resistance of almost all classes in this country to certain types of awareness is due not only to the happy continuity of its history which made possible a gradual adjustment to changing conditions, but also to a deliberate avoidance of every opportunity which might lead to a clear statement of the issues at stake. For this one cannot blame certain individuals or classes only. The conservatives were as responsible as those progressives who discussed pacifism when the enemy was at the gates. The appeasement policy of Chamberlain is just another feature of the same unwillingness to face unpleasant facts which prevailed in British Labour circles who refused to rearm when they could have foreseen the results of unpreparedness. This artificially suppressed awareness has, of course, nothing to do with 'race'. It is simply a manifestation of continuity, of gradualness in change and a certain type of education which all together developed a style of life which no doubt has great beauty and aesthetic value. But the problem to me as a sociologist is not what is its worth in itself, but whether under the entirely changed conditions this suppressed awareness can last and, if not, what will happen to it. This question, however, can only be dealt with reasonably if we have still more detailed insight into the facts that have produced it.

I shall first mention two methods prevailing in academic teaching which largely contributed to the suppression in the educated classes of what we called awareness. Later, I shall enumerate some of the more comprehensive influences which used to work in the same direction.

The first academic method which produces that lack of awareness is over-specialization. It is a method of neutralizing the genuine interest in real problems and in the possible answers to them. Specialization is necessary in an age of highly developed differentiation, but if no effort is made to co-ordinate the pieces of specialized research and of the different subjects taught in the curriculum, this can only be due to the fact that such a synthetic picture is not wanted. The student is not only unable to refuse dilettantish attempts at a synthesis, he is also rendered entirely uncritical by this method of teaching where everybody takes responsibility for a disconnected piece of research only and is, therefore, never encouraged to think of situations as a whole. Under present circumstances awareness is bound to rise and the craving for some coherent vision can no longer be completely suppressed: the great danger of the present situation, then, is that, without adequate training in the methods of synthesis, the students are bound to become an easy prey either of dilettanti or of propagandists who exploit that craving for their own or for their party's benefit.

Not only has the gradualness of change, the happy continuity of traditions, made it possible for this country to eliminate those situations in which issues become irreconcilable and therefore call for sharp definitions, but the very same social setting has developed a mental climate, a style of life which made it a principle to avoid not only overstatement but also any clear definition of the situation. If you come from the Continent to Great Britain one of the things that strikes you most is that here it seems to be a part of the accepted ways of life to leave many things unsaid which elsewhere would be plainly stated. Of course, if two Englishmen remain silent about certain things, both may know what is between the lines. But even so, it is characteristic that it is a dominant convention for many things to remain unsaid and to be present in the mind by implication only. Of course, I do not think now of sex, money and power, whose existence is not admitted by the conventions. One does not speak about them. But differences in opinion are rarely fought out in full, and hardly ever traced back to their final sources.

I admit the intrinsic value of this style of life, but I must also point to some of its disadvantages. In dealing with Continental Powers the non-committal language was very often misinterpreted.

But an even greater danger of such a collectively suppressed awareness is that it may become suicidal by not realizing those current changes in the world at large which, if they remain unchallenged, turn against the nation. To-day we realize that during the last decades a collective delusion prevailed in Western Democracies which consisted in an attitude of first ignoring and then denying the existence of menacing facts such as the rise and the growth of the Fascist régimes in Italy and Germany. One simply did not want the collective peace of mind to be disturbed, and one ostracized men like Churchill who dared to utter the truth. In that mood of suppressed awareness one denied also some of the other great changes taking place in the world. In economics one did not want to admit that the system of laissez-faire had run its course, that modern organization needs co-ordination, that a certain amount of planning is unavoidable, that a new type of State whose method is mechanized robbery was becoming the adversary.

The other factor in our academic teaching which prevented the growth of awareness was our misinterpretation of tolerance and objectivity in terms of neutrality. Neither democratic tolerance nor scientific objectivity demand that we should never take a stand for what we believe to be true, nor that we should avoid discussing the final values and objects of life.

But this was exactly what academic teaching used to aim at. The treatment of subjects by democratic teachers was very much like a carefully guided conversation in a drawing-room, where everybody avoids issues which could lead to a passionate discussion in the search of truth.

It was exactly this kind of neutralization which brought about a mental climate which from the very outset discouraged every attempt to make a distinction between essential and non-essential issues. The academic mind was proud of paying the greatest possible attention to trifles and ridiculing those who wanted first things to come first. In this connection one has also to mention the outlived educational principle that it does not matter what you learn, and that you learn only for the sake of mental discipline— a statement to which the obvious answer would be: Why should we not exactly for that reason acquire the mental discipline on those subjects which really matter? The unconscious tendency to neutralize learning and the hidden desire for self-frustration seem deliberately to avoid situations in which one would be forced to learn the essential things and to take a definite stand. This is as if one were to neglect the thorough study of the geography of one's own country from fear lest the enemy might possibly make use of the maps. The enemy will study our geography anyhow. An education and training which tried to prevent us from thinking about a subject in all its ramifications and from taking a stand somewhere is bound to create a human being incapable of offering real resistance when life surrounds him with an arsenal of doctrines and propaganda. When faced with the great issues of life, in his feeling of inferiority he will contemptuously call 'clever' everybody who tries to find a solution, and he will develop a hatred of thinking in general, and avoid all discussions, an attitude which is essentially undemocratic. As long as there was no totalitarian enemy to challenge Democracy, neutralization of everything was just a waste of human energy. But once the opponent set all his hopes on an ideological campaign the antidote to doctrine is better doctrine, not neutralized intelligence. It is here where the beginnings have to be made if we think that only militant democracy can win this war which, after all, is a war of ideas.

Of course, the militant attitude does not mean that totalitarian intolerance should take the place of free discussion, or that by removing the neutralizing effects of over-specialization we should neglect specialization altogether and should turn our teaching into propaganda. It only means that in the present situation no teaching is sound unless it trains man to be aware of the whole situation in which he finds himself, and that after careful deliberation he should be able to make his choice and come to a decision.

Apart from these merely academic methods of neutralizing the mind, there were other more fundamental causes at work. The deeper reason for pre-war democracy having avoided the creation of greater awareness was the fear that the discussion of vital issues might lead to a disintegration of that basic consensus which is a pre-condition of the functioning of democracy. Some fear this even more since the outbreak of the war, and this is the reason why they do not embark wholeheartedly upon the discussion of the problems of peace and post-war reconstruction. They are convinced that the discussion of these problems is bound to endanger that inner unity which is essential for the winning of the war. It is obvious that the people who think in these terms are caught on the horns of a dilemma. On the one hand, it is obvious that without constructive ideas they will neither inspire their own people nor those who suffer under the Fascist yoke. On the other hand, they frustrate the growth of the very same unifying ideas by being afraid of their possible effects. It is essential that we should face that issue honestly, and all the more so as our democracy, especially at the present juncture, can have a clear conscience, and has everything to gain and nothing to lose from growing awareness. When I am saying this I am not blind to the fact that it is essential both for the winning of the war and for the survival of democracy that the basic consensus should not be jeopardized. But the essential thing about true democracy is that differences in opinion do not kill solidarity as long as there is fundamental agreement on the method of agreement, i.e. that peaceful settlement of differences is better than one by violence. Democracy is essentially a method of social change, the institutionalization of the belief that adjustment to changing reality and the reconciliation of divers interests can be brought about by conciliatory means, with the help of discussion, bargaining and integral consensus.

This desire for consensus and a co-operative solution was not always quite evident in the different political parties and social groups before the outbreak of war, when too many thought that the basic dividing issue would be Capitalism—in the prevailing democratic or Fascist forms—on the one side and Communism on the other. This alternative was considered by many as irreconcilable: class war, dictatorship and complete annihilation of one's opponents seemed to have become the only methods of settling disputes.

Now my contention is that through the growth of Nazism and through the war the general situation has changed considerably. The main theme of history became different, and it is only due to a lack of awareness that all the parties still repeat their catch-phrases and do not dare to identify themselves entirely with the cause for which they make limitless sacrifice and for which they are already fighting. It is one of the remarkable features in history that the theme, the real *Leitmotif*, of its struggles may through circumstances change entirely, yet by remaining unaware of these changes people may still conceive of political alternatives in terms of their previous disctinctions and antitheses. In this respect it is obvious that such great decisions as the outbreak of a world-wide war and the issues on which it is being fought have definitely a bearing on what will be experienced for a very long time to come as the fundamental theme of our struggles.

The great change of theme seems to be that whereas before the outbreak of war in Europe it looked as though the exclusive alternative of the future would be that of Capitalism or Communism, since the outbreak of war the dividing line for the Western countries is freedom and democracy versus dictatorship. This, of course, does not mean that the social question, the problem of social reconstruction, has disappeared, but only that it ceased to be predominant. This does not mean that we have reached the happy state in which nothing is left of the former antitheses, according to which we used to expect the demand for planning and social justice to be on the one side, laissez-faire Capitalism with industrial and financial leadership on the other.

The new fact is that the irreconcilability of this alternative was mediated by an issue that seems to all the partners even more important than their previous antithesis. That new overwhelming issue is the maintenance of freedom and democratic control. What is needed to make democracy safe is not the exclusion of the social struggle, but that it should be fought out by methods of reform.

Another factor that led to a mediation of the previous, seemingly irreconcilable alternatives was that in the very struggle for victory the democratic states reconciled themselves to planning and the principle of social justice to a considerable degree. Thus the immediate effect of the war is that the struggle for victory makes planning a common necessity for all countries waging the war under modern conditions. The democratic countries are compelled to plan, and there is no real likelihood that after the war there will be a return to laissez-faire. In the same way, Britain's example is apparent in the heavy taxation, the extension of the social services, insurances against risks, compensation, etc. In all of them the principle of social justice and the idea of collective responsibility find institutional expression, and it is likely that not only a return to our pre-war society with its extreme differences in income and wealth is barred, but that these reforms will have to continue.

The result of all these changes is that the two main issues of the pre-war period, planning and social justice, which seemed to make class wars and revolutions inevitable, are being put into practice, even though in a modified and moderate form, in the democracies during the war itself. If in these countries planning is never going to become totalitarian but is restricted to the control of the key-positions in the economic life only, and if greater social justice will never lead to mechanical equalization, this will be felt by many of us as an advantage. For if there is a lesson to be learned from the experiments of the totalitarian states it is this: that ruthless regimentation leads to the enslavement of the citizen, and the mechanistic concept of equality defeats itself, as Russia's example shows, where differentiation of income and many other devices fostering social differentiation were reintroduced.

After the experiences of Russia, Germany and Italy, it seems to me that in England most of the groups on the left and the right find themselves in a less intransigent mood and will be willing to make considerable sacrifices, if reconstruction is possible without class war, revolution and dictatorship. All parties in this country (except a decreasing number of extremists) are united in the realization that the greatest evil is dictatorship.

If this is correct, it means that in the hierarchy of our values a change took place in which greater social justice and a desire for a reasonably planned order remain very important demands, but where the maintenance of freedom, the maintenance of the democratic method of change become even more essential. That means also that the planning of the transition is of even greater significance than the planning of the more distant future, because if, in the period of social reconstruction, freedom and parliamentary control are suppressed, they will probably disappear for good. It is very unlikely that if any class or group once got hold of the powerful machinery of the modern state it would ever give it up spontaneously unless there are democratic devices to check them. The chance that without war or other outside interference a totalitarian régime once established could be overthrown from within through another revolution is very slight.

At a time when the sad results of dictatorial methods become more and more apparent, the Anglo-Saxon democracies are gradually developing as an alternative to the Fascist or Communist order a Third Way, a type of planning which is not totalitarian but is under the control of the community, in which the main forms of freedom are not abolished; the fact is acknowledged that no society is possible without responsible governing groups and that a social remedy against oligarchy is not to replace an old one by a new one but to facilitate the access of the gifted from the lower ranks into the leading positions.

What we have learned from the last decades is that the aim of social progress is not an imaginary society without a governing class, but the improvement of the economic, social, political and educational opportunities for the people to train themselves for leadership, and an improvement of the method of the selection of the best in the various fields of social life.

I think I am not in the least blind to the danger-spots and to the fact that democratic awareness is needed to select from among the war-time measures those which tend to lead to the Anglo-Saxon pattern of progressive democracy, and to check those tendencies which, under the cloak of Democracy and Planning, would establish a new variety of Fascism. But I do believe that we are groping our way to a pattern of society which, once established, might, with modifications, become the basis of democratic reconstruction all over the world.

It is perhaps not by chance that the craving for social awareness is awakening exactly at a juncture when this transformation is taking place in reality. And it is hardly mere curiosity that people, young and old, again and again ask questions about man and his place in a changing society. Unconsciously they feel that all depends on their vigilance and that we need no longer be afraid to face the social situation as a whole and to develop our own social philosophy. There is no occasion for such fears: since we need not be afraid of differences still existing within our boundaries we can afford to be undogmatic. The changed situation sees to it that we should become dynamic, progressive as well as responsible. This new responsibility means that critical thought will not degenerate into destructive criticism but will remain conscious of its constructive tasks, caring at once for change and the maintenance of the basic consensus on which freedom depends.

To-day all those forces which are determined to fight the forces of evil and oppression rally round the flag of progressive democracy, which is bound to plan the New Order of Freedom and Social Justice. In this struggle we shall either be able to produce the necessary awareness, which turns the tragedy of war into a creative venture in social reconstruction—or we shall perish.

Index

[the Introduction has not been indexed]